HRM NELSON EDUCATION SERIES IN HUMAN RESOURCE MANAGEMENT

6TH EDITION

RECRUITMENT AND SELECTION IN CANADA

VICTOR M. CATANO
SAINT MARY'S UNIVERSITY

WILLI H. WIESNER
McMASTER UNIVERSITY

RICK D. HACKETT
McMASTER UNIVERSITY

SERIES EDITOR:
MONICA BELCOURT
YORK UNIVERSITY

NELSON

NELSON

Recruitment and Selection in Canada, Sixth Edition

by Victor M. Catano, Willi H. Wiesner, and Rick D. Hackett

Vice President, Editorial Higher Education:
Anne Williams

Publisher:
Jackie Wood

Marketing Manager:
David Strattron

Developmental Editor:
Toula Di Leo

Photo Researcher:
Sandra Mark

Permissions Coordinator:
Sandra Mark

Production Project Manager:
Jaime Smith

Production Service:
Cenveo Publisher Services

Copy Editor:
Kelli Howey

Proofreader:
N. Rajasekaran

Indexer:
BIM Indexing Services

Design Director:
Ken Phipps

Managing Designer:
Franca Amore

Interior Design:
Sharon Lucas

Cover Design:
Lisa Jardine

Compositor:
Cenveo Publisher Services

Printed and bound in Canada
4 5 6 7 20 19 18 17

For more information contact Nelson Education Ltd., 1120 Birchmount Road, Toronto, Ontario, M1K 5G4. Or you can visit our Internet site at nelson.com

Library and Archives Canada Cataloguing in Publication

Catano, Victor M. (Victor Michael), 1944-, author Recruitment and selection in Canada / Victor M. Catano (Saint Mary's University), Willi H. Wiesner (McMaster University), Rick D. Hackett (McMaster University). – Sixth edition.

(Nelson Education series in human resource management) Includes bibliographical references and index.ISBN 978-0-17-657031-6 (pbk.)

1. Employees–Recruiting–Canada–Textbooks. 2. Employee selection–Canada–Textbooks. I. Wiesner, Willi H. (Willi Harry), 1952-, author II. Hackett, Rick D., 1956-, author III. Title. IV. Series: Nelson Education series in human resource management

HF5549.5.R44R417
2015 658.3'11 C2014-908464-1

To my wife, Jan, and to our sons Victor and Michael and their families; you are the joy of my life. Also to Spike, my faithful cat, who once again helped me type the manuscript.
Vic Catano

To my precious wife, Linda, our children Jared (and Breanne) and Rachel (and Brian), and our grandson, Reiner. You've brought joy to my life.
Willi Wiesner

To Patti, my wife of 30 years, and my two sons, Aaron and Tyler, for their ever present unconditional love and support.
Rick Hackett

BRIEF CONTENTS

CONTENTS

ABOUT THE SERIES

The management of human resources has become the most important source of innovation, competitive advantage, and productivity, more so than any other resource. More than ever, human resources management (HRM) professionals need the knowledge and skills to design HRM policies and practices that not only meet legal requirements but also are effective in supporting organizational strategy. Increasingly, these professionals turn to published research and books on best practices for assistance in the development of effective HR strategies. The books in the *Nelson Education Series in Human Resources Management* are the best source in Canada for reliable, valid, and current knowledge about practices in HRM.

The texts in this series include:

- *Managing Performance through Training and Development*
- *Management of Occupational Health and Safety*
- *Recruitment and Selection in Canada*
- *Strategic Compensation in Canada*
- *Strategic Human Resources Planning*
- *Industrial Relations in Canada*
- *Research, Measurement, and Evaluation of Human Resources*
- *International Human Resources: A Canadian Perspective*

The *Nelson Education Series in Human Resources Management* represents a significant development in the field of HRM for many reasons. Each book in the series is the first and now best-selling text in the functional area. Furthermore, HR professionals in Canada must work with Canadian laws, statistics, policies, and values. This series serves their needs. It is the only opportunity that students and practitioners have to access a complete set of HRM books, standardized in presentation, which enables them to access information quickly across many HRM disciplines. Students who are pursuing the CHRP (Certified Human Resource Professional) designation through their provincial HR associations will find the books in this series invaluable in preparing for the knowledge exams. This one-stop resource will prove useful to anyone looking for solutions for the effective management of people.

The publication of this series signals that the HRM field has advanced to the stage where theory and applied research guide practice. The books in the series present the best and most current research in the functional areas of HRM. Research is supplemented with examples of the best practices used by Canadian companies that are leaders in HRM. Each text begins with a general model of the discipline, and then describes the implementation of effective strategies. Thus, the books serve as an introduction to the functional area for the new student of HR and as a validation source for the more experienced HRM practitioner. Cases, exercises, and endnotes provide opportunities for further discussion and analysis.

As you read and consult the books in this series, I hope you share my excitement in being involved and knowledgeable about a profession that has such a significant impact on the achievement of organizational goals, and on employees' lives.

Monica Belcourt, Ph.D., CHRP
Series Editor
October 2014

ABOUT THE AUTHORS

VICTOR M. CATANO

Dr. Catano is Professor of Industrial and Organizational Psychology at Saint Mary's University, Halifax, Nova Scotia. He is a registered psychologist in Nova Scotia and a member of the Human Resources Association of Nova Scotia.

Dr. Catano has served as President of the Association of Psychologists of Nova Scotia, member of the Nova Scotia Board of Examiners in Psychology (the body responsible for regulating the profession within Nova Scotia), and President of the Canadian Society for Industrial and Organizational Psychology. He also chaired the Canadian Council of Human Resources Association's Independent Board of Examiners, the agency that was responsible for developing and running the examinations and assessments that lead to the Certified Human Resources Professional (CHRP) designation.

He is a past editor of *Canadian Psychology* and has acted as a reviewer for numerous scholarly journals and granting agencies. He has published over 250 scholarly articles, conference papers, and technical reports. Dr. Catano's current research interests include personnel psychology, the psychology of labour relations, organizational and environmental constraints on productivity, and the impact of psychological environments on the health, safety, and productivity of workers. Dr. Catano also has extensive consulting experience in personnel selection with both private and public organizations.

In recognition of his contributions to the science and practice of psychology in Canada, Dr. Catano was elected a Fellow by the Canadian Psychological Association and an honorary member by the Canadian Forces Personnel Selection Officers Association. He is a recipient of the Canadian Psychological Association's Award for Distinguished Contributions to Education and Training and the Canadian Society for Industrial and Organizational Psychology's Distinguished Scientist Award. The Human Resources Association of Nova Scotia awarded him an honorary membership in recognition of his distinguished contributions to human resources in Canada.

WILLI H. WIESNER

Dr. Wiesner is Associate Professor of Human Resources and Management at the DeGroote School of Business, McMaster University. He has served as Institute Coordinator and President of the Canadian Society of Industrial and Organizational Psychology, and as Chair of the Human Resources and Management Area of the DeGroote School of Business at McMaster University from 1997–2008 and 2012–2013. Dr. Wiesner advises firms in both the private and public sector and gives workshops on employee selection, performance appraisal, work-team effectiveness, and other human resources areas. His recent research and publication activities have focused on employment interviewing and selection, group decision making, and work-team effectiveness.

RICK D. HACKETT

Dr. Hackett is a professor and Canada Research Chair of Organizational Behaviour and Human Performance at the DeGroote School of Business, McMaster University. He is Associate Editor of the *Journal of Business and Psychology*, past Editor-in-Chief of the *Canadian Journal of Administrative Sciences*, Fellow of the Canadian Psychological Association, and Past-President of the Canadian Society for Industrial and Organizational Psychology. From 2001 to 2003, Dr. Hackett was Visiting Scholar at the Hong Kong University of Science and Technology. As president of Hackett & Associates Human Resources Consultants Inc., he advises firms in both the public and private sector on HR assessment and selection.

PREFACE

Recruitment and Selection in Canada, Sixth Edition, is designed to meet the needs of both students and practitioners working in human resources or personnel psychology. It provides an up-to-date review of the current issues and methodologies that are used in recruiting and selecting employees to staff Canadian organizations. Over the years, the field of personnel selection and staffing has become more quantitative and subject to both federal and provincial human rights legislation. This book provides an introduction to these more technical areas in an easy-to-read style. Each chapter includes examples, cases, and other materials that illustrate how the practices discussed in the text are carried out in both private- and public-sector organizations in Canada. Many of these illustrations are drawn from current events reported in the media and presented in boxes we call *Recruitment and Selection Today*.

An important change to the Sixth Edition is the inclusion of four-colour graphics and illustrations to highlight the text. We believe this change will enhance the value of the text and make it more interesting for the students to use.

// MEETING SCIENTIFIC AND LEGAL STANDARDS

Recruitment and Selection in Canada provides an introduction to sound procedures in recruitment and selection that meet scientific, professional, and Canadian legal standards. It presents recruitment and selection as essential components of strategic human resources planning and emphasizes their role in enhancing productivity. Starting with a review of the social and economic factors that affect recruitment and selection, the text next presents key elements in a recruitment and selection system, with an emphasis on the need for a solid scientific and legal foundation on which to build that system. The text introduces job analyses and competency modelling as the keys to developing a recruitment and selection system and to understanding the relationship between improved selection systems and increased organizational productivity. Also included in this book are contemporary developments related to competencies, counterproductive work behaviours, interviewing, cognitive ability testing, personality testing, drug and honesty testing, decision making, and finalizing the deal with the selected candidate. Recognizing the constraints under which organizations operate, the text presents recruitment and selection within the context of a global market and competition.

// USE OF THE INTERNET

One of the most remarkable developments since publication of the first edition of this book has been the rise of the Internet as a resource tool and the use of social media in recruitment and selection. We have included in this sixth edition even more references to relevant websites and interactive material throughout the text and as part of the end-of-chapter exercises and cases. URLs for relevant Web links are listed near the end of each chapter. We have expanded material on the use of social media as part of the recruitment and selection process.

Many of the exercises, illustrations, and cases now require students to obtain additional information from the Web through the links we provide; many of the chapters include at least one Web-based exercise. While we have tested every link during the editorial process, the URL for a link may have changed. We suggest a quick Google search to track down the new location.

// A CANADIAN REFERENCE ON RECRUITMENT AND SELECTION

This sixth edition of *Recruitment and Selection in Canada* offers several advantages to both students and practitioners. First, it provides an up-to-date introduction to the current developments in recruiting and selecting employees within a Canadian context. The approach taken with this text has been to incorporate the Canadian material organically into the development of the text rather than "Canadianizing" a popular American text. This approach has allowed us to focus in greater detail on issues of concern to Canadian organizations and to Canadian human resources practitioners. Canadian examples and websites and links to both public and private organizations are featured wherever possible; however, we also include relevant examples from around the world.

We have attempted to provide as complete coverage as possible of current issues in recruitment and selection by integrating the role of recruitment and selection in a context of strategic human resources planning. At all stages of the recruitment and selection process, the text emphasizes the necessity of satisfying both professional and legal requirements and offers guidelines on how this can be accomplished through a feature called *Recruitment and Selection Notebook*. Each chapter includes several of these authoritative boxes.

Increasingly, both students and practitioners must understand the scientific, technical, and legal aspects that form the basis of current recruitment and selection practices. Unlike these other texts, we have provided a complete and thorough introduction to this essential material in a readable, nontechnical style that minimizes scientific jargon and emphasizes understanding of the basic concepts in a context of application. To assist understanding, we have also included learning outcomes at the start of each chapter, definitions of important concepts throughout each chapter, and both exercises and case material at the end of each chapter to illustrate important principles and concepts.

This text is designed for one-semester courses in human resources management, staffing, personnel psychology, and personnel selection. It is also ideal for short courses that form part of diploma, certificate, or professional upgrading programs. The previous five editions of *Recruitment and Selection in Canada* were adopted for courses taught as part of degree programs in colleges and universities; as well, they were used as a standard reference for graduate courses and still can be found on the bookshelves of many HR professionals.

// ADDRESSING THE NEEDS OF STUDENTS AND TEACHERS

One of the strengths of this text is the systematic integration of the different aspects of recruitment and selection with current legal and technical practices. However, the needs of students and instructors may differ across the settings in which this text may be used. Some students may already have had a substantial introduction to measurement issues in other courses that form part of their program. In those cases, parts of Chapter 2 can be omitted. Later chapters in the text, however, do refer to material contained in Chapter 2 or to concepts introduced in it, but the student can easily read the relevant sections of this chapter in conjunction with the later reference.

Similarly, Chapter 5 includes a brief discussion of issues related to performance and an expanded section on counterproductive work behaviours. It is our firm belief that students must be conversant with all aspects of the recruitment and selection system, and measurement of performance is essential to evaluating the effectiveness of any selection system. Often the problem with poor selection systems is not the selection instruments used, but how performance is measured. Performance is the bottom line and we have integrated that into the text with a very brief introduction of some performance measurement tools. We rely on other courses in performance management to present detailed instruction on the use of these tools.

// CHANGES IN THIS SIXTH EDITION

We consulted broadly with users of the fifth edition to determine how we could improve this text. We incorporated much of that feedback into the sixth edition. What's changed in this new edition? We have retained the inclusion of a vignette at the start of each chapter; however, many of these have been changed or updated. Feedback suggests that instructors and students find these to be very relevant ways of becoming engaged with the chapter's content. We have drawn these, as far as possible, from real-life situations. All of the chapters have been updated with current thinking based on the most recent theorizing and research as reflected in the HR literature.

In Chapter 1 we introduce the concept of talent management as it relates to recruitment and selection and present a recruitment and selection action plan. We also focus on the social and demographic factors related to recruitment and selection along with globalization and other factors such as unionized workplaces that affect these topics. We also included an introduction to ethical issues and expanded its coverage to professional issues. We moved a briefer section on testing issues to Chapter 7, where there is a better fit. In Chapter 2 we reduced much of the basic material on statistics and types of validation and added graphics to help understand the concepts of reliability and validity. We also included information on interpreting reliability and validity coefficients. In Chapter 3, we consolidated much of the material and provided a table of definitions of key legal terms as used in selection as well as landmark Supreme Court cases. We added material on recruiting people with disabilities and provided guidelines for non-discriminatory recruitment. Chapter 4 remains much the same although we updated it to reflect current research on both job analysis and competency modelling. We added many visual illustrations of different job analysis methods and included basic information on conducting a job analysis, including a job analysis interview protocol and critical incident reports. We also mention leadership competency models used by several provincial governments in their hiring process. In Chapter 5 we maintained the section on counterproductive work behaviours that serves as the basis for "selecting out" in later chapters. In light of current thinking we have included a section on adaptive performance apart from contextual performance in discussing performance as a multidimensional construct. Chapter 6 contains increased information on the use of social networking to attract job candidates. It also looks at factors that affect strategic recruiting. In Chapter 7 we have updated material on weighted application blanks and biographical information blanks. In Chapter 8 we added a section on employment testing and the use of employment tests. We've included the most recent information on general mental ability testing and the use of the Big Five personality measures in selection. Chapter 9 presents comprehensive, current information on the interview and the development and conduct of structured interviews. Finally, in Chapter 10 we provide information on the post-decision process: What to do to ensure you get the selected candidate on board, conditional offers of employment, and illustration of a template for an employment contract.

We retained features from the previous editions that enhanced learning opportunities and made the text more interactive, including the use of websites, expanded exercises, and case material, and the use of colour to highlight tables and figures. Web links now appear only at the end of a chapter, although URLs are included in text when relevant to a point we are making or to an example.

// RPC

In the previous editions we included relevant required professional capabilities (RPCs), which form the foundation for obtaining the Certified Human Resources Professional (CHRP) knowledge examination, at the end of each chapter. We presented only those RPCs that were related to the content of the chapter. In the sixth edition we have removed the RPCs to the ancillary material that is part of the Instructor's Guide. The reason for this is that the RPCs are under review and HR associations are using different versions of the RPCs. Some have retained older versions while others have moved on to the newer revisions. Because of this unsettled state and our hope to limit confusion, we suggest you check the CCHRA website at http://www.chrp.ca as well as the provincial HR association at the websites listed in Chapter 1 to view the current RPCs that they may be using.

// INSTRUCTOR RESOURCES

The **Nelson Education Teaching Advantage (NETA)** program delivers research-based instructor resources that promote student engagement and higher-order thinking to enable the success of Canadian students and educators. Be sure to visit Nelson Education's **Inspired Instruction** website at http://www.nelson.com/inspired/ to find out more about NETA. Don't miss the testimonials of instructors who have used NETA supplements and seen student engagement increase!

The following Instructor Resources have been created for *Recruitment and Selection in Canada*. Access these ultimate tools for customizing lectures and presentations at www.nelson.com/instructor.

NETA Test Bank: This resource was written by John Hardisty, Sheridan College. It includes an average of 40 multiple-choice questions per chapter, written according to NETA guidelines for effective construction and development of higher-order questions. Also included are true/false questions and short answer questions.

cognēro
Full-Circle Assessment

The NETA Test Bank is available in a new, cloud-based platform. **Nelson Testing Powered by Cognero®** is a secure online testing system that allows you to author, edit, and manage test bank content from any place you have Internet access. No special installations or downloads are needed, and the desktop-inspired interface, with its drop-down menus and familiar, intuitive tools, allows you to create and manage tests with ease. You can create multiple test versions in an instant, and import or export content into other systems. Tests can be delivered from your learning management system, your classroom, or wherever you want. Nelson Testing Powered by Cognero for *Recruitment and Selection in Canada* can also be accessed through www.nelson.com/instructor. Printable versions in Word and PDF are available upon request.

NETA PowerPoint: Microsoft® PowerPoint® lecture slides for every chapter have been created by Barbara Lipton, Seneca College. There is an average of 30 slides per chapter, many featuring key figures, tables, and photographs from *Recruitment and Selection in Canada*. NETA principles of clear design and engaging content have been incorporated throughout, making it simple for instructors to customize the deck for their courses.

Image Library: This resource consists of digital copies of figures, short tables, and photographs used in the book. Instructors may use these jpegs to customize the NETA PowerPoint or create their own PowerPoint presentations.

NETA Instructor's Manual: This resource was written by Barbara Lipton, Seneca College. It is organized according to the textbook chapters and addresses key educational concerns, such as typical stumbling blocks student face and how to address them. Other features include suggested answers to the exercises and cases.

Day One: Day One–Prof InClass is a PowerPoint presentation that instructors can customize to orient students to the class and their text at the beginning of the course.

MINDTAP

MindTap for *Recruitment and Selection in Canada* is a personalized teaching experience with relevant assignments that guide students to analyze, apply, and elevate thinking, allowing instructors to measure skills and promote better outcomes with ease. A fully online learning solution, MindTap combines all student learning tools–readings, multimedia, activities, and assessments–into a single Learning Path that guides the student through the curriculum. Instructors personalize the experience by customizing the presentation of these learning tools to their students, even seamlessly introducing their own content into the Learning Path.

// STUDENT ANCILLARIES

MINDTAP

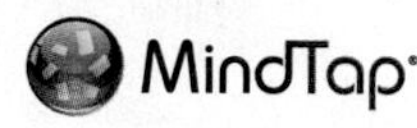

Stay organized and efficient with ***MindTap***–a single destination with all the course material and study aids you need to succeed. Built-in apps leverage social media and the latest learning technology. For example:

- ReadSpeaker will read the text to you.
- Flashcards are pre-populated to provide you with a jump start for review–or you can create your own.

- You can highlight text and make notes in your MindTap Reader. Your notes will flow into Evernote, the electronic notebook app that you can access anywhere when it's time to study for the exam.
- Self-quizzing allows you to assess your understanding.

Visit www.nelson.com/student to start using **MindTap**. Enter the Online Access Code from the card included with your text. If a code card is *not* provided, you can purchase instant access at NELSONbrain.com.

ACKNOWLEDGMENTS

The production of any book is a collaborative effort. Many people, other than the authors whose names appear on the cover, play an important role. We would like to acknowledge their assistance and to thank them for their valuable contributions to this process. We have tried to present in this book the latest scientific foundation for human resources management. We could not have done that without the research compiled by our academic colleagues throughout North America and the experience of human resources practitioners in adapting that research to the workplace. This book would not exist without their work.

We are also indebted to our past and present students who have challenged our ideas and made us be clear in the exposition of our arguments. In particular, we owe a debt to our students at Saint Mary's and McMaster universities; their feedback on earlier editions of this text was invaluable. Over the years, the book has benefited immensely from the feedback of reviewers and users at various colleges and universities across Canada. We are grateful for their thoughtful comments, which have helped to make this a better text. We hope that the sixth edition continues the improvement of the text, and wish to thank reviewers Diane White, Seneca College; John Hardisty, Sheridan College; Karen MacMillan, Western University; Judy Benevides, Kwantlen Polytechnic University; Jeff Young, Mount Saint Vincent University; Mark Podolsky, York University; Lisa Bering, Humber College; and Colleen Morrison, College of the North Atlantic.

Monica Belcourt, the editor for the series, deserves special praise. She was the glue that held everything together and kept the project on track. It is truly the case that without her efforts, this book would not have materialized. We must also acknowledge the patience and professionalism of the team at Nelson: Amie Plourde, Publisher & Team Strategist; Jackie Wood, Publisher; Rachel Eagen, Freelance Developmental Editor; Toula Di Leo, Developmental Editor; Dave Stratton, Marketing Manager; Jaime Smith, Production Project Manager; and freelance copy editor Kelli Howey.

Finally, we are most grateful to our families and friends who provided us with support and understanding throughout the long nights. They inspired us to think and write clearly.

Victor M. Catano
Saint Mary's University

Willi H. Wiesner
McMaster University

Rick D. Hackett
McMaster University

"BATFLECK"—WHAT YOU SHOULD KNOW ABOUT MAKING BAD HIRES

Hiring is hard, we know. Making sure you have the best candidate for the job is one of the most difficult and daunting tasks as a hiring manager. Even Ryan Holmes, CEO at Hootsuite, has dealt with his fair share of bad hires, and the U.S. Department of Labor estimates that the average cost of a bad hire can be 30 percent of the individual's first-year potential earnings. *Yikes.*

We're here to clear the air about bad hires, and to help us contextualize this, we'll be using recent examples buzzing around the entertainment industry.

The Bad Hire: Batfleck

Ben Affleck? As *Batman*? We, like much of the public, are extremely disappointed in this recent selection by Warner Bros., DC Comics, and [*Batman v Superman*] director Zack Snyder. Let's just put it this way—did you watch Ben kick some butt as blind superhero Daredevil? No? Well, you're not alone. That movie tanked at the box office.

We're a little disheartened to know that DC didn't reach out to us. As a leader in IT staffing and all things geek, we could've helped prevent this bad hire. We even did our research. Like any job, Batman has a list of requirements that *must* be met in order to be successful:

- 3+ years' experience driving a Batmobile
- Proficiency in employing Batarangs
- Rigorous training in martial arts (black belt or equivalent preferred)

Unfortunately, we don't think Ben meets these qualifications. It seems as though Warner Bros. is settling on Ben Affleck's Hollywood star power to balance out his inability to portray a good superhero. Is he a great actor? Absolutely. *Argo* was phenomenal. We're not judging Ben on his ability to act, but we are concerned [about his] ability to perfect the character that is Bruce Wayne/Batman … and about his ability to wear the ever-prestigious Batsuit.

Settling on a candidate who is a super hero with one of your requirements and sub-par with others isn't a wise move. Instead, hold out for someone that could be a well-rounded fit. If your candidate is "good" at a variety of skills you're looking for, it's smart to offer trainings and education to help them go from good to great. This in turn could help strengthen your manager–employee relationships.

Now, let's get back to Batman. Men like Josh Brolin or Eric Bana have that Bruce/Batman balance that fans are looking for, and we highly encourage DC to take a second look before production. *There is still time to reverse the bad hire.* For example, Tony Hsieh, CEO of Zappos, offers new hires a $2000 bonus to quit after their first week on the job—*just* to weed out bad hires. You may want to take this idea with a grain of salt, as Zappos is a very large company and consistently ranks in Fortune's 100 Best Companies to Work For list.

Now that we've discussed the very painful experience of choosing a bad hire, we can focus on what a good hire looks like. Tune in next week as we discuss a good hire example, again pulling from the same bucket—Hollywood.

Source: Gia Ciccone for Modis. Copyright August 29, 2013. Accessed May 2014. http://blog.modis.com/employers/batfleck-and-bad-hires/ Courtesy of Adecco Group North America.

// WHY RECRUITMENT AND SELECTION MATTER

An update on "Batfleck": Warner Bros. did not take the advice of thousands of potential moviegoers to replace Ben Affleck as Batman; the movie is now in production for a spring 2016 release. You will have an opportunity to decide for yourself whether Warner Bros. made a bad hire in signing Ben Affleck to play Batman.

Our purpose in writing this book is to reduce bad decisions by laying out the "best practices" in finding and hiring people who will contribute to the overall success of an organization and its products or services. Best practices are valid, reliable, and legally defensible. They must comply with relevant legislation. Throughout this book, we will focus on the best practices to recruit and select talent in a Canadian context.

CHAPTER 1

AN INTRODUCTION TO RECRUITMENT AND SELECTION

CHAPTER LEARNING OUTCOMES

This chapter introduces the topics of recruitment and selection in Canadian organizations.

AFTER READING THIS CHAPTER YOU SHOULD:

- appreciate the importance and relevance of recruitment and selection to Canadian organizations;
- know where recruitment and selection fit into the organization as a whole and the human resources management system in particular;
- understand how changes in technology, global competition, changing labour force demographics, and increasing government regulation and societal pressures for conformity to ethical, environmental, and human rights standards have an impact on recruitment and selection;
- be aware of which professional associations and groups in Canada have a stake in recruitment and selection; and
- become familiar with basic ethical and professional issues in recruitment and selection.

By definition, best practices are supported by empirical evidence that has been accumulated through accepted scientific procedures. Best practices do not involve "hunches," "guesses," or unproven practices. Best practices involve the ethical treatment of job applicants throughout the recruitment and hiring process. Best practices result from human resources (HR) professionals following the accepted standards and principles of professional associations. The inability to defend recruitment and selection practices before a judicial tribunal may have serious financial consequences for an organization.

Best practices do not have to be perfect practices. As we will see in later chapters, no selection procedures are free from error and always lead to correct decisions. However, employers must show that their procedures are fair and do not discriminate against protected groups covered by various laws. Recruitment and selection have moved far beyond the time when a manager could look over a few résumés, talk to one or two applicants (who were mostly friends of current employees), and make a hiring decision. If people are an organization's most important asset, then those responsible for recruiting and selecting personnel must be capable of finding the best person for each position in the organization.

Using "best practices" in recruitment and selection adds value to an organization and contributes to the success–including positive financial outcomes–of a company. Ployhart, Van Iddekinge, and MacKenzie[1] showed how selection of employees through an employment test of cognitive ability and personality led to increases in the human capital (i.e., a unit's composition of employees' knowledge, skills, and ability) in 238 units of a restaurant chain, and then to a unit's service performance and effectiveness.

HR is a very broad field. Figure 1.1 presents a simplified model of some of the major HR functions within an organization. By no means is the model complete; its purpose is to emphasize that recruitment and selection are but one component of the HR system. That component, however, is a very important one that helps an organization meet its goals and objectives by producing competent, committed, and effective personnel.

Figure 1.2 presents another way of looking at the functions in which human resources personnel may become involved. These functions are grouped around the broader function of **talent management**, which can be thought of as an organization's commitment to recruit, retain, and develop the most talented and superior employees. Talent management gives the line manager a significant role and responsibility in the recruitment, selection, retention, and development of superior employees with less involvement of HR. In some organizations only top potential employees are included in the talent management system; in others, talent management applies to all employees.

Talent management
An organization's commitment to recruit, retain, and develop the most talented and superior employees.

Human Resources Information Systems
Computer-based systems that track employee data, the needs of HR, and the requirements and competencies needed for different positions, among other functions.

Part of talent management involves developing an employee's career across the organization and knowing when suitable positions become vacant in the organization. To be effective with this function, larger organizations rely on **Human Resources Information Systems (HRIS)**. HRIS are computer-based systems that track employee data, the needs of HR, and the requirements and competencies needed for different positions. HRIS software is generally bundled with payroll and accounting functions. HRIS can be customized to include whatever information the organization believes is important.

We will examine only the recruitment and selection function of talent management in this book. The other books in the Nelson HR series cover the other talent management functions. You may have already taken courses in these areas. We focus on recruitment and selection because they are the means organizations use, for better

FIGURE 1.1

EXAMPLE OF A HUMAN RESOURCES SYSTEM

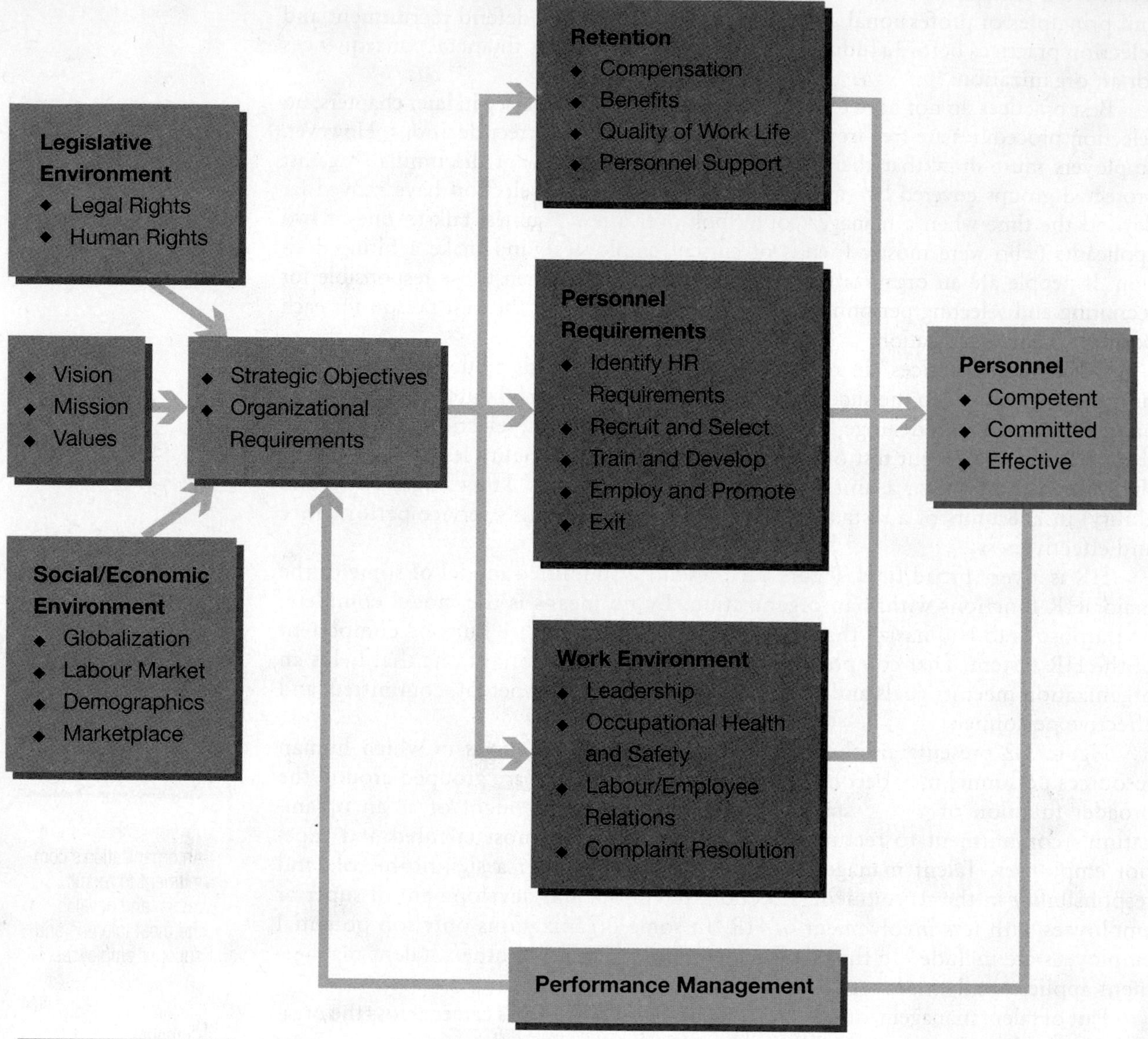

Recruitment
The generation of an applicant pool for a position or job in order to provide the required number of candidates for a subsequent selection or promotion program.

or for worse, to find and choose employees. To be effective they should follow from an organization's strategic planning. Our intent in this book is to present those best practices that will lead to the staffing of organizations with the best-qualified candidates.

Recruitment is the generation of an applicant pool for a position or job in order to provide the required number of candidates for a subsequent selection or promotion program. Recruitment is done to meet management goals and objectives for the organization and must also meet current legal requirements (human rights, employment equity, labour law, and other legislation).

FIGURE 1.2

TALENT MANAGEMENT FUNCTIONS

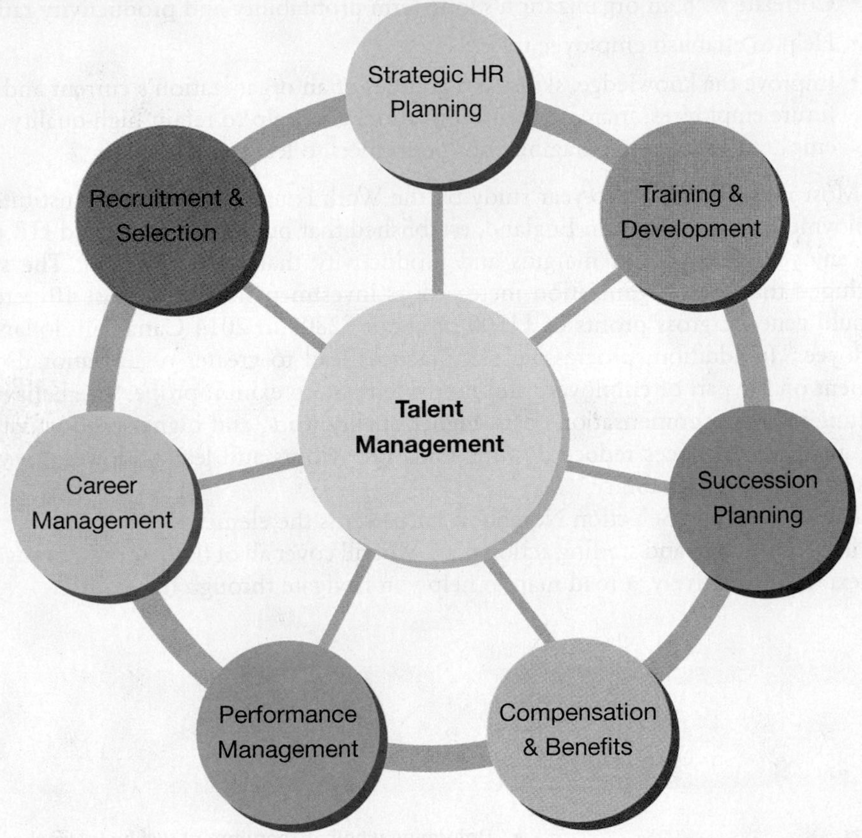

Selection is the choice of job candidates from a previously generated applicant pool in a way that will meet management goals and objectives as well as current legal requirements.

Selection
The choice of job candidates from a previously generated applicant pool in a way that will meet management goals and objectives as well as current legal requirements.

Selection can involve any of the following functions: hiring at the entry level from applicants external to the organization, promotion or lateral transfer of people within the organization, and movement of current employees into training and development programs.

Effective recruitment and selection practices can mean the difference between an organization's success or failure. As noted in the opening vignette, bad hires may cost an organization as much as 30 percent of a new hire's earnings. Differences in skills among job candidates translate into performance differences on the job that have economic consequences for an organization. Hiring people with the right skills or the highest levels of those skills leads to positive economic outcomes for the organization. Hiring a person with the wrong set of skills can lead to disaster for both the person and the organization. Effective recruitment and selection practices identify job applicants with the appropriate level of knowledge, skills, abilities, and other requirements needed for successful performance in a job or an organization.

Empirical studies demonstrate that organizations using effective recruitment and selection practices gain a competitive advantage in the marketplace. Best practices in recruitment and selection:

- Reduce employee turnover and increase productivity.[2] A one-standard-deviation increase in the use of sophisticated HR practices decreased turnover by 7 percent and increased sales by $27 000 per employee per year.[3]
- Are responsible for up to 15 percent of a firm's relative profit.[4]
- Correlate with an organization's long-term profitability and productivity ratios.[5]
- Help to establish employee trust.[6]
- Improve the knowledge, skills, and abilities of an organization's current and future employees, increase their motivation, and help to retain high-quality employees while encouraging poor performers to leave.[7]

Most importantly, a two-year study by the Work Foundation and the Institute for Employment Studies, both in England, established that businesses with good HR practices enjoyed higher profit margins and productivity than those without. The study concluded that if an organization increased its investment in HR by just 10 percent, it would generate gross profits of £1500 or about $2800 in 2014 Canadian dollars per employee.[8] In addition, progressive HR practices lead to greater organizational commitment on the part of employees and motivate them to exhibit proper role behaviour, resulting in lower compensation costs, higher quality work, and higher productivity; as well, good HR practices reduce dysfunctional behaviours and lead to lower operating costs and greater profitability.[9]

Recruitment and Selection Notebook 1.1 presents the elements that should be covered in a recruitment and staffing action plan. We will cover all of these topics throughout the text. It is, effectively, a road map to help you navigate through this course.

RECRUITMENT AND SELECTION NOTEBOOK 1.1

ELEMENTS OF A RECRUITMENT AND SELECTION ACTION PLAN

1. Develop Recruitment Strategy
   - Identify number of positions to be filled
   - Establish selection committee
   - Review organization's goals and objectives based on strategic HR plan
   - Establish budget for the recruitment process
   - Establish timelines for recruitment and selection activities
   - Develop/review job description for positions
   - Develop selection criteria
   - Develop profile of "ideal" applicant
   - Develop job advertisement/recruiting materials
2. Develop the Applicant Pool
   - Review state of the labour market
   - Consider employment equity issues
   - Determine whether recruitment will be internal or external
   - In a unionized workplace, identify any collective agreement clauses that apply
   - Identify target applicant pool
   - Identify recruitment methods to be used
   - Place ad/recruiting materials in agreed-on media
3. Screen the Applicant Pool
   - Determine whether applicant pool is large enough; if not, renew recruitment efforts
   - Screen job candidates' application forms and résumés
   - Conduct short screening interviews
   - Select "long list" of candidates for further review

4. Review and Selection of Job Applicants
    - Selection committee develops shortlist of candidates
    - Arrange visits of short-listed candidates to company
    - Conduct realistic job preview for candidates
    - Conduct valid and reliable employment tests
    - Conduct behavioural-based selection interview
    - Identify leading candidate(s) for position
    - Complete reference and background checks on leading candidates
    - Make hiring recommendation
    - Contingent on offer of employment, arrange for any required medical or physical examinations
5. Evaluate the Recruiting and Selection Effort
    - Review the recruiting and selection process: What went right? What went wrong?
    - Review the outcome of the recruiting process
    - Review the outcome of the selection process
    - Review the performance of people who were hired

Figure 1.1 presented two external factors that affect the HR system–namely, legislative requirements and the social/economic environment that play an important role in the recruitment and selection process. We will take a comprehensive look at legal and human rights issues in Chapter 3. Social/economic factors include, among others, global competition, rapid advances in information technology, changing workforce demographics, a unionized work environment, the economic context, and an organization's type and size and position in the marketplace. All of these social/economic factors have an impact on recruitment and selection procedures. Belcourt and McBey[10] present a detailed discussion of these topics in the context of strategic HR planning. We will, however, examine briefly the relationship of some of these issues to recruitment and selection.

// SOCIAL/ECONOMIC FACTORS AFFECTING RECRUITMENT AND SELECTION

GLOBAL COMPETITION

Foreign trade has always been vital to the Canadian economy, dating as far back as the trading of beaver pelts. As more than half of what is now produced in Canada is exported, we are extremely vulnerable to foreign market conditions. The KOF Swiss Economic Institute produces an annual globalization index of all countries in the world. It ranked Canada as the 12th most globalized country in the world out of the 191 countries it studied. By way of comparison, Ireland was ranked 1st and the United States was ranked 32nd. There has been a continual increase in globalization since 1970. The index is based on economic, social, and political globalization. The economic dimension of the KOF Index measures an actual trade and investment volume on the one hand, as well as the extent to which countries apply trade and capital movement restrictions to protect their own economies on the other hand. The social dimension of globalization reflects the extent of the dissemination of information and ideas, whereas the political dimension shows the degree of political cooperation between countries. Canada was near the top on the social globalization scale.[11]

Increasing globalization has changed the *level of competition* as new players enter international markets and trade barriers between countries are softened. In the retail sector, large U.S.-owned discount chains such as Costco, Walmart, and Target are serious

© iStock.com/NoDerog

© iStock.com/patty_c

threats to the survival of smaller, Canadian-owned retailers who must scramble to increase efficiencies and lower their operating costs. Canadian businesses must continually work on improving their competitiveness in providing goods and services domestically and internationally. Within the context of higher costs for HR in Canada, companies and organizations must find ways to become more efficient. One of the important ways is to find the best, most productive employees through the use of best practices in staffing that are outlined in this text.

© iStock.com/shaunl

RAPID ADVANCES IN TECHNOLOGY AND THE INTERNET

Technology is affecting every aspect of our lives, from the way we bank to the way we study and pursue our education. Employers now expect new hires to be computer literate. Employers are also using technology to a greater extent than ever before to recruit and select the best employees, including use of the Internet. Almost all recruiting by the Government of Canada is done through the Internet. Government websites offer job posting and résumé-matching services. According to the government, the benefits of e-recruiting, which we will discuss in greater detail in Chapter 6, are access to a larger pool of candidates, lower recruiting costs, eliminating printing costs and print media deadlines, and the capability for the immediate tracking of results.[12]

CHANGING WORKFORCE DEMOGRAPHICS[13]

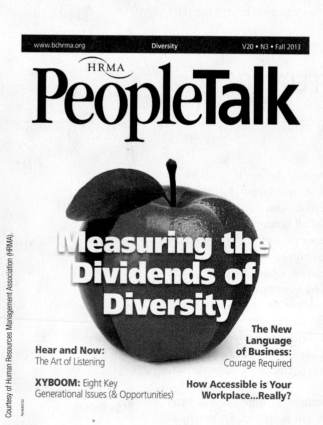

www.bchrma.org Diversity V20 • N3 • Fall 2013

HRMA PeopleTalk

Measuring the Dividends of Diversity

Hear and Now: The Art of Listening

The New Language of Business: Courage Required

XYBOOM: Eight Key Generational Issues (& Opportunities)

How Accessible is Your Workplace...Really?

Courtesy of Human Resources Management Association (HRMA).

The demographic makeup of the Canadian labour force is also undergoing significant transformations. Table 1.1 shows the age distribution of Canadians by province and territory based on the latest census data. The traditional working-age population–those between ages 18 and 64–constituted 68.5 percent of the population. The percentage of the population 65 or older grew from 13.7 percent in 2006 to 14.8 percent in 2011. Those of working age, 18–64, comprised 68.9 percent of the population with 42.4 percent between the ages of 45–64. For the first time there were more people in the 55–64 age group, where people begin to retire from the workforce, compared to those in the 15–24 age group, where people begin to enter the workforce. These changes have significant implications for human resources. The working population is getting older with fewer younger workers available.

One of the most significant changes in the Canadian workforce over the past five years has been the abolition of mandatory retirement at age 65 in most provinces and territories. Many older workers in good health see their work life continuing beyond age 65. With an aging population this trend will continue to increase. In an expanding economy, the addition of a significant number of older workers can be absorbed without much impact on unemployment rates, but in times of recession, the addition of post-65 workers leaves less room for hiring new entry-level employees.

TABLE 1.1

POPULATION ESTIMATES, AGE DISTRIBUTION AND MEDIAN AGE AS OF JULY 1, 2012, CANADA, PROVINCES AND TERRITORIES

	POPULATION	0 TO 14 YEARS	15 TO 64 YEARS	65 YEARS AND OVER	MEDIAN AGE
	Number	%			Years
Canada	**34,880,491**	**16.2**	**68.9**	**14.9**	**40.0**
Newfoundland and Labrador	512,659	14.8	68.6	16.6	44.2
Prince Edward Island	146,105	15.7	67.9	16.4	42.6
Nova Scotia	948,695	14.5	68.4	17.2	43.4
New Brunswick	755,950	15.0	68.1	17.0	43.4
Quebec	8,054,756	15.5	68.3	16.2	41.5
Ontario	13,505,900	16.3	69.1	14.6	39.8
Manitoba	1,267,003	18.8	67.0	14.2	37.6
Saskatchewan	1,079,958	19.1	66.2	14.7	37.1
Alberta	3,873,745	18.3	70.6	11.1	36.1
British Columbia	4,622,573	14.8	69.3	15.9	41.4
Yukon	36,101	17.1	73.5	9.4	39.4
Northwest Territories	43,349	21.4	72.4	6.2	32.1
Nunavut	33,697	31.7	64.9	3.3	24.7

Source: Statistics Canada, *Annual Demographic Estimates: Canada, Provinces and Territories*, Catalogue No. 91-215-X. Accessed May 20, 2014. http://www.statcan.gc.ca/pub/91-215-x/2012000/t583-eng.htm. Reproduced and distributed on an "as is" basis with the permission of Statistics Canada.

In the past, retirement at age 65 was seen as a graceful way of having employees leave the workforce without any evaluation of their performance. Post-65 workers will pose a problem for human resources. When is it time for an employee to retire and what incentives or procedures should be put in place to encourage post-65 retirement? On the other hand, this age group may present a very experienced applicant pool when the number of younger workers is decreasing, as appears to be the case now in Canada. HR departments will have to develop policies that are defensible to deal with the recruitment, selection, and evaluation of older workers and to recruit a decreasing supply of younger workers. HR policies will have to accommodate these demographic changes.

The Canadian workforce is also more gender balanced, with males comprising 70.3 percent of those between 15 and 65 and women comprising 68.5 percent. Since women live longer than men on average, it is not surprising that they comprise 15.6 percent of the population of age 65 or older with men comprising 12.6 percent of that demographic. The workforce is also more highly educated, with 64.1 percent of those between age 25 and 65 holding a certificate, diploma, bachelor's, or postgraduate degree from a trade school, college/CEGEP, or university.[14]

The Canadian labour force is more culturally diverse than at any other time in Canadian history. Table 1.2 presents the composition of the total number of visible minorities and Aboriginal people in the Canadian population, with a breakdown by major subgroups. In 2011, visible minorities comprised 19.07 percent of the Canadian population compared to 16.20 percent in 2006. Aboriginal peoples make up 4.26 percent in 2011 compared to 3.75 percent in 2006.[15]

Today, women, visible minorities, and Aboriginal people make up a significant percentage of entrants into an increasingly older Canadian labour force. Visible minorities possess expertise, skills, knowledge of foreign cultures and business practices, and

TABLE 1.2

VISIBLE MINORITY AND CANADIAN ABORIGINAL POPULATIONS BROKEN DOWN BY SUBGROUPS

2011	NUMBER	PERCENT
Total—Population by visible minority	32,852,320	100.00
Total visible minority population	6,264,750	19.07
South Asian	1,567,400	4.77
Chinese	1,324,745	4.03
Black	945,665	2.88
Filipino	619,310	1.88
Latin American	381,280	1.16
Arab	380,620	1.15
Southeast Asian	312,080	0.95
West Asian	206,840	0.63
Korean	161,130	0.40
Japanese	87,265	0.26
Visible minority, group not indicated	106,475	0.32
Multiple visible minorities	171,935	0.52
Aboriginal	1,400,685	4.26
First Nations	851,560	2.59
Metis	451,795	1.38
Inuit	59,440	0.18
Multiple identities	37,890	0.12

Source: Statistics Canada, 2011 *National Household Survey*. Accessed May 21, 2014. http://www12.statcan.gc.ca/nhs-enm/2011/dp-pd/dt-td/Index-eng.cfm. Reproduced and distributed on an "as is" basis with the permission of Statistics Canada.

natural trade links with overseas markets that are of value to employers in the current global economy.

Special challenges but tremendous opportunities emerge from having a workplace that is increasingly diverse in functional expertise, gender, age, and culture. Additionally, there exists a growing population of people who have physical or mental challenges. Employers cannot discriminate against existing or potential employees with respect to non-job-related characteristics. They must hire on the basis of an applicant possessing the knowledge, skills, and abilities or other characteristics that are necessary to perform a job. Best practices in staffing will not only find the best employees but also help to establish recruitment and selection systems that are legally defensible. In Chapter 3 we will discuss employment equity and human rights legislation that pertains to women, age demographics, visible minorities, Aboriginal people, and those with physical or mental disabilities.

THE ECONOMIC CONTEXT

The state of the economy has a profound effect on staffing. Economic booms bring with them skilled labour shortages, so recruitment and retention take on strategic importance and are given high priority. Economic slowdowns or recessions, as we have experienced in the recent past, generally lead to cutbacks in jobs, pay, and benefits, or hiring freezes. In a slowdown many qualified people are looking for jobs, so recruitment may be easier for companies that are hiring; however, there are also more unqualified applications to review. The number of people in the applicant pool has a major impact on the quality of those people who are selected for employment. If there are critical shortages of skilled labour or professionals, more emphasis must be placed on recruitment, and companies may become less selective. The controversial Temporary Foreign Workers Program was designed to address perceived labour shortages among skilled occupations. At the end of 2012, there were nearly 340 000 temporary foreign workers in Canada.[16] On the other hand, employers can take advantage of an oversupply of labour by placing less emphasis on recruitment and becoming more selective in hiring people.

TYPE OF ORGANIZATION

The public sector, both federal and provincial, tends to have more formalized recruitment and selection systems. Governments are accountable to their electorates for managing public employees and, with the exception of political appointees, have established fair recruitment and selection procedures that in most cases follow accepted professional standards. Public services tend to be highly unionized (70 percent versus 20 percent in the private sector)[17] and to follow negotiated processes for recruitment and selection.

In the private sector, recruitment and selection procedures may vary by the type and size of the business or industry. A large segment of the Canadian economy is based on small or family-run enterprises. The selection procedures in these types of business may be more informal, as the owners may not have the resources to implement sophisticated selection systems. Smaller organizations tend to rely on family and friends of current workers for recruitment of new workers and to use, at most, an unstructured interview in making a selection decision. This is one reason we use more examples from the public sector in this book. In general, larger organizations, public or private, are more likely to use formal recruitment and selection procedures. The challenge for HR is to increase the use of best practices regardless of sector or the size of an organization.

ORGANIZATIONAL RESTRUCTURING

At the same time that technology is reducing the need for labour, organizations must cope with a large segment of their workforce that is approaching retirement. To cope with these changes, employers have implemented non-age-related layoffs and early-retirement incentive packages, and have restructured or downsized their enterprises. Most notably, the traditional organizational structure of a pyramid, with a broad base of employees at entry-level positions and fewer employees at each of several higher levels, is being flattened. In the coming years, as aging "boomers" retire, will there be an adequate labour supply to replace them? In a seller's market, more emphasis will have to be placed on recruiting, as more organizations compete to hire fewer qualified candidates. Best practices in recruiting and selection will be essential in finding the right employees for an organization.

REDEFINING JOBS

In today's information era, workers are required to apply a wider range of skills to an ever-changing series of tasks. Individuals just entering the workforce may face at least three to four career changes in their lifetime. Younger workers today, unlike their parents, rarely expect to spend their entire working life with the same organization. Employers will expect workers to possess the skills and knowledge of two or three traditional employees. On the factory floor, jobs are moving targets, as they change rapidly. Workers themselves may be asked to move or rotate among positions; to do so they will need to have or be able to acquire multiple generic skills and competencies. This poses special challenges when trying to match people to jobs. Does it make sense to select people on the basis of very specific skills and abilities required by one job? Should employers redefine recruitment and selection in terms of finding people with broader skills or competencies that are of value to the organization and cut across many jobs? Using the procedures outlined in this text will help to answer these questions.

UNIONIZED WORK ENVIRONMENTS

Approximately 30 percent of employees in Canada work in a unionized environment. This figure compares to about 12 percent in the United States and over 70 percent in Europe. These figures may be misleading; looking at the rates by sector shows that employees in public or government organizations are considerably higher. In Canada about 20 percent of private organizations are unionized compared to over 70 percent of the public sector.[18]

The negotiated collective agreements in place in unionized workplaces generally address issues of recruitment and selection. Most agreements require the employer to post any job vacancies in the unit covered by the collective agreement before they can be advertised more broadly. The agreements may also specify how competitions for vacant positions are carried out including the selection procedures. In many cases, employee seniority may be a deciding factor in awarding a job to an internal applicant. Recruitment and Selection Today 1.1 provides an example of a job posting article from a collective agreement.

HR practitioners working in a unionized environment must know the requirements of any applicable collective agreement with respect to recruitment and selection

RECRUITMENT AND SELECTION TODAY 1.1

A job posting in the Collective Agreement between Thompson Rivers University and Canadian Union of Public Employees Local 4879

ARTICLE 11: FILLING OF VACANT POSITIONS

(a) Job Postings

When a position of four (4) months duration or longer in the bargaining unit is vacant or newly created, the Employer shall provide the Union President with a copy of the Job Posting and post notice of the position on the Employer's designated bulletin boards for a minimum of ten (10) working days in order that all members will know about the position and be able to make written application. The posting shall indicate that the position is open to both male and female applicants and shall contain the following information: Nature of position, qualifications required, hours of work, rate of pay and posting period.

A decision to fill or not to fill a position will be made within one month of the vacancy occurring. If the decision is made to fill a position, the appointment will be announced within one month of the close of the posting. Such announcements will be in the form of electronic mail. Employees will receive the new rate of pay at the time of filling the position or fifteen (15) working days from the date of his/her appointment, whichever first occurs.

Vacancies that are going to be filled will be posted within ten (10) working days of the decision to fill being made.

(b) Method of Making Appointments

Both parties recognize that job opportunity should increase in proportion to length of service; therefore, appointments to positions within the bargaining unit shall be made based on the applicant's seniority, qualifications, abilities and skills to perform the functions of the position. The Employer shall give consideration to an employee who does not possess all of the required skills for a position, but who is currently involved in courses or training that will enable him/her to fulfill the requirements of the position.

No external applicants shall be considered for a position within the bargaining unit until the applications of internal employees have been fully processed and the internal applicants have been issued a letter from the Human Resources Department.

Successful applicants shall be notified within five (5) working days of the completion of the selection process.

Grievances resulting from the application of this clause shall be filed in writing to the Employer within fifteen (15) working days of the notification of the Employer's decision.

(c) Trial Period

Any internal employee newly appointed to a continuing position within the bargaining unit shall work a three (3) month trial period. No later than ten (10) working days prior to the end of the trial period, the employee's supervisor will prepare a written performance evaluation which will state whether the employee has met the performance criteria necessary for the position. The supervisor shall at this time discuss the evaluation with the employee and provide the employee with a copy of the evaluation. The successful applicant shall receive the rate for the new position from the date they fill the new position or fifteen (15) work days from the date of their appointment, whichever first occurs.

(d) Result of Trial Period

If the evaluation carried out at the end of the trial period is satisfactory, the employee will continue in the position. If the evaluation is unsatisfactory, the following conditions shall apply:

(1) Employees who were previously ongoing shall return to their previous positions.

(2) Employees who were previously on the recall list shall return to the recall list where they left off.

(3) Auxiliary employees will return to the auxiliary list.

(4) After interviewing, the next senior qualified internal employee who applied for the original posting will be offered the position.

Note: Some clauses in the article related to temporary employees and positions have been deleted. The complete collective agreement may be found at http://cupe4879.ca/main/sites/default/files/CUPE%20Collective%20Agreement%202010%202014.pdf

Source: Courtesy of the Canadian Union of Public Employees Local 4879 and Thompson Rivers University. These materials contain information that has been derived from information originally made available by CUPE4879, they are not however an official version. The complete collective agreement may found at http://cupe4879.ca/main/sites/default/files/CUPE%20Collective%20Agreement%202010%202014.pdf

procedures. Failure to follow the procedures outlined in the agreement may lead to grievances and arbitration, even if the HR practitioner is concerned about the soundness of the negotiated procedures from a technical standpoint. The best way to improve the procedures is to have HR involved in the negotiating process.

BEST PRACTICES

To remain competitive, organizations must have in place HR strategies for recruiting, identifying, and selecting employees who will contribute to the overall effectiveness of the organization. With respect to recruitment and selection, the old ways of hiring on the basis of a résumé and a brief interview (or on whom you know) do not work in the new economy. Those old practices may also lead an employer astray of new legal requirements as well as to an underperforming organization.

The socio-economic changes taking place in today's workplace have an impact on HR recruitment and selection. Today, more than ever before, effective recruitment and selection matter. Figure 1.1 illustrated that recruitment and selection do not take place in isolation. They are influenced not only by the events occurring in broader society that affect the organization as a whole, but also by the somewhat narrower context of the organization itself. Recruitment and selection play an important role in the human resources management (HRM) function. Effective HRM contributes to organizational survival, success, and renewal.[19]

How do employers ensure that the people they hire will have the knowledge, skills, and abilities needed to perform the jobs for which they are being hired? How do employers decide that one candidate has "more" of the required abilities than another? More fundamentally, how do employers know that the knowledge, skills, and abilities that they seek in new hires are actually needed for a specific job? How do employers ensure that their hiring policies and procedures will treat candidates from different gender and ethnic groups fairly, as part of the recruitment and selection process? How do employers accommodate people with disabilities in both recruitment and selection? These are just a few of the questions that must be addressed by any HR manager or practitioner in setting up a recruitment and selection system. These are some of the questions we will seek to answer throughout this book.

// A SYSTEMS VIEW OF HR

Two basic principles underlie the model presented in Figure 1.1:

- **Principle 1:** HRM must carefully coordinate its activities with the other organizational units and people if the larger system is to function properly.
- **Principle 2:** Human resources managers must think in systems terms and have the welfare of the whole organization in mind.

If HR managers fail to recognize the contributions of the others in the organization or if they fail to coordinate their efforts with other system components, senior management may begin to question the added value that human resources brings to the firm. Human resources must be fully in touch with the needs of the larger organization and play a strategic role in the organization. As a staff unit, the role of human resources is to support line units pursuing the central mission of the organization. HR professionals must have an understanding and appreciation of their interdependencies with, and reliance on, other stakeholders throughout the organization. Recruitment and selection must be carried out in the context of the system, not simply as an isolated function divorced from other aspects of the organization.

Recruitment and selection set the stage for other human resources interventions. If recruitment and selection are done properly, the subsequent movement of the worker through the organizational system is made easier and the individual makes a long-term, positive contribution to organizational survival and success. When this happens, HRM makes a positive contribution to the organizational system as a whole. Conversely, if the worker enters the organization on a flat trajectory because of poor recruitment and selection, then the entire system, including HR, is adversely affected. The HRM function becomes less of an organizational asset. In today's competitive, ever-changing, and unforgiving business environment, HR must be seen as an effective change agent or face a grim (but deserved) fate at the hands of results-oriented senior managers.

// RECRUITMENT AND SELECTION AND THE HR PROFESSION

We have emphasized the need for HR staff to be aware of both the external and the internal influences that affect the working environment in which organizations operate. We have also argued that HR staff must not become isolated within the organization. There is another aspect to isolation: HR staff are professionals who must keep abreast of developments in their field through continuous learning. HR staff are responsible for knowing the latest legal and scientific information with respect to recruitment and selection. They are responsible for implementing policies and procedures that are in accordance with accepted professional standards.

Recruitment and selection activities within HRM are frequently carried out by in-house HR staff, sometimes assisted by consultants from management consulting firms. These in-house staff and consultants come to HRM from various educational

RECRUITMENT AND SELECTION TODAY 1.2

SEVERAL CAREER PATHS INTO RECRUITMENT AND SELECTION

Ms. L. became interested in HRM while taking a business program at a community college. After obtaining her college degree, she took eight courses in order to earn a certificate in Human Resources Management. Since then, Ms. L. has worked as an HR specialist in a large manufacturing plant, where she has run an assessment centre used by her employer to hire new workers. Ms. L. hopes to eventually move into a senior HRM position with her present employer or with a similar company in the manufacturing sector.

Mr. R. moved into the field after completing his degree in sociology at university. He started work in the HR department of an aircraft parts manufacturer and, over the following year, earned a Human Resources Certificate. Following completion of his HR program, he accepted a more senior HR position with a new employer. Much of his time is spent in recruitment and selection activities, especially in monitoring the results of an employment equity program put in place by his current employer.

Ms. S. obtained a bachelor's degree in psychology and became interested in personnel psychology. She went on to complete a two-year graduate program in industrial and organizational psychology. Since receiving her master's degree, Ms. S. has worked in the HR department of a major urban hospital, where her primary duties are testing and interviewing job applicants for various hospital positions. Her other duties focus on compensation and benefits.

Ms. M. also received a master's degree in industrial and organizational psychology, but continued her studies to obtain a Ph.D. She works for an internationally based consulting firm, where she designs and implements large-scale recruitment and selection systems for banks, insurance companies, and other financial institutions. She is now a partner with the consulting firm and takes regular overseas assignments to assist clients in Europe and Asia with installation and maintenance of their selection systems.

backgrounds, which are augmented by practical experience in managing HR (see Recruitment and Selection Today 1.2).

Many practitioners and consultants involved in HRM hold membership in one or more professional associations and may be certified or registered with an association or professional licensing body in their area of specialization. Recruitment and Selection Today 1.3 gives some basic information on associations having an interest in recruitment and selection practices in Canada. These associations have professional involvement well beyond recruitment and selection. With membership in these associations come certain rights and obligations, including adherence to ethical codes or standards.

Only recently has the HR field gained recognition as an independent profession. Regardless of the educational and experiential routes taken into the HR profession, today there is an increasing emphasis on HR professionals holding the Certified Human Resources Professional (CHRP) designation. Legislation in Ontario and Quebec governs use of the designation. Recruitment and Selection Notebook 1.2 gives an overview of the requirements for the new, national CHRP designation.

Maintaining memberships in professional associations keeps the HR professional from becoming isolated and provides assistance when the practitioner encounters ethical difficulties. Professional associations have developed well-thought-out codes of conduct and behaviour that are designed to protect both the HR professionals and their clients. These codes help the professional to act in a manner that will be accepted by others in the profession. Whenever possible, we will use these codes to guide our discussion on recruitment and selection practices, as should any HR professional.

RECRUITMENT AND SELECTION TODAY 1.3

LINKS TO PROFESSIONAL ASSOCIATIONS INVOLVED IN RECRUITMENT AND SELECTION

Canadian Council of Human Resources Associations (CCHRA)

(HTTP://WWW.CHRP.CA/?PAGE=ABOUT_CCHRA)

The CCHRA is a collaborative effort of provincial and specialist HR associations. Its website provides links to each member organization. The mission of the CCHRA includes establishing national core standards for the HR profession and being the recognized resource on equivalency for HR qualifications across Canada.

MEMBERSHIP QUALIFICATIONS

Practitioners and students join provincial associations, not the CCHRA. Membership requirements vary and can be found on each provincial association's website. Generally, provincial associations require completion of education and training as described under their professional certification requirements; student memberships are normally available for those taking approved courses in a postsecondary or degree program.

PROFESSIONAL CERTIFICATION OFFERED

The Certified Human Resources Professional (CHRP) designation recognizes achievement within the HR field and the holder's distinguished professionalism (see Recruitment and Selection Notebook 1.2). To receive this designation, practitioners may have to complete accredited courses, have had supervised professional experience in HR, or other requirements as specified by their provincial HR association (e.g., Human Resources Association of Nova Scotia: HRANS).

Canadian Psychological Association (including the Canadian Society for Industrial and Organizational Psychology)

HTTP://WWW.CPA.CA

The CPA is a national organization that represents all aspects of psychology, including industrial and organizational psychology and psychological testing and assessment. Psychologists, particularly practitioners, may also be members of provincial psychological associations. The CPA website contains links to provincial associations, provincial regulatory bodies, and psychology programs at Canadian universities.

The Canadian Society for Industrial and Organizational Psychology (CSIOP) comprises CPA members and other professionals with a particular interest in personnel psychology and organizational behaviour. More information on CSIOP can be found at http://psychology.uwo.ca/csiop

MEMBERSHIP QUALIFICATIONS

Master's or Ph.D. degree in psychology.

PROFESSIONAL CERTIFICATION OFFERED

Neither CPA nor CSIOP offers professional designations. Psychology is regulated at the provincial level through legislation. In order to use the designation "psychologist," an individual must be registered with a provincial regulatory body after meeting its educational, supervised practice, and other requirements.

// AN INTRODUCTION TO ETHICAL ISSUES AND PROFESSIONAL STANDARDS

Ethics
The determination of right and wrong; the standards of appropriate conduct or behaviour for members of a profession: what those members may or may not do.

Ethics are the means by which we distinguish what is right from what is wrong, what is moral from what is immoral, what may be done from what may not be done. Of course, the laws of our country also tell us what is or is not permissible by imposing penalties, such as fines or imprisonment, on violators. Ethics is a difficult subject because it deals with the large grey area between those behaviours that society punishes as illegal and

RECRUITMENT AND SELECTION NOTEBOOK 1.2

THE CHRP EDGE

There are six characteristics that define a profession:

1. A common body of knowledge;
2. Agreed performance standards;
3. A representative professional organization;
4. External perception as a profession;
5. A code of ethics; and
6. Agreed certification procedure.

Applicants for the CHRP first have to join their provincial HR association and then pass a knowledge examination of topics in HR, including recruitment and selection. After gaining experience in the profession, CHRP candidates (a designation bestowed on those who pass the first examination) are required to have their professional experience reviewed by a panel of experts.

The required professional capabilities (RPCs) form the basis of qualifications that an applicant must demonstrate before receiving the CHRP designation. Once granted the CHRP designation, HR professionals are required to keep abreast of current developments in their field through a recertification process based on continuous learning. More information on the CHRP designation process can be obtained from either your local HR association or from the national CHRP website (http://www.chrp.ca).

Why bother going to this trouble to get a CHRP designation? A CHRP identifies you as possessing the required knowledge and skills and as someone who will behave ethically. A survey of employers by the Human Resources Professionals Association of Ontario shows that CHRPs have an edge in:

- Getting jobs;
- Keeping jobs;
- Financial compensation; and
- Stakeholders' perceptions of their achievement.

Increasingly, employers are requiring the CHRP for employment of HR professionals.

Source: M. Belcourt and A. Templar. 2002. "The CHRP Edge." *HR Professional* (April/May): 30–33, 36–39. Reprinted with permission.

those that everyone readily agrees are noble and upright. A careful consideration of ethics is important because HRM requires the balancing of the rights and interests of management with those of workers, as well as the rights and interests of the HR professional with those of the larger society (see Recruitment and Selection Notebook 1.3).

Professional standards
Professional standards provide guidance on how HR professionals should behave in certain situations including the use of employment tests.

Professional standards follow from a code of ethics and provide guidance on how members should behave in certain situations. In the HR context of recruitment and selection, professional standards offer advice on things such as the appropriate use of employment tests, the standards that different tests must meet, and the qualifications of those using the employment tests.

Ethical standards regulate the behaviour of those using employment tests. In the case of psychologists, the Canadian Code of Ethics for Psychologists*[20] specifies four principles on which ethical behaviour is based:

1. respect for dignity of persons;
2. responsible caring;
3. integrity in relationships; and
4. responsibility to society.

RECRUITMENT AND SELECTION NOTEBOOK 1.3

LOOKING FOR COMMON GROUND: ETHICAL CODES

The professional associations described in Recruitment and Selection Today 1.3 have ethical codes that apply to their members. In all of these codes, members are required to obey the laws of the country, avoid conflicts of interest, and remain current in their fields of expertise. In addition, these ethics codes outline other obligations that their members have to clients, management, and workers, as well as to the larger society. One of the principles in the National Code of Ethics of the Canadian Council of Human Resources Associations, states that CHRPs shall "commit to the values of respect for human dignity and human rights, and promote human development in the workplace, within the profession and society as a whole."

The CPA's Canadian Code of Ethics for Psychologists presents the following four ethical principles, which provide a guide for individual ethical decision making: respect for the dignity of persons, responsible caring, integrity in relationships, and responsibility to society.

All of these ethical codes place constraints on what their members may and may not do when practising HRM, including recruitment and selection. However, ethical decision making is not always clear-cut; often decisions must be made in the grey areas of ethics where reasonable people differ in what they consider to be right and wrong. To complicate matters even more, an action that is considered ethical under one code might be deemed unethical under another. These inconsistencies can and do occur because the CCHRA and CPA ethical codes differ in content, scope, and emphasis. The bottom line to this discussion is that ethics is a complex matter and has the potential to be the Achilles' heel of many a promising HR career. Professionals practising recruitment and selection should read carefully the ethical codes that apply to them and their work, and then discuss the codes with colleagues.

The CCHRA National Code of Ethics can be found at: http://www.chrp.ca/?page=Code_of_Ethics. The CPA Canadian Code of Ethics for Psychologists can be found at: http://www.cpa.ca/aboutcpa/committees/ethics/codeofethics.

The ethical standards related to each of these principles apply to all testing carried out by psychologists. These ethical standards cover issues such as confidentiality of test results, informed consent, and the competence of those administering and interpreting the test results. The foremost concern is to protect the welfare and dignity of those being tested. A consumer or client may bring any concerns over a psychologist's use of tests, including selection tests, to appropriate regulatory bodies.

The Certified Human Resources Professional (CHRP) ethical code* that applies to HR practitioners specifies principles similar to those in the CPA Code of Ethics. Notably, CHRPs must:

- Support, promote, and apply the principles of human rights, equity, dignity, and respect in the workplace, within the profession, and in society as a whole.
- Adhere to any statutory acts, regulations, or bylaws that relate to the field of HRM, as well as all civil and criminal laws, regulations, and statutes that apply in one's jurisdiction.
- Not knowingly or otherwise engage in or condone any activity or attempt to circumvent the clear intention of the law.
- Strive to balance organizational and employee needs and interests in the practice of the profession.

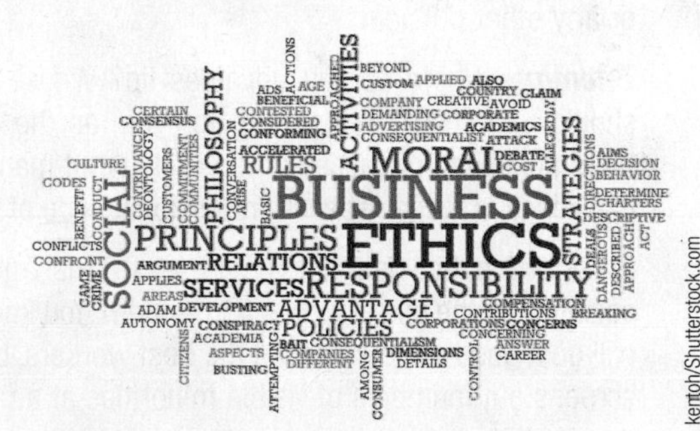

kenton/Shutterstock.com

// ETHICAL DILEMMAS IN RECRUITMENT AND SELECTION

Ethical dilemmas frequently occur during the employment testing of job applicants with various selection tools during the selection process. From a legal standpoint, an employment interview is subject to the same set of regulations and ethical considerations as any other employment test and must meet professional standards when used in making high-stakes decisions. We present three examples of ethical dilemmas in Recruitment and Selection Today 1.4 that will help to illustrate why codes of ethics are so important and why a professional may need assistance in deciding how to behave.

Ethical dilemmas raise difficult questions that cut to the very core of ethics. But such questions are unavoidable because ethics are central to any group representing itself as a professional association. Fortunately, professional HR associations in Canada have written codes and standards to provide guidance on ethical matters to their members. Violations of these codes and standards may result in professional censure, embarrassment, and, in the most serious cases, removal from the

RECRUITMENT AND SELECTION TODAY 1.4

ETHICAL DILEMMAS

1. ***Situation.*** You are a management consultant who is asked by a large employer to design and implement a system to select workers for a manufacturing plant. The plant is unionized, and there is a history of poor union–management relations. Management informs you that it intends to break the union and, as a part of this effort, you are to come up with a selection system that will screen out all new job applicants having pro-union attitudes. The idea is to skew the workforce toward management so that the union can be broken in a future decertification vote. What's more, you are to keep the purpose of the selection system a secret and are asked by management to sign a contract in which you promise not to reveal its intentions to the union, the labour board, or any other outsiders.

Dilemma. Where do your loyalties lie? Whose interests should you serve? Is it wrong for you, as the management consultant, to accept a fee to do what management is asking? Is it against your professional code of ethics?

2. ***Situation.*** Imagine that you are an HR manager who is considering the use of a selection system. You know that it will do a good job at selecting the best workers, but it also screens out members of visible minorities at a rate much greater than that for the white majority.

Dilemma. Should you use this system that will improve productivity, or try to find another that does not screen out so many members of visible-minority groups, but may not be as effective? What if the new system does not do as good a job at selecting the best workers? Should you favour societal goals of increasing visible-minority representation in the workforce or the interests of your company? Does the selection system violate your code of ethics or legal requirements?

3. ***Situation.*** You have been directed by your manager to find a way to reduce employee theft. You believe that this can be accomplished by screening out people who fail a commercially available "honesty" test. You purchase the test and administer it to all current employees and new applicants and reject or dismiss those who fail the test, including long-term employees with no history of dishonesty.

Dilemma. Should you be concerned that the test is screening out honest people? Should you be concerned about the reliability and validity of the test and whether it is appropriate to use in your situation? Should you be concerned about wrongful dismissal lawsuits on the part of employees, or human rights actions on the part of applicants? Does use of the tests violate your code of ethics, or the law? Can you defend your actions?

RECRUITMENT AND SELECTION NOTEBOOK 1.4

USEFUL HR WEBSITES

Human Resources–Related Organizations

Academy of Management	http://www.aom.org
Administrative Sciences Association of Canada	http://www.asac.ca
American Psychological Association	http://www.apa.org
BC Human Resources Management Association	http://hrcouncil.ca/hr-toolkit/Provincial HRAssociations.cfm
Canadian Council of Human Resources Associations	http://www.chrp.ca/
Canadian Psychological Association	http://www.cpa.ca
Canadian Society for Industrial & Organizational Psychology	http://psychology.uwo.ca/csiop
Employment and Social Development Canada	http://www.esdc.gc.ca
Human Resources Association of New Brunswick	http://www.hranb.org
Human Resources Association of Nova Scotia	http://www.hrans.org
Human Resources Institute of Alberta	http://www.hria.ca
Human Resources Management Association of Manitoba	http://www.hrmam.org
Human Resources Professionals Association (Ontario+)	http://www.hrpa.ca
International Personnel Assessment Council	http://www.ipacweb.org
International Public Management Association for Human Resources	http://www.ipma-hr.org
Ordre des conseillers en ressources humaines agréés	http://www.portailrh.org
Saskatchewan Association of Human Resource Professionals	http://www.sahrp.ca
Society for Human Resource Management	http://www.shrm.org
Society for Industrial and Organizational Psychology	http://www.siop.org

Human Resources Information Sources

Canadian Business	http://www.canadianbusiness.com
Canadian HR Reporter	http://www.hrreporter.com
Career Outlook	http://www.bls.gov/careeroutlook
Globe and Mail Report on Business	http://www.reportonbusiness.com
HRFocus	http://www.hrfocus.co.za
HR-Guide.com	http://www.hr-guide.com
HR Magazine	http://www.shrm.org/hrmagazine
HR Performance Solutions	http://www.hrperformancesolutions.net
People Management	http://www.cipd.co.uk/pm
Statistics Canada	http://www.statcan.gc.ca
Workforce	http://www.workforce.com

profession. Membership in the profession is based on adherence to its ethics and professional standards. Membership in the professional association is a public guarantee that the member operates in accordance with accepted principles. Naturally, these codes should factor heavily into the recruitment and selection work done by HR professionals and described in this book.

// HUMAN RESOURCES AND THE INTERNET

One of the most significant developments in recent years has been the growth of the Internet, which has made available to students and practitioners a vast array of resources and information related to every aspect of recruitment and selection. It is impossible to list every HR resource that is available on the Internet. Recruitment and Selection Notebook 1.4 lists some websites that we feel are very relevant to recruitment and selection. We have also listed throughout each chapter Web-related resources that provide more specific information on topics being discussed in the chapter. And, in Chapter 6, we provide extensive information on Internet-based recruitment and selection.

The URLs provided were correct when this edition was printed, but URLs often change. If a URL produces an error message, use the name of the association for an Internet search. In Chapter 6, we provide extensive information on Internet-based recruitment and selection. We suggest that you try out the websites we have listed. Also, in those cases where we do not list a website and you need more information, Google the key terms or phrases.

// SUMMARY

Effective recruitment and selection are important because they contribute to organizational productivity and worker growth. Recruitment and selection practices, which have found a place in organization practices, play an essential role in contemporary organizations. Effective human resource management, including recruitment and selection, must be carried out within the context of an organizational system, as well as that of the external environment. In both cases, the HR professional must not become isolated. In recognition of this, professional associations and groups exist to help HR professionals and their clients through ethical codes and standards of practice. Codes of ethics are important to HR as it continues to develop as a profession. This chapter also recognizes the increasing use of the Internet by HR professionals and provides Internet addresses for HR organizations and resources.

KEY TERMS

Ethics, p. 17
Human Resources Information Systems, p. 3
Professional standards, p. 18
Recruitment, p. 4
Selection, p. 5
Talent management, p. 3

WEB LINKS

More information on the national standards for the CHRP designation can be found at:
http://www.chrp.ca

Canadian demographic information is available at Statistics Canada:
http://www.statcan.gc.ca

The CCHRA National Code of Ethics:
http://www.chrp.ca/?page=Code_of_Ethics

The CPA Canadian Code of Ethics for Psychologists:
http://www.cpa.ca/aboutcpa/committees/ethics/codeofethics

DISCUSSION QUESTIONS

1. How can HR professionals demonstrate that they add value to a company's bottom line?
2. What are possible consequences of using poor or outdated recruitment and selection practices?
3. What are the advantages of obtaining a professional designation such as CHRP?
4. Discuss the impact that current socio-economic conditions are having on recruitment and selection practices.
5. What are ethics and how do they relate to recruitment and selection?

EXERCISES

1. Visit the Statistics Canada website to determine the current socio-economic and demographic composition of the Canadian workforce. Identify how these factors may have an impact on HR recruitment and selection. Illustrate with examples.
2. Think of a job you have held and write two brief profiles of that job. The first profile is to be that of a 95th-percentile job performer–that is, a person you have worked with who would be better than 95 out of 100 of his or her coworkers. What was that person like? What skills and abilities did he or she have? Then write a second profile of a 5th-percentile job performer–a person who was only as good as the bottom 5 percent of his or her coworkers. Compare the profiles and discuss how use of recruitment and selection might be helpful in choosing the 95th- rather than the 5th-percentile performer. How much difference would it make to have the 95th- rather than the 5th-percentile performer on the job? If you were the employer, would these differences be of sufficient value for you to invest the necessary money into recruitment and selection in order to get the 95th-percentile performer?
3. As a class or in small groups, discuss the three scenarios raised in the ethics section of this chapter. Decide what the HR professional should do in each instance, and provide an ethical justification for your decision based on the CCHRA Code of Ethics.
4. Write a brief summary of your preferred career track in HRM. What professional associations would you join and what activities would you engage in? Where do recruitment and selection fit in the mix of activities that you have planned for yourself?

CASE

The Toyota (Cambridge, Ontario) plant exemplifies the changing workplace requirements described in this chapter and their impact on HR practices. Toyota is a Japanese company that competes in the global marketplace. It has production facilities in many countries where labour costs are high, yet it strives to maintain a very efficient workforce. One reason for Toyota's ability to be an effective producer is its use of empirically proven recruitment and selection practices.

Toyota's recruitment and selection practices are designed to find the best possible people to hire, whether the job being staffed is on the shop floor or at the executive level. In 1996, Toyota received thousands of applications for 1200 blue-collar positions. As part of its hiring procedure, Toyota took prospective employees through a rigorous, comprehensive, multi-stage assessment process. According to Sandie Halyk, assistant general manager for HR, Toyota "wants people who take pride in their work and are able to work well with others. If you're not comfortable working for a team, you won't be comfortable working here."

The selection process involved realistic job previews, paper-and-pencil cognitive ability and personality assessments, tests of fine and gross motor coordination, work samples, and structured employment interviews. The work sample alone entailed a six-hour manufacturing assembly exercise that involved individual and group problem solving. Group leaders and first-line supervisors were active participants in the panel selection interview. For those "making the grade," references were checked, and health and fitness tests were undertaken by those given conditional offers of employment. The process was designed to "find out if you're able to identify problems and do something about them, and to ensure a good fit between the company and the new employee."

Source: G. Keenan. 1996. "Toyota's Hunt for 1,200 Team Players." *The Globe and Mail* (January 5): B7. Reprinted with permission from *The Globe and Mail.*

QUESTIONS

The intent of this exercise is not to have you develop detailed answers but to begin thinking about the many factors that affect recruitment and selection. We appreciate that the case does not contain detailed information but in our opinion that information is not needed to meet our primary objective. We will review in detail many of the components of Toyota's selection procedures later in this text. For now, we would like you to discuss the following points, but first you may find it useful to review Figure 1.1 and to read the article on "Candidate Glut" published by SHRM at http://www.shrm.org/Publications/hrmagazine/EditorialContent/Pages/0803frase-blunt.aspx

1. Is Toyota's elaborate selection system justified? What are appropriate criteria for assessing its effectiveness?
2. Toyota received over 40 000 applications for 1200 positions. Is this an effective approach? What is the cost, particularly the human cost, associated with reviewing all of these applications? How do you reduce the number of applicants to a reasonable number that can be run through the selection system?

3. What are some of the cultural issues that might arise with a Japanese-managed auto plant located in Ontario?
4. Provide examples of how technology might be used to facilitate and improve the recruitment and selection used by Toyota.
5. What criteria should Toyota use in selecting "team players"?

// ENDNOTES

1 Ployhart, R.E., C.H. Van Iddekinge, and W.I. MacKenzie Jr. 2011. "Acquiring and Developing Human Capital in Service Contexts: The Interconnectedness of Human Capital Resources." *Academy of Management Journal* 54: 353–68.

2 Koch, M.J., and R. Gunter-McGrath. 1996. "Improving Labor Productivity: Human Resource Management Policies Do Matter." *Strategic Management Journal* 17: 335–54.

3 Huselid, M.A. 1995. "The Impact of Human Resource Management Practices on Turnover, Productivity, and Corporate Financial Performance." *Academy of Management Journal* 38: 635–72.

4 Huselid, M.A. 1995.

5 d'Arcimoles, C.-H. 1997. "Human Resource Policies and Company Performance: A Quantitative Approach Using Longitudinal Data." *Organizational Studies* 18: 857–74.

6 Whitener, E.M. 1997. "The Impact of Human Resource Activities on Employee Trust." *Human Resource Management Review* 7: 38–39.

7 Jones, G.R., and P.M. Wright. 1992. "An Economic Approach to Conceptualizing the Utility of Human Resource Management Practices." In K.R. Rowland and G. Ferris, eds., *Research in Personnel and Human Resources Management*, vol. 10. Greenwich, CT: JAI Press.

8 Tamkin, P., M. Cowling, and W. Hunt. 2008. *People and the Bottom Line. Report 448*. London, UK: Institute for Employment Studies.

9 Wright, P.M., T.M. Gardner, and L.M. Moynihan. 2003. "The Impact of HR Practices on the Performance of Business Units. *Human Resources Management Journal*, 13, 21–36.

10 Belcourt, M., and K.J. McBey. 2010. *Strategic Human Resources Planning*, 4th ed. Toronto: Nelson.

11 Swiss Federal Institute of Technology, Zurich. 2014. "KOF Index of Globalization." Retrieved May 20, 2014, from http://globalization.kof.ethz.ch

12 Northwest Territories. "A Guide to Internet Recruiting." Retrieved May 20, 2014, from http://www.hr.gov.nt.ca/sites/default/files/documents/guidetointernetrecruiting.pdf

13 All demographic data in this section are from the 2011 census and are available from Statistics Canada at http://www12.statcan.gc.ca/census-recensement/index-eng.cfm

14 Statistics Canada, 2011 Census of Population. http://www12.statcan.gc.ca/census-recensement/index-eng.cfm

15 Ibid.

16 Canadian Council for Refugees. "Increase in Temporary Foreign Worker Numbers." Retrieved May 21, 2014, from https://ccrweb.ca/en/increase-temporary-foreign-worker-numbers

17 Perspectives on Labour and Income, 2007. Retrieved January 4, 2012, from http://www.statcan.gc.ca/bsolc/olc-cel/olc-cel?catno=75-001-X&lang=eng

18 Kelloway, E.K., V.M. Catano, and A.L. Day. 2011. *People and Work in Canada*. Toronto: Nelson.

19 Tamkin et al. 2008.

20 Canadian Psychological Association. 2000. *Code of Ethics*. Ottawa: Author. Available online at: http://www.cpa.ca/aboutcpa/committees/ethics/codeofethics/

CHAPTER 2

FOUNDATIONS OF RECRUITMENT AND SELECTION I:

Reliability and Validity

CHAPTER LEARNING OUTCOMES

This chapter develops the idea that personnel recruitment and selection strategies based on information obtained through scientific methods are more likely to benefit an organization than decisions based on impressions or intuition. The chapter begins with an illustration of a typical hiring process and goes on to examine basic concepts of reliability and validity that underlie contemporary recruitment and selection practices.

AFTER READING THIS CHAPTER YOU SHOULD:

- understand the basic components that make up a traditional personnel selection model;
- have a good understanding of the concepts of reliability and validity;
- recognize the importance and necessity of establishing the reliability and validity of measures used in personnel selection;
- identify common strategies that are used to provide evidence on the reliability and validity of measures used in personnel selection; and
- appreciate the requirement for measures used in personnel selection to evaluate applicants fairly and in an unbiased fashion.

THE "SHAM PSYCHOMETRIC TEST" CONTROVERSY

Recently, a controversy erupted in the U.K. concerning a psychometric test used by the Department of Work and Pensions. The test was developed to help unemployed people find work. The following article in *Personnel Today* gives an overview of the controversy and the nature of the test. This controversy also led to several days of questioning in Parliament. Videos of those sessions are available on YouTube, if you want to take a look at the consequences of using a test that may or may not be valid. We will deal with the issues of validity and reliability in this chapter and link them to the hiring process. Here is the article by John Hackston from *Personnel Today.*

Psychometric testing has been in the news recently, and not in a good way. According to recent reports, the Department for Work and Pensions (DWP) has required unemployed people to take "bogus" psychometric tests, and threatened to take their benefits away if they refused to do so.

A *Guardian* report and an accompanying video go on to say that the test is a "sham" and will produce the same results no matter what answers are given. Some websites and blogs go further, saying, for example, that "this 'test' is a tool for abuse and psychological torture."

It seems this particular questionnaire was developed as part of a pilot project put together by the Cabinet Office's behavioural insight team, otherwise known as the "nudge unit." This group uses two approaches that are surprisingly novel in governmental decision making. First, come up with ideas for small interventions to "nudge" individuals' behaviour in a direction that both works well for them and saves the Government money. Second, carry out randomised controlled trials to see if these interventions actually work.

One trial was in job centres, where 2,000 jobseekers were randomly assigned to one of two groups—half went through the existing system and half went through a new process. For the second group, their first visit included a conversation about getting back to work; on every subsequent visit they were encouraged to make clear plans for the next two weeks, and if they were still unemployed after eight weeks they were given further help. The results showed that after 13 weeks, the second group were 15%–20% less likely to be signing on than the first group. The project has now been expanded to larger trials.

Criticisms

So, a success story? Not quite. The psychometric test that has come in for criticism was part of this project, used at the eight-week stage to help jobseekers identify their strengths, thereby making them more able to put their best foot forward in applying for jobs. It is short (just 48 questions), is completed online and outputs a report with the respondent's five key strengths—what's not to like? Plenty, unfortunately, as the implementation of this idea is less than perfect. There are a number of issues:

Presentation. Try the test for yourself here and see what you think, but the appearance of the questionnaire does not inspire confidence. It has a very basic look and feel, the title text does not quite fit in the space reserved for it, and there is the occasional grammatical error (such as "I always look on bright side" and "Try to find a new way to use them then every day"). This may seem a little picky, but if people don't take the questionnaire seriously, they will not take any advice derived from it seriously. In the jargon of testing, it will have low face validity.

- **The questions.** Several questions are a little strange, for example: "In the last month, I have been thrilled by excellence in music, art, drama, film, sport, science or mathematics" or "I have not created anything of beauty in the last year." Some may not be easy to understand for people with lower levels of literacy or who do not have English as a first language, because of unusual phrasing or double negatives ("I hesitate to sacrifice my self-interest for the benefit of groups I am in" or "I am rarely as excited about the good fortune of others as I am about my own"). As these groups are likely to be over-represented among jobseekers, this may be an issue. Without some additional explanation or context, people will misunderstand the questions and the results will be less valid.
- **The report.** The report lists the respondent's five key strengths, based on their answers; potentially this is a very positive message. However, it is not immediately obvious that this is what the report is doing, and some additional text helping the reader to understand how

they can use the results would be extremely helpful. Some critics have even suggested that people will get the same report no matter what answers they put down; this is, in fact, not the case and different reports will be generated from different answers—although, as the reports are very similar, this is not obvious.

- **The origins of the questionnaire.** It has been reported in the press that the DWP test is a cut-down version of a much longer (120 or 240 question) "character strengths" survey published by the US-based VIA Institute on Character, and that VIA refused permission for the use of the shorter questionnaire, calling it a "non-validated version." If true, this is very worrying, as it would mean that this new version of the test is not fit for purpose.
- **The way the questionnaire appears to have been used.** This may be the biggest issue. Forcing people to complete an open personality questionnaire against their will (if this is indeed what has happened) is unlikely to have a useful outcome. Doing so on a large-scale programme in the full glare of publicity could be seen as asking for trouble. This is a real shame, because we know that accurate personality questionnaires, with specific and focused reports, can be incredibly useful in career counselling.

Can the positives outweigh the negatives?

Any personality questionnaire is a means to an end, but how it is used is just as important. Unfortunately, the world seems to have decided that the DWP questionnaire was designed from the outset to be used in a less than positive way.

Questions such as "is it reliable?" "is it valid?" or even "could it be useful?" may be drowned out—and the questionnaire, for all its flaws, is part of an approach that does seem to give results.

Errors in implementation can be corrected and a new version trialled; this is a part of the whole ethos of evidence-based policy. Let us hope that the furore does not prevent this happening, and does not detract from the many places where psychometric tools are used in a positive way to widen and inform people's career choices, to help them in the job search process, and to aid their development once in employment.

Source: John Hackston, "The Sham Psychometric Test Controversy" *Personnel Today*, May 10, 2013. http://www.personneltoday.com/hr/the-sham-psychometric-test-controversy.

The basic premise of this text is that scientific methods will enable an employer to hire job applicants who possess the **KSAOs** (knowledge, skills, abilities, or other attributes) that are required to perform a specific job. One of the concerns with the test used by the DWP is that it was never validated for an intended purpose. In fact, it is not clear what the purpose of the test is. What KSAOs identified by the test might be related to any job an unemployed person might be interested in pursuing? We argue that science-based selection will meet this goal of hiring the right people for the job and that there is a process that should be followed to identify the KSAOs and then to measure them; that is, to determine if a job applicant has the "right stuff." Figure 2.1 presents an outline of the components that make up a selection system. We will review this process and the different elements of the system over the course of this text. In this chapter we will deal with the issues of reliability and validity. These concepts are essential to the legal defensibility of any selection procedure.

KSAOs
The knowledge, skills, abilities, and other attributes necessary for a new incumbent to do well on the job; also referred to as *job, employment,* or *worker specifications.*

By using reliable and valid selection methods, HR managers save themselves and their company much aggravation and grief. The bottom line is that selection procedures that are ethical and follow professional standards are defensible, should they be challenged in court or in some employment tribunal. Science-based selection produces employees that are efficient and productive.

Using an employment test with unknown reliability and validity may lead to many uncomfortable minutes on a witness stand under cross-examination. Imagine yourself

FIGURE 2.1

JOB ANALYSIS, SELECTION, AND CRITERION MEASUREMENTS OF PERFORMANCE: A SYSTEMS APPROACH

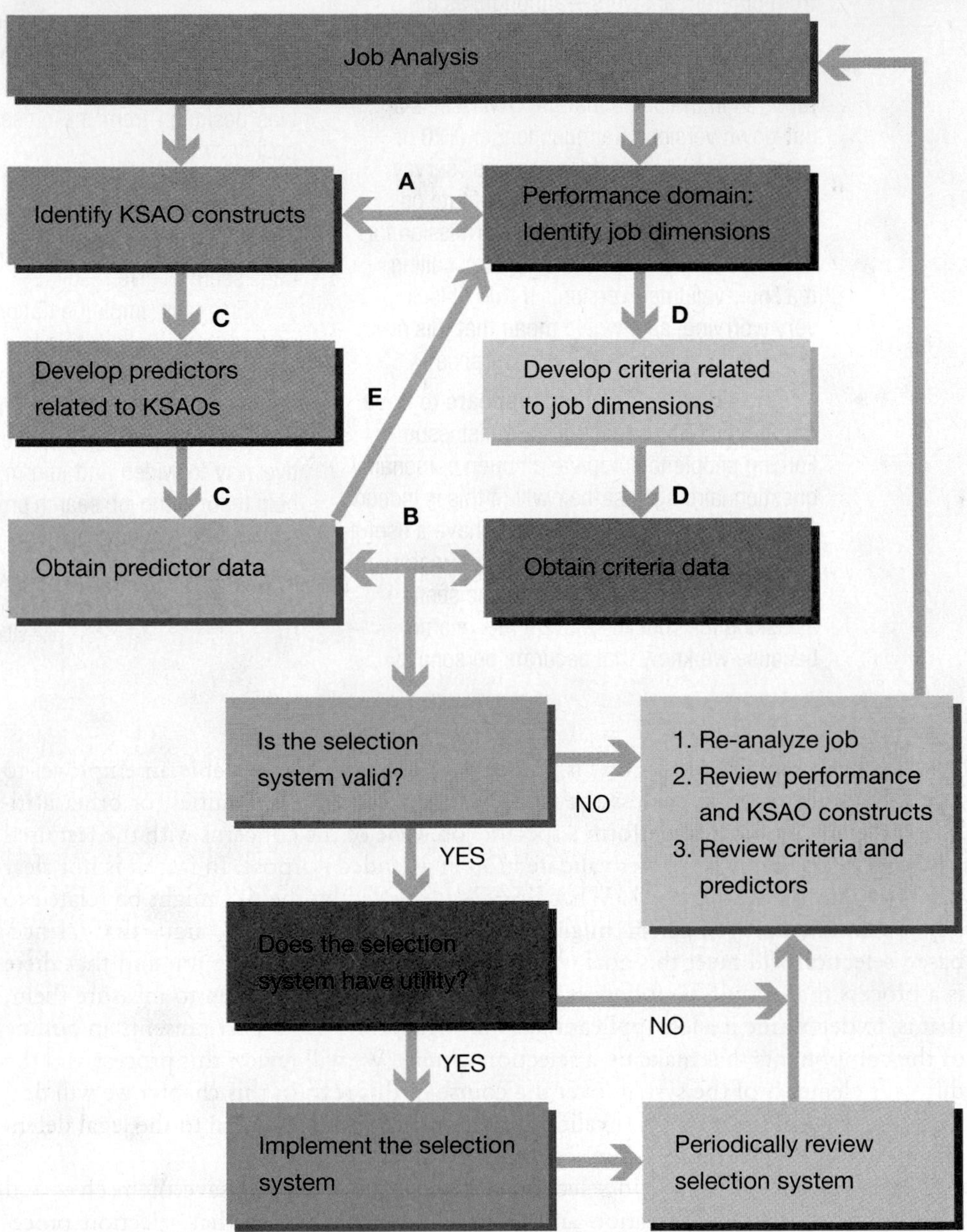

in the situation trying to defend some procedure you used to assess job applicants when you had not determined the reliability or validity of the procedure and proceeded to make employment decisions based on the procedure.

In this chapter we will develop a basic understanding of several of the measurement and validity issues that surfaced in the DWP case and with which every HR practitioner must be familiar. There are no guarantees, even when professionals attempt to follow accepted procedures, that their work will meet standards set by courts or tribunals, but HR professionals should at least know the standards they are expected to meet in order to defend their work.

// THE RECRUITMENT AND SELECTION PROCESS

In most employment situations, there are many applicants for each available job. The employer's goal is to hire an applicant who possesses the knowledge, skills, abilities, or other attributes (KSAOs) required to successfully perform the job being filled. The employer makes a guess about which applicant will perform the job most effectively. This basic decision, which is made hundreds of times each day throughout Canada, is the end result of a complex process. Correct guesses by the employer have positive benefits for the organization and the employee; bad guesses not only affect the productivity and profitability of the company but also may have negative emotional consequences for the poorly performing employee. As we saw in Chapter 1, bad hiring decisions cost an employer considerable amounts of money. In addition, bad hiring practices may lead to severe legal consequences. Recruitment and Selection Today 2.1 presents a case where a hiring manager was not using the KSAOs related to a job in selecting applicants for a waitress position.

RECRUITMENT AND SELECTION TODAY 2.1

TAKING THE MYSTERY OUT OF BAD HIRING PRACTICES

Want some free anti-harassment and anti-discrimination training? Well, have I got a deal for you! *Mystery Diners* is a reality show on the Food Network. The show's concept involves a father-daughter team who pretend to be employees and/or customers at a target restaurant in order to help the owner uncover the "leaks in the dam" so to speak.

An episode that aired last week, called "Managing Disaster," could be used as a workplace best-practices training video. In short, you could use the video to train employees that *any* of the conduct by the restaurant's manager should be considered prohibited conduct in your workplace.

Yes, it really was that bad. And I mean *bad.* Let me take a moment to run through just a few examples of conduct that occurred during the hiring process.

Candidate #1: Sarah the "Old Lady"

Two women are sent into the restaurant to interview for a waitress position. One of the women is Sarah, who is in her mid-30s and has lots of waitressing experience. She interviewed with the bad-guy-manager (we'll call him "Manager," despite he did anything but manage the employees).

During the interview, he asked her how old she was. Yes, you read that correctly. When she answered "I'm 35," Manager nearly fell out of his seat. He quickly sent her on her way and told her he'd be in touch. After she was out the door, he ran over to the bar, where he told the bartender that Sarah "was like, in her *30s*—she'd be like a mother in here!!"

Candidate #2: Destiney in a Short Skirt

The second candidate was Destiney, the daughter of the father-daughter team, who I'd guess to be *maybe* 21 years old. Destiney was young and cute and wore a short skirt to her interview. As if Manager hadn't already shown his true colors during Sarah's interview, he took it to an entirely new level with Destiney. By the end of the "interview," though, you can be sure that Destiney had been offered the job.

For starters, he made her sit on a couch for the interview, which was not only way too informal but also clearly uncomfortable for Destiney in light of her attire. When Destiney admitted that she had no real experience to speak of, Manager assured her that experience was not important—"as long as you're cute."

Ethical Standards Lower Than a Short Skirt

Seeing that he couldn't ask her about anything relevant to the duties of the job, I guess it's natural that Manager turned to other topics. In this case, Manager chose "partying," and began a series of questions about Destiney's after-hour activities, such as whether she liked to "party" and whether she liked to go clubbing, which "they" (presumably, Manager and his creepy friends), "did all of the time."

The low point of the "interview" came when Manager touched Destiney's knee as he sat way too close to her on the low-to-the-ground couch and talked about low-life topics like "partying" and assuring her that his standards for hiring were as low as his morals. What a dirt bag. And you can imagine what the father, who sat in a trailer watching the live video stream with the restaurant's owner, must have thought as he saw Manager Creepy touch Daughter Destiney's bare knee. Nice.

When Busted, Blame Others

Folks, the take-aways from this episode are, admittedly, obvious to most of us. They weren't, apparently, as obvious to Manager Creepy, who was shocked and appalled that the owner had secretly videotaped these antics. And, in a demonstration of some of the best blame-shifting skills I've perhaps ever seen, Manager Creepy, furious about the intrusion, turned the entire situation around and accused the owner of being an unsupportive boss.

Source: Margaret (Molly) DiBianca, June 27, 2012. http://www.lexisnexis.com/legalnewsroom/labor-employment/b/labor-employment-top-blogs/archive/2012/06/27/taking-the-mystery-out-of-bad-hiring-practices.aspx. Courtesy of Margaret (Molly) DiBianca.

As part of making a decision, the employer must have a good idea of both the duties that will be performed as part of the job and the level of performance required for job success. The employer must identify the knowledge, skills, abilities, or other attributes that are required for job success and measure or assess the KSAOs of all job applicants. (And, contrary to what is suggested by the behavior of the hiring manager in Recruitment and Selection Today 2.1, age and wearing short skirts do not qualify!) In Chapter 4 we will discuss different techniques that provide this necessary information. Hiring someone through an assessment of job-related attributes is based on an assumption that higher levels of attributes are linked to higher levels of job performance. Recruitment and selection need not be based on guesses on who is best suited to fill a position.

THE HIRING PROCESS

Recruitment and Selection Today 2.2 outlines the procedure used by the Toronto Police Service in selecting new recruits for the position of police constable. Candidates must meet a set of minimum requirements; they also must not have a criminal record for which a pardon has not been granted. If candidates meet the minimum requirements specified in Recruitment and Selection Today 2.2, they may proceed to register for general information sessions and undertake a series of employment tests including a test of cognitive ability (PATI), written communication (WCT), physical readiness evaluation for police (PREP), Behavioural Personnel Assessment Device for police (BPAD), and vision and hearing tests. Once the applicant has received a certificate from the Ontario Association of Chiefs of Police certifying the test results, he or she may submit an application to Toronto Police Service. After a review of testing results, competitive

RECRUITMENT AND SELECTION TODAY 2.2

SELECTION PROCESS FOR TORONTO POLICE CONSTABLES IN 2014

Minimum Qualifications

- Be a Canadian citizen or permanent resident of Canada,
- Be at least 18 years of age,
- Be physically and mentally able to perform the duties of the position, having regard to your own safety and the safety of members of the public,
- Have successfully completed at least four years of secondary school education or its equivalent. (Note: Official transcripts and diplomas will be required). Where education has been completed outside Ontario, official proof of equivalency must be obtained,
- Be of good moral character and habits, meaning that you are an individual other people would look upon as being trustworthy and having integrity.

In addition, you must:

- Have no criminal convictions for which a pardon has not been granted,
- Possess a valid driver's licence with no more than six accumulated demerit points, permitting you to drive an automobile in Ontario with full driving privileges,
- Have current certification in CPR and first aid by the time the offer of employment is given,
- Possess a valid O.A.C.P. (Ontario Association of Chiefs of Police) certificate,
- Have a minimum of 20/40 (uncorrected) vision, with normal colour acuity,
- Successfully pass the hearing standards as outlined by the O.A.C.P.,
- Be able to pass a security clearance as well as a background investigation, credit and reference checks.

Selection Process

- Complete online registration for a General Information Session (GIS),
- Attend General Information Session (GIS),
- Toronto Police Recruiter will be in contact with you,
- Complete online registration for one of our mentoring sessions,
- Attend your registered PREP, PATI or WCT mentoring session,
- Register for O.A.C.P. testing with Applicant Testing Services,
- Perform Test:
  - PATI (Police Analytical Thinking Inventory),
  - WCT (Written Communication Test),
  - PREP (Physical Readiness Evaluation for Police),
  - Vision and Hearing,
  - BPAD (Behavioural Personnel Assessment Device for police).
- Obtain O.A.C.P. Certificate of Results,
- Submit Toronto Police Service online application,
- Pre-Screening,
- Pre-Background Questionnaire (PBQ),
- Blended Interview,
- Minnesota Multi-Phasic Personality Inventory (MMPI-2),
- Background Investigation,
- Psychological Assessment,
- Conditional Offer of Employment Pending Medical Examination,
- Cadet-in-Training.

Please be advised that the process for becoming a Police Constable is competitive and as such, an applicant may be declined at any stage of the process.

Sources: http://www.torontopolice.on.ca/careers/uni_minreq.php, and http://www.torontopolice.on.ca/careers/uni_become_officer.php. Courtesy of the Toronto Police Service and the Ontario Association of Chiefs of Police.

Roy Antal/LEADER POST. Reprinted by permission.

candidates undergo a pre-screening and pre-background questionnaire followed by an extensive interview that delves into all aspects of the candidate's personal and professional life. Candidates who are considered for employment are then asked to undergo a more extensive background check and to complete a clinical personality assessment and psychological examinations. At this stage there are likely to be more qualified candidates who have passed all the steps than there are positions, so the recruiting team compares candidates and decides which applicants will receive employment offers. An offer is then made to candidates pending successful completion of a medical exam.

The Toronto Police Service selection process illustrates the major components of personnel selection that we will be discussing throughout this book. These are the components that a candidate sees; however, there is much more to the process. How does an employer know which requirements are needed to carry out the job? Should the employer be concerned if the requirements discriminate against certain groups? Under what circumstances can requirements that do discriminate against groups be used in selection? What standards must be met by the tests used in the selection procedures for the employer to be sure that they are providing valid and reliable information about the applicants? What procedures must an employer follow to ensure that its selection process is in compliance with legal and professional standards?

Every employer who makes a hiring decision follows a hiring process, even though it may not be as structured and detailed as that used by the Toronto Police Service. In many cases the hiring process is informal. The hiring system used by many employers resembles, on the surface, the selection procedure used to hire police constables in Toronto, but there are important differences. When a position becomes vacant, or is newly created, the employer may have a general idea of the duties to be performed as part of the job, which are then included in an advertisement used to recruit candidates for the position. This job advertisement may also state broad educational or experiential requirements expected from the candidates. The important difference is whether the job duties and position requirements have been determined through some systematic investigation–that is, a job analysis–or whether they represent a guess on the part of the employer's HR department.

Applicants submit résumés and, after a preliminary screening, a few may be interviewed. Based on review of the applicant's file, work references, and impressions formed during the interview, the employer makes a decision to hire one of the candidates. This decision may reflect the employer's experience, a gut feeling or intuition about a certain candidate, or simply personal preference. The employer has an *idea* of the type of person who will do well in the job or in the organization and looks for an applicant who matches this idealized employee. In any event, the employer is making a guess about which applicant will do well in the job based on information collected from the job applicant that may not, in fact, be related to the job–or it may be of questionable quality.

All too often, unfortunately, the employer's decision or guess reveals more about the biases of the employer than it does about either the requirements for the job or the qualifications and abilities of the applicants (refer to Recruitment and Selection Today 2.1). In this type of selection procedure there is little or no tracking of the performance of the people hired, and only those who happen to do well are recalled and used to reinforce the hiring process. Bad guesses may lead not only to bad hiring decisions and lower productivity, but also to legal difficulties.

Hiring decisions must be defensible; they must meet legal requirements and professional standards of reliability and validity. Defensible hiring decisions are not arbitrary; the measures used to make hiring decisions must be stable and provide job-related information. The Toronto Police Service hiring procedure outlined in Recruitment and Selection Today 2.2 illustrates how selection ought to be done, but before it or any procedure can be considered to be a model selection system, it must satisfy certain standards. Figure 2.1 represents a model of a selection system, including the components that are not seen by job applicants. The model emphasizes the need for employment decisions to be valid and to meet legal requirements. Unfortunately, practice in HR tends to lag behind the science. Far too many HR interventions, including those in selection, are based on intuition rather than empirical support. There is a stubborn reliance on intuition and use of selection procedures such as an unstructured interview even though many practitioners using this procedure know that it is not sound.[1] In a study of HR directors and managers, Lodato, Highhouse, and Brooks[2] found that practitioners who preferred intuition-based hiring were experiential thinkers who tended to make everyday decisions based on their feelings. They also tended to be less experienced than those who preferred selection tools, worked in small organizations, and did not hold professional certifications. The practitioners were consistent in using intuition

TABLE 2.1

HUMAN RESOURCES MANAGEMENT: SCIENCE VERSUS PRACTICE IN SELECTION

	SCIENCE-BASED SELECTION	PRACTICE-BASED SELECTION
TYPE OF PROCESS	ANALYTICAL	INTUITIVE
	• Job analysis identifies KSAOs • Select valid measures of KSAOs • Validate predictors and assess utility • Retain valid and useful predictors	• Untested approaches • "Fad"-based selection system • Lack of use of reliable and valid selection tools • Techniques and selection tools chosen on the basis of marketing • Selection procedures used are rarely validated
ASSESSMENT PROCEDURES	• Objective, reliable and valid measures	• Unstructured interview
DECISION MAKING	• Rational	• "Gut-feel"
IMPLEMENTATION	• System-wide	• Case-by-case basis
EVALUATION OF PROCESS	• Empirical	• Subjective
WHY IS IT USED?	• Structured procedures • Consistent process • Maintains standards	• Comfort with the process • Flexibility and speed • Fits organizational culture
POTENTIAL OUTCOMES	• Defensibility of system • Increased productivity • Effective employees	• Human rights litigation • Lack of competitiveness • Marginal employees

Source: V.M. Catano. "Empirically Supported Interventions and HR Practice." *HRM Research Quarterly* 5, 2001, pp. 1-5. International Alliance for Human Resources Research, York University. Reprinted with permission of V.M. Catano.

whether they were hiring salaried or hourly employees. In Table 2.1 we compare some of the differences between empirical evidence-based and practice-based selection processes.

A SELECTION MODEL

Figure 2.1 presented an overview of the components and process of a traditional selection system. In this model, job or work analysis information is used to identify both the performance to be carried out on the job and the KSAOs or competencies linked to that job. Job or work analysis information identifies the tasks and behaviours that make up a job and, through inference, the KSAOs that contribute to performance of these related tasks and behaviours. These inferences are based on empirical evidence demonstrating validity between the job dimensions and KSAO constructs in other situations (see Recruitment and Selection Notebook 2.1).

The HR specialist must also translate the KSAO constructs into measurable predictors. The fact that a security dispatcher sends, receives, processes, and analyzes information suggests that an applicant for this position should demonstrate a fair degree of cognitive ability. Also, that a security dispatcher must be capable of operating a variety of electronic equipment suggests the applicant should have experience operating such equipment. Similarly, if this same position requires the incumbent to remain calm under stressful conditions, applicants should demonstrate a stable emotional disposition (i.e., low neuroticism or high emotional stability).

RECRUITMENT AND SELECTION NOTEBOOK 2.1

CONSTRUCTS AND VARIABLES

Throughout this book we will refer to constructs and variables. These concepts are not as difficult as they may seem to be at first glance.

Constructs—ideas or concepts constructed or invoked to explain relationships between observations. For example, the construct "extraversion" has been invoked to explain the relationship between "social forthrightness" and sales; "learning" is a construct used to explain the change in behaviour that results from experience. Constructs are abstractions that we infer from observations and that we cannot directly observe.

Constructs are collections of related behaviours. The construct may be based on a theory. To be useful, the construct should be measurable. Intelligence, or cognitive ability, is a construct that refers to several behaviours such as verbal and numerical behaviours, spatial ability, and inductive and deductive ability, among others. There are several different theories of intelligence. The theory you adopt may guide how you measure intelligence. For example, if you believe that all you need in assessing job applicants is to know their cognitive ability and not their ability on specific components of intelligence, then you would select a test that measures cognitive ability. If you thought that several of the intelligence components were important then you would measure, for example, constructs such as verbal ability or deductive reasoning.

Variables—simply refer to how someone or something varies on the construct of interest. When we make a measurement we are assigning a numerical value to represent the degree of variation by the person or object within the construct of interest. For example, we can invent an "IQ" score to represent variability in intelligence. The test we choose to measure cognitive ability assigns a score ranging from 0 to 200 to represent "IQ." The assigned numbers will depend on the measure we use to assess intelligence. Variables allow us to make statements about constructs; e.g., "Differences in cognitive ability predict success on the job." We infer whether this statement is correct by looking at a relationship between two variables, one measure that represents cognitive ability and the second measure that represents job performance.

The HR specialists must determine how each of these KSAOs will be assessed. With respect to cognitive ability, a general cognitive ability test may be most appropriate. Information about past work history and experience may come from an application form, the candidate's résumé, or an interview, while information about the candidate's ability to deal with stressful situations may be assessed through a combination of a personality inventory and a situational interview. The predictors that are chosen must be valid measures of the KSAO constructs that have been identified as related to job performance. Keep in mind that the goal of selection is to identify job candidates who have those attributes required for success on the job. On the basis of data obtained through an assessment of job applicants, the HR team predicts which applicants will be successful in the position.

The work of the HR team does not end at this point. The team must evaluate the outcomes of its decision making. Did the applicants the team selected perform successfully? Did their decisions result in improved levels of performance and overall productivity than would be the case without such a system? Finally, any selection system must be reviewed periodically to determine whether it is still effective as jobs and organizations change.

// BUILDING A FOUNDATION

To move beyond a guess, a selection system must be built on a sound scientific foundation. In buying a house, you may not need to know how to lay a foundation, but you must be able to tell whether the house's foundation is solid. Often, HR managers are asked to adopt selection systems; this chapter provides the tools needed to determine if a selection system or procedure rests on solid footings. There are two major elements to building a sound foundation with respect to recruitment and selection. First, the system must be based on solid empirical support. HR personnel must be able to demonstrate the reliability and validity of their selection systems. Second, any selection system must operate within a legal context.

// RELIABILITY

Hardly any human characteristic can be measured in an error-free manner. The act of measuring produces a score that measures both the true score and an error component. **Reliability** is the degree to which observed scores are free from random measurement errors. Reliability is an indication of the stability or dependability of a set of measurements. Reliability refers to the consistency of a set of measurements when a testing procedure is repeated on a population of individuals or groups.[3]

Reliability
The degree to which observed scores are free from random measurement errors. Reliability is an indication of the stability or dependability of a set of measurements over repeated applications of the measurement procedure.

Think of an employer who requires each employee to punch a time clock upon arrival at work. Mr. X, Ms. Y, and Mr. Z, without fail, arrive at work each morning at 8:55 A.M., 8:56 A.M., and 8:57 A.M., respectively. If, on each day, the time clock stamped these same times, exactly, on each employee's time card, the time clock would be considered extremely reliable. The observed score–the time stamped on the time card–is the same as the true score, the time the employees arrived at work; no degree of error has been added to the measurement.

On the other hand, if the clock stamped times of 9:03 A.M., 9:00 A.M., and 9:00 A.M. for Mr. X, Ms. Y, and Mr. Z, the measurement would include an error component. Mr. X's time is off by eight minutes, Ms. Y's by four minutes, and Mr. Z's by three minutes. The time clock is not accurate, or reliable, in reporting the time people arrived for work. In this case, the error appears to be random or unsystematic; the occurrence or degree of the error does not appear to be predictable.

In terms of testing, we expect a test to provide approximately the same information each time it is given to that person. If you were given a multiple-choice test on the content of this chapter, we would expect that you would obtain approximately the same score if you were asked to retake the test. The smaller the differences between your two scores, the more reliable, or consistent, the test.

Errors may also be systematic; that is, the errors may be made in a consistent, or predictable, fashion. If the time clock were five minutes fast, it would report the three arrival times as 9:00 A.M., 9:01 A.M., and 9:02 A.M. The clock is still reliable in reporting the arrival times of the three employees, but it is systematically adding five minutes to each worker's clock-in time. The observed scores are reliable, but they do not represent the true arrival times. In other words, while the observed scores are accurate, they are not a valid indication of whether the employees started work on time.

Systematic errors do not affect the accuracy of the measurements but rather the meaning, or interpretation, of those measurements. In terms of testing, several test questions might be scored incorrectly on both the first occasion you took the test and on the subsequent administration. The incorrect scoring, which is systematic, does not affect the reliability of the test but it leads to the wrong conclusion about how well you know the material.

Figure 2.2 presents an illustration of reliability and systematic and random error. It shows the results of four different archers shooting at a target. The shots of Archer A

FIGURE 2.2

EFFECTS OF RANDOM AND SYSTEMATIC ERROR ON RELIABILITY

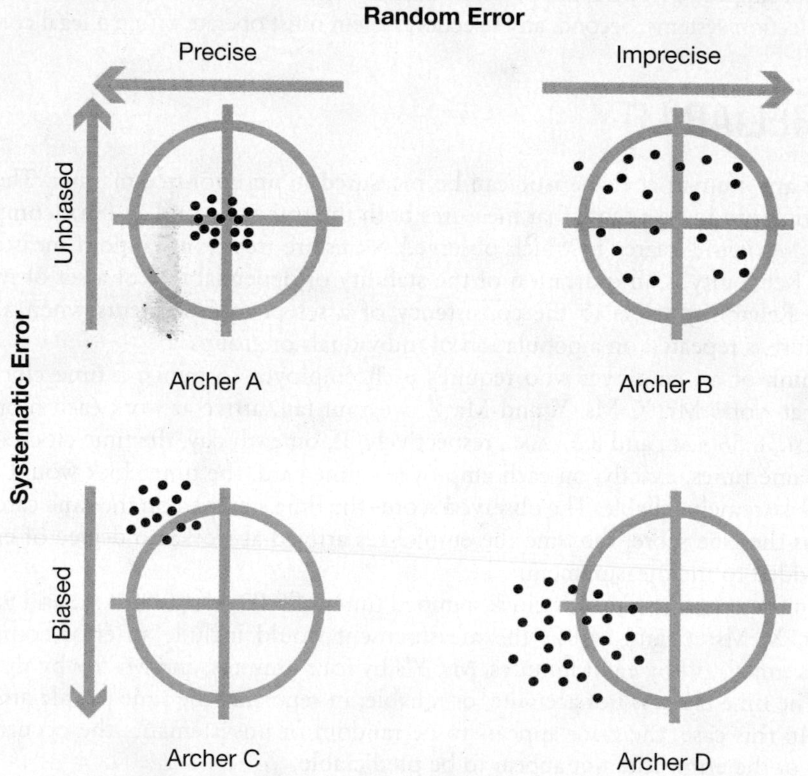

and Archer B are unbiased in that they are affected by random errors, perhaps a strong wind blows occasionally during their target practice. However, Archer A's shots on target are more precise and are still very consistent or reliable. On the other hand Archer B's shots are very imprecise and inconsistent. The reliability of Archer B's shooting is very poor; you never know where Archer B's arrow will end up. Both Archer C and Archer D are affected by some type of bias; perhaps there is a defect in the bows they are using. Nonetheless, Archer C achieves a narrow, consistent grouping of shots, but they are off the centre of the target. While Archer C's shooting is reliable we cannot make any conclusion about how well Archer C can hit the centre of the target. Archer D is also affected by systematic error, but Archer D's shots are imprecise and inconsistent. The systematic error has not changed the reliability of the two archers, but it limits what we can conclude about their target-hitting ability.

INTERPRETING RELIABILITY COEFFICIENTS

Another way to think of reliability is in terms of the variability of a set of scores. The classical measurement model,[4] which has had a major impact on personnel research, assumes that any observed score, *X*, is a combination of a **true score** and an **error score**.

True score
The average score that an individual would earn on an infinite number of administrations of the same test or parallel versions of the same test.

Error score
The hypothetical difference between an observed score and a true score.

This model assumes that the characteristic being measured is stable and that the only reason an observed score changes from one measurement to another is due to random error. Error scores are independent of the characteristic being measured; errors are attributable to the measurement process, not to the individual. That is, the magnitude of error scores is unrelated to the magnitude of the characteristic being measured. The error score for an applicant with a very high level of the critical characteristic could be very large, or very small; that same situation would hold for any level of the characteristic.

The model also assumes that true scores and error scores combine in a simple additive manner to produce the observed score. Suppose you take a test with 100 questions an infinite number of times (OK; let's say 1000 is as close to infinity as we might get!) and your average score is 80. Let's think of this as your true score; the number of questions to which you know the answer. So, any time this test is given you should make 80 correct responses; however, you take a guess on the remaining 20 questions you don't know and get 10 correct by sheer luck. The number of correct guesses is due to chance. Therefore, the score you obtain on the test, 90, is the sum of your true score, 80, plus the error score, 10, attributable to chance. We can also determine the true scores for all the students in our population. Those true scores will vary across all the students. We then administer the test one more time to all the students and determine how much variance there is in the obtained scores.

If the test is not very accurate–that is, if it adds large random error components to true scores–then the variance of the measured scores should be much larger than the variance of the true scores. Reliability can be thought of as the ratio of true score variance to observed score variance. In Figure 2.3, the normal curve marked "A" represents the distribution of true score and curves "B" and "C" represent distributions of scores obtained with two different tests designed to assess the same, stable characteristic, "A." The variance for both test distributions, as indicated by their spread, are greater than the variance of the true score distribution with the variance of Test C greater than Test B's. As illustrated in Figure 2.3, the reliability of Test B is greater than the reliability of Test C.

The reliability coefficient (r_{xx}) is also the degree that observed scores, which are made on the same stable characteristic, correlate with one another. A reliability coefficient, which is a correlation coefficient, ranges in value from 0.0 to +1.0. When a test's

FIGURE 2.3

ILLUSTRATION OF RELIABILITY OF TWO DIFFERENT TESTS OF THE SAME CHARACTERISTIC

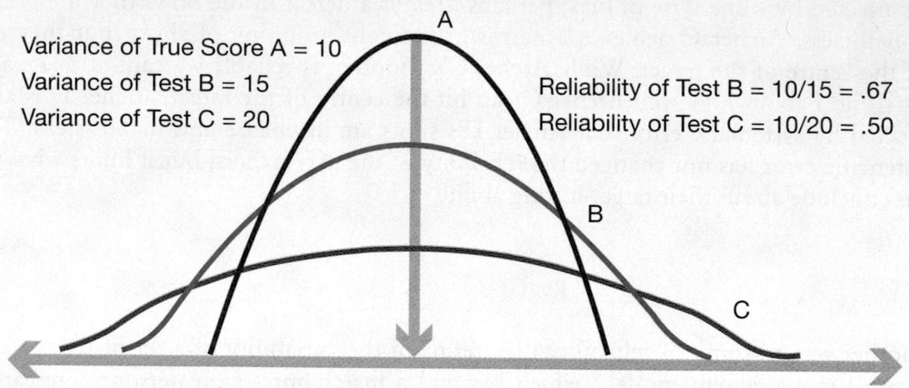

reliability coefficient is close to 0.0 all variability in obtained test scores is due to measurement error. Conversely, when a test's reliability coefficient is near +1.0, this indicates that all variability in scores reflects true score variability. The square of the reliability coefficient, $(r_{xx})^2$, represents the proportion of variance in the observed scores that is attributed to true differences on the measured characteristic. For the arrival times in our time stamp example, if $r_{xx} = .33$, then only 10 percent of the variability in the reported arrival times, $(r_{xx})^2$, is attributable to the true arrival time; the remaining 90 percent of the variability is attributable to the inaccuracy of the time clock. If the accuracy of the clock were $r_{xx} = .85$, 72 percent of the variability in arrival times is attributable to the true arrival time and 28 percent is due to error. When the time clock is systematically fast by five minutes–$r_{xx} = 1.00$–the systematic error did not affect the reliability coefficient; the scores are very reliable, but they do not tell anything about the time people actually arrived at work.

MEASUREMENT ERROR

Measurement error
The hypothetical difference between an observed score and a true score; comprises both random error and systematic error.

Measurement error can be thought of as the hypothetical difference between an individual's observed score on any particular measurement and the individual's true score. Measurement error, whether systematic or random, reduces the usefulness of any set of measures or the results from any test. It reduces the confidence that we can place in the score the measure assigns to any particular individual. Does the score accurately represent the individual's knowledge or ability, or is it so fraught with error that we cannot use it to make meaningful decisions?

Information on the degree of error present in any set of measurements must be considered when using the measurements to make employment decisions. In our example, the manager must consider the possible major sources of the error, the size of the error, and the degree to which the observed scores would reoccur in another setting or with other employees. The *standard error of measurement* is a statistical index that summarizes information related to measurement error. This index is estimated from observed scores obtained over a group of individuals. It reflects how an individual's score would vary, on average, over repeated observations that were made under identical conditions.

TABLE 2.2

GENERAL GUIDELINES FOR INTERPRETING RELIABILITY COEFFICIENTS

RELIABILITY COEFFICIENT	INTERPRETATION
.90 and up	Excellent
.80 – .89	Good
.70 – .79	Adequate
Below .70	May have limited applicability

Source: U.S. Department of Labor, *Testing and Assessment: An Employer's Guide to Best Practices.*

What degree of reliability does an employment test need to have for it to be used in making employment decisions? Professional standards simply say it should be "sufficiently high."[5] The U.S. Department of Labor[6] produced an employer's best practices guide for testing and assessment, which is now available through the O*NET Resource Center. The Guide presents guidelines for interpreting reliability coefficients, which we reproduce in Table 2.2.

The Guide goes on to say that a test should not be accepted or rejected solely based on the size of the reliability coefficient. Other considerations exist including the type of test, the type of reliability estimate reported, and the context in which the test will be used. However, many selection specialists believe that the reliability of an employment test or procedure should be at least 80.

FACTORS AFFECTING RELIABILITY

The factors that introduce error into any set of measurements can be organized into three broad categories: temporary individual characteristics, lack of standardization, and chance. Examples of these factors are given in Recruitment and Selection Today 2.3.

RECRUITMENT AND SELECTION TODAY 2.3

EXAMPLES OF FACTORS THAT MAY AFFECT RELIABILITY

Temporary Individual Characteristics

John stays awake all night cramming for his HR exam. He is nervous and loaded with caffeine when he takes the test. His performance on the test is poor. He asks his professor for a retest, arguing that the score does not reflect his true ability. The professor consents and John does much better on the retest. Factors such as health, motivation, fatigue, and emotional state introduce temporary, unsystematic errors into the measurement process.

Lack of Standardization

Mary and Faizal have been invited to interview for the same position. Mary is interviewed over lunch in a very comfortable restaurant while Faisal is interviewed in a very austere conference room. Faizal is given a few minutes to answer each question, but Mary is told to take as long as she needs. The manager, who is male, displays a lack of interest in Faizal during the interview, but reacts very positively to Mary. These are just a few of the ways that lack of standardization can enter the measurement process. Changing the conditions under which measurements are made introduces error into the measurement process.

Chance

To prevent job applicants from guessing what the interview questions might be, an HR manager randomly draws the questions from a test bank prepared for the position. The questions given to Sam are easier to answer than those asked of Sarah. By luck of the draw, Sam's interview score is higher than Sarah's. Both scores are dependent on the specific set of questions. Sam may have done as poorly as Sarah if he had been asked the questions given to her, and she may have done as well as Sam on his set of questions. This also argues for standardization of test materials. Factors unique to a specific procedure may introduce error into the set of measurements.

METHODS OF ESTIMATING RELIABILITY

One small problem exists with respect to true scores: we can never know the true score variance, as true scores are abstract constructs. But, we can estimate what the true score is likely to be. There are several ways to estimate a test's reliability. Each involves assessing the consistency of an examinee's scores over time, across different content samples, or across different scorers. The common assumption for each of these reliability techniques is that *consistent variability across the measurements represents true score variability, while inconsistency across the measurements reflects random error.*

To measure reliability, we have to estimate the degree of variability in a set of scores that is caused by measurement error. We can obtain this estimate by using two different, but parallel, measures of the characteristic or attribute. Over the same set of people, both measures should report the same score for each individual. This score will represent the true score plus measurement error. Both measures reflect the same true score; discrepancies between the two sets of scores suggest the presence of measurement error. The correlation coefficient based on the scores from both measures gives an estimate of the reliability coefficient, r_{xx}. It is extremely difficult, if not impossible, to obtain two parallel measures of the same characteristic; therefore, several strategies have been developed as approximations of parallel measures.

TEST AND RETEST

The identical measurement procedure is used to assess the same characteristic over the same group of people on two different occasions. The HR manager invites the job applicants back for a second employment interview. They are asked the same questions in the same order. The correlation of their first and second interview scores estimates the reliability of the employment interview. High correlations suggest high levels of reliability. Giving exactly the same test to students on two occasions is another example of estimating test–retest reliability.

ALTERNATE FORMS

However, having a person take the same employment interview twice may lead to a false estimate of the reliability of the interview process. The candidates may recall their original answers to the interview questions; they may also have thought of better answers after the first interview and give the improved answers on the second opportunity. To prevent the intrusion of effects from the first interview, the manager asks the applicants alternate questions during the second interview. The correlation between both interview scores again estimates reliability, with high correlations once more indicating strong reliability. Giving students two different forms of the same test is an example of estimating alternate forms reliability. The two tests cover exactly the same content but the questions are not the same on both occasions.

INTERNAL CONSISTENCY

Both test–retest and alternate forms procedures require two sets of measurements made on different occasions. In the case of employment interviews, it is quite costly in time and money to put all the candidates through a second interview procedure. Besides, isn't each question in the interview directed at measuring job-related experience? Why not consider any two questions in the interview to be an example of a test–retest situation, and determine the correlation between scores given to each item in that pair? This is the logic behind establishing reliability through internal consistency. Rather than select any particular pair of items, the correlations between the scores of all possible pairs of items are calculated and then averaged. This average estimates the internal consistency, the degree to which all the questions in the set are measuring the same thing.

These estimates are sometimes called *alpha* coefficients, or *Cronbach's alpha*, after the formula used to produce the estimate. *Split-half reliability* is a special case of internal consistency where all the items are first divided into two arbitrary groups. For example, all the even-numbered items may form one group, with the odd-numbered items placed into the second. The correlation over each person's average scores in the two groups is used as the reliability estimate.

INTER-RATER RELIABILITY

Measurement in personnel selection is often based on the subjective assessment, or rating, of one individual by another. The HR manager's assessment of job performance is a subjective measurement, as we will discuss in Chapter 5. How likely would the rating assigned by one manager be assigned by another? In assessment centres, several judges monitor and then rate the performance of candidates on multiple exercises. The correlations between these judgments estimate the reliability of the assessments. Sometimes, this index is referred to as *classification consistency* or *inter-rater agreement*. This distinction is purely semantic. As part of group projects, professors may ask all the members of the group to rate independently the contribution of all the other members of the group. The more consistent the scores, the more reliable they are as measures of a student's contribution to the group project.

CHOOSING AN INDEX OF RELIABILITY

Measures of test–retest reliability, alternate forms reliability, and internal consistency are special cases of a more general type of index called a generalizability coefficient. These three measures, however, provide slightly different views of a measure's reliability. Each

VALIDITY AND RELIABILITY EVIDENCE

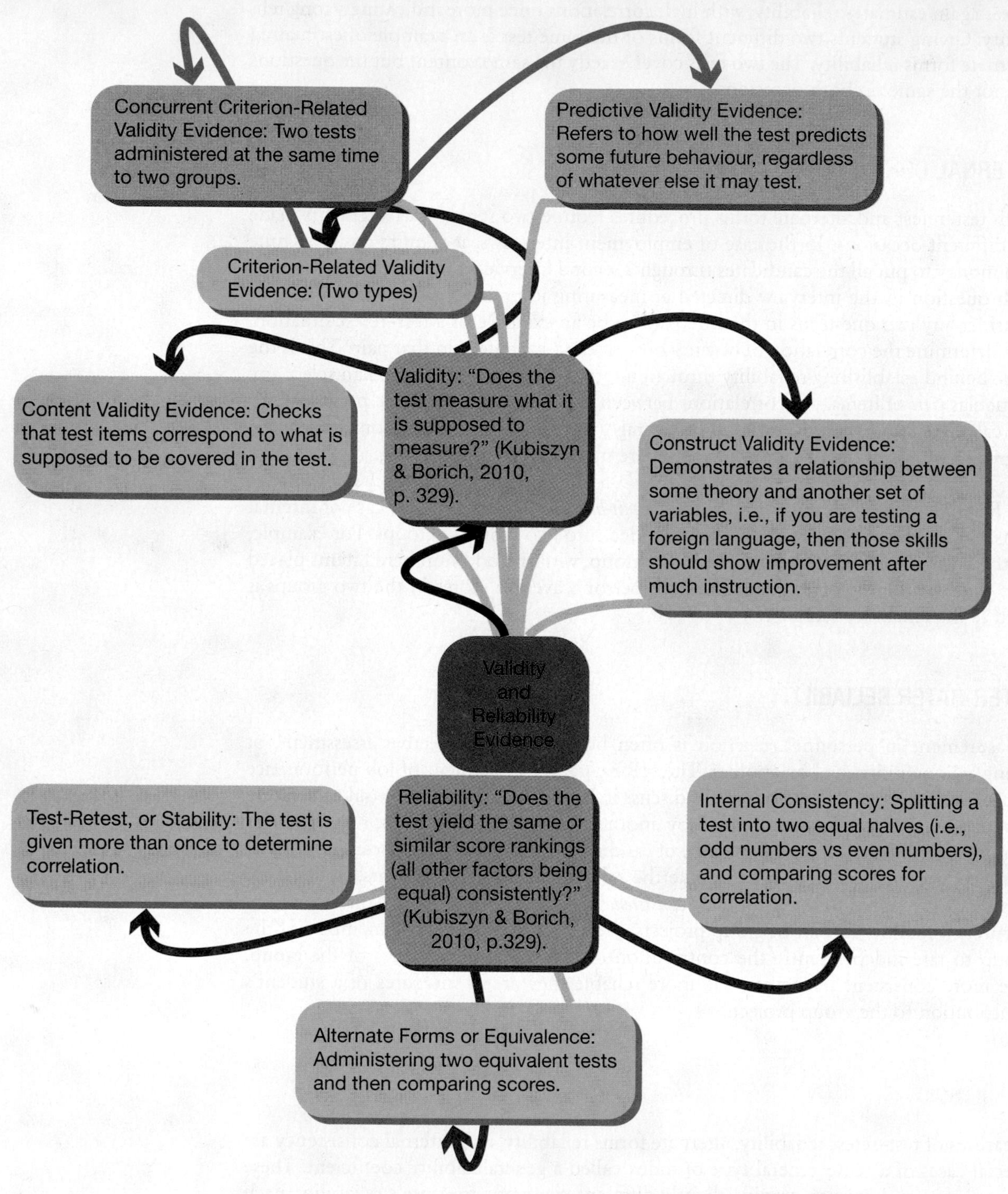

Concurrent Criterion-Related Validity Evidence: Two tests administered at the same time to two groups.
Predictive Validity Evidence: Refers to how well the test predicts some future behaviour, regardless of whatever else it may test.
Criterion-Related Validity Evidence: (Two types)
Content Validity Evidence: Checks that test items correspond to what is supposed to be covered in the test.
Validity: "Does the test measure what it is supposed to measure?" (Kubiszyn & Borich, 2010, p. 329).
Construct Validity Evidence: Demonstrates a relationship between some theory and another set of variables, i.e., if you are testing a foreign language, then those skills should show improvement after much instruction.
Validity and Reliability Evidence
Test-Retest, or Stability: The test is given more than once to determine correlation.
Reliability: "Does the test yield the same or similar score rankings (all other factors being equal) consistently?" (Kubiszyn & Borich, 2010, p.329).
Internal Consistency: Splitting a test into two equal halves (i.e., odd numbers vs even numbers), and comparing scores for correlation.
Alternate Forms or Equivalence: Administering two equivalent tests and then comparing scores.

is limited and does not convey all the relevant information that might be needed. The specific requirements of a situation may dictate which index is chosen. As well, it remains within the professional judgment of the HR specialist to choose an appropriate index of reliability and to determine the level of reliability that is acceptable for use of a specific measure. Before using any measurement to make decisions about employees, the HR specialist must consider the consequences of the decisions based on the measure. The need for accuracy increases with the seriousness of the consequences for the employee.[7]

// VALIDITY

It is important and necessary to demonstrate that a measure is reliable; it is also necessary to show that the measure captures the essence of the characteristic or attribute. Often, validity is incorrectly thought of as indicating the worth or goodness of a test or other measurement procedure. **Validity** simply refers to the legitimacy or correctness of the inferences that are drawn from a set of measurements or other specified procedures.[8] It is the degree to which accumulated evidence and theory support specific interpretations of test scores in the context of the test's proposed use. Consider the following: During an employment interview, an HR manager measures the height of each applicant with a metal measuring tape. These height measurements are likely to be very reliable. What if the manager assumes that taller applicants have more job-related cognitive ability and hires the tallest people? Are the inferences drawn from the physical height measures valid statements of cognitive ability? In other words, can the manager make a legitimate inference about cognitive ability from the height data? What if your instructor in a course on recruitment and selection in Canada gave you a test composed solely of Canadian history? Would the inferences made from that test be an accurate reflection of your knowledge of recruitment and selection?

Before using any set of measurements, it is essential to demonstrate that the measurements lead to valid inferences about the characteristic or construct under study. It is relatively easy to demonstrate that the metal tape provides valid measures of physical height. The metal tape measure can be scaled to an actual physical standard that is used to define a unit of length. The standard exists apart from the measurement process. In the case of length, the standard is a bar of plutonium maintained under specific atmospheric conditions in government laboratories.

It is more difficult to demonstrate the validity of inferences made from many psychological measurements because they deal more with abstract constructs, such as cognitive ability or intelligence. The measures may not represent important aspects of a construct (construct underrepresentation) or they may be influenced by aspects of the process that are unrelated to the construct (construct-irrelevant variance). In most of these cases, independent physical standards for the construct do not exist, making validation more difficult, but not impossible. Validation rests on evidence accumulated through a variety of sources and a theoretical foundation that supports specific interpretations of the measurements.

VALIDATION STRATEGIES

Validity is a unitary concept.[9,10] **Content**, **construct**, and **criterion-related validity** are different, but interrelated, strategies commonly used to assess the accuracy of inferences

Validity
The degree to which accumulated evidence and theory support specific interpretations of test scores in the context of the test's proposed use.

Content validity
Whether the items on a test appear to match the content or subject matter they are intended to assess; assessed through the judgments of experts in the subject area. A related concept is face validity, which is the degree to which test users or other non-experts believe that the test measures the content area.

Construct validity
The degree to which a test or procedure assesses an underlying theoretical construct it is supposed to measure; assessed through multiple sources of evidence showing that it measures what it purports to measure and not other constructs. For example, an IQ test must measure intelligence and not personality.

Criterion-related validity
The relationship between a predictor (test score) and an outcome measure; assessed by obtaining the correlation between the predictor and outcome scores.

based on measurements or tests used in the workplace. Sometimes these different strategies are mistakenly viewed as representing different types of validity. To overcome this misinterpretation, the older terms of "construct validity," "content validity," and "criterion-related validity" are no longer used in the measurement literature, although they are still used in personnel selection systems.

Both construct and content validity are validation strategies that provide evidence based on test content, while criterion-related validity provides evidence based on relationships to other variables. Our presentation is based on the *Standards for Educational and Psychological Testing*[11] and the *Principles for the Validation and Use of Personnel Selection Procedures*.[12] The latter is an important document that HR and personnel specialists rely on; it uses the traditional terms of *content*, *construct*, and *criterion-related validity* in discussing validation strategies, terms that we will continue to use in this text.

Our presentation of validation strategies is not exhaustive; we will examine only those sources of evidence for validity that are likely to be encountered in employment situations. You may want to refer to both the *Standards* and the *Principles* for a more thorough discussion of validity issues. The *Principles* can be viewed online at http://www.siop.org/_Principles/principlesdefault.aspx. The *Standards*, published in 1999, are currently being revised; they are still applicable to testing situations.

Let's assume that a company wants to hire a widget maker. The HR department performs a job analysis using one of the methods discussed in Chapter 4. Based on the job analysis, HR personnel hypothesize that cognitive ability is related to performance of the tasks or competencies associated with the position; this relationship is represented by Line A in Figure 2.4. This relationship is based on theoretical and logical analyses of expert opinion and empirical data that show, in this case, that cognitive ability is linked to the job performance of widget making. Both cognitive ability and job performance are abstract constructs, which must be operationally defined, respectively. Rather than

FIGURE 2.4

VALIDATION STRATEGIES

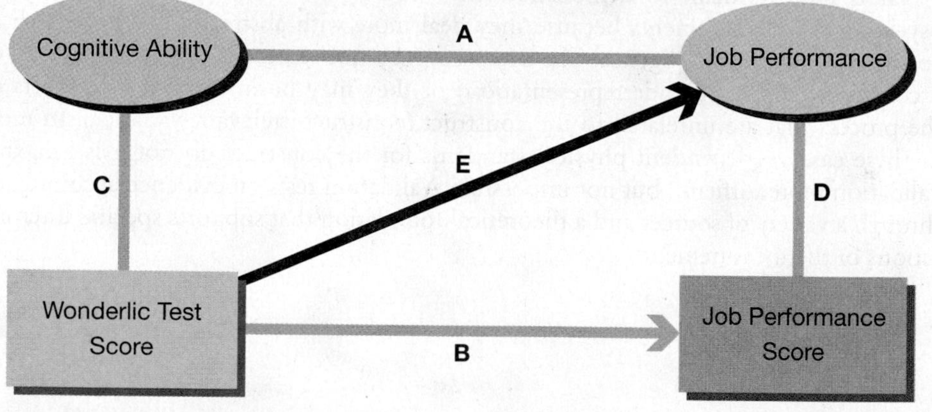

trying to develop their own measure of cognitive ability, HR personnel decide to use a cognitive ability test that is commercially available. There are many good measures of cognitive ability (see Chapter 8). They choose the Wonderlic Personnel Test (WPT), which is often used in employment situations to estimate cognitive ability. Based on research involving the WPT and information in the WPT test manual, they consider it to be both a reliable and valid measure of cognitive ability. The WPT has a relatively high correlation with other established measures of cognitive ability, e.g., the Wechsler Adult Intelligence Scale, and a relatively low correlation with the 16-PF, a measure of personality. They have established the link, Line C, between the WPT and cognitive ability based on *construct validation*.

If the HR group had decided to develop its own measure of cognitive ability, they would have had to establish its validity through a research program before they could use it to make selection decisions. Each construct has a set of associated behaviours or events. Only a relatively small handful of these behaviours are likely to be measured by any test or procedure. If the HR group had used a series of questions in their own test, a first step would be to have experts in cognitive ability assess whether the items on the test were relevant to cognitive ability. Are they the type of items you would expect on a test of cognitive ability? The experts would have to agree on what they meant by cognitive ability before they could answer this question. Doing so would be a case of *content validation*, determining that the content of their cognitive ability test represents the construct of cognitive ability. Can the HR personnel make reliable and valid conclusions about the cognitive ability of a job candidate based on scores from their test of cognitive ability?

Similarly, the HR personnel need to find a reliable and valid measure of job performance. This is usually more difficult than finding a measure of cognitive ability as the performance may be specific to the job or organization. Do all widget makers perform the same tasks or carry out the same job behaviours? Job performance is an abstract construct that involves performance of many behaviours, tasks, and competencies, and not all of these can be assessed as part of the job application process. HR must identify those tasks or competencies that are the most important, the most frequently performed, or the most critical to successful job performance. An HR specialist takes that information and turns it into a performance measure through one of the procedures discussed in Chapter 5. Whatever measure is developed to assess job performance, it should represent important work behaviours, outcomes, or relevant organizational expectations about the employee's performance. In Figure 2.4, Line D represents the relationship between the measure and construct of job performance; this is also an example of *construct validation*.

In selecting job applicants, one goal is to hire only those applicants who will perform at very high levels. If cognitive ability is associated with job performance at the construct level (Line A), then at the measurement level cognitive ability should predict job performance (Line B; the arrow indicates the direction of the prediction). We have to establish the relationship between the predictor and criterion measures empirically. This is an example of establishing the *criterion-related validity* of the WPT scores in predicting job performance scores, which is a test-relationship validation strategy. This procedure involves establishing a correlation between a predictor, in this case the WPT, and a criterion, a measure of job performance.

You may have noticed a problem with criterion-related validity strategies: the applicants have to be hired before their job performance can be measured. Two strategies get around this problem: predictive and concurrent validity strategies. Neither is a perfect solution, however both are accepted procedures for establishing the link between a predictor and criterion measures.

Predictive validation
Strategies in which evidence is obtained about a correlation between predictor scores that are obtained before an applicant is hired and criterion scores that are obtained at a later time, usually after an applicant is employed.

In **predictive validation** strategies evidence is obtained about a correlation between predictor scores that are obtained before an applicant is hired and criterion scores that are obtained at a later time, usually after an applicant is employed. If we had hired all of those who had applied for the job we could obtain data on their job performance and calculate the correlation between both variables; however, this would be at a substantial cost. We would be hiring many of the applicants with the knowledge that they would fail on the job, or that they would have to be dismissed because of that poor performance. This not only is expensive for the organization but also causes a great deal of emotional distress for those applicants who fail.

This procedure also raises serious legal and ethical considerations about the rights of job applicants and the obligations of people who make hiring decisions. To circumvent these problems, a variation on this procedure requires that hiring decisions be made without using information from the predictor measure until it is validated; the hiring decisions are made according to existing procedures, however data from the new predictor are also collected but not used until performance data are obtained from those applicants who are hired. That is, the HR specialist collects cognitive ability data from all the applicants, but the hiring decision is based solely on information contained in the applicants' résumés, employment interviews, and references. Job performance information is then collected from the group of hired applicants and correlated with their cognitive ability scores. If the correlation is high, the cognitive ability test may be used to select future job applicants. The high correlation is evidence that the measure of cognitive ability predicts a measure of job performance.

But, there is a problem with predictive validation. Validity concerns the correctness of inferences made from a set of measurements. Does the validity coefficient, which is based on only those applicants who were hired, apply to all applicants? This will be the case only if the hired applicants fairly represent the total pool of applicants; the only way this can happen is if those hired were randomly selected from the larger pool. Therefore, those who are hired on the basis of the existing selection system will likely differ from those not hired on at least one characteristic, whether or not that characteristic is related to job success.

Concurrent validation
Strategies in which evidence is obtained about a correlation between predictor and criteria scores from information that is collected at approximately the same time from a specific group of workers.

In **concurrent validation** evidence is obtained about a correlation between predictor and criteria scores from information that is collected at approximately the same time from a specific group of workers. The HR personnel have all current employees complete the cognitive ability test; at the same time, their supervisors assign a rating to the employees to reflect their job performance. A positive correlation between both sets of scores is taken as evidence for the validity of the cognitive ability test as predictor of the job performance measure. While concurrent evidence may be easier to collect, these strategies, too, are problematic. The group of existing workers used to develop the validity evidence is likely to be older, more experienced, and certainly more successful than those who apply for jobs. Unsuccessful or unproductive workers most likely are not part of the validation study as they probably were let go or transferred to other positions. The primary concern here is whether a validity coefficient based on only successful applicants can be used as evidence to validate decisions based on predictor scores obtained from a pool of job applicants who are likely to be both successful and unsuccessful on the job. An additional concern is the same one expressed with predictive strategies: does the validity coefficient computed on one group of workers apply to the pool of applicants? The current workers, who are asked to complete a battery of selection tests, may approach the whole exercise with a different attitude and level of motivation than job applicants. These differences may affect selection instruments, particularly those such as personality and integrity tests that rely on the test taker's cooperation in responding truthfully. Statistically, validity coefficients based on concurrent evidence will likely underestimate the true validity of using the predictor to make decisions within the pool of applicants. Recruitment and Selection Notebook 2.2 provides some guidance for assessing the validity of selection procedures in smaller organizations.

Despite the flaws, criterion-related validation strategies are probably the most frequently used strategies to validate selection procedures. Our interest in establishing a correlation between the predictor and the criterion makes sense only within the context of the model shown in Figure 2.4. What we really want to do is predict the job performance at the construct level from the cognitive ability scores obtained at the measurement level (Line E). That is, we want to make an inference about a job applicant's potential job performance from pre-employment measures. We want to say that job applicants with high WPT scores are likely to be employees who perform at high levels once they are hired.

Line E is the relationship that is of primary interest. Similar to Lines C and D, Line E represents a relationship between a measure and a construct; we are predicting the applicant's success on the job (not their performance score as we know what that is) from the tests we administered as part of the selection process. It is an inference or hypothesis, Line E, that can only be made after first establishing the relationships represented by Lines A, B, C, and D. We need to establish that:

- there is a theoretical or logical relationship between the predictor and criterion at the construct level (Line A);
- the predictor and criterion measures are reliable and valid measures of their respective constructs (Lines C and D); and
- there is an empirical relationship between the predictor and criterion measures (Line B).

Showing that these four relationships (Lines A, B, C, and D) exist provides evidence for the existence of Line E and allows us to use the WPT scores to select job applicants whom we believe will be successful employees. If the performance measure is based on having applicants perform a sample of the work they will actually do on the job, the performance measure itself may provide direct evidence for the relationship expressed in Line E. For example, the company has job applicants assemble widgets in a vestibule as part of the application process; this is a sample of actual job performance of building widgets. If the score from the WPT predicts the work samples test, then WPT scores directly predict job performance. However, in most situations it is difficult or expensive to obtain valid work samples, leaving Line E to be inferred indirectly.

VALIDITY GENERALIZATION

Suppose in attempting to establish the validity of cognitive ability as a predictor of specific job performance in the target organization, the HR manager discovered that many other studies also investigated measures of cognitive ability as predictors of job performance similar to widget making. Could the manager somehow combine all the information provided by these other correlation coefficients to obtain an estimate of the true validity of cognitive ability as a predictor of widget job performance in the HR manager's company? These other validity coefficients were obtained under vastly different measurement conditions and from employees who differ dramatically across these studies on a number of characteristics. The assembly of widgets might not quite be the same. Most likely, the value of the individual validity coefficients will be very inconsistent across all of these other studies. In other words, can the manager estimate the validity of cognitive ability as a predictor of job performance in the manager's work setting from the validity of inferences based on other measures of cognitive ability found in other work settings with other groups of workers? **Validity generalization** procedures allow these types of predictions to be made.

Validity generalization
The application of validity evidence, obtained through meta-analysis of data obtained from many situations, to other situations that are similar to those on which the meta-analysis is based.

Starting in the mid-1970s, Schmidt and Hunter,[13] in conjunction with several colleagues, challenged the idea that a validity coefficient was specific to the context or environment in which it was measured. They used a procedure known as *meta-analysis* to combine validity coefficients for similar predictor and criterion measures reported by different validity studies. Schmidt and Hunter argued that the relative inconsistency in validity coefficients across studies could be attributed to statistical artifacts such as the range of scores in each study, the reliability of the criterion measures, and sample size (i.e., the number of people in the validity study). In combining the data, meta-analysis weights the results from each separate validity study according to its sample. On the

RECRUITMENT AND SELECTION NOTEBOOK 2.2

VALIDITY

Validation studies require relatively large numbers of hires. This is a challenge for many Canadian organizations, particularly small businesses that do not hire many people. Several validation techniques are suited for use with small samples:

- Build a database by combining *similar* jobs *across* organizations or companies, with special care taken to ensure comparability of performance measures.
- Accumulate selection scores and performance measures *over time*, as workers leave and are replaced.
- Generalize to your particular case the mean (average) predictive validity for a test as found for jobs similar to the one to which you wish to generalize (i.e., *validity generalization*).
- Generalize to your case the *specific* validity of the test as previously established for a similar job in another setting (i.e., *validity transportability*).

Frequently, however, a *content sampling* strategy may be necessary. The steps for this process are:

1. Tasks (or activities) of the target position are identified by job experts.
2. Job experts infer, on a task-by-task basis, the required knowledge, skills, abilities, and other attributes (KSAOs).
3. Job experts independently rate the relevance of each KSAO for each task.
4. Assessment items (e.g., test questions, situational exercises, interview questions) are developed to measure the most relevant KSAOs.
5. Job experts provide independent ratings of the degree to which each assessment item is linked to the KSAOs.
6. Job experts evaluate the relationship between performance on each of the selection assessments and job success.
7. A scoring scheme is developed for the selection assessments.

The case for the validity of the selection system is then argued on the basis of an explicit systematic linking of the selection assessments (interview questions, test items, situational exercises) to the position requirements (KSAOs), as established by job experts.

Source: P.R. Sackett and R.D. Arvey. 1993. "Selection in Small N Settings." In Neal Schmitt, W.C. Borman, and Associates, eds., *Personnel Selection in Organizations.* San Francisco: Jossey-Bass, 418–47. Reproduced with permission of John Wiley & Sons Inc. via Copyright Clearance Center.

whole, the smaller the study size, the less accurate the results. Validity studies usually involve relatively small study sizes since most organizations do not hire large numbers of people. Schmidt and Hunter demonstrated that, once the effects associated with study size and the other artifacts were removed, the validity between a predictor and a criterion remained relatively stable within similar occupations. For example, the HR manager could use the Wonderlic scores to make predictions about job performance if other validity studies had linked the Wonderlic Personnel Test to job performance for similar jobs and if the Wonderlic scores were a valid measure of cognitive ability.

Should the HR specialist rely on validity generalization evidence or conduct a new validity study on-site? The answer is not straightforward. If the meta-analysis database is large and adequately represents the type of job to which it will be generalized in the local situation, there is a strong case for using the validity generalization data. On the other hand, if the database is small, the results are inconsistent, and there is little in common between the specific job and those included in the meta-analysis, then a local validity study should be carried out. If conducted properly with an adequate sample size, the local study may provide more useful information than the validity generalization data. A study carried out on the specific job in the local environment will also provide a means of corroborating questionable validity generalization data.[14]

FACTORS AFFECTING VALIDITY COEFFICIENTS

RANGE RESTRICTION

When measurements are made on a subgroup that is more homogeneous than the larger group from which it is selected, validity coefficients obtained on the subgroup are likely to be smaller than those obtained from the larger group. This reduction in the size of the validity coefficient due to the selection process is called *range restriction*. Selection results in a more homogeneous group. The applicant pool reviewed by the HR manager contains a broad range of cognitive ability. The people selected for employment are more likely to fall in the upper range of that attribute; the existing workers are also more likely to have levels of cognitive ability more similar to one another than to the applicant pool. The range of cognitive ability scores for the hired workers is narrower or more restricted than the scores of all the applicants. Statistically, the magnitude of correlation coefficients, including validity coefficients, decreases as the similarity or homogeneity of characteristics being measured increases. Figure 2.5 illustrates this effect with a plot of job performance scores against cognitive ability scores; the correlation is .55. This correlation is used in developing the regression line that is plotted through all the data points. The HR manager now requires all hires to have a score of 2.7 or higher on the cognitive ability test. The correlation between job performance and cognitive ability for the selected group is .30, which produces a flatter regression line than when calculated for all the applicants.

There are several statistical procedures that correct for range restriction and provide an estimate of what the validity coefficient is likely to be in the larger group. Range restriction is often encountered in selecting undergraduate students for graduate or professional programs. The students who apply for these positions are generally very similar with respect to their grade point averages and cognitive ability; this homogeneity generally leads to low correlation coefficients when their scores on standardized tests, such as the GRE, GMAT, LSAT, and others, are used to predict performance in graduate or professional school.

FIGURE 2.5

AN EXAMPLE OF RANGE RESTRICTION

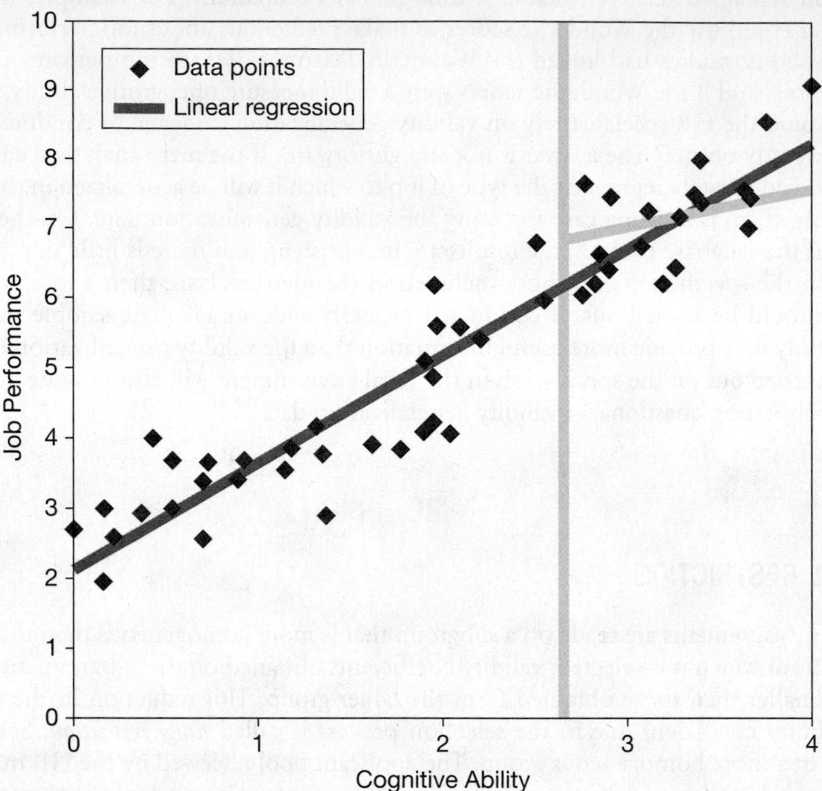

MEASUREMENT ERROR

The reliability of a measure places an upper limit on validity. Mathematically, the size of a validity coefficient cannot exceed the reliability of the measures used to obtain the data. Validity coefficients obtained from perfectly reliable measures of the predictor and criterion will be higher than those obtained with less-than-perfect measures. The decrease in magnitude of the validity coefficient associated with measurement error of the predictor, the criterion, or both, is called *attenuation*. As with range restriction, there are statistical procedures that provide an estimate of what the validity coefficient would be if it had been obtained by using measures that were perfectly reliable (i.e., $r_{xx} = 1.00$).

SAMPLING ERROR

Criterion-related validity coefficients are obtained from people who have been hired and are used to assess the accuracy of inferences that are made about individual applicants. The validity coefficient based on a sample is an estimate of what the coefficient is in the entire population; usually, it is impractical or impossible to measure the validity coefficient directly in the population. Estimates of the validity within a population may vary considerably between samples; estimates from small samples are likely to be quite variable.

CORRECTING FOR ERRORS

There are statistical procedures that can be used to correct for range restriction, attenuation, and sampling error. A validity coefficient may be corrected for any or all of these factors that may affect validity. The validity estimates produced after these corrections will almost always be higher than the uncorrected coefficients. When correction procedures are used, both the corrected and uncorrected validity coefficients should be reported along with a justification for the use of the correction.

USEFULNESS OF VALIDITY COEFFICIENTS

Figure 2.6 presents the validities for a number of employment tests or procedures with either overall job performance or training measures as the criterion. The validities range from −0.01 to 0.65.

How large should the validity of a test or procedure be for it to be used in selection? The best answer is "larger is better." The U.S Department of Labor's guide for employers on the relation of the magnitude of validity coefficients to their usefulness[15] is presented in Table 2.3. The validity coefficients in the table are uncorrected validities. This document is in use by a large number of U.S. federal departments as well as consulting firms. There is no Canadian consensus document on how large a validity coefficient should be, but the views of Canadian HR practitioners are unlikely to differ.

Mikhail Zahranichny/Shutterstock.com

The validity values in Table 2.3 are suggested guidelines. The validity a selection test or procedure rests on the integration of scientific evidence obtained through a variety of sources. It includes information that is collected from the existing scientific literature as well as data newly collected as part of the validation effort. Both existing data and theory are used to support the proposition that test scores allow accurate inferences to be made about a candidate's future job performance. The technical quality of the testing procedure (e.g., careful test development, test reliability, standardized test administration and scoring procedures, sample size, and test fairness) must also be considered along with other validity evidence. The Guide mentions that consideration must also be given to potential adverse impact, the selection ratio, the cost of a bad hire, the cost of the selection tool, and the probability of hiring a qualified applicant by chance without the aid of the tool. All of this information must be considered, along with the magnitude of the validity coefficient, in choosing an employment test or procedure.

// BIAS AND FAIRNESS

BIAS

In discussing reliability, we noted that measurement errors could be made in a consistent, or predictable, fashion. In the time clock example, five minutes were added to each worker's arrival time. What if the clock had added five minutes only to the arrival times of female employees? The observed scores are still reliable, but now they validly

FIGURE 2.6

VALIDITIES OF TESTS USED IN SELECTION

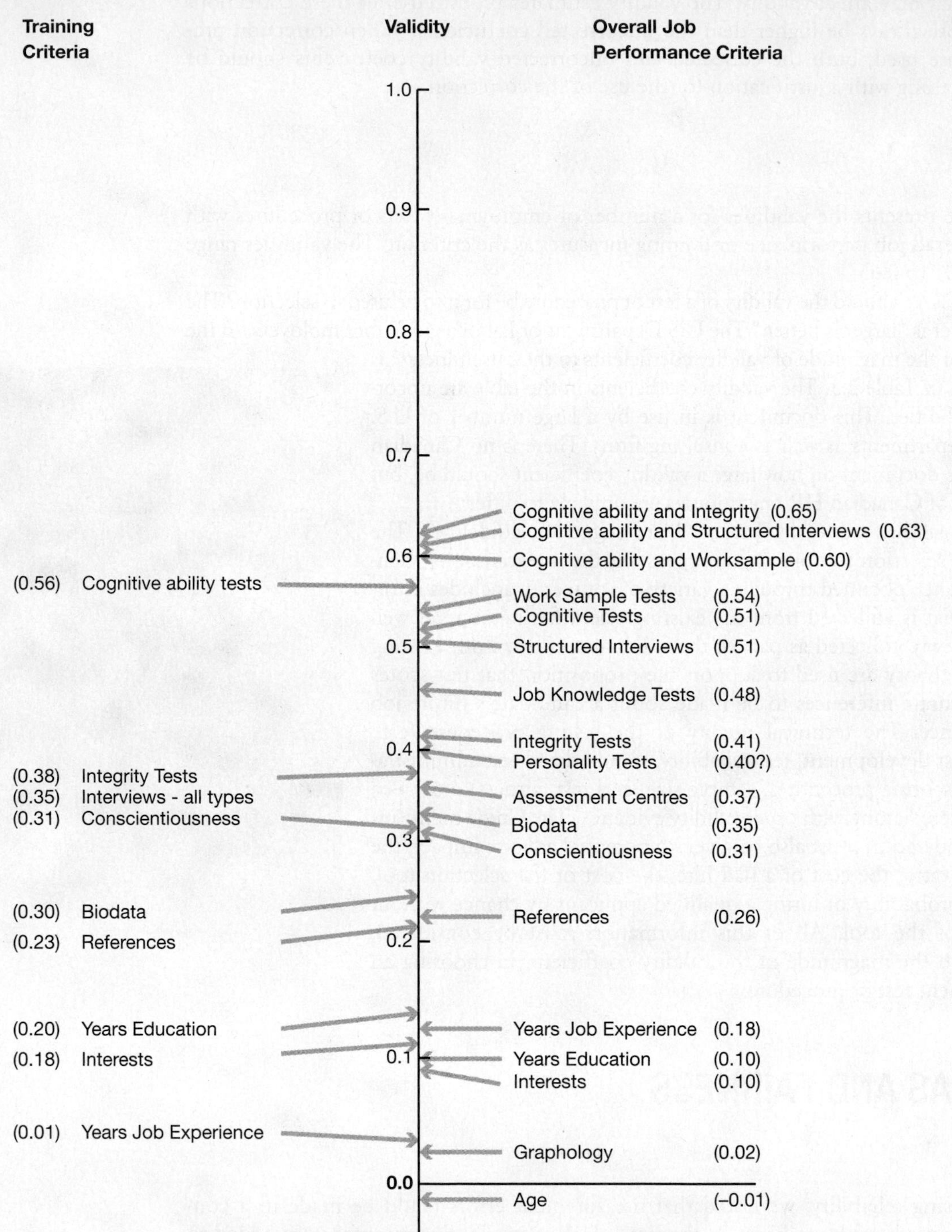

Source: Figure 1: Accuracy of Selection Methods (p. 3) in I.T. Robertson and M. Smith. 2001. "Personnel Selection," *Journal of Occupational and Organizational Psychology*, 74: 441–472. Reproduced with permission of British Psychological Society via Copyright Clearance Center.

TABLE 2.3

GENERAL GUIDELINES FOR INTERPRETING VALIDITY COEFFICIENTS

VALIDITY COEFFICIENT VALUE	INTERPRETATION
Above .35	Very beneficial
.21 – .35	Likely to be useful
.11 – .20	Depends on circumstances
Below .11	Unlikely to be useful

Source: U.S. Department of Labor, *Testing and Assessment: An Employer's Guide to Best Practices.*

represent the true arrival times for male employees, but not females. The clock is biased in measuring arrival times of female employees. **Bias** refers to systematic errors in measurement, or inferences made from measurements, that are related to different identifiable group membership characteristics such as age, sex, or race.[16] For example, suppose the cognitive ability test that is being used assigns higher test scores to females, when in fact there are no differences in cognitive ability between men and women. Inferences, or predictions, drawn from the biased measurements are themselves biased.

Bias
Systematic errors in measurement, or inferences made from those measurements, that are related to different identifiable group membership characteristics such as age, sex, or race.

The correlation between cognitive ability and job performance is used to derive a regression line that best fits the data points contained in the scatterplot shown in Figure 2.7. Figure 2.7 illustrates a hypothetical situation in which the cognitive ability scores of females are higher, on average, than those for the males, reflecting some type of systematic error. The regression line presented in Figure 2.7, using the biased cognitive ability measure as a predictor, overestimates the likely job performance of the female employees and underestimates that of males.

FIGURE 2.7

SCATTERPLOT OF COGNITIVE ABILITY AND JOB PERFORMANCE

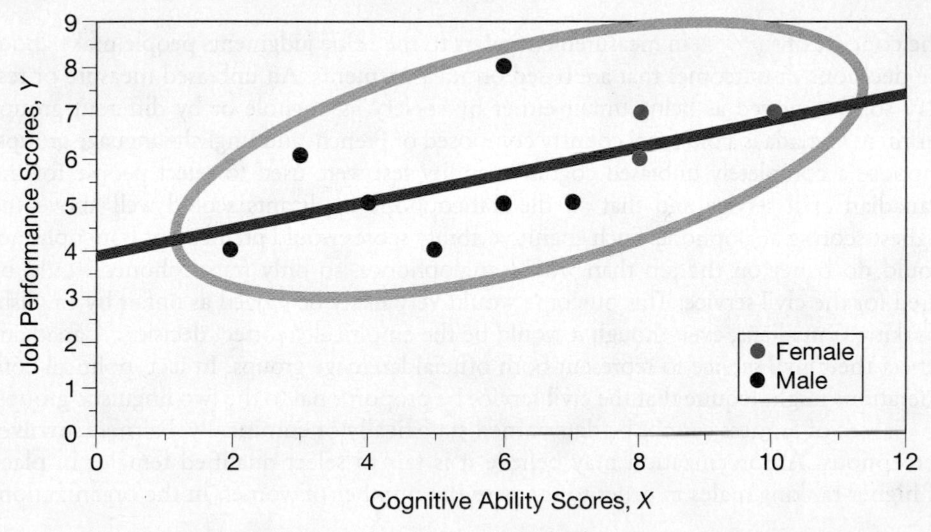

If this regression line were used to make hiring decisions (e.g., "We want employees who will obtain performance scores of 6 or better, so hire only applicants with cognitive ability scores of 8 or higher"), the predictions of successful job performance would be biased in favour of the female applicants. This type of bias is known as *predictive bias*; that is, the predicted average performance score of a subgroup, in this case females or males, is systematically higher or lower than the average score predicted for the group as a whole. This situation results in a larger proportion of the lower-scoring group being rejected on the basis of their test scores, even though they would have performed successfully had they been hired. This condition results from a less-than-perfect correlation between the predictor and criterion measures. One way to overcome this type of bias is to generate separate regression lines (i.e., separate prediction formulas) for males and females.[17] In Canadian federal organizations, separate prediction formulas are often used in selecting job applicants from anglophone and francophone linguistic groups. In U.S. federal organizations, the use of different selection rules for different identifiable subgroups (often referred to as *subgroup norming*) is prohibited by U.S. federal law.

There are other, more complicated, types of bias. *Measurement bias* occurs in a set of measurements[18] when items on a test may elicit a variety of responses other than what was intended, or some items on a test may have different meanings for members of different subgroups. For example, the Bennett Mechanical Comprehension Test contains pictures related to the use of different tools and machines that tended to be used mostly by males. Males were more likely to recognize these tools and their proper use and perform well on the test. On the other hand, females with good mechanical comprehension may not do as well on the test because of their lack of familiarity with specific tools pictured on the Bennett test. The result is that the test may underestimate the true mechanical ability of female job applicants.

The statistical procedures needed to establish predictive and measurement bias are often complicated and difficult to carry out. Nonetheless, the question of bias can be answered through empirical and objective procedures. As we will see in Chapter 3, HR professionals may have to demonstrate before courts or tribunals that the employment test or procedures they use are free from bias.

FAIRNESS

Fairness
The principle that every test taker should be assessed in an equitable manner.

The concept of **fairness** in measurement refers to the value judgments people make about the decisions or outcomes that are based on measurements. An unbiased measure or test may still be viewed as being unfair either by society as a whole or by different groups within it. Canada is a bilingual country composed of French- and English-language groups. Suppose a completely unbiased cognitive ability test were used to select people for the Canadian civil service and that all the francophone applicants scored well above the highest-scoring anglophone. Such cognitive ability scores would predict that francophones would do better on the job than would anglophones, so only francophones would be hired for the civil service. This outcome would very likely be judged as unfair by English-speaking Canadians, even though it would be the empirically correct decision. Canadians expect their civil service to represent both official language groups. In fact, political considerations might require that the civil service be proportional to the two linguistic groups.

Issues of fairness cannot be determined statistically or empirically. Fairness involves perceptions. An organization may believe it is fair to select qualified females in place of higher-ranking males in order to increase the number of women in the organization;

on the other hand, the higher-ranking males who were passed over might not agree. The *Principles for the Validation and Use of Personnel Selection Procedures*[19] states this about fairness (p. 27): "Fairness is a social rather than a psychometric concept. Its definition depends on what one considers to be fair. Fairness has no single meaning, and, therefore, no single statistical or psychometric definition." The *Principles* goes on to identify three meanings of fairness that are relevant in selection:

1. ***Fairness as equitable treatment in the testing process.*** All examinees should be treated equitably throughout the testing process. They should experience the same or comparable procedures in the testing itself, in how the tests are scored, and in how the test scores are used.
2. ***Fairness as lack of bias.*** A test or testing procedure is considered fair if it does not produce any systematic effects that are related to different identifiable group membership characteristics such as age, sex, or race.
3. ***Fairness in selection and prediction.*** This often requires a compromise between the perspective that equates fairness with lack of bias and the perspective that focuses on testing outcomes. A selection test might be considered fair if the same test score predicts the same performance level for members of all groups, but it might be considered unfair if average test scores differ across groups. The fairness of the test should, in this situation, be evaluated relative to fairness of other, non-test alternatives that could be used in place of the test.

Fairness is an even more complex topic than bias. Achieving fairness often requires compromise between conflicting interests.[20,21] This is particularly so in the case where, for whatever reason, there may be persistent differences in average test scores between different groups in the population but those differences do not necessarily indicate test bias. A test score predicts the same level of performance for members of all groups, but the average test score for one group is lower than another group's, leading to the exclusion of a larger proportion of the group with the lower average score. Lowering the selection standards to include more applicants from this group in order to make the work force more representative of the general population may come at the cost of hiring job applicants who, while they meet the minimum job qualifications, are not the most qualified candidates for the position. Presumably, the most qualified candidates bring the most return in productivity to the organization.

Does an organization have an obligation to make the enterprise as profitable as possible on behalf of its owners, or should it meet the objectives of society by providing equal employment opportunities for members of different population groups? There are no easy answers to this question. In cases such as this, one resolution is to compare the fairness of the test in question with the fairness of an alternative that might be used in place of the test.[22]

In addition to the concerns about the impact of tests on different groups, fairness issues also include the reaction of applicants to testing and personnel selection decisions. It is important from business, ethical, and legal standpoints to have tests that are scientifically sound; it is also important to have procedures that are perceived as fair. From a business perspective, the adverse reactions to selection tests and procedures may impair the ability of an organization to recruit and hire the best applicants, thereby reducing the utility of the recruitment and selection process. Applicant reactions to selection procedures may affect applicants' decision to join an organization and the degree to which they trust the organization and their behaviour once they become an employee.[23,24] In Chapter 8 we present some research on applicant reactions to different employment tests and procedures.

From an ethical view, the perceived fairness of the testing procedures may negatively affect the unsuccessful candidates. From a legal perspective, the perception of unfairness may lead unsuccessful applicants to pursue discrimination charges against the prospective employer in various legal arenas.[25]

Serious consideration should be given to the perception of a test or selection procedure from the applicant's perspective prior to its adoption. This does not mean that an employer should discard scientifically valid procedures because they may be perceived as unfair; there is far more risk for an organization that makes employment decisions on the basis of unproven methods. In the final analysis, fairness is a question of balance.

THE LEGAL ENVIRONMENT AND SELECTION

Selection programs and practices must operate within the current legal context (see Chapter 3). Ideally, they do not have adverse impact on members of protected groups. Selection programs that intentionally or unintentionally exclude job applicants using characteristics or factors that are protected under human rights legislation, unless they are bona fide occupational requirements (BFORs), run the risk of being declared unfairly discriminatory, and the organization may be subject to penalties and fines. Chapter 3 discusses in more detail the standards that must be met for selection practices to withstand legal scrutiny. Recruitment and selection procedures should yield the best-qualified candidates within the constraints imposed by the current legal environment.

// SUMMARY

Science produces information that is based on accepting as true only that objective information that can withstand continued attempts to cast doubt on its accuracy. The accuracy of scientific statements is examined empirically through methods that can be observed, critiqued, and used by others. Scientific information is dynamic and constantly evolving. One goal of personnel selection is to use scientifically derived information to predict which job applicants will do well on the job. The procedures used to select employees must meet acceptable professional and legal standards. The best way of ensuring this is to be familiar with measurement, reliability, and validity issues and to use only those procedures that will withstand legal scrutiny; that is, the selection procedures validly predict work performance in a nondiscriminatory manner.

Scientific procedures allow for the measurement of important human characteristics that may be related to job performance and are more likely than other procedures to produce results that meet legal requirements. The reliability and validity of the information used as part of personnel selection procedures must be established empirically. The methods used to establish reliability and validity can be quite complex and require a good statistical background. As a scientific process, any personnel selection system must be able to withstand attempts to cast doubt on its ability to select the best people for the job in a fair and unbiased manner.

KEY TERMS

Bias, p. 55
Concurrent validation, p. 48
Construct validity, p. 45
Content validity, p. 45
Criterion-related validity, p. 45
Error score, p. 39
Fairness, p. 56
KSAOs , p. 29
Measurement error, p. 40
Predictive validation, p. 48
Reliability, p. 37
True score, p. 39
Validity, p. 45
Validity generalization, p. 50

WEB LINKS

For more information on basic statistical procedures, go to **http://wise.cgu.edu**

Test reliability and validity information is provided at **http://www.socialresearchmethods.net/kb/relandval.php** and at **http://www.okstate.edu/ag/agedcm4h/academic/aged5980a/5980/newpage18.htm**

DISCUSSION QUESTIONS

1. Discuss why it is better to base a selection system on science than a "gut feeling."
2. Can an invalid selection test be reliable? Can an unreliable selection test be valid? (*Hint:* Consider finding Canadian history questions on your recruitment and selection exam.)
3. When should you use content, construct, or criterion-related validation strategies?
4. Does an organization have an obligation to make the enterprise as profitable as possible on behalf of its owners, or does it have an obligation to meet the objectives of society by providing equal employment opportunities for members of different population groups?
5. What is your perception of fairness?
6. Do individuals making staffing decisions have an ethical responsibility to know about measurement issues? Why or why not?

EXERCISES

1. (*Note:* Class instructors may wish to assign this exercise during the previous class and ask students to e-mail their data to them beforehand.)

   A significant portion of this chapter has dealt with tests and testing procedures. In later chapters we will explore the use of different types of employment tests that have good reputations for reliability and validity. Access to these tests is restricted for obvious reasons. They can be administered only by qualified examiners, unlike the types of "IQ" and "personality" tests that you may come across in newspapers or magazines. While these latter tests are fun to take, they may have questionable reliability and validity.

Many sites on the Internet are devoted to tests; some are serious and some are for fun. One of the better sites is Queendom Mind and Body at http://www.queendom.com. This site offers an array of tests including IQ, personality, and emotional intelligence. All of the tests are free and can be taken online and are immediately scored. Unlike some other sites, it offers statistical information on the reliability of almost all of its tests and on the validity of some. Most of the reliability data are based on measures of internal consistency.

As part of this exercise, take the Classical IQ, the Emotional Intelligence, and the Big Five Personality tests. Queendom.com will provide you with a report containing your scores and inferences from your scores about how you fare on the three constructs. Please download copies of each report as well as the statistical data provided for each test. Your instructor will arrange for you to anonymously record your scores from these tests so that data on the whole class can be accumulated for the following exercises. We will also ask you to record your sex and your cumulative grade point average or percentage (if you don't know this last item, an estimate will do).

a. *Test–Retest Reliability.* Wait at least one week after taking the three tests and then retake all three. Once all the data from the class are compiled, your instructor will compute the correlation between the first and second administration of the three tests.

   - Are each of the tests reliable? (Tests with reliability coefficients greater than 0.70 are generally considered to have acceptable reliability.)
   - How does the test–retest reliability compare with the reliability values presented online?
   - What do you think the reasons may be for any differences?
   - What factors may have led you to perform differently on each of the two testing occasions?

b. *Validity.* Examine the content of each test–that is, examine the nature of the test questions (you are allowed to download a copy of each test).

   - Do you think that the contents of each test reflect the essential nature of the construct it attempts to measure?
   - Based on other empirical and theoretical evidence, we would not expect there to be a strong relationship between the results of the Classical IQ (a measure of cognitive ability) and Extraversion/Introversion (a measure of personality) tests. Emotional intelligence has been presented as a construct, which is different from both cognitive ability and personality. There should be very low correlations among the test scores from these three tests. A high correlation between the Emotional Intelligence and Extraversion/Introversion test results might suggest that both tests are measures of the same construct. Your instructor will correlate the three test scores for the class using data from the first test administration. What is the relationship among the three test scores?
   - Cognitive ability is associated with academic performance. The Classical IQ Test measures cognitive ability, and your cumulative grade point average (GPA) is an estimate of your academic performance. GPA is a criterion. What is the correlation between the Classical IQ Test results and GPA for your class, as reported by your instructor? Does this correlation indicate that

you may make accurate inferences about academic performance from your IQ test scores? Is there a strong correlation between the Emotional IQ Test scores and GPA? Between the Extraversion/Introversion Test results and GPA? If so, what do you think these correlations suggest?

c. *Bias*. You or your instructor will have to analyze the class data separately for males and females. Compare the mean score for each group across the three tests. Compute the correlations among the three tests for men and women.
   - Do you obtain similar results for males and females?
   - Are any of the three tests biased?

d. *Fairness*. Do you believe that each of these three tests is fair? How would you react if you were given any of these three tests when you applied for your next job?

2. A marketing company is evaluating a new employment test that measures advertising aptitude of potential employees. You have used the new measure on a trial basis over the past year while you have continued to make selections using your established procedures. You have developed the following database, which includes information on gender, a score from the first administration of the test given during the selection process before the applicant was hired (Test 1), a score from a second administration of the test given at the end of the first year on the job (Test 2), and a performance score assigned by the supervisor at the end of the employee's first year of employment (Performance). You have been asked to evaluate the reliability, validity, and any gender bias of the new test. (*Note:* This exercise requires you to calculate correlation coefficients. If you do not know how to do that, your instructor will provide you with the coefficients.)

Employee	Gender	Test 1	Test 2	Performance
1	male	24	18	20
2	female	18	13	29
3	male	21	17	17
4	male	7	13	8
5	female	14	28	25
6	male	20	21	26
7	male	8	6	7
8	female	13	9	12
9	male	15	13	18
10	male	19	15	22
11	female	25	22	23
12	female	23	16	27
13	male	18	13	10
14	female	12	14	6
15	female	17	12	13
16	female	6	9	12

a. What is the reliability of the new test?
b. What is the predictive validity of the new test?
c. What is the concurrent validity of the job?
d. Is the test biased toward either males or females?
e. Would you recommend that the company adopt the new test as part of its hiring procedures?

3. Choose a specific job held by one of the people in your group. After discussing the job, choose one characteristic that you think is crucial to performing that job. How would you measure both the characteristic and job performance? Use Figures 2.1 and 2.4 to help you specify the conceptual and measurement levels. How would you establish the validity of your characteristic as a predictor of job performance?
4. *Group Project.* Each group is to choose two organizations and then interview the organizations' HR staff to identify the type of selection that is being used. Use the criteria in Table 2.1 to determine whether each organization's selection system is analytical or intuitive. Determine the validity of the selection procedures in use by each organization; that is, has the company conducted validation studies and, if so, what was the outcome? Collect any validation reports that the organizations might have produced and bring the reports back to the group for review and discussion. Each group will then present a report of its findings to the class.

CASE

A story in the *Daily Commercial News*[26] reported that a growing number of Canadian companies are using measures of emotional intelligence (EQ) as part of the screening devices administered to job applicants. These companies are looking for a measure to tap into emotions. They are seeking candidates who have the ability to inspire colleagues, to handle customers, and to be a positive influence in the office. One of the more popular measures of emotional intelligence is the Bar-On Emotional Quotient Inventory (EQi), which is distributed by Multi-Health Systems of Toronto. Steven Stein, president of Multi-Health Systems, says that IQ has to do with solving math problems and verbal ability has its place but emotional skills are much more valuable for success in the workplace. Can a measure of emotional intelligence predict job success? Lorne Sulsky, an industrial-organizational psychologist now at Wilfrid Laurier University, is skeptical because the concept is too fuzzy and EQ tests are too imprecise to be reliable. Sulsky asks, "Why should there be a relationship between job performance and EQ?"

QUESTIONS

1. What do you think? Do the data that you collected from the Queendom.com exercise help you to answer this question? Is there a relationship between job performance and EQ? Can you support your answer with any empirical data? How can the construct of EQ be improved? Is it too broad? Is EQ simply another aspect of personality?
2. If you planned to use EQ as part of your selection system, discuss the steps that you would take to ensure that you were able to make reliable and accurate inferences about job performance in your work situation. That is, what would you have to do to show that your measure was reliable and valid?

// ENDNOTES

1 Highhouse, S. 2008. "Stubborn Reliance on Intuition and Subjectivity in Employee Selection." *Industrial and Organizational Psychology* 1: 333–342.

2 Lodato, M.A., S. Highhouse, and M.E. Brooks. 2011. "Predicting Professional Preferences for Intuition-Based Hiring." *Journal of Managerial Psychology* 26: 352–365.

3 American Educational Research Association (AERA), American Psychological Association, and National Council on Measurement in Education. 1999. *Standards for Educational and Psychological Testing*. Washington, DC: American Educational Research Association.

4 Nunnally, J.C., and I.H. Bernstein. 1994. *Psychometric Theory*, 3rd ed. New York: McGraw-Hill.

5 Society for Industrial and Organizational Psychology. 2003. *Principles for the Validation and Use of Personnel Selection Procedures*, 4th ed. College Park, MD: Author.

6 U.S. Department of Labor and O*NET. 2000. *Testing and Assessment: An Employer's Guide to Good Practices*. Retrieved from http://www.onetcenter.org/guides.html

7 AERA et al. 1999.

8 Cronbach, L.J. 1971. "Test Validation." In R.L. Thorndike, ed., *Educational Measurement*, 2nd ed. Washington, DC: American Council of Education.

9 Binning, J.F., and G.V. Barrett. 1989. "Validity of Personnel Decisions: A Conceptual Analysis of the Inferential and Evidential Bases." *Journal of Applied Psychology* 74: 478–94.

10 AERA et al. 1999.

11 Ibid.

12 Society for Industrial and Organizational Psychology. 2003.

13 Schmidt, F.L., and J.E. Hunter. 1977. "Development of a General Solution to the Problem of Validity Generalization." *Journal of Applied Psychology* 62: 529–40.

14 AERA et al. 1999.

15 U.S. Department of Labor and O*NET. 2000.

16 AERA et al. 1999.

17 Ibid.

18 Sackett, P.R., and S.L. Wilk. 1994. "Within-Group Norming and Other Forms of Score Adjustment in Pre-employment Testing." *American Psychologist* 49: 929–54.

19 Society for Industrial and Organizational Psychology. 2003.

20 Gottfredson, L.S. 1994. "The Science and Politics of Race-Norming." *American Psychologist* 49: 955–63.

21 Sackett, P.R., and S.L. Wilk. 1994.

22 AERA et al. 1999.

23 Celani, A., Deutsch-Salmon, S., and Singh, P. 2008. "In Justice We Trust: A Model of the Role of Trust in the Organization in Applicant Reactions to the Selection Process." *Human Resource Management Review* 18: 63–76.

24 Saks, A.M., and J.M. McCarthy. 2006. "Effects of Discriminatory Interview Questions and Gender on Applicant Reactions." *Journal of Business and Psychology* 21: 175–91.

25 Gilliland, S.W. 1993. "The Perceived Fairness of Selection Systems: An Organizational Justice Perspective." *Academy of Management Review* 18: 694–734.

26 "Will EQ Gradually Replace IQ in Screening Candidates for Jobs?" 1998. *Daily Commercial News* 71: S2, A14.

CHAPTER 3

FOUNDATIONS OF RECRUITMENT AND SELECTION II:

Legal Issues

CHAPTER LEARNING OUTCOMES

This chapter presents an overview of the legal issues that affect the practice of recruitment and selection in Canada.

AFTER READING THIS CHAPTER YOU SHOULD:

- understand the major legal issues affecting recruitment and selection;
- know how relevant human rights and employment equity legislation and policies affect recruitment and selection in your organization;
- understand and be able to describe how legal concerns affect the practice of recruitment and selection;
- know, and be capable of explaining, the key legal concepts that have had an impact on recruitment and selection in this country; and
- be able to apply the basic concepts and principles discussed in the chapter to the development of recruitment and selection systems that meet legal requirements.

NO BABIES ALLOWED

Every Canadian organization falls under either federal or provincial/territorial legislation that has an impact on its recruitment and selection policies and practices. HR professionals may at times find themselves at odds with a manager who has responsibility for making the final hiring decision. Managers may not always be as knowledgeable of human rights issues as HR staff ought to be. Hiring decisions may run afoul of the law and leave the organization open to various criminal or civil legal prosecutions. The following incident was conveyed to us by an HR practitioner and illustrates potential problems faced by women trying to balance work and family obligations.

The manager and HR professional interviewed all of the short-listed candidates for a position. A female applicant interviewed exceptionally well and the HR professional felt that she was the strongest candidate. The manager, although agreeing that she was the best candidate, did not want to hire her. She had been previously employed by the company and was an excellent worker. When she became pregnant, she went on maternity leave; when that leave ended she resigned in order to stay home to raise her child, who is now school-aged. The manager felt that the individual had been given the chance to work for the organization once and had given up that opportunity to raise her child. He felt that the opportunity to work for the company should now be given to someone else.

The applicant clearly met all of the requirements for the position, had previous working experience in the position, interviewed well, and was the strongest candidate. A review of her previous employment record by the HR professional confirmed that the applicant was an excellent performer, had a spotless discipline record, and had indeed left the company to raise her child.

The HR professional advised the manager that not hiring this female applicant would likely constitute a human rights violation, including employment equity legislation, and lead to a complaint before the provincial human rights tribunal that the company would have to defend. The HR professional provided the hiring manager with a copy of the sections of the Human Rights Act that directly affect recruitment and employment. In addition, the HR professional pointed out to the manager that even if they were successful in defending a human rights charge, the company would be severely embarrassed by refusing to rehire an excellent former employee on the grounds that she took some time off to raise her child.

The outcome of the HR professional's intervention was that the manger changed his mind and agreed to rehire the former employee. The applicant successfully completed her training and probationary period with the company and remains a very productive employee.

Many of the illustrations in this chapter focus on areas where an organization's practices have run afoul of the applicable law. This chapter is organized into three parts. Part I describes the key legislation and legal requirements that affect recruitment and selection practices in Canada, including a review of existing legislation. Part II discusses the important legal concepts that have emerged from this existing legislation. These legal concepts require recruitment and selection programs to be nondiscriminatory with respect to hiring members of designated groups. Part III provides some practical guidance on what to do, and what not to do, in recruitment and selection to meet legal obligations. As well, the Recruitment and Selection Notebook boxes scattered throughout the chapter offer practical advice for HR practitioners with respect to these legal requirements.

We have taken many of the examples presented in this chapter from Canadian federal human rights, employment equity, employment standards, or labour laws for the following reasons. First, provincial and municipal jurisdictions often draw on federal law when drafting their own legislation and programs. Examining federal laws provides a common framework for understanding what is happening in these other jurisdictions. Second, the laws, policies, and practices vary across jurisdictions; for example, a human rights tribunal decision in British Columbia may have no applicability in any other province or territory, and vice versa. Although we present some illustrative cases from provincial rights tribunals, the rulings from these cases may not apply to your provincial situation unless those rulings have been upheld on appeal by federal courts such as the Supreme Court of Canada. Indeed, you may find two provincial human rights tribunals ruling in opposite ways on the same issue or interpreting Supreme Court of Canada decisions differently.

This chapter is not intended to be a text on Canadian employment law or labour law. Our intent is to show the impact of legal requirements, as formulated through significant legislation and case law, on the practice of recruitment and selection in Canada. We encourage you to become familiar with the human rights, employment equity, employment standards, and labour laws that apply to your provincial, territorial, and municipal jurisdictions. Keep in mind that new legislation and decisions that are made following the publication of this book may change the presentation we make in this chapter.

// PART I: A BASIC BACKGROUND IN LEGAL REQUIREMENTS FOR NONDISCRIMINATORY RECRUITMENT AND SELECTION

Discrimination
In employment, any refusal to employ or to continue to employ any person, or to adversely affect any current employee, on the basis of that individual's membership in a protected group. All Canadian jurisdictions prohibit discrimination at least on the basis of race or colour, religion or creed, age, sex, marital status, and physical or mental disability.

Four legal sources affect Canadian employment practices in recruitment and selection: (1) constitutional law; (2) human rights law; (3) employment equity legislation; and (4) labour law, employment standards, and related legislation. *Constitutional law* is the supreme law of Canada. It has a pervasive impact on employment practices, as it does on all spheres of Canadian society. *Human rights* legislation across Canada prohibits **discrimination** in both employment and the provision of goods and services (e.g., rental housing, service in restaurants). This legislation generally establishes human rights commissions or tribunals to deal with complaints, including those involving employment discrimination.

Employment equity programs are administrative mechanisms set up in many Canadian organizations in response to federal employment equity legislation initiatives and cover nearly 2 million working Canadians. Employment equity programs have a major impact on employment systems, including recruitment and selection. Employment equity programs are intended to promote the entry and retention of people from designated groups (including women, visible minorities, Aboriginal peoples, and people with disabilities).

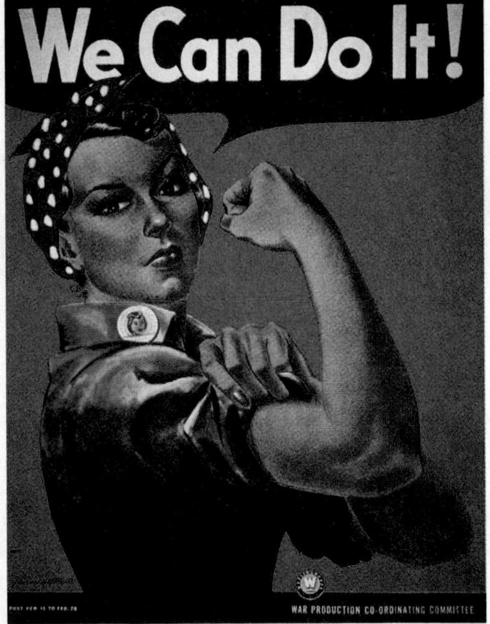

© J. Howard Miller/Corbis

Labour law, employment standards, and related legislation grant certain employment rights to both employers and employees, but also impose a wide range of employment responsibilities and obligations. Some of this legislation may have a direct impact on recruitment and selection practices in the jurisdiction where it is in force. Recruitment and Selection Notebook 3.1 illustrates some of the differences among these four types of legislation.

This chapter only hints at the complexity of the legal issues involved in recruitment and selection practices. For example, we do not discuss common law, the application of judicial precedence, or contract law, which may all have an impact on recruitment and selection decisions. As a starting point, HR professionals must understand the origins, purpose, and stakeholders of each of the fundamental legal requirements if they are to manage recruitment and selection activities in compliance with the law. They need to keep up with legislative changes on a continuing basis as the law itself is always changing.

CONSTITUTIONAL LAW

The Constitution of Canada consists of a series of acts and orders passed since 1867 by the British and Canadian Parliaments.[1] These separate acts and orders begin with the British North America Act of 1867 and end with the Constitution Act of 1982. Sections 1 to 34 of Part 1 of the Constitution Act of 1982 are called the *Canadian Charter of Rights and Freedoms*. The Constitution, taken as a whole, serves as the supreme law of Canada, as stated in subsection 52(1) of the Constitution Act of 1982:

> *52. (1) The Constitution of Canada is the supreme law of Canada and any law that is inconsistent with the provisions of the Constitution is, to the extent of the inconsistency, of no force or effect.*

All laws in Canada that come into force in a dispute between a private person and a branch of government (whether legislative, executive, or administrative) fall under the Constitution.[2] The Constitution has precedence over all the other legal means discussed in this chapter.

A section of the Constitution often cited in employment law is section 15 of the Canadian Charter of Rights and Freedoms, which lays out the principle of equality rights:

> *15. (1) Every individual is equal before and under the law and has the right to the equal protection and equal benefit of the law without discrimination and, in particular, without discrimination based on race, national or ethnic origin, colour, religion, sex, age or mental or physical disability.*
>
> *(2) Subsection (1) does not preclude any law, program or activity that has as its object the amelioration of conditions of disadvantaged individuals or groups including those that are disadvantaged because of race, national or ethnic origin, colour, religion, sex, age or mental or physical disability.*

RECRUITMENT AND SELECTION NOTEBOOK 3.1

NOT ALL LEGAL REQUIREMENTS ARE THE SAME

The four types of laws discussed in this chapter have varied historical roots and they address the needs of different stakeholder groups in society. *Constitutional law*, which has its origins in the British North America Act of 1867, spells out the division of powers between the federal and provincial/territorial governments, as well as the rights and freedoms that Canadians enjoy under governments at all levels. All citizens are stakeholders under constitutional law, and its provisions directly or indirectly affect all of us.

Human rights legislation (federal and provincial/territorial) exists in Canada partly in response to international conventions declared by the United Nations and partly because of domestic pressure to eliminate discrimination in the workplace and in other areas such as housing and provision of services. Human rights acts prohibit discrimination on protected grounds such as race or sex, and the legislation is restrictive in that its provisions have no force beyond the protected groups.

Employment equity legislation, policies, and programs have evolved in Canada as a response both to affirmative action programs in the United States and to pressures within our own country to increase workforce diversity. Employment equity addresses the concerns of designated groups (women, visible minorities, Aboriginal peoples, and people with disabilities) and has no force or effect beyond these stakeholder groups.

Labour laws in the federal and provincial/territorial jurisdictions across Canada are a response to a long history of labour union activity undertaken to improve workers' job security, wages, hours, working conditions, and benefits. These laws provide mechanisms for collective bargaining and union certification and rules for a "fair fight" between management and unions, as well as protecting the public interest.[3] Of course, the stakeholders under this legislation are unionized workers covered by collective agreements and managers in unionized workplaces.

Employment standards, both federal and provincial, trace their origins back to the British North America Act and reflect societal norms about the respective rights and responsibilities of employers and their employees, whether these employees are unionized or not. Employment standards covered in legislation across Canada include statutory school-leaving age, minimum age for employment, minimum wages, vacations and leave, holidays with pay, and termination of employment. All workers in Canada, and their managers, are stakeholders in this legislation.

Other related legislation, including regulation of federal government workers, results from unique conditions in specific sectors and is restricted to addressing the needs of those stakeholders. As a general rule, human rights and employment equity address the problem of discrimination, whereas the remainder of the legal means (labour law, employment standards, and related legislation) provide mechanisms to resolve procedural or contractual disagreements between specific stakeholders named in the legislation. (Examples of the latter would be promotion based on the merit principle for federal government employees under the Public Service Employment Act passed by Parliament, seniority rights in collective agreements for employees of Crown corporations, and other types of contractual and legal obligations between employer and employee in either the private or public sectors.) However, even this basic distinction between antidiscrimination legislation and procedural/contract enforcement legislation can blur in practice. For example, equal pay for men and women for work of equal value, which is a discrimination issue, comes under human rights acts in some provinces and territories and employment standards legislation in others.

The discrimination provision in subsection (1) of the Charter resembles provisions found in human rights legislation across Canada. Subsection (2) makes it clear that programs such as employment equity, which may favour individuals or designated groups as a means to overcome past disadvantages, are not, in themselves, discriminatory and barred by subsection (1).

As a practical matter, constitutional law does not directly affect everyday recruitment and selection activities. Constitutional law becomes an issue only when recruitment or selection practices are challenged in a human rights tribunal or court. Nevertheless, constitutional law has a pervasive, indirect impact on employment practices by setting limits and conditions on what federal, provincial/territorial, and municipal governments and courts can legally do to alter employment policies and practices. The interpretation of constitutional law through legislation and jurisprudence has an indirect, but substantial, influence on all aspects of the practice of human resources–from the development of an organization's HR policy to the conduct of an employment interview.

HUMAN RIGHTS LEGISLATION

Each province and territory, as well as the federal government, has established a human rights act or code that prohibits discrimination in employment and in the provision of goods and services. The federal or provincial/territorial acts apply to organizations that fall under their respective jurisdictions. Normally, this means that organizations are governed by the laws of the political division in which they are chartered or incorporated. For example, a company incorporated in Ontario would fall under Ontario's human rights act, while the Canadian Broadcasting Corporation (CBC), whose headquarters are in Ontario, would fall under the Canadian Human Rights Act, as it is a federally regulated organization. Federal legislation applies to all organizations in the transportation, broadcasting, and financial services sectors, as well as to any company that voluntarily chooses to register under the federal Canada Business Corporations Act. Corporations operating in more than one province/territory must register in each jurisdiction and follow the regulations that apply in that jurisdiction. HR directors must determine the legislative regime that applies to their organizations.

The Canadian Human Rights Act contains the following section[4]:

> *8. It is a discriminatory practice, directly or indirectly,*
>
> *(a) to refuse to employ or continue to employ any individual, or*
>
> *(b) in the course of employment, to differentiate adversely in relation to an employee, on a prohibited ground of discrimination.*

The Canadian Human Rights Act applies to federal government departments, Crown corporations and agencies, and businesses under federal jurisdiction, including banks, airlines, railways, the CBC and other broadcasters, and Canada Post.[5]

Section 8 of the Canadian Human Rights Act refers to "a prohibited ground of discrimination." Under this act, the following are grounds on which discrimination is prohibited[6]:

- race;
- national or ethnic origin;
- colour;
- religion;
- age;
- sex (including pregnancy and childbirth);
- marital status;
- family status;
- mental or physical disability (including previous or present drug or alcohol dependence);
- pardoned conviction; and
- sexual orientation.

The prohibited grounds of discrimination vary somewhat among jurisdictions. Table 3.1 compares prohibited grounds of discrimination across federal, provincial, and territorial jurisdictions, listing 21 prohibited grounds of employment discrimination found across these jurisdictions. There are, however, only six prohibited grounds of employment discrimination on which all jurisdictions agree: race or colour, religion or creed, age, sex, marital status, and physical/mental handicap or disability.

Human rights legislation in all jurisdictions is enforced through human rights commissions or tribunals that have the legislated power to undertake actions that may be necessary to eliminate discrimination. The Canadian Human Rights Act empowers the Canadian

TABLE 3.1

PROHIBITED GROUNDS OF EMPLOYMENT DISCRIMINATION IN CANADIAN JURISDICTIONS

PROHIBITED GROUND	JURISDICTION	COMMENTS
Race or colour	All jurisdictions	
Religion, creed, or religious beliefs	All jurisdictions	
Physical or mental disability	All jurisdictions	Quebec uses the phrase "handicap or use of any means to palliate a handicap"
Age*	All jurisdictions	• BC: 19–65 • Alberta: 18+ • Saskatchewan: 18–64 • Ontario: 18–65 • Newfoundland/Labrador: 19–65 • Quebec: Except as provided for by law
Sex (includes pregnancy and childbirth)	All jurisdictions	• BC includes breastfeeding • Alberta uses the term "gender" • Manitoba includes gender-determined characteristics • Ontario recognizes the protection of transgendered persons and accepts complaints related to "gender identity"; Ontario accepts complaints related to female genital mutilation • In Quebec, pregnancy as such is considered a ground of discrimination
Gender identity	Nova Scotia, Alberta, New Brunswick, Manitoba, NWT, Ontario	
Marital status	All jurisdictions	Quebec uses the term "civil status"
Dependence on alcohol or drugs	All *except* Yukon and NWT	• Policy to accept complaints in BC, Alberta, Saskatchewan, Manitoba, Ontario, New Brunswick, and PEI • Quebec: Included in "handicap" ground • Previous dependence only in New Brunswick and Nova Scotia
Family status or family affiliation	All *except* New Brunswick	• Saskatchewan defines as being in a parent–child relationship • Quebec uses the term *civil status*
Sexual orientation	All jurisdictions	
National or ethnic origin (including linguistic background)	All *except* BC and Alberta	• Saskatchewan and NWT use the term *nationality* • Ontario's code includes both "ethnic origin" and "citizenship"

Continued

TABLE 3.1

CONTINUED

PROHIBITED GROUND	JURISDICTION	COMMENTS
Ancestry or place of origin	Yukon, BC, Alberta, Saskatchewan, Manitoba, NWT, Ontario, and New Brunswick	
Language	Yukon, Ontario, and Quebec	• Ontario accepts complaints under the grounds of ancestry, ethnic origin, place of origin, and race • New Brunswick will accept language-related complaints filed on the basis of ancestry, although not an enumerated ground
Citizenship	Ontario	
Disfigurement	Newfoundland/Labrador	
Social condition or origin	Quebec, NWT, New Brunswick, and Newfoundland/Labrador	
Source of income	Alberta, BC, Saskatchewan, Manitoba, Quebec, Yukon, New Brunswick, PEI, and Nova Scotia	• Defined as "receipt of public assistance" in Saskatchewan • Quebec: Included under social condition
Based on association	Yukon, Manitoba, Ontario, New Brunswick, Nova Scotia, NWT, and PEI	NWT has prohibition on basis of "political association"
Political belief	Yukon, NWT, BC, Manitoba, Quebec, Nova Scotia, PEI, New Brunswick, and Newfoundland/ Labrador	Newfoundland/Labrador has prohibition on basis of "political opinion"
Record of criminal conviction	BC, Ontario, PEI, Yukon, and Quebec	Yukon's Act reads: "Criminal charges or criminal record"
Pardoned conviction	Federal, Yukon, and NWT	

**Note:* All Canadian provinces and territories, as of 2009, have legislation that prohibits employers from forcing mandatory retirement at age 65 or later. However, in some provinces, mandatory retirement is prohibited under the Act but a provision allows companies to enforce mandatory retirement under the terms or conditions of a retirement or pension plan. Also, some provinces have provisions to allow mandatory retirement for jobs where physical ability is a must, such as firefighting and police work.

Source: Reproduced with permission from the Canadian Human Rights Commission.

Human Rights Commission (CHRC) to investigate complaints, develop and deliver public information programs, undertake or sponsor research programs, liaise with other human rights commissions, and review federal legislation for conformity with the Canadian Human Rights Act. The commission has a full-time, paid staff to carry out its mandate.

The Canadian Human Rights Commission spends much of its time investigating human rights complaints. Human rights protection is predicated on the idea that individuals who believe that they are victims of discriminatory practices bear the responsibility of filing complaints with the commission. In the case of workplace disputes, a complaint would be filed after discussions with the employer failed to resolve the matter. The commission's procedure for filing and investigating discrimination complaints can be seen at http://www.chrc-ccdp.ca/eng/content/i-want-complain. Applicants who believe that they have suffered discrimination in recruitment or selection can lodge a complaint with the human rights commission that has jurisdiction over the employer. We provide a list of provincial/territorial human rights commissions at the end of this chapter in Recruitment and Selection Notebook 3.7.

Figure 3.1 and Table 3.2 provide some data on the volume and nature of complaints received by the CHRC. In 2013, the commission received 1735 complaints, with 55 percent of the complaints concerning discrimination related to disabilities and 17 percent related to sex. Table 3.2 shows that 70 percent of those complaints were employment related, with 7 percent involving employment-related harassment, 7 percent involving pay equity, and 1 percent involving trade union membership. Each complaint triggers a formal investigation and involves considerable time and energy on the part of employees, an organization's HR staff, and the CHRC itself.

Employment equity
The elimination of discriminatory practices that prevent the entry or retention of members from designated groups in the workplace, and the elimination of unequal treatment in the workplace related to membership in a designated group.

EMPLOYMENT EQUITY

Federal **employment equity** legislation requires all federally regulated employers with 100 or more employees, including organizations in industries such as banking,

FIGURE 3.1

PROPORTION OF COMPLAINTS RECEIVED IN 2013 BY GROUND OF DISCRIMINATION

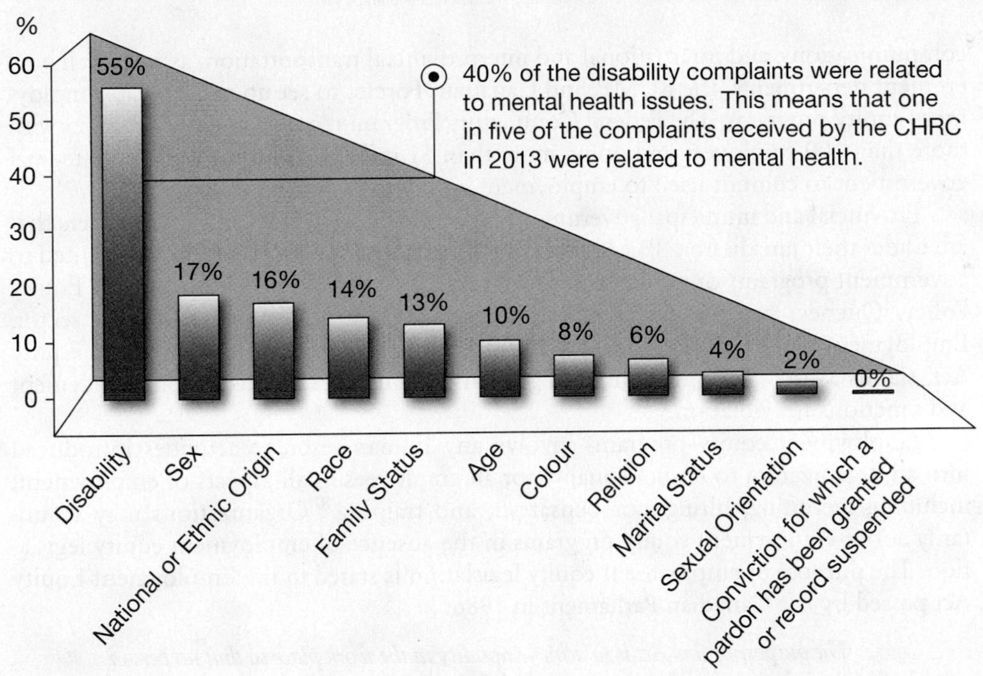

Source: Reproduced with permission from the Canadian Human Rights Commission.

TABLE 3.2

COMPLAINTS RECEIVED BY CHRC BY TYPES OF ALLEGATIONS CITED

	2011		2012		2013	
	#	%	#	%	#	%
Employment-related (sections 7, 8, 10)	2,070	71	1,658	72	1,221	70
Services-related (sections 5, 6)	435	15	390	17	321	19
Harassment—employment (section 14)	290	10	176	8	118	7
Union membership (section 9)	59	2	48	2	22	1
Retaliation (section 14.1)	36	1	32	1	22	1
Harassment—services (section 14)	33	1	7	–	17	1
Notices, signs, symbols (section 12)	–	–	3	–	7	–
Hate messages (section 13)	4	–	–	–	–	–
Pay equity (section 11)	2	–	–	–	7	–
Intimidation (section 59)	–	–	1	–	0	–
Total	2,929	100	2,306	100	1,735	100

* Total number of allegations cited exceeds the total number of complaints because some complaints dealt with more than one allegation.

Source: *Annual Report 2009.* http://www.chrc-ccdp.ca/publications/ar_2009_ra/page6-eng.aspx. Canadian Human Rights Commission, 2009. Reproduced with the permission of the Minister of Public Works and Government Services Canada, 2012. Reproduced with permission from the Canadian Human Rights Commission.

communications, and international and interprovincial transportation, as well as all government departments, the RCMP, and Canadian Forces, to set up and operate employment equity programs. The Federal Contractors Program requires any organization with more than 100 employees and doing more than $1 million of business with the federal government to commit itself to employment equity.

Provincial and municipal governments may also enact legislation for employers that fall under their jurisdiction. Provincial employment equity policies are mostly limited to government programs or public-sector workers; e.g., Nova Scotia's Employment Equity Policy. Quebec, however, extends employment equity policy to the private sector. Employment equity legislation, such as the federal government's Employment Equity Act, stands as the law of the land and generally includes mechanisms for enforcement and sanctions for violation.[7]

Employment equity programs involve any human resource activities introduced into an organization to ensure equality for all employees in all aspects of employment, including recruiting, hiring, compensation, and training.[8] Organizations may voluntarily adopt employment equity programs in the absence of employment equity legislation. The purpose of employment equity legislation is stated in the Employment Equity Act passed by the Canadian Parliament in 1986:

> *2. The purpose of this Act is to achieve equality in the work place so that no person shall be denied employment opportunities or benefits for reasons unrelated to ability and, in the fulfilment of that goal, to correct the conditions of disadvantage in employment*

experienced by women, aboriginal peoples, persons with disabilities and persons who are, because of their race or colour, in a visible minority in Canada by giving effect to the principle that employment equity means more than treating persons in the same way but also requires special measures and the accommodation of differences.

The intent of the Employment Equity Act is to address past systemic discrimination in employment systems that have disadvantaged members of the designated groups. The intent of the Act is to ensure that all selection requirements are realistic and job related. The Act provides for a review of practices that may constitute systemic barriers to the employment of members from designated groups and for establishing measures to eliminate any of the barriers. The federal Employment Equity Act of 1986 requires employers covered by the Act to implement equity, after consultation with employee representatives, by:

(a) identifying and eliminating employment practices that act as barriers to the employment of persons in designated groups; and

(b) instituting positive policies and practices and making reasonable accommodation to increase representation from designated groups among various positions in the organization to reflect the designated group's representation in either the work force or in those segments of the work force (identified by qualification, eligibility or geography) from which the employer reasonably expects to hire or promote employees.

Recruitment and Selection Notebook 3.2 outlines the steps in implementing an employment equity plan. The latest version of the Employment Equity Act came into effect on October 24, 1996. This revised act extended coverage to all private employers that fell under federal regulation and to almost all employees of the federal government. The new act gave power to the Canadian Human Rights Commission to audit all federally regulated employers' equity progress to determine if they are complying with the legislation and to require action when they fail to do so.

Employment equity programs often require an employer to undertake an extensive overhaul of the organization's recruitment and selection system. In comparison, a human rights commission may require an employer to take action only to remedy a specific complaint. Both human rights and employment equity legislation have the same ultimate goal: to eliminate discrimination in the workplace against disadvantaged

RECRUITMENT AND SELECTION NOTEBOOK 3.2

DEVELOPING AND IMPLEMENTING AN EMPLOYMENT EQUITY (EE) PLAN

1. Obtain support of senior management for the EE effort.
2. Conduct a survey to determine the present representation of designated groups in the organization's internal workforce.
3. Set future representation targets for designated groups based on availability of qualified workers in the labour market.
4. Remove systemic employment barriers to increase representation for designated groups in the internal workforce.
5. Monitor the changing composition of the internal workforce over time.
6. Make necessary changes to the EE intervention to bring designated group representation up to future targets.

groups and to improve their positions in employment systems. Human rights commissions are more reactive in nature in that they respond to complaints about alleged discrimination in the workplace. Employment equity programs are proactive in that they require employers to take action to increase the number of protected group members in the workplace. A good example of this is the Accessibility for Ontarians with Disabilities. The Act provides standards for improving accessibility for persons with disabilities in a number of areas, including employment. Employers in Ontario must be cognizant of these requirements in recruiting and selecting workers. The provisions of the Act may serve as a model for other jurisdictions. Recruitment and Selection Today 3.1 offers some advice to employers on hiring employees with disabilities.

RECRUITMENT AND SELECTION TODAY 3.1

HIRING A WORKER WITH A DISABILITY

Stuart Rudner is an HR lawyer and a founding partner of Rudner MacDonald LLP, a Toronto-based firm specializing in Canadian employment law. He wrote the following in a *Canadian HR Reporter* blog in response to the Accessibility for Ontarians with Disabilities Act.

Hiring someone with a disability should not be approached as an act of charity, but as a smart business decision. Rather than "doing someone a favour," employers should hire the best person for the job, regardless of their abilities or disabilities. Unfortunately, many employers assume a disabled worker will come with oppressive limitations, duties to accommodate and other costs that "normal" employees do not.

The reality, of course, is an individual with a disability may well be perfectly suited for a particular position, and in many cases will appreciate the opportunity far more than others—leading to a loyalty and willingness to work that exceeds the norm.

Much of my time is spent assisting employers in avoiding discrimination claims. In the hiring process, I often advise employers that "they don't want to know anything more than they have to."

This includes not asking or finding out about an applicant's age, religion, background, or disability. Otherwise, there is always the possibility a rejected applicant will allege she was discriminated against based upon a protected ground. As I advise employers, it is certainly helpful to be able to honestly say they were not even aware of the protected ground. For the full discussion, see http://www.hrreporter.com/blog/Canadian-HR-Law/archive/2012/04/03/guidelines-for-using-social-media-when-hiring

With the advent of the Accessibility for Ontarians with Disabilities Act (AODA), this becomes more difficult for employers with workers in Ontario.

Employers now have a duty to inquire about any need for accommodation in the hiring process. Once they do, and an applicant reveals a need for accommodation, the employer cannot deny knowing about it.

However, one of the pieces of advice I always offer remains valid: Do not share this information with the people making the hiring decision. Someone else can look after the accommodation inquires and arrangements, and efforts can be made to ensure that the ultimate decision-makers are not privy to it.

Of course, this is not always feasible. It will be difficult to prevent someone from seeing that an applicant is, for example, in a wheelchair. That is why I also always recommend that detailed reasons be kept supporting hiring decisions so the organization can demonstrate why an applicant was rejected for legitimate reasons.

Unfortunately, some individuals will abuse legislation that exists to protect traditionally disadvantaged groups and allege discrimination when they were, simply put, not the best person for the job. Employers need to be able to defend against such accusations.

At the same time, employers should also assess their own practices and views in order to ensure they are not rejecting qualified candidates or, even worse, preventing them from applying in the first place.

Not only is this good business practice, it will also be required as AODA comes into force in Ontario.

Employment equity legislation is often a contentious issue, subject to the political process. As times change, employment equity legislation may be delivered through different mechanisms, may be strengthened or weakened, or may even be discontinued altogether. Recruitment and Selection Notebook 3.3 provides "good practices" used by

RECRUITMENT AND SELECTION NOTEBOOK 3.3

IMPLEMENTING GOOD WORKPLACE EQUITY PRACTICES

The following "best practices" are taken from the *Employment Equity Act Annual Reports.* Under provisions of the Act, federally regulated employers must provide a statistical report on diversity issues along with a narrative report on actions they have taken to improve workplace equity. The following practices are those reported by employers in compliance with the Act.

Benefits of Implementing Employment Equity in the Workplace

- A workforce representative of Canadian culture and diversity;
- An increase in global competitiveness and productivity;
- High employee morale and decreased absenteeism;
- Amicable relationships with customers and clients;
- Enhanced corporate reputation; and
- Increased profitability and a better bottom line.

Improving Workplace Communications on Diversity Issues

- Voluntary self-identification surveys that help identify the diversity present in the workplace;
- Focus groups and committees devoted to employment equity and responsible for conducting workshops, presentations, and sessions with employees;
- Dialogue with managers concerning their positions on employment equity;
- Internal and external newsletters and magazines with sections and/or articles on employment equity;
- Internal bulletin boards where job openings and recent employment equity news items are posted;
- Company Internet websites including information concerning employment equity plans;
- Internal employment equity memos and pamphlets; and
- Exit interviews.

"Best Practices" Derived by HRSDC from Employer Reports

- Maintain an "open-door" policy that encourages and fosters a positive environment for employer and employees.
- Advertise employment opportunities in specific national or regional publications geared toward members of designated groups.
- Celebrate specific cultural holidays such as National Aboriginal Day and International Day for the Elimination of Racial Discrimination. Employers allowed flexible holiday policies so that employees could celebrate their own special days.
- Accommodate employees who needed special help, especially those with disabilities, to ease their integration into the workforce and make them comfortable in their work environment.
- Report the achievement of barrier-free workplaces through accommodation of employees. As workplaces become more complex, accommodative solutions become increasingly individualized. Employers recognized that successful accommodation involves positive encouragement from senior managers and the development of supportive workplace cultures. Some practices that employers used to meet the needs of employees included private workspaces, visual and hearing aids, job coaches, and diversity training provided to managers and staff.

Source: From Implementing *Good Workplace Equity Practices from Employment Equity Act: Annual Report 2013*, www.labour.gc.ca/eng/standards_equity/eq/pubs_eq/annual_reports/2013/index.shtml. Reproduced and distributed with the permission of Statistics Canada.

Canadian organizations to implement employment equity. These practices were compiled from reports to Human Resources and Skills Development Canada (HRSDC), recently renamed Employment and Social Development Canada (ESDC).

LABOUR LAW, EMPLOYMENT STANDARDS, AND RELATED LEGISLATION

Federal and provincial labour laws stipulate the rights of employees to organize trade unions and to bargain collective agreements with employers. Provincial labour relations acts and the Canada Labour Code establish labour relations boards to oversee union certifications and handle complaints about unfair labour practices. Collective agreements, which are legally binding and enforceable documents, cover unionized employees. Collective agreements set out the conditions under which job changes must occur and have a major impact on internal selection or internal movement of workers–for example, promotion, lateral transfer, and demotion.[9] Because closed-shop agreements–under which only union members may work for the organization–are legal in Canada, some unions have considerable control over external recruiting, even running their own hiring halls, that tend to be in the construction trades, from which the employer must hire workers. While collective agreements do restrict the freedom of the employer, unions on the whole tend to be more cooperative than adversarial in terms of HR practices such as selection.[10] However, many, if not all, collective agreements between an employer and a union specify how vacant positions are to be posted and applicants selected, with preference given to internal applicants. (Refer to Recruitment and Selection Today 1.1.)

Federal and provincial/territorial employment standards laws regulate minimum age of employment, standard hours of work, minimum wages, statutory holidays, vacations, work leaves, sexual harassment, and termination of employment.[11] You can explore the Federal Labour Standards at http://www.labour.gc.ca/eng/standards_equity/st/. As well, common law, developed through judicial proceedings, may apply to individual contracts entered into by a person and an organization. These laws have little impact on recruitment and selection practices unless the law is specifically referenced, like the Accessibility for Ontarians with Disabilities Act, and with the exception of termination, which might be considered "deselection" of people already in the organization's workforce.

Federal and provincial/territorial governments also have specialized legislation governing labour relations and setting employment standards for their own public service employees. Both the federal Public Service Employment Act and the Parliamentary Employment and Staff Relations Act illustrate the impact of this legislation on recruitment and selection. The Public Service Employment Act designates the Public Service Commission of Canada as the central staffing agency for the federal government. This Act gives candidates from the general public, as well as some public service employees, the right to request an investigation if they believe that their qualifications were not properly assessed as part of a hiring competition for a public service position.[12] The Public Service Commission resolves complaints through mediation and conciliation or through the direct intervention of the commission or a deputy head.[13] Candidates may also lodge appeals against personnel selection processes used by the Public Service Commission. (An important appeal involving the use of employment testing in the federal public service is summarized in Recruitment and Selection Today 3.2.)

RECRUITMENT AND SELECTION TODAY 3.2

PSYCHOLOGICAL TESTING IN THE FEDERAL GOVERNMENT

In 1986, an appeal board of the Public Service Commission (PSC) heard the complaints of job applicants for the job of collections enforcement clerk with the federal taxation department.[14] Four individuals who were not hired alleged that the GIT 320 (a paper-and-pencil test of cognitive ability) in use at the time for screening job applicants was (1) not properly validated; (2) had an unjustifiably high cutoff score; and (3) was gender biased. Expert witnesses, including several top personnel psychologists, testified on the technical merits of the test at the invitation of either the complainants or the commission. Based on this evidence, the appeal board concluded that the GIT 320 had been validated (using a method called validity generalization, which we discussed in Chapter 2). The two other allegations were dismissed because (1) the PSC had demonstrated the test cutoff score was reasonable and not excessively high under the circumstances and (2) the test was neither biased nor unfair to women. All three allegations about the test were dismissed and the PSC continued to use the GIT 320 in its selection work.

The *Maloley* decision is especially informative because it involves allegations of two distinct types: (1) the first two allegations claimed that the GIT 320 violated procedural rules in the PSC selection system based on the merit principle; and (2) the third allegation claimed the test was discriminatory against women. Here we see an internal appeal board, which normally would deal with procedural and technical matters only, ruling on discrimination issues customarily the prerogative of human rights commissions. This suggests that, in at least some instances, there is a blurring of the divisions separating the four legal sources discussed in this chapter. Legal issues in recruitment and selection are made even more complicated as a result.

The PSC in 2007 published a comprehensive document on *Testing in the Public Service of Canada* that outlines the standards for the development and use of tests for appointment purposes. It adheres closely to the *Standards for Educational and Psychological Testing* (1999) discussed in Chapter 2. It also demonstrates how validity and reliability apply to testing policy. The PSC also has a guide to implementing employment equity programs. Both documents are available at http://www.psc-cfp.gc.ca/plcy-pltq/frame-cadre/policy-politique/index-eng.htm

The Parliamentary Employment and Staff Relations Act provides a mechanism for collective bargaining between the federal government as employer and the various unions certified to represent federal workers. This legislation is administered by the Public Service Staff Relations Board (PSSRB), which is empowered to hear complaints under the Act and arbitrate collective bargaining disputes. PSSRB decisions that address promotion practices covered in collective agreements between the federal government and public sector unions affect recruitment and selection practices in the public sector.

// PART II: KEY LEGAL CONCEPTS IN RECRUITMENT AND SELECTION

Recruitment and Selection Today 3.3 presents landmark Supreme Court of Canada decisions that have had a profound impact on how employers recruit and select employees. Recruitment and Selection Today 3.4 presents some legal terms and concepts that follow from these decisions and other legislation that apply to selection and recruitment. We will review these cases, terms, and concepts in greater detail in this section.

Supreme Court of Canada

RECRUITMENT AND SELECTION TODAY 3.3

LANDMARK CANADIAN SUPREME COURT CASES RELATED TO SELECTION

1. *The Ontario Human Rights Commission and Bruce Dunlop and Harold E. Hall and Vincent Gray v. The Borough of Etobicoke* [1982]

This case is also known as *Etobicoke*. Harold Hall and Vincent Gray were firefighters in the Borough of Etobicoke, near Toronto. They were required to retire at age 60 by the collective agreement in place between their union and the Borough. They brought a complaint of age discrimination to the Ontario Human Rights Commission. Etobicoke defended the practice on the grounds that the retirement rule was a *bona fide occupational requirement* (BFOR) that was required to maintain an acceptable standard of firefighting performance. The case eventually came before the Supreme Court, where Justice McIntyre, writing on behalf of a unanimous court, ruled that the policy constituted age discrimination. He said that an employee or union cannot waive rights protected under human rights legislation through a collective agreement. He also specified that a BFOR must be an objective one that is supported by concrete evidence.

Source: Judgments of the Supreme Court of Canada. http://scc-csc.lexum.com/scc-csc/scc-csc/en/item/2434/index.do

2. *Ontario Human Rights Commission and O'Malley v. Simpsons-Sears Ltd.* [1985]

Theresa O'Malley was a Seventh Day Adventist whose religion forbid her to work from sundown on Friday to sundown on Saturday. She requested that Simpsons-Sears, a retailer, assign her to other shifts. Simpsons-Sears said no other full-time shifts were available and terminated her employment. Simpsons-Sears said the requirement that all employees work on Fridays and Saturdays was a neutral rule that was not intended to discriminate against Ms. O'Malley. Justice McIntyre, on behalf of a unanimous court, defined direct discrimination as, "Direct discrimination occurs in this connection where an employer adopts a practice or rule, which on its face discriminates on a prohibited ground. For example, 'No Catholics or no women or no blacks employed here.' There is, of course, no disagreement in the case at bar that direct discrimination of that nature would contravene the Act." The Court also decreed that discrimination by accident, "adverse discrimination," was just as wrong as direct discrimination, and that where adverse effect discrimination exists, the employer must take steps to accommodate an employee who has been affected short of undue hardship to the business. The Court ruled that Simpsons-Sears had discriminated against Ms. O'Malley and that it did not try to make any changes in its work schedule that would accommodate her religious requirements. It could have shuffled her work schedule without causing a problem.

Source: Judgments of the Supreme Court of Canada. http://scc-csc.lexum.com/scc-csc/scc-csc/en/item/101/index.do

3. *Canadian National Railway Co. v. Canada (Human Rights Comm.) and Bhinder* [1985]

K.S. Bhinder was a member of the Sikh religion, which required him to wear a turban and no other head covering. He was employed for four years by CN Rail and worked night shift as an electrician doing yard maintenance. CN established a safety policy that all yard employees had to wear hard hats. He refused to wear the hard hat and was fired. Mr. Bhinder argued that his religious freedom had been violated. In a split decision the Supreme Court ruled that CN's hard hat rule was a genuine bona fide occupational requirement (BFOR) and that there was no direct or adverse effect discrimination. The requirements of the job prevailed over the requirement of the employee.

Source: Judgments of the Supreme Court of Canada. http://scc-csc.lexum.com/scc-csc/scc-csc/en/item/102/index.do

4. *Canadian National Railway Co. v. Canada (Human Rights Comm.) and Action travail des femmes* [1987]

Women made up only 0.7 percent of CN Rail's unskilled workforce at a time when women comprised 41 percent of the Canadian labour force. *Action travail des femmes,* a public interest lobby group, filed a complaint with the Canadian Human Rights Commission that CN Rail violated the Canadian Human Rights Act by engaging in systemic discrimination. The Human Rights Tribunal that heard the complaint found that CN Rail had made no real effort to hire women and that it had engaged in several practices, for example the use of specific selection tools, that discouraged women from applying for blue-collar jobs. It ordered CN to start an employment equity program. CN Rail appealed the decision to the Supreme Court, which upheld the Tribunal's findings. The Supreme Court ruled that the Tribunal had the authority to impose an employment equity program on CN Rail to break the cycle of systemic discrimination.

Source: Judgments of the Supreme Court of Canada. http://scc-csc.lexum.com/scc-csc/scc-csc/en/item/6280/index.do

5. *Alberta Dairy Pool v. Alberta (Human Rights Commission)* [1990]

Jim Christie, an employee of the Alberta Dairy Pool, joined the Worldwide Church of God, which required him to take a number of days off work each week. His employer accommodated his requests until he asked to have Mondays off. His employer refused on the grounds of business necessity, that Monday was the busiest day of the week. Mr. Christie did not come to work on Monday and was fired. He alleged religious discrimination. The Dairy Pool argued that working on Monday was a bona fide occupational requirement and that it had accommodated Mr. Christie's religious beliefs to the point of undue hardship. The Supreme Court found that there had not been direct discrimination but that there was no BFOR for working on a Monday and, thus, the Dairy Pool was guilty of adverse effect discrimination. The Court expanded on the concept of undue hardship first noted in the *O'Malley v. Simpsons-Sears* case, and provided a list of factors that had to be considered in claiming that accommodation imposed undue hardship.

Source: Judgments of the Supreme Court of Canada. http://scc-csc.lexum.com/scc-csc/scc-csc/en/item/641/index.do

6. *Central Okanagan School District No. 23 v. Renaud* [1992]

Larry Renaud was a janitor working at the Central Okanagan School District. He was a Seventh Day Adventist who was required to work Friday evenings under a collective agreement that was in place. He proposed that he work Sunday through Thursday to accommodate his religious beliefs. The School Board refused his requests for accommodation and terminated Mr. Renaud. Mr. Renaud then filed a complaint of discrimination based on religion under the British Columbia Human Rights Act. Justice Sopinka, on behalf of the unanimous court, held that there was discrimination and that the employer had an obligation to accommodate Mr. Renaud to the point of undue hardship despite the existence of a collective agreement or any private contract that might be in place. This decision was important in raising the issue that contracts could not pose an impediment to accommodation and that a trade union could be held liable for discrimination in the workplace.

Source: Judgments of the Supreme Court of Canada. http://scc-csc.lexum.com/scc-csc/scc-csc/en/item/910/index.do

7. *British Columbia (Public Service Employee Relations Commission) v. British Columbia Government Service Employees' Union* [1999]

This unanimous decision is also known as the *Meiorin* case. The background of this important case is presented in Recruitment and Selection Today 3.7 later in this chapter. Why is this case significant for recruitment and selection? In it, the Supreme Court created a unified test of discrimination and did away with the distinction between direct and adverse effect discrimination. The Court ruled that while fitness tests had a valid purpose of ensuring safety, the research on which they were based must be more than impressionistic and also take into account differences between men and women when establishing performance standards. The Court articulated a new provision for establishing a bona fide occupational requirement and further specified conditions that had to be explored before claiming that accommodation would cause undue hardship.

Source: Judgments of the Supreme Court of Canada. http://scc-csc.lexum.com/scc-csc/scc-csc/en/item/1724/index.do

8. *British Columbia (Superintendent of Motor Vehicles) v. British Columbia (Council of Human Rights)* [1999]

This unanimous decision is also known as the *Grismer* case. Terry Grismer was a truck driver who incurred a visual disability after suffering a stroke. The Superintendent of Motor Vehicles cancelled his driver's licence on the grounds his disability prevented him from meeting the minimum visual standards for maintaining a licence. Mr. Grismer alleged discrimination and filed a complaint with the British Columbia Human Rights Tribunal. The Tribunal found direct discrimination on the part of the Superintendent and ordered a re-examination. The decision was appealed and went to the Supreme Court of Canada. The issue was whether a complete prohibition from driving with Grismer's visual disability was a reasonable standard under the requirements established in the *Meiorin* case. The Court upheld the Tribunal's finding of discrimination and stated that its requirement for a bona fide occupational requirement applied not only in employment situations but also in circumstances of discrimination where accommodation was available. The prohibition on driving was not reasonably necessary to accomplish the goal of protecting the public. The Superintendent failed to show that no person with the impairment could drive safely. The Superintendent was obliged to give Mr. Grismer a chance to prove he could drive safely rather than relying on an absolute standard. The cost of accommodation by individual testing did not constitute undue hardship.

Source: Judgments of the Supreme Court of Canada. http://scc-csc.lexum.com/scc-csc/scc-csc/en/item/1761/index.do

DIRECT DISCRIMINATION

In *O'Malley v. Simpsons-Sears*,[15] Justice McIntyre defined direct discrimination as occurring where an employer adopts a practice or rule that on its face discriminates on a prohibited ground. The application of this definition to HR practice is quite simple. If direct discrimination occurs, then the burden is on the employer to show that the rule is valid in application to all the members of the affected group. An employer who is hiring steelworkers for foundry work involving heavy lifting in a dirty environment may believe that this job is unsuited to women and specifies that no women will be hired. This is a clear instance of direct discrimination. If a female applicant were to complain about the blatant nature of this discrimination, the employer would have to prove to a human rights investigator that all women lack the ability to do the work—that is, that no women could perform the work successfully. If even one woman can do the job, the employer's use of the "no women allowed" rule will be struck down by a human rights tribunal or court. In all but rare circumstances, it is impossible to justify direct discrimination.

As part of recruitment and selection, no statement may be made in advertising a job that would prohibit or restrict members of a protected group from seeking that job. A statement, for example, in any job advertisement or posting that the employer is seeking "single males" constitutes direct discrimination and is illegal. During the selection process

RECRUITMENT AND SELECTION TODAY 3.4

LEGAL TERMS AND CONCEPTS THAT APPLY TO RECRUITMENT AND SELECTION

Discrimination In employment, discrimination refers to any refusal to employ or to continue to employ any person, or to adversely affect any current employee, on the basis of that individual's membership in a protected group. All Canadian jurisdictions prohibit discrimination at least on the basis of race or colour, religion or creed, age, sex, marital status, and physical or mental disability.

Direct discrimination Occurs where an employer adopts a practice or rule that, on its face, discriminates on a prohibited ground.

Indirect discrimination Occurs when an employer, in good faith, adopts a policy or practice for sound economic or business reasons, but when it is applied to all employees it has an unintended negative impact on members of a protected group

Protected groups Those who have attributes that are defined as "prohibited grounds" for discrimination under the human rights act that applies to the employing organization.

Designated groups The Employment Equity Act defines designated groups as women, visible minorities, Aboriginal peoples, and persons with disabilities.

Employment equity Refers to the elimination of discriminatory practices that prevent the entry or retention of members from designated groups in the workplace, and to the elimination of unequal treatment in the workplace related to membership in a designated group.

Adverse impact Occurs when the selection rate for a protected group is lower than that for the relevant comparison group. U.S. courts consider adverse impact to occur when the number of members selected from a protected group is less than 80 percent of the number of majority-group members selected.

Bona fide occupational requirement (BFOR) Bona fide occupational requirements are those that a person must possess to perform the essential components of a job in a safe, efficient, and reliable manner. To defend employment practice or policy on the grounds that the policy or practice may be perceived as discriminatory, the employer must show that the practice or policy was adopted in an honest and good-faith belief that it was reasonably necessary to ensure the efficient and economical performance of the job without endangering employees or the general public. BFORs are sometimes referred to as bona fide occupational qualifications (BFOQs).

Accommodation Refers to the duty of an employer to put in place modifications to discriminatory employment practices or procedures to meet the needs of members of a protected group being affected by the employment practice or procedure. As part of a BFOR defence, an employer must demonstrate that such accommodation is impossible to achieve without incurring undue hardship in terms of the organization's expense or operations.

Sufficient risk As part of a BFOR defence, an employer may argue that an occupational requirement that discriminates against a protected group is reasonably necessary to ensure that work will be performed successfully and in a manner that will not pose harm or danger to employees or the public.

Undue hardship The limit beyond which employers and service providers are not expected to accommodate a member of a protected group. Undue hardship usually occurs when an employer cannot bear the costs of the accommodation.

itself, application forms and interviews are potential sources of direct discrimination. As a result, some human rights commissions have published guidelines for questions asked by employers on employment application forms and at employment interviews. An excerpt from these guidelines published by the Canadian Human Rights Commission is given in Table 3.3. These guidelines provide practical and detailed advice on how to avoid direct discrimination in many common selection situations and should be carefully heeded by employers. The complete guide is available on the Canadian Human Rights Commission's website at http://www.chrc-ccdp.gc.ca/sites/default/files/screen_1.pdf.

TABLE 3.3

GUIDELINES TO SCREENING AND SELECTION IN EMPLOYMENT

SUBJECT	AVOID ASKING	PREFERRED	COMMENTS
Name	• About name change; whether it was changed by court order, marriage, or other reason • For maiden name		Ask after selection if needed to check on previously held jobs or educational credentials
Address	• For addresses outside Canada	Ask place and duration of current or recent address	
Age	• For birth certificates, baptismal records, or about age in general	Ask applicants if they are eligible to work under Canadian laws regarding age restrictions	If precise age is required for benefit plans or other legitimate purposes, it can be determined after selection
Sex	• Males or females to fill in different applications • About pregnancy, child-bearing plans, or child-care arrangements	Can ask applicant if the attendance requirements can be met	During the interview or after selection, the applicant, for purposes of courtesy, may be asked which of Dr., Mr., Mrs., Miss, or Ms. is preferred
Marital status	• Whether applicant is single, married, divorced, engaged, separated, widowed, or living common-law • Whether the applicant's spouse may be transferred • About the spouse's employment	• If transfer or travel is part of the job, the applicant can be asked whether he or she can meet these requirements • Ask whether there are any circumstances that might prevent completion of a minimum service commitment	Information on dependants can be determined after selection if necessary
Family status	• Number of children or dependants • About child-care arrangements	Ask if the applicant would be able to work the required hours and, where applicable, overtime	Contacts for emergencies and/or details on dependants can be determined after selection
National or ethnic origin	• About birthplace, nationality of ancestors, spouse, or other relatives • Whether born in Canada • For proof of citizenship	Since those who are entitled to work in Canada must be citizens, permanent residents, or holders of valid work permits, applicants can be asked if they are legally entitled to work in Canada	Documentation of eligibility to work (papers, visas, etc.) can be requested after selection
Military service	• About military service in other countries	Can ask about Canadian military service where employment preference is given to veterans by law	

Continued

TABLE 3.3

CONTINUED

SUBJECT	AVOID ASKING	PREFERRED	COMMENTS
Language	• Mother tongue • Where language skills obtained	Ask if applicant understands, reads, writes, or speaks languages required for the job	Testing or scoring applicants for language proficiency is not permitted unless job-related
Race or colour	• Any question about race or colour, including colour of eyes, skin, or hair		
Photographs	For photo to be attached to application or sent to interviewer before interview		Photos for security passes or company files can be taken after selection
Religion	• Whether applicant will work a specific religious holiday • About religious affiliation, church membership, frequency of church attendance • For references from clergy or religious leader	Explain the required work shift, asking if such a schedule poses problems for the applicant	Reasonable accommodation of an employee's religious beliefs is the employer's duty
Height and weight			No inquiry unless there is evidence they are genuine occupational requirements
Disability	• For listing of all disabilities, limitations, or health problems • Whether the applicant drinks or uses drugs • Whether applicant has ever received psychiatric care or been hospitalized for emotional problems • Whether the applicant has received Workers' Compensation		The employer should: • disclose any information on medically related requirements or standards early in the application process • then ask whether the applicant has any condition that could affect his or her ability to do the job, preferably during a pre-employment medical examination A disability is relevant to job ability only if it: • threatens the safety or property of others • prevents the applicant from safe and adequate job performance, even when reasonable efforts are made to accommodate the disability

Continued

TABLE 3.3

CONTINUED

SUBJECT	AVOID ASKING	PREFERRED	COMMENTS
Medical information	• Whether the applicant is currently under a physician's care • Name of family doctor • Whether the applicant is receiving counselling or therapy		• Medical exams should be conducted after selection and only if an employee's condition is related to job duties • Offers of employment can be made conditional on successful completion of a medical exam
Pardoned conviction	• Whether the applicant has ever been convicted • Whether the applicant has ever been arrested • Whether the applicant has a criminal record	If bonding is a job requirement, ask if applicant is eligible	Inquiries about criminal record or convictions are discouraged unless related to job duties
Sexual orientation	About the applicant's sexual orientation		Contacts for emergencies and/or details on dependants can be determined after selection
References			The same restrictions that apply to questions asked of applicants apply when asking for employment references

Source: *A Guide to Screening and Selection in Employment*, http://www.chrc-ccdp.ca/pdf/screen.pdf, Canadian Human Rights Commission, March, 2011. Reproduced with the permission of the Minister of Public Works and Government Services Canada, 2012. Reproduced with permission from the Canadian Human Rights Commission.

Direct discrimination is much less frequent in Canadian workplaces than it once was. Discriminatory job advertising in major daily newspapers is now quite rare, as the media may also be held accountable for running such types of ads. Direct discrimination, however, does exist to some extent in selection practices, so continued vigilance is necessary. These instances generally occur in those occupations where gender-based stereotyping persists. Despite many efforts, people still think of certain occupations as being either "female" or "male"–for example, only women make good nurses, and only men make good construction workers. Direct discrimination occurs when this stereotyping carries over into the workplace and influences recruiting and selection practices. Hopefully, such gender-based stereotyping will occur much less often in the future than in the past.

ADVERSE EFFECT DISCRIMINATION

In Chapter 2 we outlined a commonly used selection model: A job analysis is used to identify the knowledge, skills, abilities, and other characteristics (KSAOs) that are related to job performance. A situation may arise where basing selection practices on a legitimately determined KSAO has an unintended, negative impact on members of a protected group. This impact would constitute indirect discrimination and fall outside the law unless it could be shown that the selection practice was necessary to assure the efficient and economical performance of the job without endangering employees or the general public.

In the *O'Malley v. Simpsons-Sears* decision, Justice McIntyre also defined **adverse effect discrimination**–or indirect discrimination. Adverse effect discrimination occurs in recruitment and selection when an employer, in good faith, adopts a policy or practice for sound economic or business reasons that is applied to all employees but has an unintended, negative impact on members of a protected group. In recruiting, for example, employers often ask current employees for the names of friends or relatives who might be suitable for a position. An HR manager might solicit shop-floor employees for names of potential candidates to fill a welder's apprentice position. After receiving all the names, the HR manager chooses the best candidate according to a set of objective criteria. How does this recruiting strategy lead to adverse effect discrimination? If the shop-floor employees were all white males, almost all of the candidates put forward by the current employees would be white males. This recruitment practice will likely lead to the outcome of hiring a white male, to the exclusion of women or visible minorities.

Adverse effect discrimination
Refers to a situation where an employer, in good faith, adopts a policy or practice that has an unintended, negative impact on members of a protected group.

The HR manager may have believed that the strategy was a sound and effective business practice for identifying suitable candidates for the position (and as we will see in Chapter 6 on Recruitment, referrals from family or friends constitute a very popular means of recruitment). The manager did not intend to exclude members of any protected group from consideration and asked all the existing employees to nominate potential job candidates. Nevertheless, this recruitment strategy results in adverse effect discrimination by imposing penalties or restrictive conditions on women, visible minorities, and Aboriginal peoples that are not imposed on white males: women, visible minorities, and Aboriginal peoples are less likely to be nominated for the job, and less likely to be hired regardless of their qualifications. Women, visible minorities and Aboriginal peoples, groups protected under human rights legislation, may be negatively affected by the supposedly neutral recruiting practice. This is an example to illustrate a potential problem and it does not mean that all recruiting by referrals from family or friends represents indirect discrimination.

In selection, adverse effect discrimination often involves the use of a practice or use of an employment test. Suppose the HR manager, in the above example, corrected the flawed recruiting practice and subsequently obtained an applicant pool that included a proportion of women, visible minorities, and Aboriginal peoples consistent with their representation in the general population. The HR manager decides to use a mechanical comprehension test to select applicants as a welder's apprentice. Performance on the mechanical comprehension test predicts success as a welder's apprentice and will identify those applicants who are most likely to contribute to the company's overall productivity.

Could this selection strategy lead to adverse effect discrimination? Women tend to score lower, on average, on mechanical comprehension tests than do men. If the same test cutoff score were used for men and women or if applicants were offered jobs in order of their test scores (from highest to lowest), proportionately fewer women than men would be hired for the job. The use of the mechanical comprehension test would impose on women, as a group protected under human rights legislation, a penalty not imposed on men. Even though the test is applied equally to women and men, the test affects women, in a negative sense, to a greater extent than men. Even though the test predicts performance for welders' apprentices and there was no intention to discriminate against women, a human rights complaint may be launched against the employer on the grounds that use of the test had an adverse effect on women as a group and, thus, discriminated against them on that basis. The use of a selection tool that had adverse effect on women was one of the issues in the *Canadian National Railway Co. v. Canada (Human Rights Comm.) and Action travail des femmes* decision. Any employment rule, practice, or policy that has a negative effect on a group protected under human rights legislation, no matter how well intentioned by the employer, constitutes adverse effect discrimination.

ADVERSE IMPACT

Adverse impact
Occurs when the selection rate for a protected group is lower than that for the relevant comparison group.

The concept of *adverse impact* is closely related to adverse effect discrimination. At times, *adverse impact* and *adverse effect* are used synonymously.[16] In terms of recruitment and selection, the concept of adverse impact has a narrower, more technical, definition. **Adverse impact** occurs when the selection rate for a protected group is lower than that for the relevant comparison group (which has the higher selection rate). In our example of adverse effect discrimination, the mechanical comprehension test also had an adverse impact on women in that proportionately fewer women than men would be selected for the job (see Table 3.4).

Adverse impact is based on statistical evidence showing that proportionately fewer of the protected group are selected using a selection device (such as an employment test or interview) or that fewer members of the protected group pass through the selection system taken as a whole. Establishing adverse impact in selection can be very complex.[17] One rough-and-ready rule that is frequently used to establish adverse impact in selection is the *four-fifths* rule. According to this rule, adverse impact is established where the selection rate for the protected group is less than four-fifths that of the comparison group. Table 3.4 demonstrates a situation in which a mechanical comprehension test had an adverse impact on women according to the four-fifths rule. Despite its widespread adoption in Canada, the four-fifths rule has serious limitations on both rational and statistical grounds.[18]

WORKPLACE DISCRIMINATION IN THE UNITED STATES

In the United States, the primary federal legislation governing workplace discrimination is the Equal Employment Opportunity (EEO) Act of 1964, as amended in 1991. Along

TABLE 3.4

EXAMPLE OF THE FOUR-FIFTHS RULE IN DETERMINING ADVERSE IMPACT ON WOMEN: SELECTION BASED ON MECHANICAL COMPREHENSION TEST

	TOTAL APPLICANT POOL (A)	NUMBER OF PEOPLE MADE JOB OFFERS (B)	SELECTION RATE (RATIO OF B/A)
Women	10	1	0.10
Men	100	15	0.15

Minimum selection rate of women according to the four-fifths rule must be $4/5 \times 0.15 = 0.12$.

Because the selection rate of women (0.10) is less than the minimum selection rate under the four-fifths rule (0.12), we conclude that the mechanical comprehension test had adverse impact.

with the Equal Pay Act of 1963, the Age Discrimination Act of 1967, and the Americans with Disabilities Act of 1990, the EEO legislation and regulations made under it provide U.S. citizens with most of the protection against workplace discrimination afforded Canadians through the four legal sources we have discussed. In addition, significant rulings by U.S. courts have also had an impact on personnel selection standards, practices, and procedures as illustrated in Recruitment and Selection Today 3.5. Recruitment and Selection Today 3.6 provides a summary of the four most important U.S. Supreme Court cases that have had an impact on selection in the United States. While these cases do not hold any force in Canada, they do have influence in that they are used as part of legal briefs made to Canadian courts. The cases presented in Recruitment and Selection Today 3.6 have played a role in shaping the development of human rights and jurisprudence in Canada. For example, the four-fifths rule presented in Table 3.4 was fashioned in a U.S. court decision. The *Uniform Guidelines* and *Principles of Validation* that were discussed in Chapter 2 have evolved to reflect U.S. court decisions and laws. Canadian courts often use these standards in examining Canadian selection practices. These standards have also influenced professional practice in Canada.

One of the most significant differences between Canadian and U.S. legislation is the incorporation of section 15(2) into the Canadian Charter of Rights and Freedoms. Section 15(2) states that programs designed to ameliorate discrimination by favouring disadvantaged groups are not, themselves, discriminatory. In the United States, courts have often overturned programs on the grounds of "reverse discrimination." A second major difference is that there is no comparable ruling in Canada to the *Wards Cove Packing* decision. In fact, the *Meiorin* decision (discussed in Recruitment and Selection Today 3.7 and elsewhere) has set a higher standard for employers to meet before allowing discriminatory work-related practices.

DISCRIMINATION IS DISCRIMINATION

Many people have had difficulty in differentiating direct discrimination from adverse effect discrimination since the outcomes in both cases are the same: members of a

RECRUITMENT AND SELECTION TODAY 3.5

CULTURAL BIAS IN SELECTION TESTING

Much of the legislation and policy discussed in this chapter draws heavily on examples from other countries, especially the United States. Nowhere is this truer than for human rights and employment equity, which are called *equal employment opportunity* and *affirmative action* in the United States. In fact, many Canadian tribunals and courts cite American cases as precedents when making their human rights decisions. In addition, many of the same issues and concerns about recruitment and selection in this country are mirrored in the United States. For example, an article in the *U.S. News & World Report*[19] described the political upheaval in Chicago over results of a promotional examination for city police officers. Despite a cost of over $5 million paid to consultants to develop a bias-free promotional system, the multiple-choice tests used in the promotion competition still had adverse impact against African Americans and Hispanics. As a result, fewer members of these groups than whites were promoted, and city politicians were quick to line up on both sides of the controversy.

Chicago is a microcosm reflecting wider societal concerns in the United States and Canada over employment testing. The debate over adverse impact and cultural bias in selection testing continues to rage intensely on both sides of the border and is likely to do so for years to come.

RECRUITMENT AND SELECTION TODAY 3.6

LANDMARK U.S. SUPREME COURT CASES RELATED TO SELECTION

Griggs v. Duke Power (1971)

Thirteen black employees of Duke Power challenged the use of new selection requirements that included a high-school diploma, a mechanical aptitude test, and a general intelligence test on the grounds that they screened out a much higher proportion of black applicants than whites. Duke Power had no evidence to show that these requirements were job related. The Supreme Court ruled any employment practice is prohibited if it discriminates against a minority group and it cannot be shown to be valid, that is, related to job performance.

Albemarle Paper Co. v. Moody (1975)

The U.S. government established *Uniform Guidelines on Employee Selection Procedures* for use in evaluating the validity of personnel selection programs. Black employees of the Albemarle Paper Company in North Carolina claimed that the use of a seniority system, requirement for a high school diploma, and application of two tests of general cognitive ability as part of a promotion process discriminated against blacks who were employed mostly in unskilled positions and who historically had limited access to skilled jobs in the paper mill. The Court ruled that the research done to establish the validity of the tests did not meet the standards on validity set by the *Uniform Guidelines.* The Court ordered that the class of black workers were to be compensated for their discrimination, establishing the precedent for multimillion-dollar awards in subsequent cases of workplace discrimination.

Watson v. Fort Worth Bank & Trust (1988)

In reviewing candidates for promotion, Fort Worth Bank & Trust asked its supervisors to provide an assessment of each candidate in the context of the position's requirements. Clara Watson, who had been denied a promotion, challenged the system. The bank had argued that it did not have to establish that subjective evaluations such as those provided by the supervisors met the validity requirements established in previous case law for objective measures such as cognitive ability tests. The Court's ruling established that companies using subjective evaluations based on the judgment of supervisors or raters (including those based on interviews) must show that those subjective evaluations are valid, using the same standards that the Court set for more objective assessments.

Wards Cove Packing v. Antonio (1988)

Unskilled, low-paying jobs in a salmon cannery were filled mostly by members of minority groups, while skilled and nonpacking jobs were filled mostly by whites. The minority workers filed a class action suit alleging discrimination based on the racial imbalance between the two types of jobs. The Court ruled against the cannery workers. It held that the appropriate comparison for determining adverse impact was between *qualified* job applicants from the two different racial groups or between the proportions of those selected in different groups from the qualified pool of applicants. It further ruled that any racial imbalance must be attributable to an employment practice and not a result of statistical imbalances in the workforce. The Court added that where an employment practice led to adverse impact, any alternative that led to less or no adverse impact must also be as effective as the practice it was replacing in meeting the organization's legitimate business purposes. The Court's ruling made it more difficult to establish an adverse impact case.

---

protected group are subject to discrimination, although in one case the discrimination is unintentional. In a Supreme Court of Canada decision–*British Columbia (Public Service Employee Relations Comm.) v. BCGSEU*[20] (the "*Meiorin* decision")–Justice McLachlin argued that while one could differentiate between the two forms of discrimination, the distinction had little importance since the principal concern of the Court in human rights cases was the effect of an impugned law. According to Justice McLachlin, maintaining the distinction "ill serves the purpose of contemporary human rights legislation."[21]

The *Meiorin* decision is a landmark ruling that has had a substantial impact on recruitment and selection policies and practices. The case originated as a complaint to the British Columbia Human Rights Commission but wound its way through the appeal process to the Supreme Court of Canada, which took up the case under the Charter of Rights. Background on the case is presented in Recruitment and Selection Today 3.7.

RECRUITMENT AND SELECTION TODAY 3.7

THE *MEIORIN* CASE

Ms. Meiorin was employed for three years by the British Columbia Ministry of Forests as a member of a three-person Initial Attack Forest Firefighting Crew in the Golden Forest District. The crew's job was to attack and suppress forest fires while they were small and could be contained. Ms. Meiorin's supervisors found her work to be satisfactory.

Ms. Meiorin was not asked to take a physical fitness test until 1994, when she was required to pass the Government's "Bona Fide Occupational Fitness Tests and Standards for B.C. Forest Service Wildland Firefighters" (the "Tests"). The Tests required that the forest firefighters weigh less than 200 lbs. (with their equipment) and complete a shuttle run, an upright rowing exercise, and a pump carrying/hose dragging exercise within stipulated times. The running test was designed to test the forest firefighters' aerobic fitness and was based on the view that forest firefighters must have a minimum "VO2 max" of 50 ml.kg-1.min-1 (the "aerobic standard"). "VO2 max" measures "maximal oxygen uptake," or the rate at which the body can take in oxygen, transport it to the muscles, and use it to produce energy.

The Tests were developed in response to a 1991 Coroner's Inquest Report that recommended that only physically fit employees be assigned as front-line forest firefighters for safety reasons. The Government commissioned a team of researchers from the University of Victoria to undertake a review of its existing fitness standards with a view to protecting the safety of firefighters while meeting human rights norms. The researchers developed the Tests by identifying the essential components of forest firefighting, measuring the physiological demands of those components, selecting fitness tests to measure those demands and, finally, assessing the validity of those tests.

The researchers studied various sample groups. The specific tasks performed by forest firefighters were identified by reviewing amalgamated data collected by the British Columbia Forest Service. The physiological demands of those tasks were then measured by observing test subjects as they performed them in the field. One simulation involved 18 firefighters, another involved 10 firefighters, but it is unclear from the researchers' report whether the subjects at this stage were male or female. The researchers asked a pilot group of 10 university student volunteers (6 females and 4 males) to perform a series of proposed fitness tests and field exercises. After refining the preferred tests, the researchers observed them being performed by a larger sample group composed of 31 forest firefighter trainees and 15 university student volunteers (31 males and 15 females), and correlated their results with the group's performance in the field. Having concluded that the preferred tests were accurate predictors of actual forest firefighting performance—including the running test designed to gauge whether the subject met the aerobic standard—the researchers presented their report to the Government in 1992.

A follow-up study in 1994 of 77 male forest firefighters and 2 female forest firefighters used the same methodology. However, the researchers this time recommended that the Government initiate another study to examine the impact of the Tests on women. There is no evidence before us that the Government responded to this recommendation.

Two aspects of the researchers' methodology are critical to this case. First, it was primarily descriptive or "impressionistic," based on measuring the average performance levels of the test subjects and converting this data into minimum performance standards. Second, it did not seem to distinguish between the male and female test subjects.

After four attempts, Ms. Meiorin failed to meet the aerobic standard, running the distance in 11 minutes and 49.4 seconds instead of the required 11 minutes. As a result, she was laid off. Her union subsequently brought a grievance on her behalf. The arbitrator designated to hear the grievance was required to determine whether she had been improperly dismissed.

Evidence accepted by the arbitrator demonstrated that, owing to physiological differences, most women have lower aerobic capacity than most men. Even with training, most women cannot increase their aerobic capacity to the level required by the aerobic standard, although training can allow most men to meet it. The arbitrator also heard evidence that 65% to 70% of male applicants pass the Tests on their initial attempts, while only 35% of female applicants have similar success. Of the 800 to 900 Initial Attack Crew members employed by the Government in 1995, only 100 to 150 were female.

There was no credible evidence showing that the prescribed aerobic capacity was necessary for either men or women to perform the work of a forest firefighter satisfactorily. On the contrary, Ms. Meiorin had in the past performed her work well, without apparent risk to herself, her colleagues or the public.

The Court overturned Ms. Meiorin's dismissal and in the process set new legal standards for the use of employment tests that continue to influence hiring standards. The decision also articulated a unified concept of discrimination, a new requirement for establishing bona fide occupational requirements, the need for individual accommodation, and the need to consider reasonable alternatives for practices that may be discriminatory. These aspects of the Meiorin decision will be discussed throughout this chapter. The complete Meiorin decision may be found at: http://scc.lexum.org/en/1999/1999scr3-3/1999scr3-3.html

© iStock.com/digitivi

The *Meiorin* decision undermines use of the four-fifths rule as a defence to discrimination. Justice McLachlin wrote that leaving a "neutral" practice in place, even if its adverse effects were felt by only a small number of people, was questionable. The policy or practice is itself discriminatory because it treats some individuals differently from others on the basis of a prohibited ground; the size of the "affected group" is irrelevant. This suggests that the Court would not approve a selection practice that met the four-fifths rule.

In contrast to the *Wards Cove Packing v. Antonio* U.S. Supreme Court decision, the Canadian Supreme Court placed a higher onus on Canadian organizations to put in place nondiscriminatory selection procedures. The ruling laid out a unified approach for establishing whether performance standards for a job are discriminatory and reinforced the concept of individual accommodation in the workplace. Like the *Albemarle Paper Co. v. Moody* decision in the United States, this decision established new guidelines for research used in validating selection systems. These issues are addressed in greater detail in the following sections.

Bona fide occupational requirement (BFOR)
A procedure used to defend a discriminatory employment practice or policy on the grounds that the policy or practice was adopted in an honest and good-faith belief that it was reasonably necessary to assure the efficient and economical performance of the job without endangering employees or the general public. BFORs are sometimes referred to as bona fide occupational qualifications (BFOQs).

BONA FIDE OCCUPATIONAL REQUIREMENT

Most human rights acts in Canada allow an employer to defend a discriminatory policy or practice as a **bona fide occupational requirement (BFOR)** if there is a good reason for it based on the employer's need to "engage and retain efficient employees"[22] The Canadian Human Rights Act[23] states that it is not a discriminatory practice if any refusal, exclusion, suspension, limitation, specification, or preference in relation to any employment is established by an employer to be based on a bona fide occupational requirement. A BFOR is sometimes referred to as a bona fide occupational qualification (BFOQ); however, the term used in jurisprudence is BFOR.

The Supreme Court of Canada's *Etobicoke* decision[24] specified that a legitimate BFOR was imposed by an employer "honestly, in good faith, and in the sincerely held belief that it is imposed in the interests of adequate performance of the work involved with reasonable dispatch, safety and economy and not for ulterior or extraneous reasons that could defeat the Code's purpose. The qualification must be objectively related to the employment concerned, ensuring its efficient and economical performance without endangering the employee, his fellow employees and the general public." Statistical and medical evidence was to be given more weight than the impressions or persons with respect to the need for the BFOR.

This definition of a BFOR guided selection policies and human resource practices until the *Meiorin* decision, where Justice McLachlin set out a new "unified approach" to defining a BFOR for cases of both direct and adverse effect discrimination:

> *Having considered the various alternatives, I propose the following three-step test for determining whether a prima facie discriminatory standard is a BFOR. An employer may justify the impugned standard by establishing on the balance of probabilities:*
>
> *(1) that the employer adopted the standard for a purpose rationally connected to the performance of the job;*
>
> *(2) that the employer adopted the particular standard in an honest and good faith belief that it was necessary to the fulfilment of that legitimate work-related purpose; and*
>
> *(3) that the standard is reasonably necessary to the accomplishment of that legitimate work-related purpose. To show that the standard is reasonably necessary, it must be demonstrated that it is impossible to accommodate individual employees sharing the characteristics of the claimant without imposing undue hardship upon the employer.*

The "standard" referred to in this decision is the BC government's use of aerobics tests to assess forest firefighters against a minimum test score set for the "maximal oxygen uptake." This standard was believed to be necessary for firefighters to meet the physical demands required in fighting forest fires. All candidates had to meet the same minimum test score. The Supreme Court found that the standard had a prima facie discriminatory effect on women. Women have, on average, a lower aerobic capacity than men and had difficulty achieving the minimum test score that had been set for the test. Fewer women, therefore, would be hired under the standard.

The Court held that the BC government had met the first two steps of the unified approach by adopting the standard in an honest and good-faith belief that the standard was job-related and was linked to successful job performance. It failed, however, to demonstrate to the Court's satisfaction that the minimum performance standard set on the aerobics tests was reasonably necessary to the accomplishment of the legitimate work-related purpose for which it had been adopted. The employer had not demonstrated that women required the same minimum level of aerobic capacity as men to perform the job safely and efficiently; nor had the employer shown that it was impossible to accommodate women candidates without imposing undue hardship upon itself. The employer failed to demonstrate that the aerobics standard was a BFOR under the new "unified" definition and so could not successfully defend the use of the test for assessing the fitness of forest firefighters.

The three-part *Meiorin* test is now the standard under which all workplace practices, including selection testing, constitute bona fide occupational requirements. It is the test that courts, tribunals, and arbitrators use in determining whether a workplace practice can be considered to be a BFOR when considering whether those practices constitute either adverse or direct discrimination against individuals or groups.

REASONABLE ACCOMMODATION

Accommodation
The duty of an employer to put in place modifications to discriminatory employment practices or procedures to meet the needs of members of a protected group being affected by the employment practice or procedure. As part of a BFOR defence, an employer must demonstrate that such accommodation is impossible to achieve without incurring undue hardship in terms of the organization's expense or operations.

The concept of reasonable **accommodation** is incorporated into the concept of a bona fide occupational requirement. Where discrimination has occurred, the employer is under a duty to accommodate the complainant, short of undue hardship. For example, an employer who administers a standardized employment test in selection may have to demonstrate that test instructions were appropriately modified to allow persons with mental or physical disabilities a fair chance to demonstrate their ability. For example, persons with attention deficit disorders may require additional time to complete a standardized test than other job applicants. The Supreme Court of Canada, in *O'Malley* placed the employer under a burden to take reasonable steps to accommodate the complainant, with hardship occurring at the point where a policy or practice (such as modifying a selection procedure) causes undue interference in the operation of the business or unsupportable expense to the employer. In the *Central Alberta Dairy Pool* decision, the Court noted some factors that are relevant to assessing whether an employer has reasonably accommodated an individual or group protected under human rights legislation. Included among these factors that place the employer under a greater or lesser burden of accommodation are the following:

- the financial cost to the employer as a result of making the accommodation;
- disruption of an existing collective agreement;
- the impact of lowered morale on other employees;
- flexibility of workforce and facilities;
- the size of the employer's operation; and
- the magnitude of risk for workers and the general public when safety is compromised.

Later, in *Renaud*,[25] the Court held that while disruption of a collective agreement that seriously infringed on the protected rights of employees could constitute undue hardship under certain conditions, both the employer and the union had a duty to accommodate Mr. Renaud, and could not use the excuse that changing the collective agreement to accommodate him would infringe the collective rights of other employees. The *Renaud* decision is important as it established that a union could be found to have discriminated against employees and also that it had an obligation to support an employer's reasonable attempts to accommodate an employee.

INDIVIDUAL ACCOMMODATION

The concept of individual accommodation follows that of reasonable accommodation. The standard for individual accommodation has evolved over three important Supreme Court of Canada cases. In the *Bhinder* decision, the Court by majority found that once an employment policy or practice has been established as a BFOR, there was no need for the employer to accommodate the special circumstances of the individual. For example, suppose that an individual with arthritis has asked for reasonable accommodation to this disability and wants to complete a realistic work sample in place of the usual standardized manual dexterity test required of job applicants. Under the *Bhinder* decision, the employer would not be under a burden to grant the applicant's request. The minority, however, argued that finding a rule to be a BFOR did not excuse an employer from accommodating an employee to the point of undue hardship.

Five years later, the *Central Alberta Dairy Pool* decision reversed, in part, the *Bhinder* decision. The majority on the Court ruled that workplace practices that had an adverse impact on individuals were discriminatory unless the employer accommodated the individual to the point of undue hardship. It upheld *Bhinder* in stating that a workplace practice that was a BFOR and had a direct effect on individuals was not discriminatory, with no obligation on the employer to accommodate the individual. The minority on the Court argued that there was a need for accommodation whether the practice had a direct or adverse impact on individuals. In the aftermath of the *Dairy Pool* decision, an employer might show that a workplace practice such as hiring only workers with excellent manual dexterity was a BFOR. If a manual dexterity test then had an adverse impact on applicants who had arthritis in their hands, the employer would have to accommodate the arthritic job candidate, even if that person was the only candidate with that disability applying for the job. The employer might accommodate such a candidate by using a realistic work sample or job tryout in place of the standardized test. On the other hand, if the employer could show that not hiring people with arthritis was a BFOR, then the employer could state that it would not hire anyone with that condition, and that would not constitute discrimination.

Finally, in 1999, the Court's *Meiorin* decision adopted the reasoning of the minority in the *Dairy Pool* case and stipulated that adverse and direct discrimination were discrimination and that employment practices, even if they were BFORs, which resulted in either type had to be accommodated. In our example, the employer could not state that based on a BFOR it would not hire anyone with arthritis; furthermore, the employer would have to modify the testing procedures to allow for individual accommodation for any applicant with arthritis who requested accommodation. All persons with arthritis could not be treated as a group. Their unique talents needed to be assessed through a testing procedure that accommodated their disability. Recruitment and Selection Today 3.8 describes the changing need to accommodate caregiving responsibilities in the workplace based on some recent human rights cases involving accommodation based on family status. While the Federal Court of Appeal has taken a position, these cases will most likely go to the Supreme Court for a final decision. Stay tuned.

Clearly, employers can no longer apply a BFOR as a general practice or policy and by so doing disproportionately exclude members of a protected group, especially in the case of mental or physical disability. To establish a BFOR, the employer must successfully argue that accommodating the needs of the adversely affected individual would produce undue economic or administrative hardship for the organization. Justice McLachlin raised the requirements for establishing a BFOR in *Meiorin* by specifying the three-part BFOR test. Employers must now demonstrate that it is *impossible* to accommodate individual employees who are members of the protected group without imposing undue hardship on the employer. As stated by Justice McLachlin:

> *Employers designing workplace standards owe an obligation to be aware of both the differences between individuals, and differences that characterize groups of individuals. They must build conceptions of equality into workplace standards. By enacting human rights statutes and providing that they are applicable to the workplace, the legislatures have determined that the standards governing the performance of work should be designed to reflect all members of society, in so far*

RECRUITMENT AND SELECTION TODAY 3.8

ACCOMMODATION OF CAREGIVING RESPONSIBILITIES: A KEY EMPLOYMENT ISSUE

A jurisprudential logjam seems to be breaking up on the issue of the caregiving responsibilities of workers. In two recent decisions, *Canadian National Railway Co. v. Seeley* (CHRR Doc. 13-3041) and *Canada (Attorney General) v. Johnstone* (CHRR Doc. 13-3006), the Federal Court ruled in favour of women whose family childcare responsibilities conflicted with work rules.

The women were both working for employers with rotating or unpredictable schedules. When Denise Seeley, a freight train conductor whose home depot was Jasper, Alberta, did not report to Vancouver to cover a shortage because she could not arrange adequate childcare, she was fired by Canadian National. When Fiona Johnstone, a border services agent, requested a static shift so that she could make stable childcare arrangements instead of working 56-day rotating shifts, the Canadian Border Services Agency offered her only part-time hours.

For women workers the conflict between work requirements and childcare responsibilities has always been a key equality issue, and women have been penalized as workers because they are the primary caregivers for children and other family members. They have found it necessary to leave paid work, cut back hours, step aside from promotions, or avoid assignments that require travel in order to care for their family members.

Today about 60 percent of women work for pay in Canada. They are almost half the work force, and two thirds of them have children under 6. Some of them are also responsible for older parents—members of the "sandwich generation." Women (and some men too) are increasingly in conflict with employers who want them as workers, but also want them to function as though they do not have family responsibilities.

In the cases on family status discrimination, federal employers—sometimes represented by the Attorney General of Canada—have made a series of arguments: the ground "family status" does not include parental childcare obligations, since it only protects a "status" not obligations integral to it; figuring out how to balance the obligations of family life and work belongs in the home, not in the workplace; parents make choices about how to care for their children, and those personal choices are not protected by human rights legislation. In short, these federal employers take the position that families have nothing to do with them, and they do not have a duty to accommodate a worker's need to provide adequate childcare.

The B.C. Court of Appeal encouraged this resistance in its 2004 decision in *Health Sciences Assn. of British Columbia v. Campbell River and North Island Transition Society* (50 C.H.R.R. D/140). That Court ruled that to establish "family status" discrimination a complainant had to show that an employer changed a term or condition of work and the change caused a "serious interference" with a family obligation. Application of this test would defeat most family status discrimination claims.

Fortunately, there is now a line of cases that reject these arguments, including *Whyte v. Canadian National Railway Co.* (71 C.H.R.R. D/316), *Seeley,* and *Johnstone.* The ground "family status" includes childcare obligations, according to the Federal Court, and there is no reason to make the threshold for proving family status discrimination more onerous than it is for any other ground.

There is a new opportunity to address the conflicts between work rules and family obligations, and a new opening for research, study and consultation on how these conflicts affect women and men in their families and at work.

Source: *Canadian Human Rights Reporter*, "Accommodation of Caregiving Responsibilities: A Key Employment Issue", Oct. 31, 2013. http://www.cdn-hr-reporter.ca/content/accommodation-caregiving-responsibilities-key-employment-issue.

as this is reasonably possible. Courts and tribunals must bear this in mind when confronted with a claim of employment-related discrimination. To the extent that a standard unnecessarily fails to reflect the differences among individuals, it runs afoul of the prohibitions contained in the various human rights statutes and must be replaced. The standard itself is required to provide for individual accommodation, if reasonably possible. A standard that allows for such accommodation may be only slightly different from the existing standard but it is a different standard nonetheless.

REASONABLE ALTERNATIVE

The concept of reasonable alternative is also closely related to the BFOR. Under the burden of reasonable alternative, the employer must show that no reasonable or practical substitute exists for the discriminatory practice. For example, where the employer uses a cognitive ability test that has adverse impact on members of visible minorities, a tribunal may require that employer to show that no other valid selection predictor (e.g., a different employment test or a structured interview) is available that has less adverse impact. The concept of reasonable alternative can involve important elements of individual accommodation as well. As stated in the Canadian Human Rights Tribunal decision of *Andrews v. Treasury Board and Department of Transport* (1994), as part of a BFOR defence, an employer must usually explain why it was not possible to assess individually the risk presented by an employee. For example, an employer who administers a manual dexterity test to all job applicants may have to show a tribunal why it was not possible to provide a practical work sample test as a reasonable alternative to assess the ability of one particular disabled applicant to do the job. Indeed, the *Meiorin* decision placed more stringent obligations on employers to search for reasonable alternatives (see Recruitment and Selection Notebook 3.4).

RECRUITMENT AND SELECTION NOTEBOOK 3.4

SEARCH FOR REASONABLE ALTERNATIVES

The *Meiorin* decision requires an employer to address the following questions as part of establishing a defence that there were no reasonable alternatives to a practice that discriminated against individual workers. These questions are taken verbatim from the Supreme Court decision[26]:

(a) Has the employer investigated alternative approaches that do not have a discriminatory effect, such as individual testing against a more individually sensitive standard?

(b) If alternative standards were investigated and found to be capable of fulfilling the employer's purpose, why were they not implemented?

(c) Is it necessary to have all employees meet the single standard for the employer to accomplish its legitimate purpose or could standards reflective of group or individual differences and capabilities be established?

(d) Is there a way to do the job that is less discriminatory while still accomplishing the employer's legitimate purpose?

(e) Is the standard properly designed to ensure that the desired qualification is met without placing an undue burden on those to whom the standard applies?

(f) Have other parties who are obliged to assist in the search for possible accommodation fulfilled their roles? As Sopinka noted in Renaud, supra, at pp. 992–96, the task of determining how to accommodate individual differences may also place burdens on the employee and, if there is a collective agreement, a union.

ACCOMMODATING PHYSICAL AND MENTAL DISABILITY

The Supreme Court explicitly applied the *Meiorin* ruling to disability cases, such as *Grismer v. British Columbia (A.G).*[27] The Court emphasized that individualized, rather than standardized, testing must be used to accommodate individuals with disabilities.

This case did not involve the workplace but nonetheless has serious implications with respect to the accommodation of workplace disability. The *Grismer* case revolved around the Superintendent of Motor Vehicles' refusal to issue a driver's licence on the basis of a visual disability. The Supreme Court ruled that the defendants in human rights cases, here the Superintendent of Motor Vehicles, have the burden of demonstrating that the standard they have adopted "incorporates every possible accommodation to the point of undue hardship, whether that hardship takes the form of impossibility, serious risk or excessive cost." The *Grismer* case suggests that an employer must accept some moderate risk in accommodating individuals with disabilities while maintaining reasonable safety standards.

In a subsequent ruling (*Québec [Commission des droits de la personne et des droits de la jeunesse] v. Montréal [City]*),[28,29] the Court broadened the definition of disability and directed employers to take into account the social context of the impairment. The Court ruled that a person with a disability must be assessed in terms of that person's own unique abilities; the person's disability must not be viewed through any prejudice or bias, stigma, or misunderstanding on the part of the employer about the disability.

SUFFICIENT RISK

The notion of risk is important to the concepts of BFOR, reasonable and individual accommodation, and reasonable alternative. That is, the employer is obliged to accommodate workers, including job applicants, and provide reasonable alternatives up to, but not beyond, a certain level of risk. But what constitutes **sufficient risk**? Tribunals and courts have restricted the application of the risk criterion to those situations in which workplace safety is at issue. After the *Grismer* decision, each case will be judged on its own unique merits with respect to the degree of risk imposed by the disability. For example, an airline company may set a visual acuity standard for pilots, requiring that all candidates have uncorrected 20/20 full-colour vision, and defend this standard on the grounds that public safety would be compromised without it; however, a delivery company might not be able to defend not hiring a driver who was legally blind in one eye.

Sufficient risk
As part of a BFOR defence, an employer may argue that an occupational requirement that discriminates against a protected group is reasonably necessary to ensure that work will be performed successfully and in a manner that will not pose harm or danger to employees or the public.

The Supreme Court addressed the issue of sufficient risk in the *Grismer* case. While the magnitude of the risk and those who might be affected by it must be assessed, the risk must be considered in the context of human rights issues. The aim is not to lower safety standards but to find options that meet the safety standards and at the same time respect human rights. In *Grismer* the Court confirmed that risk had a limited role in determining a BFOR and that *sufficient risk* alone could not justify a discriminatory standard. Risk can still be considered under an assessment of undue hardship but not as a justification for a discriminatory action. The critical issue is whether the safety standard was reasonably necessary to ensure safety.

One area where direct discrimination might still happen with some regularity is in the area of physical or mental disability. For example, a hospital employer might screen out from the hiring process all people with HIV or with AIDS. The concern of the employer would probably centre on the safety of patients during use of invasive techniques (such as injections by syringe). If the hospital did intentionally exclude all persons with HIV/AIDS during selection, then the employer would have to establish a BFOR and show through the use of objective data that (1) people with HIV/AIDS are a sufficient safety risk; (2) all persons with HIV/AIDS present a safety risk; (3) individual testing of applicants with HIV/AIDS is impossible or impractical; and (4) that these individuals cannot be accommodated without imposing undue hardship on the employer.

The sufficient risk criterion means that the risk must be well above a minimal or nominal risk. A minimal or nominal risk criterion would, for example, suggest that a person with muscular dystrophy should not be hired because that person might be injured in a fall (an organizational policy that many human rights authorities would argue reinforces a stereotype about the physically disabled, rather than being supportable by fact). On the other hand, a severe vision disability in an airline pilot would be well above minimal or nominal risk, because a plane crash caused or contributed to by that disability could kill hundreds of people. In that instance, risk resulting from the disability might well be sufficient to justify the otherwise discriminatory action of refusing to offer the disabled person a job.

In *Québec v. Montréal (City)* the Supreme Court was quite clear in stating that the limitations imposed by a disability must be considered individually within a particular context and that some risk is acceptable. Decisions about hiring someone with a disability cannot be made on the basis of prejudice or stereotypes held about the limitations imposed by the disability.

LEGAL CONCEPTS APPLIED TO RECRUITMENT AND SELECTION

Two human rights decisions illustrate the application of the above principles to employers' recruitment or selection systems. In both decisions, each employer's system was found wanting and the court or tribunal awarded damages or remedies to the complainant. Both decisions continue to have a significant impact on recruitment and selection in Canada.

The first decision is that of *Action travail des femmes v. Canadian National* (1984). Here a women's group in Quebec lodged a complaint with the Canadian Human Rights Commission aimed at CN's recruitment and selection practices in the St. Lawrence region. *Action travail des femmes* alleged that CN's practices disproportionately excluded women from nontraditional jobs, including those of trade apprentice, brakeman, and coach cleaner, all of which were male dominated. Furthermore, the group alleged that the employment practices in question were not bona fide occupational requirements.

One selection predictor that came under scrutiny by the tribunal was the Bennett Mechanical Comprehension Test, which was used to select people for entry-level positions. The Bennett is known to have adverse impact against women, and, in addition, CN had not validated it for the jobs in question. As a result, the tribunal ordered CN to stop using the test. In addition, the tribunal ordered CN to cease a number of other discriminatory recruitment and selection practices. The tribunal also ordered CN to begin a special hiring program with the goal of increasing the representation of women in nontraditional jobs in the company. This decision was widely noted at the time and has since influenced recruitment and hiring practices in Canada.

The second decision is that of *Andrews v. Treasury Board and Department of Transport* (1994). In that decision, a Canadian Human Rights tribunal criticized a practical hearing test developed to assess a hearing-impaired applicant to the Canadian Coast Guard College. The test, which was administered in place of a maximum hearing loss standard for Canadian Coast Guard officers, was designed at a cost of over $100 000 and consisted of 14 different subtests administered to the applicant on the bridge of an operating Coast Guard ship. The subtest scenarios were administered by Coast Guard staff, who in turn supervised crew members of the ship serving as role players. The applicant's responses to the subtest scenarios were recorded and then compared against predetermined test standards.

Andrews subsequently failed the test, was declined admission to the college, and filed a complaint with the Canadian Human Rights Commission. When testifying about the test during the tribunal hearings, expert witnesses criticized it on various grounds, including incomplete technical development, lack of reliability and validity, administration under insufficiently standardized conditions, and absence of norm data against which to compare and interpret the applicant's scores. The tribunal concluded that the practical hearing test was discriminatory and granted monetary compensation to the complainant Andrews.

In the *Andrews v. Treasury Board and Department of Transport* decision, the tribunal cited the legal principles previously discussed in this chapter. The complainant, Andrews, lodged his complaint against the Coast Guard on the grounds of physical disability (hearing impairment) and also alleged both direct discrimination and adverse effect discrimination. The application of the hearing loss standard had the effect of producing adverse impact against hearing-disabled persons.

The tribunal found that the Coast Guard had discriminated against Andrews by refusing him entry to the Coast Guard College and then considered whether the Coast Guard had successfully argued a BFOR defence. The tribunal accepted the subjective element of the BFOR (that the Coast Guard had set the limitation honestly, in good faith, and in sincerity that the limitation was necessary), but rejected the Coast Guard argument that it had established the objective element of the BFOR. Importantly, the tribunal found that the Coast Guard had not established the practical hearing test as a BFOR because of the numerous technical problems associated with it; that is, the Coast Guard had failed to validate the practical hearing test according to the accepted professional standards discussed in Chapter 2. What is more, the tribunal found that Andrews could have been reasonably and individually accommodated by use of a less expensive and simpler test, which would have been a reasonable alternative to the practical hearing test. Finally, the nature of Andrews's disability did not pose sufficient risk to the safe performance of a Coast Guard navigational officer to justify denying him entry to the college to train for the job.

A comparison between these two decisions, which were made 10 years apart, illustrates that at least four important legal concepts (those of reasonable accommodation, individual accommodation, reasonable alternative, and sufficient risk) assumed greater importance in the 1990s than in the 1980s, as they do today. In 1999 the *Meiorin* and *Grismer* decisions placed an even greater emphasis on these four legal concepts. Because of the rapidly evolving character of legal issues in Canadian HRM, practitioners and HR specialists must continually upgrade their knowledge and skills in this area.

// PART III: SOME PRACTICAL GUIDELINES IN NONDISCRIMINATORY RECRUITMENT AND SELECTION

The first two parts of this chapter provided a historical and conceptual backdrop for legal issues in recruitment and selection in Canada. They reviewed important court and tribunal decisions that have affected the practice of recruitment and selection in Canada. This third part presents some practical guidelines for developing nondiscriminatory recruitment and selection practices and for reviewing and improving those practices already in place.

The guidelines presented here are exactly that–guidelines; they are not meant to be applied in a mechanical fashion. The guidelines point to the right direction and help to identify typical problem areas in recruitment and selection systems. The guidelines should stimulate critical discussion and appraisal of those systems with an eye to improvement. There are no easy answers to many of the problems discussed in this chapter; the issues are simply too complex. HR managers may need to draw on the expert help of legal and professional consultants in dealing with many of these complex issues, particularly when there is insufficient time or expertise to deal with them in-house.

KEY PRACTICAL CONSIDERATIONS IN NONDISCRIMINATORY RECRUITMENT

Recruitment is a complex HR activity. This can make it difficult to develop nondiscriminatory recruitment practices for protected group members (in the case of human rights legislation) or designated group members (in the case of employment equity). The scope of practices that must be considered is more manageable if the success or failure of recruitment is traced back to two main causes: (1) the effectiveness or ineffectiveness of the organization in contacting and communicating with target group members and (2) the positive or negative perceptions that target group members hold about the organization. (It is irrelevant whether those perceptions existed before the target group members were recruited or whether they developed during the recruiting process.)

People will not apply for a job if they are unaware that the job or organization exists or that the organization is recruiting. Getting the word out is not enough–job seekers must have a positive perception of the organization, as well as of their chances of getting the job, before they will apply. That perception is formed in at least two ways: (1) at the time the organization makes the initial contact through its **outreach recruiting**; or (2) through knowledge gained about the organization and its practices via third parties (e.g., friends, family, or news media). An organization must make a determined and persistent effort to make potential job applicants, including designated group members, aware of available positions within the employing organization.

Outreach recruiting
A recruitment practice where the employing organization makes a determined and persistent effort to make potential job applicants, including designated group members, aware of available positions within the employing organization.

Several Canadian companies have developed outreach programs to attract members of protected groups. The Royal Bank of Canada (RBC) uses three programs to attract qualified persons with disabilities. The RBC's Pursue Your Potential program helps persons with disabilities and Aboriginals to become aware of career opportunities that may be available to them, and to understand the recruitment and selection process. The RBC's Job Search Assistance program helps persons with disabilities search for a job and prepares them for interviews. Most successfully, it developed the Ability Edge Internships with RBC, where university, college, and high school students with disabilities receive paid internships with RBC. IBM also provides scholarship and internship programs for university students with disabilities who are pursuing careers in computer science, software engineering, or other areas related to information technology.[29]

Recruitment and Selection Notebooks 3.5 and 3.6 present a summary of effective and ineffective recruiting practices. They provide some practical guidance on what to do and what not to do when setting up and running recruitment programs that will meet legal requirements. As well, Recruitment and Selection Notebook 3.7 presents a list of human rights resources available on the Internet.

RECRUITMENT AND SELECTION NOTEBOOK 3.5

PRACTICES FOR NONDISCRIMINATORY RECRUITING

Effective Practices

- In employment offices, post in a conspicuous spot complete, objective, and specific information on all available jobs.
- Advertise job openings in media that are read, viewed, or listened to by protected or designated group members.
- Train employment clerical staff and recruitment officers in outreach recruiting.
- Use opportunities to visually present protected or designated group members in positive employment roles (e.g., in brochures and posters in employment office waiting areas, postings on company websites, and profiles of board members).
- Establish networks with community groups from which protected or designated group members are drawn.
- Set and advertise objectively determined selection criteria for the job.
- Base selection criteria on bona fide occupational requirements.

Ineffective Practices

- Permit receptionists and recruiters in employment offices to "pre-screen" applicants on the basis of informal criteria (e.g., appearance, dress).
- Rely on word-of-mouth advertising.
- Post job advertisements only in-house.
- Rely solely on seniority when promoting employees without regard for meeting the qualifications need for the position.
- Allow each recruiter to use and communicate idiosyncratic criteria for selecting among job applicants.
- Categorize and stream job applicants based on stereotyped assumptions about protected or designated group membership (e.g., that women are not physically strong enough for certain work).

RECRUITMENT AND SELECTION NOTEBOOK 3.6

PRACTICES THAT PROMOTE POSITIVE RECRUITING PERCEPTIONS

- Include in the job advertising role models from protected or designated groups, as well as equal opportunity statements.
- Implement management practices and policies that recognize and deal with special challenges or difficulties faced by protected or designated groups (e.g., wheelchair ramps for people with physical disabilities).
- Communicate and demonstrate the commitment of senior management to outreach recruiting.
- Actively challenge negative myths and stereotypes about protected or designated group members (e.g., through training programs).
- Bring organizational policies and procedures into line with human rights and employment equity legislation.
- Reward supervisors and managers through the pay and promotion system for success in advancing human rights and employment equity goals.
- Build outreach recruiting into departmental and organizational business plans.
- Set specific and measurable recruiting targets against which managers can work.
- Present protected and designated group members in positive roles within organization newspapers and magazines.
- Offer training and development programs to protected and designated group members to address their specific needs in adapting and progressing within the organization.

- Modify working conditions as needed to accommodate protected and designated group members.

Practices That Promote Negative Recruiting Perceptions

- Permit sexual, racial, or other forms of harassment in the organization.
- Show lack of interest by senior management in improving recruitment practices.
- Allow negative myths and stereotypes to persist regarding the capabilities of protected and designated group members.
- Leave outreach recruiting unrewarded by the pay and promotion system.
- Leave outreach recruiting out of departmental and organizational business plans.
- Tell managers to "do your best" in recruiting protected and designated group members rather than providing them with specific numerical targets.

RECRUITMENT AND SELECTION NOTEBOOK 3.7

HUMAN RIGHTS ON THE INTERNET

The following are Internet addresses for Canadian and provincial human rights tribunals and commissions, along with those for some other valuable human rights resources. On each site you will find links to other related sites and to lists of decisions or publications that can be found on the site. For example, the "Publications" link on the Canadian Human Rights Commission site will provide you with access to a list of recent reports, guides, and other materials that you can read directly from the site, print, or download. In this way, you can obtain a copy of the *Guide to Screening and Selection in Employment*. HR managers and others who engage in recruitment and selection should make a habit of reviewing recent information, including new decisions posted on these sites.

Human Rights Boards/Tribunals

Canada	http://www.chrt-tcdp.gc.ca/NS/index-eng.asp
British Columbia	http://www.bchrt.gov.bc.ca
Quebec (French)	http://www.justice.gouv.qc.ca/francais/tribunaux/trib-droi.htm
Quebec (English)	http://www.justice.gouv.qc.ca/english/tribunaux/trib-droi-a.htm

Human Rights Commissions

Canada	http://www.chrc-ccdp.ca
Alberta	http://www.albertahumanrights.ab.ca/default.asp
Manitoba	http://www.gov.mb.ca/hrc
New Brunswick	http://www.gnb.ca/hrc-cdp/index-e.asp
Newfoundland/Labrador	http://www.justice.gov.nl.ca/hrc
Northwest Territories	http://www.nwthumanrights.ca
Nova Scotia	http://www.gov.ns.ca/humanrights
Ontario	http://www.ohrc.on.ca
Prince Edward Island	http://www.gov.pe.ca/humanrights
Quebec	http://www.cdpdj.qc.ca
Saskatchewan	http://www.shrc.gov.sk.ca
Yukon	http://www.yhrc.yk.ca

Valuable Human Rights Resources on the Internet

Canadian Human Rights Reporter (CHRR) http://cdn-hr-reporter.ca

Human Rights Research and Education Centre (Ottawa) http://www.uottawa.ca/hrrec

Human Rights Information and Documentation Systems http://www.hurisearch.org

LEGAL REQUIREMENTS AND HR PRACTICE

An underlying assumption of recruitment and selection practices is that these practices are supported by empirical evidence, that they are reliable and valid procedures. Recruitment and selection practices that have an impact on careers or entry to occupations must be defensible with respect to legal requirements. That is, we expect practitioners to apply solutions that have a solid "scientific" grounding. Regrettably, HR practice too often runs ahead of research and leads to the adoption of interventions that do not have empirical support, or do not have support for the specific purposes for which they are used. Claims by a practitioner that a practice is "valid" because the practitioner "knows" it works or "it makes good business sense" will not meet legal scrutiny against the standards laid out in this chapter. Only those selection procedures that can be supported through empirical evidence will find acceptance with courts and human rights tribunals.

Adopting valid recruitment and selection practices is only part of the solution. Practitioners must ensure the proper implementation of the system and monitor it over time for any changes. It is not acceptable, for example, to show that a certain level of cognitive ability is a job requirement and then use an invalid test to measure it. Neither is it acceptable for the practitioner to use a valid test in an inappropriate manner or to lack the qualifications to use and interpret data from a valid test.

There is a need for better linkages between research and practice in HR. Practitioners must understand the need to base recruitment and selection practices on empirical evidence. These linkages have become ever more important as the field of HR moves to establish itself as an independent profession. Regulatory and credentialing systems exist to ensure the protection of the welfare of the public and clients of the practitioner and to guarantee that the practitioner operates in accordance with accepted standards of professional ethics and practice guidelines.

Practitioners are expected to use procedures and practices that not only "do no harm" but also provide benefits to the client. This is particularly important when invalid selection procedures bring the HR practitioner's organization in front of a court or tribunal and result in large-scale payouts to rectify wrongs done to employees and applicants. There are some questions that practitioners can ask to determine if the recruitment and selection procedures they are using will meet with legal acceptance:

1. Do the procedures I am using result in direct or indirect discrimination?
2. If a selection procedure I am using results in direct or indirect discrimination, can I establish that it is a BFOR by showing that:
   - I am adopting the selection procedure in good faith?
   - the selection procedure cannot be replaced by one that is valid and has less or little adverse impact?
   - the selection procedure is related to job performance or safety?
   - *all* of those people in the class excluded by the selection procedure are incapable of performing the job or present a sufficient safety risk?
   - individual testing of class members affected by the rule is impossible or impractical?
   - there are no reasonable alternatives to that testing?
   - every attempt has been made to accommodate the unique capabilities and inherent worth and dignity of every individual, up to the point of undue hardship?
3. Is the selection procedure a valid predictor of job performance?

Finally, one last thing that the HR staff may need to do is to educate management about the legal requirements that must be met in recruitment and selection. More and more Canadian organizations understand the benefits of adapting their procedures to meet legislative requirements. The intent of human rights legislation is clear: Everyone should have the opportunity to compete for the jobs available on an equal footing and on the basis of objective qualifications, regardless of group membership or employer stereotyping about what members of particular groups can and can't do. If this message has not gotten through, then HR professionals have the primary responsibility for providing the necessary education within their organizations.

Selection systems must be as legally defensible as possible. HR specialists must have the knowledge and time to collect and interpret the technical data that are essential to establishing the legal defensibility of a selection system. The best defence is a system that meets the validity and reliability requirements outlined in Chapter 2; selection based on "gut feeling," intuition, or unproven techniques will lead to embarrassment before a legal tribunal. Managers and HR staff should question and challenge each other's assumptions about what constitutes a legally defensible selection system. Even then, the legal issues are complex enough that managers and HR staff may hold differing opinions about whether a selection system is legally defensible. In those cases, legal consultation should be obtained. Nevertheless, the discussion of practical selection problems should lead to more defensible selection systems over the long run.

// SUMMARY

The Canadian workforce has always been ethnically heterogeneous, and now it is becoming increasingly diverse with regard to race, gender, and disabilities. Given that recruitment and selection are crucially important HR activities for achieving diversity, human rights and employment equity are here to stay. As well, a large segment of the Canadian workforce is unionized, which means that labour codes and related legislation will affect recruitment and selection practices in many Canadian organizations.

Legal issues in recruitment and selection are complex and take a great deal of time, study, and experience to master. What is more, the legal scene changes constantly and rapidly as new legislation, legislative amendments, human rights policies, and tribunal or court decisions are introduced. This requires practitioners in recruitment and selection to regularly update their knowledge and skills in legal issues. The legal scene will continue to grow and develop in the future as members of protected groups seek fuller participation in the Canadian labour market and as employers and employees (unionized and nonunionized) renegotiate their relationships through labour law and employment standards.

In this chapter we have presented an overview of the legal requirements that apply to recruitment and selection in Canada. We identified four main legal sources that influence the practice of HR in Canada: (1) constitutional law; (2) human rights legislation; (3) employment equity legislation and employment equity policies; and (4) labour law, employment standards, and related legislation.

The impact of these laws and policies mandates recruitment and selection practices that do not discriminate on the basis of specific characteristics. While there are differences across Canada, all human rights acts prohibit discrimination in employment with respect to race or colour, religion or creed, age, sex, marital status, and physical/mental handicap or disability. Employment equity requires proactive recruitment and selection policies to increase the number of women, visible minorities, Aboriginal peoples, and people with disabilities in the workplace by removing barriers to hiring them.

The chapter presents the most significant cases that have had a major impact on recruitment and selection. Over the past 25 years, a series of decisions by the Supreme Court of Canada and the Canadian Human Rights Commission have dealt with direct and indirect discrimination. These decisions have placed increasing restrictions on an organization's ability to use a BFOR defence against charges of discrimination, with the *Meiorin* decision dramatically changing the definition of a BFOR. Now, an organization must show that it is impossible to accommodate an individual employee or job applicant with respect to selection procedures without undue hardship to the company. This requirement is more stringent than similar requirements in the United States. The chapter also presents the obligations placed on an employer to accommodate employees and job applicants with respect to selection procedures and factors such as risk that may mitigate that obligation.

The chapter concludes with a presentation of some practical guidelines that will assist HR practitioners in developing recruitment and selection procedures that will meet with legal acceptance, should they have to address a human rights complaint. In closing, we also emphasize the need for HR practitioners to educate management about the legal requirements that recruitment and selection systems must meet and that the best way of staying out of legal trouble is to use reliable and valid selection systems, as presented in Chapter 2.

KEY TERMS

Accommodation, p. 94
Adverse effect discrimination, p. 87
Adverse impact, p. 88
Bona fide occupational requirement (BFOR), p. 92
Discrimination, p. 67
Employment equity, p. 73
Outreach recruiting, p. 101
Sufficient risk, p. 98

WEB LINKS

The Employment and Social Development Canada (formerly HRSDC) website provides extensive information on laws, regulations, and compliance issues relating to employment equity. This information can be found at
http://www.esdc.gc.ca

The Human Rights Research and Education Centre's website provides links to full-text versions of the court and tribunal decisions referenced in this chapter. You can find it at
http://www.uottawa.ca/hrrec

The complete text of the *Meiorin* decision can be found on the Supreme Court of Canada's website, as can other Court decisions mentioned in this chapter. You can find these at
http://scc.lexum.org/en/index.html

The *Queen's Human Rights Bulletin* contains summaries of cases discussed in this chapter. The *Bulletin* can be found at
http://www.queensu.ca/humanrights/legislationgroup/humanrights/bulletin.html

DISCUSSION QUESTIONS

1. Would the Canadian Charter of Rights and Freedoms prohibit an employer from putting in place a selection system that favoured women over men in the hiring process? Could such discrimination ever be justified under the Charter?
2. What are the prohibited grounds of employment discrimination in your province or territory's jurisdiction?
3. On what grounds could a Canadian employer justify the adverse impact of a selection procedure, test, or other measure?
4. What does it mean to accommodate someone to the point of undue hardship?
5. When can an apparently discriminatory selection practice be justified on the grounds of "sufficient risk"?
6. Why is basing hiring practices on a "gut feeling" risky business?

EXERCISES

1. We started this chapter with a real-life case where a manager and an HR professional disagree on whom to hire, with the HR professional arguing that the manager's reasons for not hiring a female applicant would constitute a human rights violation and providing the manager with the relevant section of their province's or territory's human rights act. Recruitment and Selection Notebook 3.7 lists the Internet URLs for most provincial and territorial human rights agencies. Download a copy of your province or territory's human rights act. (*Note:* The Nunavut government's Human Resources page provides policies in relation to a number of HR issues, http://www.nhrt.ca/splash.html.)

    a. In the context of your provincial or territorial legislation, discuss whether the HR professional was correct in arguing that not hiring the female applicant would constitute a violation of your human rights act. If so, what is the basis of the alleged violation?
    b. Review the cases and annual reports available on your provincial or territorial human rights agency's website to locate a case that may be similar to the one described at the beginning of this chapter. What was the ruling in that case? Would the ruling in that case be applicable to the situation described in our example?
    c. Would the manager ever be justified in not hiring the female applicant? If so, what would those circumstances be?

2. In the *British Columbia (Public Service Employees Relations Commission) v. BCGSEU* case, a lower appeals court had suggested that accommodating women by permitting them to meet a lower aerobic standard than men would constitute "reverse discrimination." The Supreme Court of Canada disagreed and stated that "the essence of equality is to be treated according to one's own merit, capabilities and circumstances. True equality requires that differences be accommodated. . . . A different aerobic standard capable of identifying women who could perform the job safely and efficiently therefore does not necessarily imply discrimination against men. 'Reverse discrimination' would result only if, for example, an aerobic standard representing a minimum threshold for all forest firefighters was held to be inapplicable

to men simply because they were men." What are your views on reverse discrimination? Do you agree with the views expressed by the appeals court or the Supreme Court? Why or why not? Have you ever observed or been subjected to reverse discrimination? If so, what was the situation?

3. There is considerable evidence showing that smokers are less productive than nonsmokers. Costs to organizations, besides those related to medical care, health, and life insurance, include absenteeism and loss of on-the-job time. Estimates place time loss per day due to smoking at 35 minutes a day, or 18.2 lost days per year per employee who smokes. In addition, smokers are absent, on average, three more days per year than other employees. Estimates place the cost of smoking to an employer at around $4500 per smoker per year.[30] These data suggest that it is in an employer's best interests to hire only nonsmokers or to fire smokers who cannot overcome their addiction. Would such policies, of hiring only nonsmokers and firing smokers, be acceptable under human rights legislation in your province or territory? Are smokers a "protected" group under human rights legislation? How would you defend these policies to an investigator from a human rights commission?
4. You may recall hearing about females being fired from U.S. television news anchor positions because they were too old. Clearly, this practice would be contrary to all human rights codes in Canada. However, one area of discrimination that is less clear is "lookism," in which a person is chosen for a job on the basis of his or her looks rather than his or her other qualifications. Individuals, particularly females who are overweight, tend to receive fewer job offers than others, even in cases where their appearance has no possible bearing on their work performance or where they are not involved in dealing with clients or customers. Can an employer in Canada, or in your jurisdiction, choose not to hire someone on the basis of their looks or for being overweight? Do job applicants so denied have protection under your province or territory's human rights provisions?
5. In the *Wards Cove Packing v. Antonio* decision, the U.S. Supreme Court stated that where an employment practice led to adverse impact, any alternative that led to less or no adverse impact must also be as effective as the practice it was replacing in meeting the organization's legitimate business purposes. The Court's ruling made it more difficult to establish an adverse impact case. In the *Meiorin* decision, the Canadian Supreme Court ruled that a policy or practice is itself discriminatory if it treats some individuals differently from others on the basis of a prohibited ground and that the size of the affected group was irrelevant. It also stated that an organization must accommodate individual employees to the point of imposing undue hardship upon the employer, unless it was impossible to do so. Discuss these two approaches to addressing selection practices that lead to adverse impact. Which approach do you support? Why?

CASE

Marita Smith works as a data entry clerk in a government department that is undergoing downsizing. Smith, who is severely hearing-impaired, has been a productive employee in her department for the last five years. Her performance has always been above average.

Smith has received notice that her position is being eliminated as part of the downsizing. Under her union's contract, she must be given preference for any government job that becomes available and for which she is qualified. Smith has been invited to apply for a term position in another government department, which is converting archival data from paper to an electronic database. To qualify for the position, Smith will have to pass an interview, a timed typing test, an accuracy test that involves accuracy in transcribing information from a computer screen, and another accuracy test that involves following written instructions to enter written records into the computer database. These are the same tests that all candidates for the position have had to pass to become eligible for the job.

Smith was interviewed one week prior to being administered the three skill tests. The interview protocol followed a standardized form used by all government departments. The three skill tests were administered to groups of nine applicants each. The applicants were seated at desks with computers, which were arranged in three rows of three desks each. The instructions for the tests were given verbally by the test administrator. Smith was provided with the services of a sign language interpreter during the testing and interview sessions.

Smith passed the interview but failed the skill tests. Her scores are presented in Table 3.5, along with the minimum scores that had to be obtained on each test to receive a job offer. Based on her performance on the tests, Smith did not receive an offer for the job and was laid off when her current job ended. Smith now believes that she was the victim of discrimination based on her physical disability; she claims that during the interview many references were made to her disability and that the interviewer always addressed questions to the sign language interpreter and never made eye contact with her. She feels that she was at a disadvantage in taking the skills tests.

Her prospective employer claims that had she passed the tests she would have been hired and her disability would have been accommodated. The employer argues that the testing standards were reasonably necessary for the efficient performance of the work. The standards in Table 3.5 are being justified as bona fide occupational requirements (BFORs). Smith has now filed a complaint with her provincial human rights commission.

TABLE 3.5

SMITH'S SCORES RELATIVE TO STANDARDS NEEDED TO PASS EACH TEST

	Standards	Smith
Interview	30 out of 50 points	36
Typing Test	50 words per minute with 5 errors or fewer	36 wpm 5 errors
Accuracy—Following Instructions	7 out of 10	5.5
Accuracy—Transcribing	7 out of 10	5

QUESTIONS

1. Should Smith have received a job offer? Why or why not? (In answering this and the following questions, base your arguments on the court cases presented in this chapter.)
2. Was Smith the victim of discrimination because of her disability?
3. Did she receive appropriate accommodation?
4. Are the employer's standards defensible as a BFOR?
5. Based on the material presented in this chapter, do you think the human rights commission will support her claim of discrimination?
6. If you were the employer's legal counsel, how would you defend the employer at a human rights tribunal that is called to hear Smith's complaint? What would you advise your client to do with respect to the charge?

// ENDNOTES

1 Simon, P.L.S. 1988. *Employment Law: The New Basics.* Don Mills, ON: CCH Canadian.

2 Ibid.

3 Carter, D.D., G. England, D. Etherington, and G. Trudeau. 2002. *Labour Law in Canada*, 5th ed. Markham, ON: Butterworths.

4 Canadian Human Rights Act (R.S.C., 1985, c. H-6). Retrieved from http://laws-lois.justice.gc.ca/eng/acts/h-6/

5 Canadian Human Rights Commission. 2014. *What Do I Need to Know Before Filing a Discrimination Complaint?* Retrieved from http://www.chrc-ccdp.ca/eng/content/what-do-i-need-know-filing-discrimination-complaint

6 Ibid.

7 *Employment Equity Policy in Canada: An Interprovincial Comparison.* Status of Women in Canada. ISBN 0-662-28160-8, Cat. No. SW21-46/1999E.

8 Weiner, N. 1993. *Employment Equity: Making It Work.* Toronto: Butterworths.

9 Belcourt, M., and K.J. McBey. 2010. *Strategic Human Resources Planning*, 4th ed. Toronto: Nelson.

10 Jackson, S.E., and R.S. Schuler. 1995. "Understanding Human Resource Management in the Context of Organizations and Their Environments." *Annual Review of Psychology* 46: 237–64.

11 Federal Labour Standards. Retrieved 2014 from http://www.labour.gc.ca/eng/standards_equity/st/index.shtml

12 Public Service Commission of Canada. Undated. *Investigations: An Overview.* Ottawa: Public Service Commission of Canada. Retrieved December 29, 2011, from http://www.psc-cfp.gc.ca/inv-enq/index-eng.htm

13 Public Service Commission of Canada. 2009–10. *Annual Report.* Ottawa. Retrieved December 29, 2011, from http://www.psc-cfp.gc.ca/arp-rpa/2010/index-eng.htm

14 *Maloley et al. v. Department of National Revenue.* February 1986. PSC Appeals Board. Ottawa.

15 *Ontario Human Rights Commission and O'Malley v. Simpsons-Sears Ltd.*, [1985] 2 S.C.R. 536.

16 Weiner, N. 1993.

17 Vining, A.R., D.C. McPhillips, and A.E. Boardman. 1986. "Use of Statistical Evidence in Employment Discrimination Litigation." *The Canadian Bar Review* 64: 660–702.

18 Ibid.

19 Glastris, P. 1994. "The Thin White Line: City Agencies Struggle to Mix Standardized Testing and Racial Balance." *U.S. News & World Report* (August 15): 53–54.

20 *British Columbia (Public Service Employee Relations Commission) v. British Columbia Government and Service Employees' Union (BCGSEU)*, [1999] 3 S.C.R. 3.

21 Ibid.

22 Canadian Human Rights Commission. 2007. *Bona Fide Occupational Requirements and Bona Fide Justifications under the Canadian Human Rights Act: The Implications of* Meiorin *and* Grismer. Ottawa: Canadian Human Rights Commission.

23 Canadian Human Rights Commission. 2014.

24 *Ontario Human Rights Commission et al. v. Etobicoke*, [1982] 1 SCR 202.

25 *Central Okanagan School Dist. No. 23 v. Renaud* (1992), 2 S.C.R. 970.

26 *Supreme Court of Canada. British Columbia (Public Service Employee Relations Commission) v. BCGSEU*, [1999] 3 S.C.R. 3.

27 *British Columbia (Superintendent of Motor Vehicles) v. British Columbia (Council of Human Rights) and Grismer (Estate)*, [1999] 3 S.C.R. 868.

28 *Québec (Commission des droits de la personne et des droits de la jeunesse) v. Montréal (City)*. 2000, 1 S.C.R. 665.

29 Equity and Diversity Directorate, Policy Branch, Public Service Commission of Canada. 2011. "Recruitment of Persons with Disabilities: A Literature Review." Retrieved 2014 from http://www.psc-cfp.gc.ca/plcy-pltq/eead-eeed/rprt/pwd-ph/index-eng.htm

30 Belcourt and McBey. 2010.

CHAPTER 4

JOB ANALYSIS AND COMPETENCY MODELS

CHAPTER LEARNING OUTCOMES

This chapter is divided into two parts. Part I begins with a discussion of job and work analysis and its relevance to HR development and continues with a discussion of several job analysis techniques. Part II concludes the chapter with a presentation on competency models as an alternative procedure to job analysis.

AFTER READING THIS CHAPTER YOU SHOULD:

- understand the importance of job analysis and the role it plays in recruitment and selection;
- be able to describe guidelines for conducting analyses employing a variety of job analysis techniques;
- be able to use standard tools and techniques to conduct a job analysis;
- recognize processes for identifying job specifications to be used in recruitment and selection of human resources;
- understand what competencies are;
- understand the role competencies play in recruitment and selection;
- know how to identify competencies;
- understand the need to validate competency-based systems;
- be able to distinguish competency-based HR models from those based on job analysis; and
- recognize best practices in competency modelling.

HIRING THE RIGHT PERSON

You are the HR person for a small business enterprise in charge of hiring as part of an expansion. You want to be sure that you hire the right people for the new positions. The first question that comes to mind is how to identify exactly whom you are looking for. A job analysis will help get you the necessary information. Job analysis procedures can be very elaborate; however, a job analysis is nothing more than finding answers to a series of questions about the job. Ask yourself a series of questions that will help you find the right person.

1. What do you wish your new hires to accomplish on a daily, weekly, monthly, or annual basis?
2. What are the tasks and responsibilities that you want the new employees to do as part of their jobs?
   - What equipment will the new employees use?
   - Will they supervise other employees?
   - Will they do different things on different days?
3. What knowledge, skills, abilities, or other attributes or competencies (KSAOs) should the new employees have to perform successfully for the tasks required for the position?
   - What knowledge should new employees bring with them to the job?
   - What skills must new employees have or be capable of developing?
   - What abilities should they have?
   - If the position requires the new employees to work as part of a team, what interpersonal skills should they have?
4. What do people who hold similar jobs (subject-matter experts [SMEs]) think about the tasks, requirements, and KSAOs needed for the new positions?
5. Will there be any differences between the job now and in the future?

Once you have answered these questions you will have the information needed to develop a solid job description that will be used as part of the recruiting process. The job description and its associated KSAOs will assist you in sorting through the résumés you receive to identify those applicants with the KSAOs that will lead to success on the job.

// PART I: WORK AND JOB ANALYSIS

WHAT IS WORK AND JOB ANALYSIS?

Recently researchers working in the area of personnel selection have broadened the classic definition of job analysis to reflect more contemporary approaches to this topic, although both terms can be used interchangeably. *Work analysis*, in its broadest sense, refers to any systematic gathering, documenting, and analyzing of information about the content of work performed by people in organizations, the worker attributes related to work performance, or the context, both psychological and physical, in which the work is performed.[1] The change in terminology has been made to reflect recent and important innovations[2] such as the Occupational Information Network that we will discuss later in this chapter.

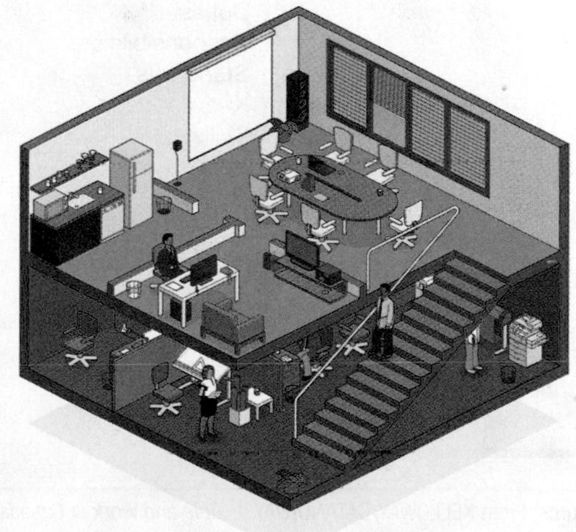

© iStock.com/exi5

Job analysis refers to the process of collecting information about jobs.[3] In its simplest terms, a job analysis is a systematic process for gathering, documenting, and analyzing data about the work required for a job. Job analysis data include a description of the context and principal duties of the job, including job responsibilities and working conditions, and information about the knowledge, skills, abilities, and other attributes required in its performance. In short, it is a method that provides a description of the job and profiles the characteristics or competencies people need to have in order to be successful in the job. It is widely accepted as the foundation of many HR activities and functions.[4] There are three key points to remember about job analysis:

1. A "job analysis" does not refer to a single methodology but rather to a range of techniques.
2. A job analysis is a formal, structured process carried out under a set of guidelines established in advance.
3. A job analysis breaks down a job into its constituent parts, rather than looking at the job as a whole.

Figure 4.1 presents an overview of the job analysis process and outcomes; it shows that job analysis data support several HR activities and can be used toward several ends (e.g., recruitment and selection, training and development, performance management, and, as we've seen, job evaluation, among several others).[5] Many activities in an organization that focus on identifying a match between a person and a job rely on accurate information produced by job analysis. Job analysis helps to ensure that decisions made with respect to HR processes are good decisions (i.e., fair and accurate), and that those employee-related decisions can be defended in courts and tribunals, if necessary. All of these HR activities are concerned with matching people to jobs within a specific

FIGURE 4.1

OVERVIEW OF JOB ANALYSIS PROCESS AND OUTCOMES

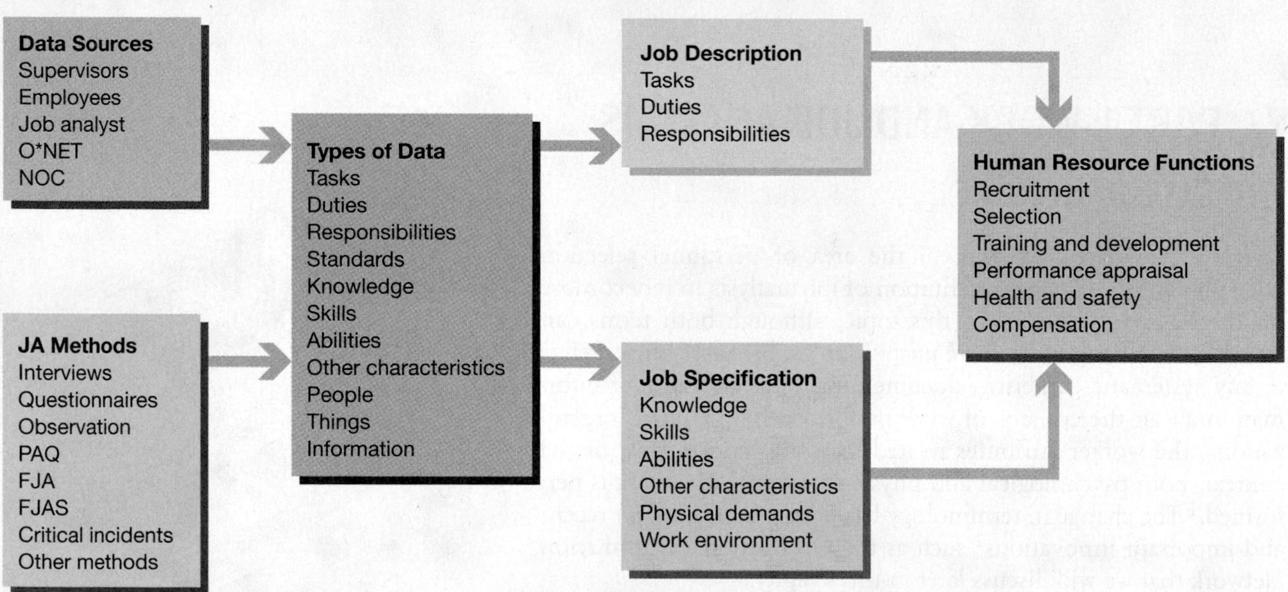

Source: From KELLOWAY/CATANO/DAY. *People and Work in Canada,* 1E. © 2011 Nelson Education Ltd. Reproduced by permission. www.cengage.com/permissions

organizational context. Job analysis is a procedure to assess the goodness of this fit between people and jobs. It provides information about both the job requirements and the KSAOs needed to do the job.

Since job analysis data have the potential for many uses, it is important to know how the information will be used before deciding on an approach or method to use in collecting the data. As we will see after we review several different job analysis methods, each has its strengths and weaknesses, and the data from a particular method may be better suited to only one or some of the above uses. It is very unlikely that one method will produce information that can be used in all of the applications where we would want to use it. In the context of employee recruitment and selection, the results of the job analysis should specify the requirements of the job that are subsequently used to establish employee selection procedures.

In Chapter 2, we presented our selection model in which job analysis was the first step in identifying job tasks and duties as well as the KSAOs needed to carry out those duties. These are the two basic products of a job analysis. The first is formally referred to as a **job description**, a written description of what the persons in the job are required to do, how they are supposed to do the job, and the rationale for any required job procedures. A job description contains a summary of job analysis data. Recruitment and Selection Today 4.1 presents a job description for a CIBC customer service representative. The second product is a **job specification**, which states the KSAOs that are required to perform the job successfully. These may include the compensable factors that are used in performing a job evaluation, such as analytical abilities, physical exertion, accountability for budgets, and unpleasant working environments. A job description like that in Recruitment and Selection Today 4.1 is typically used to recruit employees.

Job description
A written description of what job occupants are required to do, how they are supposed to do it, and the rationale for any required job procedures.

Job specification
The knowledge, skills, abilities, and other attributes or competencies that are needed by a job incumbent to perform well on the job.

Job
A collection of positions that are similar in their significant duties.

Position
A collection of duties assigned to individuals in an organization at a given time.

Job family
A set of different, but related, jobs that rely on the same set of KSAOs.

JOB VERSUS POSITION

In understanding the key concepts in this chapter, keep in mind the difference between a **job** and a **position**. A job consists of a group of tasks; a job may be held by one or more people. Many individuals perform the same job in an organization: for example, secretary, architect, or electrician. A position, on the other hand, consists of the group of tasks performed by one person in an organization at a given time. Each person in the organization is assigned a position. For example, one secretary may be assigned to the position of secretary to the HR director, while another is assigned to the position of secretary to the vice-president of finance. Both secretaries would perform the same set of general tasks, although each may be responsible for a small set of tasks that are unique to each secretary's position.

Another way of distinguishing between jobs and positions is to consider a job as a collection of positions that are similar in their significant duties and a position as a collection of duties assigned to an individual in an organization at a given time.[6] When the two sets of position-relevant tasks begin to diverge considerably from the common set of job tasks or they begin to outweigh the common job tasks, the two positions might then be considered to be different, but related, jobs. **Job family** is a term used to refer to a set of different, but related, jobs that rely on the same set of KSAOs. Jobs and positions are among the basic building blocks of any organization, and selection of individuals to fill these positions has a significant impact on the success of the organization.

RECRUITMENT AND SELECTION TODAY 4.1

JOB DESCRIPTION FOR A CIBC CUSTOMER SERVICE REPRESENTATIVE

Title: Customer Service Representative

Category: Customer Service/Customer Associate

Key Accountabilities/Activities

As the primary point of contact and "face of CIBC" for many CIBC customers, the Customer Service Rep provides exemplary customer service by serving all customers quickly, professionally, and efficiently and recognizing the appropriate time to proactively position CIBC products and services. Improve customer loyalty by identifying opportunities to promote banking products and transaction services to better meet customer needs, fulfilling or referring the opportunity, as appropriate.

Creating a positive customer experience by understanding and meeting customers' service needs quickly, professionally, and accurately is the primary responsibility of the Customer Service Representative.

Major Activities Include:

1. Create a positive client experience by understanding and meeting service transaction needs quickly, professionally, and accurately.
2. Take initiative to promote banking products and transaction services that meet client needs.
3. Recognize client needs and make quality referrals to colleagues.
4. Take ownership when clients experience a problem and take the appropriate steps to resolve the problem.
5. Balance cash holdings. Act as joint custodian of cash and securities.
6. Protect client privacy.
7. Identify client needs and sales opportunities while processing transactions quickly and providing efficient service.

Requirements:

ATTRIBUTES

- Service-oriented.
- Thorough.
- Strong interpersonal understanding.
- Initiative.
- Results orientation.
- Teamwork and partnering.

SPECIAL CONDITIONS

- Full time: 37.5 hrs./week.
- Days required to work: Monday to Saturday.
- Previous experience in customer service, retail environment an asset.
- An additional living allowance is available.

CIBC is an equal opportunity employer. It is the Company's policy to recruit and select applicants for employment solely on the basis of their qualifications, with emphasis on selecting the best-qualified person for the job. CIBC does not discriminate against applicants based on race, color, religion, sex, national origin, or disability, or any other status or condition protected by applicable federal, state or local law.

Source: From http://www.cibc.com/ca/inside-cibc/careers.html. Reprinted with permission.

Subject-matter experts (SMEs) People who are most knowledgeable about a job and how it is currently performed; generally job incumbents and their supervisors.

SUBJECT-MATTER EXPERTS

Job analysis data are collected from the people most knowledgeable about a job and how it is currently performed. In practice, this means that data are collected from job incumbents (those employees currently holding the position in question) and their immediate supervisors. Using these sources as **subject-matter experts (SMEs)** will generally result in the most accurate, and richest, information about the job. However, anyone with detailed knowledge about the job can serve as an SME. A good rule of thumb in choosing SMEs is that the closer the SME is to the job, the better the resultant information will be. However, Dierdorff and Wilson[7] report data suggesting that trained professional job analysts provide more accurate information than job incumbents when using self-report and survey instruments. Dierdorff and Wilson speculate that the trained professionals may be more objective in their assessment of what constitutes the job.

One question that must be answered is how many SMEs a particular job analysis method requires. This requirement will generally be stated in the procedures that have been established for each method. The lack of the requisite number of SMEs may argue against using a specific method. To ensure the defensibility of the job analysis results, SMEs should be representative of the target population for the job with respect to age, sex, ethnic background, and seniority in the position. Information from a diverse group of SMEs will produce job information that is likely to be more accurate, reliable, and valid.

Recall that one of the failures of the job analysis in the *Meiorin* case was lack of job information from female firefighters. If the job analysis is challenged in court, the analyst must be able to defend the procedure. A charge of unfair discrimination will be hard to defend if the analyst cannot demonstrate that the job analysis results were obtained from a sample representative of those who actually do the work.[8] Job information from a diverse group of SMEs is likely to produce a better picture of what the job is all about.

JOB ANALYSIS AND EMPLOYMENT LAW—A REPRISE

Although there are no laws that specifically require a job analysis prior to implementing recruitment and selection programs, employment decisions must be based on job-related information.[9] Job analysis is a legally acceptable way of determining job-relatedness. In 1975, the United States Supreme Court made a precedent-setting decision when it criticized the Albemarle Paper Company for its failure to use a job analysis to demonstrate the job-relatedness of its selection procedures (refer to Recruitment and Selection Today 3.6). According to Harvey, "Albemarle established job analysis as something that virtually must be done to defend challenged employment practices."[10]

We also saw in Chapter 3 the long list of precedent-setting cases in Canada that have established the need to determine that any job requirements with the potential to discriminate against members of protected groups must meet the standards set in the *Meiorin* decision (*British Columbia [Public Service Employee Relations Commission] v. BCGSEU*) for being bona fide occupational requirements. In the *Meiorin* case, the Supreme Court of Canada found that new job requirements were not based on job-related information, and that the job analysis in that case was seriously flawed. Conducting a job analysis, then, is also the first line of defence in protecting the organization if its selection procedures are challenged in court.[11,12]

A good job analysis ensures that accurate information on skill, effort, responsibility, and working conditions is specified, reducing the likelihood of impediments to equitable employment access for all Canadians. A job analysis provides objective evidence of the skills and abilities required for effective performance in the job, which can then be used to provide evidence of the relevance of the selection procedures measuring those abilities.

In *Albemarle Paper Co. v. Moody*, the U.S. Supreme Court relied heavily on the *Uniform Guidelines on Employee Selection*[13] in reaching its decision. The *Uniform Guidelines* represent a joint agreement between several U.S. government departments and agencies (the Equal Employment Opportunity Commission, Civil Service Commission, Department of Labor, and Department of Justice), outlining professional standards for employee selection procedures. Even though they are not law, the U.S. courts have granted them significant status in guiding administrative interpretations of the job analysis–job-relatedness link.[14,15]

Canadian human rights commissions and courts also recognize the *Uniform Guidelines on Employee Selection* as professional standards, unless it is established that Canadian legal precedent and professional practice deviate substantially from those set out in the *Guidelines*.[16] Furthermore, the Canadian Society for Industrial & Organizational Psychology has adopted the principles outlined in the *Guidelines* for developing equitable selection systems for use in Canada.[17] Latham explains that:

> *Countries such as Australia, Canada and the United Kingdom have been strongly influenced by Title VII of the 1964 Civil Rights Act in the U.S. In each of these countries it is now illegal to make employment decisions regarding the hiring, firing, promoting, demoting, transferring or admitting someone into a training program on the basis of the person's age, sex, race, religion, colour, national origin, sexual orientation, or physical handicap.*[18]

In practice, if not in law, the starting point for a defensible selection system is a job analysis. We next describe several job analysis methods.

JOB ANALYSIS METHODS

Harvey[19] proposes three criteria that should be considered in choosing a method: First, the goal of job analysis should always be the description of observable work behaviours and analysis of their products. Second, the results of a job analysis should describe the work behaviour "*independent of the personal characteristics or attributes of the employees who perform the job*."[20] Positions in an organization exist independently of the incumbents who fill those positions; in job analysis, it is the job (i.e., the collection of positions) that is being analyzed, not the performance of the individual incumbents. Worker specifications (i.e., the knowledge, skills, abilities, and other attributes–or KSAOs) necessary to perform successfully on the job are inferred in a separate process using the results of a job analysis. We must note that not everyone agrees with Harvey's second criteria; several worker-oriented methods we discuss below focus directly on identifying worker attributes or characteristics and not work behaviours, as do the competency models that we present in Part II of this chapter.

Finally, any job analysis must produce outcomes that are verifiable and replicable. That is, the organization must be able to produce evidence of both the validity and the reliability of each step in the job analysis process. Reliability and validity data for the job analysis method used are essential to determining the quality of the information produced by the analysis.[21] In many situations, assessing the validity of the method is redundant and an assumption is made that if reliability is acceptable, then the method is valid.[22] The basic data for job analyses are task and KSAO statements developed by a group of SMEs. One method of assuring validity of the results is to have a second group of SMEs, when appropriate, independently confirm the results of the first group.

Although the various existing job analysis techniques differ in the assumptions they make about work, they follow the same logical process when applied to the recruitment and selection of human resources. First, work activities are described in terms of the work processes or worker behaviours that characterize the job. Next, machines, tools, equipment, and work aids are defined in relation to the materials produced, services rendered, and worker knowledge applied to those ends. The job context is characterized in terms of physical working conditions, work schedules, social context and organizational culture, and financial and nonfinancial incentives for performance. Finally, job specifications are inferred by linking the job requirements identified in the analysis with the education, experience, skills, and personal attributes required for successful job performance.[23]

GETTING STARTED: GATHERING JOB-RELATED INFORMATION

In preparing for a job analysis, the first step should be to collect existing information describing the target job. The analyst mines information from organizational charts, legal requirements (e.g., the job *veterinarian* may be governed through legal statutes at the provincial level), job descriptions, union regulations, and previous data from related jobs. In addition, job-related information can be found in the National Occupational Classification (NOC) system.[24] The NOC systematically describes occupations in the Canadian labour market based on extensive occupational research and is available at the Employment and Social Development Canada website: http://www.esdc.gc.ca/eng/jobs/lmi/noc/.

racom/Shutterstock.com

Pressmaster/Shutterstock.com

FomaA/Shutterstock.com

Recruitment and Selection Today 4.2 presents the NOC description for veterinarians. The NOC profile presents both a description and specification of the job or occupation. Each occupation or job is given a four-digit code that will provide the analyst with a more extensive description related to the KSAOs associated with the job.

RECRUITMENT AND SELECTION TODAY 4.2

OCCUPATIONAL DESCRIPTION FOR VETERINARIANS

Veterinarians prevent, diagnose, and treat diseases and disorders in animals and advise clients on the feeding, hygiene, housing, and general care of animals. Veterinarians work in private practice or may be employed by animal clinics and laboratories, government, or industry.

Examples of Titles Classified in This Group

Small-animal veterinary specialist

Veterinary inspector

Veterinary physiologist

Veterinarian

Veterinary pathologist

Zoo veterinarian

Main Duties

Veterinarians perform some or all of the following duties:

- Diagnose diseases or abnormal conditions in animals through physical examinations or laboratory tests
- Treat sick or injured animals by prescribing medication, setting bones, dressing wounds, or performing surgery
- Perform routine, emergency, and post-mortem examinations
- Inoculate animals to prevent diseases
- Provide obstetrical and dental services
- Advise clients on feeding, housing, breeding, hygiene, and general care of animals
- Provide euthanasia services

Employment Requirements

- Two to four years of pre-veterinary university studies or, in Quebec, completion of a college program in health science
- A four-year university degree in veterinary medicine
- Completion of national certification examinations is required
- Provincial licensure is required
- Entry into research positions may require post-graduate study

Source: From Occupational Description for Veterinarians, from Occupational Classification (NOC), http://www5.hrsdc.gc.ca/NOC/English/NOC/2006/ProfileQuickSearch.aspx?val=3&val1=3114&val65=veterinarian. Reproduced and distributed with the permission of Statistics Canada.

Figure 4.2 presents a synopsis of the descriptors used in the NOC system, along with scales used to rate each job. For example, a rating of 3 on the "Vision" subscale in the "Physical Activities" section means that the job in question requires both near and far vision for successful completion. Full descriptions of all the scales can be found in the *Career Handbook* that is available on the NOC website. Such information, when gathered and studied in advance, will prove invaluable for organizing and conducting the ensuing analysis.

Alternative sources to the NOC have until recently included the *Canadian Classification Dictionary of Occupations* (CCDO)[25] and the *Dictionary of Occupational Titles* (DOT).[26] The CCDO, designed in 1971 by Employment and Immigration Canada, was widely used by HR professionals in Canada. Although some found the CCDO easier to use than the NOC[27] (which replaced it), the CCDO was abandoned in 1992 because its design was no longer able to accurately reflect the contemporary Canadian labour market.

Similarly, the DOT has been replaced by the O*NET system of gathering and disseminating job analysis data in the United States. O*NET, the Occupational Information Network, is an electronic database developed by the U.S. Department of Labor to replace the DOT. The occupational/skill descriptors "serve as a solid, but flexible foundation for vendors and others to develop sophisticated occupational and career information systems."[28] O*NET was first released for public use in the fall of 1998 and is available online at http://www.onetonline.org. The database grows as information becomes available on more occupations, and the U.S. Department of Labor encourages organizations to use the new database in place of the DOT, which was last updated in 1991. O*NET has also established an O*NET Resource Center at http://www.onetcenter.org that provides information on how to use the O*NET system as well as career tools and publications for HR professionals and access to the O*NET databases.

Figure 4.3 presents the conceptual foundation of the O*NET model and "provides a framework that identifies the most important types of information about work and integrates them into a theoretically and empirically sound system."[29] Peterson et al.[30] present an excellent introduction to the O*NET model and the implications for researchers and practitioners.

In addition to occupational databases, attention should be given to determining which techniques will be employed for gathering job information. Gael[31] notes that, depending on the objective of the job analysis, some techniques are better suited than others for providing job information. Analyses typically involve a series of steps, often

FIGURE 4.2

A SYNOPSIS OF DESCRIPTORS AND LABELS

APTITUDES

One of five levels assigned for each factor, with levels representing normal curve distribution of the labour force:

G General Learning Ability
V Verbal Ability
N Numerical Ability
S Spatial Perception
P Form Perception
Q Clerical Perception
K Motor Coordination
F Finger Dexterity
M Manual Dexterity

INTERESTS

Three of five descriptive factors, assigned in order of predominance and lower case rating indicating weaker representation:

D Directive
I Innovative
M Methodical
O Objective
S Social

DATA/INFORMATION, PEOPLE, THINGS

D—Data/Information		P—People		T—Things	
0	Synthesizing	0	Mentoring	0	Setting up
1	Coordinating	1	Negotiating	1	Precision working
2	Analyzing	2	Instructing—Consulting	2	Controlling
3	Compiling	3	Supervising	3	Driving—Operating
4	Computing	4	Diverting	4	Operating—Manipulating
5	Copying	5	Persuading	5	Tending
6	Comparing	6	Speaking—Signalling	6	Feeding—Offbearing
7	—	7	Serving—Assisting	7	Handling
8	Not significant	8	Not significant	8	Not significant

PHYSICAL ACTIVITIES

One of several levels assigned for each factor:

Vision
1 Close visual acuity
2 Near vision
3 Near and far vision
4 Total visual field

Colour Discrimination
0 Not relevant
1 Relevant

Hearing
1 Limited
2 Verbal interaction
3 Other sound discrimination

Body Position
1 Sitting
2 Standing and/or walking
3 Sitting, standing, walking
4 Other body positions

Limb Coordination
0 Not relevant
1 Upper limb coordination
2 Multiple limb coordination

Strength
1 Limited
2 Light
3 Medium
4 Heavy

ENVIRONMENTAL CONDITIONS

Location
L1 Regulated inside climate
L2 Unregulated inside climate
L3 Outside
L4 In a vehicle or cab

Hazards
H1 Dangerous chemical substances
H2 Biological agents
H3 Equipment, machinery, tools
H4 Electricity
H5 Radiation
H6 Flying particles, falling objects
H7 Fire, steam, hot surfaces
H8 Dangerous locations

Discomforts
D1 Noise
D2 Vibration
D3 Odours
D4 Non-toxic dusts
D5 Wetness

EMPLOYMENT REQUIREMENTS

Education/Training Indicators

1 No formal education or training requirements
2 Some high school education and/or on-the-job training or experience
3 Completion of high school
4 Completion of course work, training, workshops and/or experience related to the occupation
5 Apprenticeship, specialized training, vocational school training
6 College, technical school (certificate, diploma)
7 Undergraduate degree
8 Postgraduate or professional degree
\+ Indicating an additional requirement beyond education/training (e.g., extensive experience, demonstrated or creative ability, appointments, etc.)
R Regulated requirements exist for this group

Source: From *Career Handbook* Second Edition, http://www.5hrsdc.gc.ca/NOC/English/CH/2001/SynopsisDescriptorsLabels.aspx. Reproduced and distributed with the permission of Statistics Canada.

FIGURE 4.3

THE O*NET® CONTENT MODEL

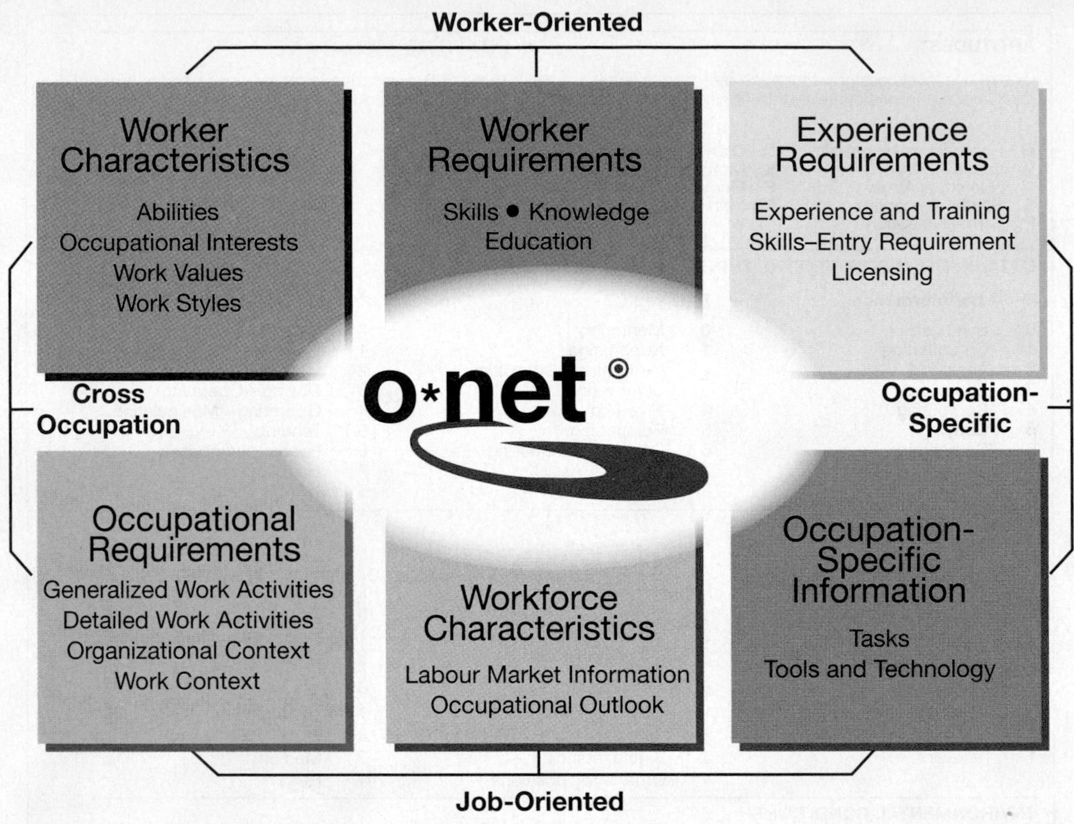

Source: The O*NET® Content Model. http://www.onetcenter.org/content.html. U.S. Department of Labor

beginning with interviews or observations that provide the information to construct a task inventory or to complete a structured questionnaire. Ideally, the job analyst employs a combination of strategies to arrive at a comprehensive and accurate description of the job in question,[32,33] although analysts operating within the very real constraints of time and funding often use a single method. Each analysis method contributes slightly different information and, by using a combination of methods, potential gaps in the results are minimized. The next section on work and worker-oriented job analysis methods illustrates the different types of information that may be obtained from job analysis procedures.

WORK AND WORKER-ORIENTED JOB ANALYSIS

There are several ways of classifying job analysis methods. One of the most complete classification schemes[34] is to categorize a job analysis technique as either work oriented or worker oriented.[35,36,37,38] Job analyses falling into either of these two categories are legally defensible. With one or two exceptions, all job analysis methods, including all of those presented here, fall into either of these two categories. In **work-oriented job analysis**, the emphasis is on work outcomes and description of the various tasks performed to accomplish those outcomes.

Work-oriented job analysis
Job analysis techniques that emphasize work outcomes and descriptions of the various tasks performed to accomplish those outcomes.

These methods produce "descriptions of job content that have a dominant association with, and typically characterize, the *technological* aspects of jobs and commonly reflect what is achieved by the worker."[39] The descriptions of tasks or job duties generated via work-oriented methods are typically characterized by their frequency of occurrence or the amount of time spent on them, the importance to the job outcome, and the difficulty inherent in executing them.[40,41] Because task inventories generated via work-oriented techniques are developed for specific jobs or occupational areas, the results are highly specific and may have little or no relationship to the content of jobs in other fields.[42]

Alternatively, **worker-oriented job analysis** methods focus on general aspects of jobs, describing perceptual, interpersonal, sensory, cognitive, and physical activities. Worker-oriented methods generate descriptions "that tend more to characterize the generalized human behaviours involved; if not directly, then by strong inference."[43] These techniques are not limited to describing specific jobs; they are generic in nature and the results can be applied to a wide spectrum of task-dissimilar jobs.[44,45,46,47]

Worker-oriented job analysis
Job analysis techniques that emphasize general aspects of jobs, describing perceptual, interpersonal, sensory, cognitive, and physical activities.

SURVEY OF WORK-ORIENTED JOB ANALYSIS METHODS

STRUCTURED JOB ANALYSIS INTERVIEWS

The interview is perhaps the most commonly used technique for gathering job facts and establishing the tasks and behaviours that define a job. It may be used as a stand-alone job analysis method or in conjunction with other approaches. This method involves questioning individuals or small groups of employees and supervisors about the work that gets done. The interview may be structured or unstructured, although for job analysis purposes, a structured format is recommended. The results of a structured job analysis interview may stand on their own, as in a formal integrated report, when there are few incumbents working within a small geographical area. Or they may provide the necessary information for completing a task inventory, structured questionnaire, or other analytic technique.[48,49]

The structured interview method is designed so that all interviewees are asked the same job-related questions. Interobserver reliability–that is, the agreement between the persons serving as interviewers–increases when interviews are structured because the individual biases of different interviewers are minimized. Whetzel et al.[50] demonstrated that a written, structured interview is a flexible and cost-effective alternative to a traditional oral structured interview and may produce very reliable job analysis information. Because it is such an important step in most job analyses, the interview should be well planned and carefully conducted. McCormick[51] and others[52,53,54,55] offer many valuable guidelines for conducting interviews. These are summarized in Recruitment and Selection Notebook 4.1.

The job analyst should record the job incumbent's or supervisor's responses by taking notes or by tape-recording the interview. Trying to remember what was said following the interview is difficult at best and likely to produce inaccurate information. Recall that the purpose of the interview is to obtain information about the work that the employee does; thus, questions should elicit information describing important job tasks, physical activities involved in the job, environmental conditions (physical and social)

RECRUITMENT AND SELECTION NOTEBOOK 4.1

GUIDELINES FOR A JOB ANALYSIS INTERVIEW

1. **Announce the job analysis well ahead of the interview date.** The impending job analysis and its purpose should be well known among employees and management. The job analysis process should be positioned as a collaborative effort, with all job incumbents and their supervisors holding valid information about the job and invited to contribute to the process.
2. **Participation in interviews should be voluntary, and job incumbents should be interviewed only with the permission of their supervisors.** The job analyst avoids creating friction within the organization and is sensitive to the use of coercion in obtaining information. In general, when analysis interviews are free from organizational politics, they can be completed in a timely manner with valid, uncontaminated results.
3. **Interviews should be conducted in a private location free from the trappings of status.** It would be unwise, for example, to conduct interviews with hourly workers in the company president's office. The job analyst is a nonpartisan party whose primary objective is to accurately describe the content of jobs; interviewees should feel comfortable and able to provide truthful information about their work and the conditions under which it is done.
4. **Open the interview by establishing rapport with the employee and explaining the purpose of the interview.** Interviews are often associated with anxiety-provoking events such as job and promotion applications and even disciplinary action. The experienced interviewer takes time at the outset to create a nonthreatening environment and alleviate any fears that interviewees might have.
5. **Ask open-ended questions, using language that is easy to understand, and allow ample time for the employee's responses.** Most people, given the opportunity, will talk in great detail about the work they do. The good analyst avoids rushing or intimidating people, does not talk down to them, and takes a genuine interest in the interviewee's responses.
6. **Guide the session without being authoritative or overbearing.** Keep the interview on topic and avoid discussions concerning worker–management relations and other unrelated topics. When discussions become tangential, the analyst can bring them back on track by summarizing relevant details and referring to the interview outline.
7. **Explain to the employees that records of the interviews will identify them only by confidential codes.** The names of interviewees and other personal information should be protected. When confidentiality is ensured, more accurate information will be obtained. The limits of confidentiality should be explained to all interviewees before they agree to participate. For example, data on age, sex, and ethnic background may have to be recorded and be made public in order to demonstrate in any subsequent court challenges that the data are based on a representative sample of the workforce.

under which the work occurs, and typical work incidents. Recruitment and Selection Notebook 4.2 provides a protocol for a structured job analysis interview that covers the essential questions needed to obtain the required information on these topics. This protocol should be considered a guide; different positions may require modification of the protocol.

An interview protocol such as that in Recruitment and Selection Notebook 4.2 prompts the interviewer to ask important questions about the job. Based on responses to the structured questions, and on the interviewer's previous knowledge of the job, the interviewer probes for more detail.[56,57] The tasks that make up each job area are identified, and the result of the interview should be a clear description of critical job domains and their related elements. Interview protocols can vary from presenting a few informal

RECRUITMENT AND SELECTION NOTEBOOK 4.2

JOB ANALYSIS INTERVIEW QUESTIONS

1. Interview information
   - Name of Employee:
   - Job Title:
   - Job Analyst:
   - Department:
   - Date:
2. Job introduction
   - Describe: location of job and any specific environmental aspects.
3. Job purpose:
   - What is the essence of work in your position? What is the job's overall purpose?
4. Job duties
   - What are the main duties and responsibilities of your position?
   - Describe your duties in the following categories: daily duties, periodic duties, duties performed at irregular intervals
   - How long do they take?
   - How do you do them?
   - Are you performing duties not presently included in your job description? Describe.
   - Do you use special tools, equipment, or other sources of aid? If so, list the names of the principal tools, equipment, or sources of aid you use.
   - Describe the frequency and degree to which you are engaged in such activities as: pushing, throwing, pulling, carrying, sitting, running, kneeling, crawling, reaching, climbing...
5. Job criteria/results
   - How would you define success in your work?
   - Have work standards been established (errors allowed, time taken for a particular task, etc.)? If so, what are they?
   - Describe the successful completion and/or end results of the job.
6. Records and Reports
   - What records or reports do you prepare as part of your job?
   - Who receives your reports?
7. Supervisor
   - Who is your supervisor?
   - What kinds of questions or problems would you ordinarily refer to your supervisor?
   - Are the instructions you receive clear and consistent with your job description?
8. Authority
   - What is the level of authority vested in your position?
   - What is the level of accountability and to whom are you accountable?
   - What kinds of independent action are you allowed to take?
9. Responsibilities
   - Are you responsible for any confidential material? If so, describe how you handle it.
   - Are you responsible for any money or things of monetary value? If so, describe how you handle it.
10. Compensation
    - In consideration of your level of productivity, do you think you are underpaid, fairly paid or overpaid?
    - In consideration of the skill level required to fulfill your responsibilities, do you think that you are: underpaid, fairly paid or overpaid?
11. Knowledge
    - What special knowledge of specific work aids is needed for this position?
    - Describe the level, degree, and breadth of knowledge required in these areas or subjects.
    - Indicate the educational requirements for the job (not the educational background of the incumbent).
    - What level of education is required for your position?
    - What type of certification and licensing is required for your position?

- Can you specify the training time needed to arrive at a level of competence on the job?
- What sort of on the job training is needed for this position?

12. Skills/ Experience

- What activities must you perform with ease and precision?
- What are the manual skills that are required to operate machines, vehicles, equipment, or to use tools?
- What is the amount of experience needed to perform your job?
- What level of experience and skills are required for your position?

13. Abilities required

- What mathematical ability must you have?
- What reasoning or problem solving ability must you have?
- What interpersonal abilities are required? What supervisory or managing abilities are required?
- What physical abilities such as strengths, coordination, and visually acuity must you have?

14. Working instruments

- Describe briefly what machines, tools, equipment or work aids the incumbent works with on a regular basis.

15. Health and safety

- Are there any safety regulations that are related to your position?
- Does your work present any type of hazardous or unusual working conditions?

16. Working conditions

- Describe your working conditions.
- Describe the frequency and degree to which you will encounter working conditions such as these: cramped quarters, moving objects, vibration, inadequate ventilation.

Source: *Job Analysis Interview Questions.* www.humanresources.hrvinet.com/job-analysis-interview-questions. Reprinted by permission of HumanResources.Hrvinet.com

prompts to very structured questions as shown here. In general, the more specific and structured the interview protocol, the more reliable will be the obtained information.

While there are no hard-and-fast rules concerning how many people should be interviewed, those that are interviewed should be representative of the employees whose job the analysis reflects. For example, when conducting a job analysis for meeting planning consultants employed in a large travel company, the analyst may obtain a stratified sample that reflects the proportion of males and females in the position. Other demographic variables such as race and ethnicity, age, physical disabilities and abilities, and native language would also be considered in a representative sample of interviewees. Supervisors should always be included in the pool of interview respondents, as they have a unique perspective on how jobs are performed and the standards for acceptable performance.

Structured interview protocols should also allow interviewees to contribute information that may not be covered in the protocol. There are certain disadvantages to job analysis interviews. First, they can be expensive and time consuming, and may be impractical for jobs with a large number of incumbents. Interviews take a great deal of time to conduct and may require a substantial number of interviewees to be truly representative of the job incumbent pool. However, the benefits of individual interviews can outweigh their relative costs. Individual employees, free from immediate social controls, are likely to respond with greater openness than when interviewed in a group. Thus, the information obtained from the individual interview may be more accurate than that obtained from interviewing the same people as part of a group. A second disadvantage of interviews is that workers may distort the information they provide about their jobs, particularly if they believe that the results will influence their pay.[58] This distortion can be overcome to some extent by making the purpose of the interview clear and by interviewing multiple incumbents and supervisors.

DIRECT OBSERVATION

Martinko makes the case that "the most effective way to determine what effective job incumbents do is to observe their behaviour."[59] In direct observation, the job analyst watches employees as they carry out their job activities. This procedure is sometimes called "job shadowing." This method allows the analyst to come into direct contact with the job; thus, the data are obtained firsthand, as contrasted with the "more remote types of information generated by questionnaires and surveys."[60]

Direct observation is most useful when the job analysis involves easily observable activities.[61] Analyzing the job of "poet" through direct observation would likely produce little of value, whereas the job of "landscaper" lends itself more readily to direct observation. Before conducting direct observations, the analyst will already have learned about the job by studying existing documents. Next, the job analyst determines the nature of the job by asking: "Does the job involve easily observable activities?" and "Is the work environment one in which unobtrusive observations can be made?" If the answer to both questions is "yes," then direct observation may be a viable analysis method.

In direct observation, systematic observations of employee activities can be recorded either in narrative format or using a customized checklist or worksheet.[62,63] Different jobs and environments will require different observation methods. A landscaper's job, one that does not occur within a complex social context, might best be observed and recorded by using a tally sheet such as the one shown in Figure 4.4. The job of residential counsellor, in which the job tasks are heavily influenced by dynamic social conditions,

FIGURE 4.4

EXAMPLE OF A FREQUENCY TALLY SHEET FOR OBSERVING A LANDSCAPER AT WORK

DATE: 15-03-15	START TIME: 10:30 A.M.	END TIME: 11:07 A.M.
	OBSERVER: LESLIE	EMPLOYEE ID: 734
TASKS (PLANTING TREES)	**CHECK IF DONE**	**TIME SPENT**
1. Measure area & mark spot	×	5 min
2. Dig hole	×	16 min
3. Move shrubbery	–	–
4. Lift trees (manually)	×	<1 min
5. Lift trees (winched)	–	–
6. Fill hole	×	7 min
7. Rake area	×	5 min

will require a recording format that enables the observer to identify important activities and the conditions under which they occur.

Figure 4.5 provides an example of a recording sheet used in observing residential counsellors at work. The form enables the observer to collect information about the job by defining the conditions under which a particular activity occurs and listing the tools and aids employed in the activity. Both recording formats permit the observer to record valuable qualitative and quantitative data.

In preparing for observations, the analyst might ask: "How many observations are enough?" or "How long should observations be?" These questions are addressed in planning the job analysis; once again, there is no rule book one can turn to for the answers. As with job analysis interviews, a representative sample of workers is needed. If the organization or department is small (e.g., Modern Builders, with only three employees in the job "electrician"), samples from all workers should be obtained. If, however, the organization or department is large (e.g., New World Residential Centres, with 10 homes employing over 120 residential counsellors), the analyst should observe a sample of workers consisting of at least 10 to 15 of the staff.[64]

Observation times should be stratified so that all shifts are covered and all work conditions are observed, ensuring that important patterns in worker activities are evident and extraneous information is eliminated. When observing at New World Residential Centres, for example, an analyst would want to observe morning, afternoon, and evening shifts during weekdays and weekends, as activities during these periods can change substantially. Similarly, when observing shift workers in a manufacturing plant, activities may change during peak and down times, and shift and day considerations will influence the observation schedule.

A variety of technological aids are available to the observer. Audio and video recording, for example, can facilitate the observation process. Each has its advantages and disadvantages. Digital audio recordings can augment observer notes with the important verbal behaviour of the worker, but they are rarely useful observation tools on their own. Important information may be lost because of poor recording quality and background noise, or because many of the behaviours of interest may be nonverbal.[65]

FIGURE 4.5

FORM FOR RECORDING WORK ACTIVITIES OF RESIDENTIAL COUNSELLORS IN A COMMUNITY GROUP HOME

OBSERVER: FAIZ	EMPLOYEE ID: 735	DATE: 15 FEB 2015	
CONDITION	**ACTIVITY**	**TOOLS**	**TIME**
Resident arrives home from school	Counsellor helps resident remove snow clothes	No special tools	5 min
Physiotherapy program	Counsellor leads resident through exercises	Walker, leg splints, physiotherapy program instructions	20 min
After meal	Medication delivery to residents	Medication recording forms, medication instructions	15 min

Video recording provides a permanent product of the verbal and nonverbal components of the observation session, which the analyst can review in private for later data collection. When the work area is small and a camera can be placed unobtrusively, videotaping is an option to consider. But, while it may be easier to make unobtrusive observations in some settings using a video recorder, the camera cannot follow workers around in large work areas without someone at the controls. As technology shrinks video recorders to increasingly smaller sizes, this becomes less of a disadvantage. Another disadvantage, reactivity to observation, may be greater during videotaped sessions than during observation sessions employing live observers.

Analysts conducting direct observation sessions should be aware that regardless of the observation technique employed, their presence may change the behaviour of the employees. Imagine yourself at work, and an unfamiliar individual with a clipboard begins to write down everything you do. Knowing you are being watched, you may respond by doing your work according to what you think the observer is looking for rather than doing it as you would in the normal day-to-day routine. This effect can be minimized when the analyst blends into the surroundings (e.g., by choosing an unobtrusive observation position) and when the employees have been informed of the purpose of the observations and are observed only with their explicit permission. Again, newer technologies may be helpful. Closed circuit television or web cams allow the analyst to observe from remote locations, which may reduce reactivity to the process. Ethically, the workers would still need to be advised that they were under observations as part of the job analysis study.

In addition to direct observation, the job analyst may ask incumbents to monitor their own work behaviour.[66,67] The workers may be asked to keep a diary of their daily activities. Martinko[68] describes several advantages that self-monitoring may have over other observation procedures. First, it is less time consuming and less expensive because the job incumbents observe and record their own behaviour. Second, self-monitoring can be used when the conditions of work do not easily facilitate direct observation by another person, as in potentially dangerous or sensitive work. Finally, self-monitoring can provide information on otherwise unobservable cognitive and intellectual processes involved in the job. The potential shortcomings of self-monitoring are that incumbents may not be reliable observers of their own behaviour, they may not accurately record or recall their activities, the self-monitoring task is an additional duty to be completed in addition to the normal workload, and some amount of training may be required in order to generate valid and reliable results from self-generated data.

ANALYZING STRUCTURED INTERVIEW AND DIRECT OBSERVATION DATA

After collecting the interview, observational, or self-monitoring data, the analyst uses the resulting notes and tally sheets to identify critical task statements, which are used to generate employee specifications. The analyst uses the task statement to describe the critical components of the job through a standard format. A **task statement** is a discrete sentence containing one action verb that concisely describes a single observable activity performed by a job incumbent. Task statements are based on data collected from a variety of sources including archival information, structured interviews, questionnaires, and direct observation. Each task statement includes:

Task statement
A discrete sentence containing one action verb that concisely describes a single observable activity performed by a job incumbent.

1. Action verb–describes the actions performed
2. Object of the verb–person, data, or things affected by the action

3. Rationale or observable work product–the intended outcome or product of the action
4. Materials, tools, procedures, or equipment used to carry out the action
5. The directions or guidelines under which the action is taken

The following task statement for a meeting planner position reflects the five parts of a task statement noted above:

> *(1) Interview (2) hotel, air, and ground transportation vendors (3) to facilitate comparisons between vendor offers for service (4) using meeting and travel reference guides (5) in accordance with client's instructions.*

The number of task statements needed to describe a job will vary with the complexity of the job, ranging from a few to a hundred or more. The goal is to describe all of the essential functions of the job to give a clear understanding of its nature and level of complexity.

Once the task statements are identified, the job analyst must identify the knowledge, skills, abilities, and other attributes (KSAOs) needed to perform each task successfully. Gatewood, Feild, and Barrick[69] proposed the following definitions of knowledge, skills, and abilities:

> ***Knowledge:*** A body of information, usually of a factual or procedural nature, that makes for successful performance of a task.
> ***Skill:*** An individual's level of proficiency or competency in performing a specific task. Level of competency is typically expressed in numerical terms.
> ***Ability:*** A more general, enduring trait or capability an individual possesses at the time he first begins to perform a task.

The "O" in KSAO stands for "other attributes" and includes personality traits and other individual characteristics that are integral to job performance. For example, some jobs may require people to work in teams and specify "cooperativeness" as a necessary characteristic, to hold a valid driver's licence, or to be fluently bilingual. Sometimes, a job description will specify physical requirements or other attributes that may be related to a person's age, sex, or race, which may bring about a legal challenge on the basis of discrimination. The job analyst must ensure that any characteristics of this type will pass legal scrutiny should they be challenged.

KSAO statements describe specific characteristics needed to carry out a task. They are not simply task statements with "knowledge of" or "ability to" tacked on at the front end. There is no formal procedure that is used to identify KSAOs. They are inferred through the knowledge and experience of the job analyst. In the case of formal job analysis procedures such as the Position Analysis Questionnaire, the vendor will have established an extensive data bank of KSAOs related to different types of tasks. KSAO statements should convey the context or effect that is expected and the level of proficiency that is required. In the case of the task statement for the meeting planner, here are KSAO examples:

> **Knowledge** of vendor pricing structures and policies to evaluate bids.
> **Skill** to type 40 words per minute without error.
> **Ability** to compile information from several sources.
> **Other:** Conscientious–completes work in a timely manner with attention to detail

There are as many KSAOs for each task statement as the job analyst can identify.

RATING TASK STATEMENTS AND KSAOS

It is good practice to have the incumbents or other SMEs rate the importance of the identified task statements and the KSAOs associated with each task after the final inventory is generated. All tasks are not equal: Some are performed more frequently than others, some are more important, and some require a degree of difficulty to perform. A task may be performed frequently but have little importance and not require a great deal of skill, while another may be performed rarely but have extreme importance attached to it. Table 4.1 presents an example of one task statement for the job of "meeting planner." The SMEs would rate this task, and all of the others, with respect to frequency, importance, and difficulty. Evaluation of the ratings obtained from all the SMEs helps the job analyst to fully understand what goes on in the job.

The KSAOs, as well, must be rated, as these will ultimately be sampled by the selection measures used in choosing new employees or assigning current employees to new positions. Each of the KSAOs must be rated by the SMEs with respect to at least its importance in performing the specific task and its proficiency (i.e., whether it is required upon entry to the job). Table 4.1 presents KSAOs for the sample task statement for the meeting planner job. Keep in mind that the SME would perform the ratings for all the KSAOs identified for each task statement. Reviewing the proficiency information helps to set the selection standards for entry into the job. They are also useful in establishing training standards for the new hires to show what the person must be capable of doing after a period of learning either through courses or on-the-job training.

The job analyst finally integrates the information by compiling a Task × KSAO matrix,[70] illustrated in Table 4.2. Several tasks may require the same KSAOs. The job analyst develops a table similar to the one shown in Table 4.2. We've omitted the first steps in which the analyst would produce two tables, one with the actual importance ratings for the KSAOs, and the second with the proficiency ratings. With our 0 to 5 point scale, we might take the position that only those KSAOs with an average score of 3.0 or higher are important for a given task. Next we would review the proficiency data. In developing the selection system, we want to identify those KSAOs applicants should have upon their hiring. Based on our scale, we want KSAOs with a rating of 1.0 or higher on proficiency. In Table 4.2 the rows represent task statements and KSAOs that the job analysis has identified for the target job. Each cell in the matrix states whether the KSAO applies to a task; that is, if the KSAO met both the importance and proficiency cutoffs for the task statement, we entered a "Y" for Yes in the matrix. In Table 4.2, K3 (knowledge of reference guides) applies to all eight tasks that have been identified for the meeting planner, while S2 (interviewing skills) applies to five of the eight tasks, A1 (verbal comprehension) applies to all eight, and O2 (conscientiousness) applies to four of the eight tasks. In developing selection instruments, the HR staff might wish to concentrate on the KSAOs that apply to the most tasks in the matrix. In the case of Table 4.2, these would be K2, K3, S2, A1, A4, and O2, which are bolded in the table. The Task × KSAO matrix provides a linkage between the KSAOs that are needed to perform tasks effectively; it also provides the basis for developing a defensible selection system.

The rating methods illustrated in Tables 4.1 and 4.2 do not apply only to data collected through interviews, observation, and self-report techniques. They can be used with any procedure that generates task statements that are used to derive KSAOs. A limitation of this approach is that it may be very time consuming when there are large numbers of task statements and KSAOs.

TABLE 4.1

TASK STATEMENT AND ASSOCIATED KSAOS WITH RATING SCALES

TASK STATEMENT	FREQUENCY	IMPORTANCE	DIFFICULTY
Interview hotel, air, and ground transportation vendors to facilitate comparisons between vendor offers for service using meeting and travel reference guides in accordance with client's instructions.	0 – Never 1 – A few times a year 2 – Once a month 3 – Once a week 4 – Once a day 5 – Several times a day	0 – None 1 – Little importance 2 – Some importance 3 – Moderate importance 4 – Very important 5 – Extremely important	0 – Never perform 1 – Very easy 2 – Easy 3 – Average difficulty 4 – Very difficult 5 – Extremely difficult
	0 1 2 3 4 5	0 1 2 3 4 5	0 1 2 3 4 5

	IMPORTANCE	PROFICIENCY
	0 – None 1 – Little importance 2 – Some importance 3 – Moderate importance 4 – Very important 5 – Extremely important	0 – Not needed 1 – Needed upon entry to job 2 – Essential for job
KNOWLEDGE		
K1. Knowledge of service provided by vendors as part of their offers.	0 1 2 3 4 5	0 1 2
K2. Knowledge of previous negotiated goods and services agreements from vendors in comparing offers.	0 1 2 3 4 5	0 1 2
K3. Knowledge of facility and travel reference guides to identify best features of hotels and airlines.	0 1 2 3 4 5	0 1 2
K4. Knowledge of vendor pricing structures and policies to evaluate bids.	0 1 2 3 4 5	0 1 2
SKILLS		
S1. Skill in typing 40 words per minute without error.	0 1 2 3 4 5	0 1 2
S2. Skill in interviewing vendors to obtain best offers.	0 1 2 3 4 5	0 1 2
S3. Skill in using computer spreadsheets to compile bid information.	0 1 2 3 4 5	0 1 2
ABILITIES		
A1. Ability to comprehend verbal information obtained over the telephone.	0 1 2 3 4 5	0 1 2
A2. Ability to organize work assignments to ensure deadlines are met.	0 1 2 3 4 5	0 1 2
A3. Ability to use airline reservation systems to identify availability of flights.	0 1 2 3 4 5	0 1 2
A4. Ability to compile information from several sources.	0 1 2 3 4 5	0 1 2
OTHER		
O1. Emotional stability—remains calm under pressure from vendors.	0 1 2 3 4 5	0 1 2
O2. Conscientiousness—completes work in a timely manner with attention to detail	0 1 2 3 4 5	0 1 2
O3. Honesty—does not accept vendor kickbacks.	0 1 2 3 4 5	0 1 2

TABLE 4.2

TASK STATEMENT BY KSAO MATRIX

	KNOWLEDGE				SKILLS			ABILITY				OTHER		
TASK STATEMENT	K1	K2	K3	K4	S1	S2	S3	A1	A2	A3	A4	01	02	03
T1	Y	N	Y	N	Y	Y	N	Y	N	N	Y	Y	N	N
T2	N	N	Y	N	N	Y	N	Y	N	Y	Y	N	Y	N
T3	Y	Y	Y	N	N	Y	N	Y	Y	Y	N	N	Y	N
T4	N	Y	Y	N	Y	Y	N	Y	Y	Y	Y	N	Y	Y
T5	Y	Y	Y	N	Y	N	N	Y	N	N	Y	N	Y	N
T6	N	Y	Y	N	N	N	Y	Y	Y	N	Y	Y	N	N
T7	N	Y	Y	Y	N	Y	N	Y	N	N	Y	N	N	N
T8	N	N	Y	Y	N	N	N	Y	N	N	Y	N	N	N

"Y" in a cell means that the KSAO in the column applies to the task statement listed in the row. "N" means that the KSAO does not apply to the specified task.

STRUCTURED JOB ANALYSIS QUESTIONNAIRES AND INVENTORIES

Structured job analysis questionnaires and inventories require workers and other SMEs to respond to written questions about their jobs. Respondents are asked to make judgments about activities and tasks, tools, and equipment and working conditions involved in the job. These can be off-the-shelf questionnaires and inventories that can be used for a variety of jobs, such as the worker-oriented *Position Analysis Questionnaire* (PAQ),[71] or they can be developed by the analyst for the specific job and organization in question using the critical incident technique,[72] functional job analysis,[73,74] or other inventory methods. As well, the interview protocol shown in Recruitment and Selection Notebook 4.2 can easily be turned into a written questionnaire administered to a larger number of SMEs.

TASK INVENTORIES

Task inventories
Work-oriented surveys that break down jobs into their component tasks.

Task inventories are structured work-oriented surveys that break down jobs into their component tasks and ask job incumbents and supervisors to make judgments about activities and tasks, tools and equipment, and working conditions involved in the job. A well-constructed survey permits workers to define their jobs in relation to a subset of tasks appearing on the inventory.[75] Drauden[76] indicates that certain task inventory methods were developed in response to the *Uniform Guidelines* criteria for job analysis. According to these criteria, job analysis should assess (1) the duties performed, (2) the level of difficulty of job duties, (3) the job context, and (4) the criticality of duties to the job. An inventory comprises task statements that are objectively based descriptions of what gets done on a job. Tasks are worker activities that result in an outcome that serves some specified purpose.[77,78] The task inventory is next used to identify a list of relevant KSAOs as outlined above. These inventories are typically developed for specific jobs or occupations. Task inventories are advantageous in that they are efficient to use with large numbers of employees and are easily translated into quantifiable measurements. On the other hand, they can be time consuming to develop and thus can be expensive. Motivating incumbents to participate in the rating process may also be a problem with long inventories. When the task inventory procedure and analysis are well planned, the results can be extremely valuable in developing HR selection programs. Task inventories are unique to a specific job in contrast to worker-oriented methods that permit application of survey instruments to a wide variety of unrelated jobs.

FUNCTIONAL JOB ANALYSIS (FJA) FJA is conducted by an experienced job analyst who has attended FJA training workshops and who has been certified as an FJA analyst. The analyst convenes a focus group of approximately six job incumbents who have a broad range of experience in the position. The focus of the workshop is on obtaining two types of information, specifically what a worker does and how a task is performed. Under the guidance of the analyst, the focus group collects information on (1) the outputs of the job for which they are paid, (2) the KSAOs required to perform their job, and (3) the tasks that they need to do to perform their job. After identifying the job outputs and KSAOs, much of the time is spent writing task statements that clearly define what needs to be done to get the work performed.

The task statement is the basic unit of analysis. Task statements follow the same format we presented earlier in this chapter. The focus group writes as many task statements as possible. Generally, 20 to 30 task statements are sufficient to describe the essential job components, although with complex jobs the number needed may go as high as 100. This bank of task statements should cover at least 95 percent of the work that the job entails. The task bank is then edited by the analyst to ensure clarity and conformity to the format and then sent to the focus group participants for their feedback and evaluation.

Next, the task bank is distributed to a sample of job incumbents and other experts, who are asked to rate each task on seven scales that assess the complexity of the task. The Data scale assesses worker involvement with ideas, information, facts, and statistics; the Things scale assesses the employee's use of equipment and tools; and the Person scale assesses the worker's interaction with other humans. Table 4.3 presents the descriptors that serve as a guide in making these three ratings. These scales are those used in the *Dictionary of Occupational Titles*, the *Canadian Classification Dictionary of Occupations*, and the *National Occupational Classification* (refer to Figure 4.2).

The remaining four scales assess Worker Instructions, the amount of discretion a worker has over the specific methods of task performance, and three General Educational Development scales: Reasoning Development, which assesses problem-solving and decision-making demands of a task; Mathematical Development, which assesses the math operations required by a task; and Language Development, which assesses the oral and written materials related to the task. The results of these four scales are used to develop the KSAOs related to the tasks.

An optional last step in the FJA is to ask workers to rate the frequency, importance, and difficulty of each task (refer to Table 4.1). Fine[79] notes that the usefulness of the latter three ratings is dubious: "The critical issue is really whether the task needs to be performed to get the work done. If it is necessary, then it is important and critical, and frequency does not matter." A worker in a nuclear power facility may, for example, be required to enter and conduct rescues in radiologically contaminated confined spaces. While such a rescue operation is rarely, if ever, necessary in the life of a job, it is essential that certain workers be able to perform to stringent standards at any given time, so this is a critical component in employee selection.[80,81]

TABLE 4.3

THE DATA, PEOPLE, THINGS SCALES USED IN FUNCTIONAL JOB ANALYSIS

	DATA	PEOPLE	THINGS
HIGH COMPLEXITY ↑	Synthesizing	Mentoring	Setting up
	Coordinating	Negotiating	Precision working
	Analyzing	Instructing	Operating/controlling
	Compiling	Supervising	Manipulating
	Computing	Diverting	Tending
	Copying	Persuading	Feeding/offbearing
	Comparing	Speaking/signalling	Handling
		Serving	
		Taking instructions/helping	
LOW COMPLEXITY			

The mean employee ratings from the seven scales are used to summarize each task in the task bank. The mean ratings are used to develop the job requirement and specifications. There is no agreed-upon formula for how to do this. However, Gatewood, Feild, and Barrick[82] suggest that at least 75 percent of the employees must perform the task and their mean ratings on a scale are above the mean and have a relatively low standard deviation (i.e., more agreement among the raters). For example, on a 5-point scale, the task should have a mean rating of greater than 3 and a standard deviation of less than 1. Tasks whose ratings reflected these values would be used in listing the job requirements and specifications. This is similar to the strategy we used in developing the Task × KSAO matrix in Table 4.2. The resultant tasks and their KSAOs form the basis for the subsequent selection measurements.

CRITICAL INCIDENT TECHNIQUE Critical incidents are examples of effective and ineffective work behaviours that are related to superior or inferior performance. The critical incident technique generates behaviourally focused descriptions of work activities. It was originally developed as a training needs assessment and performance appraisal tool.[83] The critical incident technique provides important, contextually rich examples of job behaviours that are particularly useful in developing behaviourally anchored rating scales (BARS; see Chapter 5) and behavioural interviews (see Chapter 9), as well as being the basis for situational judgment tests and assessment centre exercises such as role-plays and in-basket tests (see Chapter 8).[84]

The first step in this method is to assemble a panel of job experts, usually consisting of people with several years' experience who have had the opportunity to observe both poor and exemplary workers on the job. The job of the panel is to gather critical incidents. Flanagan[85] defined an incident as an observable human activity that is sufficiently complete to facilitate inferences and predictions about the person performing the act. Panel members describe incidents, including the antecedents to the activity, a complete

FIGURE 4.6

CRITICAL INCIDENT REPORT FORM

1. What was the situation leading up to the event? (Describe the context)

2. What did the person do? Describe the actions taken.

3. What was the outcome or result of the action?

Circle the number below that best reflects the level of performance that this event exemplifies.

1	2	3	4	5	6	7
Highly **Ineffective**						Highly **Effective**

description of the behaviour, the results of the behaviour, and whether the results were within the control of the worker. All of the incidents are then rated by the panel in terms of whether they represent effective or ineffective behaviour on the part of the employee. Figure 4.6 presents an example of a form used to collect critical incidents.

After the incidents are gathered, they are edited and reviewed by a panel of SMEs who sort the incidents into themes or dimensions that they believe characterize the complete set of incidents. These dimensions may have been predetermined or they may be inferred from the incidents. At least 60 percent of the SMEs must agree that an item belongs in a dimension; if this criterion is not met, the item is dropped. Catano and Harvey[86] used this technique to develop a new measure to evaluate teaching based on competencies. From close to 500 critical incidents they identified nine competencies (dimensions) that formed the new scale: communication, availability, creativity, individual consideration, social awareness, feedback, professionalism, conscientiousness, and problem solving. Examples of ineffective and effective incidents for four of the competencies are presented in Table 4.4.

The dimensions or competencies, rather than tasks, are used to describe the job. The performance dimensions and the rated incidents are used to derive KSAOs and to identify appropriate selection methods. If we were hiring teachers we might consider selecting them on the basis of their communication skills and the personality factors of openness and conscientiousness, as suggested by Table 4.4. The rated incidents within each dimension can be used to develop the anchors for the BARS instruments, situational judgment tests, and structured interviews that are discussed in later chapters.

The critical incident technique has the advantages of being flexible and collecting data from employees in their own words. It identifies rare events that may help to define

TABLE 4.4

EXAMPLES OF EFFECTIVE AND INEFFECTIVE CRITICAL INCIDENTS SORTED BY DIMENSION

AVAILABILITY

The teacher is a part-time instructor and is rarely seen on campus. The teacher was never available during office hours. The teacher did not provide an e-mail or other means of contact. There was no support for the students who required extra assistance or supplementary information to understand the material and assignments.

The course material in the class was very difficult, and students were concerned that the lectures were not helping them to understand the material. The professor took time out of his schedule and offered tutorial sessions. The students greatly appreciated this and felt that they received higher marks in the class because of it.

COMMUNICATION

The professor was new at teaching and was very nervous. The professor's style was to read off the PowerPoint slides and she was so uncomfortable when she spoke that it was difficult to understand what she was saying. The result was that the students felt they did not learn as much as they could.

The student told the professor that the professor could not be heard properly from the back of the room. The professor thanked the student and proceeded to conduct the lecture in a louder voice. The student was able to fully hear the professor and to take better notes.

CONSCIENTIOUSNESS

The professor arrived early for class and listed on the blackboard the concepts that would be covered that day. Beside the concepts were small but effective descriptions for each concept. The class was extremely organized, and was taught succinctly. The student understood what the professor was talking about, and was able to generate extremely efficient notes.

The professor did not give out a syllabus explaining what would be covered during the semester and when it would be covered. The student was not sure what to read for class or what would be covered during the class. This made it very difficult to keep up with the readings.

INDIVIDUAL CONSIDERATION

A student approached the teacher to discuss some concerns about the class. The teacher was very cold and uninterested. The student felt very uncomfortable, and did not receive any support from the teacher. The student never returned to discuss issues regarding the class.

Because of the death of a family member, a student had to leave for an extended period of time during the semester. The teacher kept the student updated in order to prevent the student from falling too far behind. As a consequence, the student was accommodated and obtained a good grade for the course.

the work situation. It is relatively inexpensive compared to other methods, and provides rich behavioural data that can be used in selection interviews and performance evaluations. On the other hand, the focus on critical incidents may miss important routine tasks. The critical incidents rely on memory and often only recent events are recalled. It may take a while to collect enough critical incidents to describe a job. CIT develops rich qualitative data that provide great insights but are relatively labour-intensive to develop.[87]

WORKER-ORIENTED JOB ANALYSIS METHODS

POSITION ANALYSIS QUESTIONNAIRE (PAQ) The PAQ is a structured job analysis questionnaire that focuses on the general behaviours that make up a job. It assumes that all jobs can be characterized in terms of a limited number of human abilities. The PAQ includes 195 items, called *job elements*, organized into 32 job division dimensions that may be further organized into 6 dimensions–*information input, mental processes, work output, relationships, job context,* and *other job characteristics*–and 13 *overall* dimensions.[88] Figure 4.7 presents a sample of the PAQ items used in assessing information input from visual sources.

The PAQ can be used for many jobs. Figure 4.8 shows the scores on the PAQ job dimensions provided by job analysts to four very different occupations. The scores are percentiles and represent comparisons for the dimension with normative data from the PAQ database of over 300 000 job analyses. For example, ratings for homemakers on *demanding situations* were equal to or greater than ratings on this dimension for 85 percent of jobs in the PAQ database. Figure 4.8 illustrates how comparisons may be made across a number of jobs.

FIGURE 4.7

SAMPLE OF PAQ ITEMS

A. Information Input

A1. Visual Sources of Job Information

Using the response scale at the left, rate each of the following items on the basis of the extent to which it is used by the worker as a source of information in performing the job.

Extent of Use

0 Does not apply
1 Nominal/very infrequent
2 Occasional
3 Moderate
4 Considerable
5 Very substantial

1. Written materials
E.g., books, reports, office notes, articles, job instructions, or signs

2. Quantitative materials
Materials that deal with quantities or amounts, e.g., graphs, accounts, specifications, or tables of numbers

3. Pictorial materials
Pictures or picture-like materials used as sources of information, e.g., drawings, blueprints, diagrams, maps, tracings, photographic films, x-ray films, or TV pictures

4. Patterns or related devices
E.g., templates, stencils, or patterns used as sources of information when observed during use (Do not include materials described in item 3.)

5. Visual displays
E.g., dials, gauges, signal lights, radarscopes, speedometers, or clocks

6. Measuring devices
E.g., rules, calipers, tire pressure gauges, scales, thickness gauges, pipettes, thermometers, or protractors used to obtain visual information about physical measurements (Do *not* include devices described in item 5.)

7. Mechanical devices
E.g., tools, equipment, or machinery that are sources of information when observed during use or operation

Source: PAQ Services, Inc.

FIGURE 4.8

PAQ DIMENSION SCORES FOR FOUR OCCUPATIONS

PAQ DIMENSION	JOB			
	COUNTER CLERK	HOME-MAKER	SECRETARY	FOOD SERVER
1. Decision/Communication/Social responsibility	16	69	25	21
2. Skilled activities	22	34	21	11
3. Physical activity/Environment conditions	65	87	33	59
4. Equipment/ Vehicle operation	44	65	31	62
5. Information processing	67	28	79	65
6. Visual input from devices	24	46	33	16
7. Perceptual interpretation	45	29	35	33
8. Information from people	54	73	39	85
9. Visual input from distal sources	30	31	58	52
10. Physical information evaluation	64	63	40	38
11. Environmental awareness	86	98	38	57
12. Aware of body movement	18	27	40	35
13. Decision making	10	52	14	11
14. Information processing	36	26	85	63
15. Machine/ Process control	56	26	85	40
16. Manual control activities	42	52	25	32
17. Control/ Equipment operation	28	69	33	22
18. General body activity	30	70	34	56
19. Handling/Manipulating	93	79	61	85
20. Finger dexterity/Physical activity	48	16	74	40
21. Skilled/Technical activities	25	50	36	32
22. Communication decisions/judgments	16	67	37	20
23. Job information exchange	81	46	16	80
24. Staff-related activities	27	77	64	15
25. Superior/ Subordinate relations	81	18	33	51
26. Public-related contact	90	64	16	81
27. Unpleasant/Hazardous environment	29	45	23	30
28. Demanding situations	35	85	42	47
29. Businesslike situations	48	17	72	63
30. Attentive/Discriminating	09	32	06	09
31. Structured work	78	17	60	64
32. Regular work schedule	13	05	62	10

Note. Entries are percentile ranks for each job on the relevant PAQ dimension; dimensions 1–5 are the overall PAQ factors, whereas dimensions 6–32 are division dimensions.

Source: Butler, S.K. and Harvey, R.J. 1988. "A comparison of Holistic Versus Decomposed Ratings of Position Analysis Questionnaire Work Dimensions" *Journal of Applied Psychology*, 41: 761–771. American Psychological Association.

The PAQ can be completed by trained job analysts, HR practitioners, or job incumbents and supervisors; trained job analysts produce the most accurate and reliable results in the least amount of time.[89] The PAQ ratings can be combined in several different ways to provide excellent information for selection, job descriptions, job evaluations, and compensation. It has good reliability and is available "off-the-shelf" for immediate use. It can be used with a small number of SMEs. PAQ Services provides computerized scoring and uses the thousands of jobs in its database as benchmarks. The PAQ provides straightforward information for developing selection procedures. Finally, the PAQ has been rated as one of the most cost-efficient job analysis methods.[90]

There are drawbacks, however, including serious questions about the readability of the statements in the inventory (refer to Figure 4.7) with the suggestion that a job analyst complete the inventory after interviewing job incumbents and supervisors. The PAQ requires a college-level reading ability. Having the job analyst complete the inventory increases the time and cost of administering the PAQ. The content of the PAQ makes it more suitable for blue-collar jobs. It does not quantify what work actually gets done on a job. Because of its focus on behaviours rather than tasks and on de-emphasizing job context, important differences between jobs may not be picked up.

Recently, the PAQ has been updated to include items that meet a wider variety of human resource needs, including those related to disabilities. It has also produced a separate version of the PAQ that is designed for use with occupations involving professional and managerial work. The PAQ offers free services, materials, and sample scoring reports to classes in HR and I/O psychology.

More information on the Position Analysis Questionnaire is available on the PAQ website at http://www.paq.com.

WORKER TRAITS INVENTORIES

Worker traits inventories
Methods used to infer employee specifications from job analysis data.

Worker traits inventories do not provide information on the job as a whole or any tasks associated with it, but only certain requirements needed to carry out the job. For this reason some researchers argue that worker traits inventories are not legitimate job analysis methods.[91] However, these methods are widely used to infer employee specifications from work or job analysis data and are useful for selection and training purposes. These methods are commonly included in the job analysis literature and accepted by most practitioners as legitimate work or job analysis methods. Worker traits inventories are designed to identify the traits or KSAOs that predict job success. The identification of these KSAOs is made by SMEs, who are most familiar with the job or occupation. In many ways, worker traits inventories are similar to procedures used to identify worker competencies that we discuss in Part II of this chapter.

FLEISHMAN JOB ANALYSIS SURVEY (F-JAS) The Fleishman Job Analysis Survey (F-JAS)[92] is a system for identifying which and to what degree an array of empirically derived ability constructs are critical to perform a specific job effectively. It assumes that job tasks differ with respect to the abilities required to perform them successfully and that jobs can be classified according to the abilities required to perform them. Fleishman and his colleagues,[93,94] using factor analysis methods, identified 52 human ability categories, such as "oral comprehension" and "multi-limb coordination" and "night vision." In the F-JAS booklet (F-JAS-1) these abilities are grouped into four clusters: cognitive, psychomotor, physical, and sensory/perception. The methodology employs a minimum of 10 raters familiar with the job to assess the job with behaviourally anchored rating scales ranging from a high of 7 to a low of 1 on that ability requirement level. The average of these 10 rater scores is obtained to provide a statistically significant value for the degree of expertise that job requires of that ability. These 52 abilities are now used by O*NET in describing the level of abilities required by jobs in its database. Caughron, Mumford, and Fleishman[95] and Wilson, Bennett, Gibson, and Alliger[96] provide additional information on the development and uses of the F-JAS.

Figure 4.9 provides the rating scale used for the ability "Oral Comprehension." Unlike many other rating systems, this scale and those shown in Figure 10 and Figure 11 include definitions of the ability and how it differs from others. The scale is anchored with behaviours that help the rater to determine the level of the ability needed for the job.

FIGURE 4.9

THE F-JAS ABILITY SCALE FOR ORAL COMPREHENSION

1. Oral Comprehension This is the ability to listen and understand spoken words and sentences.

How Oral Comprehension Is Different From Other Abilities		
Oral Comprehension: Involves **listening** to and **understanding** words and sentences spoken by others.	vs.	*Written Comprehension*: Involves **reading** and **understanding written** words and sentences.
		Oral Expression and *Written Expression*: Involve **speaking** or **writing** words and sentences so others will understand.

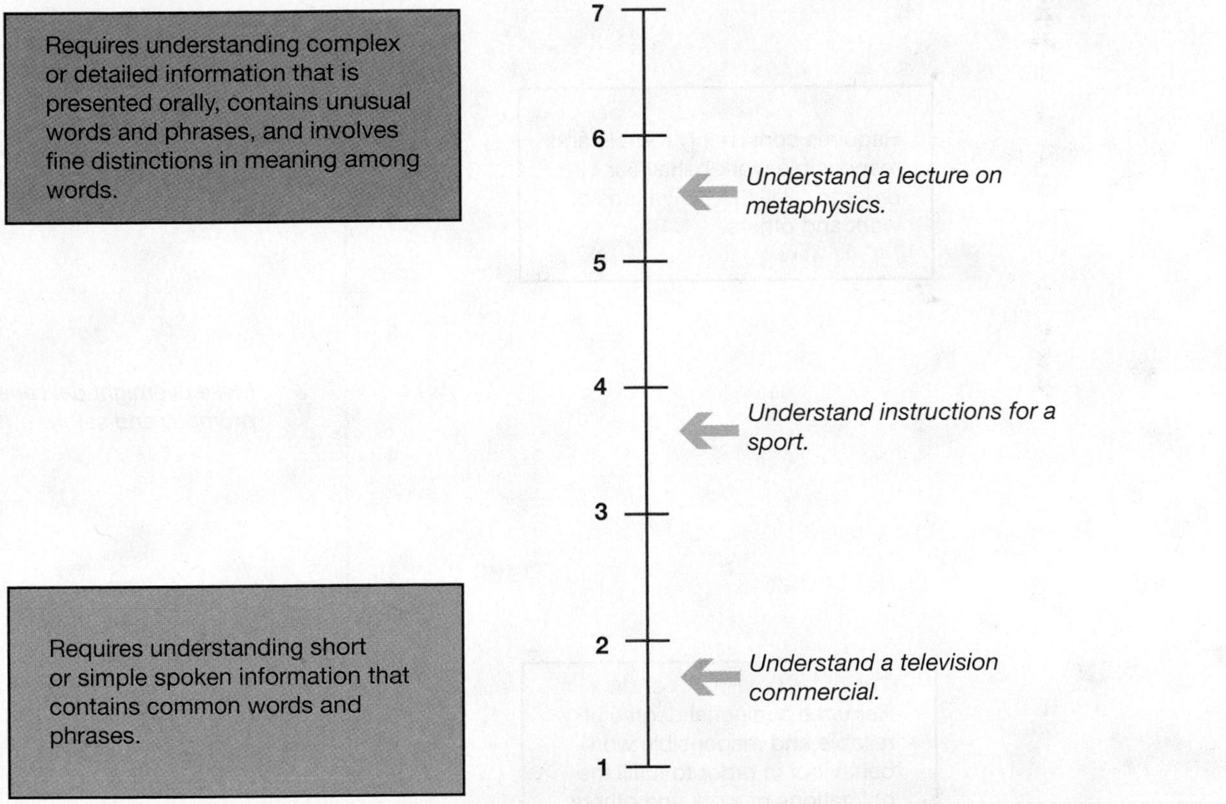

Requires understanding complex or detailed information that is presented orally, contains unusual words and phrases, and involves fine distinctions in meaning among words.

7

6

Understand a lecture on metaphysics.

5

4

Understand instructions for a sport.

3

Requires understanding short or simple spoken information that contains common words and phrases.

2

Understand a television commercial.

1

Source: Copyright © Management Research Institute http://www.managementresearchinstitute.com/

More recently, Fleishman and his colleagues extended this work to the development of F-JAS-2, which provides 21 job-related social and interpersonal abilities. A number of these abilities, such as dependability and assertiveness, reflect the current research on the role of personality variables in selection and job performance. Administration of the F-JAS-2 requires that same sample of subject-matter experts, the job incumbents, supervisors, and others, be presented with the job description and assess it against the component social and interpersonal abilities. The methodology offers job analysts the flexibility to rate the extent that each ability is required at the job as a whole level or at more specific levels of inquiry such as task statements or dimensions of the job.

Figure 4.10 provides an example of the rating scale for "Dependability."

FIGURE 4.10

THE F-JAS ABILITY SCALE FOR DEPENDABILITY

4. Dependability

This is the ability to be reliable and responsible to others. This ability involves being disciplined, conscientious, and trustworthy in fulfilling obligations and tasks expected by others.

Scale	Anchor description	Example
7	Requires consistently reliable and responsible work behaviour in order to fulfill the obligations of work and others.	
		Remain alert on guard duty near enemy territory. (between 6 and 7)
6		
5		
		Make overnight deliveries promptly and safely. (between 4 and 5)
4		
3		
		Return a telephone call. (between 2 and 3)
2		
1	Requires a minimal degree of reliable and responsible work behaviour in order to fulfill the obligations of work and others.	

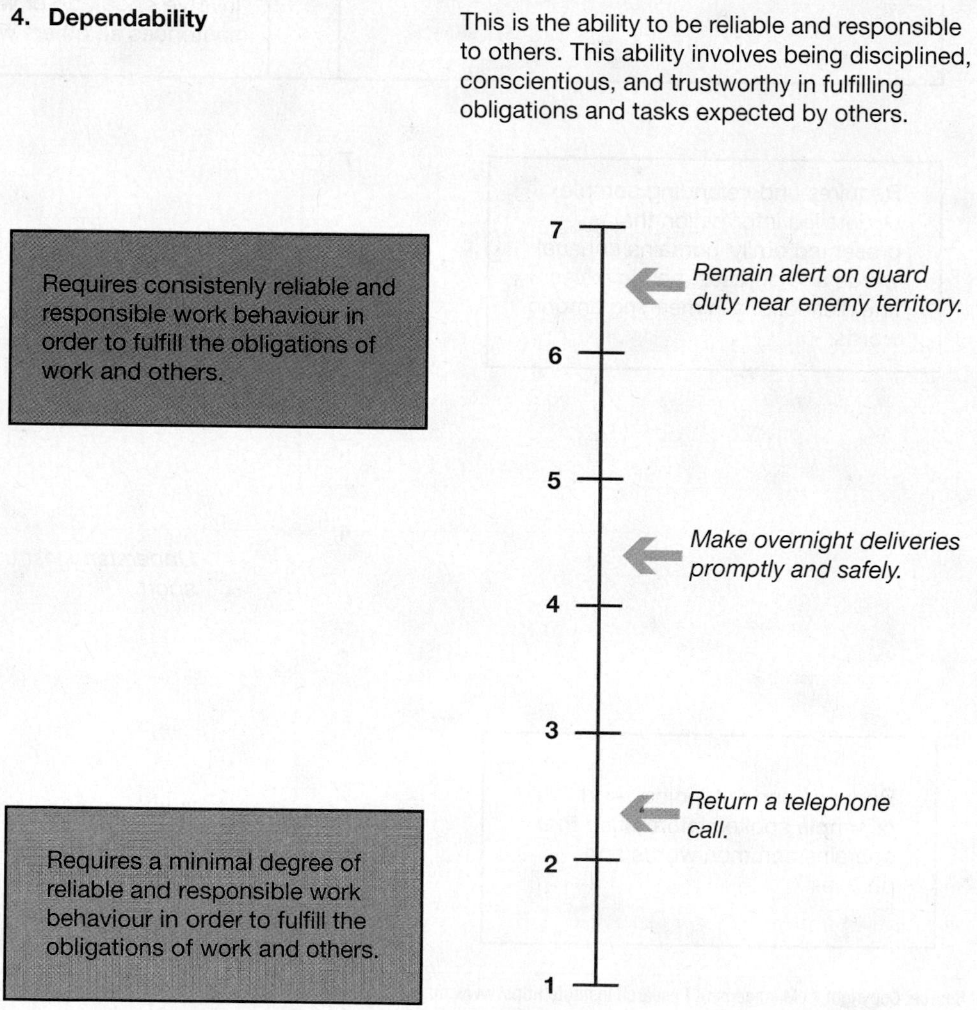

In addition to F-JAS-1 (ability requirements) and F-JAS-2 (social requirements), Fleishman, Costanza, and Marshall-Mies[97] have developed an additional F-JAS-3 component to cover the 49 major knowledge and skill requirements of jobs, using the same rating scale formats as the F-JAS.

Figure 4.11 provides an example of the rating scale for "Personnel/HR Knowledge."

Fleishman and Reilly[98] have produced a companion handbook that provides a compilation of commercially available assessment instruments designed to measure each of the specific abilities required of job incumbents.

More information on the F-JAS can be found at http://www.managementresearchinstitute.com.

FIGURE 4.11

THE F-JAS ABILITY SCALE FOR PERSONNEL/HR KNOWLEDGE

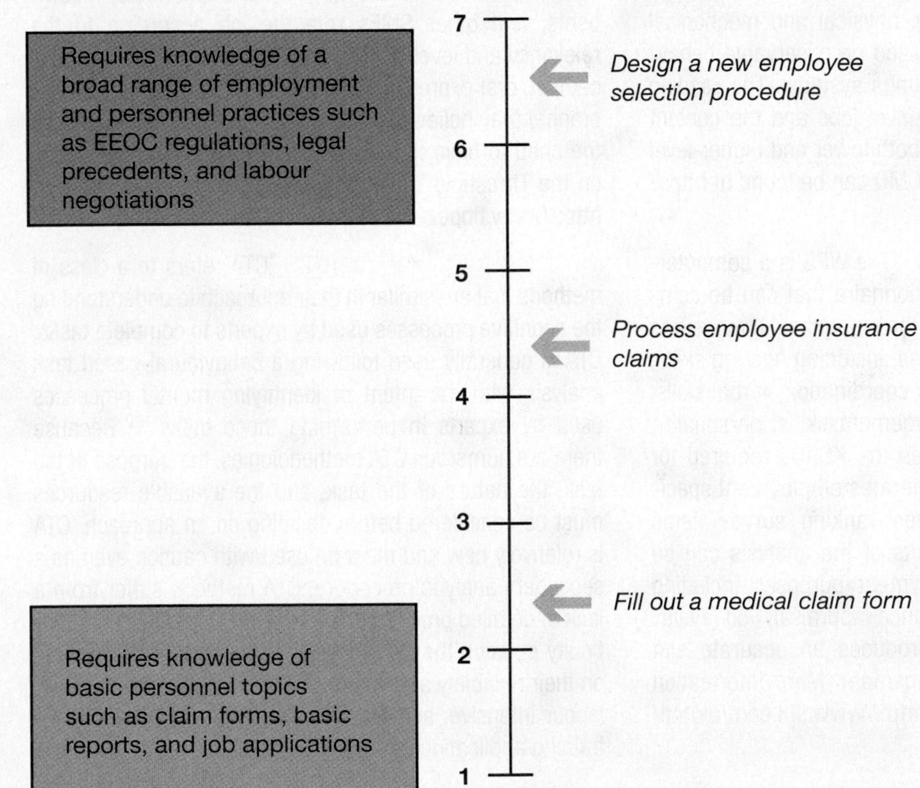

OTHER JOB ANALYSIS METHODS

There are many other job analysis methods that are available for general or specific purposes. It is impossible to cover all of these. Recruitment and Selection Notebook 4.3 presents brief information on some of the more popular of these methods.

BEST PRACTICE IN CHOOSING JOB ANALYSIS METHODS

Throughout this chapter we have discussed several different job analysis methods. Recruitment and Selection Notebook 4.4 presents the advantages and disadvantages of the methods we covered in this chapter.

Each of these methods has advantages and disadvantages, so which method is the best one? Which one should we choose for use? There is no real answer to these questions. It depends on the purpose for which you are doing the job analysis: selection,

RECRUITMENT AND SELECTION NOTEBOOK 4.3

OTHER JOB ANALYSIS METHODS

Common-Metric Questionnaire (CMQ) The CMQ[99] is a structured, off-the-shelf job analysis questionnaire that captures information about the job's background, contacts with people, decision making, physical and mechanical activities, and work setting, based on observable behaviour rather than subjective ratings systems. The reading level is appropriate for lower-level jobs and the content appears to be appropriate for both lower and higher-level jobs. More information on the CMQ can be found at http://commonmetric.com.

Work Profiling System (WPS) The WPS is a computer-administered structured questionnaire that can be completed and scored online or in the workplace. It measures ability and personality attributes, including hearing skills, sight, taste, smell, touch, body coordination, verbal skills, number skills, complex management skills, personality, and team role.[100] WPS defines the KSAOs required for effective performance and generates employment specifications based on the highest-ranking survey items across respondents. The results of the analysis can be used for a variety of employment purposes including employee selection, performance appraisal, job evaluation, and restructuring. It produces an accurate and efficient system for HR management. More information on the WPS can be found at http://www.shl.com/uk/intl/canada-english.

Threshold Traits Analysis System The Threshold Traits Analysis System[101] is designed to identify worker traits that are relevant to the target job. Supervisors, incumbents, and other SMEs rate the job according to the relevancy and level of 33 worker traits (e.g., stamina, perception, oral expression, adaptability to pressure, and tolerance) they believe are necessary to perform the job and the need to have the traits upon hiring. More information on the Threshold Traits Analysis System can be found at http://www.flopez-associates.com/services.html.

Cognitive Task Analysis (CTA) CTA refers to a class of methods that are similar in their approach to understanding the cognitive processes used by experts to complete tasks. CTA is generally used following a behavioural-based task analysis with the intent of identifying mental processes used by experts in performing those tasks.[102] Because there are numerous CTA methodologies, the purpose of the task, the nature of the task, and the available resources must be considered before deciding on an approach. CTA is relatively new and must be used with caution even as a secondary analytic procedure. CTA methods suffer from a lack of detailed procedural information, complexity and difficulty in using the procedures, and lack of sufficient data on their reliability and validity. CTA is also time consuming, labour intensive, and expensive. CTA is more suitable for training applications rather than selection.

RECRUITMENT AND SELECTION NOTEBOOK 4.4

ADVANTAGES AND DISADVANTAGES OF COMMONLY USED JOB ANALYSIS METHODS

METHOD	ADVANTAGES	DISADVANTAGES
Existing Documentation O*NET NOC Job descriptions Job specifications Training manuals	• Easy to use • Existing data • O*NET and NOC provide rich, detailed information • May be used to suggest information that is needed • Useful for several purposes	• May not cover job of interest • Information may not be up to date or relevant • Job may have changed
Structured interview	• Job incumbents describe work • Information obtained from persons most familiar with the job • May provide unexpected information	• Requires experienced interviewer • Requires well-designed questions and probes • Provides qualitative data that may be difficult to combine and analyze • Time consuming • Interviewees may distort information
Direct observation	• Analyst sees first hand what the job involves • Useful for blue-collar work • Simple to use • May verify data from other sources	• Observations may not cover all time periods in which job is performed • Time consuming • Not useful for jobs involving cognitive tasks • Observation may bias performance • Validity and reliability may be problematic
Structured questionnaires	• Job incumbents describe work • Information obtained from persons most familiar with the job • Access information from large number of workers • Relatively inexpensive	• Only a portion of workers may respond • Respondents may not answer honestly • Questions are fixed and do not allow flexibility • May not capture points that the worker believes are important
Functional job analysis	• Provides task bank of standardized task statements • Identifies the level of involvement with people, data, and things • Used to develop job descriptions • Helps to identify KSAOs related to task statements • Produces reliable and valid data, if data collected by trained analyst	• Only trained analysts may use the method • Very costly for analyst training • Very time consuming, laborious, and costly to collect task statements

Continued

METHOD	ADVANTAGES	DISADVANTAGES
Critical incident technique	• Analysis based on observable behaviour • Work described in workers' own words • Relatively easy to collect data • Perceived as relevant and practical • Has good reliability and validity • Good cost–benefit ratios • Provides rich behavioural data • Best used for selection	• Does not require training for the analyst • May not capture all the dimensions critical for job performance • Relies on memory of recent events • Reliability and validity may be lower than off-the-shelf inventories
Position Analysis Questionnaire	• Allows standardized comparisons between jobs in PAQ data bank • Information is not task specific • Information includes KSAOs related to selection • Mostly suited to blue-collar jobs • Relatively inexpensive • Has very good reliability • Requires only a small number of SMEs	• Requires an experienced job analyst • Statements are lengthy and detailed • Requires an above average reading level on the part of the person completing the inventory
Fleishman Job Analysis Survey	• Easy to administer • Can be used with task statements or the whole job • Cost efficient • Does not require trained analyst to collect data • Ratings are behaviourally anchored • Provides rich data for writing worker specification • Useful for both blue- and white-collar jobs • Has good reliability	• Needs at least 10 SMEs • Does not provide task statement or information on the job duties • Task information needs to be obtained through another process

job evaluation, compensation, pay equity, and so on. Some methods are better suited to one purpose than another. Levine and his colleagues[103] identified 11 criteria that could be used in assessing job analysis methods. These are presented in Recruitment and Selection Notebook 4.5.

An important issue that must be addressed as part of selecting a job analysis method is the reliability or accuracy of the information that the method will provide. Dierdorff and Wilson[104] used a meta-analysis of 299 reliability estimates that were from different job analyses involving a variety of occupations. They concluded that methods that gathered specific task data (e.g., "replaces ink cartridges in desktop printers") did so with greater accuracy than methods that assessed generalized work activity (e.g., "supervises work of office staff"). They also reported that professional job analysts made more accurate assessments than did job incumbents who made self-reports or surveys. Finally, their

RECRUITMENT AND SELECTION NOTEBOOK 4.5

CRITERIA FOR CHOOSING A JOB ANALYSIS METHOD

The following criteria were developed by Levine and his colleagues to evaluate seven job analysis techniques. They remain a useful set of questions for any HR practitioner to use in deciding among various procedures.

- **Operational status:** Has the method been tested and refined sufficiently?
- **Availability:** Is it available off the shelf?
- **Occupational versatility:** Is it suitable for analyzing a variety of jobs?
- **Standardization:** Is it possible to compare your results with others that have been found elsewhere?
- **User acceptability:** Is the method acceptable to the client and the employees who will have to provide the information?
- **Training requirements:** How much training is needed and available to use the method; must one receive special certification in the procedure to use it? Can it be done "in-house"?
- **Sample size:** From how many employees must data be collected for the method to provide reliable results?
- **Reliability:** Will the method give results that are replicable?
- **Cost:** What are the costs of the method in materials, consultant fees, training, and person-hours?
- **Quality of outcome:** Will the method yield high quality results (e.g., legally defensible)?
- **Time to completion:** How many calendar days will the data collection and analysis take?

Source: E.L. Levine, R.A. Ash, H. Hall, and F. Sistrunk. 1983. "Evaluation of Job Analysis Methods by Experienced Job Analysts." *Academy of Management Journal*, 26: 339–48.

analysis showed that SMEs made the most reliable estimates when using "importance" and "frequency" scales rather than other types of measurements.

This information should be of value to practitioners in designing job analysis projects: "For instance, when only a certain amount of financial resources are procurable to conduct a job analysis, one could use the information presented herein to provide an estimate of how much reliability could be expected from using 25 incumbents versus five trained analysts rating tasks as opposed to [generalized work activity]."[105] Dierdorff and Wilson's findings do not imply that only task-oriented job analysis methods should be used. The value of a job analysis lies in how the information from the analysis will be used. For some uses, such as training and development, task data may be necessary, while for some other uses, such as designing a performance management system, a more holistic method may be acceptable. The practitioner must take the intended use into consideration when choosing a method.

Recently, job analysis proponents have debated the best way to assess the reliability and validity of different job analysis methods. Sanchez and Levine[106] have taken the position that traditional methods of assessing reliability are inappropriate for assessing job analysis data in that they are of little practical value. They propose that job analysis data be evaluated in terms of their consequences: "Thus, the evaluation of [job analysis] data should focus on (1) the inferences derived from such data; and (2) the rules governing the making of such inferences." They note that Levine et al.[107] showed that four very different job analysis methods, which likely had very different degrees of accuracy, led HR professionals to develop very similar selection strategies.

Morgeson and Campion[108] echo these arguments by endorsing an inferential approach to validation, similar to our presentation in Chapter 2 (refer to Recruitment and Selection Notebook 2.2). In their model at the conceptual or construct level, the analyst identifies job performance and job-related psychological constructs. SMEs produce a job description outlining tasks and duties that is made by inference from the job performance construct. Similarly, job specifications, in terms of KSAOs, are inferred from the job-related psychological constructs. An operational linkage is assumed to tie the KSAOs to the tasks and duties. Validation rests on verifying the different inferences.

Harvey and Wilson[109] take issue with these approaches; they maintain the position that a procedure that focuses only on job specifications or the consequences of those specifications is not a true job analysis procedure. They argue that holistic ratings, or direct inferences of KSAOs from psychological constructs rather than from job tasks, will always produce inferior data. However, the position of Harvey and Wilson runs directly counter to the procedures used to develop competency-based models that we discuss in Part II of this chapter. There is little empirical evidence at this time on which to judge the merits of these two competing positions to provide guidance to an HR practitioner. The best advice that we can give is to be aware of these two differing views toward assessing reliability and validity of job analysis systems and the implications for legal defensibility.

Recruitment and Selection Notebook 4.6 presents guidelines developed by Thompson and Thompson[110] to determine whether a job analysis procedure would meet legal standards. The guidelines are based on U.S. court decisions but represent what HR professionals could expect from Canadian courts and tribunals when they evaluate the information produced by a job analysis. Although the guidelines are a bit

RECRUITMENT AND SELECTION NOTEBOOK 4.6

ASSESSING THE LEGAL DEFENSIBILITY OF A JOB ANALYSIS

Based on U.S. court and tribunal decisions, Thompson and Thompson identified the following factors that influence the defensibility of job analysis data used as evidence in legal proceedings:

- A job analysis must be performed according to a set of formal procedures. It is not acceptable to rely on what "everyone" knows about a job since that knowledge may be based on inaccurate stereotyped notions of the job demands.
- The job analysis must be well documented; it is not enough to simply carry around job information in the analyst's head.
- The job analysis should collect data from several up-to-date sources. This suggests using several different methods of job analysis.
- The sample of people interviewed should be sufficient in number to capture accurately the job information. The sample should also represent the full diversity of job incumbents (e.g., ethnic and gender groups, people with and without formal qualifications) to ensure the validity of the data.
- The job analysts should be properly trained in the different techniques to ensure that they collect objective information and are as free from bias as possible.
- The job analysis should determine the most important and critical aspects of the job, and it is on these that the key attributes and selection and evaluation for the job should be based.

Source: D.E. Thompson and T.A. Thompson. 1982. "Court Standards for Job Analysis in Test Validation," *Personnel Psychology*, 35: 872–73. Reproduced with permission of Blackwell Publishing, Inc. via Copyright Clearance Center.

dated, they are still relevant, but they may change with the adoption of new laws or standards or what is considered to be acceptable professional practice.

No guarantee exists that any job analysis method will find acceptance before the courts. The best that can be said is that having done a formal job analysis, regardless of method, is better than not having done one, and having carried it out properly will increase the probability that the courts will accept its results. Given the limitations of different methods and their suitability to different HR management functions, it is not unusual for an organization to use several job analysis techniques. Often, such multi-method approaches are needed to understand the complexity of today's jobs where the dividing lines between job, worker, and job-related behaviours become blurred.

Using a variety of approaches is a form of "triangulation" and provides different perspectives on the job that when synthesized produce the best information for matching people to jobs. Ultimately, what the HR practitioner must decide is (1) Which job analysis method best serves the intended purpose of the job analysis (i.e., Will the data be used for selection, performance appraisal, job evaluation, etc.)? (2) Can the job analysis be carried out reliably given the number of positions to be assessed, the availability of SMEs, the time allowed to complete the project, and the cooperation of job incumbents? (3) Which job analysis method has the best track record with respect to technical adequacy and legal defensibility?[111]

Recruitment and Selection Notebook 4.7 summarizes the information we have presented on job analysis in this part of the chapter, and presents guidelines on conducting a job analysis. These are guidelines as the specific nature of how the analysis is carried out may depend on many specific issues. We present a procedure that we believe will meet the requirements of legal defensibility while producing important, job-relevant information.

RECRUITMENT AND SELECTION NOTEBOOK 4.7

GUIDELINES FOR CONDUCTING A JOB ANALYSIS

1. **Determine the purpose** of the job analysis. Is the job analysis to be used for selection, job evaluation, compensation, or other purposes? Different job analysis methods are more suited to some of these purposes than others.
2. **Determine the resources** that are available and those needed for the job analysis.
   a. What is the budget for the job analysis?
   b. How many job incumbents are there in each job position of interest?
   c. Are subject matter experts available to assist?
   d. Will consultants be involved?
   e. Where is the job analysis worksite, one or several locations?
   f. What is the deadline for completing the process?
3. **Review available documentation/information** for the position or job in question. This may include job or position descriptions, recruitment information, past job analyses, and website information, e.g., O*Net, NOC.
4. **Determine the job analysis method** to be used. The choice of a job analysis depends on answers to Points #1 and #2. Review these points in the context of the criteria for choosing a job analysis method in Recruitment and Selection Notebook 4.5. Does the job analysis method require special training on the part of the analyst?
5. **Identify subject-matter experts (SMEs) and incumbents** who will participate in the job analysis. SMEs used in the job analysis process should include first-level supervisors or hiring managers.

Additionally, previous employees or trainers may be appropriate. A good SME has direct knowledge of the job and knows what is required to succeed in the job. The number and role of incumbents depends on the job analysis method; in most cases they should be top performers who know the job.

6. **Conduct the job analysis** to obtain task and/or KSAO statements. The type of statement will depend on the job analysis method. Some methods, for example, will not produce task statements.
7. **Confirm the task and KSAO statements.** Have a second SME panel review the output of the job analysis. Such a review increases the accuracy of the statements and adds validity to the job analysis process. The task and KSAO statements should include important aspects of the job.
8. **Compile the task and KSAO statements** into a job analysis questionnaire (JAQ). Administer the JAQ to SMEs and job incumbents to obtain individual ratings for the tasks and KSAOs. For each task, rate (1) the importance of the task to successful job performance, (2) the frequency of the task performance, and (3) the difficulty or criticality of the task in job performance. Similarly rate each KSAO in terms of (1) how important the KSAO is to successful job performance, and (2) whether the KSAO is essential and required on the first day of the job.
9. **Establish cutoff criteria** to determine the critical tasks and KSAOs necessary to successfully perform the job. In addition, identify the tasks and KSAOs with ratings that did not meet the cutoff criteria. These statements may be useful for other purposes other than selection (e.g., training needs analyses).
10. **Develop a Task × KSAO matrix** to link tasks to KSAOs and to identify those KSAOs that relate directly to performing the job. Organize the critical tasks and KSAO statements into logical content areas, performance domains, or competencies such as oral and written communication, machine operation program management, leadership, decision making, safety, and so on. This becomes the basis for the choice of selection instruments related to critical job functions.
11. **Select employment selection method(s)** that are the most effective way to measure the KSAOs that are essential to job performance. In some cases more than one instrument may be chosen to measure a KSAO.
12. **Document the job analysis** through a report that summarizes the specific methodology used to gather all relevant information about the job, how the job content was analyzed, and how appropriate selection modalities were identified to assess job candidates in terms of KSAOs relevant to successful job performance. In an appendix present all of the data from the job analysis.

// PART II: THE ROLE OF COMPETENCIES IN RECRUITMENT AND SELECTION

Today's workplace is in the midst of unprecedented change as it struggles to adapt to increasing global competition, rapid advances in information technology, multitasking, and changing workforce demographics. Emerging from this turbulence are worker requirements unlike any we have seen in the past. With many of the routine aspects of work now done by machines, jobs have been redefined, with greater emphasis given to the management of technology.

In this post-industrial information era, workers are required to apply a wider range of skills to an ever-changing series of tasks. Individuals just entering the workforce will face at least three to four career changes in their lifetime. Workers will be expected to possess the skills and knowledge of two or three traditional employees.[112] On the factory floor, jobs change rapidly, and workers constantly rotate among positions, acquiring multiple and generic skills. Today's workplace poses special challenges when trying to match people to jobs.

For many workers, these changes mean that the tasks performed today may be radically different from those required a few months from today. Skill requirements for employees may be increased or decreased, depending on the type of technology employed.[113] Task and job instability create a growing need for hiring people with an already-learned set of skills and the ability to make decisions and adapt to changing organizational demands. The results of a job analysis may hold for only as long as the job remains configured as it was at the time of the job analysis.[114] For example, today there is a greater emphasis on the strategic role played by HR professionals than in the past. Singh[115] argues that with decreasing specialization and shifting of shared work assignments typical of today's work, traditional methods of job analysis may not be appropriate as they do not present a strategic approach to defining work. That is, they are simply inconsistent with the new management practices of cross-training assignments, self-managed teams, and increased responsibility at all organizational levels. A job analysis should be linked to an organization's strategic focus.

The evolution toward rapidly changing jobs and organizations that demand flexibility of their workers has led some HR practitioners to search for alternatives to traditional job analysis techniques. In order to recruit, select, and promote flexible workers who are able to make their own rules and adjust to the changing demands of work, HR specialists are faced with the ever-increasing need to adjust their methods to ensure that people are hired based on the needs of the organization, while remaining within legal boundaries. One approach that HR practitioners are using in a rapidly changing environment is to select employees through work-related **competencies** that are thought to be related to successful job performance. A growing number of U.S. and Canadian organizations have implemented competency-based management strategies. Stone, Webster, and Schoonover[116] surveyed 48 HR and I/O practitioners in 2011 and found that 69 percent of their organizations had used competency modelling for five or more years; this represented an increase from 33 percent in a similar survey conducted in 2000. The practitioners noted several concerns over the use of competencies:

Competencies
Groups of related behaviours or attributes that are needed for successful job performance in an organization.

1. Some organizations that adopt competency models do not know how to implement them;
2. There are challenges in linking or integrating different applications when different competency models are developed for different HR functions;
3. Competencies may be too broad and cannot be measured, while some are too detailed for use and acceptance by employees;
4. Changes in top organizational leadership may lead to changes in the competencies and instability in their application to HR functions; and
5. Organizations often fail to validate their competency model in predicting job performance, particularly when adopting an off-the-shelf competency dictionary.

WHAT IS A "COMPETENCY"?

Boyatzis[117] popularized the term "competency" in *The Competent Manager* and defined it as a combination of a motive, trait, skill, aspect of one's self-image or social role, or a body of relevant knowledge. This definition left much room for debate and has been followed since by a plethora of definitions that tend to reflect either individual or specific organizational concerns. Stevens[118] presents a comparison of some of these various definitions of what constitutes a competency. Definitions generally contain three elements. First, most suggest that competencies are the KSAOs or behaviours that underlie effective and successful job performance; second, the KSAOs or behaviours must be observable or measurable; and third, the KSAOs or behaviours must distinguish between superior and other performers.[119] Competencies, then, are measurable attributes or behaviours that distinguish outstanding performers from others in a defined job context. In practice, competencies at times have been based on "average" performance; nonetheless, we will base our discussion on the original intent: to distinguish competencies that identify superior performance, while recognizing that organizations may have to modify the definition of a competency to meet their own needs.

Competencies are used to identify the KSAOs that distinguish superior performers from others. All of these definitions require the identification of KSAOs from behaviours displayed by superior employees. In one case, the KSAOs are labelled "competencies," and in the other, the term is applied to the behaviours. In both cases, we are concerned with identifying and measuring the KSAOs that underlie what the organization considers to be successful job performance, whether that performance is recognized as average or superior.

Competency-based selection systems take the view that employees must be capable of moving between jobs and carrying out the associated tasks for different positions.[120] In the competency-based approach, the HR specialist attempts to identify those KSAOs that distinguish superior performers from others and that will allow an organization to achieve its strategic goals. By selecting people who possess KSAOs that lead to superior performance, organizations are attempting to establish a closer connection between organizational success and individual performance. Recall that worker traits systems identify or describe KSAOs for specific jobs; competency-based approaches initially sought to identify KSAOs valued by the organization *regardless* of job. However, this has changed and many competency-based systems now identify job-level KSAOs as well as those that apply at the organizational level.

COMPETENCY FRAMEWORK OR "ARCHITECTURE"

Competency model
A collection of competencies that are relevant to performance in a particular job, job family, or functional area.

Competency framework
A broad framework for integrating, organizing, and aligning various competency models that are based on an organization's strategy and vision.

Many of the early **competency models** identified a single, target job in the organization to describe the key job requirements and KSAOs. The information obtained from this approach could not be applied to other jobs in the organization. In other cases, a common set of competencies was identified for a broad range of jobs and became the basis for recruitment and selection.[121] This common set of competencies did not describe any one job because it had to be sufficiently generic to describe a broad range of jobs. In effect, the KSAOs for a specific job are de-emphasized. Both of these approaches had limited value in selection and led to criticism of competency models. Would you want to fly in an airplane where an airline selected both pilots and flight attendants using only the competencies of leadership, motivation, trust, problem solving, interpersonal skills, and communication and ignored the specific skills required for either position?

More recently, organizations that use competency models have recognized that they must include the competencies required at the specific job level. Today, organizations that use competency models mostly develop a three-tiered **competency framework** or architecture. They identify competencies that apply across all jobs in the organization (core competencies), those that apply to a group of similar jobs (functional competencies), and those that apply to a single class of jobs (job-specific competencies).

COMPETENCY CATEGORIES

Core competencies are those characteristics that apply to every member of the organization regardless of position, function, or level of responsibility within the organization. Core competencies support the organization's mission, vision, and values. They are organizational KSAOs and behaviours that are required for organizational success.[122] Core competencies are what an organization or individual does or should do best; they are key strengths that organizations and individuals possess and demonstrate.[123] An airline could require that all employees from the chief executive officer down to pilots and flight attendants and on to the lowest-level employee exhibit the common core competencies of leadership, motivation, trust, problem solving, interpersonal skills, and communication.

Core competencies
Characteristics that every member of an organization, regardless of position, function, job, or level of responsibility within the organization, is expected to possess.

Functional competencies are characteristics shared by different positions within an organization that belong to a common job group or occupational family or by employees performing a common function. They are the common characteristics shared by different positions within the job group. They describe the KSAOs that are required for any job within the job group. For example, pilots and navigators may share the same KSAOs of map reading and developing flight plans, while flight attendants and ticket agents must both exhibit courtesy and a service orientation.

Functional competencies
Characteristics shared by different positions within an organization (i.e., a group of related or similar jobs). Only those members of an organization in these positions are expected to possess these competencies.

Job-specific competencies are characteristics that apply only to specific positions within the organization. These are competencies that are associated with a position in addition to core and functional competencies. A pilot needs a wide range of skills to fly a plane; a navigator does not have to have those skills even though the jobs may be part of the same occupational family. Similarly, a ticket agent needs to operate the computerized reservation system; the flight attendant does not need those skills. Employees need to know the competencies that are required for them to do their own jobs successfully.

Job-specific competencies
Characteristics that apply only to specific positions within the organization. Only those people in the position are expected to possess these competencies.

Core, functional, and job-specific competencies comprise the architecture of a company's competency model. Core competencies are the foundation on which to build functional competencies, which in turn serve as the base for job-specific competencies (see Figure 4.12). In practice, the architecture may vary across organizations, with some companies increasing or decreasing the number of layers. As well, organizations may choose to use different names for the layers in the competency model; for example, referring to "organizational" competencies in place of "core" competencies, "group" or "role" in place of "functional," and "task" in place of "job-specific."

COMPETENCY DICTIONARIES

A **competency dictionary** lists all of the competencies that are required by an organization to achieve its mandate. It includes the core and all functional and job-specific competencies identified throughout the organization and defines each competency in terms of the behaviours and KSAOs related to it. As part of developing a competency framework, an organization must develop a competency dictionary. The HR specialist and SMEs, using an accepted procedure, identify the competencies they believe are most relevant to the organization's success. The critical incident technique described in Part I is often used in developing the competency dictionary; however, there is no agreed-upon methodology for doing this.

Competency dictionary
A listing of all of the competencies required by an organization to achieve its mandate, along with the proficiency level required to perform successfully in different functional groups or positions.

In some cases, the HR specialist will start with a generic list of competencies that has not been tailored to any particular company or position and then adapt those generic competencies to its own needs. This shortcut procedure saves time and money but may not be as valid as initially identifying competencies specific to the organization. Simply selecting

FIGURE 4.12

A COMMON ARCHITECTURE FOR COMPETENCY MODELS

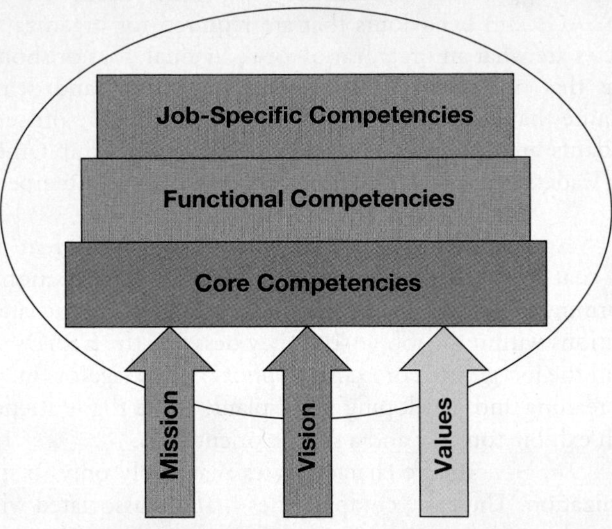

competencies from a generic competency dictionary may fail to capture those competencies that are not in the generic dictionary but are critical for successful job performance.

> **Proficiency level**
> The level at which competency must be performed to ensure success in a given functional group or position.

A competency dictionary also includes information on the **proficiency level** needed to successfully perform each competency for each position in the organization. All organization members are expected to exhibit all of the core competencies; however, they are not expected to do so to the same degree. Similarly, individuals may need the same functional and job-specific competencies, but each competency may require a different level of proficiency, depending on the organizational level of the individual.[124] As employees take on more responsibility in an organization, they may be required to become more proficient with respect to any competency if they are to perform effectively.

For example, risk management might be identified as a core competency; however, the behavioural expectations for risk management may vary across positions in the organization. Figure 4.13 provides an example from the competency dictionary developed by the Police Sector Council for use by police forces across Canada. The structure of a dictionary listing includes a definition of the competency, the proficiency level and expected performance, and behavioural indicators of the competency. As shown in Figure 4.13, the level of proficiency increases with organizational level. A senior constable would be expected to have a greater proficiency in risk management than a rookie police officer. Those at the higher levels are expected to be capable of expressing the behavioural demands at all of the lower levels before moving on to a higher-ranking position. That is, the levels are cumulative. Organizations using a competency model identify the proficiency levels on the required competencies for each position in the organization. The organization assesses each employee or potential employee with respect to the required proficiency levels and then uses these for selection, development and training,

RCMP Competency Dictionary

October 2008 Page 1 © RCMP-GRC 2008

FIGURE 4.13

EXAMPLE OF A COMPETENCY FROM A COMPETENCY DICTIONARY

Competency name & definition

RISK MANAGEMENT **Manages situations and calls to mitigate risk and maintain a safe environment for self and others.**				
Level 1	**Level 2**	**Level 3**	**Level 4**	**Level 5**
Participates in the management of situations and calls	**Manages a limited range of situations and calls with minimal guidance**	**Manages a full range of situations and calls**	**Manages highly sensitive and complex situations and calls**	**Develops best practices, strategies and procedures to manage situations and calls**
• Analyses implicatio[illegible] proposed [illegible] of action to mitigate risk to self and others • Participates in the implementation of contingency plans in low complexity situations where errors have a low level of consequence	[illegible] information • Implements emergency contingency plans in low complexity situations where errors have a low level of consequence	• Fully assesses the risks involved in a full range of situations and calls • Implements courses of actions and plans in situations of medium complexity where errors have a medium level of consequence	• Conducts risk assessment when identifying or recommen[illegible] strategic and tactical option[illegible] • Develops and implements contingency plans in highly complex and sensitive situations where errors have a high level of consequences	• Develops broad strategies that reflect in-depth understanding [illegible]sment [illegible]nal, [illegible]ntal and social realities and risks. Adapts strategies to take into account evolving trends, best practices and stakeholders

Proficiency level & expected performance

Behavioural indicator

Source: Police Sector Council. 2013. *A Guide to Competency-Based Management in Police Services.* http://www.policecouncil.ca/wp-content/uploads/2013/03/Competency-Based-Management-Guide.pdf

and promotion purposes. The competency dictionary for an organization includes definitions for each core, functional and job-specific competency, structured as the one shown in Figure 4.13, for every position in the organization.

Proficiency scales, like that represented in Figure 4.13, are included in the competency dictionary. The proficiency scale is independent of any position. The levels in a proficiency scale reflect real, observable differences from one organizational level to another. The proficiency scale is not a tool to assess employees; rather, it presents a series of behaviours that are expected at specific levels of a competency. Figure 4.13 presents a competency dictionary entry for a "Risk Management" competency, along with its associated proficiency scale. The behavioural indicators listed on the scale in Figure 4.13 are there simply to illustrate the concept. An actual scale might have considerably more indicators at each proficiency level as well as having more rating levels. The proficiency

> **Proficiency scale**
> A series of behavioural indicators expected at specific levels of a competency.

scale would be developed to meet the needs of the organization; normally, proficiency scales are based on four- or five-point rating scales.[125,126]

COMPETENCY PROFILES

Competency profile
A set of proficiency ratings related to a function, job, or employee.

A **competency profile** is a set of core, functional and job-specific competencies related to a function, job, or employee expressed in terms of the expected level of the proficiency. Since core competencies apply to all functions and jobs, they are included as part of functional and job-specific profiles. The proficiency level required on the core competencies, however, would vary across functions and positions. A functional competency profile would include the proficiency levels for all of the core and functional competencies related to the occupational family that form the functional group. A job-specific profile adds the proficiency levels required for a specific position within the functional group. Figure 4.14 presents a competency profile developed by Human Resources and Skills Development Canada (now ESDC) for its citizen service agents.[127] The number in parentheses following each competency represents the proficiency level required for that competency for successful job performance.

FIGURE 4.14

A COMPETENCY PROFILE FOR AN HRSDC CITIZEN SERVICE AGENT

Citizen Service Agent (PM–01)

Competency Profile

Core Competencies
- Communication (4)
- Thinking Skills (4)
- Using Technology (3)
- Changing and Learning (3)
- Client Focus (4)
- Initiative (3)
- Positive Attitude (4)
- Working with Others (3)
- Knowing Our Business (3)

Group Competencies (Primary)
- Applying Principles and Procedures (4)
- Diagnostic Information Gathering (4)
- Verification and Accuracy (4)
- Interpersonal Awareness (4)

Task Competencies
- Knowledge of Service Canada Programs and Services (3)

Source: Arieh Bonder. 2008. *A Blueprint for the Future: Competency-Based Management in Human Resources and Skills Development Canada* (HRSDC). Unpublished presentation, HRSDC.

An employee profile represents the proficiency level demonstrated by an employee on each competency that is included in the competency dictionary. A match between an employee profile and a job-specific or functional profile suggests that the employee is suitable for holding the specific position or a position in the functional group. Once they know their own profile, employees can match it to other jobs in the organization and determine the positions or functional areas for which they meet the minimum proficiency level on the required competencies. In cases where they are deficient, comparing their profile to that of a position of interest suggests where they need to undertake developmental activities.

An organization that decides to use competency models must have the capability to identify the required competencies and then to assess accurately the competency level of each employee with respect to the competency. It must also have in place an information management system that is capable of storing all of the required competency information for each position and for each employee. It must also allow accessibility to managers and employees to track the competency profiles for positions and for themselves.

LEGAL DEFENSIBILITY OF COMPETENCY MODELS

Competency modelling can be defended. Most likely courts will use past precedents for judging the acceptability of any particular model. Courts and tribunals in both Canada and the United States have ruled that HR systems must be supported by empirical evidence that there is a link between selection measures and the essential duties of a job (refer to Chapter 3). There is no agreed-upon methodology for developing competency models. Whether a competency-based system is deemed to meet legal standards may well depend on the methodology chosen to develop the competency dictionary, the resultant competency profiles, and their links to jobs. More rigorous competency methodologies that incorporate job analysis procedures are more likely to withstand legal scrutiny.[128,129] Competency models that fail to establish, and to document, the necessary link to work performance may not survive a legal challenge. An additional concern is the lack of reliability and validity data for most competency-based inferences; professional standards and guidelines have an expectation that selection systems have reasonable psychometric properties.

Stevens[130] makes the cogent point that legal defensibility of a competency model depends on its intended use. A company using it to align training and organizational development with strategic objectives may not require a great deal of rigour or validation.[131] On the other hand, using the model to select and hire job applicants or for internal selection (promotion) will require rigorous methods that meet psychometric standards. In a highly litigious environment, it may be better to use a traditional job analysis method, or to include some type of work analysis into the competency model.[132]

Recruitment and Selection Notebook 4.8 presents a methodology that should meet those standards. Recruitment and Selection Notebook 4.9 presents a set of best practices regarding competency modelling that are based on experiences and lessons learned over time from academic, applied, and professional perspectives.[133] Campion and colleagues provide detailed examples on each of the 20 practices listed in Recruitment and Selection Notebook 4.9. Following these best practices in developing a competency framework also helps to ensure legal defensibility against challenges to decisions based on the framework.

RECRUITMENT AND SELECTION NOTEBOOK 4.8

STEPS IN DEVELOPING A COMPETENCY-BASED MANAGEMENT FRAMEWORK

1. Obtain executive-level support, including sufficient human and financial resources, to develop a competency model.
2. Review the organization's mission, vision, and values statements.
3. Adopt a competency definition that meets the needs of the organization (e.g., average versus superior performance issue; KSAOs versus behaviour).
4. Determine the HR functions for which competencies will be used (e.g., selection, training, compensation).
5. Determine the architecture of the competency model (core, functional, job-specific layers?) that best meets the intended functions for which it will be used.
6. Develop the competency dictionary.
7. Define the profiling methodology.
   a. Conduct advance planning and preparation.
      - Review jobs and data collection techniques most appropriate for use.
   b. Consult key stakeholders in the organization.
   c. Identify SMEs for each level in the competency model.
      - Specify the competencies and proficiency levels.
   d. Validate the draft competency profiles.
      - Use focus groups or surveys to ensure that profiles accurately reflect the critical competencies required for the function and/or job.
   e. Confirm compatibility of draft competency profile and HRM information system.
   f. Revise and finalize competency profiles based on feedback from key stakeholders.
8. Identify reliable and valid assessment strategies to determine employee competency profiles.
9. Document all steps in the development and implementation of the system and the rationale for key decisions, in case these are needed as evidence before tribunals or courts.
10. Evaluate the system on an ongoing basis to ensure that the competency profiles continue to predict successful job performance.

ASSESSING EMPLOYEE COMPETENCIES

Developing reliable and valid ways of measuring employee competencies is crucial to the success of the competency model and to its legal defensibility. At some point, an HR manager must determine whether a job applicant possesses the required competencies or whether an internal candidate is qualified to hold or be promoted into a position. An organization must adopt an assessment strategy for assessing employee proficiency levels. A variety of assessment methods may be used to assess employee competencies. The choice of method depends on how the results will be used. For example, assessment of competencies for selection and promotion decisions must be carried out with methods that are fair, reliable, and valid. Chapters 7, 8, and 9 examine the different techniques that have been developed over the years to make assessments that meet these criteria. The behavioural statements associated with a proficiency level for a given position should be used by SMEs to identify the relevant KSAOs that are used in the selection process. This is identical to identifying KSAOs from behavioural statements identified through a critical incident technique. The behavioural statements can also serve as the basis of structured interview questions discussed in Chapter 9.

RECRUITMENT AND SELECTION NOTEBOOK 4.9

BEST PRACTICES IN COMPETENCY MODELLING

Analyzing Competency Information (Identifying Competencies)

1. Considering organizational context
2. Linking competency models to organizational goals and objectives
3. Starting at the top
4. Using rigorous job analysis methods to develop competencies
5. Considering future-oriented job requirements
6. Using additional unique methods

Organizing and Presenting Competency Information

7. Defining the anatomy of a competency (the language of competencies)
8. Defining levels of proficiency on competencies
9. Using organizational language
10. Including both fundamental (cross-job) and technical (job-specific) competencies
11. Using competency libraries
12. Achieving the proper level of granularity (number of competencies and amount of detail)
13. Using diagrams, pictures, and heuristics to communicate competency models to employees

Using Competency Information

14. Using organizational development techniques to ensure competency modelling acceptance and use
15. Using competencies to develop HR systems (hiring, appraisal, promotion, compensation)
16. Using competencies to align the HR systems
17. Using competencies to develop a practical "theory" of effective job performance tailored to the organization
18. Using information technology to enhance the usability of competency models
19. Maintaining the currency of competencies over time
20. Using competency modelling for legal defensibility (e.g., test validation)

Source: Table 2 in Michael A. Campion. 2011. "Doing competencies well: Best practices in competency modelling," *Personnel Psychology*, 64: 225–262. Reproduced with permission of Blackwell Publishing, Inc. via Copyright Clearance Center.

VALIDATING COMPETENCY-BASED SELECTION SYSTEMS

Since 1973, when McClelland first introduced the concept of competency modelling, nearly 2000 professional and business articles have been written on competency-based models[134]; however, most of these articles offer only theoretical or anecdotal descriptions of competencies. These articles are short on details describing the process used to establish the competencies or how they were assessed as part of a selection process. Rarely do any of these articles present data showing the impact of competency-based selection on job or organizational performance.

Only 68 articles looked at the current practices in competency modelling from a scientific or applied perspective. The reliability and validity of competency models used in selection must be established. Both Rodriguez et al.[135] and Catano et al.[136] provide similar procedures that can be used to build in reliability and validity to a competency model. Both studies showed how ratings of frequency and criticality by supervisors and incumbents could be built into a competency model followed by validation against supervisor measures of performance and assessment of inter-rater reliability. As well, Bonder and his colleagues[137] describe how Service Canada developed a competency-based framework that incorporated into the competency model information obtained through job analysis, particularly information on KSAOs. Keep in mind the criticisms of Harvey[138,139] that without knowing something about the tasks associated with a position, the inferences of competencies, or KSAOs, in a holistic fashion will produce less reliable data. More research, however, is needed on defining the psychometric properties of competency models particularly in the use of selection and promotion. More consideration must be given to the role that training of raters plays in enhancing reliability and validity as well as the nature of the competencies that are rated. Is the reliability and validity of inferences based on narrow, behaviourally based competencies better than that for broad strategic ones? These questions remain to be answered.

COMPETENCY MODELLING VERSUS JOB ANALYSIS

Concern over the increasing use of competency models led the Professional Practice Committee and the Scientific Affairs Committee of the Society for Industrial and Organizational Psychology to form the Job Analysis and Competency Modeling Task Force. The task force, which was composed of advocates of both traditional job analysis and competency-based procedures, identified 10 technical criteria on which it evaluated both approaches. Job analysis was judged superior on 9 of the 10 criteria. The only criterion where competency modelling was seen to have an edge was with respect to a more transparent linkage between business goals or strategies and the information provided by the competency-based approach. In all other instances, both proponents of job analysis and competency modelling rated the traditional job analysis methods as more rigorous, particularly in providing more reliable information.[140]

The task force also identified other, less technical criteria and concluded that competency approaches were more likely to focus on generic personal characteristics that are common across a broad range of jobs. It viewed competency approaches as being closely aligned with worker-oriented job analyses. The emphasis on these types of characteristics gave competency modelling higher levels of "face validity" with organizational decision makers. Executives typically commented that competencies provided them with a common language. As organizations continue to "de-complicate" business processes, the increased face validity of competency modelling procedures and their focus on core competencies holds wide appeal. However, these factors have resulted in decreased quality of the technical information needed for legal defensibility purposes.[141]

More recently, Sanchez and Levine[142] compared traditional job analyses and competency models along six dimensions which are shown in Table 4.5. These comparisons help to differentiate the two methodologies. Each method has its strengths and weaknesses. They should be viewed as being complementary to one another, with each providing unique information about jobs. Bonder[143] and his colleagues make the point that even though competencies may seem to be the primary focus of many organizations, job analysis is still important because it provides an objective picture of the job, not the person performing the job, and provides fundamental information to support HR functions such as recruitment and selection, among others.

TABLE 4.5

A COMPARISON OF JOB ANALYSIS AND COMPETENCY MODELLING

DIMENSION	JOB ANALYSIS	COMPETENCY MODELLING
Primary purpose	To better understand work assignments.	To influence how work assignments align with an organization's strategy.
View of job	The essential elements of a job do not change from one job incumbent to another.	A job is a role to be interpreted and then enacted by each job incumbent.
Focus	The focus of job analysis is solely on the job.	Competency modelling cuts across jobs and places value on common behavioural themes.
Time orientation	Job analysis provides a descriptive, objective account of work activities and associated job requirements.	Competency models prescribe the manner in which work activities should be carried out in alignment with an organization's strategy.
Performance level	Job analysis is based on typical job performance described in a job description as performed by an average worker.	Competency models are based on maximal performance as reflected in a strategic interpretation of the job that identifies behaviours related to strategic themes.
Measurement approach	Job analysis captures sound, unitary constructs that define job performance and lend themselves to quantitative measurement.	Competency models capture "fuzzy," multiple constructs that are best suited to global, clinical judgments.

A GENERIC COMPETENCY FRAMEWORK

Bartram[144] analyzed 29 competency studies through a meta-analysis. He presented a model of performance that was based on eight broad competency factors. The eight factors were based on analyses of self-ratings and manager ratings of workplace performance. The "Great Eight" factors aggregate 112 sub-competencies. These eight generic factors and their definitions are presented in Table 4.6, along with likely predictors of those competencies.

Much more work must be done toward specifying the predictors of these eight competencies. It is most likely that there will be several different predictors for each competency. Practitioners must be prepared to use a variety of selection tools to capture the essence of work-related behaviours. Bartram[145] argues that practitioners need to remember why we measure different characteristics: performance at work and the outcomes of that performance. In the next chapter, we will examine different models of performance and ways of measuring performance.

TABLE 4.6

"GREAT EIGHT" COMPETENCIES AND THEIR DEFINITIONS AND LIKELY PREDICTORS

FACTOR	COMPETENCY	COMPETENCY DEFINITION	PREDICTOR
1	Leading and deciding	• Takes control and exercises leadership • Initiates action, gives direction, and takes responsibility	Need for power and control, extraversion
2	Supporting and cooperating	• Supports others and shows respect and positive regard for them in social situations • Puts people first, working effectively with individuals and teams, clients, and staff • Behaves consistently with clear personal values that complement those of the organization	Agreeableness
3	Interacting and presenting	• Communicates and networks effectively • Successfully persuades and influences others • Relates to others in a confident, relaxed manner	Extraversion, general mental ability
4	Analyzing and interpreting	• Shows evidence of clear analytical thinking • Gets to the heart of complex problems and issues • Applies own expertise effectively • Quickly takes on new technology • Communicates well in writing	General mental ability, openness to new experiences
5	Creating and conceptualizing	• Works well in situations requiring openness to new ideas and experiences • Seeks out learning opportunities • Handles situations and problems with innovation and creativity • Thinks broadly and strategically • Supports and drives organizational change	Openness to new experiences, general mental ability
6	Organizing and executing	• Plans ahead and works in a systematic and organized way • Follows directions and procedures • Focuses on customer satisfaction and delivers a quality service or product to the agreed standards	Conscientiousness, general mental ability
7	Adapting and coping	• Adapts and responds well to change • Manages pressure effectively and copes well with setbacks	Emotional stability
8	Enterprising and performing	• Focuses on results and achieving personal work objectives • Works best when work is related closely to results and the impact of personal efforts is obvious • Shows an understanding of business, commerce, and finance • Seeks opportunities for self-development and career advancement	Need for achievement, negative agreeableness

Source: D. Bartram. 2005. "The Great Eight Competencies: A Criterion-Centric Approach to Validation," Table 1. *Journal of Applied Psychology*, 90, 1185–1203. American Psychological Association. Reprinted with permission.

LEADERSHIP COMPETENCY MODELS

Leadership competencies are one of the fastest growing areas in competency modelling. Leadership competencies contribute to superior performance on the part of those leading organizations in both the private and public sectors. The Canadian government as well as provinces of British Columbia, Saskatchewan, and Nova Scotia have all developed competency models for their senior executives. IBM, PepsiCo, and 3M have developed their own customized leadership competency models, as have many other private companies. The leadership competency model is based on the company's strategic vision and business goals. The competency model identifies the relevant competencies along with a definition of each. The number of leadership competencies ranges from as few as four to as many as 67. The norm seems to be 8 to 10 competencies.

It is impossible to list all the competencies that have been identified as leadership competencies. To give you an idea of what leadership competencies are we reviewed different sets of leadership competencies. The following appear to be common among the different government and private organizational leadership competency models. In some models components of the competencies are cited as separate competencies. We have integrated them to what we believe are the essential eight leadership competencies and recognize that there will be differences of opinion on this.

1. **Integrity and Ethics**–Serving with respect; being honest; ensures integrity in personal and organizational practices. Builds a respectful workplace. This is the basis for other leadership competencies.
2. **Strategic Thinking**–Visioning the future and building plans and making decisions to get there. Aligns program policy with the strategic direction of the organization.
3. **Engagement**–Showing passion for the job. They engage people, organizations, and partners in developing goals, executing plans, and in delivering results. They follow and lead across boundaries to engage broad-based stakeholders, partners, and constituencies in a shared agenda and strategy.
4. **Innovation**–Thinks creatively; is open to new ideas and technologies. Champions organizational change. Is flexible and adaptable in meeting changing demands of clients, stakeholders, and public.
5. **Accountability**–Accepts and creates a culture of accountability; fosters personal growth; takes personal ownership and inspires others to do the same. Is self-aware and demonstrates a commitment to ongoing learning and development.
6. **Building the Organizational Team**–Recognizes that the leader alone cannot get the job done; surrounds self with excellent talent. Builds successful relationships with individuals, staff stakeholders, and partners.
7. **Effective Communication**–Fosters open communication, listens to others, speaks effectively, and prepares written communication so that messages are clearly understood.
8. **Results Focus**–Action-oriented. Maximizes organizational effectiveness and sustainability. Aligns people, work, and systems with the business strategy to harmonize what they do and how they work to meet organizational objectives. Responsible for human and financial resources.

The primary benefit of leadership competencies is that they communicate a view of leadership to the public in terms that can be easily understood. They provide a unifying mechanism for leadership at all levels of the organization. As is the case with any competency, profiles are developed that identify the behaviours needed at different leadership levels. Leadership competencies, to be useful and defensible, must meet the same standards we have discussed that apply to any competency model.

// SUMMARY

This chapter began with a discussion of job analysis and its relevance to employee recruitment and selection, continued with a discussion of several job analysis methodologies, and ended with an introduction to competency-based models as alternatives to job analysis. As the workplace rapidly changes with the introduction of new technologies and global competition, HR practitioners will need to combine organizational and job analysis techniques to develop employee selection programs that lead to the selection and hiring of the best job candidates. At the organizational level, objectives for success are defined relative to delivery of products or services to paying customers. At the job level, the analyst describes collections of positions that are similar in their significant duties, which when taken together contribute to process outputs. Job analysts must link job requirements to organization functioning to optimize recruitment and selection systems.

Job analysis is a process of collecting information about jobs and encompasses many methods, which fall into two broad categories: work-oriented and worker-oriented methods. Work-oriented methods result in specific descriptions of work outcomes and tasks performed to accomplish them. Worker-oriented methods produce descriptions of worker traits and characteristics necessary for successful performance. There is no one right way of conducting a job analysis; all methods follow a logical process for defining employment or worker specifications (KSAOs). While job analysis is not a legal requirement for determining KSAOs and selecting employees, the employer must demonstrate job-relatedness of selection criteria if challenged in court.

Regardless of the method used, a good job analysis begins with collection of background information. Gathering job descriptions defined in the NOC or O*NET is a recommended first step. It is also good practice for the analyst to employ a combination of methods, typically beginning with interviews or observations of employees on the job. The resulting information can then be used to construct a task inventory or provide a backdrop for completing structured questionnaires. Employment specifications are generated by identifying the most frequently occurring activities or requirements in interviews and observations or by identifying those items in an inventory or questionnaire receiving the highest ratings of criticality.

A wide variety of techniques are available for analyzing jobs. While some focus primarily on the work that gets done, others focus on generic human behaviours that are relevant to all work. Deciding which of these techniques to use is based on the goal of the analysis, the resources available to the analyst, and the needs of the organization. No one method will be completely acceptable for all selection needs in an organization. Job analysts must themselves be adaptable in the methods they apply. Recruitment and Selection Notebook 4.10 presents a list of job analysis resources available on the Internet.

Organizations that compete in a global environment that is often unpredictable and unstable have to change quickly in order to survive. To meet these demands, some organizations are placing more emphasis on the competencies of individual workers rather than on the specific tasks that those workers will perform. These organizations expect all employees to possess core competencies that are related to the organization's mission or goals, as well as functional and job-specific competencies, which are related to successful performance in a position or job. This emphasis on competencies has taken place in the absence of an agreed-upon definition of what constitutes a "competency" and of an agreed-upon methodology for identifying competencies. In several respects, competency-based systems are similar to worker-trait job analysis methods in providing information about the KSAOs and behaviours needed for successful job performance, but without identifying the tasks that workers are required to do in their jobs.

Competency-based systems must provide information that is valid and meets legal requirements, just as more traditional job analysis methods must. The chapter provides several guidelines that should help in choosing job analysis or competency-based methods to identify KSAOs. In deciding between the two approaches, competency-based models may "speak the language of business" but they may provide technically inferior information. HR practitioners must decide which of these factors is most relevant to their situation.

RECRUITMENT AND SELECTION NOTEBOOK 4.10

JOB ANALYSIS ON THE INTERNET

These Web addresses provide useful resources to help students and professionals learn about and conduct job analyses. The sites provide information on job analysis methods and their uses, along with links to other relevant sites. The most comprehensive site, HR-Guide.com, also provides links for users to research legal issues, tips for conducting job analyses, and FAQs, along with up-to-date descriptions of commonly used interview, observation, and structured questionnaire methods. Official websites for the NOC, DOT, and O*NET are sources of standard occupational dictionaries and employment specifications. The NOC site, for example, contains a search engine enabling the user to retrieve information by searching job titles, aptitudes, interests, and other work characteristics. Sites for specific job analysis tools enable users to review the tools and learn about their applications, scoring, and commercially available services.

General Information Sites

HR Guide.com contains links to Web-based resources for HR professionals and students	http://www.hr-guide.com/jobanalysis.htm
Harvey's Job Analysis & Personality Research Site	http://harvey.psyc.vt.edu
HR Zone	http://www.hrzone.com

Sites for Job Classification Systems

NOC	http://www.esdc.gc.ca/eng/jobs/lmi/noc
O*NET	http://online.onetcenter.org

Sites for Job Analysis Tools

PAQ	http://www.paq.com
F-JAS	http://www.managementresearchinstitute.com/f-jas.aspx
CMQ	http://commonmetric.com
WPS	http://www.shl.com
Job-Analysis.net	http://www.job-analysis.net

KEY TERMS

Competencies, p. 151
Competency dictionary, p. 153
Competency framework, p. 152
Competency model, p. 152
Competency profile, p. 156
Core competencies, p. 153
Functional competencies, p. 153
Job, p. 115
Job description, p. 115
Job family, p. 115
Job specification, p. 115
Job-specific competencies, p. 153
Position, p. 115
Proficiency level, p. 154
Proficiency scale, p. 155
Subject-matter experts (SMEs), p. 116
Task inventories, p. 133
Task statement, p. 129
Worker-oriented job analysis, p. 123
Worker traits inventories, p. 140
Work-oriented job analysis, p. 123

WEB LINKS

The CCHRA website is at
http://www.chrp.ca

The National Occupational Classification (NOC) system can be accessed at
http://www.esdc.gc.ca/eng/jobs/lmi/noc

The DOT is available at
http://www.oalj.dol.gov/libdot.htm

O*NET can be accessed at
http://online.onetcenter.org

Additional PAQ information can be found at
http://www.paq.com

For more information about the CMQ, go to
http://commonmetric.com

More information about the WPS can be found at
http://www.shl.com

DISCUSSION QUESTIONS

1. Why is a job analysis essential to the defence of any selection process or selection system?

2. What is the difference between a job analysis and a job evaluation? Can different jobs be equated? Are the "compensable" factors the best way of equating jobs?
3. What is the relationship of a "position" to a "job" and a "job" to a "job family"?
4. Why do some researchers argue that worker traits inventories are not job analysis techniques?
5. What are the major differences between a competency-based selection system and one developed through job analysis?
6. What is a competency? Defend your answer.
7. Discuss why you might not wish to fly in an airplane if the pilot were selected on the basis of only core competencies.
8. What is the difference or similarity between a proficiency level and a skill?

EXERCISES

1. (*Note:* You must identify the position you will be analyzing before using the *Position Description Questionnaire Program*.) Develop a questionnaire using the online *Position Description Questionnaire Program* located at http://www.job-analysis.net/G908.htm. Use the questionnaire you develop to interview a job incumbent or supervisor. You may choose to interview a parent or sibling about his or her work, a coworker or supervisor from your workplace, or a classmate. Make careful notes during the interview in the spaces provided. Submit your completed questionnaire for review.
2. Use the interview protocol in this chapter to conduct a job analysis. Select a job for which you can find three or more incumbents willing to provide job analysis data. These may be jobs held by family, friends, or classmates. Conduct the analysis and provide a summary report that includes a list of task statements and describes the requisite abilities for your chosen job.
3. Catano and Harvey identified nine competencies related to teaching through use of the critical incident technique. Either as a class as a whole or in groups of five, generate as many critical incidents as you can about teaching performance. Keep in mind that you are focusing on teaching only, and not other aspects of a professor's or instructor's duties, such as research or administration activities. Sort your critical incidents into categories or competencies. Compare the competencies your class or group has identified with those identified by Catano and Harvey. (*Note:* This exercise can be carried out for any occupation, but teaching is used since it is an occupation with which all students will have some familiarity. Other occupations, such as doctor or dentist, may be substituted.)
   a. If several groups have completed the exercise, compare the labels each has assigned to their competencies. Are the groups using different labels for the same set of behaviours? Are they different from those used by Catano and Harvey?
   b. Specify the KSAOs that are critical to successful teaching performance.
   c. Develop a competency profile for a superior teacher.
4. Job analysis is useful for describing many job types, even those that you know well and can describe objectively.
   a. Identify a job that you are familiar with and list the tasks associated with it. Now, using the O*NET website, search the job title and compare the task inventory listed there to the one that you wrote down.

b. How does O*NET function as an SME?

c. What are the benefits to using the O*NET database as opposed to conducting a full-scale job analysis? What are the costs?

5. Can you place the leadership competencies described in the text into the "Great Eight" competencies identified by Bartram? Which ones, if any, don't fit Bartram's model?

CASE

Root of the Problem Landscaping is a small yard-maintenance company that got its start in 2006. The company specializes in small-scale operations, including installing and maintaining flower beds, ponds, hedges, and lawns. The company employs five site supervisors and approximately 30 groundskeepers. The owner, Daniel Black, is himself involved in the work performed at most sites and is the sole negotiator of terms with clients.

Originally serving only Halifax, Nova Scotia, the company has grown to accommodate clients as far away as the Moncton, New Brunswick, area. Now in its third season of operation, however, Black has noticed a decline in his company's rate of growth because the gains associated with opportunities afforded by new clients have been offset by the loss of older ones and also because he is having difficulty maintaining lasting employer–employee relationships.

You have been hired on a consulting contract by Root of the Problem Landscaping to investigate why business growth has stalled. You begin by interviewing Black and his site supervisors to establish what, if any, customer feedback they have received, to find out what qualifications both Black and the supervisors have, and to investigate the state of employment satisfaction.

Some negative customer feedback is associated with lack of knowledge and skills on the part of both the supervisors and the groundskeepers. Clients have noted that there have been instances where flowers have been removed that should not have been and weeds have gone unnoticed. In addition, there have been some instances where trees and shrubs were not properly planted and cared for. There has been a lack of attention paid to sun/shade and/or depth considerations, so some plants did not survive the winter. Most negative feedback that has resulted in a lack of repeat business is associated with job sites where Black had little or no involvement in the actual landscaping.

You notice a tendency for Black to attribute customer dissatisfaction to the customers' own personality flaws as opposed to anything his company may be doing wrong. The supervisors can provide little or no additional information because, as instructed by Black, they rarely communicate with clients.

Your interview with Black has revealed that he has extensive knowledge and skills associated with landscaping as a result of a lifetime of hands-on experience. He is also passionate about his work. You also notice that he doesn't know where his knowledge came from and sometimes thinks specialized knowledge that he has should be common sense to others.

Black's employees have limited knowledge of landscaping compared to Black's knowledge, and what they have seems to have been gained by learning on the job with Root of the Problem Landscaping. You have noticed that many of the employees seem to be dissatisfied with their workplace environment, and some report that they find Black to be unprofessional and inconsiderate as an employer. Jobs are often interrupted or delayed because of a lack of proper inventory procedures, resulting in frequent trips to hardware stores, etc.

You notice some employees having difficulty with lifting tasks and the operating of machinery. Some employees are working with two gloves and others with only one or none. Some employees seem to be suffering from aches and pains, and you can see bad sunburns on their bodies because of a lack of sunscreen use. Some older and less agile employees seem to be attempting physically demanding tasks while the younger, fitter employees are engaged in less strenuous activity.

You have been observing Root of the Problem Landscaping both when Black is there and when he is not. When Black is present, the job seems to get done, but you notice he often has to go back and work on tasks that were not completed properly by his employees. When fixing a problem, he tends to complain to the employees but does not instruct them on how to do it properly in the future. You observe instances where Black is unduly harsh in his criticisms of the employees and seems to lack some people skills. There is evidence that the employees do not have respect for Black and his business when you observe them "cutting corners" on the job when he is absent.

QUESTIONS

1. If Black had conducted a job analysis prior to employee selection, how might his company have benefited? Include considerations of employer, employees, and clients.
2. Using the O*NET website, if you type "landscaper" into the space provided for the occupational quick search, a list of job titles appears. Select the "first-line supervisors/managers of landscaping" job title and review the knowledge, skills, and abilities listed. Which of these does Black currently possess? Which of these is he lacking? What about the employees?

// ENDNOTES

1 Pearlman, K., and J.I. Sanchez. 2010. "Work Analysis." In J.L. Farr and N.T. Tippins, eds., *Handbook of Employee Selection* (pp. 73–98). Routledge.

2 Morgeson, F.P., and E.C. Dierdorff. 2010. "Work Analysis: From Technique to Theory." In S. Zedeck, ed., *APA Handbook of Industrial and Organizational Psychology. Vol. 2: Selecting and Developing Members for the Organization* (pp. 3–41). Washington, DC: American Psychological Association.

3 Wilson, M.A., W. Bennett, Jr., S.G. Gibson, and G.M. Alliger. 2012. *The Handbook of Work Analysis: Methods, Systems, Applications and Science of Work Measurement in Organizations.* New York: Routledge/Taylor & Francis Group.

4 Sackett, P.R., and R.M. Laczo. 2003. "Job and Work Analysis." In W.C. Borman, D.R. Ilgen, and R.J. Klimoski, eds., *Handbook of Psychology,* Vol. 12 (pp. 21–38). Hoboken, NJ: John Wiley and Sons.

5 Levine, E.L., R.A. Ash, and N. Bennett. 1980. "Exploratory Comparative Study of Four Job Analysis Methods." *Journal of Applied Psychology* 65: 524–35.

6 Harvey, R.J. 1991. "Job Analysis." In M.D. Dunnette and L.M. Hough, eds., *Handbook of Industrial and Organizational Psychology,* Vol. I (pp. 71–163). Palo Alto, CA: Consulting Psychologists Press.

7 Dierdorff, E.C., and M.A. Wilson. 2003. "A Meta-Analysis of Job Analysis Reliability." *Journal of Applied Psychology* 88: 635–46.

8 Thompson, D.E., and T.A. Thompson. 1982. "Court Standards for Job Analysis in Test Validation." *Personnel Psychology* 35: 872–73.

9 Sparks, C.P. 1988. "Legal Basis for Job Analysis." In S. Gael, ed., *The Job Analysis Handbook for Business, Industry and Government*, Vol. I (pp. 37–47). New York: John Wiley and Sons.

10 Harvey, R.J., 1991.

11 Ash, R.A., 1988.

12 Levine, E.L., J.N. Thomas, and F. Sistrunk. 1988. "Selecting a Job Analysis Approach." In S. Gael, ed., *The Job Analysis Handbook for Business, Industry and Government*, Vol. I (pp. 339–52). New York: John Wiley and Sons.

13 *Uniform Guidelines on Employee Selection Procedures.* 1978. Federal Register 43: 38290–39315.

14 Levine, E.L. 1983. *Everything You Always Wanted to Know About Job Analysis.* Tampa, FL: Mariner Publishing Company.

15 Sparks, C.P. 1988.

16 Cronshaw, S.F. 1988. "Future Directions for Industrial Psychology in Canada." *Canadian Psychology* 29: 30–43.

17 Latham, G.P., and C. Sue-Chan. 1998. "Selecting Employees in the 21st Century: Predicting the Contribution of I-O Psychology to Canada." *Canadian Psychology* 39: 14–22.

18 Latham, G.P. 2001. "Minimizing Legal Challenges to Hiring and Promotion Decisions." http://www.hr.com/en/communities/human_resources_management/minimizing-legal-challenges-to-hiring-and-promotio_eacukgay.html. © Copyright 2014 HR.COM Limited. All rights reserved.

19 Harvey, R.J. 1991.

20 Ibid.

21 Peterson, N.G., and P.R. Jeanneret. 2007. "Job Analysis: An Overview and Description of Deductive Methods." In D.L. Whetzel and G.R. Wheaton, eds., *Applied Measurement: Industrial Psychology in Human Resources Management* (pp. 13–56). Mahwah, NJ: Lawrence Erlbaum Associates.

22 Peterson, N.G., and P.R. Jeanneret. 2007.

23 McCormick, E.J. 1979. *Job Analysis: Methods and Applications.* New York: AMACOM.

24 Human Resources and Skills Development Canada. "About the NOC." http://www5.hrsdc.gc.ca/noc/english/noc/2011/aboutnoc.aspx

25 Employment and Immigration Canada. 1989. *Canadian Classification and Dictionary of Occupations Guide.* Ottawa: Canadian Government Publishing.

26 *Dictionary of Occupational Titles (DOT).* Washington, DC: U.S. Department of Commerce: http://www.oalj.dol.gov/libdot.htm

27 Human Resources and Skills Development Canada. "About the NOC." http://www5.hrsdc.gc.ca/noc/english/noc/2006/aboutnoc.aspx

28 DOL Office of Policy and Research. 2000. "O*NET Project." http://www.doleta.gov/programs/ONet

29 O*NET Resource Centre. "The O*NET Content Model." http://www.onetcenter.org/content.html

30 Peterson, N.G., M.D. Mumford, W.C. Borman, P.R. Jeanneret, E.A. Fleishman, K.Y. Levin, M.A. Campion, M.S. Mayfield, F.P. Morgeson, K. Pearlman, M.K. Kowing, A.R. Lancaster, M.B. Silver, and D.M. Dye. 2001. "Understanding Work Using the Occupational Information Network (O*NET): Implications for Practice and Research." *Personnel Psychology* 54: 451–91.

31 Gael, S. 1988. "Interviews, Questionnaires, and Checklists." In S. Gael, ed., *The Job Analysis Handbook for Business, Industry and Government*, Vol. I (pp. 391–418). New York: John Wiley and Sons.

32 Cascio, W.F. 1998. *Applied Psychology in Human Resources Management.* 5th ed. Toronto: Prentice Hall Canada.

33 Harvey, R.J. 1991.

34 Peterson, N.G., and P.R. Jeanneret. 2007. "Job Analysis: An Overview and Description of Deductive Methods." In D.L. Whetzel and G.R. Wheaton, eds., *Applied Measurement: Industrial Psychology in Human Resources Management* (pp. 13–56). Mahwah, NJ: Lawrence Erlbaum Associates.

35 Harvey, R.J. 1991.

36 McCormick, E.J. 1979. *Job Analysis: Methods and Applications.* New York: AMACOM.

37 McCormick, E.J., P.R. Jeanneret, and R.C. Mecham. 1972. "A Study of Job Characteristics and Job Dimensions as Based on the Position Analysis Questionnaire (PAQ)." *Journal of Applied Psychology* 56: 347–67.

38 McCormick, E.J., P.R. Jeanneret, and R.C. Mecham. 1972.

39 Ibid.

40 Gael, S. 1983. *Job Analysis: A Guide to Assessing Work Activities.* San Francisco, CA: Jossey-Bass.

41 Ghorpade, J.V. 1988. *Job Analysis: A Handbook for the Human Resource Director.* Englewood Cliffs, NJ: Prentice Hall.

42 McCormick, E.J., and P.R. Jeanneret. 1991. "Position Analysis Questionnaire (PAQ)." In S. Gael, ed., *The Job Analysis Handbook for Business, Industry and Government*, Vol. II (pp. 825–42). New York: John Wiley and Sons.

43 McCormick, E.J., P.R. Jeanneret, and R.C. Mecham. 1972.

44 Harvey, R.J. 1991.

45 McCormick, E.J. 1979.

46 McCormick, E.J., and P.R. Jeanneret. 1991.

47 McCormick, E.J., P.R. Jeanneret, and R.C. Mecham. 1972.

48 Gael, S. 1983.

49 Gael, S. 1988.

50 Whetzel, D.L., L.E. Baranowski, J.M. Petro, P.J. Curtin, and J.L. Fisher. 2003. "A Written Structured Interview by Any Other Name Is Still a Selection Instrument." *Applied HRM. Research* 8: 1–16.

51 McCormick, E.J. 1979.

52 Fine, S.A., and S.F. Cronshaw. 1999. *Functional Job Analysis: A Foundation for Human Resources Management.* Mahwah, NJ: Lawrence Erlbaum and Associates.

53 Gael, S. 1988.

54 Gatewood, R.D., H.S. Feild, and M. Barrick. 2008. *Human Resources Selection.* Mason, OH: Thomson/South-Western.

55 Levine, E.L. 1983.

56 Gael, S. 1988.

57 Ghorpade, J.V. 1988.

58 Cascio, W.F. 1998.

59 Martinko, M.J. 1988. "Observing the Work." In S. Gael, ed., *The Job Analysis Handbook for Business, Industry and Government*, Vol. I (pp. 419–31). New York: John Wiley and Sons.

60 Martinko, M.J. 1988.

61 Cascio, W.F. 1998.

62 Ibid.

63 Martinko, M.J. 1988.

64 McPhail, S.M., P.R. Jeanneret, E.J. McCormick, and R.C. Mecham. 1991. *Position Analysis Questionnaire: Job Analysis Manual.* Rev. ed. Palo Alto, CA: Consulting Psychologists Press.

65 Martinko, M.J. 1988.

66 Harvey, R.J. 1991.

67 Martinko, M.J. 1988.

68 Ibid.

69 Gatewood, R.D., H.S. Feild, and M. Barrick. 2008.

70 Tenopyr, M.L. 1977. "Content-Construct Confusion." *Personnel Psychology* 30: 47–54.

71 McCormick, E.J., P.R. Jeanneret, and R.C. Mecham. 1989. *Position Analysis Questionnaire.* Palo Alto, CA: Consulting Psychologists Press, Inc.

72 Harvey, J.L., L.E. Anderson, L.E Baranowski, and R. Morath. 2007. "Job Analysis: Gathering Job-Specific Information." In D.L. Whetzel and G.R. Wheaton, eds., *Applied Measurement: Industrial Psychology in Human Resources Management* (pp. 57–96). Mahwah, NJ: Lawrence Erlbaum Associates.

73 Fine, S.A., and S.F. Cronshaw. 1999.

74 Ibid.

75 Christal, R.E., and J.J. Weissmuller. 1988. "Job-Task Inventory Analysis." In S. Gael, ed., *The Job Analysis Handbook for Business, Industry and Government*, Vol. II (pp. 1036–50). New York: John Wiley and Sons.

76 Drauden, G.M. 1988. "Task Inventory Analysis in Industry and the Public Sector." In S. Gael, ed., *The Job Analysis Handbook for Business, Industry and Government*, Vol. II (pp. 1051–71). New York: John Wiley and Sons.

77 Levine, E.L., R.A. Ash, H. Hall, and F. Sistrunk. 1983. "Evaluation of Job Analysis Methods by Experienced Job Analysts." *Academy of Management Journal* 26: 339–48.

78 McCormick, E.J., and P.R. Jeanneret. 1991.

79 Fine, S.A. 1988. "Functional Job Analysis." In S. Gael, ed., *The Job Analysis Handbook for Business, Industry and Government*, Vol. II (pp. 1019–35). New York: John Wiley and Sons.

80 Fine, S.A., and S.F. Cronshaw. 1999.

81 Fine, S.A., and M. Getkate. 1995. *Benchmark Tasks for Job Analysis: A Guide for Functional Job Analysis (FJOB ANALYSIS) Scales.* Mahwah, NJ: Lawrence Erlbaum Associates.

82 Gatewood, R.D., H.S. Feild, and M. Barrick. 2008.

83 Bownas, D.A., and H.J. Bernardin. 1988. "Critical Incident Technique." In S. Gael, ed., *The Job Analysis Handbook for Business, Industry and Government*, Vol. II (pp. 1120–37). New York: John Wiley and Sons.

84 Harvey, J.L., L.E. Anderson, L.E Baranowski, and R. Morath. 2007.

85 Flanagan, J.C. 1954. "The Critical Incident Technique." *Psychological Bulletin* 51: 327–58.

86 Catano, V.M., and S. Harvey. 2011. "Student Perception of Teaching Effectiveness: Development and Validation of the Evaluation of Teaching Competencies Scale (ETCS)." Assessment and Evaluation in Higher Education 36: 701–717. doi:10.1080/02602938.2010.484879

87 Pearlman, K., and J.I. Sanchez. 2010.

88 McCormick, E.J., P.R. Jeanneret, and R.C. Mecham. 1989.

89 McPhail, S.M., P.R. Jeanneret, E.J. McCormick, and R.C. Mecham. 1991.

90 Levine, E.L., R.A. Ash, and N. Bennett. 1980.

91 Harvey, R.J. 1991.

92 Fleishman, E.A., and M.E. Reilly. 1992. *Handbook of Human Abilities: Definitions, Measurements, and Job Task Requirements*. Potomac, MD: Management Research Institute.

93 Fleishman, E.A., and M.D. Mumford. 1988. "Ability Requirement Scales." In S. Gael, ed., *The Job Analysis Handbook for Business, Industry and Government*, Vol. I (pp. 917–35). New York: John Wiley and Sons.

94 Fleishman, E.A., and M.K. Quaintance. 1984. *Taxonomies of Human Performance: The Description of Human Tasks*. Orlando, FL: Academic Press.

95 Caughron, J.J., M.D. Mumford, and E.A. Fleishman. 2012. "The Fleishman Job Analysis Survey: Development, Validation, and Applications." In M.A. Wilson, W.J. Bennett, S.G. Gibson, and G.M. Alliger, eds., *The Handbook of Work Analysis: Methods, Systems, Applications and Science of Work Measurement in Organizations* (pp. 231–246). New York: Routledge/Taylor & Francis Group.

96 Wilson, M.A., W.J. Bennett, S.G. Gibson, and G.M. Alliger. 2012.

97 Costanza, D.P., E.A. Fleishman, and J.C. Marshall-Mies. 1999. "Knowledges." In N.G. Peterson, M.D. Mumford, W.C. Borman, P.R. Jeanneret, and E.A. Fleishman, eds., *An Occupational Information System for the 21st Century: The Development of O*NET*. Washington, DC: American Psychological Association.

98 Fleishman, E.A., and M.E. Reilly. 1992.

99 Personnel Systems and Technologies Corporation. 2000. "The Common-Metric System." http://commonmetric.com

100 SHL Group. http://www.shl.com/SHL/americas/Products/Access_Competencies/Competency_Questionnaires/Competency_Questionnaires_List/WorkProfilingSystem.hm

101 Lopez, F.M. 1988. "Threshold Traits Analysis System." In S. Gael, ed., *The Job Analysis Handbook for Business, Industry and Government*, Vol. I (pp. 880–901). New York: John Wiley and Sons.

102 Schraagen, J. M., S.F. Chipman, and V.L. Shalin. 2000. *Cognitive Task Analysis.* Mahweh, NJ: Lawrence Erlbaum Associates.

103 Levine, E.L., R.A. Ash, H. Hall, and F. Sistrunk. 1983.

104 Dierdorff, E.C., and M.A. Wilson. 2003.

105 Ibid.

106 Sanchez, J.I., and Levine, E.L. 2000.

107 Levine, E.L., R.A. Ash, and N. Bennett. 1980.

108 Morgeson, F.P., and M.A. Campion. 2003. "Work Design." In W.C. Borman, C. Walter, D.R. Ilgen, and R.J. Klimoski, eds., *Handbook of Psychology: Industrial and Organizational Psychology*, Vol. 12 (pp. 423–52). Hoboken, NJ: John Wiley and Sons.

109 Harvey, R.J., and M.A. Wilson. 2000.

110 Thompson, D.E., and T.A. Thompson. 1982.

111 Peterson, N.G., and P.R. Jeanneret. 2007.

112 Greenbaum, P.J. 1996. "Canada's Hiring Trends: Where Will Canadian Jobs Come From in the Next Millennium?" *HR Today* (July). Ottawa: Canadian Institute of Professional Management.

113 Methot, L.L., and K. Phillips-Grant. 1998. "Technological Advances in the Canadian Workplace: An I-O Perspective." *Canadian Psychology* 39: 133–41.

114 Cascio, W.F. 1998.

115 Singh, P. 2008. "Job Analysis for a Changing Workplace." *Human Resource Management* 18: 87–99.

116 Stone, T.H., B.D. Webster, and S. Schoonover. 2013. "What Do We Know About Competency Modeling?" *International Journal of Selection and Assessment* 21: 334–338.

117 Boyatzis, R.E. 1982. *The Competent Manager: A Model of Effective Performance.* New York: John Wiley and Sons.

118 Stevens, G. 2012. "A Critical Review of the Science and Practice of Competency Modeling." *Human Resource Development Review* 12: 86–107.

119 Catano, V.M. 2002. "Competency-Based Selection and Performance Systems: Are They Defensible?" Summary. *Canadian Psychology* 43(2a): 145.

120 Reitsma, S.J. 1993. *The Canadian Corporate Response to Globalization.* Report No. 10693. Ottawa: Conference Board of Canada.

121 Mansfield, R.S. 1996. "Building Competency Models." *Human Resource Management* 35: 7–18.

122 Prahalad, C., and G. Hamel. 1990. "The Core Competence of the Corporation." *Harvard Business Review* (May–June): 79–91.

123 Lahti, R.K. 1999. "Identifying and Integrating Individual Level and Organizational Level Core Competencies." *Journal of Business and Psychology* 14: 59–75.

124 Trainor, N.L. 1997. "Five Levels of Competency." *Canadian HR Reporter* 10: 12–13.

125 Bonder, A., C.-D. Bouchard, and G. Bellemare. 2011. "Competency-Based Management–An Integrated Approach to Human Resource Management in the Canadian Public Sector." *Public Personnel Management* 40: 11–24.

126 Campion, M.A., A.A. Fink, B.J. Ruggerberg, L. Carr, G.M. Phillips, and R.B. Odman. 2011. "Doing Competencies Well: Best Practices in Competency Modelling." *Personnel Psychology* 64: 225–62.

127 Bonder, A. 2003. *A Blueprint for the Future: Competency-Based Management in HRDC*. Unpublished presentation, HRDC Canada.

128 Bonder, A. et al. 2011.

129 Campion, M.A. et al. 2011.

130 Stevens, G. 2012.

131 Sanchez, J.I., and E.L. Levine. 2009. "What Is (Or Should Be) the Difference between Competency Modeling and Traditional Job Analysis?" *Human Resource Management Review* 19: 53–63.

132 Stevens, G. 2012.

133 Campion M.A. et al. 2011.

134 Stevens, G. 2012.

135 Rodriguez, D., Patel, R., Bright, A., Gregory, D., and Gowing, M.K. 2002. "Developing Competency Models to Promote Integrated Human Resource Practices." *Human Resource Management* 41: 309–324.

136 Catano, V.M., W. Darr, and C.A. Campbell. 2007. "Performance Appraisal of Behavior-Based Competencies: A Reliable and Valid Procedure." *Personnel Psychology* 60: 201–230.

137 Bonder, A. et al. 2011.

138 Harvey, R.J. 1991.

139 Harvey, R.J., and M.A. Wilson. 2000.

140 Shippmann, J.S., R.A. Ash, M. Battista, L. Carr, L.D. Eyde, B. Hesketh, J. Kehoe, K. Pearlman, and E.P. Prien. 2000. "The Practice of Competency Modeling." *Personnel Psychology* 53: 703–40.

141 Shippmann, J.S. et al. 2000.

142 Sanchez, J.I., and Levine, E.L. 2009.

143 Bonder, A. et al. 2011.

144 Bartram, D. 2005. "The Great Eight Competencies: A Criterion-Centric Approach to Validation." *Journal of Applied Psychology* 90: 1185–1203.

145 Ibid.

CHAPTER 5

RECRUITMENT, SELECTION, AND JOB PERFORMANCE

CHAPTER LEARNING OUTCOMES

This chapter examines job-related performance as an integral part of the recruitment and selection process. Job performance is presented as a multidimensional construct that is composed of task, contextual, adaptive and counterproductive work behaviours. Each of these job-related behaviours is linked to factors that should be considered during recruitment and selection.

This chapter also discusses measures of job performance that may be used as criteria in validating selection systems. Criteria related to task, adaptive and contextual performance are used to "select in" job applicants while criteria related to counterproductive work behaviours are used to "select out" job applicants. Valid performance measures play an essential role in developing a defensible selection system. This chapter does not cover material on performance appraisal as that material is covered extensively in other HR courses; however, we present a brief overview of several types of performance appraisal systems.

AFTER READING THIS CHAPTER YOU SHOULD:

- appreciate the important role played by job performance in selection and assessment;
- be able to define the differences among task, contextual, adaptive, and counterproductive work behaviours;
- understand the different types of counterproductive work behaviours;
- be able to describe the importance of developing and using scientifically sound measures of job performance in selection and assessment;
- understand what constitutes acceptable criteria that may be used to assess performance;

- understand the relationship among individual performance measures, criteria, and performance dimensions related to a job; and
- appreciate the technical aspects of measuring job performance.

USING FACEBOOK TO MAKE HIRING DECISIONS

Organizations are increasingly using Facebook and other social networking websites (Twitter, LinkedIn, etc.) when recruiting and hiring employees. Over 90 percent of employers say they use some form of social networking when recruiting applicants, with nearly half to two-thirds of employers using Facebook during the recruiting process. And according to CareerBuilder, close to 40 percent of companies search applicant's Facebook or other social media profiles during the recruiting process. Employers use this information for a variety of reasons: to see if a candidate is qualified for the job, fits the company culture, and/or to look for possible reasons not a hire candidate. The use of Facebook or other social networking websites in the recruiting process is now pervasive, yet a key question remains: is this an effective way of recruiting candidates and can it predict whether an applicant will be successful on the job?

Recent research suggests that the answer to this question is a clear and resounding NO. A forthcoming study in the Journal of Management found that recruiter ratings of candidate Facebook profiles were not related to that candidate's actual performance on the job, nor to the candidate's turnover intentions – both of which are key outcomes generally tracked by recruiters. These researchers looked at a sample of undergraduate students who were on the job market and then had recruiters and HR managers assess each of the student's Facebook profiles along three dimensions: employability, intelligence, and job-related skills. One year later, the researchers followed up with the students and asked them to report their current employment status and whether they planned to stay at that job. At the same time, the researchers also contacted the employed students' current supervisor to get a rating of their performance on the job. Results revealed that none of the ratings of the Facebook profiles predicted supervisor-rated performance on the job, nor actual turnover, nor employee-reported turnover intentions.

The recruiter ratings of applicant's Facebook profiles were not only ineffective at predicting job performance, but they also suggested possible bias in using such ratings. Specifically, the researchers found that ratings of white applicants were significantly higher than ratings of African-Americans and Hispanics, and that ratings of women were significantly higher than ratings of men. The ethnicity and gender differences suggest the possibility of legal problems for employers that use Facebook to recruit candidates. A bias could be particularly damaging for recruiters, as organizations are responsible for demonstrating the validity of recruitment policies in situations in which adverse impact exists. And the results from the study suggest that establishing the validity of these practices could be difficult.

If using Facebook to recruit candidates isn't a valid way to predict performance on the job, are there other uses of this method in the recruitment process? One possibility is that employers use Facebook profiles to assess the personality of job candidates. Research from a sample of undergraduate students in the United States and Germany suggests that ratings of an individual's Facebook profile are accurate predictors of that individual's personality. The profiles, in other words, were not being used to project a glorified image of one's ideal self (i.e., an attempt to be a more socially desirable person). Facebook profile ratings were especially predictive of an individual's extraversion (e.g., sociability, gregariousness, assertiveness) and openness to experience (e.g., creativity, imagination, willingness to try new things). This suggests that Facebook profiles could be used in jobs in which these personality traits might be particularly relevant. Say, for a sales job where sociability is important (extraversion), or for jobs involving innovation or creativity (openness to experience).

In general, the results suggest that recruiters should be very hesitant to use Facebook and other social networking websites in the recruiting process. And while using Facebook profiles may provide a window into understanding an applicant's personality, given the potential privacy and legal ramifications, recruiters looking to assess personality should instead use validated personality inventories such as the Big 5 or the host of personality inventories used by consultants. As a first step, recruiters need to test and validate methods for using Facebook in the recruiting process to show that such methods can actually predict important outcomes such as job performance and turnover. At the very least, as the researchers of the Journal of Management study suggest, recruiters who use Facebook need to develop clear policies and methods for doing so.

As for potential job applicants, given the prominent use of Facebook by recruiters, you may want to block access to your Facebook profile (and most users don't), as a recruiter may find something unrelated to performance on the job that prevents you from getting hired.

// JOB PERFORMANCE

As the opening story shows, recruitment, selection, and job performance are inextricably linked. Recruiters must be attuned to job-related KSAOs and not act on "intuition" concerning which characteristics are important to job performance. The KSAOs must be reliable and valid and identified through the procedures outlined in the previous chapters; they must be capable of predicting actual job performance. We started out this book by presenting an overview of an HR system in Figure 1.1. We presented recruitment and selection as influenced by several variables including the mission, vision, and values of the organization. Recruitment and selection carried out properly, in conjunction with other organizational factors, lead to personnel who are competent, committed, and effective. We presented performance management as a feedback loop that allowed the organization to monitor the quality of employees who were being recruited and selected.

We continued this discussion in Chapter 2 by showing the necessity of evaluating performance as part of validating a selection system and the specific KSAOs that will be used to select employees. In Chapter 4 we examined different job analysis systems and competency models that could be used to identify those KSAOs and job-related aspects of performance. All HR staff personnel must have an understanding of the role that performance plays in developing valid recruitment and selection strategies, unless they are unconcerned about a total systems failure. Job performance and performance management are complex topics in and of themselves. Our goal in this chapter is to introduce the current thinking on performance measurement so that those working in HR may appreciate the need to measure performance as part of a recruitment and selection system. Selection is not simply interviewing and testing employees. The HR person must know that the selection tools being used are related to job performance, and that they are appropriate and valid measure of job performance.

To manage performance, organizations and companies must take job performance seriously. Performance measurement is a means to emphasize and reinforce an organization's core values in addition to identifying performance differences between employees. Performance measurement is used to transform companies into results-oriented organizations. It provides a means of identifying employees who need improvement and development.[1] Measuring performance is easier said than done. The organization, or its HR manager, must decide what performance to measure and the level of performance needed to attain organizational excellence.

Job performance
Behaviour (the observable things people do) that is relevant to accomplishing the goals of an organization.

Criteria
Measures of job performance that attempt to capture individual differences among employees with respect to job-related behaviours.

Job performance is behaviour–the observable things people do–that is relevant to accomplishing the goals of an organization. As we saw in Chapter 4, rarely if ever do jobs involve the performance of only one specific behaviour. Also, individuals may perform at different levels of proficiency across job-related tasks or competencies (see Chapter 4). Measures of job performance that attempt to capture these differences are called **criteria**.[2] They are the performance standards for judging success or failure on the job. Criteria also provide guidance on the standards that must be met by someone placed into a job. A lack of standards may lead to the selection of inappropriate job candidates.

Choosing a criterion or performance measure may be rather complex. Suppose you are a personnel selection officer in the Canadian Forces and are placed in charge of selecting military engineering officers. You are responsible for recruiting and selecting men and women who will perform successfully in places such as Afghanistan, Rwanda, Bosnia, and Somalia. Do you recruit and select people on the basis of their job-related technical skills, or do you also consider core competencies such as leadership, courage, loyalty, selflessness, and self-discipline? What, then, constitutes successful performance

© Bettmann/CORBIS

by a military engineer? What if someone is judged to be a success as a leader but a failure in the technical aspects of engineering, or vice versa? Are any of the competencies on which we select people more important than others? And what about self-discipline–how does that enter into the equation?

Job performance is a complex, multidimensional construct.[3,4] We can break job behaviour into four subcategories: **task performance**, **contextual performance**, **counterproductive work behaviours**,[5] and **adaptive performance**.[6] Previously adaptive behaviour was included as part of contextual performance; however, recent empirical evidence shows it to have different predictors than task or contextual behaviour.[7] Task performance includes the direct production of goods and services and direct contribution to the efficient functioning of the organization and is, perhaps, closest to traditional definitions of "job performance."[8] Task performance behaviours contribute to the core activities of an organization and include producing goods, selling merchandise, acquiring inventory, and managing and administering the enterprise.[9] Contextual performance is closely related to the notion of organizational citizenship behaviour.[10] Generally, contextual performance has included both interpersonal job performance and job dedication.[11,12] Contextual performance contributes to the culture and climate of the organization; it is the context in which the organization's core activities take place.[13] Employees who are proficient in job-related task and contextual behaviours lead to productive organizations.

Adaptive performance encompasses an employee's reaction to changes in the work environment and their role in the organization. It is the extent to which a worker is capable of adapting to changes in the workplace. It includes being capable of solving problems

Task performance
Duties related to the direct production of goods and services and to the direct contribution to the efficient functioning of the organization that form part of a job. These duties are part of the worker's formal job description.

Contextual performance
The activities or behaviours that are not part of a worker's formal job description but that remain important for organizational effectiveness.

Counterproductive work behaviours
Voluntary behaviours that violate significant organizational norms and in so doing threaten the well-being of an organization, its members, or both.

Adaptive Performance
A worker's behavioural reactions to changes in a work system or work role.

creatively, dealing with unpredictable work situations, learning new technologies and procedures, and adapting to other individuals, cultures, or physical surroundings.[14] Due to changing and dynamic work environments, the need for adaptive employees is extremely important.[15] Adaptive performance exists across many different types of jobs, although various names may be used to describe this dimension of job performance.

Counterproductive behaviour is in some sense the opposite of organizational citizenship, although the two are clearly distinct constructs.[16,17] Counterproductive work behaviours include both deviance and aggression.[18] Counterproductive behaviours on the part of/among employees lead to decreased performance and less productive organizations. The fundamental issue that an organization must address when it develops an integrated recruitment and selection system is which aspect or aspects of performance should drive recruitment and selection. How an organization answers this question determines whom the organization will recruit and hire. Obviously, organizations wish to be productive and to select into the organization those job applicants who possess job-related task and contextual behaviours and not to select those with counterproductive work behaviours.

Figure 5.1 presents these four types of job performance along with behavioural indicators for each dimension. We will consider each of these types with respect to how they influence recruitment and selection, and discuss the types of KSAOs that, based on the behavioural indicators, may predict each type of performance.

FIGURE 5.1

COMPONENTS OF INDIVIDUAL WORK PERFORMANCE

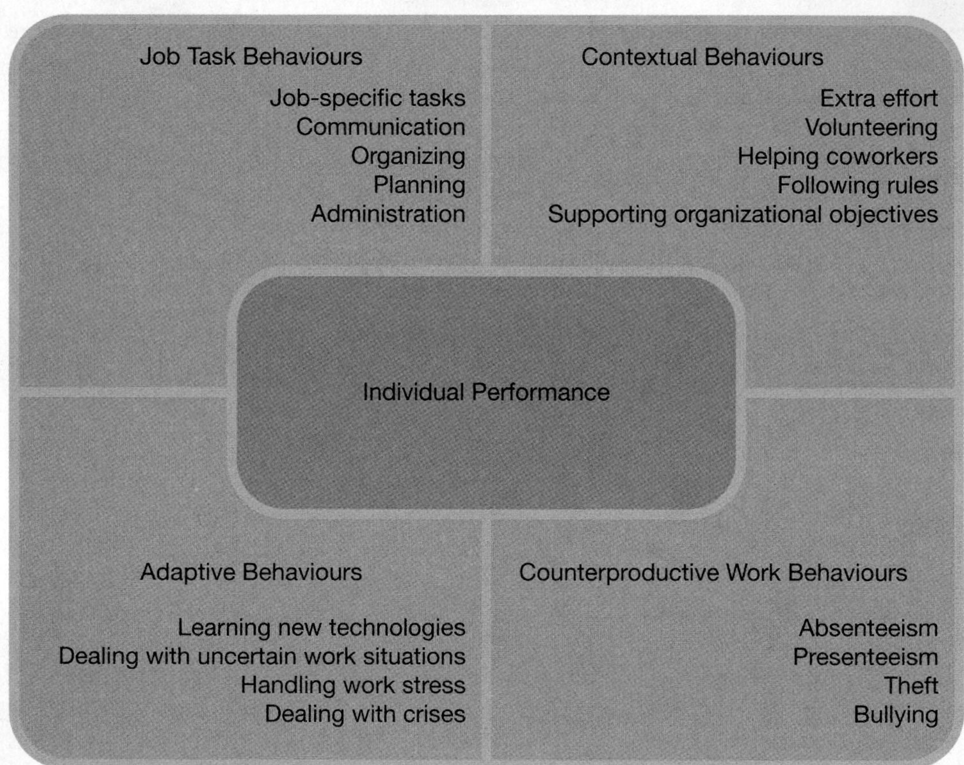

JOB PERFORMANCE AS A MULTIDIMENSIONAL CONCEPT

In the early part of the 20th century, job performance meant the performance of a set of tasks that were specifically related to a job. Job performance was synonymous with task performance. Over the past 30 years, definitions of job performance have broadened to include all activities or behaviours that may affect, positively or negatively, organizational effectiveness.[19,20] We should consider not only individual outputs for a specific set of job tasks, but also the contributions of those outputs to meeting the goals of the organization. Job performance depends on the specific job requirements as they relate to the goals of the organization and the value that the organization places on contextual factors such as teamwork and cooperation.[21,22]

Recently, a number of job performance models have argued for a multidimensional conceptualization of job performance that includes nontask behaviours that may be important to job success. Figure 5.2 presents an example of a possible **job performance domain** for an airplane pilot that is composed of task, contextual, adaptive, and counterproductive work behaviours. Job performance is behaviour (i.e., the observable things people do) that is related to accomplishing the goals of the organization, or the unit, in which a person works. The goals pursued by an organization are value judgments on the part of those empowered to make them. Goals are defined for employees who hold specific positions within the organization. Individual performance must contribute to achieving the organizational goals. The activities or behaviours needed to accomplish goals may vary considerably from job to job, or across levels in organizations. It becomes a matter of *expert* judgment whether particular actions or behaviours are relevant for particular goals. Performance is *not* the consequence or result of action; it is the action itself.[23]

Job performance domain
The set of job performance dimensions (i.e., behaviours) that is relevant to the goals of the organization, or the unit, in which a person works.

Performance dimensions
Sets of related behaviours that are derived from an organization's goals and linked to successful job performance.

PERFORMANCE DIMENSIONS

Job behaviours can be grouped into categories, called **performance dimensions**. Performance dimensions are sets of related behaviours that are derived from an

FIGURE 5.2

A JOB PERFORMANCE DOMAIN FOR AN AIRPLANE PILOT

Performance Domain—Air Pilot							
Job Task Behaviours			Contextual Behaviours		Adaptive Behaviours	Counter-productive Behaviours
Take-off and Landing	Navigation	Managing Air Crew	Mentors Junior Pilots	Promotes Safety Procedures	New Computer Flight System	Self-Discipline

organization's goals and linked to successful job performance. In Figure 5.2, a pilot must be capable of performing many job task behaviours. Some of these behaviours are related to taking off and landing an aircraft, another set of task behaviours might be related to navigating the plane from one location to another, while a third set of task behaviours are needed to manage and direct the flight crew under the pilot's command. The pilot performs all of these task behaviours within a specific organizational context that emphasizes senior pilots serving as mentors for their juniors and promoting safety rules and regulations. All of the pilot's behaviours directed at these last two dimensions may not be strictly necessary to flying an airplane, but they are valued job behaviours. Consider the very real situation where the pilot's company has recently changed the planes it flies. The new models have an increased level of computer technology that controls more of the piloting functions. Pilots must adapt to the new technology and their role in flying the aircraft. The performance domain also contains negative, counterproductive work behaviours that interfere with job performance. Successful employees are expected not to exhibit counterproductive work behaviours. The pilot is expected to maintain self-discipline by showing up for work on time and not drinking alcohol while on flight duty.

A MULTIDIMENSIONAL MODEL OF JOB PERFORMANCE

One of the most significant developments has been the attempt by John Campbell and his associates to specify a theory of work performance.[24] Campbell proposes that the behaviours people are expected to exhibit as part of their job appear to fall into eight job performance dimensions, which together specify the job performance domain. These eight performance dimensions, as identified by Campbell,[25] are as follows:

1. *Job-specific task proficiency* reflects the degree to which an individual can perform technical tasks that make up the content of the job. A petroleum engineer and an accountant must perform different behaviours as part of their specific jobs. Within jobs, individuals may vary in their level of competence. One engineer may be more technically proficient than another, just as one accountant may be more technically proficient than some other accountants.
2. *Non-job-specific task proficiency* reflects the degree to which individuals can perform tasks or behaviours that are not specific to any one job. Both the engineer and accountant may have to have a good understanding of the business environment in which their company operates.
3. *Written and oral communication task proficiency* is the degree to which an individual can write or speak, independent of the correctness of the subject matter. Both the engineer and accountant make oral reports to people they deal with on the job; both also make written reports on the work they perform.
4. *Demonstrating effort* reflects the degree to which individuals are committed to performing all job tasks, to working at a high level of intensity, and to working under adverse conditions. How willing are the engineer or accountant to work overtime to complete a project? Do they begin their workdays earlier than expected? Can they be relied on to give the same level of effort day in and day out? Do they show initiative?
5. *Maintaining personal discipline* characterizes the extent to which negative behaviours are avoided. Do either the engineer or the accountant drink on the job?

Do they follow the appropriate laws, regulations, or codes that govern their professions? Do they show up for scheduled assignments?

6. *Facilitating peer and team performance* is the degree to which an individual supports coworkers, helps them with job problems, and keeps them working as a team to achieve their goals. Is the engineer or accountant available to give the others a helping hand? Do either or both offer new trainees the benefit of their experience? Do they keep their colleagues focused on completing the work team's goals?
7. *Supervision/leadership* includes behaviours that are directed at influencing the performance of subordinates through interpersonal means. Does the engineer, accountant, or both set goals and performance standards for people they direct? Do they use whatever influence is at their disposal, including the authority to reward and punish, to shape the behaviour of subordinates?
8. *Management/administration* includes all other performance behaviours involved in management that are distinct from supervision. Do the engineer and accountant contact clients and arrange appointments? Do they schedule work in the most efficient manner? Do they complete all the paperwork related to a project?

Job-specific task proficiency, demonstrating effort, and maintaining personal discipline are major performance components of every job[26]; however, not all eight dimensions have to be present in every job. Few, if any, management skills are required by an assembly-line worker in an auto plant; on the other hand, the requirements and attributes of the CIBC customer service representative (see Recruitment and Selection Today 4.1) fit nicely into this framework. The pattern of differences in these eight dimensions can be used to classify jobs and is consistent with the job classification schemes used by the *Canadian Classification Dictionary of Occupations*, the Canadian *National Occupational Classification* system, and the U.S. *Dictionary of Occupational Titles*.

There are other models of job performance dimensions[27]; however, Campbell's is the most complete and overlaps with dimensions proposed in other models, except for adaptive performance. In Table 5.1 we map Campbell's eight job dimensions onto the four types of job behaviour we have presented here. Note that the three components Campbell states are present in each job–job task proficiency, demonstrating effort, and maintaining discipline (the lack of it)–correspond respectively to task, contextual, and counterproductive behaviours. Arguably, each of these three types of job behaviours is present in every job. We believe that facilitating team and peer performance requires an individual to display adaptability in dealing with other workers. It remains for each employer to determine which of the four job behaviours is most important in terms of recruitment and selection and other organizational outcomes.

What determines individual differences on these eight job performance components? That is, why does one pilot perform more efficiently than another? Campbell and his associates[28] showed that the eight job dimensions are influenced by three factors: declarative knowledge, procedural knowledge and skill, and motivation. *Declarative knowledge* is knowledge about facts and things including knowledge of rules, regulations, and goals. It is technical knowledge necessary to do a job properly. *Procedural knowledge and skill* are attained when declarative knowledge, knowing what to do, is combined with knowing how to do it. One pilot knows all about landing procedures but lacks the appropriate skills to perform a smooth landing every time. Procedural knowledge and skill include cognitive, psychomotor, physical, perceptual, interpersonal, and

TABLE 5.1

THE RELATIONSHIP OF CAMPBELL'S EIGHT JOB DIMENSIONS TO TASK, CONTEXTUAL, ADAPTIVE, AND COUNTERPRODUCTIVE BEHAVIOUR

JOB TASK BEHAVIOURS
Job-Specific Behaviours
Non–Job-Specific Behaviours
Leadership/Supervision
Management/Administration
CONTEXTUAL BEHAVIOURS
Communication Proficiency
Demonstrating Effort
ADAPTIVE WORK BEHAVIOURS
Facilitating Peer and Team Performance
COUNTERPRODUCTIVE WORK BEHAVIOURS
Maintaining Personal Discipline

self-management skills. *Motivation* is defined in terms of choice to perform, level of effort, and persistence of effort.

Job performance is some combination of these three factors; performance cannot occur unless there is both a choice to perform at some level and at least a minimal amount of knowledge and skill. In later chapters on selection we will see how different selection tools are related to the most important dimensions in an effort to predict those job applicants who will be the most effective job performers.

TASK PERFORMANCE

In Chapter 4 we saw that the identification of job tasks was one of the functions of job analysis. Employees who have the requisite KSAOs must successfully complete the tasks that comprise a job. Task performance, as previously discussed, is fundamental to job performance in every job performance model.[29]

CONTEXTUAL PERFORMANCE

Campbell's job dimensions specify what people do as part of their jobs. Borman and Motowidlo[30] make the point that work performance extends beyond performing tasks that are related to the job. Employees are called on to perform activities that are not part of their formal job duties; the activities are, however, part of the context in which those job tasks are performed. Contextual performance involves activities or behaviours that are not part of a worker's formal job description but that remain important for organizational effectiveness.

While job performance is closely related to underlying knowledge, skills, and abilities, contextual performance supports the organizational, social, and psychological environment in which the job is performed. Contextual activities are not related to a specific job or role but extend to all jobs in an organization. Contextual performance often reflects organizational values. For example, many Canadian companies actively support worthwhile causes as part of their desire to be good corporate citizens and may expect their employees to contribute time or money to these projects. The United Way campaign is one fundraising activity that enjoys strong corporate support. Volunteer fundraising activities on the part of employees are not related to specific jobs but may advance the goals of the organization.

Contextual performance appears to fall into five major categories[31]:

1. Persisting with enthusiasm and extra effort as necessary to complete one's own task activities successfully.
2. Volunteering to carry out task activities that are not formally part of one's own job.
3. Helping and cooperating with others.
4. Following organizational rules and procedures.
5. Endorsing, supporting, and defending organizational objectives.

Contextual performance is closely related to organizational citizenship behaviour (OCB).[32,33] OCB is individual behaviour that is discretionary, that is not directly recognized by a formal reward system, and that, overall, promotes the effective functioning of the organization. The difference between contextual performance and OCB is that OCB is considered to be beyond the role requirements of a job and, thus, not rewarded. Contextual performance, on the other hand, is not required to perform specific job tasks, but it is behaviour, much like core competencies, that an organization wishes all of its employees to exhibit. Contextual performance is regarded as part of an employee's role in an organization and is often rewarded through pay increases or promotion.[34]

In many ways, the contextual performance dimensions appear to be extensions of the eight job performance dimensions included in Campbell's model.[35] As we show in Table 5.1, several of Campbell's job dimensions can be deemed to be aspects of contextual performance. For example, "persisting with enthusiasm and extra effort" appears to be related to "demonstrating effort"; "volunteering to carry out tasks not part of one's job" to "facilitating peer and team performance"; "following organizational rules and procedures" to "maintaining personal discipline"; and "endorsing, supporting, and defending organizational objectives" to "supervision/leadership." We would categorize "helping and cooperating with others" as adaptive performance; however, keep in mind that some researchers would argue that adaptive behaviour is a form of contextual performance.

Campbell's job dimensions relate to specific jobs, while contextual performance may relate to broader organizational roles taken on by an employee without reference to specific job-related tasks. However, this distinction is becoming increasingly blurred. Hoffman and his colleagues[36] did an extensive review of the relationship of organizational citizenship behaviour in relation to job task behaviour. They concluded that the various components of OCB could be mapped onto a single dimension that was distinct from, but strongly related to, task performance. They also concluded that because the OCB factor correlated with several job attitudes such as job satisfaction and commitment, OCBs should be considered when assessing job performance.

Contextual performance activities may represent important criteria for jobs in many organizations because of their relationship to organizational effectiveness. Contextual performance dimensions may not all have the same degree of relevance or importance across organizations. Organizations are likely to emphasize those that are most compatible with their values and goals. Contextual performance is not a substitute for job task performance; it represents *additional* factors that may be considered in developing personnel selection criteria.

Contextual performance by itself does not get the job done; in evaluating staff, managers place more emphasis on task performance than on contextual performance.[37] In fact, Rotundo and Sackett[38] found that managers placed the least weight on contextual or citizenship behaviours. Managers from 15 different organizations that were geographically dispersed across the United States fell into one of three categories when asked to rate the three types of job behaviour. The first group rated task performance the highest over the other two, the second group felt that counterproductive work behaviours were the most important, and the third group of managers rated task and counterproductive work behaviours higher than citizenship (contextual) behaviours. The managers were a diverse group that came from five different occupational groups. An increasing number of North American companies, such as Apple Computer, GE, Honeywell, and 3M, assess how well employees fit the organization in addition to how well they can do the job.[39] Organizational fit between an employee, the organizational culture, and the desired environment predicts an employee's contextual performance.[40] In Chapter 6, we will review person–organization fit in the context of recruitment.

ADAPTIVE WORK PERFORMANCE

Campbell's taxonomy of job performance did not explicitly include adaptive performance as job behaviour. Pulakos[41] and her colleagues showed that an important behaviour among employees was their ability to adapt to ongoing changes in the workplace. Other researchers noted the relevance of this characteristic to job performance, but used a variety of names, such as role flexibility, in describing it. Based on nearly 9500 critical incidents collected across 21 jobs and 11 organizations, Pulakos et al. defined adaptive performance as comprising eight dimensions:

1. Handling emergencies or crisis situations
2. Handling work stress
3. Solving problems creatively
4. Dealing with uncertain and unpredictable work situations
5. Learning work tasks, technologies, and procedures
6. Demonstrating interpersonal adaptability
7. Demonstrating cultural adaptability
8. Demonstrating physically oriented adaptability

Table 5.2 presents the definitions for these eight dimensions of adaptability. Similar to Campbell's dimensions, not all eight aspects of adaptability are required on every job, and where required the level of the aspect needed may vary across jobs. In the O*NET system, these adaptability dimensions are included under *work context* and *work styles* factors. Pulakos and her colleagues recognized that different predictors might be needed for these adaptability aspects when used as part of a selection program. For example, cognitive ability might be used to predict problem solving while the personality factor of emotional stability might predict handling work stress.

TABLE 5.2

DEFINITIONS OF THE EIGHT DIMENSIONS OF ADAPTIVE PERFORMANCE

DIMENSION TITLE	DIMENSION DEFINITION
Handling emergencies or crisis situations	Reacting with appropriate and proper urgency in life threatening, dangerous, or emergency situations; quickly analyzing options for dealing with danger or crises and their implications; making split-second decisions based on clear and focused thinking; maintaining emotional control and objectivity while keeping focused on the situation at hand; stepping up to take action and handle danger or emergencies as necessary and appropriate.
Handling work stress	Remaining composed and cool when faced with difficult circumstances or a highly demanding workload or schedule; not overreacting to unexpected news or situations; managing frustration well by directing effort to constructive solutions rather than blaming others; demonstrating resilience and the highest levels of professionalism in stressful circumstances; acting as a calming and settling influence to whom others look for guidance.
Solving problems creatively	Employing unique types of analyses and generating new, innovative ideas in complex areas; turning problems upside-down and inside-out to find fresh, new approaches; integrating seemingly unrelated information and developing creative solutions; entertaining wide-ranging possibilities others may miss, thinking outside the given parameters to see if there is a more effective approach; developing innovative methods of obtaining or using resources when insufficient resources are available to do the job.
Dealing with uncertain and unpredictable work situations	Taking effective action when necessary without having to know the total picture or have all the facts at hand; readily and easily changing gears in response to unpredictable or unexpected events and circumstances; effectively adjusting plans, goals, actions, or priorities to deal with changing situations; imposing structure for self and others that provide as much focus as possible in dynamic situations; not needing things to be black and white; refusing to be paralyzed by uncertainty or ambiguity.
Learning work tasks, technologies, and procedures	Demonstrating enthusiasm for learning new approaches and technologies for conducting work; doing what is necessary to keep knowledge and skills current; quickly and proficiently learning new methods or how to perform previously unlearned tasks; adjusting to new work processes and procedures; anticipating changing work demands and searching for and participating in assignments or training that will prepare self for these changes; taking action to improve work performance deficiencies.
Demonstrating interpersonal adaptability	Being flexible and open-minded when dealing with others; listening to and considering others' viewpoints and opinions and altering own opinions when it is appropriate to do so; being open and accepting of negative or developmental feedback regarding work; working well and developing effective relationships with highly diverse personalities; demonstrating keen insight of others' behavior and tailoring own behavior to persuade, influence, or work more effectively with them.
Demonstrating cultural adaptability	Taking action to learn about and understand the climate, orientation, needs, and values of other groups, organizations, or cultures; integrating well into and being comfortable with different values, customs, and cultures; willingly adjusting behavior or appearance as necessary to comply with or show respect for others' values and customs; understanding the implications of one's actions and adjusting approach to maintain positive relationships with other groups, organizations, or cultures.
Demonstrating physically oriented adaptability	Adjusting to challenging environmental states such as extreme heat, humidity, cold, or dirtiness; frequently pushing self physically to complete strenuous or demanding tasks; adjusting weight and muscular strength or becoming proficient in performing physical tasks as necessary for the job.

Source: Table 1 in Pulakos, E. D., Arad, S., Donovan, M. A. and Plamondon, K. E. (2000) "Adaptability in the Workplace: Development of a Taxonomy of Adaptive Performance". *Journal of Applied Psychology*, 85:612–624. Published by American Psychological Association. Reprinted with permission.

COUNTERPRODUCTIVE WORK BEHAVIOURS

Productivity is the end result of a complex interaction of task, contextual, adaptive and counterproductive work behaviours. For example, in highly technical and complex occupations (e.g., air traffic controller) the role of contextual performance to the organizational effectiveness may be less critical than task performance,[42] but counterproductive work behaviours on the part of the controller could have devastating consequences. In most cases, contextual and adaptive behaviours should lead to increases in productivity that are primarily influenced by task behaviour, while counterproductive work behaviours detract from it. How individuals differ in terms of knowledge, skill, motivation, and other factors such as personality may determine how they ultimately perform in the workplace. Counterproductive work behaviours are intentional acts by employees intended to harm their organization or the people in it. Counterproductive work behaviours include acts of both physical and psychological violence.[43] Counterproductive work behaviours lead, ultimately, to decreases in productivity through loss of efficiency and effectiveness.

A complete conception of the performance domain must also include an understanding of behaviours that have negative impacts on organizational effectiveness. Robinson and Bennett define counterproductive work behaviours as "voluntary behaviours that violate significant organizational norms and in so doing threaten the well-being of an organization, its members or both."[44] Examples of these behaviours include lying, theft, property damage, violence, engaging in risky behaviours, harassment of coworkers, and sabotage, among others.[45] Perhaps the most negative work behaviour is withdrawal from the job. We will take a closer look at these different types of counterproductive work behaviours (CWBs) in the next section and then follow up with a discussion of whether we can predict counterproductive work behaviours in Chapter 8.

TYPES OF COUNTERPRODUCTIVE WORK BEHAVIOURS

Table 5.3 presents definitions of the most common types of CWBs. The following sections discuss these different CWBs in greater detail.

WITHDRAWAL BEHAVIOURS

TARDINESS AND ABSENCE

Counterproductive work behaviours include withdrawal behaviours such as tardiness, i.e., being late for work; absence, i.e., not showing up for scheduled work[46]; and voluntary turnover, i.e., quitting the job permanently. Withdrawal also includes psychological withdrawal where employees show up for work on time, don't miss a day of work and have no intention of quitting, but withhold effort and do not perform to their fullest capabilities. Psychological withdrawal may also take the form of drug and alcohol use in the workplace during working hours.

Tardiness and absenteeism lead to loss of productivity and cost organizations money. Tardiness is more prevalent than previously thought. In a 2013 report to the Conference Board of Canada, Stewart[47] placed the direct cost of absenteeism in Canada at $16.6 billion annually. This cost does not include the impact of absence on replacement workers, administration related to absenteeism, team performance and coworker

TABLE 5.3

COMMON TYPES OF COUNTERPRODUCTIVE WORK BEHAVIOURS

TARDINESS	Being late for work
ABSENCE	Not showing up for scheduled work
PRESENTEEISM	A measure of lost productivity that occurs when employees show up for work but are not fully engaged in their jobs because of personal health and life issues
WORKPLACE DEVIANCE	The voluntary violation of significant organizational norms in a way that threatens the well-being of the organization, coworkers, or both
PRODUCTION DEVIANCE	Primarily passive acts of an employee directed against the organization
PSYCHOLOGICAL WITHDRAWAL	Where employees withhold effort and do not perform to their fullest capabilities
EMPLOYEE THEFT	A form of workplace property deviance where the goal is not to destroy property but to steal the organization's property, including money, for oneself
WORKPLACE AGGRESSION AND VIOLENCE	Behaviours directed toward other employees that are intended to cause either physical or psychological harm
BULLYING	Offensive, intimidating, malicious, or insulting behaviour directed at another; an abuse or misuse of power through means intended to undermine, humiliate, denigrate, or injure an intended victim

morale, reduction in productivity, and customer satisfaction. On average, each full-time Canadian worker was absent 9.3 days; this rate was fairly constant over the past decade. The highest rates were among health care and social assistance workers at 14.0 percent, with the lowest among professional, technical, and scientific workers at 5.8 percent. The drivers of absenteeism were societal influences, personal characteristics, and organizational influences. These drivers lead to stress, health issues, disengagement, and entitlement, and ultimately either voluntary or non-voluntary absence. Stewart summarizes these factors in the model presented in Figure 5.3.

Figure 5.3 shows that there are many reasons for being absent from work; some of these involve legitimate reasons related to health and family issues where the absence

FIGURE 5.3

DRIVERS, PREDICTORS, AND CAUSES OF ABSENTEEISM

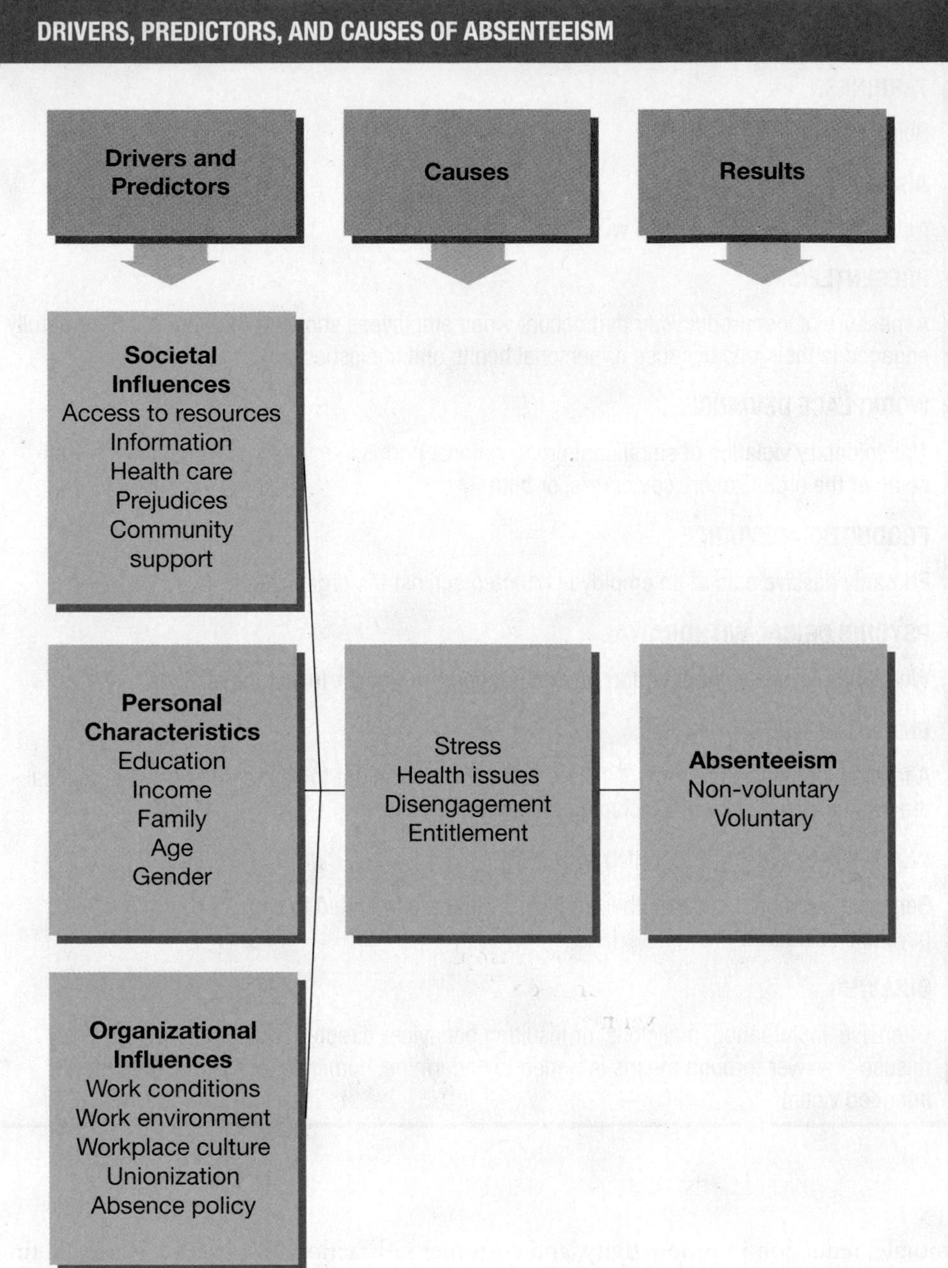

Source: "Missing in Action: Absenteeism Trends in Canadian Organizations" by Nicole Stewart. The Conference Board of Canada, 2013.

is taken with the employer's knowledge, if not approval, and are of a long-term nature. These types of absence are believed not to be under the control of the employee. The forms of absenteeism that fall under counterproductive work behaviours are those of a very short-term nature of one to three days where the employee does not show up for work when scheduled and calls in with some excuse, including being ill.

PRESENTEEISM

Ines Bazdar/Shutterstock.com

Presenteeism is a relatively new concept. It is defined as a measure of lost productivity that occurs when employees show up for work but are not fully engaged in their jobs because of personal health and life issues. The employees show up for work out of fear of losing their income or their jobs and may be prone to making catastrophic mistakes as well as transmitting illness among other employees.[48] In cases where the employee believes that the organization is less tolerant of absenteeism, the employee will show up for work but engage in a minimum of work. Being "present" is used as a screen for poor performance. Presenteeism may pose more of a problem than absenteeism. Robertson Cooper[49] reports that 25 percent of 39 000 workers in the United Kingdom reported going to work while sick. The study argued that presenteeism could have damaging and costly effects on the economy. In a Canadian study, Johns found that workers reported an average of 3.0 days of presenteeism compared to 1.8 days of absenteeism.[50] In a study carried out in Quebec, Brun estimated presenteeism days at 9.9 compared to 7.1 days of absenteeism.[51] Looking at both studies it appears that the ratio is two days of productivity loss due to presenteeism to one day lost to absenteeism.

VOLUNTARY TURNOVER

Voluntary turnover is the most extreme form of employee withdrawal behaviour. The employee withdraws completely from the organization. In some cases, the employee's withdrawal may be welcomed by the organization; however, turnover, whether voluntary or involuntary, carries with it considerable costs. The departing employee needs to be replaced, incurring recruiting, selection, and training costs for the replacement. During this period other employees may be asked to work overtime to pick up work that was to be performed by the departing employee. The departure may also lead to withdrawal on the part of the remaining employees, resulting in a drop in productivity. There is also likely to be a dropoff in productivity while the replacement is brought up to speed.[52] Voluntary turnover may have positive effects for the organization if poor or dysfunctional employees choose to leave and if they can be easily replaced. On the other hand, if the best performers are leaving and there is difficulty in finding replacements, then productivity will suffer. A good performance management system will help organizations to identify the good and poor performers and to take action to retain the former and to let the latter go, either voluntarily or involuntarily.

WORKPLACE DEVIANCE

Workplace deviance generally involves the voluntary violation of significant organizational norms in a way that threatens the well-being of the organization, coworkers, or both.[53] Robinson and Bennett produced a typology of deviant workplace behaviours that classified those behaviours according to whether they were directed against the organization or people, and the severity of the action. Their typology included psychological withdrawal, production deviance, workplace property deviance, and interpersonal workplace deviance.

Psychological withdrawal occurs where employees withhold effort and do not perform to their fullest capabilities. Presenteeism is a good example of psychological withdrawal. Psychological withdrawal also includes the employee leaving early, taking excessive breaks, and wasting resources. These examples are a form of production deviance in that they are primarily passive acts directed against the organization and not other employees. They are qualitatively different from the more serious workplace property deviance behaviours such as actively sabotaging equipment or production or stealing from the company. Interpersonal workplace deviance generally involves aggression against other people, such as bullying.

WORKPLACE PROPERTY DEVIANCE

EMPLOYEE THEFT Employee theft is a form of workplace property deviance where the goal is not to destroy property but to steal the organization's property, including money, for oneself. The nature of the theft may range from small supply items such as a pack of printer paper to theft of petty cash to embezzlement of corporate or client funds. These losses are sometimes called "inventory shrinkage." In a 2012 retail security survey, PricewaterhouseCoopers[54] placed the cost of shrinkage at $10.8 million per shopping day; this figure included losses due to theft by customers and organized crime, inventory and accounting errors, as well as employee theft, which was not separated out in the survey. In response to this problem, many retailers have established "loss prevention" departments; they have emphasized employee training and workplace improvements as well as installing procedures for controlling inventory. Many organizations have also initiated programs designed to select people who not only are capable of doing the job but also are honest, reliable, or of high integrity. We will discuss selection procedures designed to assess honesty or integrity in Chapter 8.

INTERPERSONAL WORKPLACE DEVIANCE

Acts of interpersonal workplace deviance are directed against people rather than the organization and generally involve coworkers, supervisors, or clients. We will briefly examine the more serious forms of interpersonal workplace deviance.

WORKPLACE AGGRESSION AND VIOLENCE Acts that fall into these categories involve aggression or abuse against others. These behaviours are intended to cause either physical or psychological harm. The aggression may range from shouting obscenities to actual physical assaults. Behaviours that do not involve any type of physical contact are classified as psychological aggression. Physical assaults of any type are examples of physical violence. Workplace aggression is a broader term than workplace violence as not all forms of aggression involve violence. Schat, Frone, and Kelloway[55] report data on workplace deviance taken from a random, national telephone survey of over 2500 employed adults in the United States. They assessed the frequency of exposure to psychological aggression and to physical violence. Over 41 percent of those surveyed reported experiencing psychological aggression at least once in the last 12-month period, with 13 percent experiencing it on a weekly basis. Those figures translate into 15 million workers experiencing some form of psychological aggression on a weekly basis. The aggressive behaviours reported by Schat et al. included being shouted at in anger, being the target of obscenities, being insulted or called names, or being threatened with violence.

Moreover, when survey participants were asked if they had experienced some form of physical violence in the workplace during the past year, 6 percent said they had, with 0.7 percent (785 586 workers) reporting that they were actually attacked with a knife, gun, or another weapon. The Schat et al. data are consistent with Statistics Canada data, which found in 2004 that 17 percent, or 365 000, of all violent incidents involving sexual assault, robbery, and physical assault occurred at the respondent's place of work. The U.S. Bureau of Labor Statistics reported that workplace homicides accounted for 475 deaths in 2012.[56] Statistics Canada reported that on average 356 000 incidents of workplace violence occur each year in the workforce. The annual cost of workplace violence in Canada is around $7.6 billion.

Regrettably, violence in the workplace has given rise to the term "going postal" after an incident where a U.S. Postal Service worker opened fire on his coworkers, killing one person and himself. Of course, these workplace incidents are not limited to the postal service or to the United States. A number of "going postal" incidents have occurred in Canada, including one at OC Transpo in Ottawa. Eight provinces have legislation that addresses workplace violence. Bill 168 amended the Ontario Occupational Health and Safety Act to require any employer with more than five employees to provide protection to workers from violence and harassment.[57] The new protections require employers to:

- develop and maintain an unambiguous program to implement workplace violence and harassment policies;
- designate a person as a workplace coordinator with respect to workplace violence and workplace harassment, and set out the duties of the coordinator;
- take every reasonable precaution in the circumstances to ensure the protection of a worker should the employer become aware, or ought reasonably to be aware, that domestic violence that would expose a worker to physical injury may occur in the workplace;
- provide information and instructions to the employees on the contents of the policy and program with respect to workplace violence and harassment; and
- set out a fair and transparent process for investigating complaints.

BULLYING AT WORK Bullying can be defined as offensive, intimidating, malicious, or insulting behaviour, which is an abuse or misuse of power through means intended to undermine, humiliate, denigrate, or injure the intended victim of the bullying behaviour. Bullying does not have to take place face-to-face. It may take place by written communications, e-mail (so called "flame-mail" or cyber bullying), phone, and automatic supervision methods–such as recording telephone conversations. Bullying can often be hard to recognize–it may not be obvious to others, and may be insidious. The victim may think "perhaps this is normal behaviour in this organization." She may be anxious that others will consider her weak, or not up to the job, if she finds the actions of others intimidating. She may be accused of overreacting, and worry that she won't be believed if she does report incidents. People being bullied may appear to overreact to something that seems relatively trivial but may be the "last straw" following a series of incidents. There is often fear of retribution if they do make

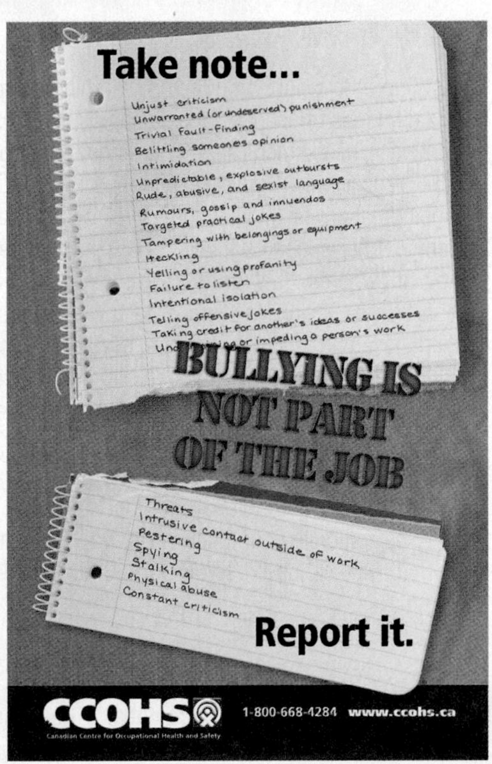

Canadian Centre for Occupational Health and Safety / Government of Canada

a complaint. Colleagues may be reluctant to come forward as witnesses, as they too may fear the consequences for themselves, or may be so relieved not to be the subject of the bully themselves that they collude with the bully as a way of avoiding attention.[58]

Workplace bullying is a significant occurrence in most organizations. In the United Kingdom and Australia, 10 percent to 20 percent of employees label themselves as being bullied.[59] In the United States, there is a slightly higher incidence, while Sweden has about half the rate found in the United Kingdom.[60] In part, the lower Swedish rate may be due to the Swedish National Board of Occupational Safety and Health passing ordinances on the actions that employers must take to prevent workplace bullying. Depending on the country, 50 percent to 80 percent of bullying is done by someone in authority over the victim, often their boss.[61] In the remainder of the cases, bullying is carried out by a coworker. Rarely is a person in authority bullied by a subordinate.[62]

Recruitment and Selection Today 5.1 presents two cases of harassment and threats of violence. In the first, the matter arose out of the RCMP Act and in the second, Bill 168. Both decisions have consequences for employers in dealing with harassment and bullying in the workplace.

PSYCHOLOGICAL HARASSMENT Bullying behaviour can be thought of as one type of psychological harassment. In 2004, Quebec became the first jurisdiction in North America to prohibit psychological harassment in the workplace through the Quebec Labour Standards

RECRUITMENT AND SELECTION TODAY 5.1

THE COST OF HARASSMENT AND BULLYING

Sulz v. Attorney General of Canada

The Supreme Court of British Columbia awarded Nancy Sulz damages of nearly $1 million as compensation for the workplace harassment she experienced. Ms. Sulz was an RCMP officer with 12 years' experience. She experienced an ongoing pattern of vulgar, aggressive, and demeaning comments by her superiors that left her clinically depressed to the point where in the future she would only be able to work in part-time positions in stress-free environments. The Court ruled, based on medical evidence, that the harassment and bullying had a negative impact on Ms. Sulz's mental health, affecting not only her ability to work, but also her ability to enjoy her life and to function as a member of her family and community. The Crown appealed the decision but the Appeal Court refused to hear the appeal.

The complete Court decision is available at http://www.courts.gov.bc.ca/jdb-txt/sc/06/00/2006bcsc0099.htm

Under Bill 168

Two days after attending an anger management workshop, a long-term employee of the City of Kingston, Ontario, attended a meeting to discuss a back-to-work plan with her manager, an occupational health nurse, and the president of her union local. The meeting was to discuss how to accommodate restrictions that had been placed on the employee. During the discussions the employee threatened the union president's life. The employee also became verbally abusive to the other participants in the meeting. After an investigation of the incident, the City moved to terminate the employee. The case went to arbitration, where the arbitrator held that the Employer had an obligation under Bill 168 amendments to the Occupational Health and Safety Act to react to an allegation of a threat, and not to trivialize the incident. The arbitrator found that the Employer acted in accordance with Bill 168, but that nothing in the bill mandated automatic termination. It is ultimately up to the Employer following an investigation to consider various options for dealing with the employee. Because of the employee's long history of harassment in the workplace, the arbitrator decided that the Employer's action of termination was justified.

The complete arbitration decision is available at http://www.canlii.org/t/fmq99

Act. The act defined psychological harassment as "any vexatious behaviour in the form of repeated and hostile or unwanted conduct, verbal comments, actions or gestures, that affects an employee's dignity or psychological or physical integrity and that results in a harmful work environment for the employee. A single serious incidence of such behaviour that has a lasting harmful effect on an employee may also constitute psychological harassment."[63] The Act also guaranteed every employee the right to "a work environment free from psychological harassment. Employers must take reasonable action to prevent psychological harassment and, whenever they become aware of such behaviour, to put a stop to it."[64] The Quebec Act has national importance. It squarely places the onus on the employer to prevent or stop psychological harassment from occurring in the employer's workplace. It is legislation that sets the standard for the rest of Canada. Increasingly, the act will be used by human rights tribunals and labour arbitrators as the standard against which employers are judged and the type of workplace behaviour that is acceptable.

PREDICTING TASK, CONTEXTUAL, ADAPTIVE AND COUNTERPRODUCTIVE JOB PERFORMANCE

Individuals differ considerably in their job performance. One worker may be several times more productive than a coworker. Can we predict who will be the most productive employee? Should we be concerned about predicting each type of job behaviour? Productivity may be the end result of an interaction among all four types of job behaviours. In highly technical and complex occupations (e.g., air traffic controller), the role of contextual performance to the organization's effectiveness may be less critical than task performance; however, adaptive behaviour may be essential in dealing with stressful situations. Counterproductive work behaviours on the part of the air traffic controller could have devastating consequences. Figure 5.1 presented several behavioural indicators for each type of job performance. We can use these indicators to suggest predictors for each.

TASK PERFORMANCE

Cognitive ability appears to be the best predictor of task performance across all job situations,[65,66] although it may carry with it some adverse impact on protected groups.[67] When used by itself as a predictor cognitive ability has a validity of around 0.50. This relationship appears to be culturally invariant in Western countries, as it occurs in North America, the U.K., and European countries. The validity increases with job complexity. We will examine measures of cognitive ability in Chapter 8.

Knowledge is related to task performance. Campbell et al.[68] proposed that declarative and procedural knowledge, two aspects of job knowledge, were determinants of job performance. There is a strong positive correlation between job content knowledge tests (declarative knowledge) and job performance ratings of 0.48.[69] Measures of procedural knowledge have a slightly lower correlation with job performance of 0.34.[70] Job experience knowledge has weak correlation with task performance, 0.13.[71]

CONTEXTUAL PERFORMANCE

Contextual performance appears to be linked to different aspects of personality and motivation. When opportunities for advancement within an organization are limited, employees may perform contextual acts because they are conscientious; however, when there are opportunities for advancement, employees may engage in contextual acts because they are ambitious.[72]

Personality measurement improves the ability to predict contextual performance among sales and service representatives.[73] The increasing emphasis on organizational citizenship behaviour and contextual performance as performance dimensions may require the addition of personality measures as part of the selection process. We will return to the use of personality in selection in Chapter 8.

ADAPTIVE PERFORMANCE

Few studies have examined predictors of adaptive performance. Pulakos et al.[74] found that aspects of personality such as openness to experience, achievement motivation, and emotional stability were related to adaptive performance.

COUNTERPRODUCTIVE WORK BEHAVIOURS

CWBs appear to be caused by work stress and triggered by negative emotions such as boredom, frustration, anxiety, and lack of self-control; others propose that differences in personality may be linked to counterproductive work behaviours.[75] Different aspects of personality appear to predict violence and aggression and drug and alcohol use as well as predicting an individual's honesty or integrity.[76] In Chapter 8 we will review integrity and honesty tests along with other procedures that have been developed to predict whether a job applicant or employee is likely to engage in specific types of counterproductive behaviour, with the intent to screen out job applicants or employees with those behaviours. Testing that selects out, including testing for honesty or integrity, is a very controversial procedure.

// MEASURING PERFORMANCE

The usefulness of selection measures is assessed by how well they predict performance. Typically, a supervisor's rating of the employee's performance is used for this purpose. Hard measures of performance, such as dollar sales, units produced, and absenteeism data, are less frequently available. Performance measures need to capture the contributions workers make as they move from one assignment to another, and from team to team. Frequently, performance measurements will have to come from multiple sources (e.g., peers, customers, supervisors).

In validating selection measures, we will need to decide whether we wish to predict one or more performance dimensions or types of performance, or some overall composite measure of performance. Are we interested in task, contextual, adaptive, or counterproductive work behaviours? If we assess several competency or performance dimensions, then we need to determine which aspects of performance contribute most to the success of the organization and what weights should be given to the different dimensions.[77,78] If we want an overall measure of performance, then we must find a method for combining the performance data that we obtain from different sources.

Most efforts directed at improving selection systems have focused on the measurement of job-related KSAOs or competencies. Until recently, relatively less thought has been given to improving the measurement of job performance. Most organizations rely on criterion-related validity studies to defend the appropriateness of their selection systems before human rights and other tribunals. No matter how accurately the organization measures KSAOs or competencies, the criterion-related validity will still be low without improvement in performance measurement. There remains a need to use valid criterion measures and to develop a better understanding of what constitutes job performance.[79] Fortunately, more companies and HR managers are beginning to appreciate the linkage between selection and performance measurement.[80] Performance measures, however, are still too often chosen because the pressure of getting things done leads to choosing the most convenient measure at hand and hoping it will turn out all right.

The performance measurement or criterion problem is really one of defining what is meant by performance and choosing a measure or set of measures that best capture the essence of that complex job-related performance. Without a clear understanding of what constitutes job performance in a specific organizational position (i.e., task, contextual, adaptive, or counterproductive behaviour), the best measurement systems will never be able to effectively measure performance at work. We need first to define job performance before we can attempt to assess it.[81] One implication of a multidimensional conception of job performance is that any performance management system should include measures of task, contextual, adaptive, and counterproductive work behaviours.

Performance measurement plays an important role in developing strategies for effective recruitment and selection. Rather than simply choosing a measure and hoping it works, the first step is to specify job performance in terms of measurable behaviours; the next step is to find valid measures of those behaviours. The criterion or performance measure must be a valid indicator of job performance as determined by job analysis. There is an important difference in contemporary approaches to establishing criteria. Desired job-related behaviours and outcomes are those that secure organizational goals. Increasingly, companies are looking for a fit between the person and the organization; this search for a person–organization fit often drives the company's recruitment process. (We will discuss the person–organizational fit in more detail in Chapter 6.)

We discussed the need to validate selection measures to establish that they are meeting legal requirements. We also need to establish validity to assure ourselves that the people we are hiring will be the "best" or "most productive." Improvements in selection procedures can lead to substantial increases in productivity. For example, in sales occupations replacement of invalid selection procedures with valid procedures produces an average increase in sales of $60 000 per employee for each year that the employee stays on the job.[82] To evaluate the effectiveness of selection systems, we must find a way to measure those task, contextual, adaptive, and counterproductive work behaviours we identify as important for job success. Criterion measurement plays an essential part in recruitment and selection. Measuring performance is easier said than done; criterion measurement is a complex and technical process.

EFFECTIVE PERFORMANCE MEASURES

Once job analysis has identified the major performance dimensions, the next step is to measure employee performance on those dimensions. How will we measure job task proficiency, supervision, or helping and cooperating with others? We can think of these job dimensions as labels that are constructed to describe different aspects of job performance. Before we can measure any job dimension, we have to define that dimension in terms of specific, measurable activities or behaviours. For example, supervision includes giving orders to subordinates, accomplishing organizational goals, and teaching employees the proper way to do a job, among many other things. One person may be better at "giving orders to subordinates" than "teaching subordinates"; our view on that person's supervisory performance will depend on which of these behaviours we include in our measure of supervisory performance. Smith[83] established general guidelines to help identify effective and appropriate performance measures, based on relevancy, reliability, and practicality.

RELEVANCY

Relevancy requires that a criterion must be not only relevant, but also not deficient or contaminated. **Criterion relevance** is the degree to which a criterion captures behaviours or competencies that constitute job performance. A criterion must be a valid measure of the performance dimension in question. Suppose we develop a measure of a sales associate's performance based on an overall rating assigned by a supervisor. This measure might be relevant to sales performance in that it captures behaviours related to service orientation, communication, and interpersonal relations. However, the measure may be deficient in not measuring competencies such as achievement, business orientation, self-discipline, and organizing, which may also be related to success in sales. **Criterion deficiency** refers to those job performance behaviours or competencies that are not measured by the criterion. Additionally, the criterion may be influenced by problem solving, learning, and management competencies that are not critical for success in this particular job, resulting in **criterion contamination**–the degree to which the criterion is influenced by, or measures, behaviours or competencies that are not part of job performance. As a criterion measure, a supervisor's rating may be contaminated in that it is measuring things other than the sales associate's performance. These three aspects of criterion measurement are illustrated in Table 5.4.

Criterion relevance The degree to which the criterion measure captures behaviours or competencies that constitute job performance.

Criterion deficiency Those job performance behaviours or competencies that are not measured by the criterion.

Criterion contamination The degree to which the criterion measure is influenced by, or measures, behaviours or competencies that are not part of job performance.

RELIABILITY

Reliability involves agreement between different evaluations, at different periods of time, and with different, although apparently similar, measures; that is, the measurements that

TABLE 5.4

ILLUSTRATION OF CRITERION RELEVANCY FOR PERFORMANCE IN A SALES ASSOCIATE POSITION

UNMEASURED COMPETENCIES	**RELEVANT TO SALES PERFORMANCE**	Criterion Deficiency Business Orientation Self-Management Organizing
MEASURED COMPETENCIES	**RELEVANT TO SALES PERFORMANCE**	Criterion Relevance Service Orientation Communication Interpersonal Relations
	NOT RELEVANT TO SALES PERFORMANCE	Criterion Contamination Problem Solving Learning Management

are produced by the criterion measure must meet scientific and professional standards of reliability. Reliability is the degree to which observed scores are free from random measurement errors (i.e., the dependability or stability of the measure). Criterion or performance measurements are subject to the same errors as any other kind of measurement. There is no such thing as error-free criterion measurement; some criteria, however, are more reliable than others. Reliable criterion measures will tend to produce similar scores when the same behaviour is measured on more than one occasion. The reliability of any criterion measure must be established, as part of its use in a personnel selection system, through the procedures discussed in Chapter 2.

PRACTICALITY

Practicality means that the criterion measure must be available, plausible, and acceptable to organizational decision makers. The supervisor's rating of the sales associate's performance must mean something to those responsible for evaluating the sales associate. It must also be a number that can be readily obtained from the supervisor with little cost in time or money. It should also be a plausible indicator of individual performance. That is, the criterion measure must have meaning and credibility for those who will use the measurements in making decisions.

Practicality
The degree to which a criterion measure is available, plausible, and acceptable to organizational decision makers.

There is a danger of being seduced by practicality and choosing criteria that, while readily available, do not meet standards of validity and reliability. These two requirements cannot be traded off in favour of practicality. For example, the supervisor may be tempted to use the number of units sold in a month to evaluate the sales associate's performance. This is a very practical measure; however, it may be neither reliable nor valid. The sales volume may be affected by a number of factors outside the sales associate's control, such as the state of the economy, sales campaigns by the competition, and so forth. As well, the records of the number of sales attributed to the associate may not be accurate or entered consistently into a database. That is, while the monthly sales volume may be an easy-to-use, practical measure, it may not meet acceptable standards for reliability and validity. Criteria must be practical as well as being reliable and valid measures of job performance.

IDENTIFYING CRITERION MEASURES

Several issues must be considered as part of the process of identifying a criterion or a set of criterion measures for use in a selection system. Criteria are "dynamic, multidimensional, situation-specific, and serve multiple functions."[84] Although progress has been made on these issues, there are still gaps between research and practice when it comes to designing a selection system.[85] The resolution of these issues influences which measures are selected as criteria and when measurements are made.

MULTIPLE, GLOBAL, OR COMPOSITE CRITERIA

THE ULTIMATE CRITERION

The first issue is one that has generated a great deal of controversy over the years—namely, how criteria should be measured. In large part this controversy arises through

Ultimate criterion
The concept that a single criterion measure reflects overall job success.

misunderstanding of the job performance domain. At one time, criterion research was dominated by a concern to find the ultimate criterion for a given job. The **ultimate criterion** is the concept of a single criterion measure that could reflect overall job success. The idea of an ultimate criterion implies that job performance is a unitary concept, that one measure could be found that assessed a person's overall job performance.

Even Thorndike,[86] who developed the idea, recognized that an ultimate criterion would rarely, if ever, be found in practice: "A really complete ultimate criterion is multiple and complex in almost every case. Such a criterion is ultimate in the sense that we cannot look beyond it for any higher or further standard in terms of which to judge the outcomes of a particular personnel program." Unfortunately, many who followed Thorndike did not heed his advice and wasted considerable time trying to find ultimate measures of job performance. It is unlikely that you will ever find one measure that will tell you everything about performance in a specific job, considering the complexity of measuring task, contextual, adaptive, and counterproductive work behaviours.

GLOBAL VERSUS MULTIPLE CRITERIA

Job analysis procedures used by most organizations are inductive: the job analyst infers the dimensions that make up the overall job performance domain from specific empirical data. Other approaches deduce performance dimensions from organizational goals with or without the help of job analysis data.[87] As we saw in Chapter 4, many organizations are turning directly to deriving competencies without going through a traditional job analysis procedure and building competency profiles. If there is a need, then, to compare the relative performance of employees in the same occupational group, is it appropriate to combine the scores on each dimension into an overall composite score, or should a new criterion be developed to measure overall performance?

Many practitioners, heavily influenced by the controversy surrounding the search for the ultimate criterion, would answer "No." They would emphasize that the multidimensionality of job performance requires the use of multiple, independent criteria to measure performance. They would say that independent criteria, reflecting independent performance dimensions, should not be combined into an overall composite measure of job performance. Combining *navigational skills, managing air crew,* and *self-discipline* to understand a pilot's performance would be, to use Smith's[88] analogy, like adding toothpicks to olives to understand a martini. Furthermore, these practitioners would not believe it was appropriate to obtain a separate, overall measure of performance because such a global criterion measure would lose the rich information contained in the multiple performance dimensions.

Our discussion of task, contextual, adaptive, and counterproductive job performance supports this position. Nonetheless, there is still support for use of a global criterion measure, particularly if there is a need to make a global, overall assessment: "If you need to solve a very specific problem (e.g., too many customer complaints about product quality), then a more specific criterion is needed. If there is more than one specific problem, then more than one specific criterion is called for. But in most situations, a global measure will serve quite well."[89]

The difficulty is in identifying those situations where the global measure is best suited. In practice, the best strategy will be to collect multiple criteria data to measure important, diverse dimensions. In Chapter 10 we will review different methods of decision making; that is, how to make use of the data we collect from our personnel selection system. As part of decision making we can require that job candidates meet minimum requirements on each of the multiple criteria that we used in the selection process. Multiple data can always be combined into a composite score.

COMPOSITE VERSUS MULTIPLE CRITERIA

We have emphasized the multidimensionality of job performance and the requirement of assessing those different dimensions through multiple criterion measures. Nonetheless, there may be times when a single, all-inclusive criterion measure is needed in making employment decisions and no global criterion measure is available. Not everyone agrees that it is inappropriate to combine individual criterion measures into a single composite.[90] There seems to be general agreement on how to proceed. Since performance measurements will be used for a variety of purposes, it makes sense to collect scores from each criterion separately. That information can be combined to compute a composite score as needed for different administrative decisions.

The weights assigned to the separate performance scores in creating a composite measurement should reflect the priority of the different performance dimensions as set by the organization's goals. Implicit in this position is a recognition that the priority of organizational goals may change over time. If separate performance scores have been maintained, it is a relatively straightforward exercise to recompute the composite to reflect the new organizational, and economic, realities. Caution should be taken; creating a composite averages performance across all the performance dimensions. Performance on one dimension may be so critical that deficiencies cannot be made up by excellent performance on other dimensions. In this case, a composite criterion is inappropriate.

CONSISTENCY OF JOB PERFORMANCE

In discussing reliability as a requirement for criterion measurement, we assumed that the employee's behaviour was more or less consistent at the time the observations were made. Of course, people's job performance may change over time. This is a substantially different issue from the random, daily fluctuations in performance. Changing performance levels may affect criterion measurements.

TRAINING VERSUS JOB PROFICIENCY CRITERIA

Do you obtain the same criterion results if you measure performance very soon after a person is placed in a job as opposed to several months or years later? Generally, early performance in a job involves informal learning or systematic training. Workers are continually evaluated during training or probationary periods. Performance measures taken during early training will be very different from those taken later when workers are more proficient. Criterion measurements taken during training periods may produce validity coefficients that overestimate the selection system's ability to predict later job proficiency.[91] Nonetheless, the convenience of short-term performance measures, rather than their relevance to long-term performance, dictates their use in many situations as criteria. Training criteria remain very popular performance measures.

TYPICAL VERSUS MAXIMUM JOB PERFORMANCE

Maximum performance occurs in situations where individuals are aware that they are being observed or evaluated, or where they are under instructions to do their best. Their performance is measured over a short time period when their attention remains focused on performing at their highest level. Typical performance is the opposite of maximum performance, in which individuals are not aware that their performance is being observed and evaluated, in which they are not consciously attempting to perform to the best of their ability, and in which performance is monitored over an extended period of time.

There is very little relationship between performance under typical and maximum performance situations, for either inexperienced or experienced workers. Performance measurements taken during training assess maximum performance and may be inappropriate if a selection system is to predict long-term typical performance. Motivational factors play a larger role in typical, everyday performance. In maximum performance, motivation is probably at high levels for everyone; in typical performance situations in the actual work setting, motivation is likely to differ among individuals.[92,93]

The use of typical or maximal criteria has important implications for selection decisions. First, each of these types of criteria seemed to have different relationships with predictors. Marcus and colleagues,[94] using supervisory ratings as data for typical performance and assessment centre evaluations for maximal data, found that cognitive abilities were more strongly correlated with maximal performance than with typical performance, while personality variables were more closely related to typical performance. The obvious implication is that predictors based on cognitive ability will have a greater degree of validity when used with maximal criteria, while personality measures may be more useful in predicting typical criteria.

DYNAMIC VERSUS STABLE CRITERIA

Employee performance appears to decrease over time regardless of the employee's experience or ability. These changes may reflect the effects of many personal, situational, and temporal factors. Early job performance may be limited only by ability and experience since every new employee is motivated to do well, while later job performance may be influenced more by motivation.[95,96]

IDENTIFYING CRITERION MEASURES: SUMMARY

Early job performance, which may occur under more rigorous scrutiny than later performance, is ability driven and is a better estimate of what individuals can maximally achieve rather than how they will typically perform on the job. Performance will decrease over time, generally reflecting changes in motivation. Training criteria are acceptable performance measures for estimating maximum performance, but will overestimate typical performance. To be safe, several performance measures should be taken at different times when validating selection systems.

JOB PERFORMANCE CRITERIA AND PERFORMANCE APPRAISAL

It is very unlikely that any two workers doing the same job will perform at exactly the same level. Factors such as knowledge, skill, and motivation are likely to cause variation in job performance within and between workers. As we saw in our discussion of competencies in Chapter 4, the essence of a competency profile is the specification of the proficiency level required on each competency to successfully perform a job and then being able to assess those employee proficiencies in a reliable and valid manner. Two employees doing exactly the same job, although they meet the minimum proficiency required for a job, may not perform at the same level. Most likely, any two pilots would not perform exactly at the same level on all critical job dimensions; nor is it likely that any one engineer would perform at the same level on all dimensions that applied to the engineer's work. Every employee has strengths and weaknesses.

How do we actually measure these differences in performance between employees on the relevant job dimensions? How do we determine that they meet the performance requirements for a position? How do we determine areas in which an employee needs training and development? What do we actually use as the criterion data necessary for validating selection systems? Performance appraisals or evaluations often provide the answers to the above questions.

OBJECTIVE PERFORMANCE APPRAISAL MEASURES

Because of the importance of performance appraisals to organizational productivity, this topic is covered in stand-alone courses in many HR programs. We will not review that material here except to note, briefly, some common criteria that are used as part of appraisal systems. There are two broad categories that are used to measure job performance. The first, **objective performance measures**, involves using production, sales, and personnel data to assess individual performance. The second, **subjective performance measures**, involve the use of rating scales. Recruitment and Selection Today 5.2 lists some of the more common examples of objective performance measures.

Objective performance measures
Production, sales, and personnel data used in assessing individual job performance.

Subjective performance measures
Ratings or rankings made by supervisors, peers, or others that are used in assessing individual job performance.

All of these measures are prone to contamination and deficiency when used as criteria. For example, insurance companies use the total dollar value of insurance sold in a month to measure an agent's performance. One agent may sell more insurance in a month than another because one's territory includes a compact city district populated by upper-income professionals, while the other's includes a sparsely populated rural county of low-income farm workers. Both the opportunity to make sales and the amount of insurance sold may have more to do with the sales territory than the sales ability of either of the agents. The total dollar value of insurance sold may not measure how safely the agents drove to their territories, the oral communication skills needed to explain the complex insurance policies, or how accurately they completed the necessary paperwork to initiate the policy and to bill for its premiums. Recruitment and Selection Today 5.3 lists potential constraints on individual performance that may affect the more objective measures of job performance.

SUBJECTIVE PERFORMANCE APPRAISAL: RATING SYSTEMS

As a person's job becomes removed from actual production or sales work, it becomes more difficult to associate objective measures to the employee's performance. Upper-level jobs in an organization may involve more administration, leadership, team building, and decision making–dimensions that are not easily measured in objective terms. The

RECRUITMENT AND SELECTION TODAY 5.2

EXAMPLES OF OBJECTIVE MEASURES OF JOB PERFORMANCE*

Production of Sales Measures

QUANTITY

- Number of items produced
- Volume of sales
- Time to completion
- Number of calls processed each day
- Average size of sales orders
- Words typed per minute
- Speed of production

QUALITY

- Number of errors
- Dollar cost of errors
- Number of customer complaints
- Number of spelling and grammatical mistakes
- Degree of deviation from a standard
- Number of cancelled contracts

TRAINABILITY

- Time to reach standard
- Rate of increase in production
- Rate of sales growth

Personnel Data

ABSENTEEISM

- Number of sick days used
- Number of unscheduled days off work
- Number of times late for work

TENURE

- Length of time in job
- Voluntary turnover rate
- Involuntary turnover rate

RATE OF ADVANCEMENT

- Number of promotions
- Percentage increase in salary
- Length of time to first promotion

ACCIDENTS

- Number of accidents
- Cost of accidents
- Number of days lost to accidents
- Number of safety violations

*These are measures that have been used over time; inclusion in this list does not necessarily mean that these are the best objective measurements of individual or group performance.

Relative rating system
A subjective measurement system that compares the overall performance of one employee to that of others to establish a rank order of employee performance.

issues of criterion relevance, deficiency, and contamination become even more serious. How should an organization evaluate the performance of an accountant's supervisor? Most likely, the supervisor's own manager, peers, and perhaps even subordinates will be asked to rate, or judge, the supervisor's performance on relevant job dimensions. Without a doubt, performance ratings are the most frequently used criteria.

There are two classes of subjective performance measures. The first are those relative rating systems that compare the overall performance of an employee with that of others to establish a rank order of employee performance. **Relative rating systems** are also known as comparative rating systems for obvious reasons. There are several different types of relative rating systems.

RECRUITMENT AND SELECTION TODAY 5.3

SOME POTENTIAL CONSTRAINTS ON INDIVIDUAL PERFORMANCE

- Lack of supplies/materials
- Lack of needed staff
- Absenteeism of critical personnel
- Failure to receive material/assemblies from other units
- Poor working conditions
- Inadequate physical facilities
- Poor leadership
- Excessive bureaucracy
- Unpredictable workloads
- Overextended staff
- High stress levels in workplace
- Change in policies, procedures, and/or regulations
- Peer pressure to limit production
- Poor communication of goals and objectives
- Lack of necessary equipment
- Inadequate training of new hires
- Too many inexperienced staff in unit
- Lack of support staff
- Budget restrictions/cost-saving measures

RANK ORDER

In rank ordering, the rater arranges the employees in order of their perceived overall performance level. For a group of 10 workers, the best performer would be assigned rank 1 and the worst, rank 10.

PAIRED COMPARISONS

In paired comparisons, the rater compares the overall performance of each worker with that of every other worker who must be evaluated. In rating four employees, their supervisor compares every possible pair of workers: Employee 1 versus Employee 2, Employee 1 versus Employee 3, and so on. The workers are then ranked on the basis of the number of times they were selected as the top-rated performer over all of the comparisons.

FORCED DISTRIBUTION

Rather than rank workers from top to bottom, the system sets up a limited number of categories that are tied to performance standards. For example, the rater may be given a scale with the categories excellent, above average, average, below average, and poor to evaluate each worker overall or on specific job dimensions. The rater is forced to place a predetermined number or percentage of workers into each of the rating categories on the basis of a normal frequency distribution. That is, only a specified percentage of workers may be called excellent or above average and another percentage must be called poor or below average.

RELATIVE PERCENTILE METHOD

The relative percentile method (RPM)[97,98] overcomes one of the major shortcomings of other comparative rating systems by allowing raters to compare individuals on job performance dimensions that have been derived through job analytic procedures. The

RPM requires raters to use a 101-point scale (0 to 100), with a score of 50 representing *average* performance. For each performance dimension, or for the global comparison, a rater uses the 101-point scale to assess each ratee relative to one another. The rating scale anchors each rater's comparisons to an absolute standard and, thus, allows meaningful comparisons among ratings obtained from different raters.

ABSOLUTE RATING SYSTEMS

Absolute rating systems
Compare the performance of one worker with an absolute standard of performance; can be used to assess performance on one dimension or to provide an overall assessment.

Absolute rating systems compare the performance of one worker with an absolute standard of performance. These methods provide either an overall assessment of performance or assessments on specific job dimensions. A rating scale is developed for each dimension that is to be evaluated. Over the years, a variety of formats have been developed to assess performance in absolute terms. While these rating scales may have important qualitative differences, they usually lead to the same administrative decisions. One rating system may provide more effective feedback, while supervisors are more likely to favour another and support its use. The ratings assigned to employees by either rating system are likely to be highly correlated, once measurement errors are taken into account. The particular ratings scale format may not make much difference in the relative order of scores derived for each employee. However, different rating formats may not have the same degree of validity or meet relevant legal requirements.[99] We present three examples of commonly used absolute rating scales.

GRAPHIC RATING SCALES

Graphic rating scales can be produced to assess an employee on any job dimension. The scale usually consists of the name of the job component or dimension, a brief definition of the dimension, a scale with equal intervals between the numbers placed on the scale, verbal labels or anchors attached to the numerical scale, and instructions for making a response. Figure 5.4 presents samples of graphic rating scales that have been designed to rate effort. The presence or absence of elements such as a definition, instructions on how to make a response, and the subjectivity of labels attached to different numerical values on the scale help to distinguish between the relative goodness of the scales. The poor rating scale presented in Figure 5.4(a) does not provide the rater with a definition of effort. Each rater may define this term in a different way or have a different understanding of the characteristic, leaving open the possibility that different raters are not assessing the same thing. The better example in Figure 5.4(b) provides a definition of the performance dimension and instructions on how to make a response.

BEHAVIOURALLY ANCHORED RATING SCALES

Behaviourally anchored rating scales (BARS) use the critical incident technique discussed in Chapter 4 to empirically derive job behaviours that are rated and then used to anchor the values placed on a rating scale. Although this procedure sounds simple, it is actually quite complex and time consuming. Figure 5.5 shows a behaviourally anchored rating scale developed for the competency of communication. In Figure 5.5, statements such as "Makes interesting and informative presentations," "Uses e-mail effectively and replies in a timely fashion," and "Explains complicated points in different ways to ensure understanding"

FIGURE 5.4

EXAMPLES OF GRAPHIC RATING SCALES

a) A Poor Rating Scale: The scale does not provide a definition of the trait or characteristic being measured, and it provides little if any instruction on how to make a response. The labels for values "1" and "5" are subjective and open to interpretation by different raters. Does the "X" represent a value of "2," "3," or somewhere in between?

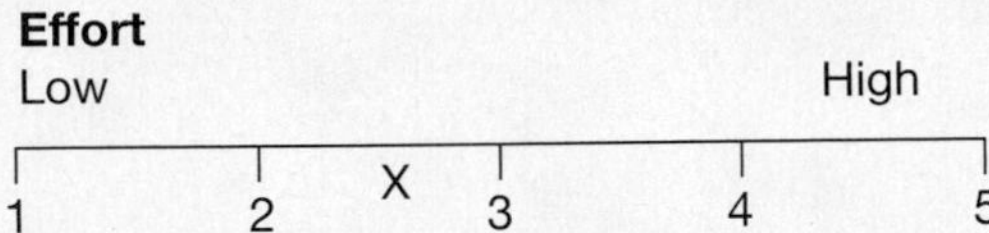

b) A Better Rating Scale: The scale offers a definition of "Effort" and provides instructions on how to rate, but the value labels are still subjective and open to different interpretations by different raters.

EFFORT – Consider the amount of energy brought to the job to complete the work in a professional manner. Circle the number that best reflects the employee's effort on the job.				
1	2	3	4	5
Poor	Below Average	Average	Above Average	Excellent

would have been assigned similarly high ratings by SMEs. A rating scale like this could then be used to evaluate an employee's level of proficiency with respect to communication.[100]

BEHAVIOUR OBSERVATION SCALES

Behaviour observation scales (BOS) are very similar to BARS in that the starting point is an analysis of critical job incidents by those knowledgeable about the job to establish performance dimensions.[101] Once the list of behaviours that represent different job dimensions is constructed, supervisors are asked to monitor the frequency with which employees exhibit each behaviour over a standardized time period. Next, the frequency data are reviewed through an *item analysis*, where the response to each item is correlated to a performance score for a dimension. This performance score is obtained by summing all of the items that belong to a particular dimension. Only those items that attain high correlations with the total score are retained for the performance appraisal measurement. This procedure assures a high degree of internal consistency for each dimension. An example of a BOS used in evaluating the performance of a security dispatcher is presented in Table 5.5.

FIGURE 5.5

BEHAVIOURAL ANCHORS USED TO ASSESS COMMUNICATION COMPETENCY

Communication involves communicating ideas and information orally and/or in writing in a way that ensures the messages are easily understood by others; listening to and understanding the comments and questions of others; marketing key points effectively to a target audience; and speaking and writing in a logical, well-ordered way. Circle the rating that best represents the degree of communication exhibited by the employee you are rating.

5 — **Excellent**

Makes interesting and informative presentations; explains complicated points in different ways to ensure understanding; written reports are concise, understandable, and lead to defendable and convincing conclusions; uses e-mail effectively and replies in a timely fashion; actively listens to others to ensure understanding of what they said; uses humour to capture and maintain attention of audience; makes effective use of nonverbal communication; provides feedback to ensure comprehension of messages that are received.

4 — **Above Average**

Written and oral communication exhibit excellent grammar and vocabulary; maintains eye contact with audience during oral presentations; speaks with confidence and authority; written and oral presentations are well organized; gets to the point in oral presentations; accurately summarizes positions taken during group discussions; listens carefully to opinions and concerns of others.

(3) — **Average**

Performs well in a structured setting; actively participates in group discussions; presents unpopular positions in a nonthreatening manner and acknowledges opposing points of view; asks for feedback from audience; makes presentations in a clear and concise manner.

2 — **Below Average**

Oral presentations are factual and accurate but lose the attention of the audience; presentations are overly long; leaves out important points in both oral and written reports; e-mail messages are confusing; performs other tasks while listening to people and does not hear what was said; needs to repeat points to get them across to an audience; does not make an effort to obtain feedback from audience.

1 — **Unsatisfactory**

Has difficulty establishing a relationship with the audience; uses inappropriate grammar and vocabulary; responds inappropriately to what has been said; does not make an effort to ensure that presentation was understood; ideas are presented in a disorganized manner; written communication and e-mails are brief and incomplete.

TABLE 5.5

BEHAVIOURAL OBSERVATION SCALE USED TO EVALUATE A SECURITY DISPATCHER

JOB-SPECIFIC TASK PROFICIENCY				
Properly secures lost and found articles	Almost Never	1 2 3 4 5	Almost Always	
Controls visitor access to buildings	Almost Never	1 2 3 4 5	Almost Always	
Monitors multiple surveillance devices	Almost Never	1 2 3 4 5	Almost Always	
Ensures confidentiality and security of information	Almost Never	1 2 3 4 5	Almost Always	
Activates appropriate emergency response teams as needed	Almost Never	1 2 3 4 5	Almost Always	
				Total Score_____
6–16 Very Poor	17–19 Unsatisfactory	20–21 Satisfactory	22–23 Excellent	24–25* Superior

*Management sets performance standards.

MANAGEMENT BY OBJECTIVES (MBO)

Management by objectives is a performance measurement system that emphasizes completion of goals that are defined in terms of objective criteria such as quantity produced or savings realized. It is a results-based system. MBO starts with the identification of organizational goals or objectives and uses these to specify goals for each employee's job performance. Before any goals can be set, the job-related behaviours must first be identified through a job analysis. The employee plays an important role in this process. Once both the employee and supervisor understand the job, both meet to develop a mutually agreeable set of goals that are outputs of the employee's job. Once the goals are established, the supervisor uses them to evaluate the employee's performance. Over the review period there are several meetings between employee and supervisor to review progress. At the end of the review period, there is a final meeting to assess whether the employee met the established goals and to set the goals for the next review period.

Strengths of this system involve the linkage between organizational and individual goals, frequent analysis and discussion of the employees' progress toward meeting the goals, and immediate feedback about performance. The employees know, from the objective criteria, whether they are performing up to expectations. Because the system is based on objective or hard criteria, the system suffers from all the problems inherent in the use of that type of performance measure. The emphasis on task performance through hard criteria mostly ignores contextual performance that may be as critical to the organization's success. In addition, the process can be as time-consuming as a BARS procedure to develop, with managers at different levels in the organization having conflicting views on what constitutes appropriate goals. The process may stifle creativity because of its emphasis on short-term results. It leads to the emphasis on personal goals, which may impede the development of teamwork.[102]

BALANCED SCORECARD

A balanced scorecard approach, like MBO, links higher-level strategic goals to individual performance. It provides feedback around both the internal business processes and external outcomes in order to continuously improve strategic performance and results. The balanced scorecard approach is an approach to describing and communicating strategy and selecting performance measures linked to strategic outcomes.[103] The balanced scorecard approach provides a measurement system for evaluating organizational effectiveness as well as providing a management framework for aligning activities with an organization's mission, vision, and strategy. The basic premise of the balanced scorecard system is that organizational effectiveness is a multidimensional concept and that the major elements of the system, including individual performance, must be in alignment with accepted organizational objectives.

The balanced scorecard incorporates performance feedback around internal business process *outputs* and the *outcomes* of business strategies. Measurement is key to improvement and the success of the system. Measures and indicators are developed for the strategic plan's priorities. The selected measures and indicators provide the necessary information on the organization's progress toward meeting its strategic objectives. Processes are then designed to collect information relevant to these metrics and reduce it to numerical form for storage, display, and analysis. Decision makers examine the outcomes of various measured processes and strategies and track the results.

The balanced scorecard approach is a useful method for clarifying the multiple performance dimensions of a job that should be the basis of evaluation. It also establishes the linkages of any one job or position to other components of the organization. For example, a human resources professional's job may involve contact with specific employees, service to other organizational units, interaction with budgeting and finance, working with the training department to establish development plans for employees or groups, and so forth. In the case of teams, the balanced scorecard can be used to track team performance with respect to key objectives or activities. Actions or processes that are under the control of individual team members can be tracked and can help the team to take corrective action in support of individual members. The approach can help the team to identify ongoing problems and to address those issues to avoid further complications.[104] More information on the balanced scorecard approach can be found at http://www.balancedscorecard.org.

PERCEIVED FAIRNESS AND SATISFACTION WITH RATING SYSTEMS

An important consideration in the choice of a rating system is not only the validity and reliability of the system, but also its acceptance by those it will be used to evaluate. Acceptance of the rating system by those subject to evaluation by the system is critical to the system's successful implementation and continued use.[105] The perceived fairness and perceived justice of the performance appraisal process plays a central role in determining employee reactions. Rating systems that are perceived to be fair and those that produce a high degree of satisfaction among the ratees are more likely to find acceptance.[106] Both the BOS and BARS produce greater degrees of satisfaction and perceived fairness than trait scales. Managers do not view trait scales as an acceptable measurement instrument, particularly when they are used to assess their own performance by other managers.[107] Most importantly, organizations are more likely to win cases involving performance evaluation when they can show a court or tribunal that the performance appraisals were fair and carried out with due process.[108]

CREATING A JOB PERFORMANCE DATABASE

Throughout this chapter we have discussed the necessity of organizations obtaining performance data to develop criteria that can be used to validate selection systems. We started off by describing the different types of performance and then moved on to discuss issues involving job performance measures used as criteria. Finally we briefly looked at some ways of assessing employee performance. There may be considerable individual variation in how employees carry out their jobs. This individual performance data must be recorded to help employees identify strengths and weaknesses and to improve through training but also to assist the organization in recruiting and selecting people who meet the KSAOs or competency profile for a specific position. Many organizations use a Human Resource Information System (HRIS) to carry out these functions.

HRIS is generally an online, centralized set of standardized and specialized software packages that track existing employee data including personal histories, skills, capabilities, accomplishments, and salary. HRIS management modules record basic demographic data and information on selection, training and development, competencies and skill management, and compensation. The data can be used in recruitment, selection, performance appraisal, promotion, and compensation. Some systems have an "employee self-serve module" that is interactive; for example, employees may query the system about their attendance record and to upload achievements relevant to their KSAOs and competencies, as well as uploading other changes to their personal information. In this latter case, sophisticated HRIS can match the qualification of employees with requirements of positions in creating succession plans or identifying potential candidates for promotion. The HRIS also contains the performance appraisal data collected by supervisors. HRIS also contains other modules that go beyond the needs of recruitment and selection.

// HUMAN RIGHTS AND PERFORMANCE APPRAISAL

Ever since *Griggs v. Duke Power*,[109] which we discussed in Chapter 3, personnel practices in the United States and Canada have been increasingly subject to review by judiciary or human rights tribunals. Although the Canadian legal precedents have occurred more recently, they have been influenced by U.S. case law.[110,111] Reviews of U.S. decisions related to criterion-related validity studies and performance measurement systems emphasize that the defensibility of performance measures rests on the ability to demonstrate that they are job related.[112] This point was emphasized in the Supreme Court of Canada's *Meioren* decision.[113] The court ruled that a standard–that is, a criterion–must be reasonably related to the accomplishment of work-related purposes (see Chapter 3).

The absence of a job or work analysis as part of criterion development will likely cast suspicion on any performance measurement system subject to judicial review.[114] In *B.L. Mears v. Ontario Hydro*,[115] a tribunal under the Ontario Human Rights Commission decided that black employees were unfairly ranked for layoffs, compared with white employees, through the use of vague and undefined criteria (e.g., productivity, safety, quality of work, attendance, and seniority). Additionally, the ranking system was informal, as no written records of productivity or quality of work were kept. In reviewing U.S. court decisions involving performance appraisal systems, Barrett and Kernan[116] also note the requirement for written documentation regarding performance measurements. They go on to advise employers to maintain a review mechanism through which employees can appeal performance assessments they believe to be unfair or discriminatory.

Increased critical examination of performance measurement practices by Canadian human rights commissions and courts will mean strict adherence to accepted professional standards of criterion development.[117] These standards will include those that apply in the United States unless it can be shown that professional standards in Canada seriously deviate from those in the United States, or that Canadian legislation or case law has established practices that vary from U.S. standards. At present neither of these conditions hold. The most explicit statement on criteria is contained in the "Uniform Guidelines,"[118] which were jointly developed by the U.S. Equal Employment Opportunity Commission, Civil Service Commission, Department of Labor, and Department of Justice[119]:

> *Whatever criteria are used should represent important or crucial work behavior(s) or work outcomes. . . . The bases for the selection of the criterion measures should be provided, together with references to the evidence considered in making the selection of criterion measures. A full description of all criteria on which data were collected and means by which they were observed, recorded, evaluated, and quantified should be provided. If rating techniques are used as criterion measures, the appraisal form(s) and instructions to the raters should be provided as part of the validation evidence or should be explicitly described and available. All steps taken to insure that criterion measures are free from factors which would unfairly alter the scores of members of any group should be described.*

A performance measurement system must meet both legal and professional practice standards to satisfy human rights requirements. Reviews of legal decisions and research suggest that the steps outlined in Recruitment and Selection Notebook 5.1 must be included in a performance measurement system to meet those requirements.

RECRUITMENT AND SELECTION NOTEBOOK 5.1

DESIGNING A PERFORMANCE MEASUREMENT SYSTEM TO MEET LEGAL AND PROFESSIONAL STANDARDS

1. Conduct a job and organization analysis to describe the job performance domain and competencies that are necessary for successful completion of the organization's goals.
2. Select criteria that are valid, reliable, and practical measurements of the job performance dimensions or competencies. Document the development of the criteria and measurement scales as well as their validity.
3. Identify the performance standards and goals or expected results that will be used to evaluate employees on the selected criteria. These standards should be made known to employees in understandable terms at the beginning of the review period. These standards must be work related and bona fide occupational requirements.
4. Train people in the use of the performance measurement system, particularly when they will be called on to make judgments about employee performance. This training should include a review of the criteria, the measurement scales, and the standards.
5. Provide written instructions to all assessors on the proper use of the measurement system, particularly if the system involves the use of rating procedures.
6. Provide feedback from the performance evaluation to the employees. Assist those employees who receive

poor evaluations to improve their performance. Raters should be trained in the effective use of feedback.

7. Establish a formal review mechanism, which has responsibility for the appraisal system and for any appeals arising from the evaluation process.

8. Document all steps in the development of the appraisal system and its use, as well as all decisions affecting employees that result from using the performance measurement data.

// SUMMARY

This chapter illustrates the important role that job performance plays in recruitment and selection. The premise of the chapter is that a solid understanding of job performance and its measurement is an integral part of building a selection system that will meet professional and legal standards. A key to validating selection systems, whether competency based or the more traditional type, is to understand the nature of the job performance that is being predicted by the competencies or KSAOs. Job performance is linked to an organization's mission, values, and goals. One useful approach to understanding job performance is to recognize that job performance is a multidimensional construct composed of task, contextual, adaptive, and counterproductive work behaviours.

The chapter uses the performance model developed by Campbell[120] that categorizes jobs in terms of their performance requirements into eight performance dimensions to illustrate the role that contextual, adaptive, and counterproductive work behaviours play in any job. Understanding the factors that underlie job performance is necessary to its measurement. The Campbell model emphasizes that declarative knowledge, procedural knowledge, and motivation underlie job performance. The chapter uses these concepts to illustrate likely predictors of different aspects of job behaviour, particularly contextual, adaptive, and counterproductive work behaviours.

The usefulness of any selection system is determined by how well it predicts job performance as measured by job-related criteria. Any criteria chosen as a measure of job performance must be valid, reliable, practical, and capable of withstanding legal challenge. A construct validation strategy such as that outlined by Campbell[121] will help to satisfy legal requirements. Once job-related performance dimensions or competencies have been identified, the type of criterion measure that most validly represents each performance dimension or competency should be selected. Most likely there will be different measures for different performance dimensions or competencies.

The chapter reviews different factors that affect criteria and the pros and cons of combining different criterion measures to form composites. It also assesses the stability of performance measures over time. Current research suggests that training criteria are acceptable performance measures for estimating maximum performance. However, to obtain a better understanding of possible changes in validities over time, repeated measures of performance should be taken over time. Data from the various criterion measures should be collected in an uncollapsed form and formed into composites when necessary. The weighting of composites should reflect the priority assigned by the organization to the different goal-related behaviours. All the procedures used in establishing the performance dimensions or competencies, their measures, and data collection and analysis should be documented. The chapter ends with a brief review of objective and subjective performance appraisal tools.

KEY TERMS

Absolute rating systems, p. 206
Adaptive Performance, p. 179
Contextual performance, p. 179
Counterproductive work behaviours, p. 179
Criteria, p. 178
Criterion contamination, p. 198
Criterion deficiency, p. 198
Criterion relevance, p. 198
Job performance, p. 178
Job performance domain, p. 181
Objective performance measures, p. 203
Performance dimensions, p. 181
Practicality, p. 199
Relative rating system, p. 204
Subjective performance measures, p. 203
Task performance, p. 179
Ultimate criterion, p. 200

WEB LINKS

The National Occupational Classification (NOC) system is available online at
http://www.esdc.gc.ca/eng/jobs/lmi/noc

Resources on performance measurement can be found by Googling the term. One of the better resources is
http://www.performance-measurement.net/news-list.asp

Information on workplace violence from the Workplace Violence Research Institute can be found at
http://www.workviolence.com

The CareerBuilder.com website provides useful information on workplace issues at
http://www.careerbuilder.com/JobSeeker/Resources/CareerResources.aspx

DISCUSSION QUESTIONS

1. Why is it important to understand performance as part of the recruitment and selection process?
2. In this chapter we discuss task performance, contextual performance, adaptive behaviour, and counterproductive behaviour. Discuss the role that each of these plays in developing a recruitment and selection system.
3. If you were limited in selecting employees on the basis of only one of the four types of performance discussed in this chapter, which one would you choose? Why?
4. Discuss Campbell's performance taxonomy. Can you think of a job that does not fit that model?
5. Compare Campbell's model to the "Great Eight" competencies presented in Chapter 4. What are the differences/similarities?

6. Discuss the distinction among criterion relevance, criterion contamination, and criterion deficiency.
7. What are the characteristics of a good criterion measure?

EXERCISES

Many of the forms used by colleges and universities to assess teaching performance suffer from all the defects of graphic rating scales. For this exercise:

1. Obtain a copy of the teaching assessment form used by your institution and critique it using the information presented in this chapter. If a teacher were dismissed solely on information obtained from this instrument that indicated the person was a poor teacher, would the decision stand up before a court or labour arbitration board?
2. Assume that teaching involves the following major activities: lecture preparation and organization; communication skills; use of examples and exercises; use of audio-visual materials/PowerPoint/Internet; grading; course-related advising and feedback; interaction with students; and maintaining class and office hours.
   a. Place these activities into the job performance dimensions developed by Campbell as well as the "Great Eight" competencies. More than one activity may be placed in a dimension.
   b. Identify the major behaviours and/or KSAOs for each dimension.
3. (May be done as a group exercise.) For each job dimension or competency, construct a behaviourally anchored rating scale of the type shown in Figure 5.5. You do not have to follow all the steps required to construct a BARS. Act as your own SME and then have a classmate rate the different behaviours for their importance. Shaw, Schneier, and Beatty[122] present useful information for constructing a BARS.
4. Compare your scale with the one used in your institution. Which one would you prefer to use? Which does your professor prefer? Why?
5. What are your views on performance appraisal? Do you believe that individual performance feedback has an impact on improving team or organizational performance?

CASE

As part of restructuring, a television network decided to close one of its local stations in Cape Breton. Several different unions represented the employees at the station. Employees were given severance packages or opportunities to transfer to the network's Halifax station if they were qualified for any available positions. Two electronic news-gathering (ENG) camera operators received layoff notices and requested transfer to Halifax, where two ENG positions were open. Two ENG operators–two ENG positions to fill. No problem? Not quite. A recent hire at the Halifax station also applied for one of the two positions. Under the terms of the ENG operators' collective agreement, during any restructuring the employer had the right to fill positions with employees deemed to be the best performers.

The network had never employed any type of performance assessments with its unionized employees and was at a loss as to how to determine which two of the three were the best, other than through their supervisors' opinions. The collective agreement, however, called for an "objective" assessment. The network's HR director recalled that a few years previously its Toronto station had had to prepare for compliance with pay equity legislation and had developed a rating system to evaluate all its Toronto employees, from secretaries to on-air news anchors. The survey was a graphic rating scale very similar to the type shown in Figure 5.4(b). It listed 12 traits or characteristics, including "effort," as shown in Figure 5.4(b). The 12 traits were very general characteristics such as "knowledge," "willingness to learn," and so on. The HR director asked two different managers who had worked with the three employees to use the form to rate the employees' performance. The new hire received the highest rating and was offered a position. The two potential transfers received low ratings and neither was offered a position.

Under the terms of the collective agreement, the two laid-off employees had the right to grieve the decisions, and their union carried the case to arbitration. The arbitration panel was composed of a neutral chairperson, who was mutually selected by the other two members of the panel, one of whom was appointed by the employer and the other by the union. In presenting its case to the arbitration panel, the union's lawyer decided to call an expert in HR to comment on the performance measure that had been used to assess the employees. After hearing the expert's opinion, which was not challenged by the employer, the arbitration panel threw out the decision based on the performance measure and declared that the two laid-off employees must be offered the two vacant positions.

QUESTIONS

1. What did the expert most likely tell the arbitration panel?
2. If you were that expert, what would you tell the arbitration panel? Be as detailed as possible and call upon all the material that has been covered in previous chapters.
3. Do you think an "off-the-shelf" measure that was designed for one purpose can be used to assess performance in another context?
4. After rejecting the performance measure, the arbitration panel itself was charged with assessing which of the three employees were the best performers. What would you advise the panel to do in this situation? How should they evaluate the employees' performance?

// ENDNOTES

1 "Best Practices in Performance Appraisals." 2000. *HR Focus* 2: 8.

2 Austin, J.T., and P. Villanova. 1992. "The Criterion Problem: 1917–1992." *Journal of Applied Psychology* 77: 836–74.

3 Borman, W.C., and S.J. Motowidlo. 1993. "Expanding the Criterion Domain to Include Elements of Contextual Performance." In N. Schmitt and W.C. Borman, eds., *Personnel Selection in Organizations* (pp. 71–98). San Francisco: Jossey-Bass.

4 Campbell, J.P., M.B. Gasser, and F.L. Oswald. 1996. "The Substantive Nature of Job Performance Variability." In K.R. Murphy, ed. *Individual Differences and Behavior in Organizations* (pp. 285–99). San Francisco: Jossey-Bass.

5 Rotundo, M., and P.R. Sackett. 2002. "The Relative Importance of Task, Citizenship and Counter Productive Performance to Global Ratings of Job Performance: A Policy-Capturing Approach." *Journal of Applied Psychology* 87: 66–80.

6 Sonnentag, S., J. Volmer, and A. Spychala. 2008. "Job Performance." In J. Barling and C.L. Cooper, eds., *Sage Handbook of Organizational Behavior*, Vol. 1 (pp. 427–447). Thousand Oaks, CA: Sage.

7 Koopmans, L., C.M. Bernaards, V.H. Hildebrandt, W.B. Schaufeli, H.C.W. de Vet, and A.J. van der Beek. 2011. "Conceptual Frameworks of Individual Work Performance: A Systematic Review." *Journal of Occupational and Environmental Medicine* 53: 856–866.

8 Motowidlo, S.J., W.C. Borman, and M.J. Schmit. 1997. "A Theory of Individual Differences in Task and Contextual Performance." *Human Performance* 10: 71–83.

9 Motowidlo, S.J., and M.J. Schmit. 1999. "Performance Assessment in Unique Jobs." In D.R. Ilgen and E.D. Pulakos, eds., *The Changing Nature of Performance* (pp. 56–86). San Francisco: Jossey-Bass.

10 Coleman, V.I., and W.C. Borman. 2000. "Investigating the Underlying Structure of the Citizenship Performance Domain." *Human Resource Management Review* 10: 25–44.

11 Conway, J.M. 1999. "Distinguishing Contextual Performance from Task Performance for Managerial Jobs." *Journal of Applied Psychology* 84: 3–13.

12 VanScotter, J.R., and S.J. Motowidlo. 1996. "Interpersonal Facilitation and Job Dedication as Separate Facets of Contextual Performance." *Journal of Applied Psychology* 81: 525–31.

13 Motowidlo, S.J., and M.J. Schmit. 1999.

14 Koopmans et al. 2011.

15 Pulakos, E.D., S. Arad, M.A. Donovan, and K.E. Plamondon. 2000. "Adaptability in the Workplace: Development of a Taxonomy of Adaptive Performance." *Journal of Applied Psychology* 85: 612–624.

16 Kelloway, E.K., C. Loughlin, J. Barling, and A. Nault. 2002. "Self-Reported Counterproductive Behaviors and Organizational Citizenship Behaviors: Separate But Related Constructs." *International Journal of Assessment and Selection* 10: 143–51.

17 Sackett, P.R., C.M. Berry, S.A. Wiemann, and R.M. Laczo. 2006. "Citizenship and Counterproductive Behavior: Clarifying the Relationship between Them." *Human Performance* 19: 441–64.

18 Robinson, S.L., and R.J. Bennett. 1995. "A Typology of Deviant-Workplace Behaviors: A Multidimensional Scaling Study." *Academy of Management Journal* 38: 555–72.

19 Organ, D.W., and J.B. Paine. 1999. "A New Kind of Performance for Industrial and Organizational Psychology: Recent Contributions to the Study of Organizational Citizenship Behavior." *International Review of Industrial and Organizational Psychology* 14: 337–68.

20 Borman, W.C. 1991. "Job Behavior, Performance, and Effectiveness." In M.D. Dunnette and L.M. Hough, eds., *Handbook of Industrial and Organizational Psychology,* Vol. 2, 2nd ed. (pp. 271–326). Palo Alto, CA: Consulting Psychologists Press.

21 Motowidlo, S.J., and M.J. Schmit. 1999.

22 Murphy, K.R., and A.H. Shiarella. 1997. "Implications of the Multidimensional Nature of Job Performance for the Validity of Selection Tests: Multivariate Frameworks for Studying Test Validity." *Personnel Psychology* 50: 823–54.

23 Campbell, J.P. 1990. "Modelling the Performance Prediction Problem in Industrial and Organizational Psychology." In M.D. Dunnette and L.M. Hough, eds., *The Handbook of Industrial and Organizational Psychology*, Vol. 1, 2nd ed. (pp. 687–732). San Diego: Consulting Psychologists Press.

24 Campbell, J.P., R.A. McCloy, S.H. Oppler, and C.E. Sager. 1993. "A Theory of Performance." In N. Schmitt, W.C. Borman, and Associates, *Personnel Selection in Organizations*. San Francisco: Jossey-Bass.

25 Campbell, J.P. 1990.

26 Ibid.

27 Koopmans et al. 2011.

28 McCloy, R.A., J.P. Campbell, and R. Cudeck. 1994. "Confirmatory Test of a Model of Performance Determinants." *Journal of Applied Psychology* 79: 493–505.

29 Sonnentag et al. 2008.

30 Borman, W.C., and S.J. Motowidlo. 1993.

31 Ibid.

32 Coleman, V.I., and W.C. Borman. 2000.

33 Organ, D.W. 1997. "Organizational Citizenship Behavior: It's Construct Cleanup Time." *Human Performance* 10: 85–97.

34 Organ, D.W. 1997.

35 Campbell, J.P., M.B. Gasser, and F.L. Oswald. 1996.

36 Hoffman, B., C. Blair, J. Meriac, and D. Woehr. 2007. "Expanding the Criterion Domain? A Quantitative Review of the OCB Literature." *Journal of Applied Psychology* 92: 555–66.

37 Conway, J.M. 1999.

38 Rotundo, M., and P.R. Sackett. 2002.

39 Bowen, D.E., G.E. Ledford Jr., and B.R. Nathan. 1991. "Hiring for the Organization, Not the Job." *Academy of Management Executive* 5: 35–51.

40 Goodman, S.A., and D.J. Svyantek. 1999. "Person–Organization Fit and Contextual Performance: Do Shared Values Matter?" *Journal of Vocational Behavior* 55: 254–75.

41 Pulakos et al. 2000.

42 Griffin, M.A., A. Neal, and M. Neal. 2000. "The Contribution of Task Performance and Contextual Performance to Effectiveness: Investigating the Role of Situational Constraints." *Applied Psychology: An International Review* 49: 517–33.

43 Spector, P., S. Fox, and T. Domagalski. 2006. "Emotions, Violence, and Counterproductive Work Behaviors." In E.K. Kelloway, J. Barling, and J.J. Hurrell, Jr. *Handbook of Workplace Violence* (pp. 29–46). Thousand Oaks, CA: Sage.

44 Robinson, S.L., and R.J. Bennett. 1995.

45 Gialacone, R.A., and J. Greenberg. 1997. *Antisocial Behavior in Organizations*. Thousand Oaks, CA: Sage.

46 Johns, G. 2002. "Absenteeism and Mental Health." In J. C. Thomas and M. Hersen, eds., *Handbook of Mental Health in the Workplace* (pp. 437–55). Thousand Oaks, CA: Sage.

47 Stewart, N. 2013. *Missing in Action: Absenteeism Trends in Canadian Organizations*. Ottawa: The Conference Board of Canada.

48 Böckerman, P., and E. Laukkanen. 2010. "What Makes You Work While You Are Sick? Evidence from a Survey of Workers." *European Journal of Public Health* 20: 43–46.

49 Robertson Cooper. 2010. "'Presenteeism' on the Rise as an Estimated Quarter of UK Employees Admit to Working When Ill." Retrieved April 26, 2010, at http://www.robertsoncooper.com/news/1-latest-news/167-presenteeism-on-the-rise-as-an-estimated-quarter-of-uk-employees-admit-to-working-when-ill http://www.robertsoncooper.com/news/presenteeism.aspx

50 Johns, G. 2011. "Attendance Dynamics at Work: The Antecedents and Correlates of Presenteeism, Absenteeism, and Productivity Loss." *Journal of Occupational Health Psychology* 16: 483–500.

51 Brun, J.P. 2009. "Missing Pieces: 7 Ways to Improve Employee Wellbeing and Organizational Effectiveness." Montréal: Les Éditions Transcontinental.

52 Sagie, A., A. Birati, and A. Tziner. 2002. "Assessing the Costs of Behavioral and Psychological Withdrawal: A New Model and an Empirical Illustration." *Applied Psychology: An International Review* 51: 67–89.

53 Robinson and Bennett. 1995.

54 PricewaterhouseCoopers. 2012. "Stealing Retailer's Thunder: PwC Estimates Canadian Retailers Are Losing over $10 million a Day to Shrinkage." Retrieved from http://www.pwc.com/ca/en/media/release/2012-10-31-canadian-retailers-losing-ten-million-a-day-shrinkage.jhtml

55 Schat, A.C.H., M.R. Frone, and E.K. Kelloway. 2006. "Prevalence of Workplace Aggression in the U.S. Workforce." In E.K. Kelloway, J. Barling, and J.J. Hurrell, Jr. *Handbook of Workplace Violence* (pp. 47–89). Thousand Oaks, CA: Sage.

56 U.S. Bureau of Labor Statistics. 2014. "Revisions to the 2012 Census of Fatal Occupational Injuries (CFOI) Counts." Retrieved from http://www.bls.gov/iif/oshwc/cfoi/cfoi_revised12.pdf

57 Ministry of Labour. 2010. "Protecting Workers from Workplace Violence and Workplace Harassment." Fact Sheet #2. Toronto: Ontario Ministry of Labour. Retrieved January 9, 2012, at http://www.labour.gov.on.ca/english/hs/pdf/fs_workplaceviolence.pdf

58 Raynor, C., and C.L. Cooper. 2006. "Workplace Bullying." In E.K. Kelloway, J. Barling, and J.J. Hurrell, Jr., eds., *Handbook of Workplace Violence* (pp. 121–46). Thousand Oaks, CA: Sage.

59 Raynor and Cooper. 2006.

60 Ibid.

61 Ibid.

62 Ibid.

63 *Act Respecting Labour Standards*. (2004). R.S.Q. c. N-1.1, ss. 81.18-81.20 and 123.6–123.16.

64 Ibid.

65 Schmidt, F.L., and J.E. Hunter. 1998. "The Validity and Utility of Selection Methods in Personnel Psychology: Practical and Theoretical Implications of 85 Years of Research Findings." *Psychological Bulletin* 124: 262–74.

66 Schmidt, F.L. 2002. "The Role of General Cognitive Ability and Job Performance: Why There Cannot Be a Debate." *Human Performance* 15: 187–210.

67 Outz, J.L. 2002. "The Role of Cognitive Ability Tests in Employment Selection." *Human Performance* 15: 161–171.

68 Campbell et al. 1993.

69 Hunter, J.E., and R.F. Hunter. 1984. "Validity and Utility of Alternative Predictors of Job Performance." *Psychological Bulletin* 96: 72–98.

70 McDaniel, M.A., F.P. Morgeson, and F.B. Finnegan. 2001. "Use of Situational Judgment Tests to Predict Job Performance: A Clarification of the Literature." *Journal of Applied Psychology* 86: 730–740.

71 Sonnentag et al. 2008.

72 Hogan, J., S.L. Rybicki, S.J. Motowidlo, and W.C. Borman. 1998. "Relations between Contextual Performance, Personality, and Occupational Advancement." *Human Performance* 11: 189–207.

73 McManus, M.A., and M.L. Kelly. 1999. "Personality Measures and Biodata: Evidence Regarding Their Incremental Predictive Value in the Life Insurance Industry." *Personnel Psychology* 52: 137–48.

74 Pulakos, E.D., N. Schmitt, D.W. Dorsey, S. Arad, J.W. Hedge, and W.C. Borman. 2002. "Predicting Adaptive Performance: Further Tests of a Model of Adaptability." *Human Performance* 15: 299–324.

75 Daw, J. 2001.

76 D.S. Ones, C. Viswesvaran, and S. Dilchert. 2005. "Personality at Work: Raising Awareness and Correcting Misconceptions." *Human Performance* 18: 389–404.

77 Murphy, K.R., and A.H. Shiarella. 1997.

78 Rotundo, M., and P.R. Sackett. 2002.

79 Austin, J.T., and P. Villanova. 1992.

80 "Best Practices in Performance Appraisals." 2000.

81 Sulsky, L.M., and J.L. Keown. 1998. "Performance Appraisal in the Changing World of Work: Implications for the Meaning and Measurement of Work Performance." *Canadian Psychology* 39: 52–59.

82 Farrell, S., and R. Hakstian. June 2000. *A Meta-Analytic Review of the Effectiveness of Personnel Selection Procedures and Training Interventions in*

Sales Occupations. Paper presented at the annual meeting of the Canadian Psychological Association, Ottawa.

83 Smith, P.C. 1976. "Behaviours, Results, and Organizational Effectiveness: The Problem of Criteria." In M.D. Dunnette, ed., *Handbook of Industrial and Organizational Psychology* (pp. 745–76). Chicago: Rand McNally.

84 Austin, J., and P. Villanova. 1992. "The Criterion Problem: 1917–1992." *Journal of Applied Psychology* 77: 836–74.

85 Austin, J., and T. Crespin. 2006. "Problems of Criteria in Industrial and Organizational Psychology: Progress, Pitfalls, and Prospects." In W. Bennett, Jr., C.E. Lance, and D.H. Woehr, eds., *Performance Measurement: Current Perspectives and Future Challenges* (pp. 9–48). Mahwah, NJ: Lawrence Erlbaum Associates.

86 Thorndike, R.L. 1949. *Personnel Selection: Test and Measurement Technique*. New York: Wiley.

87 Austin, J., and P. Villanova. 1992.

88 Smith, P.C. 1976.

89 Guion, R.M. 1987. "Changing Views for Personnel Selection Research." *Personnel Psychology* 40: 199–213.

90 Landy, F.L. 1989. *Psychology of Work Behavior*, 4th ed. Pacific Grove, CA: Brooks/Cole.

91 Ghiselli, E.E. 1966. *The Validity of Occupational Aptitude Tests*. New York: Wiley.

92 Sackett, P.R., S. Zedeck, and L. Fogli. 1988. "Relations between Measures of Typical and Maximum Job Performance." *Journal of Applied Psychology* 73: 482–86.

93 Sackett, P. 2007. "Revisiting the Origins of the Typical-Maximum Performance Distinction." *Human Performance* 20: 179–85.

94 Marcus, B., R. Goffin, N. Johnston, and M. Rothstein. 2007. "Personality and Cognitive Ability as Predictors of Typical and Maximum Managerial Performance." *Human Performance* 20(3): 275–85.

95 Deadrick, D.L., and R.M. Madigan. 1990. "Dynamic Criteria Revisited: A Longitudinal Study of Performance Stability and Predictive Validity." *Personnel Psychology* 43: 717–44.

96 Austin, J., and P. Villanova. 1992.

97 Goffin, R.D., I.R. Gellatly, S.V. Paunonen, D.N. Jackson, and J.P. Meyer. 1996. "Criterion Validation of Two Approaches to Performance Appraisal: The Behavioral Observation Scale and the Relative Percentile Method." *Journal of Business and Psychology* 11: 23–33.

98 Goffin, R.D., and Olson, J.M. 2011. "Is It All Relative? Comparative Judgments and the Possible Improvement of Self-Ratings and Ratings of Others." *Perspectives on Psychological Science* 6: 48–60.

99 Greene, L., H.J. Bernardin, and J. Abbott. 1985. "A Comparison of Rating Formats after Correction for Attenuation." *Educational and Psychological Measurement* 45: 503–15.

100 Catano, V.M., W. Darr, and C.A. Campbell. 2007. "Performance Appraisal of Behavior-Based Competencies–A Reliable and Valid Procedure." *Personnel Psychology* 60: 201–230.

101 Latham, G.P., and K.N. Wexley. 1981. *Increasing Productivity through Performance Appraisal*. Reading, MA: Addison-Wesley.

102 Bowman, J.S. 1999.

103 Kaplan, R.S., and D.P. Norton. 1996. *The Balanced Scorecard: Translating Strategy into Action*. Boston: The Harvard Business School Press.

104 Meyer, C. 1998. "How the Right Measures Help Teams Excel." In *Harvard Business Review on Measuring Performance* (pp. 99–122). Boston: HBS Publishing.

105 Hedge, J.W., and M.S. Teachout. 2000. "Exploring the Concept of Acceptability as a Criterion for Evaluating Performance Measures." *Group & Organizational Management* 25: 22–44.

106 Smither, J.W. 1998. "Lessons Learned: Research Implications for Performance Appraisal and Management Practice." In J.W. Smither, ed., *Performance Appraisal: State of the Art in Practice*. San Francisco, CA: Jossey Bass.

107 Latham, G.P., and G.H. Seijts. 1997. "The Effect of Appraisal Instrument on Managerial Perceptions of Fairness and Satisfaction with Appraisals from Peers." *Canadian Journal of Behavioural Science* 29: 278–82.

108 Werner, J.M., and M.C. Bolino. 1997. "Explaining U.S. Courts of Appeals Decisions Involving Performance Appraisal: Accuracy, Fairness, and Validation." *Personnel Psychology* 50: 1–24.

109 *Griggs v. Duke Power*. 1971. 401 U.S. 424.

110 Cronshaw, S.F. 1986. "The Status of Employment Testing in Canada: A Review and Evaluation of Theory and Professional Practice." *Canadian Psychology* 27: 183–95.

111 Cronshaw, S.F. 1988. "Future Directions for Industrial Psychology in Canada." *Canadian Psychology* 29: 30–43.

112 Barrett, G.V., and M.C. Kernan. 1987. "Performance Appraisal and Terminations: A Review of Court Decisions since *Brito v. Zia* with Implication for Personnel Practices." *Personnel Psychology* 40: 489–503.

113 *British Columbia (Public Service Employee Relations Commission) v. BCGSEU*. Supreme Court of Canada decision rendered September 9, 1999.

114 Landy, F.L. 1989.

115 *B.L. Mears, Gifford Walker, George Wills, Hollis Trotman, Thomas Atherly, Hubert Telphia and Leon Francis v. Ontario Hydro and Jack Watson, A. Watkiss, T. Ouelette and Mossis Loveness*. 1984. *Canadian Human Rights Reporter,* 5, D/3433 (Ontario Human Rights Commission Board of Inquiry, December 1983.

116 Barrett, G.V., and M.C. Kernan. 1987.

117 Cronshaw, S.F. 1988. "Future Directions for Industrial Psychology in Canada." *Canadian Psychology* 29: 30–43.

118 "Uniform Guidelines on Employee Selection Procedures." 1978. *Federal Register* 43: 38290–315.

119 Ibid.

120 Campbell, J.P. 1990.

121 Ibid.

122 Shaw, D.G., C.E. Schneier, and R.W. Beatty. 1991. "Managing Performance with a Behaviorally Based Appraisal System." In J. Jones, B.D. Steffy, and D.W Bray, eds., *Applying Psychology in Business: The Handbook for Managers and Human Resource Professionals* (pp. 314–25). New York: Lexington Books.

CHAPTER

6

RECRUITMENT:

The First Step in the Selection Process

CHAPTER LEARNING OUTCOMES

This chapter reviews the role played by recruitment in HR planning. We present this topic from the perspective of recruitment as the first step in selection. The first part of the chapter looks at recruitment as part of a human resources strategy along with the factors that influence the strategy. The second part reviews different recruitment methods and their overall effectiveness. The third part of the chapter reviews factors that may attract job applicants and influence them to apply for jobs with an organization. The chapter ends with a discussion of points to consider in evaluating the success of recruitment strategies.

AFTER READING THIS CHAPTER YOU SHOULD:

- be able to discuss recruitment as part of an organization's strategic planning;
- understand the link between recruitment and selection;
- appreciate how the characteristics of the job and organization are influential in attracting job applicants;
- know the role that accurate expectations play in developing a fit between a person and an organization;
- be able to discuss why a realistic job preview may benefit both the job seeker and the organization;
- be aware of the internal and external factors that influence an organization's recruitment strategy;
- be able to design and implement a recruitment action plan;

- be aware of the different methods that can be used to recruit internal and external job applicants;
- understand the increasingly important role played by the Internet and social media in recruiting; and
- appreciate the need to evaluate the effectiveness of different recruitment methods.

EMPLOYERS BREW UP NEW WAYS TO RECRUIT TALENT

Big Rock Brewery of Calgary has attracted a Facebook and Twitter following among fans of its premium craft beers. Sellout crowds attend its annual awards for the best amateur beer commercials.

Brewmaster Paul Gautreau's blog promotes the latest product offering, Gopher Lager, and throws in recipes to pair with Big Rock ales: Guacamole, with Big Rock Lime; an Italian sausage dish with Grasshopper, a wheat ale; and—"I know it sounds weird"— apple pie, with Big Rock's Traditional Ale served at 5 degrees Celsius, or even warmer.

And then there's what HR specialists refer to as the "employer brand," which gives prospective employees a taste of what the work environment is like.

"Imagine taking your work home with you," the brewery posts on its careers Web portal. "If you're the type of person who thinks that making exceptional beers for discriminating customers while working for an underdog that takes on the big multi-nationals describes your perfect job, please send us your resume."

"Our website gets a lot of hits; it's very popular," said Lynn Thomson, supervisor of human resources and administration at Big Rock Brewery Income Trust. "So we have had a lot of success hiring from our website. We posted three opportunities in March and the response was overwhelming, just overwhelming."

Companies have always focused on their brand to win over customers. Now, many—like Big Rock—are finding they can gain an edge in the war for talent by focusing on their "employment branding" as well.

Another way companies are recruiting people is through social media sites such as LinkedIn, which has become a fertile hunting ground for employers on the prowl, said Bill Greenhalgh, chief executive officer of the Human Resources Professionals Association. "Social [media] networks in general in the recruitment industry are a game-changer, there's no question about that."

"They allow potential recruits to check out what other people feel about an organization, and they allow organizations to identify people who are not necessarily looking for jobs but might be amenable to being approached."

LinkedIn, which members use primarily for business networking purposes, has emerged as a favourite with recruiters, he said. "A lot of people who go on LinkedIn and put their information on there are surreptitiously looking for jobs. They don't want to broadcast it too broadly, but of course they are always open to offers and approaches."

Neil Crawford, leader of Hewitt Associates' Best Employers in Canada study, said that for employers, Facebook and LinkedIn are "valuable ways to connect with people and get your message out, particularly for companies that are not household names."

But once employers have tapped into this pool of prospective candidates, they need some sort of process to determine which candidates will be the best fit, Mr. Crawford said.

Right Management Canada, a career and talent management company, has found more employers seeking help with the assessment process as the economic recovery gains traction. They are now hiring again, but very selectively, Bram Lowsky, the firm's senior vice-president and general manager, said in an interview.

Employers are looking for candidates who have the capability and technical expertise to do the job, "but ultimately the cultural fit is going to be the driver of success, and the more senior the role, the more critical that becomes," Mr. Lowsky said.

When Ms. Thomson posts a position at Red Rock—listing all the requirements of the job in question—those candidates whose resumes address every single point in the posting warrant a second look. If a current employee recommends one of the applicants, even better. Who you know still counts—a lot.

"It's important," said Ms. Thomson, who places a lot of weight on employee referrals. "If an employee comes forward, they are putting their reputation on the line."

"We look for people we feel will blend in with the close-knit staff, because we are a modest size," she said of the company, which has 120 employees. "Attitude and the ability to blend in and fit the culture is really paramount."

Mr. Greenhalgh said it has always been the case that more than 70 per cent of positions are never advertised. The Internet just makes it that much easier to find someone who might know someone who would be ideal for the job.

Ms. Thomson herself was recommended to Big Rock by a former business acquaintance—now in a senior role at the brewery—with whom she had kept in touch by e-mail.

"I was interviewed by the president and the brewmaster," said Ms. Thomson, who joined the company in March.

Source: © Virginia Galt. Special to *The Globe and Mail.* Published Wednesday, Jun. 09, 2010

© iStock.com/Robert Churchill

Recruitment is the first step in the selection process. People apply for jobs in organizations on the basis of their interest in the job and their belief that they have the required knowledge, skills, abilities, or other attributes and competencies needed to do the job well. They also hope that the organization will provide a hospitable environment in which to spend their working hours. Obviously, this is an idealized view of the world; in bad economic times, when jobs are at a premium, people may change their perceptions of jobs and organizations, as well as their willingness to work in either. In hard economic times, people may value the security of having a job and the income it provides above everything else. However, security and income, although important considerations, are not always the most influential factors in attracting applicants to jobs or organizations.

The ultimate goal of a job-related selection system is to bring people into the organization who will perform at above-average levels and who will increase the productivity of the organization. The goal of **recruitment** is to attract a large pool of qualified candidates (an **applicant pool**) from whom the organization can select the best-qualified people for the position. Recruitment is done to meet management goals and objectives for the organization and must also meet current legal requirements (human rights, employment equity, labour law, and other legislation).

Recruitment
The generation of an applicant pool for a position or job in order to provide the required number of qualified candidates for a subsequent selection or promotion process.

Applicant pool
The set of potential candidates who may be interested in, and who are likely to apply for, a specific job.

Only within the last 30 years or so has recruitment received serious attention for the important role it plays in the selection process. Previously, recruitment was simply a means of attracting a large enough pool of candidates from which the organization could select the best-qualified people, without much thought as to how that was done or what factors influenced applicants to become part of that pool of candidates.[1] The quality and quantity of the applicant pool is related to the source and nature of the recruiting information an applicant receives.[2] In the past, though, the availability of a job and the need for money were assumed to be motivation enough to attract candidates. Hardly any consideration was given to the possibility that candidates were using the recruiting process to select the organization. Job applicants are not passive organisms; during the recruitment and selection process, they form opinions about the organization, the selection process, the people they meet, and the desirability of working in the organization.

In Part I of this chapter, we discuss strategic recruitment as the end product of HR planning and link recruiting to an organization's business strategy. We discuss the relevance of both job and organizational analysis in developing a recruitment action plan. Part II discusses the sources that an organization uses as part of its recruitment strategy, and provides an assessment of those sources. E-recruitment is now playing an increasingly important role in recruitment and is a major focus of Part II. In Part III, we review those organizational factors that attract job candidates and procedures that can be used to ensure job candidates are provided with accurate information about the job and organization. Accurate information and expectations help to prevent recruitment failures and promote the staffing of organizations with people who not only are qualified for the job but also have a good understanding of the organization in which the job takes place.

// PART I: STRATEGIC RECRUITMENT

Recruitment takes place within a strategic HR management context; that is, the interrelated practices, policies, and philosophies that are linked to organizational or business strategies. Figure 6.1 presents a simplified view of this model in which recruitment is an outcome of HR planning. The decision to recruit candidates for jobs in an organization is based on (1) an assessment of the internal and external factors affecting the organization, (2) an organization analysis based on those factors, (3) a job analysis that identifies worker behaviours and characteristics to aid in selecting candidates who are qualified for the position, and (4) forecasts about the supply of labour with the requirements to fill vacant positions. We will take a more detailed look at external and internal factors, organizational analysis and HR planning functions that influence the development of a recruitment action plan.

EXTERNAL FACTORS

In Chapter 1 we discussed a number of factors that influenced recruitment and selection: global competition, technological advances, changing workforce demographics, and the economic environment. You may wish to review that section of Chapter 1 before proceeding further. Recruitment is also influenced by two external factors over which the organization has little control: (1) the labour market which is a function of the economic environment, and (2) the laws and regulations that pertain to recruitment and selection.[3]

LABOUR MARKETS AND RECRUITING

Organizations must develop a recruiting campaign that makes sense in the context of a specific labour market. Labour markets and economic conditions impose different constraints. The overall nature of the economy may influence an organization's decision to hire or not to hire, but once a decision to hire is made, the nature of the labour market determines how extensively the organization will have to search to fill the job with a qualified candidate. In 1996, Toyota Canada was in the enviable position of having more than 50 000 people apply for 1200 positions that were being created as part of an expansion at its Cambridge, Ontario plant. The jobs paid $20 per hour plus benefits in a geographic area that had an 8.3 percent unemployment rate. Toyota had 11 000 applications on file before it had run a single advertisement or posted the jobs with employment centres.[4]

When qualified labour is scarce, the organization must broaden its recruiting beyond its normal target population. This includes going beyond normal recruiting

FIGURE 6.1

RECRUITMENT AS PART OF THE HR PLANNING PROCESS

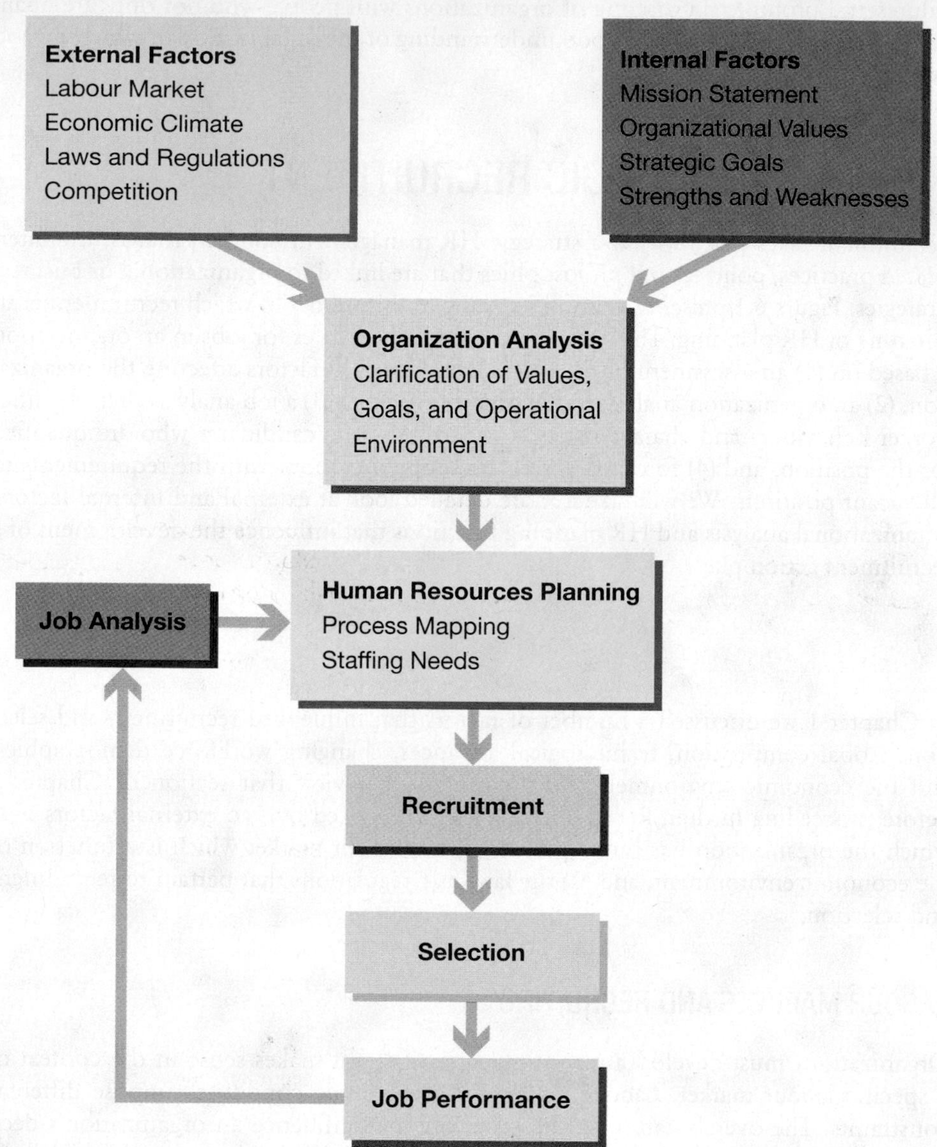

channels to attract applicants it might not seek in more favourable times. For example, if there is a shortage of chartered accountants, the organization may take a look at hiring finance majors with a background in accounting who may develop into the accounting position with some additional training. The organization may also recruit outside its normal territory, emphasizing those geographic regions with high unemployment rates or low economic growth. The controversial Temporary Foreign Workers program was designed to address labour shortages in certain sectors where it was difficult to find Canadian workers even in times of high unemployment. It has been used extensively by the restaurant and fast food industries, farming, and fish plant operators to meet labour shortages.

In favourable labour markets, the organization may advertise the accounting position only in one or two professional journals. In a poor market, it may decide to use a variety of media to attract as many qualified applicants as possible. With poor labour markets, the organization may make the job more attractive by improving salary and benefits, training and educational opportunities, and working conditions. In poor markets, the organization may spend additional resources to overcome the shortage of qualified applicants and to increase the attractiveness of the organization and the job. These considerations become even more important when the organization must compete with its rivals for scarce human resources. Recruiting when the labour market is poor is an expensive proposition.

Organizations must be prepared to alter their recruiting strategy to match labour market conditions. Internal demand and external supply of job candidates may vary considerably, causing firms to change their recruiting strategies. As well, job applicants who perceive that they have fewer or more choices are likely to react differently to different recruiting strategies.[5]

PART-TIME LABOUR MARKETS AND RECRUITING In response to today's global economy, more and more companies are employing low-wage, entry-level workers on a part-time basis. Temporary or contingent jobs have shown tremendous growth over the last decade. Nearly 2 million people go to work each day in North America on a part-time basis. North American retailing giants such as Sears, Walmart, and K-Mart have made part-time work their industry norm.

Recruiting and retaining the best part-time workers present unique problems to companies choosing to go this route. Workers who receive lower pay and benefits are less likely to feel committed to their organization or to go out of their way to get the job done. Many part-time workers are unskilled and poorly educated. Companies such as Whirlpool have responded to the need to recruit part-time workers by restructuring their pay and benefits, as well as by providing training and educational opportunities for them. Others, such as Taco Bell, have attempted to restructure the work environment to meet the needs of their part-time employees.[6]

Increasingly, temporary work is serving as a training ground for more permanent positions. On the other hand, ever-greater numbers of skilled professionals and retired workers are taking jobs on a part-time or contract basis.[7] A recent survey found that over two-thirds of temporary workers reported that they gained new skills while in their temporary positions. Organizations that depend on part-time workers will need to develop recruiting methods to attract and retain contingent employees. Indeed, some workers prefer part-time status, and when these employees are placed in part-time positions, they tend to be satisfied and committed to the organization. They also tend to remain longer.

However, placing them into full-time positions leads to less satisfaction and more turnover. The same effects occur when workers who desire full-time jobs are placed into part-time positions: less satisfaction and commitment and higher turnover.[8] The contingent or part-time status of jobs should be clearly indicated in all recruiting materials.

Outsourcing
Contracting with an outside agent to take over specified HR functions.

OUTSOURCING **Outsourcing** is the practice of contracting with an outside agent to take over specified HR functions, specifically, recruitment. Companies that need workers on a temporary or short-term basis often turn to temporary help agencies to provide them with contingent workers. In these cases, the workers are employees of the temporary help firm, not of the organization in which they do their work. The employee is actually "leased" from the outside firm. The individual is employed by the outside agency but assigned to a position with the client organization.

The outside firm assumes all payroll responsibilities (pay and benefits), but charges the client administration and placement costs, usually prorated to salary. If the client chooses to hire the individual for a full-time permanent position, then additional fees are paid to the employment agency. Some Canadian banks now meet part of their staffing needs through these arrangements. Client organizations benefit from increased workforce flexibility and savings in administrative costs. They also get to see the worker on the job over a period of time before any decisions to hire directly are made.

Investigations in both Canada and the United States suggest that some temporary help agencies may be willing to accommodate their client organizations' requests that the agency not send blacks, people with accents, or unattractive women.[9,10] Often, the client organizations have the mistaken notion that since they are not the legal employer, they are immune to charges of discrimination and free from any employment equity obligations. By allowing temporary workers on their premises and directing their work, the client organization can be subject to discrimination claims, unless it can show that the assignment based on group membership was a bona fide occupational requirement.[11]

Current information on the state of the Canadian labour market and the availability of different skill sets can be found at http://www.jobbank.gc.ca/home-eng.do?lang=eng. The website provides information for Canada as a whole and each province or territory. It also tracks the availability of specific skills and abilities and jobs that require them.

THE LEGAL ENVIRONMENT

Any organizational recruitment program must comply with the legal and regulatory requirements that apply to its operation. Chapter 3 presented some of the landmark cases and legislation that govern employment in Canada. In the United States, employment laws and regulations are assumed to affect both recruitment practices and outcomes.[12] It is likely that Canadian employment legislation has similar effects on recruitment in Canadian organizations. The most important considerations are employment equity and pay equity legislation. Any recruitment campaign that intentionally or unintentionally excludes members of groups that are protected under human rights legislation runs the risk of being declared discriminatory, with the organization subject to penalties and fines. The best defence against charges of **systemic discrimination** is to document that every attempt has been made to attract members from the protected groups.

Systemic discrimination
In employment, the intentional or unintentional exclusion of members of groups that are protected under human rights legislation through recruiting, selection, or other personnel practices or policies.

DIVERSITY RECRUITMENT In Canada, employment equity legislation seeks to eliminate discrimination in the workplace for women, visible minorities, Aboriginal peoples, and people with disabilities.

Organizations may be required, particularly if they wish to do business with the federal government, to demonstrate that they have actively sought to recruit members from these four groups. Good-faith recruitment efforts mean that the organization must use a variety of communication channels to get its message to members of different groups and to present its recruiting message in a way that interests different audiences. The recruitment effort must make members from these groups feel welcome in the organization, even when they are working there on a temporary basis.

Organizations perceived as hostile to workplace diversity will see the effectiveness of their recruitment efforts significantly compromised, and the quality of their overall applicant pool adversely affected. Diversity advertising focuses on how firms present diversity. To recruit women and minorities, organizations must communicate that they value diversity, fairness, and inclusion. Job advertisements depicting diversity and emphasizing equal employment opportunities for minorities tend to make the organization more attractive to members of minority groups.[13]

Many Canadian communities have made an effort to recruit women and visible minorities for employment as police officers. Most of these efforts have been relatively unsuccessful. For example, black police applicants often perceive a lack of fit between their attitudes and the demands of modern policing that is related to racial prejudice on the part of serving police officers and the community.[14] To help overcome these types of barriers, women, visible minorities, Aboriginal peoples, and people with disabilities should participate as front-line recruiters to help send a clear message that equal employment opportunities and a welcoming environment will be provided.[15]

Organizations must think very carefully about the messages they convey to job applicants when they seek to increase workplace diversity. While members of minority groups react favourably to efforts to recruit them, white males tend to react negatively.[16] All job candidates, however, react negatively to questions about their age, marital status, gender, or ethnicity,[17] which we noted in Chapter 3 as violating various human rights legislation. Efforts to recruit minorities may lead to reduced self-esteem on the part of the minority hires and reduced perceptions of their competence (i.e., perceptions that they were hired because they were from a minority group and not because of their fit to the job and organization).

White males often see a process that emphasizes group membership as a factor in hiring as unfair where unqualified people are hired in place of those more qualified. These negative issues, for members of both minority and majority groups, seem to decrease when merit is central to the decision-making process.[18] When organizations seek to recruit members from minority groups, they should emphasize that hiring decisions are merit based.

The sources used to recruit minorities may also be very important to the success of attracting them to apply for jobs with an organization. Ryan, Horvath, and Kriska[19] demonstrated that the informativeness of the source was related to whether individuals who were interested chose to apply for a firefighter's job. Applicants who received more and better information about a job were more likely to apply for the job and saw themselves as a good fit with the job and organization. Often minorities do not choose to apply for positions as they see themselves as a poor fit with the organization, no matter how well qualified they are. One strategy to improve diversity would be to ensure the use of highly informative recruitment sources when recruiting minorities.

INTERNAL FACTORS

While it is clear that different organizations take different approaches to recruiting new employees, very little is known about how organizational characteristics produce differences in recruiting practices, processes, or outcomes. Partly, this is the result of most research focusing on job seekers rather than on the employing organizations.[20] Many possible organizational characteristics could influence a job seeker's perception of the organization during the job search phase (e.g., the type of industry, size of the organization, profitability, growth, and financial trends). These characteristics may influence both the number and the quality of applicants who apply for a position with the organization. They may also influence how the organization recruits candidates and how competitive the organization is in making offers to the best applicants.[21]

BUSINESS STRATEGY

A company's business strategy or plan has a major impact on its recruitment strategy. To be effective, the recruitment strategy must be linked to the business plan. A company's business plan is its action plan for managing the company. The business plan or strategy includes a statement of its mission and philosophy, recognition of its strengths and weaknesses, and a statement of its strategic goals and objectives for competing in its economic environment. A business plan addresses those aspects of the external environment that affect how the company does business and influences the company's recruiting process. For example, Company A wants to be a market leader on price and carefully controls labour costs. Company A's recruiting is primarily at the entry job level for mostly unskilled workers. Company A's recruitment is likely to be by word of mouth or by applicants applying on-site, thus saving the costs of more expensive recruiting sources. Company B wants to be a leader in producing unique, quality consumer products. It needs employees who are innovative and creative. Company B's recruitment efforts would be directed at identifying people with the skills and abilities it needs to produce its products. It is likely to recruit through the Internet and through specialized, professional magazines. A company's business plan also influences the degree to which it fills vacancies with internal or external applicants.[22] Rarely do organizations like Company A fill entry-level positions with internal candidates; vacant higher level positions in Company A are mostly filled through internal promotions. It is quite common for organizations like Company B to bring someone in from the outside to fill a vacant position at both lower and higher organizational levels.

There may also be factors other than a business plan that influence how companies staff vacant positions. Some companies may insist, as a matter of organizational policy, that internal candidates be given preference as a means of motivating employees and ensuring that the successful candidate knows and shares the organization's philosophy, values, goals, and attitude toward achieving a return on investment in both human capital and material resources. As we discussed in Chapter 1, collective agreements that apply to a workplace may require that internal applicants be given first consideration for positions for which they are qualified. Other organizations may have policies that insist external candidates be given preference for jobs in order to expose the company to new ideas and to new ways of doing business. Still other organizations may insist that the best candidate be given the job offer, regardless of whether that person is an internal or external applicant.

JOB LEVEL AND TYPE

As we saw with Company A and Company B, both the type of occupation and the nature of the industry in which it is involved may influence an organization's recruiting strategy.[23] In some industries or occupations, people are recruited in a particular way not so much because that method is very effective, but because it is the norm. It is how recruiting is done for that type of work, and how it is expected to be done. For certain executive-level positions, vacancies are never advertised but are instead given to a consulting company to carry out an executive search. Such "headhunting" firms generally have a list of potential executive candidates that they have developed over time through contacts in many different organizations. The search firm knows the organization and works to find a match with one of its candidates. Rarely, if ever, are such firms used to recruit production or service workers; vacancies for those types of positions are filled by candidates who respond to local newspaper advertisements or job postings with Service Canada's Job Bank or who are referred by other employees, as was the case with the 50 000 applicants for the production jobs at Toyota Canada.[24]

ORGANIZATION ANALYSIS

Organization analysis is an important step in the recruitment and selection process. When designing and implementing recruitment and selection programs to fill jobs within their organization, human resources specialists must be aware of the mission, goals, and business strategy of the organization. Although there are many ways to conduct an organization analysis, most methods share the common goals of describing and understanding the design and structure, functions and processes, and strategies and missions of organizations. An organization analysis highlights areas of strength and weakness useful to human resources planning. For example, recruitment efforts might be directed to addressing perceived weaknesses in skills.

Organization analysis
An important step in the recruitment and selection process in which human resources specialists consider the design and structure, functions and processes, and strategies and missions of organizations to highlight areas of strength and weakness useful to human resources planning.

Recruitment and selection must be linked to the strategic goals of the organization. When the guiding principles of an organization are laid out as goals, and the environment in which the organization operates is defined, recruitment and selection processes can most effectively contribute to the overall success of the organization. Different organizational goals lead to different recruitment strategies. Similarly, an organization's philosophy and values influence whether it actively seeks to recruit women, visible minorities, Aboriginal peoples, and people with disabilities, or whether its approach to employment equity is one of minimal compliance. Organization analysis helps to clarify these issues. In developing recruiting strategies, one must decide whether to concentrate recruiting efforts on internal or external candidates. Organization analysis reveals the likelihood of finding suitable internal candidates, and the extent to which qualified internal candidates can fill the job openings, by providing an inventory of skills and abilities that exist within the company as well as indicating the potential for advancement among current employees. In conjunction with job analysis, this information gives a good indication of the likelihood of finding the right internal people for the job and the need for external recruiting. Unfortunately, relatively few companies inventory their employees' skills and abilities; such inventories are expensive to develop and to maintain.

JOB ANALYSIS

Before you can recruit employees, you must have an idea of the KSAOs or competencies that they should have now or after training. To what extent do these KSAOs or competencies exist among our current workers? Map these KSAOs or competencies of current employees onto the KSAOs or competencies needed to implement the strategic business plan. Are there any gaps in the attributes your current employees have and those needed to meet your strategic goals? Recruitment should seek to narrow any gaps that result from this assessment.

One of the most important pieces of information that both a recruiter and job candidates rely on throughout the recruiting process is a description of the job and worker requirements. The recruiter needs to know what type of applicant to seek out and applicants need to have a clear idea of the duties and tasks that they will perform on the job and the resources that they will need to bring to the job. It is very difficult to recruit job applicants without knowing the essential characteristics of the position or the worker requirements. Job descriptions that are up to date and based on a job analysis lead to accurate expectations on the part of the job candidate. Both applicants and recruiters should have a clear idea of the qualifications needed by people in the position. Often recruiters are told to seek the "best person" for the job, instead of being told to find the "best-qualified person" for the job. Recruitment and Selection Today 4.1 in Chapter 4 presented a job description for a CIBC customer service representative. This description, used in recruiting, is sufficiently detailed to provide both the job candidate and the recruiter with a clear idea of what the position entails and how it fits into the organization. It also suggests the type of person who will best fit with the values and culture of CIBC.

HUMAN RESOURCES PLANNING

Human resources planning is the process of anticipating and providing for the movement of employees into, within, and out of an organization.[25] It is an effort to forecast the net requirement for personnel by determining the demand for and supply of human resources now and in the future. This planning process integrates the results from both the organizational analysis and job analysis, as seen in Figure 6.1, resulting in a forecast of the number and type of employees required to meet the business plan's objectives. Through organization and job analyses, the planning process identifies the human resources needed to carry out the business plan, both those resources that exist within the organization and those that must be secured through a recruiting program.

HR planning must also evaluate the potential supply of job applicants with the desired attributes. You need to consider the demographics of the workforce that is available, including likely educational attainment, mobility, and unemployment rates. As well consideration must be given to any relevant laws such as equity that will have an impact on recruitment. The final step in the planning process is to determine how to balance your demand for employees with the supply of people with the attributes you are seeking. This final evaluation should determine the type of people you are recruiting, the number you want to hire, if there is an adequate supply, and whether you will hire full- or part-time employees. Human resources planning develops an action plan based on this analysis.

RECRUITMENT ACTION PLAN

Recruitment is the end product of human resource planning. In Chapter 1 we presented a fairly detailed overview of the elements involved in recruitment and selection; you may want to review that example now. HR planning should have developed a number of questions that resulted from the integration of the job and organizational analyses. Answers to these questions form an action plan that is in accordance with the organization's business strategy. These questions include the following but may expand to include others specific to an organization. These questions are just a guide.

- Based on your business plan, how many positions will we need to staff? How many will be full-time vs. part-time?
- Based on your business plan, what are the levels and types of positions you are seeking to fill?
- Based on your job analysis, what is the job description for the positions to be filled?

- Based on your job analysis, what qualifications (knowledge, skills, abilities, experience, competencies) must job candidates possess to do the job successfully?
- Based on your organization analysis, what percentage of the positions can, or should, be staffed with internal candidates?
- Based on your analysis of the labour market, is there an available supply of qualified external candidates?
- Based on the labour market, how extensively will we have to search for qualified applicants? Will we have to search beyond our normal geographic boundaries? Will we have to take special measures to locate our target applicant population?
- What sources or methods should we use to reach the potential applicants?
- Based on your policies and philosophy and legal considerations, what are the employment equity and diversity goals?
- What is your recruiting budget?
- Who will do the recruiting?
- Based on the business plan, organization analysis, and job analysis, is it feasible to recruit at this time?

TIMING OF RECRUITMENT INITIATIVES

In many organizations, recruiting occurs in response to need. An employee leaves for one reason or another and, if the position is retained, must be replaced either through internal or external hiring. In cases like this, there is little organizational control over timing. Delays in hiring may lead to delays in production, with unrealistic demands placed on the remaining employees. The recruitment goal is to hire someone qualified to do the work as soon as possible, even if hiring at a later date may have led to finding someone who was better qualified for the position. In other organizations, where there is a systematic turnover of employees, recruiting may follow a well-defined pattern.

This pattern occurs most often in large organizations, which recruit heavily from among college and university graduates.[26] The availability of such graduates in the spring of each year often determines when organizations implement their recruiting strategy; it influences when they send information to campus employment centres, place advertisements in campus newspapers, visit the schools, meet with the potential applicants, extend invitations to visit the organization, and make their job offers. If an organization is late in recruiting, top candidates may have already accepted offers from the competition. To remain competitive, the organization must synchronize its recruiting to when the best candidates are likely to be available. This means that the HR team must have a good working knowledge of the labour market and an effective recruitment and staffing plan (see Recruitment and Selection Notebook 6.1).

In competing for qualified candidates, particularly when supply is weak, organizations are starting to incorporate in their recruiting strategies knowledge of how job candidates evaluate jobs and make choices. There is evidence to suggest that job seekers prefer early job offers as a way of reducing anxiety and uncertainty about other offers; there is also evidence to suggest that more-qualified candidates generate offers earlier and more easily than less-qualified candidates.[27] If this is so, then organizations may have to begin recruiting as early as possible if they want to hire the most-qualified candidates. Instead of waiting until the spring to recruit college and university graduates, an

RECRUITMENT AND SELECTION NOTEBOOK 6.1

ELEMENTS OF A RECRUITMENT AND STAFFING ACTION PLAN

1. Develop Recruitment Strategy
   - Establish selection committee.
   - Review organization's goals and objectives.
   - Establish budget for the recruitment process.
   - Establish timelines for recruitment and selection activities.
   - Review job description for position.
   - Develop selection criteria.
   - Develop profile of "ideal" applicant.
   - Develop job advertisement/recruiting materials.
2. Develop the Applicant Pool
   - Review state of the labour market.
   - Consider employment equity issues.
   - Determine if recruitment will be internal or external.
   - Identify target applicant pool.
   - Identify recruitment methods to be used.
   - Place ad/recruiting materials in agreed-on media.
3. Screen the Applicant Pool
   - Determine whether applicant pool is large enough; if not, renew recruitment efforts.
   - Screen job candidates' application forms and résumés.
   - Conduct short screening interviews.
   - Select "long list" of candidates for further review.
4. Conduct Review of Job Applicants
   - Selection committee develops shortlist of candidates.
   - Arrange visits of short-listed candidates to company.
   - Conduct realistic job preview for candidates.
   - Conduct employment tests.
   - Conduct selection interview.
   - Identify leading candidate(s) for position.
   - Complete reference and background checks on leading candidates.
   - Make hiring recommendation.
   - Contingent on offer of employment, arrange for any required medical or physical examinations.
5. Evaluate the Recruiting Effort
   - Review the recruiting process: What went right? What went wrong?
   - Review the outcome of the recruiting process.
   - Review the performance of people who were hired.

organization may begin the process earlier in order to make job offers before the end of the fall semester.

Some organizations are also beginning to pursue college and university students before they enter the job market. Companies often use summer job placements, internships, or cooperative education as early-recruitment programs.[28] These strategies are designed to have candidates accept an early job offer that meets their minimum standards rather than waiting to make a choice between competing offers.

The timing of events within a recruiting program is important. The recruiting process can extend over a considerable period of time, with several candidates evaluated for each vacancy. Job candidates do not stop their job search activities while waiting for a decision. An organization that does not provide candidates with timely feedback about their progress through the recruitment and selection process may risk losing top candidates. Job seekers may take lack of contact as a lack of interest and accept an early offer from a less-preferred company. Job candidates may not stop their job search activities even after accepting an early offer from an organization. They may continue to receive interest from other companies that were late off the mark in recruiting and, if they receive an attractive offer, they may change their minds about accepting the first offer. Maintaining contact with the candidate after an offer is accepted helps to forestall such reversals. Organizations must maintain contact with high-quality, viable candidates during all phases of the recruiting process until a job offer is tendered and accepted.[29]

LOCATING AND TARGETING THE APPLICANT POOL

In an ideal world, an organization could search as broadly as possible until it found the most suitable applicant. However, extensive recruiting is an expensive proposition that few organizations can afford. It is also questionable whether the benefits of extensive recruiting surpass its associated costs. A more effective plan is to target recruiting efforts on a specific pool of job applicants who have the appropriate knowledge, skills, abilities, competencies, and other talents needed to perform the job. This applicant pool may be concentrated in one geographic area or spread widely throughout the country. The HR team must know where to find the appropriate applicant pool.

If a company wants to hire electronics technicians, it makes more sense to concentrate on recruiting graduates from electronics training programs or from areas where there is a concentration of electronics technicians rather than search broadly throughout the country. The HR team must know which colleges or institutes offer training in electronics, and must know where electronics industries are concentrated. If a company were recruiting experienced miners, it would be more appropriate to target Cape Breton as a source for this applicant pool rather than Metropolitan Toronto. On the other hand, recruiting upper-level executives might require a nationwide search to find the best candidate.

Targeting a specific applicant pool allows the organization to tailor its message to that group, to understand where that applicant pool is likely to be located, and to attract applications from that pool. In limiting its recruiting to a target applicant pool, however, an organization must be careful not to systematically exclude members of protected groups. In fact, organizations may target members of minority groups to increase organizational diversity and to comply with legal mandates.[30]

// PART II: RECRUITMENT SOURCES

Once the target applicant pool has been identified and located, the HR team must choose the most appropriate recruitment methods or sources for reaching all potential job applicants, including members of protected groups. The following sections describe some of the more popular recruiting methods that have been used to contact members of different applicant pools. We review first more traditional recruiting sources followed by Internet and social networking recruiting.

TRADITIONAL RECRUITMENT SOURCES

INTERNAL CANDIDATES

Internal candidates provide the organization with a known source of labour. Many of the activities carried out as part of HR planning provide the organization with information about the best-qualified internal applicants. Internal applicants are likely to have more realistic expectations about the job or organization and to have more job satisfaction and organizational commitment, but there is a risk that recruiting through internal sources may lead to a workforce that is less diversified with respect to minority applicants. We briefly review some common sources used to attract internal applicants.

INTERNAL JOB POSTINGS

Internal job postings can be notices posted on bulletin boards, ads placed in company newsletters, announcements made at staff meetings, or notices circulated through departments. The intent of the posting is to make internal employees aware of the vacancy and to allow them an opportunity to apply for the position. As a matter of policy, some organizations seek to fill positions through internal sources before going to the external market. Other organizations may have agreed, through a collective agreement with employees, to give first consideration to internal candidates for any vacant position that falls under the collective agreement. In these cases, the jobs are posted for a period of time in specified locations. Internal postings generally provide information on the job, its requirements, and the compensation associated with the position. Internal job postings make the vacancy known to all employees, which is an important consideration when implementing employment equity programs throughout different levels of the organization.

There are, however, disadvantages to internal job postings. Internal postings lengthen the time needed to fill the position, as external searches generally do not begin until after all internal candidates are first evaluated. Internal candidates who are unsuccessful may become less motivated, or may initiate a job search outside the organization. Placing an internal candidate in a vacant position sets off a sequence of events that brings with it a degree of instability and change: The position the employee leaves must itself be posted and filled. The effects of filling the first position with an internal candidate reverberate through several layers of the organization before the process comes to an end.

SUCCESSION PLANS/REPLACEMENT CHARTS

Organizations expect that vacancies will occur through death, illness, retirement, resignation, or termination and, as part of the HR planning function, develop a succession plan for filling vacancies with existing employees. Organizations have a good idea of the talent in other positions that can step in to fill a vacancy, either on a short- or long-term basis. Succession/replacement charts, like organizational charts, list each job with respect to its position in the organizational structure, particularly its relationship to positions above and below it. The replacement chart lists the incumbent for the position and the likely internal replacements for the incumbent. The chart includes information on the present job performance of each potential successor (e.g., "excellent performer"), an assessment of the successor's potential and readiness to step into the position (e.g., "needs more experience in present position"), and a rank-ordering of each as the incumbent's replacement. Sometimes a chart will also include a photo of the individual holding the position. We caution against this as the use of a photo may lead to a discrimination charge by an employee who is lower ranked on the chart. Figure 6.2 presents an example of a succession plan for a Chief Financial Officer.

Replacement charts provide a quick, visual presentation of an organization's human resources, but they give little information beyond that of a candidate's performance

FIGURE 6.2

EXAMPLE OF A SUCCESSION/REPLACEMENT PLAN FOR A CHIEF FINANCIAL OFFICER

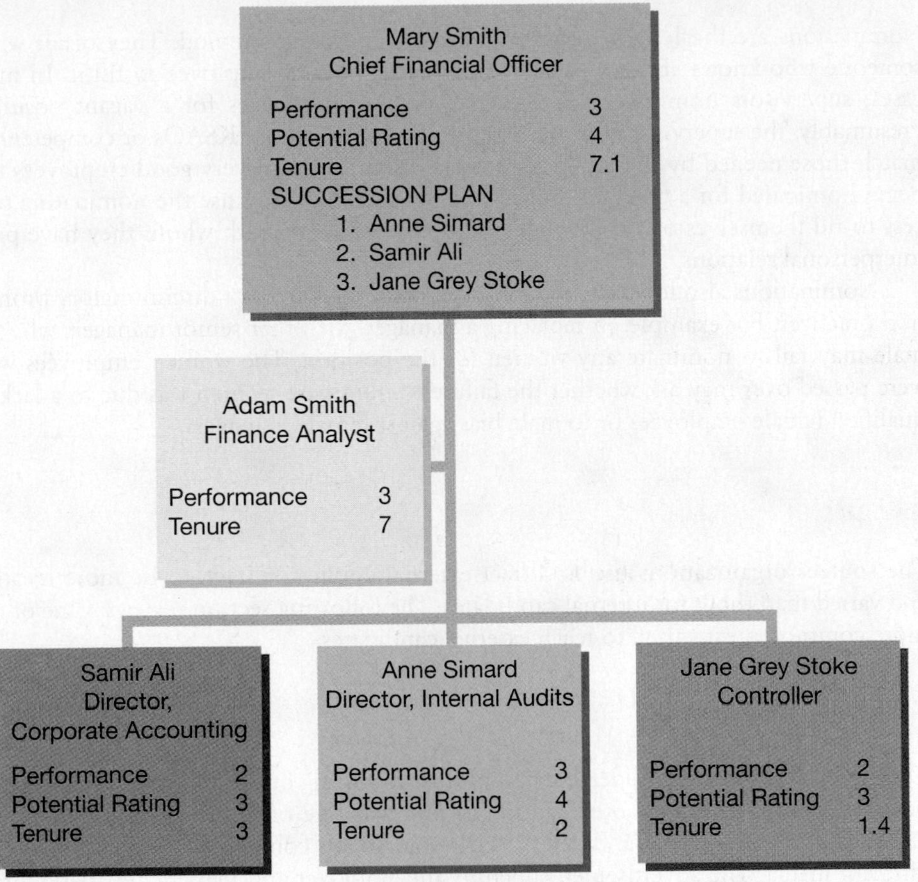

and promotability. These charts are limited by the constraints imposed by the organizational chart. Employees are evaluated for positions one level above theirs in the chain of command. They are not evaluated for positions that are horizontal or lateral to theirs, although in contemporary organizations, employees are expected to have skills and competencies that are transferable to jobs that are related to their position.

HUMAN RESOURCES INFORMATION SYSTEMS (HRIS)

As we discussed previously, human resources planning often involves the creation of a comprehensive computerized database that contains the job analysis information on each position, including information on the required KSAOs. This computerized inventory also contains information on employee competencies and KSAOs, along with employee work histories, experiences, and results of performance evaluations. Internal candidates for a vacant position may be found through a HRIS match of the person's characteristics with those required by the job. The match does not give any indication of employee interest in the position or motivation to take on the new job. It is simply a first cut of employees who qualify for the position.

NOMINATIONS

Nominations are the least systematic internal recruitment method. They occur when someone who knows about a vacancy nominates another employee to fill it. In most cases, supervisors nominate one or more of their employees for a vacant position. Presumably, the supervisor nominates those employees whose KSAOs or competencies match those needed by the job. This process often results in very good employees not being nominated for a position. Supervisors or managers may use the nominating process to rid themselves of a problem employee or someone with whom they have poor interpersonal relations.

Nominations also leave the organization open to charges of discriminatory promotion practices. For example, in replacing a manager, the other senior managers who are male may fail to nominate any women for the position. The women employees who were passed over may ask whether the failure to nominate women was due to a lack of qualified female employees or to male bias against female managers.

EXTERNAL CANDIDATES

The sources organizations use to attract external applicants have to be more creative and varied than those for internal candidates. The following section reviews some of the more common means used to reach external candidates.

JOB ADVERTISEMENTS

Organizations spend a considerable part of their recruiting budgets on advertising vacant positions, and the "help-wanted" ad in the past was one of the most commonly used methods of recruiting job candidates.[31] Help-wanted ads come in various forms and use different media. The advertisements identify the employer and may include basic information on the job and compensation, the job requirements, and how to apply (including closing dates for applications). The ad may also contain information on the organization's employment equity program. The ad should not include any statements that could lead to charges of discrimination (e.g., "The ideal applicant will be between 25 and 30 years old"), unless those statements can be supported as bona fide occupational requirements.

Organizations also use job advertisements to enhance their image with potential candidates. Image concerns may dictate the size of the advertisement, where it is placed, and the content of the ad as much as the information needed to attract qualified candidates.

Job advertisement campaigns should also be designed with the target applicant pool in mind:

- Who are we trying to reach? Who is in our target applicant pool?
- How large is the target applicant pool and what portion of it do we need to reach to obtain a reasonable number of applicants?
- How many applicants do we need to fill the position with qualified people?
- What type of ad content will attract the target applicant pool's attention?
- What advertising media are likely to reach the target applicant pool?

The answers to most of these questions are very complex and depend on consideration of many factors, including the nature of the organization, the job, and the target applicant pool. One of the most important decisions is choosing the media for the advertising campaign.

Newspapers offer a quick and flexible means of contacting potential applicants. Newspapers need only a short lead time before an ad is published. The ad can be placed in the classified ads section listing employment opportunities or prominently displayed in another section of the paper. Often managerial and professional positions are advertised in a newspaper's business section. Newspaper ads attract the interest of people who are actively searching for a job and who happen to see the advertisement before it disappears. There is some evidence that newspaper ads are not a very effective means of attracting very qualified applicants,[32] particularly scientific and technical personnel.[33] Newspaper ads tend to be less effective in attracting candidates than other recruiting methods.[34]

Professional periodicals and trade journals allow the organization to reach very specialized groups of applicants. Many professional and trade associations publish newsletters or magazines that are distributed to each member. These publications carry job advertisements. The association, and the distribution of its publication, may be international, national, or regional. Publications of this type are the best means of reaching people with specific skills or qualifications. Ads in these types of publications often require a long lead time before the ad appears. For example, an advertisement appearing in the March issue of a journal may have an early January deadline for ad copy. With the growth of the Internet, many professional and trade associations have reduced the publication lag by posting job ads in their online publications as the ads are received; the ads are also published in the print edition later.

Radio and television job advertising, in comparison to print media, has not been used extensively, although these media offer the potential to reach large numbers of the target applicant pool. Radio and television advertising directors have detailed demographic information on the audience for specific shows and can place the advertisement during shows likely to be watched or listened to by the target applicant pool. Nonetheless, organizations appear reluctant to use these methods for job advertisements and limit their use to image advertising. The cost of radio and television advertising, particularly on a national scale, may be quite high even for a 15- or 30-second commercial. The short duration of most commercials prevents the inclusion of essential job information. Many organizations now place ads on the Internet, including YouTube, with the expectation that they will reach a wider audience at little cost. In fact some organizations rely solely on the Internet rather than running ads on broadcast outlets.

Courtesy of A&W Food Services of Canada Inc.

Public displays attempt to bring job vacancies to the attention of the target applicant pool through the use of advertisements that range from help-wanted notices to display ads placed in buses, trains, and subway stations. Service and retail employers rely on help-wanted signs posted in their windows or near service counters to attract job applicants. Most positions advertised through these types of notices are at the entry level and do not require extensive skills or abilities on the part of the applicant. These ads are directed at recruiting employees from among the employer's normal range of customers. Display ads in public transportation stations and vehicles attempt to reach a broader population than service and retail help-wanted ads, but they are also directed at attracting people for low-skill or limited-ability entry-level positions. Public display ads tend to be low in cost relative to the number of people that they reach.

Direct mail advertising attempts to bring the organization's recruiting message directly to members of the target applicant pool. The potential employer sends each person on the mailing list recruiting information about the organization and the job, reaching both those who are actively seeking jobs and those who may become interested through reading the materials. The keys to this type of advertising are the acquisition or development of a mailing list consisting of names and addresses of the target applicant population, the attractiveness of the recruiting materials, and the ease with which follow-up contacts can take place. Often, mailing lists can be obtained from various professional associations. The costs of direct mailings are high with the Internet offering a better way to reach an audience. Direct mail is rarely used to fill a specific job vacancy; rather it is used to draw attention to openings in an organization.

Open houses involve inviting potential job applicants from the local community to visit the company facilities to view demonstrations or videos about the company and its products, and to meet the organization's employees informally over refreshments. The invitations are advertised through local print and electronic media, and company websites. Sometimes, the organization may choose to hold the affair offsite at a trade centre or hotel because of security or other concerns. Open houses work best when an organization has several jobs to fill and when there are tight labour markets.

Job fairs involve several organizations seeking to hire from the same target applicant pool having arranged to recruit in conjunction with an ongoing event. For example, a trade or professional association may invite employers to hold a job fair as part of its annual convention. The employers, who pay a fee to participate, have access to all of the convention delegates, both those who are actively seeking jobs and those who may become interested through meeting an organization's representative. The convention delegates represent the ideal target applicant pool. The job seekers make contact with organizations, while the employers meet many prospective employees in a short period of time at a relatively low cost. The disadvantage is information overload, where the candidate is bombarded with too much information from too many organizations.

Employee referral is word-of-mouth advertising that relies on current employees telling their friends and relatives about job vacancies in their company. This is a low or no-cost method of advertising. It assumes that the employees know other people with skills and abilities similar to their own, that the employees refer people with good work habits and attitudes similar to their own, and that current employees are the best representatives of the organization. In some companies, employees are paid a bonus for each successful referral.

The referred candidate is likely to have been given an accurate representation of the job and organization by the friend or relative.[35,36] There is some evidence that employees recruited by referral remain with the organization longer than employees recruited through other means and have more positive organizational outcomes.[37,38] The greatest concern with using referrals as a recruiting method is the probability that it may produce charges of discriminatory hiring practices. In referring friends and relatives, employees are likely to refer individuals from their own ethnic, racial, or gender groups; this could work against meeting employment equity goals. Referrals, however, are a very popular means of attracting job applicants.[39,40]

Networking is a cross between a recruiting method (such as referrals and nominations) and a job search technique. For professionals, networking is deemed to be vital to career advancement and is promoted by career transition experts as the best way for a professional to find a job. Job seekers are encouraged to join industry groups and professional organizations, join study groups, read journals, and attend conferences.

Networking also involves joining college or university alumni associations; keeping in touch with family, friends, professors, advisors, coaches, and tutors; and joining social clubs or volunteer groups. It also includes activities such as meeting an old friend for coffee to obtain information on career opportunities or asking a friend's father to put in a good word for you at his company.

Networking contacts can keep the job seeker informed about what life is like in a company from the perspective of an insider. At the same time, the networking contact is aware that the job seeker is looking for employment or for a new position and can forward that information to appropriate people in the company. Monster.ca (http://career-advice.monster.ca/Job-Hunt-Strategy/Professional-Networking/jobs.aspx) and CareerKey.com (http://www.careerkey.com/career_resources.htm#networking) are two examples of Internet recruiting sources that have established websites that provide advice on networking. In Recruitment and Selection Today 6.1 two recruiters discuss the importance of networking referrals in the context of social media.

WALK-INS

In the external sources described above, the organization makes every attempt to contact members of the target applicant pool. The recruitment is initiated by the employer. Walk-in recruitment is initiated by the job seeker, who visits an organization's personnel office and requests to fill out an application for employment, even though the company may not have any job vacancies. The *write-in* method is a variation of this approach; rather than visiting the company, job seekers send their résumés to the company. The company usually holds the applications and résumés for a period of time (e.g., three months), in case vacancies do occur. Walk-in and write-in methods are inexpensive ways to fill entry-level positions, although they are less effective than referrals.[41]

EMPLOYMENT AGENCIES

Employment agencies are independent organizations that attempt to find a match between a person and a job. Their success depends on the willingness of both the job seeker and the organization to use their services. We will look at the major types of employment agencies: Service Canada's Job Bank, private employment agencies, executive search firms, in-house recruiters, and temporary help agencies.

Service Canada Centres throughout the country provide no-charge access to the online Job Bank for both job seekers and employers. As soon as employers post a job vacancy, the position is listed in the Job Bank at http://www.jobbank.gc.ca. Available jobs across the country are listed by province to facilitate the job search for workers who want to remain in their home provinces or who want to relocate. The job seeker selects a job category, and all of the available jobs in that category are displayed, along with the salary (if specified) and location of each job. Clicking on one of the job titles produces a detailed description of the job, including a list of the skills, education, and credentials required. The manner in which a job application is to be made is specified (e.g., in person, mail, e-mail, fax, or website).

As noted later in this chapter in Recruitment and Selection Today 6.5, the Job Bank site also offers information about effective job search strategies and even a "Job Seeker" feature (http://seekers.jobbank.gc.ca/commun-common/connection-login.aspx), for which applicants have to register to gain access. The effectiveness of the Job Bank is

RECRUITMENT AND SELECTION TODAY 6.1

IS THE RÉSUMÉ DEAD?

The way businesses select and hire potential employees has been evolving for decades—especially with the introduction of social media. But is this the way of the future? Is the current format by which we recruit and hire a thing of the past?

To further delve into this topic, *The Globe and Mail* asked two experts in the field to offer their predictions: Karen Scott, vice-president of human resources at Acosta Mosaic Group, a Jacksonville, Fla.-based marketing company, and Lisa Kramer, director of campus recruiting at Royal Bank of Canada.

How has social media affected the recruitment process for your companies?

Karen Scott: Social media has had a great impact for our organization because it took a lot of the things that we were already doing and gave us better, faster opportunities to communicate. The things we've been able to do with things like our Facebook page around what it's like to work at Mosaic, giving job seekers tips, and further connecting to what I call a "warm-candidate" population. It was just a whole lot easier to do on Facebook than it was on our traditional website. We use the term "extended experience"; we've been able to take all of the things that we did offline and put a lot of them online, which has been great. We use three of the main, traditional social media elements of Twitter, Facebook and LinkedIn.

Lisa Kramer: For us at RBC, I would have to 100-percent agree that social media has definitely impacted our recruitment process, more from an education piece. It allows us to start the conversation with candidates much earlier in the recruiting process than we would have before. We're able to educate them on the different opportunities we have with different platforms across the bank. In some cases it allows candidates to direct themselves to the appropriate area or career path within the bank that matches their skill set. In the past, without social media, [students] were waiting until we came to campus to get that information. [Social media] allows us to answer those questions and then brand and promote the opportunities that we have to the right subset of students.

How important are referral programs going to become in the next five to six years?

KS: Referral programs in networking, and sharing referrals, have been a part of how people have gotten jobs for the last 200 years. In the next five, I think referral programs and the concept of referring people for jobs has just heightened with the ability to do it in a very easy way because of things like social media. I think referrals will remain a critical part of successful hiring. We have our recruitment methods and one of our biggest successes is our word-of-mouth recruitment, which centres around some core referral programming. The tactics with which you go out and get referrals, I think they'll probably ebb and flow. I think there will be some different options you can use to get to referrals faster and with better candidates.

LK: It's really, as Karen said, going beyond the referrals. It's that whole networking piece. We've spent time in going back to campus and working with students to really understand how they can effectively network and make those connections. It's not enough now to just wait for the job posting to show up in their inbox and go in and apply—it's candidates being proactive and networking. We know that great employees know great candidates and that's why referral programs are so effective. Really working your network, maybe uncovering those opportunities that maybe aren't posted or you didn't know existed, that's going to happen through that process.

Source: Daina Lawrence, Special to *The Globe and Mail*. June 5, 2014. http://www.theglobeandmail.com/report-on-business/economy/is-the-resume-dead/article18988834/ Reprinted by permission of the Canadian Writers Group.

somewhat mixed; most of the job placements are in sales, clerical, and service industries, with very few in managerial and professional occupations.

Private employment agencies bring together job seekers and hiring organizations. These agencies charge a fee for their services. Most provinces regulate employment agency fees and prohibit the agency from charging job seekers for placing them with employers. The agency fees are paid by the employing organization, usually in the form of a commission tied to a percentage of the job candidate's starting salary. Employment agencies may use any of the recruiting methods we've discussed, but they tend to rely on walk-ins, newspaper advertising, and lists of potential job seekers compiled over time. Employment agencies tend to have a fair degree of success in finding both skilled and managerial workers.

Executive search firms are private employment agencies that specialize in finding executive talent. These firms charge the organization for their services, whether or not they are successful in filling a position. The major difference between search firms and employment agencies is that search firms rarely advertise positions, although they will do so if requested by their clients. Rather, they seek out candidates who are not actively searching for jobs through an extensive list of contacts that they have developed over time. Their main supply of talent comes from executives who are already employed by other organizations; consequently, these search firms are also known as "headhunters." More recently, search firms have started to use online recruiting websites as a source for their referrals. The major disadvantages of using search firms are their cost and the likelihood that some firms develop specific recruiting philosophies that lead them to look for the same type of executive to fill all positions.

Hiring any type of search firm does not absolve the company of all responsibilities for the hiring process. A successful search depends on the company working with the search firm and doing its homework about the nature of the position to be filled and the required KSAOs and competencies before the search firm is called on to begin the search. Headhunters Canada provides an online directory of executive search firms across Canada listed by province and specialty area (http://headhunters-canada.com).

In-house recruiters are usually executive-level employees or highly respected professionals who hold an executive title such as vice-president or director. They are similar to headhunters in that they seek to recruit upper-level executives and professionals, except that they work only for their own company and do not recruit for any other company. In-house recruiters know the opportunities that exist in their organization; as well, they know the strengths of the local community and the social environment in which the new recruits are likely to live. Relying on networking to identify potential candidates, in-house recruiters are typically used to recruit professionals who are in high demand and in short supply. In the health-care industry, many hospitals use nurses and physicians as in-house recruiters to travel across the country seeking to recruit other health-care professionals for their hospitals.

In-house recruiters do have some disadvantages. Most companies use them to reduce the costs associated with an executive search firm. However, unless in-house recruiters take time to become familiar with different recruiting methods, they may limit their work to posting notices on different Internet sites. In-house recruiters may also suffer from "tunnel vision" in looking only for certain types of candidates and ignoring a broader range of qualified job seekers.

Temporary help agencies are similar to private employment agencies except that they specialize in providing organizations with short-term help. In most cases, the worker remains employed by the temporary help firm, but carries out duties under the direction and control of the temporary help firm's client organization. These agencies provide clients with temporary help, contract workers, and seasonal and overload help in certain specialized occupations, such as secretaries, computer experts, labourers, and executives, among others. Temporary help agencies are an example of outsourcing, which we discussed earlier in this chapter. These agencies rely on inventories of talent pools they have developed over the years and are capable of filling their clients' needs within a reasonable amount of time. However, as discussed previously, the client organizations may be liable for any discrimination claims incurred through the control and direction of the temporary employee.

RECRUITING AT EDUCATIONAL INSTITUTIONS

Technical schools, colleges, and universities are common sources of recruits for organizations seeking entry-level technical, professional, and managerial employees. Many schools provide their students with placement services, which assist the recruiting efforts of visiting organizations. Recognizing educational institutions as a good source of target applicants, organizations have well-established campus recruiting programs that involve both campus advertising and campus visits by company recruiters. Campus recruiting is one of the most popular ways in which graduates find their first job. It is also an expensive proposition in terms of both time and money. It becomes even more expensive considering that, on average, about 50 percent of recruits may leave the organization within the first few years of employment.[42]

Many research studies have tried to identify factors that produce successful recruiting campaigns at educational institutions. In a recent meta-analysis, Chapman and his associates found that while job–organization characteristics, recruiter behaviours, perceptions of the recruiting process, perceived fit, and hiring expectancies predicted applicant attraction to an organization, the recruiter demographics, such as age, gender, and race, did not.[43] Rynes and Cable[44] reviewed the post-1991 research on recruiter effects and came to much the same conclusion as previous research: that "recruiters probably do not have a large impact on actual job choices."[45]

E-RECRUITING: USE OF THE INTERNET AND SOCIAL NETWORKS

In a few short years, the Internet has transformed recruiting and become an important job search tool for job hunters.[46] Traditionally, a company used one of the means we just described to reach potential job applicants. The company may have placed an advertisement in the print media, made use of referrals and nominations from current employees, or participated in job fairs. Applicants who happened to become aware of the vacancy submitted their résumés by mail or fax, or dropped them off in person. Staff in the HR department reviewed the applications. Candidates whom the staff judged to be qualified on the basis of that review were invited for an interview and possible further review through employment tests. Eventually, one of these applicants might be offered a position. The remaining applications were likely discarded, with perhaps a few kept on file. This process could take weeks or months from the initial announcement of the position to an offer. The Internet has changed everything. We review two ways that the Internet is used in recruiting. The first is the more established use of a company's own website and job boards while the second approach focuses on social networks.

Internet recruiting
The use of the Internet to match candidates to jobs through electronic databases that store information on jobs and job candidates.

INTERNET RECRUITING

With **Internet recruiting**, a company can place notice of a vacancy on its website or list it with one of the online job or career websites (see Recruitment and Selection Today 6.2).

RECRUITMENT AND SELECTION TODAY 6.2

CANADIAN JOB AND CAREER WEBSITES

General Job and Career Sites

CanadianCareers.com	http://www.canadiancareers.com
CareerBuilder	http://www.careerbuilder.ca
CareerXchange.com	http://www.careerexchange.com
Monster.ca	http://www.monster.ca
Service Canada Job Bank	http://www.servicecanada.gc.ca/eng/sc/jobs/jobbank.shtml
Service Canada	http://www.jobsetc.gc.ca
Workopolis.com	http://www.workopolis.com

Sites Designed for High School, College, and University Students

College Grad Job Hunter	http://collegegrad.com
Public Service Commission	http://jobs-emplois.gc.ca/index-eng.htm
Youth Canada	http://www.youth.gc.ca

The job or career site does a keyword search of résumés in its database and forwards those that match the position requirements to the company. For example, the Government of Canada conducts external recruitment almost exclusively online and provides online application blanks on the Public Service Commission's website (http://jobs-emplois.gc.ca/index-eng.htm). Some sites alert job seekers who are listed with it by e-mail when a job is posted that exactly matches their qualifications. Some HR practitioners argue that someday online recruiting will be the only job hunting source[47] and that it is driving the integration of other HR functions.[48]

Once a company receives résumés or applications from a posting on its own website or from an Internet job site, it begins its review. It may decide to continue its search or to invite a few of the applicants for interviews, after which it may make job offers. The interviews may take place on-site at the company or through videoconferencing if the candidate is outside the company's geographic area. Any employment testing that the company wishes to do may also be carried out online with an HR consultant. Videoconferencing and online testing are becoming increasingly popular since the Internet has no geographical boundaries. A company may receive applications from far outside its normal territory. The whole process may take just a few days from placing the notice of the vacancy to making an offer. Recruitment and Selection Today 6.3 presents the experience of NAV CANADA with Internet recruitment. Using the Internet significantly increased the number of applications and reduced time to selecting job candidates for further screening and training; as well, it helped develop the brand image of NAV CANADA.

Large national or international Internet sites (e.g., Service Canada's Job Bank) may list tens of thousands of jobs. The job seeker usually has the option of limiting the search to specific geographic areas or types of work, occupations, or industries. Some sites are limited to specific regions of the country. Certain sites are specific to an industry or profession; for example, prospective university professors can find out about job postings by checking the Canadian Association of University Teachers website at http://www.academicwork.ca. Job seekers interested in working in the not-for-profit sector can go

RECRUITMENT AND SELECTION TODAY 6.3

E-RECRUITING AT NAV CANADA

Michelle Gauthier is the national manager of candidate selection at NAV CANADA. She provided the following information on NAV CANADA's experience with e-recruitment.[49]

"NAV CANADA is the country's air navigation services provider, responsible for delivering essential air traffic control services to pilots and airlines that operate in Canadian airspace. Following a period of 10 years where the Recruitment and Selection function was managed by an external contractor, NAV CANADA made a strategic decision in early 2008 to bring recruitment and selection functions for air traffic control and flight service specialist careers in-house. For those 10 years, the third-party contractor was responsible for the screening, testing, and interviewing of prospects. As part of the recruiting function, the contractor was also responsible for the marketing and branding component related to building awareness of air traffic control and flight service specialist careers. The third party used an online application system that was very limited in its functionality and relied heavily on traditional forms of marketing, such as print ads and participating in career fairs. Under this process the third-party contractor averaged about 4500 applicants per year.

"NAV CANADA immediately focused on e-recruitment as it was consistent with our philosophy, which was to focus on an integrated approach and leverage technology to improve efficiencies and effectively target our audience. Utilizing the power of social media avenues and linking them to our Candidate Tracking System, we were able to draw key metrics on the performance of these methods. However, in order to achieve this, the entire process had to be cohesive in its design and also focus on understanding our target audience. Social media avenues have afforded us the ability to attract our target market and drive them to the Career microsite. Our main goal was to build awareness of these career opportunities at NAV CANADA, which means increasing traffic to our http://takecharge.navcanada.ca microsite. Social media tools have the ability to select demographic information (age, location, interests) on prospects and allow your ad to reach your audience much more effectively.

"From these ads, prospects are launched to our http://takecharge.navcanada.ca microsite where they can learn about these careers, the company, the training, the selection process, eligibility requirements, and gain access to the application system.

"Interested prospects then begin the selection process, by gaining access to the Prospect System. This system allows them to complete their application information (Contact, Work History, Education, etc.), and complete two pre-screening tests; prospects also have the ability to follow their progress through the entire process, up to and including the offer stage. This system truly took into account the needs of our prospects, and their need to follow their progress and provide key information on upcoming hurdles and requirements.

"The ability to attract prospects to NAV CANADA careers is one thing, but the key to success of an e-recruitment platform is the ability to manage application information from the business point of view. The Applicant Candidate Trainee Tracking System (ACT System) allows NAV CANADA to manage these prospects through the various selection hurdles to ensure consistency of the process/program, ensure constant communication with those involved in the selection of prospects, and the ease to access information. A strong recruitment system which incorporates the necessary workflows reduces time to process an applicant, bearing in mind the balance between supply and demand (i.e., the number of interested applicants versus the number of trainees required).

"The e-recruitment system has increased our number of interested candidates to 16 000 registrations per year, of which 6900 candidates complete the application process including the pre-screening testing requirements. Depending on the individual, it takes between 1 and 1-1/2 hours to complete both the application portion and the initial screening requirements.

"The initial screening takes place online, and there are two requirements that need to be completed:

1. Application Requirements (depending on the individual and level of work experience and education, this process can take anywhere from 30–60 minutes to complete; there is also an essay question that must be completed).

2. Online testing (there are two tests that are administered: the first test is a personality test, that does not have a time limit associated with it; the second test is a short-form general cognitive ability test that is timed at eight minutes—prospects typically average 30 minutes to complete both testing requirements).

"Once the tests are completed and submitted, the system informs the candidate, typically within minutes, of their overall results, i.e., successful/unsuccessful. At this point, NAV CANADA screens in a total of 35% of applicants who then move on to the next hurdles, which are administered for security and other reasons at NAV CANADA testing sites.

"We believe that e-recruiting has the following advantages:

1. Ad creation and utilization is uncomplicated and cost effective, with much more rapid turnaround compared to previous methods.
2. Brand building and awareness—reach is far greater using social media methods; our Facebook fanpage enables the Company to build brand loyalty and build a connection with interested prospects.
3. Ability to reach a more diverse population.
4. Higher quality of candidate simply because you can reach greater numbers of the required target audience, especially taking advantage of the targeting capability in today's social networks, with the ad placements and automated screening-in process.
5. The metrics that are available when using these avenues are invaluable. Google Analytics is a powerful tool and can provide some key insights about your site, visitors and ad effectiveness; and trend reporting is done with a simple click.
6. Increased workforce efficiencies through the use of technology with the integration of the online application process and the internal workflow management system.
7. Provides prospects with access 7 days a week, 24 hours a day to career information and the application system.

"E-recruiting does have disadvantages:

1. May not reach the more remote areas in Canada; for these areas NAV CANADA also incorporates traditional forms of marketing.
2. Too many unqualified applicants; however, NAV CANADA sees this as an opportunity to continue with building the brand and awareness of careers in air traffic control and flight service.

"We have received countless positive comments from applicants relating to the ease of applying, the transparency of the information both on the microsite and discussion boards on Facebook, the quality of information that is available to candidates, but most importantly the ability of a prospect to view their status online through the Prospect System and view information related to upcoming hurdles. A 'positive candidate experience' is one of our goals and will continue to be one of our goals."

Source: Reprinted with permission of NAV CANADA.

to http://www.charityvillage.com; those interested in working in the arts can review the postings at http://www.workinculture.ca. Each provincial human resources association has a members-only location on its website for HR-related job postings. Increasingly, newspapers and professional journals are placing copies of classified ads for job openings on their websites to run either before or at the same time as print ads.

Internet recruiting has several advantages for both the employer and the job seeker. The biggest advantage to the company is that it can reach a potentially limitless talent pool at minimal cost and beyond its normal geographic location. It allows the company to provide more information about the position to job seekers than does a typical print ad. Internet recruiting also allows companies to provide up-to-date information on their corporate image. New jobs can be posted on a daily basis rather than being at the mercy of a newspaper's or journal's publication schedule. Most of all, it speeds up the process of finding good prospective employees by facilitating searches of thousands of résumés stored in data banks. It facilitates finding the right candidate for the job in a cost-efficient manner. Internet recruiting is relatively inexpensive and provides more opportunities for smaller firms.[50]

From the job seekers' perspective, Internet recruiting allows them to apply for many jobs quickly at no cost other than that of an Internet connection. It gives job seekers access to a larger geographic area than other recruitment sources and provides them with a feel for the labour market. Job seekers can use the Internet systems 24/7 with the advantage of time savings and quick turnaround time on their applications. It allows job seekers to target specific searches.[51] Also, résumés posted on a job search website can be accessed by an unlimited number of potential employers. Their résumés remain in the database for a specified length of time, and résumés can usually be modified at any time. In addition, job seekers registered with some Internet job sites receive information about new job openings as they become available. Internet recruiting does not appear to affect job seekers' perceptions of the realistic nature of the information they find on the Internet; they perceive it to be as realistic as information provided by other means.[52] Recruiting on the Internet does appear to influence perceptions of whether the applicant is a good fit for the organization[53] or the applicant's attraction to the organization.[54] In the latter case, applicant attraction may be influenced by the design features of the organization's website.

Internet recruiting is not without its disadvantages. The ease of submitting résumés coupled with the sheer number of websites devoted to jobs and careers means that a company may be flooded with applications. According to the Internet Business Network,[55] there are now more than 100 000 career websites on the Internet. Whatever savings a company makes through Internet recruiting may be eroded by the costs of dealing with the large volume of applications.

The disadvantages of Internet recruiting for job seekers take a different form. First, given a choice, some job seekers prefer to read job postings in traditional paper formats, as opposed to Web-based postings. Job seekers are also turned off by low-quality websites.[56] Internet recruiting brings with it an overwhelming number of applicants, many of whom are unqualified. The cost savings from using the Internet are soon consumed by staff time required to sift through the résumés that are received. Next, Internet recruiting and job searching are available only to job seekers who have access to the Internet and the expertise to use computers and related software. This restriction may impede an organization's ability to attract candidates from different population subgroups and meet employment equity goals; it may be seen as discriminatory.[57]

Perhaps the major concern of job seekers is related to privacy.[58] When a résumé is included in a database, or when it is circulated, it becomes more or less a public document. Often, job seekers who are employed do not want their current employer to know they are looking for other work; they should first assure themselves of the privacy policy of the website before submitting an application through the site. Some employers now routinely have staff or agencies comb through job and career sites to find out if any of their employees are on the job market. Corporate recruiters regularly "mine" job sites using sophisticated technology to gather lists of prospects. They also mine news articles and corporate websites for candidates, even though those individuals may not be seeking employment elsewhere.[59]

Although managerial and professional jobs appear to be particularly well suited to Internet recruiting, people in these types of positions have concerns about their résumés appearing in databases and having others know that they are "shopping around." Except for a few high-tech firms, most companies have not abandoned more traditional forms of recruiting. Internet recruiting is used as part of a mix of methods to obtain the "best" candidates. With the phenomenal growth of the Internet, this may change very rapidly as more companies start to rely solely on Internet recruiting.

SOCIAL NETWORK RECRUITING

Social networking has grown from a fad to a powerful recruiting source. Social networks offer almost instant contact between HR professionals and potential job applicants, particularly those who may not be actively engaged in a job search. A June 2013 survey of 1600 recruiting and HR professionals carried out by Jobvite[60] found that 94 percent of respondents intended to recruit through social networks; this was an increase from 78 percent in 2008. Seventy-three percent indicated that their company would increase spending on social networking recruiting compared to 39 percent increases in spending on job boards. Over 90 percent also reported that they routinely reviewed social profiles that are available on social networking sites. Recruitment and Selection Today 6.4 presents recruiter and HR professionals' reactions to types of information observed on applicant pages on social media.

RECRUITMENT AND SELECTION TODAY 6.4

REACTIONS TO JOB CANDIDATES' SOCIAL PROFILES

SOCIAL RECRUITING SURVEY RESULTS

93% of recruiters are likely to look at a candidate's social profile.

Q. How would you react to these possible items discovered by reviewing a candidate's social network profile?

	Positive	Neutral	Negative
References to doing illegal drugs	1%	7%	83%
Posts/tweets of a sexual nature	1%	16%	71%
Profanity in posts/tweets	4%	20%	65%
Spelling/grammar errors in posts/tweets	3%	29%	61%
References to guns	1%	31%	51%
Pictures of consumption of alcohol	1%	39%	47%
Volunteering/donations to charity	65%	26%	1%
Poltical posts/tweets	2%	65%	18%
Overtly religious posts/tweets	2%	55%	28%

42% have reconsidered a candidate based on content viewed in a social profile, leading to both positive and negative re-assessments.

More recruiters react negatively to profanity (65%) and grammar and punctuation errors in posts/tweets (61%) than references to alcohol use (47%).

Jobvite Social Recruiting Survey Results 2013 8

Source: From 2013 *Social Recruiting Survey Results*, p. 8. http://web.jobvite.com/rs/jobvite/images/Jobvite_SocialRecruiting2013.pdf Reprinted with permission from Jobvite, Inc.

Almost 78 percent of the companies surveyed reported that they had successfully hired new employees through social networking sites, with 92 percent using LinkedIn, 24 percent Facebook, and 14 percent Twitter. Despite this growing popularity as a recruitment source, many questions remain to be answered, including the validity and usefulness of information found on social networking sites.[61] As discussed at the start of Chapter 5, low recruiter ratings based on negative perceptions from Facebook may not indicate candidates will be poor performers as employees. Information gathered from social media sites should not be used alone in making decisions about candidates.

Social networks
Internet sites that allow users to post a profile with a certain amount of information that is visible to the public.

WHAT ARE SOCIAL NETWORKS? **Social networks** are Internet sites that allow users to post a profile with a certain amount of information that is visible to the public. The more popular sites for recruiters include LinkedIn, Facebook, and Twitter. These sites allow users to share information online including photos and videos. With respect to recruiting, the Jobvite survey found that 94 percent of the companies surveyed used LinkedIn, followed by 65 percent for Facebook and 55 percent for Twitter. Another 15 percent of companies used YouTube as a recruiting tool.

BENEFITS OF SOCIAL NETWORK RECRUITING HR professionals who have engaged in social network recruiting believe that the people hired through social networks perform better on the job and stay with the company for longer periods of time. The costs associated with social networking are confined to the HR staff charged with the recruiting. Unlike job boards, there is no cost to joining a social network. Thus, the returns on investment for social network recruiting can far exceed those associated with other recruiting sources. Additionally, social network recruiting can identify "passive" applicants, those not actively seeking a new job but who can be targeted by the recruiter because of their apparent skills and abilities.

THE DOWNSIDE OF SOCIAL NETWORK RECRUITING The most significant disadvantage of social network recruiting is that it may have adverse impacts on members of protected groups. While data for Canada are lacking, studies in the United States show that Hispanics and African-Americans participate in LinkedIn to a lesser degree than members of those groups in the total U.S. population–2 percent versus 15.4 percent for Hispanics and 5 percent versus 12.8 percent for African-Americans.[62] Most likely, the participation rates for other social networks are similar. Recruiting only from social networks may leave a company open to charges of systemic discrimination.

A related issue is the use of social networks in screening job candidates, either those being recruited or those candidates who may be about to receive a job offer. There are numerous media reports about job candidates who were about to receive job offers until HR staff reviewed their social media accounts. The Jobvite 2013 Social Recruiting Survey found that 42 percent of personnel involved in recruiting reconsidered a candidate based on the content of their social media pages. They reacted most negatively to profanity and poor grammar, punctuation, and spelling in posts. Postings on social media can be unreliable, with users tending to boast about their activities, including drug and alcohol use. Users post photos and videos, sometimes placing themselves in compromising positions; photos may also indicate that the job candidate has a disability. Users may indicate their sexual orientation or make antigay remarks. In all cases, reviewing this material may place HR in contravention of legal and ethical issues. As we have noted in previous chapters, HR personnel cannot ask certain questions, yet viewing photos on Facebook identifies the race of the candidate. Age, religious preference, and other private information can also be identified. Using information from these sources to eliminate job candidates leaves the organization open to charges of discrimination.[63]

SOCIAL NETWORK RECRUITING GUIDELINES Social networks are becoming an integral part of recruiting and there is every indication that their popularity will increase. It is essential that HR staff use them properly and avoid the pitfalls that may lead to charges of discrimination. The following guidelines are offered as a means of avoiding those charges.

1. Develop a written policy on the use of social networks in recruiting and screening.
2. Document your use of the social network sites; keep detailed records of your searches that can be used to show that hiring decisions were related to job-relevant criteria.
3. Do not use social networking sites as the only recruiting source; doing so may lead to charges of adverse impact by members of protected groups.
4. Avoid using social networks for screening candidates unless you can be assured that the information on those sites is reliable and accurate.
5. Disclose to candidates that you will review social networking sites. If you discover negative information about a job candidate, give the candidate an opportunity to respond to that information.

COMPARISON OF RECRUITMENT METHODS

Table 6.1 summarizes the advantages and disadvantages of different recruitment methods. Internal recruitment has the advantage of dealing with known quantities. Internal job applicants already have realistic expectations of life in the organization. They are, or should be, aware of the organizational goals and values. Likewise, the organization is familiar with the internal applicant's work history and performance record. Internal recruitment is also relatively inexpensive. Most middle-level jobs in an organization are filled through this means. External recruitment, on the other hand, is used mostly to staff jobs at either the entry or executive levels. External recruitment brings needed skills and competencies to an organization and prevents organizations from becoming "inbred." It exposes companies to new people, new ideas, and new ways of doing things. External recruitment may be the only means through which employment equity programs succeed. External recruitment can be very time consuming and expensive.

RECRUITING AND INTERNATIONAL ASSIGNMENTS

With the spread of globalization, Canadian organizations increasingly need to staff foreign operations. Most of this recruitment has focused on managerial-level personnel. Recruiting someone to head a project in another country is very important if a company is to expand its business into foreign markets. Typically, Canadian organizations have recruited internally or domestically for foreign assignments and have paid the recruits up to three times their normal salaries for accepting foreign postings.[64] Use of North American expatriates to staff the operations of North American firms overseas, however, has not been successful in many cases. One reason for this is that international recruiting tends to rely on domestic hiring practices with some cosmetic changes.[65] Problems

TABLE 6.1

COMPARISON OF RECRUITMENT METHODS

METHODS	ADVANTAGES	DISADVANTAGES
INTERNAL RECRUITMENT		
Job postings	• Inexpensive • Rewards performance • Discovers talent	• Time consuming • Produces instability • Demoralizing process
Succession/ replacement charts	Based on known human resources	Limited by organizational chart and structure
Information systems (HRIS)	Known KSAO database linked to job	• Expensive • Rarely used by companies
Nominations	Based on known human resources	• Random process • May lead to discrimination
EXTERNAL RECRUITMENT		
Newspaper ads	• Quick and flexible • Specific market	• Expensive • Short lifespan for ads
Periodicals/journals	Targets specific groups or skills	• Long lead time for ads • Expensive
Radio and TV	• Mass audience • Targets specific groups • Image advertising	• Very expensive • Short ad duration • Provides little information
Public displays	• Inexpensive	• Provides little information
Direct mail	• Targets specific groups and skills • Can provide much information	• Expensive and inefficient • Requires mailing list • Often not read
Special events: open house, job fairs	• Useful for filling multiple jobs • Relatively inexpensive • Targets job pool	• Shares job pool with competition • Information overload/stress
Employee referrals	Inexpensive	May lead to discrimination and inbreeding
Networking	Inexpensive	May lead to discrimination and inbreeding
Walk-ins	Inexpensive	Random process; inefficient
Canada Employment Centres	Inexpensive; job–KSAO fit	Success limited to certain occupational categories
Private employment agency	Person–job fit	Expensive

Continued

TABLE 6.1

CONTINUED

METHODS	ADVANTAGES	DISADVANTAGES
Executive search firm	Known talent pool	Very expensive
In-house recruiter	Knows company	Limited knowledge of recruiting methods
Temporary help agency	• Access to short-term labour pool • Few recruiting demands	• Exposure to risk of discrimination claims • Mostly unskilled and poorly educated talent pool
Recruiting at schools	• Known talent pool • Pretrained applicants	Time consuming; very expensive
Internet	• Mass audience • Inexpensive • Specific audience	• Random process • Unknown audience
Social networks	• Targets "passive" applicants • High rate of return on investment	• Potential for discrimination • Information may be unreliable

associated with family adjustment to new cultures and the manager's lack of personal adjustment to the foreign business environment often lead to failure.[66]

Moore[67] makes the point that international recruitment involves defining the assignment and the person requirements needed for the position, and then developing a recruitment campaign to attract people with the needed skills. Dowling and Welch[68] identified four myths about international recruiting:

1. There is a universal approach to management.
2. People can acquire multicultural behaviours without outside help.
3. There are common characteristics shared by all successful international managers.
4. There are no impediments to mobility.

Holding on to these myths is a recipe for failure in the international arena. International recruitment is context dependent; it is difficult to predict who will do well. However, giving recruitment careful consideration may reduce the risk of failure.[69]

Canadian firms must do a much better job of identifying, recruiting, and selecting individuals based on those competencies related to success abroad. With the development of the borderless job-search websites and résumé data banks, companies may have an easier time finding job applicants from around the world who have the requisite knowledge of the laws and culture of the host country.

FREQUENCY OF USE OF RECRUITING METHODS

Table 6.2 presents data from an online survey conducted by Bissonnette in 2011.[70] She sampled both U.S. and Canadian adults employed in 13 different industries. Internet

TABLE 6.2

PERCENTAGE OF RESPONDENTS FINDING JOBS THROUGH DIFFERENT RECRUITING SOURCES

RECRUITING SOURCE	2011 SURVEY (%) (N=455)[a]	2005 WES (%) (N=25.000)[b]
Internet postings	53.2	7.2
Employee referrals (e.g. company insider)	47.5	—
Network of contacts (e.g. professional associations, colleagues)	45.7	—
Help wanted ads	42.2	14.5
Family and friends	37.4	39.5
Prior experience	32.2	—
Recruiting agency	26.2	3.1
Walk-in	23.3	21.9
Government recruiting agency	17.6	4.0
Job fair	13.4	0.4
On-campus recruitment	11.0	2.6
Union posting	7.9 %	0.7
Directly recruited by employer	—	13.5

[a] A. Bissonnette and V.M. Catano. 2007. *Recruitment Source Over Time: Correlations, Perceptions, Interpretations and Future Directions.* Paper presented at the annual meeting of the Administrative Association of Canada, Ottawa. Reprinted with permission of V.M. Catano.
[b] Bissonnette, A.B., and V.M. Catano. 2007. "Recruitment Source over Time: Correlations, Perceptions, Interpretations and Future Directions." Paper presented at the annual meeting of the Administrative Association of Canada, Ottawa. Reprinted with permission of V.M. Catano.

postings were the most frequently used source to finding a job, with 53.2 percent of the respondents having done so. This compared to only 7.2 percent in the 2005 survey conducted by Statistics Canada as part of its Workplace and Employee Survey (WES). The difference in use between 2005 and 2011 may not be entirely due to increased use of the Internet, but rather the types of jobs included in the survey. The WES was based on primarily blue-collar jobs, while the 2011 survey sampled more professional and technical employees. Family and friends were used by about 39 percent of employees in both samples to find a job. Employee referrals and networks were used by about 46 percent of employees to find a job in 2011. The WES survey did not ask questions related to these two sources. Although the Internet was used extensively in 2011, help wanted ads and other print media were used by 42 percent as part of their job search activities. The 2011 sample also used employment agencies to a greater extent than those in the WES sample. Again, the difference is likely due to a greater number of professional and technical workers in the 2011 survey.

Zottoli and Wanous[71] reviewed over 50 years of research on recruiting source effectiveness, as measured through job turnover/survival and job performance. Referrals by family and friends and current employees, in-house job postings, and rehiring of former employees were the most effective methods in filling positions. Walk-ins were slightly less effective, with the least effective sources consisting of newspaper ads, placement services, and employment agencies, whether private or government-run. The Internet was not used as a recruiting source in the reviewed research. As the most popular recruiting methods also have the potential to produce systemic discrimination, HR practitioners must be particularly alert to this undesirable outcome.

// PART III: ATTRACTING JOB APPLICANTS

Recruiting is a two-way street. Organizations wish to attract high quality job applicants, but at the same time applicants are evaluating the organization as a place of employment. Breaugh and Starke[72] present a model of how job expectations on the part of an applicant influence attitudes and behaviours toward an organization and a job (see Figure 6.3).

Because of their experience, many job candidates conclude that they do not want to work in a particular organization, or that they will not fit in; they may also form other attitudes, which last through their early work experience.[73] A study of over 3500 police applicants showed that those who self-selected out of the process and those who stayed differed in their perceptions of the organization, expectations about the job, and the opinions of family and friends about joining the police.[74]

In the long run, such **self-selecting out** may be in the best interests of both the applicant and the organization, if that decision is based on accurate information and a realistic perception of the job and the organization. On the other hand, if these early decisions are based on inaccurate information, both the candidate and the organization may be worse off. Ryan and colleagues[75] found that the perceptions of women and blacks who withdrew from the police application process differed from the majority group, posing difficulties for organizations trying to increase their diversity.

Self-selecting out
Occurs during the recruitment and selection process when candidates form the opinion that they do not want to work in the organization for which they are being recruited.

THE ORGANIZATIONAL CONTEXT

Individuals become job applicants after forming an opinion on the desirability of working in a particular job within a specific organization.[76] Organizational characteristics such as location, size of the enterprise, and type of industry may steer individuals away from applying for jobs no matter how attractive the job or how qualified they are to do it.[77] For example, a physician is unlikely to apply for a position in Yukon if she is concerned about her aging parents living in Nova Scotia, regardless of pay or career opportunities. Location may be the main factor in deciding whether to apply for the position.

In today's rapidly changing workplace with a highly educated workforce, jobs providing autonomy, decision-making authority, and opportunities for self-development win out over those that lack these attributes. Moreover, with the increase in dual-career couples, single-parent families, and female representation in the workforce, organizations that offer special accommodations and flexible work arrangements gain

FIGURE 6.3

THE FORMATION OF JOB EXPECTATIONS AND THEIR INFLUENCE ON JOB APPLICANT ATTITUDES AND BEHAVIOURS

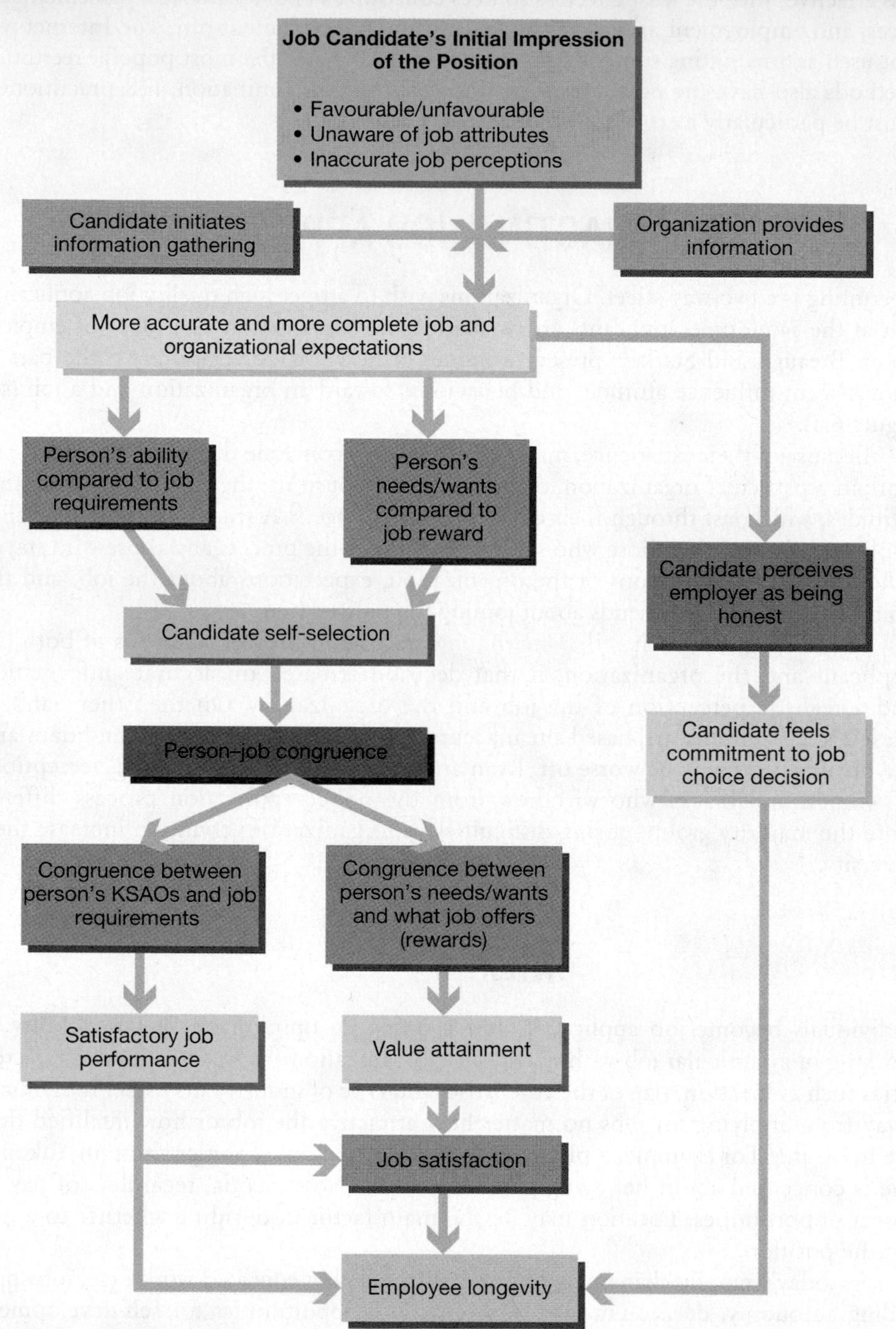

Source: J.A. Breaugh and M. Starke. 2000. "Research on Employee Recruitment: So Many Studies, So Many Questions," Figure 2. *Journal of Management*, Vol. 26, Issue 3: 405–34. Copyright © 2000 SAGE Publications, Inc. Reprinted by Permission of SAGE Publication.

competitive advantages in recruiting. For positions requiring geographical relocation of candidates, employers that assist working spouses to secure local employment gain further advantage.

Ultimately, the **interests and values** of the job applicant influence the relative importance of different organizational attributes and whether an individual will apply for a specific job. Interests and values do not indicate whether a person is qualified for a job; they only suggest the type of work a person may find satisfying. Potential job applicants must also have the knowledge, skills, abilities, or other attributes and competencies (KSAOs) that are required for the job. Nonetheless, the degree of satisfaction with a job is one of the many factors that influence job turnover, especially in good economic times when jobs are plentiful.[78]

Interests and values
An individual's likes and dislikes and the importance or priorities attached to those likes and dislikes.

The Department of National Defence actively recruits members for both civilian and military jobs in the Canadian Forces through its website (http://www.forces.ca/en/home), which includes a Jobs menu that provides information on specific jobs and occupations in the Canadian Forces, particularly those "in demand." The site also includes information on the working environment and requirements for entry and training for the different positions.

NAV CANADA owns and operates Canada's civil air navigation service. It coordinates the safe and efficient movement of aircraft in domestic international air space assigned to Canada. Information on careers available with NAV CANADA, for example air traffic controllers, can be seen at http://takecharge.navcanada.ca/en.

Many professional associations also provide information on careers in their professions and the KSAOs and credentials needed for entry. These sites also list positions that are available. A good example, which deals with chartered accountants, is http://www.casource.com.

The size of an organization influences its attractiveness to prospective employees, as well as the organization's recruitment strategies. A study of 119 small-business employers and 184 large employers showed that job seekers have distinct preferences regarding firm size that influence their job search behaviours to such an extent that one might argue large and small firms comprise separate labour markets.[79] Job seekers appear to tailor their **job search** to match the recruiting strategies used by large or small organizations. Large firms, particularly when recruiting college or university graduates, tend to have more formal and bureaucratic recruiting practices, while smaller firms rely on more informal methods.

Job search
The strategies, techniques, and practices an individual uses in looking for a job.

Large firms tend to start recruiting earlier and to use trained recruiters and campus placement offices. They also are more likely to base their decisions on a candidate's objective qualifications and the results of employment tests. Smaller firms tend to rely more on traditional sources such as advertising and internal referrals to fill their positions and to base their decisions on an interview. Students who prefer a large firm start their job search earlier and make use of recruiting sources, such as the campus placement office, that are used by larger firms. Students who prefer smaller firms are less intense in their search efforts and rely on traditional sources of information about jobs.[80] The strategies and information that people use in forming preferences and opinions about organizations are by no means clear. In some cases, information is based on preconceived stereotypes or information obtained from inaccurate sources. In other cases, people may undertake extensive job searches before applying for employment with an organization. They may consult a variety of published documents for information about the organization, including annual reports and stories about the company and its employees in newspapers and business periodicals. Also, they might check companies' Internet sites for job opportunities.

Internet employment-related websites offer profiles on the various companies that use their sites. For example, Monster.ca (http://www.monster.ca) provides information on the company, its major products or services, the number of people it employs, its location, and current employment opportunities. The Government of Canada now uses the Internet extensively to recruit people for different positions throughout Canada. Job listings can be found at http://jobs-emplois.gc.ca/index-eng.htm. Selecting a specific job posting provides a wealth of information about the job and its organizational environment. Also, job applicants sometimes seek out employees of an organization or friends or acquaintances who have worked for a company to obtain personal views on what it is like to work there and what the employees are like as coworkers. Recruitment and Selection Today 6.5 provides more information on Service Canada's Internet job sites.

CORPORATE IMAGE AND APPLICANT ATTRACTION

Often, the reputation of an organization is an important concern to job applicants. Corporate image predicts the likelihood of interest on the part of a job seeker: The better the image, the more attractive the organization is.[81] Job seekers may not even consider applying for jobs in organizations that have a negative image. This lack of attractiveness may be particularly troublesome in tight labour markets, when there is a scarcity of qualified job applicants. In the case of high reputation firms, there is likely to be a steady stream of job applicants, regardless of the labour market, making selection rather than recruitment the key to successful staffing.[82]

RECRUITMENT AND SELECTION TODAY 6.5

GOVERNMENT-SPONSORED INTERNET JOB SITES

One of the most useful tools in conducting a job search is the Internet, where there are thousands of sites related to work and occupations. One of the best is the Job Bank site operated by Service Canada at http://www.jobbank.gc.ca/home-eng.do?lang=eng on behalf of Employment and Social Development Canada (ESDC). The Job Bank provides a wealth of information not only about jobs available across Canada, but also about effective job search strategies, including information on preparing a résumé. Available jobs are listed by province and territory, and there are also links to numerous other public- and private-sector employment sites.

Service Canada also has a "Training, Career, and Worker Information" site at https://www.jobsetc.gc.ca/eng/home.jsp. This site has an interactive feature that takes the user through a series of quizzes to help identify possible career choices (choose "Career Exploration" and then "Identify your career options"). After you choose a resulting identified occupation, the Career Navigator will provide you with information (wages, number of jobs available, and employment prospects, etc.) to help you make an informed career decision. The quizzes relate to:

- Abilities
- Data, people, things
- Work preference
- Work values
- Multiple intelligence
- Seeing, hearing, doing

The variety and depth of the information provided, plus the links to many excellent relevant sites, means that spending time at the Service Canada website before beginning a job search will be time well invested.

What influences organizational attractiveness? One of the most prominent factors is the job applicant's degree of familiarity with the organization. The more familiar applicants are with the company, the more likely they will hold a positive image of it.[83,84] The profitability of a company and its pay level positively influence attractiveness and reputation,[85] with pay strongly predicting whether a job applicant will pursue a job with an organization.[86] There are other considerations on the part of younger workers who compare their values with those of the organization. Organizations that express positive corporate social policies, those that include concern for the environment, promoting community relations, improving labour relations, and improving diversity, are more attractive to job applicants.[87] As well, job advertisements that present an organization as one that is psychologically healthy, in that it cares about the health of its employees, help the organization to be seen as very attractive by job seekers.[88] On the other hand, job applicants rate vacant positions as less attractive when the company's help-wanted advertisements contain minimal information about both the attributes of the position and the pay associated with it.[89]

Organizations often initiate activities designed to enhance their image and reputation. Providing job applicants with more information about an organization appears to influence job applicant behaviour; organizational familiarity, and thus attractiveness, seems to increase when an applicant receives more information about a company through employment advertisements and other recruitment materials.[90] A company's recruitment image is also affected by the advertisements it places for products or services.[91] Many companies undertake **image advertising** to raise the profile of their organizations in a positive manner to attract interest from job seekers, as well as increasing interest in their services and products.[92] A good example of image advertising is the sponsorship of the many summer jazz festivals and other cultural events by Canadian companies. The hope is that associating their names with high-profile events will improve the corporate image and result in greater interest in the company.[93] Presumably, working for companies with positive images raises the self-esteem of employees, and this prospect is attractive to potential employees.[94]

Image advertising
Advertising designed to raise an organization's profile in a positive manner in order to attract job seekers' interest.

Similar to image advertising, another strategy that corporations use to enhance their identity in the marketplace and to sell the organization is "branding." Companies use branding to establish certain perceptions about the corporation in the public's mind through associating the organization with high-profile celebrities or being known as one of the best 100 employers in Canada. Again, these strategies may backfire. Many retail companies used Tiger Woods, who had a positive reputation as a golfer, to enhance their own identity through associating him with many of their own products. After Woods was embroiled in a sex scandal, these same companies scrambled to disassociate themselves from him.

An organization that is having trouble attracting qualified candidates should investigate how it is perceived by job candidates and take corrective action, if necessary. One of the difficulties is identifying the components that influence an organization's image, as different individuals may have different perceptions of the same company; job seekers and company executives may hold very different perceptions of the organization's image. Image advertising must present an accurate and consistent picture of the organization. Image advertising that creates misperceptions will lead to mismatches in the fit between person and organization. Image advertising should be designed to improve the attractiveness of the organization on the basis of an accurate representation of its characteristics. Recruitment and Selection Notebook 6.2 provides a few guidelines for organizational recruiting.

RECRUITMENT AND SELECTION NOTEBOOK 6.2

GUIDELINES FOR EFFECTIVE RECRUITING

- Ensure that candidates receive consistent and noncontradictory information about important features of the job and its environment from all people involved in the recruiting process.
- Recognize that the behaviour of recruiters and other representatives gives an impression of the organization's climate, efficiency, and attitude toward employees.
- Ensure that all recruiting information and materials given to job applicants present accurate and consistent information, whether positive or negative.
- Present important information on the job and the organization to job candidates by several different, reliable, and credible sources.
- Give serious consideration not only to the content of information presented to candidates but also to the context in which it is presented.
- Take extreme care in preparing recruiting materials and selecting advertising media, and also in choosing the recruiters who will interact with job applicants.

Person–job fit
Occurs when a job candidate has the knowledge, skills, abilities, or other attributes and competencies required by the job in question.

Person–organization fit
Occurs when a job candidate fits the organization's values and culture and has the contextual attributes desired by the organization.

// THE PERSON–ORGANIZATION FIT

No matter how desirable or compatible a job and organization appear to the candidate, it is all for naught unless the candidate receives an offer of employment. During the recruitment process, the organization, through its representatives, is seeking to learn as much as it can about the candidate. Recruiters assess potential employees in terms of their fit with both the job and the organization. **Person–job fit** concerns whether the job applicant has the knowledge, skills, abilities, or other attributes and competencies required by the job, while **person–organization fit** is the recruiter's belief that the candidate fits with the organization's values and culture; that is, the candidate has the contextual attributes that the company is looking for.

Recruiters distinguish between these two types of "fit" and tend to make decisions early in their interview with a candidate on whether the candidate matches what the organization is looking for.[95] The recruiter's perception that the applicant fits the job appears to be based mainly on an assessment of the candidate's skills and experience, derived from information gathered during the recruiting process. These sources are likely to include a review of the candidate's résumé and a brief screening interview. In some cases, candidates may also be asked to take employment tests at this stage. These screening and selection procedures are the focus of Chapters 7, 8, and 9. The recruiter's perception of a person–organization fit is mostly based on an assessment by the recruiter of the candidate's work experience, personality, and values.

© iStock.com/mevans

An applicant's résumé plays an important role in determining whether the applicant will proceed to the next stage of the hiring process. Organizational recruiters use the content of job applicants' résumés to make inferences about the suitability of applicants for both P-O and P-J fit. As noted above, they use information about the candidate's work experience and educational background to assess person–job fit. Recruiters go on to use work experience and extracurricular activities that are noted on the résumé to make an assessment of the applicant's person–organization fit. Résumé content influences the recruiter's hiring decision.[96]

Both the perception of person–job fit and of person–organization fit predict whether the company will make a job offer. The perception of a poor person–organization fit, however, will reduce the likelihood that a person with a good job fit will receive a job offer. Recruiters form and use perceptions of a candidate's organizational fit as part of the hiring process.[97] Hiring by Zappos, a retail clothing company owned by Amazon, is based solely on P-O fit and not an assessment of job fit. We don't have any data on how successful Zappos is in hiring successful employees, but the empirical evidence is not good. Unfortunately, predictions based only on P-O fit are not very accurate. Meta-analysis has shown that P-O fit is not a good predictor of job performance (r=.15), although a somewhat better predictor of job turnover (r=.24).[98] P-O fit and P-J fit do a much better job at predicting several attitudinal variables such as job satisfaction and organizational commitment. Both are also negatively related to intentions to quit and indicators of strain.[99] Table 6.3 presents the results from two meta-analyses supporting these conclusions.

The assessment of fit and the decision of the company to make an offer and the candidate to accept it are based on the exchange of information, including the résumé, that takes place over the recruitment process. If the job candidate does not make an adequate investigation of the job or organization, or if the organization does not represent itself accurately through the people involved in recruiting and selection, the probability of a person–organization mismatch increases. Mismatches can be quite costly in terms of absenteeism, low productivity, and turnover. A major goal of any recruitment campaign should be to improve the chance of making a good fit between candidates and the organization.

COMMUNICATION AND PERCEPTION

Based on information that was available or obtained during the recruitment process, the candidate and the organization form a perception of each other. If the perceptions of

TABLE 6.3

THE CORRELATION OF P-O FIT AND P-J FIT WITH VARIABLES LISTED IN THE FIRST COLUMN

	PERSON–ORGANIZATION FIT	PERSON–JOB FIT
Job performance[a, b]	.15	.20
Intentions to quit[b]	–.35	–.46
Job satisfaction[b]	.44	.56
Organizational commitment[b]	.51	.47
Coworker satisfaction[b]	.39	.32
Supervisor satisfaction[b]	.33	.33
Indicators of strain[b]	–.27	–.28

Sources of data:
[a] Arthur et al. 2006
[b] Kristof-Brown et al. 2005

both are positive ("This is the right candidate," "This is the right job for me"), a job offer is made and accepted. If the perceptions of one do not match those of the other, a job offer is either not made or, if made, not accepted. Figure 6.4 presents the possible outcomes from this process. In all cases, there is a possibility that the perceptions formed by the candidate and/or the organization are wrong. Candidates, particularly, may develop overly positive perceptions of the organization.[100]

Perceptions are based on communication. During the recruiting process both the candidate and the organization try to control the flow of information from one to the other. One party may not wish to share some information with the other. An organization may fear losing top-quality candidates by revealing that it is not the perfect workplace; candidates may fear losing a job offer by admitting they do not plan to stay with the organization for a long period of time. Both may misrepresent their attributes or characteristics. An organization may exaggerate the chances for promotion to attract a candidate; candidates may exaggerate their experience. Both the organization and the candidate evaluate each other during the recruitment process.[101]

Inaccurate, incomplete, or distorted information leads to misperceptions and inaccurate decisions. A primary goal of recruitment should be to increase the accuracy of the perceptions that each party holds about the other.

ACCURATE EXPECTATIONS

By developing a systematic job search strategy, job candidates will come into contact with information on jobs and organizations. Many of the initial expectations that candidates develop are based on the accuracy of this preliminary information, as well as the more extensive information that accumulates during the recruiting process. For example, accuracy of information received from the recruiting source and the organization directly influenced the length of time that Canadian students stayed in seasonal jobs, as well as

FIGURE 6.4

MATCHING THE CANDIDATE'S AND ORGANIZATION'S PERCEPTIONS: JOB OFFER OUTCOMES

		Candidate's Perception of the Organization	
		Positive	Negative
Organization's Perception of the Candidate	Positive	Job offer made by organization and accepted by candidate.	Job offer made by organization and rejected by candidate.
	Negative	Job offer not made by organization but would have been accepted by candidate.	Job offer not made by organization and would not have been accepted by candidate.

their commitment to the organization and their job satisfaction.[102] Candidates actively evaluate the merits of any message they receive.[103] Organizations, however, have no control over whether candidates search for any information, or which information they select and use in forming an opinion about the job or organization.

Newcomers in an organization often develop overly high expectations about the job and organization, and these initial expectations may substantially influence the long-term relationship between the candidate and the organization.[104] Organizations do, however, have control over the accuracy and the completeness of the information they present when recruiting job candidates (see Recruitment and Selection Notebook 6.3). During the United States' first war with Iraq, many military personnel who were recruited into the U.S. Reserve Forces were shocked and outraged to learn that they were liable for combat duty; they claimed that they had never been made aware of such a possibility before signing on.[105] Unmet expectations on the part of new hires leads to lack of both job satisfaction and organizational commitment.[106] Adding more relevant information about the job and organization to job postings can lead to an applicant's greater attraction to the job while a lack of information may lead to negative inferences and lower attraction to the job.[107]

Courts in both Canada and the United States have held employers accountable for the accuracy of information they present to job candidates as part of the recruiting process. False promises and misrepresentations made in recruiting candidates to work

RECRUITMENT AND SELECTION NOTEBOOK 6.3

CREATING ACCURATE EXPECTATIONS

Four factors play an influential role in creating accurate expectations that candidates hold about prospective jobs:

1. **Source of information.** In describing a job or position, the organization should present information to job candidates that accurately describes the job and its context.
2. **Communication media.** Recruitment media differ in their effectiveness. Organizations should use as many different types of communication media as they can afford, including newer technologies such as job postings on their websites or on Internet employment sites.
3. **Content of information.** The content of information provided throughout the recruitment process is the most important factor in creating accurate job expectations and should be:
   - Accurate—Job candidates should be given both positive and negative information about the job and the organization.
   - Specific—Job candidates should be given detailed information that will allow them to make an informed decision.
   - Broad—Job candidates should be given information about a wide range of job and organizational attributes, not only information related to a narrow range of topics.
   - Credible—Job candidates must believe that the information they receive is reliable and accurate.
   - Important—Job candidates should be given information that is important to their decision making and which they are unlikely to receive through other means.
4. **Nature of the job candidates.** The organization must know something about the audience that it wants to respond to the information. This includes knowledge of the social and demographic characteristics of the target group. The content of the message should be compatible with its intended audience and address their needs and interests. It should be placed in media most likely to be used by the target group.

for a company may result in a damage award. Recruiters must be very careful in statements they make to job applicants concerning issues such as time to promotion and pay increases.[108] Employees who believe that they were misled about the nature of their working conditions or their working environment are likely to take legal action against their employers to the extent that they are injured through reliance on the false or misleading statements.[109] As part of orienting newcomers into an organization, a company may wish to initiate a set of procedures that are designed to lower the expectations of the new hire to more realistic and accurate perceptions of the organization, apart from that individual's specific job.[110]

REALISTIC JOB PREVIEWS

Realistic job preview A procedure designed to reduce turnover and increase satisfaction among newcomers to an organization by providing job candidates with accurate information about the job and the organization.

Recruitment programs can be designed to increase the accuracy of the expectations that job candidates hold about the job and the organization. One such program, **realistic job previews** (RJPs), is intended to improve the possibility of identifying a fit between the job candidate and the organization. The primary goal of RJPs is to reduce turnover among newcomers to an organization by providing job candidates with accurate information about the job and the organization.[111] Other hoped-for outcomes of the RJP are (1) that the job candidates will develop realistic perceptions of what it is like to work in the organization, (2) that they will view the organization in a more credible light, and (3) that, if they accept the job offer, they will be more satisfied with their job and committed to the organization. Extensive research shows that while RJPs accomplish their goals, they do so at a modest level.[112]

Rather than have a candidate accept a job on the basis of unrealistic expectations, only to quit after discovering a mismatch with the organization, RJPs give the candidate an accurate preview of the job before the job offer is accepted (e.g., weekend work, limited promotional opportunities). In this way, candidates who discover a mismatch self-select out, or remove themselves from the competition, saving themselves the aggravation of having made a bad decision and the organization the cost of hiring and training them. There are some concerns that the realism also discourages very qualified candidates from accepting job offers from the organization[113]; however, the number of withdrawals from the applicant pool after an RJP is not great.[114]

The more exposure a job applicant has to a job, the more likely it is that the applicant may overemphasize the negative aspects of the job and refuse a job offer; this aspect of RJPs may prove problematic in extremely competitive job markets.[115] The negative information in the RJP appears to influence the job applicant's decision and may have a greater adverse impact on the best-qualified applicants,[116] requiring greater compensation to attract them to the position.[117]

On the other hand, presenting negative information as part of the RJP may have positive effects. In addition to lowering job candidates' expectations and attraction to the organization, RJPs may increase perceptions of the trustworthiness of the organization and facilitate a person–organization match more so than a traditional job preview.[118] Similarly, RJPs enhance a job candidate's perception that the organization is a caring one that is concerned for its employees.[119] There is some evidence that RJPs lead to increased commitment and reduced turnover through perceptions of employer concern and honesty.[120] Recruitment and Selection Today 6.6 outlines the use of RJPs in the Canadian Forces.

RJPs remain one of the most intriguing aspects of the recruiting process. Notwithstanding the methodological flaws in RJP research,[121] RJPs lead to accurate

RECRUITMENT AND SELECTION TODAY 6.6

REALISTIC JOB PREVIEWS IN THE CANADIAN FORCES

The Canadian Forces (CF) uses RJPs as part of its recruitment program. The program was designed to reduce early attrition of new recruits by improving identification of both the person–job fit and person–organization fit. RJPs are carried out throughout the Canadian Forces as a matter of policy. They are embedded in a comprehensive counselling system designed to match the goals, interests, and abilities of applicants to the characteristics and conditions of service associated with specific trades in the CF.

By using advertising media and recruiting visits to schools and public places such as shopping malls, the CF raises the interest of potential applicants in the military as a career and attracts them to recruiting centres. The applicant is met by a recruiting officer, who presents the candidate with brochures and information on the CF and determines initial suitability of the candidate for a CF career. Applicants who pass this first screening then view an orientation video, which depicts the careers of two candidates from recruitment through basic and trades training, and on to their first job postings. The video provides a realistic preview of life in the forces in general and includes information on both the positive and negative aspects of military life. For example, it may portray the personal and social support offered to CF members and their families as well as the hazards and physical demands of military duty.

Following the orientation video, the candidate meets with a military career counsellor and has an opportunity to raise any questions or concerns stimulated by the video. At this point, the candidate must make a decision about whether to continue the process by completing an application form and a series of ability and aptitude tests. Candidates are next shown up to five trade/lifestyle videos for entry-level positions for which they qualified through ability and aptitude testing. These videos are based on interviews with personnel from each trade they represent; they contain both verbal descriptions and live-action footage of what it is like to work in that trade in a military environment. The speakers not only provide a description of what the trade is like but also express their views about their work.

Following these videos, the candidate meets once again with a military career counsellor to review all aspects of the different trades and the military lifestyle. If the candidate remains interested in one of the selected trades, if there is an appropriate vacancy in that specialty, and if the candidate has passed a series of employment tests and interviews, the candidate is given an offer to enroll in the Canadian Forces. This offer is made conditional on the candidate's meeting appropriate medical and physical requirements.

Internet versions of some of the initial RJP material can be found on the Canadian Forces website at http://www.forces.ca/en/jobexplorer/browsejobs-70. Scroll down the page to see a list of available CF jobs. If you select "Personnel Selection Officer," a function similar to many HR positions, a written description of the job is provided, along with photos and a video that illustrate the working environment.

As illustrated by this example, RJPs, when done right, require an extensive array of resources during their development and implementation. The cost to produce an RJP that is done well may place it beyond the reach of many small to medium-sized organizations.

expectations on the part of job candidates, to reductions in turnover, and to improvements in job satisfaction[122]; however, the magnitudes of these significant effects are small, raising questions about whether the costs and time needed to develop an RJP are balanced or offset by its benefits. Rynes and Cable[123] do not expect RJPs to remain a major priority for recruitment research, given the modest effects found by Phillips in her meta-analysis.[124] Saks agreed that RJPs had only a modest effect on turnover reduction.[125] Breaugh, on the other hand, argued that Phillips's conclusions that RJPs produce very small or modest effects may have been premature due to the small number of studies in the meta-analysis, failure to consider different types of RJPs, and an improper application of RJP theory.[126] A more recent meta-analysis confirmed many of the previous conclusions about RJPs but also found that the RJP link to reduced voluntary turnover was mediated by an instilled sense of organizational honesty. The most effective RJPs were those that were oral or written and delivered post-hire, as opposed to pre-hire, and that were designed to signal organizational honesty.[127]

Nonetheless, when prospective employees know more about an organization, whether through an RJP or other means, there appear to be more positive outcomes for the employees with respect to their job satisfaction and organizational commitment. Moser[128] found that job applicants who were recruited by an organization through referrals from family and friends, internships, or in-house notices had fewer unmet expectations about the job and expressed more job satisfaction and organizational commitment. Moser argued that the internal recruitment sources provided the applicants with more and better information about the organization and the jobs, much like an RJP.

EXPECTATION-LOWERING PROCEDURES

Today's increasingly educated workers have higher expectations about their workplaces and their jobs. They expect greater opportunities for skill development and empowerment (i.e., input into decision making). However, many of these expectations may be unrealistic. Realistic job previews may be a valuable tool in helping to lower these expectations to more reasonable levels and to improve communications and trust. There is another step an organization can take to ensure accurate expectations once job applicants become new hires. Many companies have new hires go through an orientation procedure to learn about the policies and practices of the company. The inclusion of material designed to lower expectations as part of this orientation will also lead to a reduction in some of the negative outcomes experienced by new hires. These expectancy-lowering procedures (ELPs) focus on the expectations of the new hires rather than on specific aspects of the job or organization, which are typically included in an RJP.

An ELP workshop could present information showing (1) how important it is to have realistic expectations at the start of a job and how expectations are formed, (2) how unrealistically high expectations are related to negative organizational outcomes, and (3) how unrealistically high expectations that remain unfulfilled lead to dissatisfaction with work and turnover. Buckley and his colleagues[129] demonstrated that an ELP such as this led to less dissatisfaction and turnover and recommended that organizations use it as a complement to RJPs.

Subsequently, Buckley and another team of researchers[130] assessed the effectiveness of an ELP, RJP, or both together in predicting the number of days worked by applicants for telemarketing jobs, which are notorious for high turnover rates. The combination of RJP and ELP given to all job applicants resulted in the largest number of days worked by candidates who were hired, compared to applicants who were given only one of the procedures or no preview at all. The RJP by itself did not increase the number of days worked beyond that of the group not given any preview.

DECISION-MAKING TRAINING

Decision-making training (DMT) operates on the assumption that any actions that improve the decision-making process on the part of job candidates, either by providing accurate information or enhancing decision-making skills, will lead to the party delivering the actions being seen as helpful.[131] In DMT, candidates are taught how to identify and weigh positive and negative outcomes from a set of alternatives. The message is similar to that conveyed by RJPs except that the message need not include negative information; the intention is to establish that the organization wants candidates to make decisions that are good for them even if those decisions are at the expense of the organization in losing the candidate.

DMT may be a viable, less costly alternative to RJP that produces longer-lasting benefits. Because the DMT does not contain information about the company, let alone negative information, it avoids the negative spinoffs of RJP. DMT may prove to be a good means for determining person–organization fit but, because it does not convey job information, it may be less appropriate for determining person–job fit. DMT is a relatively new concept that is primarily used in career counselling with high school and college students. Relatively few studies have looked at DMT as part of recruitment; much more research is needed.

// EVALUATING RECRUITING EFFORTS

We started this chapter with the proposition that recruitment is the first step in the selection process through which an organization finds the best-qualified people to fill job vacancies. It is quite obvious that recruiting can be very expensive and time consuming. While it is important to know the effectiveness of different recruiting methods, organizations that engage in recruiting should also be concerned that their money and time are well spent. They should want to know not only whether the job advertisements paid off in more applications, but also whether better-qualified candidates were hired, what it cost to recruit the new employees, whether the new recruits are more productive or have a more positive attitude about the organization, and whether they stay with the organization for a longer period of time.

Unfortunately, many companies do not bother to ask these questions or evaluate the effectiveness of their recruiting efforts, the quality of the people they recruited, or the recruits' success on the job. Their primary criteria for judging the success of recruiting appear to be the number of applications received and whether the vacant jobs were filled. Very few organizations track the performance and behavioural outcomes of people recruited into the organization or the costs associated with the recruiting campaign, including advertising costs.[132] Without doubt, recruiters will increasingly be required to demonstrate the effectiveness of their programs. It is essential that HR practitioners demonstrate the effectiveness, and worth, of recruiting.[133]

Recruiting should not be taken at face value but should be evaluated on the basis of specific criteria. Recruiting efforts should be evaluated separately from the selection system. The criterion measures that an organization uses to evaluate its recruiting program should be consistent with the goals that were set for that effort. If the organization wanted to recruit the best possible candidates available, it would be unfair to evaluate the recruiting program on the cost involved in finding those candidates. The appropriate measure would be whether the best possible candidates were hired. If the organization used recruiting to generate a large applicant pool, then an appropriate criterion measure might be the number of applications that were received rather than the quality of the people hired.

RECRUITMENT AND SELECTION TODAY 6.7

EXAMPLES OF CRITERIA USED TO EVALUATE RECRUITING METHODS

Behavioural Measures

- Time to fill position
- Turnover rates
  - within 6 months
  - within 12 months
  - within 24 months
- Absenteeism
- Recruitment Costs

Performance Measures

- Quality of hire
- Performance ratings
- Sales quotas
- Performance potential

Attitudinal Measures

- Job satisfaction
- Job involvement
- Satisfaction with supervisor
- Commitment to organization
- Perceived accuracy of job descriptions

Sources: S.L.Rynes. 1991. "Recruitment, Job Choice, and Post-Hire Consequences." In M.D. Dunnette and L.M. Hough, eds., *Handbook of Industrial and Organizational Psychology*, Vol. 2 (pp. 399–444). 2nd ed. Palo Alto, CA: Consulting Psychologists Press; J.P. Wanous and A. Colella. 1989. "Organizational Entry Research: Current Status and Future Directions." In K.M. Rowland and G.R. Ferris, eds., *Research in Personnel and Human Resource Management*, Vol. 7 (pp. 59–120). Greenwich, CT: JAI Press.

Many different criterion measures can be used to evaluate recruiting efforts; some of them are shown in Recruitment and Selection Today 6.7.[134,135] These criteria can be grouped into three broad categories: behavioural measures, performance measures, and attitudinal measures.

Employment equity
Policies and practices designed to increase the presence of qualified women, visible minorities, Aboriginal people, and people with disabilities in the workforce.

One final criterion, **employment equity**, should be considered as part of evaluating any recruitment efforts. The organization must review whether its recruiting campaign has produced an increased presence of qualified women, visible minorities, Aboriginal people, and people with disabilities in its workforce. In the context of Canadian employment equity legislation, as discussed in Chapter 3, recruiting efforts must be judged on this basis as well as the more traditional outcome measures.

RECRUITMENT AUDIT

Ryan and Tippens[136] developed an audit of recruitment practices to help HR managers determine if their recruitment practices reflected best practices based on research. The questions that form that audit are presented in Recruitment and Selection Today 6.8. Review of the audit questions can assist HR professionals in identifying gaps in their recruitment practices.

RECRUITMENT AND SELECTION TODAY 6.8

AN AUDIT OF RECRUITMENT PRACTICES

- Have we determined which applicant groups to target?
- Are efforts being made to recruit a diverse applicant pool?
- Are efforts being made to have a low selection ratio (i.e., a low number of people selected relative to the total number of applicants)?
- Are we considering combinations of tools to achieve the highest validity and lowest adverse impact?
- Have we considered how our ordering of tools affects validity and adverse impact?
- Are we considering all aspects of job performance in choosing tools?
- Have we determined which recruiting sources provide the best yield?
- Are we providing applicants with the specific information they desire?
- Have we selected recruiters who are warm and friendly?
- Is appropriate attention being given to early recruitment activities?
- Are applicants being processed quickly?
- Do we solicit feedback from applicants on satisfaction with the staffing process?
- Are applicants being provided with information about the job-relatedness of the selection process?
- Are applicants provided with accurate information on which to judge their fit with the position?
- Do we have evidence that selection procedures are job related?
- Are applicants treated with respect?
- Is the selection process consistently administered?
- Does the process allow for some two-way communication?
- Is feedback provided to applicants in an informative and timely manner?

Source: A.M. Ryan and N.T. Tippens. 2004. "Attracting and Selecting: What Psychological Research Tells Us," *Human Resource Management*, 43:4 305–18. *Human Resource Management* by University of Michigan. Reproduced with permission of John Wiley & Sons, Inc. via Copyright Clearance Center.

// SUMMARY

Recruitment is the first step in the hiring or staffing process, but, unlike other aspects of this process, the actions and decisions of the job seeker play a major role. A recruitment process, no matter how brilliantly conceived, is a failure if it does not attract qualified job applicants. A recruitment strategy must be based not only on the actions and decisions of job seekers but also on the organization's strategic planning.

In developing a recruitment strategy, HR planners must consider both the internal and external constraints on the organization. All recruitment is influenced by external factors over which the organization has little control (e.g., the labour market and the legal environment), as well as internal factors that it can influence (e.g., its compensation strategy, business plan, and values). Recruitment strategies and materials, which are grounded in organization and job analysis, establish both realistic expectations among job applicants and the availability of qualified internal and external job candidates.

Every recruitment strategy must contain an action plan, which schedules recruiting initiatives and provides a means of identifying and locating the target applicant pool. The action plan must also identify the appropriate methods for contacting the target applicant pool. The action plan should also include a method for evaluating the effectiveness of the recruitment campaign.

HR professionals must know the effectiveness of different recruiting methods and build into their recruitment strategy plans for evaluating the recruiting outcomes. They also must know the appropriate recruitment source for the target pool of applicants. In cases where informal methods such as referrals and job postings are used, care must be taken to avoid systemic discrimination. In evaluating outcomes, the quantity of applicants should not be the only criterion, as the quality of the applicants attracted to the organization is an even more important factor.

Recruitment campaigns are a success when they understand what organizational characteristics attract job seekers. The recruitment process must take into account the strategies that job seekers use to investigate jobs and organizations. The process should provide job candidates with information they need to make appropriate job choices. Job candidates should receive information about the job, the organization, and the organization's approach to compensation. For example, job candidates will want to know whether the company will meet market pay rates, whether compensation is related to performance, and what reward systems are in place, among other issues.

Recruitment campaigns should be based on the principle of improving the fit between job candidates and the organization. Organizations can help to achieve this by presenting an accurate image of both the job and the organization to job seekers. The organization should use communications in a way that develops accurate expectations and perceptions on the part of job applicants. One method that appears capable of doing this is a realistic job preview.

KEY TERMS

Applicant pool, p. 226
Employment equity, p. 270
Image advertising, p. 261
Interests and values, p. 259
Internet recruiting, p. 246
Job search, p. 259
Organization analysis, p. 233
Outsourcing, p. 229
Person–job fit, p. 262
Person–organization fit, p. 262
Realistic job preview, p. 266
Recruitment, p. 226
Self-selecting out, p. 257
Social networks, p. 252
Systemic discrimination, p. 230

WEB LINKS

For information on careers in the military, check out the Canadian Forces site at **http://www.forces.gc.ca**

Job postings can be found at
http://www.monster.ca, http://www.engineeringjobs.com, and http://www.cpasource.com

Check out government-sponsored job posting and job search information sites at
http://www.jobbank.gc.ca, http://jobs-emplois.gc.ca/index-eng.htm, and http://www.workingincanada.gc.ca/content_pieces-eng.do?cid=1

Networking resources can be found at
http://career-advice.monster.ca and http://www.careerkey.com

DISCUSSION QUESTIONS

1. Discuss the relationship between recruitment and selection.
2. Why is organizational strategy important in recruitment?
3. Discuss how the characteristics of the job and organization influence job seekers.
4. Why is it important that job seekers develop accurate expectations of what their position/role will be in an organization before accepting employment there?
5. Why does a realistic job preview benefit both the job seeker and the organization?
6. What are the internal and external factors that influence an organization's recruitment strategy?
7. What are the elements of an effective recruitment and staffing action plan?
8. What are the different methods that can be used to recruit internal and external job applicants?
9. Is the Internet an effective recruiting method? Why or why not?
10. What are the advantages and disadvantages of social network recruiting?

EXERCISES

1. Choose an organization in your community and schedule a meeting with its HR manager (or designate). Using the material in this chapter as a guide, interview the HR representative on the organization's recruiting efforts (e.g., determine the role that job and organization analysis played in developing the strategy). Ask whether the organization considers how potential applicants would react to the recruiting materials. Ask if the organization uses the Internet and social media as part of its recruiting efforts. Prepare a report on the organization's recruiting strategy and its effectiveness.
2. Examine the organization's recruiting program (the one chosen for Exercise 1) from a job candidate's perspective. With the assistance of the HR representative, interview a recently hired employee who was an external applicant. Ask the employee about the employee's job search strategy, perceptions of the organization, the recruiting process, requirements for pay and benefits, what influenced the decision to take the job, and whether that decision changed after being in the organization for a period of time. Prepare a report summarizing this interview.
3. Using the information presented in this chapter and the information obtained from your interviews in Exercises 1 and 2, develop a comprehensive recruitment strategy for the organization based on the job of the new employee whom you interviewed.

4. How did the organization advertise the position? Identify the best ways for reaching the target applicant pool for this job.
5. Prepare an advertisement for the position of the person you interviewed. Compare the costs of running this advertisement in some of the commonly used media discussed in this chapter.
6. Use the NOC or O*NET to find a job description for a position that is of interest to you. Write an effective job advertisement for that position.
7. For the position you identified above, prepare a recruitment plan to fill that position through both the Internet and social networks.

CASE

When qualified applicants are scarce, recruiting becomes extremely competitive, particularly when two companies go after the same candidate, as often happens in the case of searching for professionals.

After interviewing three short-listed candidates, a high-tech company, Company X, made an offer to one and advised the other two candidates that they were unsuccessful. The successful candidate was given one week to consider the offer. The candidate asked for a week's extension to consider the offer but was granted only an additional three days.

At the end of the time period, the candidate verbally accepted the offer and was sent a contract to sign. Rather than returning the signed contract, the candidate informed Company X that he had accepted a position at Company Y. He had received the second offer after verbally accepting the first position at Company X. The second company knew that the candidate had verbally accepted Company X's offer.

Before accepting Company Y's offer, the candidate had consulted a respected mentor who advised him to ignore his verbal commitment to Company X and to accept Company Y's offer. There were no substantial differences in the salaries being offered by each company or in the work that each would expect the candidate to perform. The candidate simply saw Company Y as the more prestigious of the two employers.

QUESTIONS

1. Did the candidate act in an appropriate manner?
2. What should the candidate have done?
3. What would you have done if you had been in the candidate's position?
4. Did Company Y act ethically, knowing that the candidate had verbally accepted another offer?
5. Does a verbal acceptance constitute a legal and binding contract?
6. What should the candidate's mentor have advised him to do?
7. Should Company X take any action to enforce the verbal commitment? Should it take any legal action against the candidate or Company Y? Why or why not?
8. How can situations like this be avoided?
9. Describe what Company X should have done to maintain the candidate's interest in the position.

// ENDNOTES

1 Guion, R.M. 1976. "Recruiting, Selection, and Job Placement." In M. Dunnette, ed., *Handbook of Industrial and Organizational Psychology* (pp. 777–828). Chicago: Rand-McNally.

2 Ryan, A.M., and Delaney, T. 2010. "Attracting Job Candidates to Organizations." In J.L. Farr and N.T. Tippens, eds., *Handbook of Employee Selection* (127–50). New York: Routledge.

3 Rynes, S.L. 1991. "Recruitment, Job Choice, and Post-Hire Consequences." In M.D. Dunnette and L.M. Hough, eds., *Handbook of Industrial and Organizational Psychology,* Vol. 2, 2nd ed. (pp. 399–444). Palo Alto, CA: Consulting Psychologists Press.

4 Keenan, G. 1996. "Toyota Swamped in Rush for Jobs." *The Globe and Mail* (February 21): A1, A7.

5 Dineen, B.R., and S.M. Soltis. 2011. "Recruitment: A Review of Research and Emerging Directions." In S. Zedeck, ed., *APA Handbook of Industrial and Organizational Psychology, Vol. 2: Selecting and Developing Members for the Organiation* (pp. 43–66). Washington, DC: American Psychological Association.

6 Greengard, S. 1995. "Leveraging a Low-Wage Work Force." *Personnel Journal* 74 (January): 90–102.

7 Flynn, G. 1995. "Contingent Staffing Requires Serious Strategy." *Personnel Journal* 74 (April): 50–58.

8 Holton, B.C., T.W. Lee, and S.T. Tidd. 2002. "The Relationship between Work Status Congruence and Work-Related Attitudes." *Journal of Applied Psychology* 87: 903–15.

9 Galt, V. 1992. "Agencies Still Refer Whites Only." *The Globe and Mail* (September 8), B1.

10 Castro, J. 1993. "Disposable Workers." *Time* (March 29): 43–47.

11 Ryan, A.M., and M.J. Schmit. 1996. "Calculating EEO Statistics in the Temporary Help Industry." *Personnel Psychology* 49: 167–80.

12 Rynes, S.L. 1991.

13 Dineen, B.R., and S.M. Soltis. 2011.

14 Perrott, S.B. 1999. "Visible Minority Applicant Concerns and Assessment of Occupational Role in the Era of Community-Based Policing." *Journal of Community and Applied Social Psychology* 9: 339–53.

15 Avery, D.R., and P.F. McKay. 2006. "Target Practice: An Organizational Impression Management Approach to Attracting Minority and Female Job Applicants." *Personnel Psychology* 59: 157–87.

16 Kravitz, D.A., and S.L. Klineberg. 2000. "Reactions to Two Versions of Affirmative Action among Whites, Blacks, and Hispanics." *Journal of Applied Psychology* 85: 597–611.

17 Saks, A.M., J.D. Leck, and D.M. Saunders. 1995. "Effects of Application Blanks and Employment Equity on Applicant Reactions and Job Pursuit Intentions." *Journal of Organizational Behavior* 16: 415–30.

18 Heilman, M.E., W.S. Battle, C.E. Keller, and R.A. Lee. 1998. "Type of Affirmative Action Policy: A Determinant of Reactions to Sex-Based Preferential Selection?" *Journal of Applied Psychology* 83: 190–205.

19 Ryan, A.M., M. Horvath, and S.D. Kriska. 2005. "The Role of Recruiting Source Informativeness and Organizational Perceptions in Decisions to Apply." *International Journal of Selection and Assessment* 13: 235–49.

20 Rynes, S.L. 1991.

21 Ibid.

22 Ibid.

23 Ibid.

24 Keenan, G. 1996.

25 Belcourt, M., G. Bohlander, and S. Snell. 2011. *Managing Human Resources*, 6th Canadian edition, Toronto: Nelson.

26 Barber, A.E., M.J. Wesson, Q.M. Roberson, and M.S. Taylor. 1999. "A Tale of Two Job Markets: Organizational Size and Its Effects on Hiring Practices and Job Search Behaviour." *Personnel Psychology* 52: 841–68.

27 Rynes, S.L. 1991.

28 Ibid.

29 Dineen, B.R., and S.M. Soltis. 2011.

30 Avery, D.R., and P.F. McKay. 2006.

31 Arthur, D. 2001. *The Employee Recruitment and Retention Handbook*. New York: AMACOM.

32 Decker, P.J., and E.T. Cornelius. 1979. "A Note on Recruiting Sources and Job Survival Rates." *Journal of Applied Psychology* 64: 463–64.

33 Breaugh, J.A. 1981. "Relationships between Recruiting Sources and Employee Performance, Absenteeism and Work Attitudes." *Academy of Management Journal* 24: 142, 147–48.

34 Zottoli, M.A., and J.P. Wanous. 2000. "Recruitment Source Research: Current Status and Future Directions." *Human Resource Management Review* 10: 353–82.

35 Taylor, S.G. 1994. "The Relationship between Sources of New Employees and Attitudes toward the Job." *Journal of Social Psychology* 134: 99–111.

36 Wanous, J.P., and A. Colella. 1989. "Organizational Entry Research: Current Status and Future Directions." In K.M. Rowland and G.R. Ferris, eds., *Research in Personnel and Human Resource Management*, Vol. 7 (pp. 59–120). Greenwich, CT: JAI Press.

37 Taylor, S.G. 1994.

38 Moser, K. 2005. "Recruitment Sources and Post-Hire Outcomes: The Mediating Role of Unmet Expectations." *International Journal of Selection and Assessment* 13: 188–97.

39 Zottoli, M.A., and J.P. Wanous. 2000.

40 Bissonnette, A., and V.M. Catano. 2003. *Revisiting the Efficacy of Recruiting Methods*. Paper presented at the 11th Congress of the European Association of Work and Organization Psychology, Lisbon, Portugal.

41 Zottoli, M.A., and J.P. Wanous. 2000.

42 Dolan, S.L., and R.S. Schuler. 1994. *Human Resource Management: The Canadian Dynamic*. 2nd edition. Scarborough, ON: Nelson Canada.

43 Chapman, D.S., K.L. Uggerslev, S.A. Carroll, K.A. Piasentin, and D. A. Jones. 2005. "Applicant Attraction to Organizations and Job Choice: A Meta-Analytic Review of the Correlates of Recruiting Outcomes." *Journal of Applied Psychology* 90: 928–44.

44 Rynes, S.L., and D.M. Cable. 2003. "Recruitment Research in the Twenty-First Century." In W.C Borman, D.R. Ilgen, and R. Klimoski, eds., *Handbook of Psychology: Industrial and Organizational Psychology*, Vol. 12 (pp. 55–76). New York: John Wiley and Sons.

45 Rynes, S.L. 1991.

46 Ployhart, R.E. 2006. "Staffing in the 21st Century: New Challenges and Strategic Opportunities." *Journal of Management* 32: 868–97.

47 Capelli, P. 2002. "Making the Most of On-Line Recruiting." *Harvard Business Review* (March): 139–46.

48 Cullen, B. 2001. "E-Recruiting Is Driving HR Systems Integration." *Strategic Finance* 83: 22–26.

49 Email communication from Michelle Gauthier, June 28, 2011.

50 Verhoeven, H., and S. Williams. 2008. "Advantages and Disadvantages of Internet Recruiting: A UK Study into Employers' Perceptions." *International Review of Business Research Papers* 4: 364–73.

51 Verhoeven and Williams. 2008.

52 Rozelle, A.L., and R.S. Landis. 2002. "An Examination of the Relationship between Use of the Internet as a Recruitment Source and Student Attitudes." *Computers in Human Behavior* 18: 593–604.

53 Dineen, B.R., S.R. Ash, and R.A. Noe. 2002. "A Web of Applicant Attraction: Person–Organization Fit in the Context of Web-Based Recruitment." *Journal of Applied Psychology* 87: 723–34.

54 Cober, R.T., D.J. Brown, L.M. Keeping, and P.E. Levy. 2004. "Recruitment on the Net: How Do Organizational Web Site Characteristics Influence Applicant Attraction?" *Journal of Management* 30: 623–46.

55 Pearsall, K. 1998. "Web Recruiting Complicated by Sheer Numbers." *Computing Canada* 24: 11, 14.

56 Zusman, R.R., and R.S. Landis. 2002. "Applicant Preferences of Web-Based versus Traditional Job Postings." *Computers in Human Behavior* 18: 285–96.

57 Verhoeven and Williams. 2008.

58 Ibid.

59 Piturro, M. 2000. "The Power of E-cruiting." *Management Review* 89: 33–37.

60 Jobvite Social Recruiting Survey. 2013. Retrieved July1, 2014, from http://web.jobvite.com/Q313_SocialRecruitingSurvey_LandingPage.html?utm_campaign=SEM_Social_Recruiting_Survey

61 Kristl Davison, H., C. Maraist, and M.N. Bing. 2011. "Friend or Foe? The Promise and Pitfalls of Using Social Networking Sites for HR Decisions." *Journal of Business and Psychology* 26: 153–59.

62 *Workforce Management Magazine*. Retrieved January 11, 2012, from http://www.workforce.com/section/06/feature/26/68/67/

63 Kristl Davison et al. 2011.

64 Ondrack, D. 1996. "Global Warning." *Human Resources Professional* (May): 27–29.

65 Moore, F. 2006. "Recruitment and Selection of International Managers." In T. Edwards and C. Rees, eds. *International Human Resource Management*. London, UK: Pearson.

66 Ondrack, D. 1996.

67 Moore, F. 2006.

68 Dowling, P., and D. Welch. 2004. *International Resource Management: Managing People in a Multinational Context*. London, UK: Thompson.

69 Moore, F. 2006.

70 Bissonnette, A.B. 2011. *Job Information Sources and Applicant Perceptions: Antecedents, Correlates, and Outcomes*. Unpublished doctoral dissertation, Saint Mary's University, Halifax, NS.

71 Zottoli, M.A., and J.P. Wanous. 2000.

72 Breaugh, J.A., and M. Starke. 2000. "Research on Employee Recruitment: So Many Studies, So Many Questions." *Journal of Management* 26: 405–34.

73 Rynes, S.L. 1993. "Who's Selecting Whom? Effects of Selection Practices on Applicant Attitudes and Behaviour." In N. Schmitt, W.C. Borman et al., eds., *Personnel Selection in Organizations* (pp. 240–74). San Francisco, CA: Jossey-Bass.

74 Ryan, A.M., J.M. Sacco, L.A. McFarland, and S.D. Kriska. 2000. "Applicant Self-Selection: Correlates of Withdrawal from a Multiple Hurdle Process." *Journal of Applied Psychology* 85: 163–79.

75 Ibid.

76 Schwab, D.P., S.L. Rynes, and R.J. Aldag. 1987. "Theories and Research on Job Search and Choice." In K.M. Rowland and G.R. Ferris, eds., *Research in Personnel and Human Resource Management*, Vol. 5 (pp. 129–66). Greenwich, CT: JAI Press.

77 Turban, D.B., J.E. Campion, and A.R. Eyrung. 1995. "Factors Related to Job Acceptance Decisions of College Recruits." *Journal of Vocational Behavior* 47: 193–213.

78 Carsten, J.M., and P.E. Spector. 1987. "Unemployment, Job Satisfaction, and Employee Turnover: A Meta-Analytic Test of the Muchinsky Model." *Journal of Applied Psychology* 72: 374–81.

79 Barber, A.E., M.J. Wesson, Q.M. Roberson, and M.S. Taylor. 1999. "A Tale of Two Job Markets: Organizational Size and Its Effects on Hiring Practices and Job Search Behavior." *Personnel Psychology* 52: 841–68.

80 Barber, A.E., et al. 1999.

81 Lemmink, J., A. Schuif, and S. Streukens. 2003. "The Role of Corporate Image and Company Employment Image in Explaining Application Intentions." *Journal of Economic Psychology* 24: 1–15.

82 Dineen, B.R., and S.M. Soltis. 2011.

83 Turban, D.B. 2001. "Organizational Attractiveness as an Employer on College Campuses: An Examination of the Applicant Population." *Journal of Vocational Behavior* 56: 293–312.

84 Cable, D.M., and M.E. Graham. 2000. "The Determinants of Organizational Reputation: A Job Search Perspective." *Journal of Organizational Behavior* 21: 929–47.

85 Ibid.

86 Aiman-Smith, L., T.N. Bauer, and D.M. Cable. 2001. "Are You Attracted? Do You Intend to Pursue? A Recruiting Policy-Capturing Study." *Journal of Business and Psychology* 16: 219–37.

87 Highhouse, S., E.E. Thornbury, and I.S. Little. 2007. "Social-Identity Functions of Attraction to Organizations." *Organizational Behavior and Human Decision Processes* 103: 134–46.

88 Catano, V.M., and H. Morrow. 2010. *Psychologically Healthy Workplaces, Corporate Social Responsibility and Applicant Attraction.* Paper presented at the European Academy of Occupational Health Psychology, Rome, Italy.

89 Yuse, P., and S. Highhouse. 1998. "Effects of Attribute Set Size and Pay Ambiguity on Reactions to 'Help Wanted' Advertisements." *Journal of Organizational Behavior* 19: 337–52.

90 Cable, D.M., L. Aiman-Smith, P.W. Mulvey, and J.R. Edwards. 2000. "The Sources and Accuracy of Job Applicants' Beliefs about Organizational Culture." *Academy of Management Journal* 43: 1076–85.

91 Gatewood, R.D., M.A. Gowan, and G.J. Lautenschlager. 1993. "Corporate Image, Recruitment Image, and Initial Job Choices." *Academy of Management Journal* 36: 414–27.

92 Magnus, M. 1985. "Recruitment Ads at Work." *Personnel Journal* 64: 4–63.

93 Gil, A. 2003. "It's Party Time at Film Festival." Report on du Maurier's sponsorship of a Toronto Film Festival event. *The Globe and Mail* (September 23): A13.

94 Ashforth, E., and G. Kreiner. 1999. "'How Can You Do It?' Dirty Work and the Challenge of Constructing a Positive Identity." *Academy of Management Review* 24: 413–34.

95 Kristof-Brown, A.L. 2000. "Perceived Applicant Fit: Distinguishing between Recruiters' Perceptions of Person–Job Fit and Person–Organization Fit." *Personnel Psychology* 53: 643–71.

96 Tsai, W-C, N-W. Chi, T-C. Huang, and A-J. Hsu. 2011. "The Effects of Applicant Résumé Contents on Recruiters' Hiring Recommendations: The Mediating Roles of Recruiter Fit Perceptions." *Applied Psychology: An International Journal* 60: 231–54.

97 Kristof-Brown, A.L. 1998. "The Goldilocks Pursuit in Organizational Selection: How Recruiters Form and Use Judgments of Person–Organization Fit." *Dissertation Abstracts International Section A: Humanities and Social Sciences* 58(11-A): 4345.

98 Arthur, W., Jr., S.T. Bell, A.J. Villado, and D. Doverspike. 2006. "The Use of Person-Organization Fit in Employment Decision Making: An Assessment of Its Criterion-Related Validity." *Journal of Applied Psychology* 91: 786–801.

99 Kristof-Brown, A.L., R.D. Zimmerman, and E.C. Johnson. 2005. "Consequences of Individual's Fit at Work: A Meta-Analysis of Person–Job, Person–Organization, Person–Group, and Person–Supervisor Fit." *Personnel Psychology* 58: 281–342.

100 Wanous, J.P., and A. Colella. 1989.

101 Rynes, S.L. 1993.

102 Saks, A.M. 1994. "A Psychological Process Investigation for the Effects of Recruitment Source and Organization Information on Job Survival." *Journal of Organizational Behavior* 15: 225–44.

103 Wanous, J.P., and A. Colella. 1989.

104 Buckley, M.R., D.B. Fedor, D.S. Marvin, J.G. Veres, D.S. Wise, and S.M. Carraher. 1998. "Investigating Newcomer Expectations and Job-Related Outcomes." *Journal of Applied Psychology* 83: 452–61.

105 Buckley, M.R., D.B. Fedor, and D.S. Marvin. 1994. "Ethical Considerations in the Recruiting Process: A Preliminary Investigation and Identification of Research Opportunities." *Human Resource Management Review* 4: 35–50.

106 Moser, K. 2005.

107 Yuce, P., and Highhouse, S. 1997. "Effects of Attribute Set Size and Pay Ambiguity on Reaction to 'Help Wanted' Advertisements." *Journal of Organizational Behavior, 19*, 337–52.

108 Hansen, F. 2007. "Avoiding Truth-in-Hiring Lawsuits." *Workforce Management Online.* Retrieved May 13, 2011, from http://www.workforce.com

109 Buckley, M.R., D.B. Fedor, and D.S. Marvin. 1994.

110 Buckley, M.R., et al. 1998.

111 Wanous, J.P. 1980. *Organizational Entry: Recruitment, Selection, and Socialization of Newcomers.* Reading, MA: Addison-Wesley.

112 Phillips, J.M. 1998. "Effects of Realistic Job Previews on Multiple Organizational Outcomes: A Meta-Analysis." *Academy of Management Journal* 41: 673–90.

113 Rynes, S.L. 1991.

114 Phillips, J.M. 1998.

115 Meglino, B.M., E.C. Ravlin, and A.S. DeNisi. 1997. "When Does It Hurt to Tell the Truth? The Effect of Realistic Job Reviews on Employee Recruiting." *Public Personnel Management* 26: 413–22.

116 Bretz, R.D., Jr., and T.A. Judge. 1998. "Realistic Job Previews: A Test of the Adverse Self-Selection Hypothesis." *Journal of Applied Psychology* 83: 330–37.

117 Saks, A.M., W.H. Wiesner, and R.J. Summers. 1996. "Effects of Job Previews and Compensation Policy on Applicant Attraction and Job Choice." *Journal of Vocational Behavior* 49: 68–85.

118 Travagline, A.M. 2002. "Online Recruiting: Implementing Internet-Based Realistic Job Previews." *Dissertation Abstracts International: Section B: The Sciences and Engineering* 63 (1-b): 579.

119 Meglino, B.M., A.S. DeNisi, and E.C. Ravlin. 1993. "Effects of Previous Job Exposure and Subsequent Job Status on the Functioning of a Realistic Job Preview." *Personnel Psychology* 46: 803–22.

120 Hom, P.W., R.W. Griffeth, L.E. Palich, and J.S. Bracker. 1999. "Revisiting Met Expectations as a Reason Why Realistic Job Previews Work." *Personnel Psychology* 52: 97–112.

121 Rynes, S.L. 1991.

122 Phillips, J.M. 1998.

123 Rynes, S.L., and D.M. Cable. 2003.

124 Phillips, J.M. 1998.

125 Saks, A. 2005. "The Impracticality of Recruitment Research." In A. Evers, N. Anderson, and O. Voskuijl, eds., *Handbook of Personnel Selection* (pp. 47–72). Malden, MA: Blackwell.

126 Breaugh, J.A. 2008. "Employee Recruitment: Current Knowledge and Important Areas for Future Research." *Human Resource Management Review* 18: 103–18.

127 Earnest, D.R., Allen, D.G., and Landis, R.S. 2011. "Mechanisms Linking Realistic Job Previews with Turnover: A Meta-Analytic Path Analysis." *Personnel Psychology* 64: 865–897.

128 Moser, K. 2005.

129 Buckley, M.R., et al. 1998.

130 Buckley, M.R., T.A. Mobbs, J.L. Mendoza, M.M. Novicevic, S.M. Carrahar, and D.S. Beu. 2002. "Implementing Realistic Job Previews and Expectation-Lowering Procedures: A Field Experiment." *Journal of Vocational Behavior* 61: 263–78.

131 Ganzach, Y., A. Pazy, Y. Ohayun, and E. Brainin. 2002. "Social Exchange and Organizational Commitment: Decision-Making Training for Job Choice as an Alternative to the Realistic Job Preview." *Personnel Psychology* 55: 613–37.

132 Rynes, S.L., and J.L. Boudreau. 1986. "College Recruiting in Large Organizations: Practice, Evaluation, and Research Implications." *Personnel Psychology* 39: 729–57.

133 Grossman, R.J. 2000. "Measuring Up, Appropriate Metric Help: HR Proves Its Worth." *HR Magazine* 45: 28–35.

134 Rynes, S.L. 1991.

135 Wanous, J.P., and A. Colella. 1989.

136 Ryan, A.M., and N.T. Tippens. 2004. "Attracting and Selecting: What Psychological Research Tells Us." *Human Resource Management* 43: 305–18.

CHAPTER 7

SELECTION I:
APPLICANT SCREENING

CHAPTER LEARNING OUTCOMES

This chapter introduces procedures commonly used in applicant *screening*, which refers to the early stages of a sequential selection process in which applicants who fail to meet the minimally required qualifications associated with a target job are eliminated so that more detailed consideration can be given to the remaining candidates. Occasionally, screening also may refer to a cursory, quick selection process that does not involve the use of additional assessments.[1] Screening takes on increasing importance as the ratio of applicants to positions increases (or conversely, as there are fewer to be selected for hire as a percentage of the total applicant pool—the *selection ratio*). As the most resource-intense assessments are typically reserved for the most promising candidates, a well developed and implemented screening process reduces overall applicant processing costs and results in time savings for both the job seeker and employer.

We will review common traditionally used screening procedures, including use of information obtained from application blanks, biographical information forms, résumés, and reference checks. More recent technology-enabled tools, such as social networking site searches, video résumés, and virtual career fairs, will also be considered. Then, Chapter 8 covers the assessment methods that are typically given only to applicants who survive the screening process. Chapter 9 focuses on the employment interview per se which, while occasionally used for screening, is typically reserved for screened applicants only. Note that all screening and post-screening tools, from the most basic to the most sophisticated, must satisfy both psychometric (Chapter 2) and legal requirements (Chapter 3).

AFTER READING THIS CHAPTER YOU SHOULD:

- be able to differentiate between employee screening and employee selection;
- know the advantages and disadvantages associated with widely used screening tools, including the use of information collected from application forms, biographical information blanks, reference/background checks, résumés, video résumés, social networking sites, and virtual job auditions;
- be able to cite the legal status of these screening tools and the extent to which they are predictive of performance in the target job;
- be able to design an effective multiphase screening program appropriate to the position requirements for any target job.

SALES GROWTH TRENDS AT LIVING HEALTHY INC. IN POOR HEALTH

Ray Stevens was having a bad day. As the head of closely held Living Healthy Inc. (LHI), a Vancouver-based retailer of outdoor recreational gear and sporting goods, Ray had overseen the expansion of LHI from three West Coast stores to 30 locations in major cities across Canada. After several years of strong growth, Ray had just learned that same-store sales at LHI were down for the third quarter in a row. He knew that a turnaround in sales was crucial to the willingness of private investors to continue funding the expansion.

There was some good news. Recently conducted market research revealed that name recognition for LHI was high. In terms of cost control, Marie Squires, Len's Chief Operations Officer, had been able to renegotiate downward the leasing costs at 12 locations as the contracts had come up for renewal. Sales through the LHI website had also continued to grow. Overall, though, Ray was frustrated. He had been confident that the recent expansion of men's and women's clothing, including yoga gear and eco-conscious offerings, would be helpful to sales.

In considering the current state of affairs, Marie commented, "we haven't thought much about it, but since you used your industry connections to initially place managers at most of our locations, more than half of them have left." "So what?" Ray replied. "Haven't we been moving our best salespeople into those management positions as they open up?" "We have," countered Marie, "but Glen in Human Resources has always warned that the best salespeople don't necessarily make for the best managers." Marie continued, "We also can't seem to keep our front-line staff; many of them leave within three months. As soon as we get them trained, they're gone!" "Well, let's get Glen in here," interjected Ray impatiently.

The next day, in a meeting with Ray and Marie, Glen commented, "It's no surprise to me we have a high turnover rate—it's very common in the retail industry. But, there is a major opportunity here for HR to contribute to the business beyond the record keeping and benefits administration we've been taking care of." Ray said, "Well, I've never cared much for the touchy-feely aspects of people management; I think you count on the judgment of the store managers to bring good people in, and they either sink or swim in a sales environment." "But we can do a much better job of screening the people the company hires into sales without a lot of added cost," countered Glen. "We ought to be using the same screening process across all of our locations—not only to increase efficiency and effectiveness, but also to keep us out of legal difficulties." Glen continued, "We use our website as another venue to boost sales, but could also use it to receive applications and résumés, paired with software to scan and identify candidates that are a good fit based on background experience, interests, education, and store location. The most promising applicants could then be called into the local store for a screening interview, though we might be able to conduct online screening interviews and save the more intense behaviourally focused selection interview for on-site."

Marie said, "Glen, you have been wary about promoting our best salespeople into store manager positions as they open up. Why is that a problem?" "Sales positions and management positions are fundamentally different," Glen quickly responded. "Screening people for jobs is more of a science than an art, requiring procedures designed specifically with each position in mind. I'm sure I can develop a cost-effective proposal on this, including anticipated performance outcomes and financial returns. I'll have it ready for you both to review within a week."

// APPLICANT SCREENING

Screening
The first step of the selection process; involves identifying individuals from the applicant pool who lack the minimum qualifications for the target position(s). Candidates "passing" this first hurdle then undergo more extensive assessment.

Minimum qualifications (MQ)
Knowledge, skills, abilities, and experience, deemed necessary for minimally acceptable performance in one or more positions; designed for making the "first cut" in screening applicants, and sometimes referred to as *selection criteria.*

Designated targeted groups
The four groups (women, visible minorities, Aboriginal peoples, and people with disabilities) designated in the federal government's Employment Equity Act that receive legal "protection" in employment policies and practices because of their under-representation in the workforce.

Selection ratio
The proportion of applicants for one or more positions who are hired.

False positives
Individuals who, based on their screening outcomes, are expected to perform well in the target job, but who do not.

Screening is the first phase of selection, in which a "rough cut" of the larger applicant pool is undertaken. Typically, the goal is to identify and eliminate the candidates who do not meet the **minimum qualifications** (MQs) established for a position. MQs often consist of educational requirements, experience, and closely related personal attributes that are required in order for a person to have a reasonable chance of performing the target job satisfactorily.[2] Candidates who fall short of the minimum standards receive no further consideration for the target position. MQs critically affect the entire selection process, and are often closely scrutinized for adverse impact against **designated targeted groups**. Accordingly, they should be systematically and carefully established. Levine et al.[3] provide a clear, step-by-step description of how MQs can be developed and validated to withstand legal challenge for selected jobs in a large mental health facility, which is a useful guide for establishing MQs in other contexts.

RECRUITMENT, SCREENING, AND SELECTION

Lucian Milasan/Shutterstock.com

Figure 7.1 shows the relationship among recruitment, screening, and selection in terms of the key considerations at each step. The aim of *recruitment* is to acquire a sufficient number of qualified applicants; *screening* eliminates applicants who fail to meet minimum requirements, while *selection* identifies the remaining candidates who are most likely to be successful in the target job. The relationship between the number of people ultimately hired and the number who initially applied for a position is expressed as a proportion, called the **selection ratio**. For example, 200 applicants for 10 positions would yield a selection ratio of 0.05 (10/200 = 0.05, or one position for every 20 applicants).

Well-designed screening tools quickly and inexpensively identify applicants who do not meet the MQs. Sometimes the decisions involved are quite straightforward, as, for example, when a high school degree is required for the job. Nonetheless, decisions concerning other MQs, such as work experience, can be subjective because the meaning of applicant claims must be accurately interpreted. Two types of errors—**false positives** and **false negatives**—can be made in the screening process. False positives, those who inappropriately pass the screening process, are likely to be eliminated through more extensive testing at the selection stage (see Chapters 8 and 9). The implications of false negatives—those who have the MQs but are inappropriately eliminated—are more serious, depending on the nature of the job involved. For example, competitive advantage is at stake if a research scientist inappropriately eliminated during screening turns up at a competitor and is a successful innovator. Moreover, applicants who are false negatives may take legal action if they believe the screening procedure was discriminatory and based on factors unrelated to job performance. The legal implications and psychometric properties associated with screening tools should be carefully evaluated to avoid litigation, bad publicity, and loss of competitive advantage.

FIGURE 7.1

THE RELATIONSHIP AMONG RECRUITMENT, SCREENING, AND SELECTION

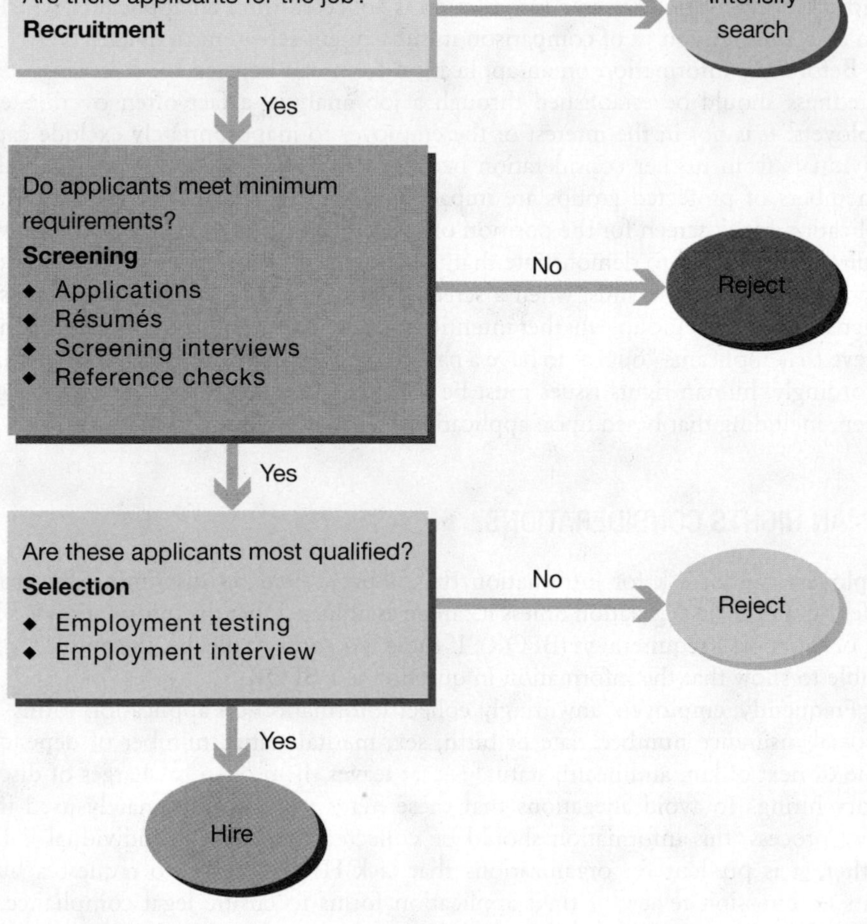

False negatives
Individuals who, based on their screening outcomes, are expected to be unsuccessful in the job, but who nonetheless would have performed satisfactorily if given the chance.

SCREENING METHODS

We now consider the common traditionally used screening procedures, including the review of information obtained from application forms, biographical information blanks, résumés, and reference and background checks, as well as the evaluation of applicant work experience. More recent technology-enabled tools, such as social networking site searches, virtual career fairs, and virtual job auditions, will also be considered. Well designed and implemented screening tools identify and eliminate applicants who lack the MQs for the position in a manner that is cost effective and legally defensible.

APPLICATION FORMS

Application blank
A form completed by job candidates that provides a prospective employer with basic information concerning such things as applicant knowledge, skills, education, and previous work experience.

Applicants at large organizations especially are almost always asked to complete an employment application form, commonly referred to as an **application blank**, which requests information related to the MQs for the position in question. The questions often involve educational background, job experience, special training, and other areas deemed relevant to job performance. For example, successful completion of a course on CPR (cardiopulmonary resuscitation) may be an MQ for a security dispatcher position.

Regardless of the specific format used, information from application forms provides a preliminary pre-employment screen that addresses position-related MQs. Use of a standard form ensures the same information is collected from all applicants, which can then be a common point of comparison in subsequent screening activities.

Before any information on an application form can be used for screening, its job-relatedness should be established through a job analysis–a fact often overlooked by employers. It is not in the interest of the employer to inappropriately exclude capable individuals from further consideration because there is the potential of legal liability if members of protected groups are impacted. For example, if CPR were used as an application blank screen for the position of security dispatcher, a court challenge would require the employer to demonstrate that the training is meaningfully related to performance in the position. Thus, when a screen has adverse impact against members of a designated minority group, whether intentional or otherwise, it is *not* sufficient to merely believe that applicants "ought" to have a particular level or type of education or training. Accordingly, human rights issues must be considered when developing and using any screen, including that based upon application form information.

HUMAN RIGHTS CONSIDERATIONS

Employers cannot ask for information that is prohibited on discriminatory grounds under human rights legislation unless it can be established that the information is a bona fide occupational requirement (BFOR). If there is a court challenge, the employer must be able to show that the information in question is a BFOR.

Frequently, employers unwittingly collect information on application forms–such as social insurance number, date of birth, sex, marital status, number of dependants, name of next of kin, and health status[4,5]–that leaves them open to charges of discriminatory hiring. To avoid allegations that these items were inappropriately used in the hiring process, this information should be collected only *after* an individual is hired. Further, it is prudent for organizations that lack HR specialists to request a human rights commission review of their application forms to ensure legal compliance. The review and approval can then be noted on the application form itself, thereby decreasing the likelihood of complaints. A template job application provided by the Ontario Human Rights Commission is found here: http://www.ohrc.on.ca/en/human-rights-work-2008-third-edition/appendix-d-%E2%80%93-sample-application-employment. Also, guidelines concerning legally inappropriate application form content are provided by the Canadian Human Rights Commission (http://www.chrc-ccdp.ca/sites/default/files/screen_1.pdf; also see, for example, Chapter 3, Table 3.3), and by other jurisdictions throughout Canada. The *Canadian Human Rights Reporter* (http://www.cdn-hr-reporter.ca) is a useful source of information for human rights cases and legal guidelines for recruitment, screening, and assessment.

When it is necessary to collect information concerning applicant status with regard to protected classes to monitor applicant flow as prescribed by employment equity legislation, this should be done using a form and a process that is separate from screening wherein applicants are assured that the information collected is per government requirements, and will not be accessible to those making hiring decisions. Specific guidelines for collecting sensitive information are available from government employment equity officers.

With regard to the decisions concerning application form content, the following questions should be considered:

- What is the purpose of including the item and how will the information be used?
- Does the item conflict with provincial, territorial, or federal human rights guidelines concerning questions that cannot be asked on an application form (see Chapter 3)?
- If the item-based information is used in the screening decision, is it likely to have an adverse impact on a protected minority group?
- Is it more appropriate to obtain the information only after making a job offer?
- Has the job-relatedness of the item been established?

Independently of legal considerations per se, it is important to note that employers can put themselves at a disadvantage, in tight labour markets especially, by using a poorly designed application form. For example, candidates who complete forms containing discriminatory questions tend to view the employer as less attractive and less just; they also express higher litigation intentions than those who complete legally compliant forms, especially when the employer fails to provide an explanation of the screening process.[6] Finally, candidates encountering application forms with discriminatory questions are less likely to pursue employment with the organization, less likely to accept a job offer, and less likely to recommend the organization to a friend.[7]

While respecting the rights and interests of job candidates, employers also need to protect their own interests by verifying the information applicants provide. Failure to do so can be embarrassing for all parties. For example, at the Massachusetts Institute of Technology (MIT), Marilee Jones, the Dean of Admissions, was forced to resign for falsely claiming both a bachelor's and a master's degree on her résumé.[8] In anticipation that applicants may distort their credentials, it should be explicitly and visibly stated on the application form that the data provided will be checked thoroughly for accuracy. For example: "I understand that providing any false, misleading, or incomplete information is grounds for immediate discharge from employment."[9] This will help discourage misrepresentation and provide grounds for dismissal should a candidate be hired and found subsequently to have embellished credentials.

WEIGHTED APPLICATION BLANKS

Sometimes information concerning a single item on an application form is sufficient to screen out a candidate, such as when successful completion of a bar exam is essential for positions involving the practice of law. However, for many applicants and many positions, a single piece of information on the application will not provide for a simple error-free determination. Instead, the screener must use personal judgment and experience to evaluate the entirety of the information provided, much like a person might review the voting record of a candidate for political office.

An alternative to this subjective approach involves the development of a formal scoring key for responses to many of the items on the application form. For example, lawyers who have not passed the bar exam might be given a score of 0, while those who have passed receive a 1. Similarly, weights are assigned to other item responses with the higher numbers being reflective of answers provided by applicants who subsequently proved to be successful in the target job. Adding all the assigned weights together produces a total score for each applicant. Use of a formal scoring procedure of this kind is referred to as a **weighted application blank (WAB)** and is analogous to the process bank managers use to evaluate loan applications, as there are personal indicators, financial and otherwise, that reliably predict loan repayment.

Weighted application blank (WAB)
A formal method for quantitatively combining information from application blank items by assigning weights that reflect the value of each item in the prediction of job success.

Like any selection instrument, the WAB must exhibit good psychometric properties. Accordingly, the scoring for WABs is developed in relation to aspects of employee performance that matter to the employer. For example, the level of absenteeism might be important for a security dispatcher's position, such that the HR manager would use the maximum permissible days absent per year to divide the current and previous dispatchers into groups that fall above and below the acceptable number. The application forms they submitted would then be reviewed for the pattern of item responses that best differentiated between the low- and high-absenteeism groups. For example, it may be that 80 percent of security dispatchers with only a high school education fall into the good attendance category, while the remaining 20 percent have poor attendance. The 60 percent difference (i.e., 80 – 20 = 60) is the basis of the "net weight" for "high school graduate." Similarly, for university graduates, if 60 percent have a low absenteeism rate and 40 percent have a high rate, the 20 percent difference would be the "net weight" for "university graduate." The net weight derived for each education level is then transformed into a specific score. For instance, applicants with a high school education *alone* would be given a higher score (e.g., 3) than university graduates (e.g., 1).

Note that there are a variety of outcomes in addition to absenteeism that are important to the employer and which might be used as the basis to separate employees into acceptable and unacceptable groups. Regardless of the specific outcome chosen, the variable used to form the groups is referred to as the **criterion measure**.

Criterion measures
Measures of employee job-related outcomes important to the employer (e.g., absenteeism, turnover, supervisory ratings of performance) used to establish the validity (i.e., the appropriateness and meaningfulness) of screening and selection tools.

Because establishing weights and specific scores is complex, tables have been developed to facilitate the process for the vertical percentage method exemplified above, as well as for other approaches[10,11] such as the correlational method.[12]

BENEFITS OF WABS

Well-constructed WABs are good predictors of certain aspects of work, such as absenteeism and accidents. They also have been shown to reduce employee turnover in the hospitality industry[13,14] and among clerical employees.[15] Once developed, they are both easy and economical to use especially when applications are collected digitally, such that computer algorithms can quickly and efficiently score them at low cost. Importantly, well-constructed WABs are unlikely to be considered intrusive or threatening, as most job applicants expect to complete one.

CONCERNS ABOUT WABS

Some cautions are associated with the use of WABs. First, WAB scoring keys are typically derived to predict one specific, often narrow, outcome (e.g., turnover, absenteeism, or accident rates) as opposed to broad multifaceted measures of performance. While there is evidence that WABs can also predict success in training and overall job proficiency,[16] care should be taken not to automatically make generalizations beyond the purpose for which the WAB was designed.

Second, WABs require data from a large number of employees to obtain percentages that are stable estimates of the targeted weights. Several years of data collection might be required to develop the system, and changes in the job, applicants, or organization over time may produce weights that poorly reflect the first- and last-hired employees in the sample. Further, weights derived from the original sample should be applied to a second independent sample from the same population of workers (i.e., cross-validated) to ensure they are stable. Weights based on biographical information have shown good stability.[17]

Finally, while WABs enable employers to predict certain work outcomes,[18] often the *reasons* for the relationships found are not immediately evident, which is bothersome.[19] This criticism is less of an issue when the WAB items used are derived *rationally* from a systematic job analysis. For example, it is well known that if people have realistic expectations for a job at the outset, they are less likely to leave. Thus, a business looking to reduce turnover among its sales positions may include items, targeted to those without experience, concerning the degree to which the applicant has close friends or relatives who are in sales positions, with the expectation that they would be better informed concerning the nature of the work.[20] Nonetheless, and somewhat surprisingly, a purely statistical analysis of application blank items results in better prediction of work outcomes than rationally (or quasi-rationally) derived approaches.[21]

WHEN TO USE WABS

WABs are often used for quick, cost-effective screening and may also be used in combination with other types of predictors (e.g., personality or cognitive ability; see Chapter 8) to improve the final selection decisions. This is especially appropriate when there is a large number of applicants for a single position,[22] or when large numbers of applicants are hired for similar kinds of jobs, because the same item set is likely to be useful across the entire applicant group. Also, given their capability to predict turnover, WABs are often used for positions requiring long and costly training where turnover costs are especially high.

BIOGRAPHICAL DATA

A typical application form requires job candidates to provide information about their knowledge, skills, and education, as well as a narrow range of job-related information. The use of biographical data addresses a wider range of content than the typical application form, by addressing, for example, educational experiences, hobbies, family relationships, leisure-time pursuits, personal accomplishments, and early work experiences. Whereas an application form focuses on a narrower set of factual and verifiable information concerning educational background, training, and work experience, biographical data addresses a wider array of more subjective issues.[23] Thus, as we detail later, aspects of biographical data collection may run afoul of privacy and human rights legislation.

Biographical data are synonymous with, or frequently referred to as, "autobiographical data," "personal or life history information," "background data," or more simply "biodata." Such data can be collected in a relatively unstructured manner using, for example, interviews and life history essays. However, use of the **biographical information blank (BIB)** is the most common, wherein candidates are required to answer a series of multiple-choice or short-answer essay questions.[24,25] BIBs, also known as *life history* or *personal history inventories*, are based on the assumption that past behaviour is the best

Biographical information blank (BIB)
A pre-selection questionnaire that requires applicants to provide detailed job-related information concerning their personal background and life experiences.

predictor of future behaviour. Thus, the intent of BIB content is to obtain job-related insights from the past that provide clues concerning applicant's future interests and capabilities. Recruitment and Selection Today 7.1 presents an example of a BIB developed for use with applicants for a managerial position. As with the WAB, the scoring procedure developed for a BIB on an initial sample should be evaluated using a second independent group before it is used operationally. Relative to the WAB, a well-designed BIB provides greater insight concerning the type of individuals likely to experience success in the target job.

RECRUITMENT AND SELECTION TODAY 7.1

EXAMPLE OF A BIOGRAPHICAL INFORMATION BLANK

Personal Information

Name: ______________________ ______________________
Last First

Mailing Address: ____
Street, City, Province, Postal Code

How long have you lived at your current address? __________

Do you consider your net worth to be low ____ moderate ____ or high _____?

Have you ever been turned down for a loan? Yes ________ No ________

How many credit cards do you have? ________

Education and Training

Highest level of education completed:

High School _______ Vocational ______ College ______ University _______ Postgraduate _______

What educational degrees do you have? Diploma/Certificate ______ B.A. ______ B.Sc. ______ B.Comm. ______

M.B.A. ______ Master's ______ Other (Identify) _______

What subjects did you major in? ________________ ________________

What was your grade-point average in college or university? A ___ B ____ C ___ D ____

Did you graduate with honours? Yes ________ No ________

Did you receive any awards for academic excellence? Yes ______ No ______

Did you receive any scholarships? Yes ________ No ______

List the extracurricular activities you participated in during school: ______________________________

Information about You

Did you find school stimulating ______ boring ______?

Did you hold a job while attending school? Yes ______ No ______

How did you pay for your post–high school training? (Check as many as appropriate)

Parents paid ______ Loans ______ Scholarships ______ Paid own way ______

Have you ever held a job where you earned commissions on sales? Yes ______ No ______

If "Yes," were your commissions low ______ moderate ______ high ______?

Five years from now, what do you expect your salary to be? ____________

Do you enjoy meeting new people? Yes ______ No ______

How many social phone calls do you receive a week? ______

Do people count on you to "cheer up" others? Yes _____ No ________
How many parties do you go to in a year? ______
Do you enjoy talking to people? Yes ______ No ______
Rate your conversational skills:
Excellent ______ Very Good ______ Good ______ Fair ______ Poor ______
How often do you introduce yourself to other people you don't know?
Always ______ Sometimes ______ Never ______
Do you enjoy social gatherings? Yes ______ No ______
Do you go to social gatherings out of a sense of duty? Yes ______ No ______
How many times a year do you go out to dinner with friends? ______
Do you enjoy talking to people you don't know? Yes ______ No ______
What are your hobbies?______________________________
What sports, recreational, or physical activities do you engage in?____________
How confident are you in your ability to succeed?
Very Confident ______ Confident ______ Somewhat Confident ______

As another example, for more than 70 years the life insurance industry in Canada and the U.S. has used **biodata** to help screen millions of candidates for sales representative positions using materials developed and distributed by the Life Insurance Marketing Research Association (LIMRA). Life insurance sales positions are demanding because agents typically are not provided with "leads," but are expected to prospect for customers among friends, family, and acquaintances. Since most contacts do not produce a sale, agents must be "thick skinned" and persevering to be successful. Approximately half of those selected leave the position within the first year before training costs can be recouped. Thus, the Career Profile+ combines biodata and personality items designed originally to identify individuals with previous industry experience who would be most suited to life-insurance sales.[26] It targets insurance-related experiences; belief in the value and importance of insurance; number of friends, relatives, and personal contacts in the industry; knowledge of the position; financial and occupational stability; and commitment to one's present situation (e.g., ties to one's current job). See: http://www.limra.com/Solutions/Assessment/Sales_Assessment_Tools/Sales_Representatives/Career_Profile.aspx.

Biodata
Biographical data gathered from applicant BIBs, application blanks, or other sources.

BIB DIMENSIONS

As reflected in the work of LIMRA, BIBs can cover a wide range of information and are typically reflective of between 13 and 15 separate areas of content.[27] Although a complicated process is required to compare the content areas of BIBs that have been developed for different positions,[28] subject comparison suggests eight areas of commonality[29]:

- school achievement (academic success and positive academic attitude);
- higher educational achievement (holding a degree from a post-secondary school);
- drive (motivation to be outstanding, to attain high goals, to achieve);
- leadership and group participation (involvement in organized activities and membership in groups);

- financial responsibility (financial status and handling of finances);
- early family responsibility (assuming accountability for certain roles/tasks);
- parental family adjustment (happy parental home experience); and
- situational stability (mid-life occupational stability).

The above analysis highlights the fact that when BIBs are used operationally, the focus should be on broad content areas, such as drive and financial responsibility, rather than the specifics of the applicant's goals or financial status. The particular content area(s) of interest will also likely vary depending on the criteria (aspects of performance) the employer is most interested in predicting.[30] Finally, BIB items have also been written to reflect each of five broad dimensions of personality (covered in Chapter 8) as an alternative to direct self-reports concerning personality, which may be more subject to distortion (i.e., "faking" or "impression management").[31]

CONCERNS OVER THE USE OF BIODATA

Despite the evidence supporting the predictive validity of biodata there are some cautions associated with its use, including legality, invasiveness, fakability, and generalizability. With respect to legality and invasiveness, many BIB items may request personally sensitive information concerning family background and experiences that border on violations of human rights legislation.[32] Thus, the items in question should be used only if the employer can demonstrate that they are job-related–by, for example, showing that they are predictive of certain aspects of job performance. In the United States, each BIB item must be shown to be free of adverse impact on members of protected groups.[33] Importantly, differences in accessibility to the life experiences measured by biodata items may give rise to variation in how applicants from different groups (e.g., gender and race) respond to them, though these individuals may not, in fact, differ on the broader construct that underlies the items.[34] The use of certain types of biodata item responses can cause problems with regard to ethnicity as well.[35]

The above examples notwithstanding, when biodata items are carefully developed and systematically scored, they tend to have less adverse impact on women and other designated minority groups than many other types of selection measures.[36] For example, the Canadian insurance industry adjusted its BIB to comply with human rights legislation without any loss in its usefulness; the Canadian biodata form developed by LIMRA predicts both the retention of life insurance agents and their sales.[37,38]

Many other items on a BIB delve into areas that are not protected by legislation but do raise issues of privacy. For example, job applicants may feel it inappropriate to share information about their financial status and the number of credit cards they have. This matters because, as noted earlier, applicants form perceptions of the organization and its values based on the screening processes, which can influence a variety of their decisions including whether or not to accept a job offer.[39]

Both professionals and nonprofessionals view certain types of biodata items as invasive, such as those that are relatively less verifiable, less transparent in purpose, and relatively personal.[40] Complicating matters is that the perceived acceptability of specific BIB items is somewhat context specific. For example, items concerning home, spousal, and parental situations, recreation and hobbies, as well as interest in travel and in new experiences were all perceived as more job-relevant, fair, and appropriate when used to select applicants for international postings rather than for domestic positions.[41] This is likely because the information was seen as relevant to coping with the demands of international assignments.[42] Relatedly, increasing the transparency concerning the purpose of biodata items improves their perceived acceptability.[43]

Another caution associated with the use of BIBs is that managers often express concern that job applicants are less than honest in completing them, especially with regard to the reporting of negative information. The evidence concerning fakability is mixed. On the positive side, in a study involving applications for positions in a Florida police department, there was very high correspondence between applicant answers and actual events.[44] Having applicants elaborate on their answers to biodata questions (i.e., through providing written support) can also reduce faking.[45,46,47] Applicants who expect their answers to be verified are more likely to tell the truth. Nonetheless, some distortion on BIBs should be expected. Even with regard to responses on traditional application forms, the information may be inaccurate in up to 25 percent of cases.[48] Similarly, the degree of inaccuracy or misrepresentation found in application materials supplied by job candidates is 33 percent.[49] Finally, reports of the prevalence and severity of "faking" or deception in assessments for entry-level positions are particularly pronounced where special measures are taken to ensure anonymity of responses.[50]

As with the WAB, the predictive validity of a BIB is typically initially established for a large pool of applicants for a specific job. As noted earlier, over time LIMRA's work concerning life insurance agents has involved millions of applicants throughout North America. Thus, small- to medium-sized organizations would likely need a consortium-based effort to gain access to a large enough sample for validation purposes.[51] Their development also requires technical expertise in test validation. These drawbacks likely account for the relatively infrequent use of BIBs in North America, despite good predictive validity and minimal adverse impact.[52,53,54]

Sometimes a biodata instrument can be used outside the specific organization for which it was developed and remain useful for years.[55] For example, the biodata component of the *Manager Profile Record* (MPR), which was developed in a single organization, predicted managerial progress (e.g., rate of promotion; $r = 0.53$, $SD = 0.05$) in 24 other organizations over an 11-year period.[56] Similarly, a biodata instrument that proved helpful in selecting graduates into the accounting profession proved to have good predictive validity across a wide range of firms over a 5-year period.[57] Also, biodata scoring keys used in the insurance industry were uniformly applicable across the United States, the United Kingdom, and the Republic of Ireland.[58] Thus, some biodata items appear to have generic validity for a given job, assuming their content remains stable.[59] Nonetheless, generic biodata instruments tend to have lower validities than those developed for specific jobs in specific organizations.[60] The applicability of scoring keys sometimes varies depending on whether or not the applicants completed high school,[61] which illustrates the sensitivity of the applicability of biodata scoring keys to the specifics of an applicant's developmental experiences.[62] In all, generalizability of the validity of BIBs developed on a specific sample is not to be assumed.

PREDICTIVE VALIDITY OF BIODATA

As noted above, BIBs can be an effective, noninvasive, and defensible means of improving HR selection decisions. They have shown comparable levels of predictive validity for similar jobs across organizations and over time. Similar to the findings concerning WABs, biodata can accurately predict various types of job behaviour, such as absenteeism, turnover, job proficiency, supervisory effectiveness, and job training, in a wide range of occupations.[63–73] On average, corrected correlations between scores on

Validity coefficient The correlation between assessment scores and job performance measures.

biodata instruments and job-relevant criteria range from 0.30 to 0.40.[74,75,76] **Validity coefficients** for biodata have sometimes exceeded 0.50.[77] Validity estimates for job performance and performance in training are .35 and .30, respectively.[78]

The effectiveness of BIBs is thought to be grounded in the use of past behaviours and experiences as *indirect* reflections of preferences, values, personality, opportunities, constraints, and so forth, which can in turn be matched to the needs of the job and to the culture of the employer.[79] This indirect approach is appropriate to the screening stage, since use of more direct assessments (e.g., personality scales, preference/interest inventories, etc.; see Chapter 8) of the content thought to be reflected in biodata would be more costly and time consuming.

In addition to being predictive of a wide range of criteria,[80] BIBs sometimes yield meaningful prediction beyond other types of assessments, such as cognitive ability and personality (see Chapter 8), that have also been collected during the screening and selection effort.[81,82,83] Moreover, biodata may be most predictive in complex as opposed to nonskilled, simpler jobs,[84] where the dollar gains associated with effective screening and selection are typically even more substantial. As noted earlier, compared to other screening and selection tools biodata tends to have little or no adverse impact.[85,86,87] The generalizability of many of these findings remains a concern, however, because with few exceptions[88] samples of current employees, rather than groups of applicants, are used for developing and validating of BIBs.[89]

WHEN TO USE BIBS

Biodata has been used within and across a variety of contexts (e.g., work, education) and fields (clinical, developmental, and social psychology).[90] As with WABs, BIBs are especially appropriate for organizations hiring large numbers of employees for similar kinds of jobs, where relatively few will ultimately be hired (i.e., when there is a low selection ratio).[91]

Deerfield Photo/Shutterstock.com

RÉSUMÉS

Résumés are another source of biographical information. Of course, unlike with application forms and BIBs, here it is the applicant who decides what to provide and how to present it, as part of an effort to give a brief, written self-introduction to the employer. Not surprisingly, résumé information often overlaps with that requested by the employer on application blanks or BIBs. Employers often presume that résumé information is job related and will help them to determine if a candidate satisfies the MQs. However, job applicants may inadvertently include information that the employer might rather not see (e.g., citizenship, national origin, height, weight, and marital status); that, if used as part of selection, would violate employment laws. It would likely be quite difficult for an employer to prove that prohibited information on a résumé did not influence their decision making.

FIRST IMPRESSIONS

The résumé, including biographical information, is often the basis of the first impression an employer forms of the applicant. In addition to the content, the résumé's style, neatness, organization, layout, vocabulary, and phrases used each convey candidate information. For example, when business professionals selected the two individuals they would invite for interviews from among seven sets of four résumés, one-page résumés fared better than two-page offerings; specific objective statements were better regarded than general ones; listing a 3.00 GPA was better than omitting GPA information; a 3.5 GPA was regarded as significantly better than a 2.75; listing relevant course work was better than not listing any; and listing accomplishments was better than omitting them.[92] Similarly, listing relevant job experience and education enhanced business managers' evaluations of résumés, as did candidate listings of *concrete* examples of their accomplishments.[93] However, *general* impression-management tactics such as the use of self-descriptive adjectives such as "excellent," "extremely hard working," and "energetic" (e.g., not tied to specific accomplishments) led to *negative* impressions.[94]

Studies also suggest that HR managers consider résumé characteristics as reflections of different aspects of the applicant in much the same way as a projective personality test (see Chapter 8). For example, applicants' résumé information as evaluated by recruiters may, to some extent, predict candidate cognitive ability and personality.[95,96] Perhaps not surprisingly, recruiters who infer from résumé characteristics that candidates are conscientious consider them as especially suited to conventional jobs (e.g., accounting), whereas recruiters' inferences of extraverted applicants resulted in perceived good matches to "enterprising" jobs (e.g., marketing).[97] Nonetheless, while recruiters at times are able to draw moderately accurate inferences concerning candidates' extraversion from résumé content, their ability to do so for other personality characteristics is poor.[98] Accordingly, it is not recommended that an applicant's personality be inferred from a résumé; instead, it should be assessed directly (see Chapter 8).

To build a favourable first impression with a résumé, it should be accompanied by a well-written cover letter. In a survey of 100 senior executives from the largest Canadian companies, 93 percent indicated that cover letters are valuable in assessing job candidates. Executive Director Dave Willmer of OfficeTeam, a firm specializing in placing highly skilled professionals into administrative jobs, who contracted the survey, commented: "Submitting a résumé without a cover letter is like not shaking hands when meeting someone for the first time." He notes that a cover letter should reveal the applicant's knowledge of the company, highlight relevant skills and work experience, and explain résumé anomalies (e.g., extended employment gaps).[99] Indeed, a representative survey of 140 U.S. and multinational firms revealed a preference (56%) for the inclusion of a cover letter.[100]

OfficeTeam (http://www.roberthalf.com/officeteam) provides the following seven tips to help job seekers develop strong cover letters:

1. Address your letter to the specific hiring manager rather than using a generalized introduction.
2. Research the company online and clearly communicate how your knowledge and skills fit the job and could benefit the organization.
3. Address any potential concerns (e.g., employment gaps).
4. Limit your cover letter to two or three short paragraphs.
5. Show your excitement for the position and conclude by identifying next steps (e.g., "I'll follow up next week to discuss in person").
6. Review (and have others review) your cover letter for typos and grammatical errors.
7. When applying through online job boards, always choose the option to add your cover letter to your résumé. When e-mailing application materials to a hiring manager, paste your cover letter within the body of your message.[101*]

WRITING A RÉSUMÉ

Many people have difficulty writing a good résumé. Vocational guidance and employment counsellors often provide useful help in résumé writing as part of their services. Most libraries have references concerning résumé preparation as well. Résumés should include the applicant's name, address, and phone number(s), education and training, employment history, names of references with contact information, and a brief statement of employment objectives. Information regarding hobbies and interests should be included only if relevant to career goals. For example, a candidate for a forest ranger position could note an interest in hiking.

The résumé should be well organized and highlight key information. The typeface size (e.g., a 10-, 11-, or 12-point font) and style (e.g., Arial) should make for easy and quick reading. Use electronic delivery if possible (i.e., via e-mail or the company's website) rather than sending a scanned résumé.[102] Although relatively few multinationals (7%) desire a paper copy of a résumé,[103] when required these should be generated using printers of high quality.

Generally, use of unusual fonts, small type, excessive italics, or too much single-line spacing (all of which make the résumé congested and difficult to read) should be avoided. As electronic résumé submission has become common, some career and employment counsellors recommend listing a keyword summary at the start, using appropriate nouns reflective of words that HR software is likely to search for (see Recruitment and Selection Today 7.2). Recruitment and Selection Notebook 7.1 offers steps to writing an effective business résumé; Recruitment and Selection Notebook 7.2 provides an example business résumé. Crosby and Liming also provide helpful and detailed information on preparing effective cover letters and résumés, including samples of each.[104]

---

*Source: http://www.officeteam.com

RECRUITMENT AND SELECTION TODAY 7.2

USING THE INTERNET TO SCREEN JOB CANDIDATES

In Chapter 6, we discussed the impact of the Internet on recruiting through online job sites such as Workopolis.com and Monster.ca. One disadvantage of these recruiting methods is that they typically generate many more applications and résumés (hundreds daily) than the employer needs. Accordingly, sophisticated software has been developed to create and manage applicant databases to promote quick, effective screening.

With the appropriate software, client companies can access application service agencies for potential hires, such as Workstream Inc. (http://uat.workstreaminc.com/products_services/recruitment.asp). Clients using this software can screen online applications and spot an excellent prospect in a matter of minutes. In addition to submitting a résumé, a candidate may be asked to complete a questionnaire specific to the prospective employer that solicits information not likely to be presented in a general résumé. Some companies will accept an application and résumé only if the candidate provides the additional information requested. For example, for a global company, the additional questions might include "Can you travel immediately?" and "Do you have a passport?"

Some questionnaires intended for screening beyond general résumé submissions are comparable to BIBs in that they may include multiple-choice items related to skills or experience (e.g., "How much experience have you had using a programming language?") or short essays (e.g., "How would you handle a programming problem that you could not solve by yourself?"). Some software offerings assign points to the answers submitted.

Source: Ann Kerr. 2000. "Sophisticated Software Does the Job for On-Line Recruiters: The More Complex Programs Manage Everything from Posting Positions to Pre-Screening Applicants and Keeping Tabs on Future Prospects." *The Globe and Mail* (June 30). Reprinted with permission from *The Globe and Mail.*

RECRUITMENT AND SELECTION NOTEBOOK 7.1

FIVE STEPS TO WRITING AN EFFECTIVE BUSINESS RÉSUMÉ

1. Complete a Self-Assessment and Create a Skills Inventory: evaluate past activities that have been most important in making you unique and valuable. Consider: successful accomplishments, school contributions, achievements at work and other proud moments.
2. Define Your Accomplishments: use the STAR (situation, time, action, result) method to show achievements and accomplishments. By highlighting the results of your actions, as well as your skills, attributes, and experiences, employers will see not only what you did, but how well you did it. Example: *Supervised over 12 students in daily activities, which also included developing and facilitating sports skill workshops in basketball and soccer, creating a heightened sense of team spirit and a fun environment.*
3. Use Résumé Sections/Headings to Emphasize Your Value: organize your résumé according to the following sections:

Header

Begin your résumé with your name, address, email address, LinkedIn URL (optional), and phone number(s). It is preferable not to include any personal information such as birth date, marital status, or health.

Section 1: Education

Education represents the top one-third of your résumé. Academic experience should be listed in reverse chronological order, to indicate the most recent program first, including dates (e.g., expected date of completion: April 2017). A representative survey of 140 U.S. and multinational firms revealed a preference that résumé material be presented in chronological order.[105] Do not include coursework/special projects unless it is relevant to the role.

Section 2: Work Experience

This section appears directly after Education. Use accomplishment-oriented bullet-points (what, where, how well etc. . . .) to describe your STAR stories. Begin each job description bullet with an action verb that describes exactly what you did (e.g., *analyzed, performed, directed, produced, managed* etc. . . .). Try not to use phrases such as "responsible for"; that is, be skills oriented, not duty oriented. Avoid unsubstantiated self-describing general statements, such as "I'm creative, dynamic, a quick learner, a hard worker," and so on. Use factual statements rather than inferential ones; for example, "Was commended for my creativity in developing a new marketing strategy."

Section 3: Career Related Skills

Include computer related skills (program software) with your level of knowledge and proficiency. List achievements that directly enhance your brand and relate to the role. If you have second language skills (oral or written), include this information and your proficiency.

Section 4: Volunteer Experience

Highlight relevant volunteer activities, especially if they demonstrate leadership and job-related competencies.

Section 5: Extracurricular Activities and Interests

Include extracurricular experiences that link to job-related competencies and your overall personal brand. If an organization is linked to the stated activities, include its name, with the appropriate city and province. Sharing such interests offers a "well-rounded" appearance.

4. Five Ps to Consider—to ensure your résumé is easy to read and error-free, review the *packaging, positioning, power information, personality* and *professionalism*!

   i. Packaging:

   - Paper should be white or light coloured; do not use graphics or colour
   - Use a readable, professional looking font in 10, 11, or 12 pt (Tahoma, Arial, Verdana) and only use **one** font type throughout; your name should be no larger than 16 pt (header)
   - Do not use templates; create your own Word document
   - Single spacing should be used within each section and margins should be no less than 0.5" and no greater than 1"

   ii. Positioning:

   - Résumé should read in reverse chronological order under each section/heading
   - Education: degree, major/specialization on first line in **bold**; university name, location, and date (positioned at right margin) on second line, not bold
   - Employment: position title and department should appear on first line in **bold**; company name, location, and date (at right margin) on second line, not bold

   iii. Power Information:

   - Make use of STAR statements to demonstrate what, why, how, when, and the result
   - Work experience should include results/outcomes; quantify these where possible (i.e., "Increased sales by 10 percent"; "Handled cash up to $10K per shift"; "Supervised a five-member team")
   - Do not list duties or tasks; instead use past-tense action verbs
   - Use bullet points (3–5 per work experience) and one sentence per point
   - Most significant and/or relevant aspects of the role should be listed first, followed by inserted bullets in descending order of importance

   iv. Personality:

   - To the extent that volunteer/activities/interests are related to the job, include them to demonstrate your well-roundedness

- Do not underestimate the value of volunteer or summer employment; these experiences offer many transferrable skills
- Avoid undue repetition of the same word(s) and do not use more words than necessary to communicate an idea (i.e., use "to" rather than "in order to")

v. Professionalism:

- Double-check for spelling and grammatical errors; then ask a friend to do the same—a single mistake on a résumé can get you screened out
- Spell out numbers one to ten and use numbers for 11 and above
- Spell out months and university degrees completely, and avoid using abbreviations except for provinces and states (i.e., ON, AB, NY)
- If using acronyms, spell out the related term followed by the acronym in brackets upon initial use; the acronym can then be used throughout the remainder of the document

5. Getting your Résumé Market Ready: consider: *Does my résumé reflect the brand I want to represent and does it effectively communicate this brand to employers?* To ensure your résumé is market ready and attractive to recruiters, use the following exercise:

- List the key competencies you regard as essential to the role.
- Does your résumé effectively highlight these competencies?
- Are there any gaps? What do you lack? Which skills are missing?

A Note Concerning Social Media and Your Online Brand:

While it is optional for candidates to include a LinkedIn URL within the résumé header, a Facebook URL is **not** recommended because it is a social network rather than a professional association. Moreover, candidates must be aware of their online brand at all times. Ensure that privacy settings are in place to prevent public profile viewing and that any viewable profile pictures are professional.

Source: Business Career Services, Michael G. DeGroote School of Business, McMaster University. Reprinted with permission.

SCREENING RÉSUMÉS

The unique format and content of each résumé makes standardized screening and scoring difficult, if not impossible, which is a major reason that employers develop their own application blanks and BIBs. Nonetheless, all of the psychometric and legal considerations that apply to application forms and biodata apply equally when résumés are used for screening and selection purposes. The following are example guidelines for screening a résumé[106]:

- Think of what the company needs for excellent job performance in terms of its job performance criteria.
- Read each résumé with reference to the organization's criteria of job performance.
- Check résumés for work experience, chronology, and history.
- Examine résumés for concrete accomplishments and identifiable skills.

As detailed in Recruitment and Selection Today 7.2, computer software is used in many cases to enhance the speed and accuracy of résumé screening.[107]

Advances in technology have also enabled the use of video résumés, wherein candidates send employers a video self-presentation of their skills, experiences, credentials, and accomplishments. Much like the unwanted inclusion of certain types of information

RECRUITMENT AND SELECTION NOTEBOOK 7.2

AN EXAMPLE OF A BUSINESS RÉSUMÉ

Jane M. Smith
Address, City, Province A1B 2C3
(905) XXX-XXXX • janesmith@mcmaster.ca • http://ca.linkedin.com/in/~smith

---

Education

HONOURS BACHELOR OF COMMERCE, LEVEL 4

DeGroote School of Business, McMaster University, Hamilton, ON September 2012–Present

- Area of focus: Accounting, Pursuing Minor in Economics
- Entrance Scholarship, 2012
- Dean's Honour List, 2013
- Member of Golden Key Honour Society, September 2010–present
- Participated in 16-month Commerce Internship, IBM
- Expected date of completion: April 2016

Work Experience

SALES AND OPERATIONS SUPPORT

IBM Canada, Markham, ON May 2010–August 2012

- Conducted and distributed midweek metrics and forecasting to Canadian Mid-market TeleCoverage sales force, which improved forecasting accuracy.
- Implemented and trained four new sales representatives on new Forecasting template and sales growth strategy for 2010, which allowed individuals to update and manipulate data as required.
- Prepared Personal Business Commitment packages for representatives and Manager, improving internal customer relations.
- Created e-contact customer list and new tracking system in Microsoft Access identifying new business leads for national sales force.
- Recognized in Thanks! Award Program, for "Excellent Sales Support and Willingness to Learn," and for "Quickly Picking up the Role and Adding Value to the Team.

SHIFT SUPERVISOR

Starbucks Coffee, Hamilton, ON September 2008–August 2010

- Led and directed team of 12; received MUG (Moves of Uncommon Greatness) award for receiving 99 percent store 'Snapshot' based on excellent service provided to secret shopper.
- Delegated tasks such as brewing coffee, cashier, cleaning front or barista based on personal strengths and interests to a team of six shift employees, which motivated them to perform tasks to best of ability.
- Brainstormed with other supervisors to design and implement new strategies to improve store dynamic; created communication log, increasing consistency in delivery of store and promotions announcements.
- Coached 16 new employees, one-on-one and delegated responsibility with respect, resulting in increased speed and service to patrons.

- Analyzed inventories of coffee and paper supplies, created stock orders, and partnered with suppliers, ensuring shipments delivered on time.

EMPLOYMENT CLERK/TYPIST, OFFICE ADMINISTRATION AND BUSINESS DEPARTMENTS

Mohawk College, Hamilton, ON April–August 2008

- Completed typing, printing, and assembly of custom courseware manuals and course outlines to optimize the operations of the office.
- Prepared databases and performed merges for large mail-outs using Word, ensuring timely distribution to external clients.
- Handled reception of visitors, transfer of calls, answered general inquiries, delivering quality customer service and upholding the brand standard of the college.

Skills and Qualifications

- Proficient in Microsoft Office Suite, including Excel, Word, PowerPoint, and Access
- Basic knowledge of HTML programming
- French: Strong understanding of written communications with basic competency in oral

Volunteer Experience

Volunteer, Hamilton Cancer Assistance Program, Hamilton, ON March 2009–August 2010

- Worked with Coordinator to organize four annual events and raised over $1K annually for the Hamilton Cancer Society.
- Recruited and trained over nine student volunteers for telethon promotions, allowing organization to meet monthly targets for fundraising.

Administrative Assistant, Ontario Ball Hockey League, Hamilton, ON June 2009–September 2010

- Organized practice and tournament dates and collected fees from players to ensure smooth execution of the league each week.

Extracurricular Activities

Participant—Trader-in-Residence, Gould Trading Floor September 2012–Present

- Attended presentations by finance industry professionals to enhance industry knowledge and network with professionals

Participant, McMaster DECA U Business Competition January 2013

- Competed in a marketing simulation business case with a team of four; designed marketing plan and promotional strategy for fictional company in the consumer packaged goods industry; team placed in the Top 3.

Interests

- Sports—recreational swimming, snowboarding
- Travel—backpacked across India and Turkey May–August 2011

Source: Business Career Services, Michael G. DeGroote School of Business, McMaster University. Reprinted with permission.

on traditional résumés, videos reveal cues concerning age, gender, ethnicity, religion (e.g., wearing a turban, hijab, sari, kippah), and handicap (e.g., speech impediment) that could leave an employer open to allegations of discrimination. Moreover, not all candidates may have access to the technology required to produce their own videos, and when they do, the production quality may vary widely but have little to do with the suitability of the candidate. Analogous to the paper-based résumé, standardization of presentation structure, format, length, and content are lacking, making a fair, objective comparison of applicants difficult. Given the potential for bias, many firms appear reluctant to embrace the video résumé.[108] Relative to traditional options, video résumés can result in differing assessments of applicant traits and lower evaluations of their skills and abilities. It may be wise for employers to avoid them pending further study of their efficacy and fairness.[109] Candidates should check employer preferences before sending any type of résumé or referring potential employers to personal blogs.[110]

Despite their potential drawbacks, the number of services available for building and distributing video résumés is growing.[111] Video Resume Now offers a service to create video résumés and to provide a connection to potential employers (http://videoresumenow.com). Sample video résumés may be viewed on the Video Resume Now website.

HONESTY AND THE RÉSUMÉ

While striving to develop an effective résumé, honesty is an important consideration in avoiding overly exaggerated qualifications or accomplishments. There is often a fine line between presenting oneself in the "best possible light" and intentional misrepresentation. As noted earlier, there have been embarrassingly high-profile job losses associated with exaggerated and/or untrue claims concerning job qualifications. Yet, surveys indicate that approximately one-third of job candidates exaggerate or fabricate résumé information related to educational credentials, grade point averages, current or previous salaries, and past experiences and accomplishments.[112,113]

As noted earlier, the likelihood of applicants fabricating or embellishing credentials is lessened considerably when they believe that the information provided will be verified; employers should include a statement to this effect in the application materials.[114] Also, those conducting résumé screening must learn how to "read between the lines" of résumés (see Recruitment and Selection Today 7.3). Later phases of selection should also provide for opportunities to probe the credibility of applicant information.

RECRUITMENT AND SELECTION TODAY 7.3

WHAT TO LOOK FOR WHEN EXAMINING A RÉSUMÉ

- Unexplained gaps in work or education chronology.
- Conflicting details or overlapping dates.
- Career regression, or "downward" trend.
- Use of qualifiers such as "knowledge of," and "assisted in" to describe work experience.
- Listing of schools attended without indicating receipt of a degree or diploma.
- Failure to provide names of previous supervisors or references.
- Substantial periods in a candidate's work history listed as "self-employed" or "consultant."

PREDICTIVE VALIDITY OF RÉSUMÉS

Information of the type typically included in résumés has relatively low usefulness for predicting job success.[115] Experience has the highest validity ($r = 0.18$), followed by academic achievement ($r = 0.11$) and education ($r = 0.10$). Nonetheless, a résumé and accompanying cover letter remain the primary means by which most job applicants introduce themselves to an employer and they are usually required before a person can receive serious consideration. Also, the relatively low predictive validities associated with the résumé information are not especially problematic as this typically represents only the initial stage of a more complete selection process.

REFERENCE CHECKS

Applicants are often asked to provide supporting references, including past or present colleagues and supervisors, who may be asked to verify information or comment on the candidate's traits, characteristics, and behaviours. A **reference check** can be distinguished from employment verification, wherein the focus is on the accuracy of the job history information provided by the applicant (in the application, résumé, or verbally), including matters such as dates, salary, and job title.

Reference check
Information gathered about a job candidate from supervisors, coworkers, clients, or other people named as references by the candidate. The information is usually collected from the written references and/or from contacts over the phone.

Since reference checks are typically collected only for applicants who make it through earlier stages of screening, they tend to be conducted near the end of the screening process. This minimizes the time and costs and protects the confidentiality of candidates who prefer that their current employer is kept unaware of their job search. Although applicants implicitly grant their permission to contact those listed as references, the prospective employer should explicitly (in writing) secure such permission. Web-based tools are beginning to appear that make it easier for employers to obtain standardized references from multiple sources in a timely manner.[116] Whether obtained on the phone or in writing, the credibility of the reference will, of course, likely vary with the length of tenure and the degree of direct contact the parties had in the employment relationship; and also with the extent to which the work completed in the past is similar to the target job.[117]

PHONE-BASED REFERENCE CHECKS

Many employers are reluctant to give references in writing, preferring instead to provide them over the phone. As part of the late stages of the screening process, many employers directly contact those who have provided the written references. Since prospective employers should not be considering age, race, sex, family status, and disability (among other protected classifications) in their decisions, information concerning these matters should not be sought in reference checking. Further, a standard list of questions should be followed to help ensure the same information is collected concerning all the candidates for a given position. Care should be taken to use questions that yield as much objective information as possible, while minimizing the need for the contact to make undue judgments and inferences. Typical questions include:

- How long, and in what capacity, have you known the applicant?
- What sort of employee is the applicant?
- Does the applicant show initiative? If so, how?
- How did the applicant get along with other employees, supervisors, and clients?

- Did the applicant meet deadlines? Get work done on time?
- Was the applicant punctual? Were there attendance problems?
- Were you satisfied with the applicant's performance; if your worst employee is given a rating of 1 and your best a rating of 10, what rating would this candidate receive?
- Why did the applicant leave your company (if applicable)?
- Is there anything you feel I should know about this candidate?
- Would you rehire the applicant?

A reference check conducted over the phone provides an ideal opportunity to obtain confirmation of information provided by candidates that the prospective employer deems to be especially important. References should also be probed for more information when their answers sound overly qualified or overly general in nature. Ask for specifics that include behaviorial examples–for example, "Describe a situation in which the candidate performed exceptionally well or exceptionally poorly." Many of the techniques discussed in Chapter 9 for developing structured, behaviour-based interview questions can and should be adapted for use in reference checks. As is the case with interviewing for selection, the use of job-related, behaviour-based questions is likely to increase the meaningfulness and appropriateness of information obtained through the reference check.

Standardized, targeted questions aside, it is not a simple matter to use reference checks with previous employers to screen out applicants who lack work records because there is a hesitancy to make strong, negative statements about current or former employees. Consider the following situation:

> *You receive a call concerning an unproductive employee who has applied for a job with another company. You want to be honest and helpful, yet you do not want to say anything that will discourage another organization from taking a relatively poor employee off your hands; accordingly, you are truthful, but do not volunteer negative information. Nonetheless, you are aware that if you are specifically asked about problem behaviours and you intentionally mislead the caller, or cover up the problems, you could be liable for economic losses or hardship suffered attributable to the hiring of this employee.*[118,119]

To avoid the types of issues reflected in the above example, it is not uncommon for employers to have a policy of verifying name, position, and length of service only when speaking to others about former employees.[120,121] On the other hand, this could be unfair to people with favourable performance records and, in the case of problematic employees, could result in harm to the future employer. Moreover, the failure to give a deserved favourable reference can present legal problems for Canadian employers if it is seen as having impeded a job search. For example, in a precedent-setting case in 1977, the Supreme Court of Canada ruled that employers have an obligation to act in good faith when an employee is terminated: Jack Wallace, the plaintiff, was awarded 24 months of salary when it was found that his former employer, United Grain Growers, neglected to provide a reference letter within the timeframe required for him to secure a new job.[122] Court awards such as this suggest that employers should provide honest written and oral references for their former employees.

Although the legal risks associated with providing references are real, as a practical matter in Canada it is extremely difficult for a former employee to win a suit for libel or slander due to a poor reference, even if it contains some inaccuracies. Specially, the

Canadian courts have endowed employment reference providers with the protection of the law of "qualified privilege," such that employers cannot be sued if the comments are "honestly made." Thus, the former employee would have to prove that the referee did not believe the facts as asserted (e.g., that she *knowingly* fabricated information, acted maliciously, or in bad faith).[123]

While it is unlikely that Canadian employers will be sued for honestly providing unfavourable references, they are quite vulnerable in cases where they knowingly hold back unfavourable information, especially if the former employee subsequently causes harm to the new employer or its clientele. Under these circumstances, the new employer could sue for damages for "negligent misrepresentation."[124] The intent is to prevent cases like the one in the U.S. involving Charles Cullen, a nurse, who for 16 years was able to move from hospital to hospital, intentionally killing patients at each facility. Although Cullen had been under investigation in seven hospitals and been fired or forced to resign in several of them, none of these institutions provided a bad reference.[125]

NEGLIGENT HIRING

Employers can be held legally liable if an employee causes harm to other employees or to clientele if it is found that pre-hire references were not adequately reviewed. Circumstances of this type are referred to as negligent hiring–"where an employer places an unfit or unqualified person in an employment situation which puts others at an unreasonable risk of harm. Establishing liability for negligent hiring stems primarily from whether the employer *knew or should have known* that the employee was unfit for the job at the time of hiring."[126] Guidelines for avoiding negligent hiring are provided in Recruitment and Selection Notebook 7.3.

RECRUITMENT AND SELECTION NOTEBOOK 7.3

GUIDELINES FOR AVOIDING NEGLIGENT HIRING

Yosie Saint-Cyr provides the following guidelines to employers on ways to avoid negligent hiring.[127]

- Train staff on selection and hiring, and implement a hiring and reference check policy.
- Require applicants to sign an authorization form giving you the right to contact and check references. To encourage previous employers to provide complete references, consider requiring job applicants to sign a release and provide it to the prior employer.
- Conduct reference checks in keeping with employment and human rights legislation. Canadian human rights legislation recommends that background checks only be conducted after the applicant has been given a conditional offer of employment, to help ensure that the reference is not given undue weight and to protect the employer against complaints from unsuccessful candidates.
- Don't merely ask for references, actually check all of them thoroughly and document the outcomes in employee files.
- Certain positions may require checking additional sources, e.g., employers should check the driving records of prospective delivery persons. Some occupations are governed by statute or professional standards requiring more extensive background checks. Positions in sensitive occupations, such as banking or health care, may require checks of potential employee credit and/or criminal histories.
- Question applicants about any gaps in employment history, they may for example, reflect prison for violent crime.

- Ask former employers about the applicant's reliability, honesty, and tendencies toward anger or violence. Even if these questions go unanswered the attempt will help in a defence against negligent hiring claims, since it will be hard to prove the employer "knew or should have known" the employee's unfitness at the time of hiring, when you sought the information but [were] refused an answer.
- Use an employment application that advises applicants that the discovery of an omission, misrepresentation, or falsification of information will result in rejection of the application or subsequent termination of employment.
- Establish a policy manual and employee handbook, including a disciplinary policy and procedure section for any violation of any policy; outline your disciplinary actions and follow them as needed.
- In an employee's file, document each and every time they are disciplined.
- Conduct formal performance reviews on an annual basis, more frequently as needed, and document the outcomes. Do not retain incompetent employees. Deal with noticeable problems immediately. Discipline, re-train, demote, reassign, or replace them. Liability for negligent retention—retaining an employee after the employer became aware of the employee's unsuitability, thereby failing to act on that knowledge—is a valid legal concept.
- Do not be negligent in your supervision of employees. Negligent supervision results in failing to provide the necessary monitoring to ensure that employees perform their duties properly.
- Apply adequate, sufficient, effective, and consistent security. Inadequate security is inconsistent with potential threat(s) to employees, customers and members of the public.
- If you outsource reference checking to a third party carefully review their services for quality and completeness. Ensure they comply with all applicable rules and legislation. Companies that go directly to the source, i.e., courthouse, educational institutions, former employers, and credit bureaus are more reliable than those who rely on a stored database that may be outdated.

Source: Saint-Cyr, Y. (2007). Negligent Hiring-How it affects the employer. HRinfodesk: *Canadian Payroll and Employment Law at Work.* http://www.hrinfodesk.com/preview.asp?article=7961

PREDICTIVE VALIDITY OF REFERENCES

Written references obtained from past supervisors have a low to moderate association with job performance ratings of new hires.[128,129] The mean corrected validity coefficient against job performance criteria is 0.23, while incremental validity beyond general mental ability alone is 0.12.[130] The range of validity coefficients for personal references ranges from a low of 0.16 for promotion criteria to a high of 0.26 for supervisor rating criteria.[131] Thus, predictive validity of written references is low relative to both biodata and many of the employment test alternatives discussed in Chapter 8. Accordingly, references and reference checks should be used only to screen out especially weak or potentially problematic candidates, not for final *hiring* decisions.[132,133]

REASONS FOR POOR VALIDITY OF REFERENCES

In accounting for the relatively low validity of personal references, it is important to note that it is highly unlikely an applicant would knowingly offer the name of someone who would provide a bad reference. In fact, before listing someone as a reference, applicants should consider asking the person involved if the reference would be a positive one. In any case, the tendency of references to be uniformly positive limits their usefulness in discriminating among candidates and explains why mention of the slightest negative in a reference eliminates an applicant from further consideration.[134] Thus, range restriction as discussed in Chapter 2 is in play, contributing to low validity.

One way to improve the predictive validity of reference information is to use standardized reference forms. For example, the *relative percentile method* requires references to indicate the relative standing of candidates on a 100-point scale and has shown predictive validity on 520 recruits for the Canadian military.[135]

BACKGROUND CHECKS

Background checks are conducted to obtain confirming evidence concerning information obtained from the applicant's BIB, résumé, or interview, which are more comprehensive and in-depth than a typical phone reference. Especially thorough background checks, reserved for sensitive government positions, security-related jobs such as the RCMP, and top-level managerial appointments, are sometimes referred to as field investigations. Given the time-consuming nature and possible legal sensitivities, background checks and field investigations are typically contracted out to specialists.

One type of information often sought as part of a background check concerns the credit status of the applicant. In 2010, 60 percent of respondents to an employer survey indicated that they conducted background credit checks on some or all job candidates. The commonly held assumption is that those with more favourable credit scores are more conscientious, are higher in integrity, and are less likely to engage in deviant behaviour. Indeed, there is evidence that conscientiousness positively predicts credit score ratings, which in turn positively predicts both task performance and organizational citizenship.[136] Surprisingly, agreeableness (reflecting a preference to avoid conflict and a desire for others to like them) related negatively to credit scores, which did not predict workplace deviance. While there are few studies supporting the validity of the practice, credit score information will likely continue being used for screening, especially for positions that provide access to large sums of money and/or for jobs likely to attract bribes. Still, caution is warranted since using credit scores in screening is likely to adversely impact certain protected minority groups,[137] which could bring in legal challenge.[138]

Common résumé misrepresentations uncovered through background checks include listing family members as former supervisors; gaps in employment; errors concerning start and end dates; false academic credentials; and incorrect job titles.[139] Among 2.6 million background checks conducted in 2001, ADP Screening and Selection Services (https://www.adpselect.com) found that 44 percent of applicants lied about their work histories, 41 percent lied about their education, and 23 percent falsified credentials or licences.[140] Thus, employers who do not conduct background checks are at risk for negligent hiring. The Public Service Commission of Canada provides guidelines for conducting a thorough, legally defensible reference check: see http://www.psc-cfp.gc.ca/plcy-pltq/guides/checking-verification/index-eng.htm#app1. A "how-to guide for employers" to comply with background reference check rules for all Canadian jurisdictions (updated 2013) is available at http://www.firstreference.com/guides/RefCheck-sample.pdf.

enterlinedesign/Shutterstock.com

WORK EXPERIENCE

In screening applicants using résumés, preliminary interviews, or reference checks the emphasis is on formal credentials, including formal training (e.g., licence, diploma, or degree) and work experience. Since most jobs involve a given level of education and/or formal training among the MQs, some applicants are easily and appropriately screened out on this basis. Unfortunately, judgments concerning work experience are typically less straightforward.

Work experience refers to the applicant's past employment, which can be evaluated for its relatedness to the target position using a wide variety of dimensions including its length, the number of employers and contexts involved, and of course the number and type of tasks performed.[141,142,143]

For many jobs, there are important *quantitative* indicators of the work experience. In evaluating the past employment of a car salesperson, for example, length of time, types of dealerships worked for, number of vehicles sold, and annual dollar sales would be important considerations.

While the quantitative aspects noted above are important, they might be misleading without also considering a variety of *qualitative* factors concerning, for example, the level, diversity, and complexity of the job. Continuing with car sales, there can be variation in (a) the level of autonomy provided agents in negotiating with customers; (b) the number and complexity of models for sale; (c) the level of staff assistance provided; and (d) the extent to which technology was available and used. The demographics of the target market (e.g., age, gender, ethnicity, socio-economic status) is another important aspect in evaluating the qualitative aspect of work experience. Qualitative assessments are typically made during a screening interview, though they can also be inferred to some degree from résumé content.

Accurate evaluation of work experience becomes more complex, but even more crucial, as the level and responsibilities associated with the position increase. Research has shown that the nature of experience accumulated by executives across roles, responsibilities, and work activities, combined with measures of their cognitive ability, proved highly predictive of their competency in strategic thinking.[144]

False negatives can occur in screening if the focus is on years of experience only. Two applicants with equal job and organizational tenure can differ greatly in the level of challenge and complexity they encountered in their task assignments.[145] Accordingly, screening interviews and reference checks should include some qualitative probing, for example with behavioural questions (see Chapter 9). Evaluation of work experience should align not only with that aspect of performance you wish to predict, but also with the context of the new work environment within which the successful applicant will be placed. For example, a highly regarded long-tenured employee, working mostly alone and independently in a static environment with a high level of hierarchical control, may not perform as well under the same job title in a team-based, profit-sharing, dynamic environment where empowerment is emphasized. Contextual elements such as these can be easily missed in standard job descriptions, though they should be accounted for in recruiting, screening, selection, and development.

PREDICTIVE VALIDITY OF WORK EXPERIENCE

Job tenure–the most widely used measure of experience–relates positively to job performance because it is usually a quantitative reflection of increased job knowledge and skill competency.[146,147] For example, the length of time spent as an engine mechanic was predictive of performance on three different sets of job-related tasks.[148] More broadly, the validity coefficients involving work experience (defined in terms of job tenure) predicted job performance in the range of 0.18 to 0.32.[149,150,151] The relationship is higher ($r = 0.41$) when work experience is defined at the task (versus job) level (e.g., "number of times performing a task" or "level of task") and with regard to performance measure type (e.g., standardized work samples $r = .39$ or supervisory ratings, $r = .24$).[152]

Besides its association with formally defined performance aspects of target jobs,[153] work experience, defined by organizational tenure, associates positively with organizational citizenship–that is, performance-related behaviours that are not formally required, but promote the smooth functioning of a unit (e.g., helping coworkers). These relationships endured when chronological age was controlled. Moreover, the positive tenure–performance associations were higher for certain demographics, such as younger workers, including those of college age, women, and non-Caucasians. On the other hand, though the relationship between organizational tenure and job performance is positive in general, its *strength* decreases as tenure increases. That is, the performance-enhancing benefits of increasing organizational tenure, while remaining positive, appear to diminish over time.[154] Finally, tenure with the organization is positively associated with some negative behaviours as well, such as non-sickness absences.[155]

Since most of the findings cited above are based on studies of employees at the same organization, much less is known about the degree to which experience in the same industry or occupation transfers *between* organizations. Most of the research that has been conducted suggests that the experience–performance relationship is more complex than originally thought, such that work experience is associated with both potential benefits and potential costs to prospective employers.[156] Specifically, task-relevant work experiences enhance task-relevant knowledge and skills which, in turn, positively predict effectiveness in similar tasks performed with a new employer. However, when the knowledge and skill advantage is controlled for, work experience relates *negatively* to performance. This may reflect experienced workers bringing into their new work environments old habits and established ways of doing things that often prove less effective in their new organization. Such negative effects, however, were weaker among new hires who were rated as adaptable by their supervisors, and for employees who indicated that they were an especially "good fit" with their new employer. Overall, then, the positive effects of prior work experience are realized through acquiring task-relevant knowledge and skills, which enhance performance of similar tasks with a new employer. This advantage can compensate for the negative effects of work experience grounded in the bad habits or rigidities employees may bring from their past employment. Accordingly, it appears that employers can enhance the organizational benefits of hiring experienced workers by selecting the most adaptive among them, while ensuring their past work experiences fit with their new workplace environment. This can be facilitated through well designed and executed selection, orientation, and mentorship programs.

SOCIAL MEDIA NETWORKS

As use of social networking (e.g., Facebook, Twitter, MySpace, and LinkedIn) has grown, employers are accessing these sites, mostly during the screening process,[157] for information concerning the social, political, and leisure activities of applicants.[158] For example, 45 percent of hiring managers in the U.S. indicated that they searched social network sites (SNSs) for information on job applicants; moreover, 35 percent of this same group made a decision "not to hire" based on this information.[159] Similarly, a 2013 CareerBuilder survey conducted online in Canada and the United States (involving polling 5518 job seekers and 2775 hiring managers) revealed that 44 percent of the respondents reviewed applicant profiles on Facebook, while 27 percent monitored Twitter accounts.[160] Of the employers that screened applicants online, 65 percent were interested in the professionalism of the candidate; 51 percent were assessing cultural fit; 45 percent were looking for information concerning qualifications; and 12 percent were looking for a reason *not* to hire.[161]

Caveats associated with using SNSs for screening are that (a) the available information typically varies across candidates, such that any review is necessarily incomplete and unstandardized; (b) the available information was not created for the purposes of employer screening or selection and is therefore likely of questionable job relevance; (c) information that is discovered on race/ethnicity, gender, national origin, religion, marital status, pregnancy status, union membership, political affiliation, or disability status could inappropriately be used in screening and hiring decisions, leaving the employer vulnerable to legal liabilities; (d) a statistically meaningful relationship between SNS-based content and performance in an employment context has yet to be demonstrated; (e) a large segment of the population (i.e., potential applicant pools) do not use SNSs (e.g., those lacking ready access to a computer), and therefore may be subject to an inappropriate disadvantage; and (f) employers alienate desirable candidates who object to companies accessing their sites (i.e., perceived invasion of privacy).[162] Finally, the job-relatedness of SNS content can be compromised when people present "digital personas" that do not align with their true character (i.e., impression managing through their SNS).

In all, reliance on SNSs for candidate screening, especially relative to known effective alternatives, could easily result in erroneous judgments, abetted by the subjective, nonstandardized, nonstructured nature of cyber-profiling. In any case, applicants must be sensitive to the information they make accessible on SNSs. There are websites, such as www.reputation.com, that scour the Internet for information related to one's public profile, which can be used to help manage online reputation.

Since use of SNS for screening is relatively recent, there have been few formal evaluations of the outcomes. When self-report measures of personality were compared to the rating others provided these same individuals based on them evaluating Facebook pages, the judgments were only modestly related, ranging from 0.3 to 0.5. However, even these modest correlations were obtained through aggregating across multiple judges, who were provided with clear definitions of each trait. In practice, of course, recruiters would typically be making their judgments without the benefit of carefully developed and shared definitions of the traits evaluated.[163] In another more promising study, the average overall "hirability" rating collected from multiple raters of individuals' Facebook pages correlated 0.28 with job performance ratings.[164] Unfortunately, the sample size was small (N=56) and the hypothetical position on which raters based their evaluations was distinctly different from the jobs the people being evaluated were actually performing. Physical attractiveness conveyed through personal pictures on SNSs has also been shown to positively influence hiring decisions.[165]

The opening vignette to Chapter 5 presented one of the most rigorously designed and executed studies on the relationship between SNS evaluations and job performance at the time of this writing. Recruiters from several employers rated information obtained from the Facebook profiles of 416 college students who were applying for full-time jobs.[166] When these evaluations were compared with supervisory ratings of performance obtained after the students had obtained jobs, there was no relationship between the two. Moreover, the Facebook ratings favoured female and Caucasian applicants over male and non-Caucasians, raising litigation concerns.[167]

In addition to the early indications of poor predictive validity and adverse impact associated with SNS-collected information when used for screening and selection, there are legislative actions that limit using SNS for employment screening. For example, as reported in the Huffington Post,[168] Maryland passed the "Password Protection Act," prohibiting employers form asking job candidates to provide them with usernames or passwords to their Facebook and other SNS accounts.

In Canada, the Information Privacy Commission of Ontario has published "Reference Check: Is Your Boss Watching? Privacy and Your Facebook Profile" (2012), containing guidelines for protecting one's SNS presence from abuse by employers (see http://www.ipc.on.ca/images/Resources/facebook-refcheck-e.pdf). At the federal level, the Privacy Commissioner of Canada issued the Personal Information Protection and Electronic Documents Act (PIPEDA), which provides rules governing how "private sector organizations can collect, use, or disclose personal information in the course of commercial activities." It states that if organizations wish to collect, use, or disclose information about you, personal consent is required. Even where consent is given, the organization must disclose the purpose for which the personal information is being used, and *how* it is being used. Further, you, as the targeted individual, have the right to see what personal information is being used and must be given the opportunity to correct misinformation. The document is available at: http://www.priv.gc.ca/resource/fs-fi/02_05_d_16_e.asp.

Clearly, organizations are being discouraged from using SNSs as part of their recruitment or selection processes, and applicants need not oblige employers that ask for access to their sites. If SNS-sourced information is eventually found to be helpful for employment screening, it is more likely to come from more structured sites, such as LinkedIn, which is intended to facilitate employment networking opportunities.[169]

Notwithstanding the above-noted limitations and caveats, and the availability of more effective and legally defensible alternatives, the Chartered Institute of Professional Development (CIPD) offers guidelines for how recruiters can avoid litigation should they insist on using SNSs for recruitment and selection (http://www.cipd.co.uk/hr-resources/guides/pre-employment-checks.aspx).

VIRTUAL CAREER FAIRS

Employers are increasingly turning to electronically administered career fairs to recruit and screen job candidates. Digital career fairs electronically match position openings to posted candidate profiles. Chat lines are often available to allow employers to share information about the hiring process and the company; any interested candidate can view the content and post follow-up questions. Within this infrastructure, separate and private one-to-one exchanges can be arranged online, to allow for further screening prior to any arranged in-person interviews. Indeed, many colleges and universities have adopted this relatively new technology-enabled platform as it efficiently and effectively services recruiter and applicant needs. See http://blogs.wsj.com/atwork/2014/04/03/so-long-interview-suit-here-comes-the-virtual-career-fair.

VIRTUAL JOB AUDITIONS

Another relatively recent development involving the application of technology to the screening process involves Select International (http://www.selectinternational.com)

and Toyota Motor Engineering and Manufacturing of North America, who partnered to develop and use virtual job auditions.[170] Specifically, applicants for assembly positions at the Toyota Tundra plant in San Antonio, Texas are required to participate in an online work simulation requiring, for example, that candidates read dials and gauges, spot safety problems, and interactively engage in general problem-solving activities. Candidates passing this virtual simulation get invited to a hands-on tryout, involving the lifting of 23-kilogram car parts, bolting nuts with an airgun, and spray-painting vehicles. It is likely that the use of virtual reality technology in employee screening, selection, and development will grow exponentially over the next few years as the depth and richness of the software applications continue to improve and the cost declines.

// SUMMARY

Organizations should be staffed with people capable of performing their assigned jobs well. The primary role of recruiting is to secure an adequate supply of job applicants, while screening identifies and eliminates applicants lacking minimal qualifications. The remaining applicants are then referred for additional assessments involving tools that are relatively more time consuming and costly.

Effective screening tools are: (a) grounded in organization and job analysis, (b) relatively inexpensive to use; (c) predictive of job-relevant criteria, (d) legally defensible, and (e) perceived as acceptable (fair) by job candidates.

Information used for screening can be collected from various sources, including application forms, biographical information blanks, résumés, reference and/or background checks, and the analysis of past work experience. Reliable, valid screening systems are rooted in job-relevant past behaviours, interests, and experiences being predictive of future performance criteria.

Professionally developed BIBs are among the most effective screening options, but they are typically applicable only in situations where there are large numbers of applicants and a large number of similar positions to be filled. Careful, critical analysis of the amount and type of past work experience is also among the more effective screening tools. Reference checks are among the least effective options in that they are useful only for screening out the most undesirable candidates.

Advancements in technology have resulted in some relatively new screening options. Some employers now review social networking sites for information they perceive as useful, but research suggests that these reviews are unrelated to future job performance. This is not especially surprising since most social networking sites are not intended for job screening purposes. More promising technology-enabled screening tools include virtual career fairs and virtual job auditions.

KEY TERMS

Application blank, p. 285
Biodata, p. 291
Biographical information blank (BIB), p. 289
Criterion measures, p. 288

Designated targeted groups, p. 284
False negatives, p. 285
False positives, p. 284
Minimum qualifications (MQ), p. 284
Reference check, p. 303
Screening, p. 284
Selection ratio, p. 284
Validity coefficient, p. 294
Weighted application blank (WAB), p. 288

WEB LINKS

To view updated news releases and a list of publications of the Canadian Human Rights Commission, visit
http://www.chrc-ccdp.ca

A useful source of information about human rights cases and legal guidelines for recruitment, screening, and assessment is the *Canadian Human Rights Reporter* at
http://www.cdn-hr-reporter.ca

Visit Internet-based recruitment and applicant screening service provider HRsoft at
http://www.hrsoft.com

For examples of firms that provide applicant background checks, go to
https://www.csiscreening.com and http://www.infocubic.net

To view examples of sites for creating, posting, and/or viewing video résumés, visit Video Advantage and Devon James Associates at
http://www.videoadvantage.ca and http://www.devonjames.com

DISCUSSION QUESTIONS

1. What are the differences between employee screening and selection?
2. What are the advantages and disadvantages of using the following screening devices?
   a. biographical data
   b. application forms
   c. résumés
   d. background reference checks
3. What is negligent hiring? Provide an example. What can employers do to guard against this?
4. How best can an employer avoid legal challenges arising against its use of screening procedures?
5. Describe an effective screening program that you could use to deal with a large number (over 1000) of job applications for the position of public bus operator.
6. What are applicant behaviours that give rise to positive (or negative) employer impressions of job applicants?

EXERCISES

1. Prepare your own personal résumé using the résumé presented in this chapter as a model. Exchange your résumé with one of your classmates. Critique each other's document in terms of organization, clarity of information, style, and presentation. Write a short paragraph describing the impressions you formed from reading your classmate's résumé.
2. Develop a set of questions based on the security dispatcher's job description that can be used to screen applicants for that position.
3. Suppose that you are managing a Swiss Chalet franchise and need to recruit table servers for your store. List in priority order the three things you would be most inclined to screen for, how you would do the screening, and provide a rationale for each.
4. In reference to Exercise 3 above, develop a set of three questions that could be useful in your background reference checks on applicants for the Swiss Chalet table server position and explain their use.
5. Think of the key activities of a job that you have held (part-time or full-time). From these key activities, list biodata items that could be helpful in predicting success in this job. A brief rationale should accompany each item. Develop a one-page biodata questionnaire by phrasing each item in question format.
6. With respect to the vignette that opens this chapter, Glen, the HR director, has recommended a number of interventions concerning recruitment, screening, selection, and retention. Drawing on your reading of the current chapter, recommend specific procedures/tools likely to be effective in these areas and argue your case. In forming your recommendations, be sure to consider the different jobs involved (i.e., store manager versus salespeople), the implications of LHI's growth, and the degree to which various decisions should be made at the store level and at the company level.

CASE

ABC Glass, a Canadian-based manufacturer of glass with a dominant share of the international market, seeks to fill a newly created position of "director of communications." This person will be responsible for both internal and external communications of the company, including writing corporate newsletters, communicating with the press in a public relations function, coaching senior officers on ways to improve their presentation skills, communicating orally and in writing the corporate directions (mission statements) and policies to employees, and soliciting news from employees for reporting in corporate newsletters to enhance cohesiveness and morale following the merger of French- and English-speaking companies. The president of the merged company has hired you to recruit and screen for this position, referring to him the top three candidates. He, along with the HR director, will select their top candidate from among these three, using one or more focused assessments. The position requirements for this appointment, developed from the job analysis workshop, include:

- fluency in both written and spoken French and English;
- excellent oral and written communication skills;
- ability to manage interpersonal conflict;
- ability to work under tight timelines, with multiple conflicting demands;

- ability to plan and organize;
- ability to remain calm when demands considered unreasonable are being made by one's boss;
- ability to solicit information and cooperation from others and overcome personal obstacles;
- ability to extract relevant information from an abundance of reports and summarize it;
- ability to present relatively difficult material in an easily understandable way;
- ability to provide effective coaching to senior officers for improving their presentation skills;
- ability to motivate others to embrace and execute corporate policies; and
- willingness to "go above and beyond the call of duty."

The president has contracted you to (1) establish a recruitment plan, specifying the specific recruitment outlets; (2) propose a screening strategy, outlining each stage of screening and the tools to be used; (3) describe a post-screening selection assessment; and (4) speak to the merits of your proposal. Finally, develop biodata items that are likely to be useful for screening for this position and provide your rationale for each. (Of course, before using such items, you would need to determine empirically whether they are appropriate.)

QUESTIONS

1. Should background checks be mandatory for all jobs or only for certain jobs? Explain your reasoning.
2. Describe a procedure that could be used for doing background checks in a tight labour market.
3. Should background checks be made before a candidate receives a job offer? If so, how do you avoid obtaining information that may be used to discriminate against the candidate (see Table 3.1).
4. How can the Internet be used to do background checks and to speed up the process? Are there any risks in this process?
5. Explain why background checks may be an invasion of a job applicant's right to privacy.
6. If you discover that a job applicant has a criminal record, can you disqualify the candidate solely on that ground and without fear of violating the candidate's human rights?
7. What is the value of a degree from a prestigious university on a résumé? Would such a degree influence your hiring decision if everything else were equal among candidates? Should it? Why or why not?
8. What should you do if you discover someone has fudged her application form information or résumé or lied during the screening interview? Does it matter how big the lie is? Explain and argue your case.

// ENDNOTES

1 Anastasi, A. 1988. *Psychological Testing*. 6th ed. New York: Macmillan.

2 Levine, E.L., D.M. Maye, A. Ulm, and T.R. Gordon. 1997. "A Methodology for Developing and Validating Minimum Qualifications (MQs)." *Personnel Psychology* 50: 1009–23.

3 Ibid.

4 Kethley, B.R., and D.E. Terpstra. 2005. "An Analysis of Litigation Associated with Use of the Application Form in the Selection Process." *Public Personnel Management* 34 (4): 357–76.

5 Wallace, C.J., and S.J. Vodanovich. 2004. "Personnel Application Blanks: Persistence and Knowledge of Legally Inadvisable Application Blank Items." *Public Personnel Management* 33(3): 331–49.

6 Wallace, C.J., E.E. Page, and M. Lippstreu. 2006. "Applicant Reactions to Pre-Employment Application Blanks: A Legal and Procedural Justice Perspective." *Journal of Business and Psychology* 20(4): 467–88.

7 Saks, A.M., J.D. Leck, and D.M. Saunders. 1995. "Effects of Application Blanks and Employment Equity on Applicant Reactions and Job Pursuit Intentions." *Journal of Organizational Behavior* 16: 415–30.

8 Winstein, K.J., and D. Golden. 2007. "MIT Admissions Dean Lied on Résumé in 1979, Quits." *Wall Street Journal* (Eastern edition) (April 27): B1.

9 Solomon, B., 1998. "Too Good to Be True?" *Management Review* 87(4) (April): 27.

10 Owens, W.A. 1976. "Biographical Data." In M.D. Dunnette, ed., *Handbook of Industrial and Organizational Psychology,* 1st ed. (pp. 609–50). Chicago: Rand-McNally.

11 Telenson, P.A., R.A. Alexander, and G.V. Barrett. 1983. "Scoring the Biographical Information Blank: A Comparison of Three Weighting Techniques." *Applied Psychological Measurement* 7: 73–80.

12 Hogan, J.B. 1994. "Empirical Keying of Background Data Measures." In G.A. Stokes, M.D. Mumford, and W.A. Owens, eds., *Biodata Handbook* (pp. 109–107). Palo Alto, CA: Consulting Psychologists Press.

13 La Lopa, J.M., J. Beck, and R. Ghiselli. 2009. "The Role of Biodata and Career Anchors on Turnover Intentions among Hospitality and Tourism Educators." *Journal of Culinary Science and Technology* 7(2): 196–206.

14 Kaak, S.R., H.S. Feild, W.F. Giles, and D.R. Norris. 1998. "The Weighted Application Blank: A Cost Effective Tool That Can Reduce Employee Turnover." *Cornell Hotel and Restaurant Administration Quarterly* 39: 18.

15 Lee, R., and J.M. Booth. 1974. "A Utility Analysis of a Weighted Application Blank Designed to Predict Turnover for Clerical Employees." *Journal of Applied Psychology* 59: 516–18.

16 Ghiselli, E.E. 1966. *The Validity of Occupational Aptitude Tests*. New York: Wiley.

17 Rothstein, H.R., F.L. Schmidt, F.W. Erwin, W.A. Owens, and C.P. Sparks. 1990. "Biographical Data in Employment Selection: Can Validities Be Made Generalizable?" *Journal of Applied Psychology* 75: 175–84.

18 Mitchell, T.W., and R.J. Klimoski. 1982. "Is It Rational to Be Empirical? A Test of Methods for Scoring Biographical Data." *Journal of Applied Psychology* 67: 411–18.

19 Guion, R.M. 1998. *Assessment, Measurement and Prediction for Personnel Decisions*. London: Lawrence Erlbaum Associates.

20 Barrick, M.R., and R.D. Zimmerman. 2005. "Reducing Voluntary, Avoidable Turnover through Selection." *Journal of Applied Psychology* 90: 159–66.

21 Cucina, J.M., P.M. Caputo, H.F. Thibodeaux, C.N. MacLane, and J.M. Bayless. 2013. "Scoring Biodata: Is It Rational to Be Quasi-Rational?" *International Journal of Selection and Assessment* 21(2): 226–232.

22 England, G.W. 1971. *Development and Use of Weighted Application Blanks*, rev. ed. Minneapolis: University of Minnesota Industrial Relations Center.

23 Gatewood, R.D., H.S. Field, and B. Murray. 2008. *Human Resource Selection*. 6th ed. Mason, Ohio: Thomson/South-Western

24 Owens, W.A., and L.F. Schoenfeldt. 1979. "Toward a Classification of Persons." *Journal of Applied Psychology* 65: 569–607.

25 Owens, W.A. 1976.

26 McManus, M.A., and M.L. Kelly. 1999. "Personality Measures and Biodata: Evidence Regarding Their Incremental Predictive Value in the Life Insurance Industry." *Personnel Psychology* 52(1): 137–48.

27 Owens, W.A. 1976.

28 Klimoski, R.J. 1993. "Predictor Constructs and Their Measurement." In N. Schmitt and W.C. Borman, eds., *Personnel Selection in Organizations*. San Francisco: Jossey-Bass, 99–134.

29 Owens, W.A. 1976.

30 Rynes, S.L. 1993. "Who's Selecting Whom? Effects of Selection Practices on Applicant Attitudes and Behavior." In N. Schmitt et al., eds., *Personnel Selection in Organizations* San Francisco, CA: Jossey-Bass, 240–74.

31 Sisco, H., and R.R. Reilly. 2007. "Development and Validation of a Biodata Inventory as an Alternative Method to Measurement of the Five Factor Model of Personality." *The Social Science Journal* 44: 383–89.

32 Mael, F.A., M. Connerley, and R.A. Morath. 1996. "None of Your Business: Parameters of Biodata Invasiveness." *Personnel Psychology* 49: 613–50.

33 *State of Connecticut v. Teal*. 457 U.S. 440, 1981.

34 Imus, A., N. Schmitt, B. Kim, F.L. Oswald, S. Merritt, and A.F. Wrestring. 2011. "Differential Item Functioning in Biodata: Opportunity Access as an Explanation of Gender- and Race-Related DIF." *Applied Measurement in Education* 24(1): 71–94.

35 Dean, M.A. 2013. "Examination of Ethnic Group Differential Responding on a Biodata Instrument." *Journal of Applied Social Psychology* 43(9): 1905–1917.

36 Mitchell, T.W. 1994. "The Utility of Biodata." In Garnett S. Stokes, Michael D. Mumford, and William A. Owens, eds., *Biodata Handbook* (pp. 492–93). Palo Alto, CA: CPP Books.

37 McManus, M.A., and M.L. Kelly. 2006. "Personality Measures and Biodata: Evidence Regarding Their Incremental Predictive Value in the Life Insurance Industry." *Personnel Psychology* 52(1): 137–48.

38 McManus, M.A., and S.H. Brown. 2006. "Adjusting Sales Results Measures for Use as Criteria." *Personnel Psychology* 48(2): 391–400.

39 Saks, A.M., J.D. Leck, and D.M. Saunders. 1995.

40 Mael, F.A., M. Connerley, and R.A. Morath. 1996.

41 Elkins, T.J., and J.S. Phillips. 2000. "Job Context, Selection Decision Outcome, and Perceived Fairness of Selection Tests: Biodata as an Illustrative Case." *Journal of Applied Psychology* 85(3): 479–84.

42 Elkins, T.J., and J.S. Phillips. 2000.

43 Mael, F.A., M. Connerley, and R.A. Morath. 1996.

44 Cascio, W.F. 1975. "Accuracy of Verifiable Biographical Information Blank Response." *Journal of Applied Psychology* 60: 767–69.

45 Schmitt, N., and C. Kunce. 2002. "The Effects of Required Elaboration of Answers to Biodata Questions." *Personnel Psychology* 55: 569–87.

46 Schmitt, N., F.L. Oswald, B.K. Kim, M.A. Gillespie, L.J. Ramsay, and T. Yoo. 2005. "Impact of Elaboration on Socially Desirable Responding and the Validity of Biodata Measures." *Journal of Applied Psychology* 88: 979–88.

47 Levashina, J., F.P. Morgeson, and M.A. Campion. 2012. "Tell Me Some More: Exploring How Verbal Ability and Item Verifiability Influences Responses to Biodata Questions in a High-Stakes Selection Context." *Personnel Psychology* 65(2): 359–383.

48 Goldstein, I.L. 1971. "The Application Blank: How Honest Are the Responses?" *Journal of Applied Psychology* 71: 3–8.

49 "Looking at Job Applications? Remember–It's Hirer Beware." 1994. *Canadian Banker* 101 (May/June): 10.

50 Donovan, J.J., S.A. Dwight, and G.M. Hurtz. 2003. "An Assessment of the Prevalence, Severity and Verifiability of Entry-Level Applicant Faking Using the Randomized Response Technique." *Human Performance* 16(1): 81–106.

51 Harvey-Cook, J.E., and R.J. Taffler. 2000. "Biodata in Professional Entry-Level Selection: Statistical Scoring of Common Format Applications." *Journal of Occupational and Organizational Psychology* 73(1): 631–64.

52 Donovan, J.J., S.A. Dwight, and G.M. Hurtz. 2003.

53 Hammer, E.G., and L.S. Kleiman. 1988. "Getting to Know You." *Personnel Administrator* 34: 86–92.

54 Terpstra, D.E., and E.J. Rozell. 1993. "The Relationship of Staffing Practices to Organizational Level Measures of Performance." *Personnel Psychology* 46: 27–48.

55 Thacker, J.W., and R.J. Cattaneo. 1992. "Survey of Personnel Practices in Canadian Organizations: A Summary Report to Respondents." Working Paper W92-04, Faculty of Business, University of Windsor.

56 Carlson, K.D., S.E. Scullen, F.L. Schmidt, H. Rothstein, and F. Erwin. 1999. "Generalizable Biographical Data Validity Can Be Achieved Without Multi-Organizational Development and Keying." *Personnel Psychology* 52(3): 731–55.

57 Harvey-Cook, J.E., and R.J. Taffler. 2000.

58 Dalessio, A.T., M.M. Crosby, and M.A. McManus. 1996. "Stability of Biodata Keys and Dimensions across English-Speaking Countries: A Test of the Cross-Situational Hypothesis." *Journal of Business and Psychology* 10(3): 289–96.

59 Breaugh, J.A. 2009. "The Use of Biodata for Employee Selection: Past Research and Future Directions." *Human Resource Management Review* 19: 219–231.

60 Bleisener, T. 1996. "Methodological Moderators in Validating Biographical Data in Personnel Selection." *Journal of Occupational and Organizational Psychology* 69: 107–20.

61 Steinhaus, S.D., and B.K. Waters. 1991. "Biodata and the Application of a Psychometric Perspective." *Military Psychology* 3: 1–23.

62 Mumford, M.D., and W.A. Owens. 1987. "Methodological Review: Principles, Procedures, and Findings in the Application of Background Data Measures." *Applied Psychological Measurement* 11: 1–31.

63 Asher, J.J. 1972. "The Biographical Item: Can It Be Improved?" *Personnel Psychology* 25: 251–69.

64 Ghiselli, E.E. 1966.

65 Hunter, J.E., and R.F. Hunter. 1984. "Validity and Utility of Alternative Predictors of Job Performance." *Psychological Bulletin* 96: 72–98.

66 Maertz, C.P., Jr. 1999. "Biographical Predictors of Turnover among Mexican Workers: An Empirical Study." *International Journal of Management* 16(1): 112–19.

67 Rothstein, H.R., F.L. Schmidt, F.W. Erwin, W.A. Owens, and C.P. Sparks. 1990.

68 Stokes, G.S., and L.A. Cooper. 1994. "Selection Using Biodata: Old Notions Revisited." In G.S. Stokes, M.D. Mumford, and W.A. Owens, eds., *Biodata Handbook*. Mahwah, NJ: Erlbaum, 103–38.

69 Vinchur, A.J., J.S. Schippmann, F.S. Switzer, III, and P.L. Roth. 1998. "A Meta-Analytic Review of Predictors of Job Performance for Salespeople." *Journal of Applied Psychology* 83(4): 586–97.

70 Breaugh, J., J. Labrador, K. Frye, D. Lee, V. Lammers, and J. Cox. 2014. "The Value of Biodata for Selecting Employees: Comparable Results for Job Incumbent and Job Applicant Samples?" *Journal of Organizational Psychology* 14(1): 40–51.

71 Becton, J.B. 2012. "Using Biodata as a Predictor of Errors, Tardiness, Policy Violations, Overall Job Performance, and Turnover among Nurses." *Journal of Management and Organization* 18(5): 714–727.

72 Rothstein, H.R., F.L. Schmidt, F.W. Erwin, W.A. Owens, and C.P. Sparks. 1990.

73 Breaugh, J., J. Labrador, K. Frye, D. Lee, V. Lammers, and J. Cox. 2014.

74 Reilly, R.R., and G.T. Chao. 1982. "Validity and Fairness of Some Alternative Employee Selection Procedures." *Personnel Psychology* 35: 1–62.

75 Hunter, J.E., and R.F. Hunter. 1984.

76 Schmitt, N., R.Z. Gooding, R.A. Noe, and M. Kirsch. 1984. "Meta-Analysis of Validity Studies Published between 1964 and 1982 and the Investigation of Study Characteristics." *Personnel Psychology* 37: 407–22.

77 Asher, J.J., and J.A. Sciarrino. 1974. "Realistic Work Samples Tests: A Review." *Personnel Psychology* 27: 519–23.

78 Schmidt, F.L., and J.E. Hunter. 1998. "The Validity and Utility of Selection Methods in Personnel Psychology: Practical and Theoretical Implications of 85 years of Research Findings." *Psychological Bulletin* 124: 262–74.

79 Breaugh, J.A. 2009. "The Use of Biodata for Employee Selection: Past Research and Future Directions." *Human Resource Management Review* 19: 209–13.

80 Becton, J.B., M.C. Matthews, D.L. Hartley, and D.H. Whitaker. 2009. "Using Biodata to Predict Turnover, Organizational Commitment, and Job Performance in Healthcare." *International Journal of Selection and Assessment* 17: 189–202.

81 Mount, M.K., L.A. Witt, and M.R. Barrick. 2000. "Variance in Faking across Noncognitive Measures." *Journal of Applied Psychology* 85: 812–21.

82 Allworth, E., and B. Hesketh. 2000. "Job Requirements Biodata as a Predictor of Performance in Customer Service Roles." *International Journal of Selection and Assessment* 8: 137–47.

83 Dean, M.A. 2004. "An Assessment of Biodata Predictive Ability across Multiple Performance Criteria." *Applied H.R.M.* 9: 1–12.

84 Becton, J.B., M.C. Matthews, D.L. Hartley, and D.H. Whitaker. 2009.

85 Becton, J.B., M.C. Matthews, D.L. Hartley, and D.H. Whitaker. 2009.

86 Hough, L.M., F.L. Oswald, and R.E. Ployhart. 2001. "Determinants, Detection and Amelioration of Adverse Impact in Personnel Selection Procedures: Issues, Evidence and Lessons Learned." *International Journal of Selection and Assessment* 9: 152–94.

87 Barrick, M.R., and R.D. Zimmerman. 2005. "Reducing Voluntary, Avoidable Turnover through Selection." *Journal of Applied Psychology* 90: 159–66.

88 Breaugh, J., J. Labrador, K. Frye, D. Lee, V. Lammers, and J. Cox. 2014.

89 Breaugh, J.A. 2009.

90 Schmitt, N., and J. Golubovich. 2013. "Biographical Information." In K.F. Geisinger, B.A. Bracken, J.F. Carlson, J-I Hansen, N.R. Kuncel, S.P. Reise, and M.C. Rodriguez, *APA Handbook of Testing and Assessment in Psychology, Vol. 1: Test Theory and Testing and Assessment in Industrial and Organizational Psychology* (pp. 437–455). Washington, DC: American Psychological Association.

91 England, G.W. 1971.

92 Thoms, P., R. McMasters, M.R. Roberts, and D.A Dombkowski. 1999. "Résumé Characteristics as Predictors of an Invitation to Interview." *Journal of Business and Psychology* 13(3): 339–56.

93 Knouse, S.B. 1994. "Impressions of the Résumé: The Effects of Applicant Education, Experience and Impression Management." *Journal of Business and Psychology* 9: 33–45.

94 Knouse, S.B., R.A. Giacalone, and P. Hinda. 1988. "Impression Management in the Résumé and Its Cover Letter." *Journal of Business and Psychology* 3: 242–49.

95 Cole, M.S., H.S. Feild, and W.F. Giles. 2003. "What Can We Uncover about Applicants Based on Their Résumés? A Field Study." *Applied HRM Research* 8(2): 51–62.

96 Cole, M.S., H.S. Feild, and W. Giles. 2003. "Using Recruiter Assessments of Applicants' Résumé Content to Predict Applicant Mental Ability and Big Five Personality Dimensions." *International Journal of Selection and Assessment* 11(1): 78–88.

97 Cole, M.S., H.S. Feild, W.F Giles, and S.G. Harris. 2004. "Job Type and Recruiters' Inferences of Applicant Personality Drawn from Résumé Biodata: Their Relationships with Hiring Recommendations." *International Journal of Selection and Assessment* 12(4): 363–67.

98 Cole, M.S., H.S. Field, W.F. Giles, and S.G. Harris. 2009. "Recruiters' Inferences of Applicant Personality Based on Resume Screening: Do Paper People Have a Personality?" *Journal of Business and Psychology* 24: 5–18.

99 "Cover Letters Still Play a Valuable Role in Hiring Decisions, Survey Suggests." 2008. *CNW Group.* Retrieved January 11, 2012, from http://www.newswire.ca/en/releases/archive/June2008/26/c8058.html

100 Schullery, N.M., L. Ickes, and S.E. Schullery. 2009. "Employer Preferences for Résumés and Cover Letters." *Business Communication Quarterly* 72(2): 163–76.

101 Ibid.

102 Schullery, N.M., L. Ickes, and S.E. Schullery. 2009.

103 Schullery, N.M., L. Ickes, and S.E. Schullery. 2009.

104 Crosby, O., and D. Liming. 2009. *Resumes, Applications, and Cover Letters.* Government Printing Office.

105 Schullery, N.M., L. Ickes, and S.E. Schullery. 2009.

106 Wein, J. 1994. "Rifling through Résumés." *Incentive* 168: 96–97.

107 Bachler, C. 1995. "Résumé Fraud: Lies, Omissions, and Exaggerations." *Personnel Journal* 74(6): 50.

108 Cywinski, M. 2008, August. "Video Résumés: To Use or Not to Use?" *CanadaOne*: http://www.canadaone.com/ezine/briefs.html?StoryID=08Aug16_1

109 Waung, M., R.W. Hymes, and J.E. Beatty. 2014. "The Effects of Video and Paper Resumes on Assessments of Personality, Applied Social Skills, Mental Capability, and Resume Outcomes." *Basic and Applied Social Psychology* 36(3): 238–251.

110 Roberts, J. 2006. "Didn't Get the Job? Could It Be Your Name?" *The Globe and Mail* (August 2): C1.

111 Pedrasa, I.M.J.P. 2008. "Filipino Video Résumés Set to Go Global." *BusinessWorld* (January 4): 1.

112 Akkad, O.E. 2006. "Confronting the Fib No Easy Task for Boards." *The Globe and Mail* (February 20): B12.

113 Luciw, R. 2007. "In Résumés, Cutting the Fiction Reduces the Friction: It's Okay to Sell Your Strengths (and Admit Your Weaknesses), But Recruiters Prefer You Back It Up with Hard Facts." *The Globe and Mail* (February 24): B10.

114 Donovan, J.J., S.A. Dwight, and G.M. Hurtz. 2003.

115 Hunter, J.E., and R.F. Hunter. 1984.

116 Hedricks, C.A., C. Robie, and F.L. Oswald. 2013. "Web-Based Multisource Reference Checking: An Investigation of Psychometric Integrity and Applied Benefits." *International Journal of Selection and Assessment* 21: 99–110.

117 Gatewood, R.D., H.S. Feild, and B. Murray. 2008.

118 Leavitt, H. 1992. "Should Companies Be Hesitant to Give Ex-Employees References?" *The Toronto Star* (July 20): C3.

119 Clark, L., and P. Snitzer. 2005. "'Speak No Evil' Is a Risky Policy: Reference Checks on Former Workers Can Be Tricky for Healthcare Employers." *Modern Healthcare* 35: 49.

120 Ibid.

121 Hutton, D. 2008. "Job Reference Chill Grows Icier: Employers' Growing Reluctance to Talk about Former Employees Frustrates Both Those Doing the Hiring and Those Trying to Get Hired." *The Globe and Mail* (June 18): C1.

122 Hutton, D. 2008.

123 Hutton, D. 2008.

124 "The Legalities of Providing a Reference Check on a Former Employee." 2007. *AXIOM International Reference Checking Service*. http://www.axiom-int.com/survey_legalities.htm

125 Clark, L., and P. Snitzer. 2005.

126 Saint-Cyr, Y. 2007. "Negligent Hiring–How It Affects the Employer." HRinfodesk: Canadian Payroll and Employment Law at Work. Retrieved January 12, 2012, from http://www.hrinfodesk.com/preview.asp?article=7961

127 Ibid.

128 Mosel, J.N., and H.W. Goheen. 1958. "The Validity of the Employment Recommendation Questionnaire in Personnel Selection: I. Skilled Traders." *Personnel Psychology* 11: 481–90.

129 Mosel, J.N., and H.W. Goheen. 1959. "The Validity of the Employment Recommendation Questionnaire: III. Validity of Different Types of References." *Personnel Psychology* 12: 469–77.

130 Schmidt, F.L., and Hunter, J.E. 1998. "The Validity and Utility of Selection Methods in Personnel Psychology: Practical and Theoretical Implications of 85 Years of Research Findings." *Psychological Bulletin* 124: 262–74.

131 Hunter, J.E., and R.F. Hunter. 1984.

132 Solomon, B., 1998.

133 Kabay, M. 1993. "It Pays to Be Paranoid When You're Hiring." *Computing Canada* (April 26): 21.

134 Knouse, S.B. 1983. "The Letter of Recommendation: Specificity and Favorability of Information." *Personnel Psychology* 36: 331–42.

135 McCarthy, J.M., and R.D. Goffin. 2001. "Improving the Validity of Letters of Recommendation: An Investigation of Three Standardized Reference Forms." *Military Psychology* 13(4): 199–222.

136 Bernerth, J.B., S.G. Taylor, H.J. Walker, and D.S. Whitman. 2012. "An Empirical Investigation of Dispositional Antecedents and Performance-Related Outcomes of Credit Scores." *Journal of Applied Psychology* 97(2): 469–478.

137 Gallagher, K. 2006. "Rethinking the Fair Credit Reporting Act: When Requesting Credit Reports for Employment Purposes Goes Too Far." *Iowa Law Review* 91: 1593–1621.

138 Smith, A. 2007. "Unnecessary Credit Checks Challenges." *HRM Magazine* 52(5): 22–24.

139 Humber, T. 2003. "Name, Rank and Serial Number." *Canadian Human Rights Reporter* 16(10): G1, G7.

140 Babcock, P. 2003. "Spotting Lies: As a First-line Defense, HR Can Take Steps to Weed Out Dishonest Applicants." *HR Magazine* 48(10): 46.

141 Quinones, M.A., J.K. Ford, and M.S. Teachout. 1995. "The Experience between Work Experience and Job Performance: A Conceptual and Meta-Analytic Review." *Personnel Psychology* 48: 887–910.

142 Rowe, P.M. 1988. "The Nature of Work Experience." *Canadian Psychology* 29: 109–15.

143 Tesluk, P.E., and R.R. Jacobs. 1998. "Toward an Integrated Model of Work Experience." *Personnel Psychology* 51: 321–55.

144 Dragoni, L., I-S Oh, P. Vankatwyk, and P.E. Tesluk. 2011. "Developing Executive Leaders: The Relative Contribution of Cognitive Ability, Personality, and the Accumulation of Work Experience in Predicting Strategic Thinking Competency." *Personnel Psychology* 64: 829–864.

145 Ford, J.K., M.A. Quinones, D.J. Sego, and J. Speer-Sorra. 1992. "Factors Affecting the Opportunity to Perform Trained Tasks on the Job." *Personnel Psychology* 45: 511–27.

146 Schmidt, F.L., J.E. Hunter, and A.N. Outerbridge. 1986. "Impact of Job Experience and Ability on Job Knowledge, Work Sample Performance, and Supervisory Ratings of Job Performance." *Journal of Applied Psychology* 71: 432–39.

147 Borman, W.C., M.A. Hanson, S.H. Oppler, E.D. Pulakos, and L.A. Whilte. 1991. "Job Behavior, Performance, and Effectiveness." In M.D. Dunnette and L.M. Hough, eds., *Handbook of Industrial and Organizational Psychology*, Vol. 2, 2nd ed. (pp. 271–326). San Diego: Consulting Psychologists Press.

148 Vance, R.L., M.D. Coovert, R.C. MacCallum, and J.W. Hedge. 1989. "Construct Models of Task Performance." *Journal of Applied Psychology* 74: 447–55.

149 Hunter, J.E., and R.F. Hunter. 1984.

150 Quinones, M.A., J.K. Ford, and M.S. Teachout. 1995.

151 McDaniel, M.A., F.L. Schmidt, and J.E. Hunter. 1988. "Job Experience Correlates of Job Performance." *Journal of Applied Psychology* 73: 327–30.

152 Quinones, M.A., J.K. Ford, and M.S. Teachout. 1995.

153 Ng, T.W.H., and D.C. Feldman. 2010. "Organizational Tenure and Job Performance." *Journal of Management* 36(5): 1220–1250.

154 Ibid.

155 Ibid.

156 Ibid.

157 Bohnert, D., and H.R. Ross. 2010. "The Influence of Social Networking Web Sites on the Evaluation of Job Candidates." *Cyberpsychology, Behavior and Social Networking* 13: 341–347.

158 Olzak, T. 2009. "Cyber-Profiling: Benefits and Pitfalls, Olzak on Business Continuity." Retrieved January 12, 2012, from http://blogs.csoonline.com/cyber_profiling

159 Stamper, C. 2010. "Common Mistakes Companies Make Using Social Media Tools in Recruiting Efforts." *CMA Management* 84(2): 12–14.

160 Grasz, J. 2013. "New CareerBuilder Study Reveals Nine Lessons for Job Seekers and Recruiters That May Surprise You." Career Builder Press Release.

161 Nguyen, N.T. 2014. "Employer's Use of Social Networking Sites in Applicant Screening: An Unethical and Potentially Illegal Practice." *Business & Financial Affairs* 3:e138 doi:10.4172/2167-0234.1000e138

162 Stoughton, J.W., L.F. Thompson, and A.W. Meade. In Press. "Examining Applicant Reactions to the Use of Social Networking Websites in Pre-Employment Screening." *Journal of Business and Psychology.* doi:10.1007/s10869-013-9333-6

163 Kluemper, D.H., and P.A. Rosen. 2009. "Future Employment Selection Methods: Evaluating Social Networking Web Sites." *Journal of Managerial Psychology* 24: 567–580.

164 Kluemper, D.H., P.A. Rosen, and K. Mossholder. 2012. "Social Networking Websites, Personality Ratings, and the Organizational Context: More Than Meets the Eye." *Journal of Applied Social Psychology* 42: 1143–1172.

165 Tews, M.J., K. Stafford, and J. Zhu. 2009. "Beauty Revisited: The Impact of Attractiveness, Ability, and Personality in the Assessment of Employment Suitability." *International Journal of Selection and Assessment* 17: 92–100.

166 Van Iddekinge, C.H., S.E. Lanivich, P.L. Roth, and E. Junco. In Press. "Social Media for Selection? Validity and Adverse Impact Potential of a Facebook-Based Assessment." *Journal of Management.*

167 Seibert, S., P.E. Downes, and J. Christopher. 2012. "Applicant Reactions to Online Background Checks: Welcome to a Brave New World." In R.N. Landers, *The Role of Social Media and On-line Resources in Selection.* Boston: The Academy of Management Annual Meetings.

168 http://www.huffingtonpost.com/2012/04/20/maryland-becomes-first-st_n_1439866.html

169 Van Iddekinge, C.H., S.E. Lanivich, P.L. Roth, and E. Junco. In Press.

170 Winkler, C. 2006. "Job Tryouts Go Virtual: Online Job Simulations Provide Sophisticated Candidate Assessments." *HRMagazine* 51(9): 131–33.

CHAPTER

8

SELECTION II:

TESTING AND OTHER ASSESSMENTS

CHAPTER LEARNING OUTCOMES

This chapter describes testing and other assessments in HR selection, providing information on the technical, ethical, and legal requirements governing their use.

AFTER READING THIS CHAPTER YOU SHOULD:

- have a good understanding of commonly used assessments in HR selection;
- know the advantages and disadvantages of using these assessments;
- understand the importance of the validity and utility of HR assessments;
- be aware of assessee perceptions of HR assessment tools and processes and how such perceptions impact views of organizational attractiveness; and
- know the legal issues surrounding the use of HR assessments.

LISTENING TO THE AIRPORT GURU

My name is Aaron. I am the HR director for a large CD retail operation. Tyler, the CEO, said he couldn't understand why we had to spend so much time and money on our selection procedures. He felt that our computer software and electronics retail business had to hire people in the 19–34 age group, about the same demographic as most of our customers. He wanted to hire people who are likely to have hands-on experience with the latest computer software and electronics rather than sales knowledge alone.

He kept showing me all these articles he read on the airplane; you know the ones, where the newest management guru has the quick fix to all your problems (for a small fee). He brought in this one guy he read about to give us a seminar on the best way to hire people. The guru had a method that was guaranteed to work. It involved hiring only those applicants who had a high "developmental quotient," or DQ. You brought the candidate in, sat the person down in a quiet room, and asked a series of questions about his childhood and adolescence.

The guru claimed that most people were stuck in the adolescent stage and your goal was to find candidates who had progressed to the adult level, which was difficult to do since very few people had attained that level. You could hire people who were at the pre-adult stage if you sent them to his training seminar to learn how to advance to the next stage. He trained people to identify a person's "developmental quotient" based on the person's answers to the interview questions.

After the seminar, Tyler pulled me aside and said he wanted to change our selection procedures to the "DQ" method. I laughed and told him what I thought of the procedure. He said I would either implement the "DQ" selection system and a training program to increase "DQ" levels or look for a new job. I knew I should have stood up for what was right and for what I believed in, but I couldn't afford to lose my job at my age with a mortgage to pay. I convinced myself that the new system met the selection standards outlined by my professional association and decided to give it a try.

I now spend most of my time preparing for court and tribunal hearings. Some of our job candidates found out we were hiring only people between the ages of 19 and 34. They filed a complaint with the human rights tribunal that we were discriminating against them. We also had another problem with the "DQ" system when some female applicants thought some of the questions about their adolescent experiences were too intimate and suggestive. They filed a sexual harassment suit.

These cases became so costly we had to hire two lawyers to deal with them. We wound up paying these people hundreds of thousands of dollars when our lawyers brought in external consultants who told us there was no way we could legally defend the "DQ" test as a valid and reliable selection instrument. The lawyers told us to cut our losses and settle the suits. Of course, as the HR director, I took the fall for all these problems and was fired by Tyler.

// WHAT DO YOU KNOW ABOUT EMPLOYMENT TESTING?

Many of you will be aiming to become an HR professional. HR professionals are responsible for improving organizational effectiveness through the recruitment, selection, development, and motivation of organizational members. Yet, many organizations often do not adopt practices that have been established through credible research as effective,[1] or continue to use practices for which there is little empirical support.[2]

Rynes, Colbert, and Brown[3] surveyed 5000 HR professionals who were members of the Society for Human Resource Management (SHRM). Each HR professional was asked to answer 39 true-or-false questions from different HR content areas, including staffing, which included personnel selection. How did the HR professionals do? Their average score was 57 percent. How would you have answered the following true-or-false questions from the survey? Write your answers (T or F) beside each question as you read each item. We will then present you with the correct answers (don't peek!).

1. Despite the popularity of drug testing, there is no clear evidence that applicants who score positive on drug tests are less reliable or productive employees.
2. There are only four basic dimensions of personality as captured by the *Myers-Briggs Type Indicator* (MBTI).
3. High intelligence is actually a disadvantage in a low-skilled job.
4. There is little difference among personality inventories in predicting job performance.
5. Integrity tests that try to predict whether employees will steal, be absent, or otherwise take advantage of an employer don't work well in practice because so many people lie on them or fake their answers.
6. Employees of companies that screen job applicants for values perform better than do employees screened for intelligence.
7. On average, conscientiousness is a better predictor of job performance than is intelligence.*

So, how did you do? Only the first of the above items is "true." Fewer than 50 percent of HR professionals passed the section on HR staffing. After having mastered the material in this chapter, you will know more about HR assessment than many of today's practising HR professionals. So, do not be discouraged if you did not score well.

EMPLOYMENT TESTING

A major function in recruitment and selection is to find the best job candidate. When there are many applicants, organizations typically use a variety of assessments to inform their selection decision. The best and most legally defensible HR assessments are standardized and meet professional standards concerning their psychometric properties and predictive validities (e.g., demonstrated ability to predict important work-related criteria, including job performance), as noted in Chapter 2.

In most hiring situations, there are more applicants than there are positions to be filled. The goal is to select those candidates who best possess the knowledge, skills, abilities, or other attributes and competencies (KSAOs) that bring value to the organization. To demonstrate their value, the KSAOs must be shown to predict important work-related criteria (e.g., success in training, job performance, tenure, organizational citizenship behaviour, promotion through the ranks). Recruitment and Selection Notebook 8.1 presents information on the use of employment tests.

CHOOSING A TEST

Recruitment and Selection Notebook 8.2 presents some points that should be considered in selecting commercially available employment tests. These points reflect the technical considerations discussed above. Anyone who has the responsibility for choosing

*Rynes, S.L., A.E. Colbert, and K.G. Brown. 2003. "HR Professionals' Beliefs About Effective Human Resource Practices: Correspondence Between Research and Practice." *Human Resource Management*, 41: 149–74.

RECRUITMENT AND SELECTION NOTEBOOK 8.1

USE OF EMPLOYMENT TESTS

The central requirement for assessments used in selection is that they accurately assess an individual's capacity to perform the essential components of the target job safely, efficiently, and reliably, without discriminating against protected group members except where the KSAO can be established as a bona fide occupational requirement (BFOR). The use of employment tests must comply with the following:

Testing Standards

Employment assessments must be reliable, valid, unbiased, and fair. The psychometric properties of the test must be established before it is used for decision-making purposes.

Professional Guidelines

Professional bodies have developed guidelines for the development and use of tests. Employment testing should adhere to the guidelines from the *Standards for Educational and Psychological Testing*, published by the American Psychological Association and two other organizations. These standards have been adopted by the Canadian Society for Industrial and Organizational Psychology as contained in the *Principles for the Validation and Use of Personnel Selection Procedures* (http://www.siop.org/_Principles/principlesdefault.aspx).

Who Can Test?

The availability of employment tests and computerized scoring and interpretation systems often tempts unqualified people to administer tests and to interpret results from them. Proficiency in employment testing requires a considerable degree of training and experience. Reputable test publishers require purchasers to establish their expertise in using a test before allowing its purchase. These safeguards help protect the public against misuse of tests and information collected through testing. The CHRP National Code of Ethics requires HR professionals to recognize their own limits and to practise within the limits of their competence, culture, and experience.

Cautions in Using Employment Tests

1. ***Informed consent.*** Job applicants must be told why they are being tested; they must be informed in clear language that the test results may be provided to a prospective employer and that those results may be used in making employment decisions.
2. ***Access to test results.*** Whenever possible and feasible, job applicants should receive feedback on their test performance and on any decisions that are based on those tests, unless this right has been waived by the applicant or if it is prohibited by law or court order.
3. ***Privacy and confidentiality.*** Job applicants reveal information about themselves during the job selection process, but there is no justification for obtaining any information that is not job related. Applicants have a right to privacy, so information that is provided by job applicants must be held in confidence.
4. ***Language and culture.*** Job applicants have the right to be tested in a language in which they are fluent. Administering a test to applicants who do not have good command of the language in which the test is written will lead to test bias; the test results will be confounded by incomprehension of the language.
5. ***Accommodation.*** Employers are expected to make reasonable accommodation to meet the needs of employees or applicants with disabilities who meet job requirements. Employment tests should be given to an applicant in a way that accommodates the applicant's disability, even at the expense of changing standardized testing procedures.

employment tests should be knowledgeable about the various standards and technical documents related to their use. Goffin[4] states that there is a tendency for HR professionals to choose "the flavor of the month" when it comes to pre-employment tests rather than taking a serious look at actual job requirements and the demonstrated ability of the test to assess candidates against these requirements.

RECRUITMENT AND SELECTION NOTEBOOK 8.2

POINTS TO CONSIDER IN SELECTING A TEST

1. Do a job analysis to determine the knowledge, skills, abilities, or other qualities that have been related to job success.
2. Consult an information resource on testing to identify tests that are relevant to your job needs. Obtain information from several sources including test publishers or developers and human resources consultants knowledgeable about testing.
3. Obtain information on several tests related to what you want to measure. Read through the materials provided by the test developers. Reject out of hand any test for which the publisher or developer presents unclear or incomplete information.
4. Read the technical documentation to become familiar with how and when the test was developed and used. Does the technical documentation provide information on the test's reliability and validity? Does it address the issue of test fairness? Does it include normative data based on sex, age, and ethnicity that are comparable to your intended test takers? Does it include references for independent investigations of the test's psychometric properties? Eliminate from consideration any tests whose documentation does not allow you to answer "yes" to these questions.
5. Read independent evaluations of the tests that you are considering adopting. Does the independent evidence support the claims of the test developers? Is the test valid and reliable? Eliminate those tests that are not supported by this evidence.
6. Examine a specimen set from each of the remaining tests. Most publishers will sell a package that includes a copy of the test, instructions, test manual, answer sheets, and sample score report at a reasonable cost. Is the test format and reading level appropriate for the intended test takers? Is the test available in languages other than English? Can the test accommodate test takers with special needs? Is the content of the test appropriate for the intended test takers? Eliminate those tests that you do not feel are appropriate.
7. Determine the skill level needed to purchase the test, to administer the test, and to interpret test scores correctly. Do you have the appropriate level of expertise? Does someone else in your organization meet the test's requirements? If not, can you contract out for the services of a qualified psychologist or human resources professional who does?
8. Select and use only those tests that are psychometrically sound, that meet the needs of your intended test-takers, and that you have the necessary skills to administer, score, and interpret correctly.

Information on thousands of psychological tests, including employment tests, can be found on the Internet. One of the best sites is the Buros Center for Testing (http://buros.org). This site presents reviews of an extensive list of tests by experts. The remainder of this chapter presents an introduction to the wide variety of employment assessments used in Canadian organizations. Recruitment and Selection Notebook 8.3 lists some of the more common tests used to select employees. Examples of cognitive ability, personality, and emotional intelligence assessment items can be found at http://www.queendom.com, although some of these assessments may not meet the psychometric standards required for actual use in employee selection.

ABILITY AND APTITUDE TESTS

As we have seen in earlier chapters, job-related KSAOs, including competencies, play an important role in successful job performance. For example, applicants for a position of

RECRUITMENT AND SELECTION NOTEBOOK 8.3

EXAMPLES OF PSYCHOLOGICAL ASSESSMENTS USED TO SELECT EMPLOYEES

Personality Inventories

- California Psychological Inventory
- Guilford-Zimmerman Temperament Survey
- Hogan Personality Inventory
- Jackson Personality Inventory
- NEO-FFI and NEO-PI-R
- Personal Characteristics Inventory (PCI)
- Sixteen Personality Factor Questionnaire (16PF)
- Work Personality Index (WPI)
- Work Profile Questionnaire (WPQ)

Honesty/Integrity Inventories

- Hogan Personality Inventory–Reliability Scale
- Inwald Personality Test
- London House Personnel Selection Inventory
- PDI Employment Inventory
- Reid Report
- Stanton Survey

Tests of Emotional Intelligence

- Bar-On Emotional Quotient Inventory (EQi)
- Emotional Competence Inventory (ECI)
- Mayer-Salovey-Caruso Emotional Intelligence Test (MSCEIT)
- Work Profile Questionnaire–emotional intelligence (WPQei)

Vocational Interest Inventories

- Jackson Vocational Interest Survey
- Kuder Preference and Interest Scales
- Occupational Preference Inventory
- Self-Directed Search
- Strong Interest Inventory
- Vocational Preference Inventory

Cognitive Ability Tests

- Otis-Lennon Mental Ability Test
- Stanford-Binet Intelligence Scale
- Watson-Glaser Critical Thinking Appraisal
- Wechsler Adult Intelligence Scale (WAIS)
- Wonderlic Personnel Test

Aptitude Tests

- Comprehensive Ability Battery (CAB)
- Differential Aptitude Tests (DAT)
- General Aptitude Test Battery (GATB)
- Multidimensional Aptitude Battery–II

Psychomotor Tests

- General Aptitude Test Battery (GATB)
    - Subtest 8—Motor Coordination
    - Subtests 9 and 10—Manual Dexterity
    - Subtests 11 and 12—Finger Dexterity
- O'Connor Tweezer Dexterity Test
- Purdue Pegboard Test
- Stromberg Dexterity Test

Physical Ability and Sensory/Perceptual Ability Tests

- Dynamometer Grip Strength Test
- Ishihara Test for Colour Blindness
- Visual Skills Test

electronic repair technician might be expected to have a high degree of finger dexterity (to perform repairs on circuit boards), colour vision (to tell the difference between different wires), and a potential for acquiring knowledge related to electronics (to achieve an understanding of basic circuit theory).

Selection programs seek to predict the degree to which job applicants possess the KSAOs related to the job. Many different tests have been developed to measure specific human abilities and aptitudes. In the case of electronic repair technicians, we would seek to employ those applicants with the highest levels of finger dexterity and colour vision, and the most aptitude for learning electronics.

ABILITY TESTS

Abilities are attributes that an applicant brings to the employment situation–the enduring, general traits or characteristics on which people differ. It is of no importance whether ability has been acquired through experience or inheritance. Abilities are simply general traits that people possess and bring with them to the new work situation. For example, finger dexterity is the ability to carry out quick, coordinated movements of fingers on one or both hands and to grasp, place, or move very small objects.[5]

Abilities
Enduring, general traits or characteristics on which people differ and which they bring to a work situation.

Ability can underlie performance on a number of specific tasks; finger dexterity might be required to operate a computer keyboard and to assemble electronic components. One keyboard operator may have taken several months of practice to develop the finger dexterity needed to type 100 words per minute; another may have come by that ability naturally. Both have the same ability, regardless of how it was acquired. Ability exists in individuals at the time they first begin to perform a task, whether that task is operating a keyboard or assembling electronic components.

Skill, on the other hand, refers to an individual's degree of proficiency or competency on a given task, based on both ability and practice, which has developed through performing the task. Two keyboard operators may have the same level of finger dexterity; however, one may have learned to type with hands raised at an inappropriate angle in relation to the keyboard. As a result, the two have different skill levels, or proficiencies, in using a keyboard despite having the same ability. Similarly, a keyboard operator and an electronics assembler might have the same level of finger dexterity but the keyboard operator might be more skilled at word processing than the assembler is at wiring circuit boards.

Skill
An individual's degree of proficiency or competency on a given task, which develops through performing the task.

Aptitude
A specific, narrow ability or skill that may be used to predict job performance.

Cognitive abilities
Intelligence, general mental ability, or intellectual ability.

Aptitude can be thought of as a specific, narrow ability or skill. Measurements or tests of different aptitudes are used to predict whether an individual will do well in future job-related performance that requires the ability or skill being measured.

Based on a test of finger dexterity, a human resources manager might predict that a job applicant has an aptitude for operating a keyboard, or for assembling electronic components. Over the years, Fleishman and his associates[6] have identified 52 distinct human abilities, which can be grouped into four broad categories: cognitive, psychomotor, physical, and sensory/perceptual abilities. Over time, many psychometrically sound tests have been developed to assess these different abilities.

COGNITIVE ABILITY TESTS

Cognitive abilities are related to intelligence or intellectual ability. These abilities include verbal and numerical, reasoning, memory, problem solving, and processing information, among others. The first wide-scale, systematic use of cognitive ability testing took

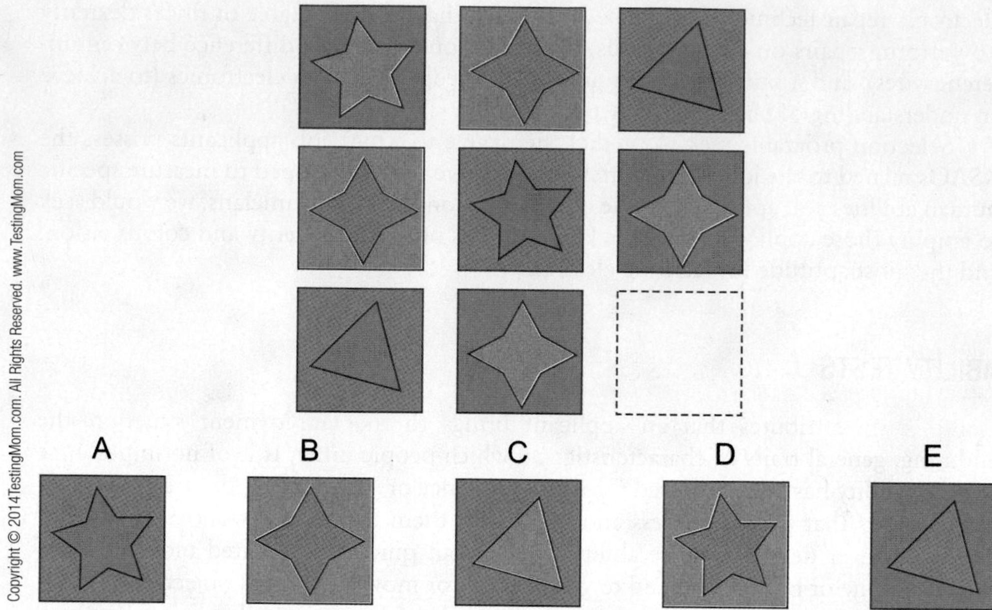

place during World War I, when a group of industrial psychologists developed the U.S. Army Alpha Intelligence Test. This was a paper-and-pencil test that could be efficiently administered to groups of army recruits to determine how those recruits could best be employed. The Army Alpha test sought to measure intellectual or basic mental abilities that were thought to be essential to performing military duties.

Today, an extensive array of tests is available to measure specific cognitive abilities. Most likely you have taken one or more of them. The Personnel Psychology Centre (PPC) of the Public Service Commission of Canada (PSC) offers federal government departments and agencies a range of professional assessment products and services that can be used for recruitment and selection or personnel development. These include "general competency tests," a form of cognitive ability testing that assesses verbal and quantitative abilities, spatial relations, and analytical and logical reasoning. Sample test questions from their General Competency Test Level 1 (GTC2-207) and General Competency Test Level 2 (GCT2-314) are available online along with other tests used by the PSC-PPC (go to http://www.psc-cfp.gc.ca/ppc-cpp/psc-tests-cfp/tst-by-par-lvl-nivo-eng.htm). See Recruitment and Selection Today 8.1 for sample items from their General Competency Test GCT1.

More recently, there has been a move away from assessing many individual, specific abilities to a more general cognitive ability assessment. General cognitive ability (or general mental ability, abbreviated as *g*, GCA, or GMA), is thought to be the primary ability underlying intellectual capacity. General cognitive ability is believed to promote effective learning, efficient and accurate problem solving, and clear communications. GMA can be thought of as a manager of other, specific cognitive abilities, similar to a computer's operating system managing software programs. It is essentially the ability to learn.[7] GMA has been related to successful job performance in many different types of occupations.[8] It predicts how easily people can be trained to perform job tasks, how well they can adjust and solve problems on the job, and their satisfaction with job demands.[9]

A test of GMA can provide a quick and efficient basis for selecting applicants for more extensive, and costly, testing. The National Football League (NFL) has given the

RECRUITMENT AND SELECTION TODAY 8.1

GENERAL COMPETENCY TEST: LEVEL 1

GCT 1 Sample Questions

The **General Competency Test: Level 1** (GCT1) contains three types of questions: understanding written material, solving numerical problems, and drawing logical conclusions.

A sample question of each type is provided below.

Type I—Understanding Written Material

This type of question involves reading a short passage, which is usually in memorandum format, and answering a question about the information in the text.

QUESTION 1

Government of Canada MEMORANDUM	Gouvernement du Canada NOTE DE SERVICE

TO: All employees

FROM: Manager

Please note that the answer sheets currently being used will be replaced with new ones next year. The existing supply of answer sheets should be used from now until the end of the year. It is important that the new sheets are used next year because they will enable the collection of additional information that will be required at this time.

The main purpose of this memorandum is to:

(1) Indicate the need for new answer sheets.

(2) Notify employees that new answer sheets will replace the existing ones.

(3) Notify employees that the current answer sheets are inadequate.

(4) Indicate the need for additional information.

Type II—Solving Numerical Problems

This type of question involves choosing the correct answer to a practical numerical problem.

QUESTION 2

You are in charge of financial services and must calculate overtime pay for employees in your division. Due to a heavy workload, an employee had to work 35 hours of overtime in two weeks. For 28 of these hours, the employee was paid at one and one-half times the hourly rate. For the remaining hours, the employee was paid at twice the usual hourly pay. The employee's hourly pay is $10. How much overtime money should the employee be paid for the two-week period?

(1) $340 (3) $560

(2) $420 (4) $760

Type III—Drawing Logical Conclusions

In this type of question, the task is to choose the correct answer to a practical problem.

QUESTION 3

One of your duties is the selection and disposal of boxes of obsolete files. According to regulations, ordinary files become obsolete after 24 months, protected files after 36 months, and classified files after 48 months. Which of the following boxes of files can be discarded?

(A) A box containing ordinary files dated 26 months ago and classified files dated 34 months ago.

(B) A box containing ordinary files dated 38 months ago and protected files dated 28 months ago.

(1) A only (3) Both A and B

(2) B only (4) Neither A nor B

Answers

(2)

(3)

(4)

Source: *General Competency Test Level 1*. http://www.psc-cfp.gc.ca/ppc-cpp/psc-tests-cfp/gct1-ecg1-q-eng.htm. Public Service Commission of Canada, 2011. Reproduced with the permission of the Minister of Public Works and Government Services Canada, 2014.

Wonderlic Personnel Test, a test of general cognitive ability, to potential recruits since 1968. According to Charles Wonderlic, president of the testing company, "The test measures a person's ability to learn, solve problems and adapt to new situations."[10] Wonderlic test scores, along with information on the candidate's physical prowess and ability, are available to each NFL team for use in drafting players (i.e., making selection decisions). The Wonderlic has a maximum possible score of 50. The average score for factory workers is 17, for lawyers, 30, and for NFL prospects, 21, which is the overall average for the test. A low score on the test does not eliminate an NFL prospect but red-flags him as someone who may not be able to meet the demands of a game that is becoming ever more cognitively complex. The Wonderlic is used as part of a battery of tests to develop a psychological profile on each candidate. Recruitment and Selection Today 8.2 presents a case where an organization was actually looking for applicants with scores *below* a specific level on the Wonderlic!

Measurements of GMA, which have an average validity coefficient of 0.50, are among the best predictors of success in training and job performance for a variety of occupational groups, ranging from retail clerks to skilled workers to managers and

RECRUITMENT AND SELECTION TODAY 8.2

WHAT? I'M TOO SMART FOR THIS JOB?

When job applicants are asked to take a cognitive ability test, there is an underlying assumption that those with the best scores will qualify for a job offer. Job applicants do their best to achieve a high score on the test. What if the company or organization is actually looking for applicants whose cognitive ability falls *below* a specific level? The company may feel that people with high cognitive ability will become bored in the job, dissatisfied with the work, and soon leave. What are the likely consequences of adopting such a procedure?

The Boston Globe reported a case in which the Southeastern Connecticut Law Enforcement Consortium rejected a police force applicant, Robert Jordan, who scored 33 out of 50 points on the *Wonderlic Personnel Test.*[11] Jordan was disqualified from the competition along with 62 other high-scoring applicants. The Wonderlic test manual recommends that applicants for police officer positions have a score in the range of 20–27. The New London, Connecticut, police chief was quoted as saying, "Police work, believe it or not, is a boring job. What happens if you get certain people who can't accept being involved in that sort of occupation is it becomes very frustrating. Either the day they come in they want to be chief of police, or they become very frustrated and leave."

Jordan went to federal court but lost his case. After reviewing evidence about the validity of the Wonderlic and job analysis requirements for "police officer," the judge ruled that it was reasonable to reject people who scored higher than the requirements set out for the position. Jordan may have had the last laugh, as the report quotes him as saying, "I made them the laughingstock of the country. Jay Leno made up this great song. The theme music was 'Dumb cops, dumb cops, whatcha gonna do, with a low IQ.' People can't get over it that they want to cultivate this kind of department."

Laughter and questions of legality aside, there is an important consideration here for practitioners. Is it ethical to seek applicants with average or less-than-average intelligence when applicants expect that doing well on a test will lead to a job offer? It may be, provided there is strong job analysis data to support that position. But then another problem arises: Applicants taking employment tests are to be fully informed of the purpose of the test and how it will be used. The applicants would have to be told that, contrary to expectations, those with high scores would be disqualified.[12] In that circumstance, how many applicants are likely to do well on the test? Furthermore, while a high IQ might predict high turnover in certain jobs, it also strongly predicts job performance: Higher cognitive ability, higher performance. Turnover may not be the most appropriate criterion in cases like this. So, maybe Jay Leno was right.

executives.[13,14] Ones and Dilchert[15] reviewed and integrated various meta-analyses (statistical compilation of predictive validity studies) of the relationship between general cognitive ability and performance in training and on the job, reporting mean "corrected" correlations of .68 and .47 respectively. Further, though some research has reported cognitive ability to be a stronger predictor of performance for high versus low complex jobs,[16,17,18] other research has not supported these findings.[19,20]

For all jobs, regardless of complexity or skill level, cognitive ability is a primary predictor of performance.[21] Schmidt[22] presents a comprehensive review of the major meta-analyses that conclusively demonstrate that GMA, as well as specific abilities tests, predicts both training and job performance across many different occupations. Salgado, Anderson, Moscoso, Bertua, and de Fruyt[23] did a meta-analysis of data from 10 European Community countries that varied in language, culture, religion, and social values and found even stronger validities for these European countries as compared to those reported for North American samples.

Similarly, Bertua, Anderson, and Salgado[24] reviewed 283 studies done in the United Kingdom that used cognitive ability as a predictor of job and training performance. Their results were very similar to those of Salgado et al. in that validities ranged from 0.50 to 0.60, with higher validities associated with more complex occupations. In the context of globalization, the results of Salgado et al. and Bertua, Anderson, and Salgado suggest that cognitive ability transcends language and culture and can be used as a valid HR selection test in many countries of the world.

In a 2014 meta-analysis, Gonzalez-Mulé and colleagues showed that personality does a much better job predicting counterproductive work behaviour (CWB; e.g., lateness, absence, sabotage, theft) than does GMA, but that GMA and personality are about equally predictive of organizational citizenship behaviour (OCB; e.g., helping coworkers, keeping one's work station tidy, working outside of formal job requirements in ways that benefit the organization or one's coworkers). GMA, however, does a better job than personality at predicting task and overall job performance. The implications of these findings for developing optimal selection systems are discussed by the authors.[25]

In reviewing the most common criticisms of cognitive ability testing in education and employment and drawing from the cumulative empirical literature, Sackett, Borneman, and Connelly[26] concluded that (1) ability tests are valid for their intended uses in predicting a wide variety of aspects of short-term and long-term academic and job performance; (2) the validity of these tests is not an artefact of socio-economic status (i.e., the predictive validity holds within and across different social economic groups); (3) coaching is not a major determinant of test performance; (4) ability tests are not biased in that they do not underpredict minority group member performance, and (5) test-taking motivation is not a major determinant of test performance in most high-stakes settings.

The political controversy over the use of cognitive ability testing in employee selection is rooted primarily in differences in mean test performance between majority and minority group members, especially with regard to blacks and Hispanics who generally score lower than their white counterparts. Yet, the cumulated psychometric literature until very recently had produced a growing consensus in psychology and related fields (e.g., education, human resource management) that such mean differences (resulting in adverse impact in hiring) do not reflect test bias. Test bias occurs where there is either over- or underprediction of performance, using test scores, for the minority group relative to the majority group. Years of test bias research results have converged in finding that test bias that is disadvantageous to minority group members is seldom found; that differences in test scores between minority and majority group members accurately and equally predict differences in their subsequent job performance for both groups; and that in the few cases where bias is found, it is usually shown to benefit minority group members (e.g., test scores overpredict for minorities).[27]

This common wisdom in the literature on employee selection–that cognitive ability testing is not biased against minority group members–is now being challenged. Specifically, a compelling argument, supported by large-scale Monte Carlo simulations conducted by Aguinis, Culpepper, and Pierce, suggests that the findings on which conclusions of no test bias were reached can be explained in terms of statistical artefacts, especially to the low sample sizes of the minority groups on which the analyses were based.[28] More specifically, much larger sample sizes than those typically used in these studies are required to provide the "statistical power" necessary for detecting the between-group differences that would allow one to find evidence of test bias. That is, Aguinis et al. contend that there are insufficient data to conclude confidently that cognitive ability tests are not biased against racial/ethnic minorities.

Notwithstanding the claim by Aguinis et al. with regard to data limitations (especially with respect to small sample sizes of minority groups on which analyses were based), Berry, Clark, and McClure[29] provided the largest test to date of racial/ethnic differential validity for cognitive ability tests. Specifically, their meta-analysis included more than one million participants aggregated across and within the literatures on educational admissions, civilian employment, and selection into the military. They found the criterion-related validity for cognitive ability tests to be stronger for whites (mean $r = .33$; $N = 903\ 779$) and Asians (mean $r = .33$; $N = 80\ 705$) than for blacks (mean $r = .24$; $N = 112\ 194$) and Hispanics (mean $r = .30$; $N = 51\ 205$). While the trend toward lower predictive validities for blacks compared to whites was evident in all three study domains (education, civilian employment, military employment), it was strongest in military samples. Stronger validities for whites over Hispanics were evident within the educational domain only. Further, Berry et al. found that in civilian employment settings, mean black validity was less than mean white validity for subjective measures of performance (i.e., supervisor ratings) but not for more objective criterion measures, raising the question as to whether bias in performance ratings underlie the group differences in validities. Adding to the complexity of their findings, and the need for further research on racial/ethnic bias associated with using cognitive ability testing in high-stakes selection, Berry et al. also found that predictive validities were stronger for blacks than for whites when their analysis excluded studies in which cognitive ability was measured by the General Aptitude Test Battery (GATB).

The growing demands on workers to learn new tasks quickly as they move among assignments and encounter ever-changing technology will not diminish. Accordingly, the power of GMA to predict job success is likely to strengthen. Cognitive ability testing is extremely cost-effective and has, to date, withstood court challenges both in Canada and the United States, although it tends to be one of the more frequently challenged selection tools in U.S. courts.[30,31,32]

To be sure, there is compelling evidence of cognitive ability measurements serving as a consistent predictor of performance in training and on the job. At the same time, the more recent studies reported above suggest that differential prediction and bias by race and ethnicity associated with the use of cognitive ability in high stakes selection cannot be ruled out. This creates a dilemma that is only exacerbated by the substantial adverse impact that cognitive ability measurements have been shown to have on blacks and Hispanics.[33] While the bulk of research showing such adverse impact has been conducted in the United States, similar findings have been reported using Canadian samples. For example, mean differences in favour of whites (relative to visible minorities) were uncovered among police officer applicants on two commonly used measures of cognitive ability (the General Aptitude Test Battery and Raven's Standard Progressive Matrices [SPM]).[34] Two other studies conducted in Canada have shown similar effects, one of municipal bus operators[35] and the other involving police services recruits.[36] In their survey of 154 organizations across Canada, Ng and Sears[37] found that an organization's reported use of cognitive ability testing in selection was positively associated with lower levels of minority group representation in the organization as a whole, and in management ranks (after having statistically controlled for other diversity management practices). They also found that firms covered under employment equity legislation were less likely to use cognitive ability tests compared to those organizations not covered by such legislation. This latter finding may well reflect the desire of organizations covered under employment equity legislation to avoid using selection tests likely to result in adverse impact against Canadian minority group members.

In light of the above, should cognitive ability tests be used in high stakes selection? While such tests are strong predictors of performance in training and on the job, and are likely to become increasingly predictive given the changing nature of work, there is increasing evidence that they could disadvantage members of visible minority groups. Outtz[38] suggested that the adverse impact associated with using cognitive ability tests could be reduced by replacing them with structured interviews, biodata, and personality measures that have lower validities than cognitive ability tests but also considerably less adverse impact. However, depending on their content and structure, some of these alternative measures may have a strong cognitive component. Given the rising importance of cognitive ability for many of today's knowledge-based jobs (with unskilled work being transported overseas), Canadian employers are likely best to continue measuring cognitive ability, but lessening its potential adverse impact by including it among a battery of other assessments that are predictive of performance, and that have much less or no adverse impact (e.g., personality). This approach has been shown to reduce adverse impact associated with using cognitive ability test scores alone.[39,40,41] This strategy is especially recommended when an applicant pool includes members of different racial groups, which is likely to be the case for many Canadian employers.

Another strategy for lessening adverse impact is to perhaps first determine the nature of the job and then consider whether verbal ability is a bona fide occupational requirement. Most measurements of cognitive ability are verbal measurements in that they require a fair degree of reading ability. If verbal ability is not essential, it may be appropriate to base employment decisions on nonverbal measurements of cognitive ability. Vanderpool and Catano[42] demonstrated that members of First Nations living in remote areas of Manitoba performed as well as predominantly white recruits undergoing military training on nonverbal cognitive tests such as the SPM mentioned above, but at a much lower level on verbal measurements such as the Wonderlic Personnel Test. If enrollment decisions into the Canadian Forces and subsequent occupational assignments were made solely on the basis of the verbal cognitive tests, adverse impact most likely would occur; First Nations members might not qualify for enrollment in the Forces or, if they were to qualify, they might be assigned to the lowest-status jobs. The study suggested that nonverbal tests of cognitive ability could be substituted for verbal cognitive ability tests with little loss in predictive ability for occupations involving a high degree of spatial ability. However, more research here is needed because, as noted above, Hausdorf et al. found adverse impact on visible minority applicants for police constable positions with respect to the SPM.[43]

Overall, the political controversy over the use of cognitive ability testing in employment decisions remains, though use of such tests has withstood legal scrutiny in both the

United States and Canada. Those employers who continue to use cognitive ability testing in selection despite the associated controversy likely do so because of the large economic benefits associated with having in place a workforce capable of quickly acquiring new knowledge demanded of fast-changing jobs, and one that is quick to process information efficiently and accurately to facilitate decision making and problem solving, in work roles that increasingly lack clear structure and that change quickly. Rather than dismissing the use of cognitive ability testing in employee selection, we need to better understand and address the sources of the lower cognitive ability performance of certain minority group members relative to their nonminority member counterparts.

Beyond job performance, GMA positively predicts overall career success (e.g., income and occupational prestige). Judge, Klinger, and Lauren[44] showed that the careers of people high in GMA rose more steeply over time than was the case for people low in GMA, attributable to the former group attaining more formal education, completing more job training, and taking up more complex jobs. Moreover, even where people of lower GMA pursued higher education, completed job training, and were employed in more complex jobs, this did not translate into the same level of career success (income, occupational prestige) for them as it did for their higher GMA counterparts. Further, GMA relates directly and indirectly (through healthy behaviours and occupational prestige) to physical well-being (health) and wealth, which in turn relate to overall subjective well-being.[45] Clearly, the societal importance to understanding differences in GMA between minority and majority group members is high.

MULTIPLE APTITUDE TEST BATTERIES

Over the years, a number a specific cognitive abilities have been identified; for example, verbal and numerical ability and inductive and deductive reasoning (see Fleishman and Reilly[46] for a comprehensive list). Psychometrically sound tests are available for these specific cognitive abilities. But will assessing specific abilities provide improvement in prediction over GMA? One line of research downplays the importance of specific abilities in prediction, suggesting that they add only marginally to predictions based on GMA alone.[47] Others argue for measuring specific abilities, noting that such tests provide statistically significant, though small, increases in prediction beyond general cognitive ability.[48] As well, tests of specific abilities (e.g., verbal, numerical, and reasoning) have provided validity coefficients in the same range as GMA.[49] Proponents of GMA suggest that the validities of specific ability tests occur because they and GMA measure the same construct.[50]

Different theories exist as to why measurements of specific abilities may improve on predictions based on overall GMA. Carroll[51] proposed a hierarchical model in which GMA, at the apex, is the most general level of cognitive ability and underlies performance across a broad spectrum of cognitively demanding tasks. The next level down contains broad abilities that apply to performance on clusters of tasks. These broad abilities include visual perception, auditory perception, and cognitive speediness, among others. At the lowest level in the hierarchy are more specific abilities that are more homogeneous and narrower than those at the broad ability level. For example, spatial relations, sound discrimination, and perceptual speed, respectively, would relate to the above-noted broader abilities.

Other researchers[52] have proposed a nonhierarchical model of general mental ability, one referred to as the "nested-factors model." At the risk of oversimplifying, this model does *not* assume that GMA alone explains one's standing on each of a number of more specific cognitive abilities. Rather, it assumes (1) that both GMA and the narrower cognitive abilities directly (and uniquely) explain variance (differences) in performance on cognitive ability tests; and (2) GMA has no causal effect on cognitive abilities, and therefore, GMA is not a "higher order factor" (as per the hierarchical model noted above). With respect to this nested model, then, specific cognitive abilities develop to varying strengths, depending less on GMA and more on genetic and environmental differences among people. Where one person may have high resources (from genetics or environmental exposure) for memory processes, another may have high resources for spatial relations, and during development such resource advantages facilitate development of other cognitive resources. This means that people with different types of initial resource advantages will develop high performance on a broad variety of cognitive abilities, whereas others without such initial resource advantage will not. For a more complete explanation of the differences between the hierarchical and nested-factors model of cognitive abilities see Lang, Kersting, Hulsheger, and Lang.[53]

Whether one subscribes to the hierarchical or the nested-factors model will determine the data analytic strategy most appropriate for determining the relative importance of GMA and specific cognitive abilities as predictors of job performance. In using a data analytic approach most suited to the nested-factors model (relative importance analysis), Jonas et al. found[54] that GMA accounted for between 10.9 percent and 28.6 percent of the total variance explained in job performance and, importantly, though GMA was an important predictor, so was verbal comprehension (a specific ability). Their analyses drew from a meta-analytic intercorrelation matrix they constructed from a large body of studies that used a German ability test battery (the Wilde Intelligence Test), suggesting their results to be quite robust (i.e., reliable).

On the face of it, it seems reasonable that job applicants who do well on GMA may not possess the narrower abilities particularly important to performance. If a set of specific abilities is likely essential for successful performance, then inclusion of predictors related to those abilities in selection systems should lead to improved validity.

The Canadian Forces uses cognitive ability testing as part of its selection process. Potential recruits into the Forces complete the Canadian Forces Aptitude Test (CFAT), which validly predicts performance in a wide range of military occupations. (For examples and practice questions, see http://www.publicserviceprep.com/public/full_pkg_canadianforces.aspx. Click on "sample questions" at the bottom of the page to work through a sample aptitude test based on the CFAT.) The CFAT is an example of a multiple aptitude test battery.

Is the small increase in validity that testing specific abilities may provide over GMA worth the time and money spent in assessing them, particularly since they tend to be highly correlated with measurements of GMA?[55] Although the bulk of evidence supports the view that in most instances measuring specific abilities will not provide much in improved prediction over GMA alone,[56] it appears that in some cases measuring specific abilities in addition to GMA could prove helpful. Such cases could include those where specific abilities are of particular importance to task performance (i.e., nonsubstitutable or noncompensable)[57,58] such as vigilance and spatial relations for air-traffic controllers, or figural reasoning and spatial relations for architects (or students applying to advanced studies in architecture). Likewise, some basic level of numerical ability is likely required for bank customer service representatives (i.e., "tellers"). Of course, multiple aptitude test batteries, such as the GATB, provide specific aptitude scores that are used in deriving an overall GMA score, allowing HR practitioners to ensure that job candidates score "well" on the specific cognitive abilities deemed most relevant to the target job.

When considering which assessments to include in employee selection, costs, applicant reactions, perceived fairness, organizational goals, managerial acceptance, and legal concerns all need to be considered.[59] Some selection experts have suggested that using measures of specific cognitive abilities rather than a GMA test may improve applicant reactions, in that specific measures are often more transparently related to what applicants, managers, and other stakeholders deem job relevant.[60,61] Also, selecting for specific abilities (in lieu of reliance on GMA) may offer another way in which potential adverse impact of cognitive ability tests could be reduced. These considerations strengthen the case for measuring specific cognitive abilities in employee selection.

PRACTICAL INTELLIGENCE AND JOB KNOWLEDGE

Practical intelligence
The ability to apply ideas in "real world" contexts.

Sternberg and his associates[62,63] distinguish practical intelligence from intellectual or academic ability. The distinction between academic intelligence and **practical intelligence** is similar to the difference between declarative knowledge and procedural knowledge described in Chapter 5. Practical knowledge is related to knowing how to get things done. Some characterize it as "street smarts" or "common sense" in contrast to academic intelligence or "book smarts."[64] For example, consider two department managers competing to increase their respective budgets. Both have the intellectual ability to put together a rational proposal based on facts and figures to support their positions. The successful manager knows that the proposal alone will not succeed; the successful manager will know how to craft the report to show that the budget increase will also accomplish the goals of the decision makers and will know whom to lobby within the organization for support of the proposal.

Tacit knowledge
Knowledge that is derived from experience when learning is not the primary objective.

Tacit knowledge is an important component of practical knowledge or procedural knowledge that is used to solve practical, everyday problems. It is knowledge that is derived from experience when learning is not the primary objective. It is knowledge about how to perform tasks in different situations and knowledge that an individual uses to help attain specific goals.[65] Tacit knowledge is typically measured through situational judgment tests (SJTs, discussed later in this chapter) that consist of a series of questions and response options on how best to behave in a number of situations representative of the sorts of situations one is likely to encounter if hired and placed in the job.[66]

Measurements of tacit knowledge or practical intelligence have predicted performance of bank managers, salespeople, and military personnel.[67,68,69] Other evidence, however, does not provide support for practical intelligence as a predictor of job success.[70] Taub[71] compared GMA and practical intelligence as predictors of success among a sample of university students. Taub found that intellectual and practical intelligence were, indeed, independent constructs, but he could not find that practical intelligence was a better predictor of real-world success than GMA. Lobsenz[72] found results similar to Taub's when he used a measurement of practical intelligence to predict job performance of entry-level telecommunications managers. Practical intelligence did not improve on the predictions that could be made from GMA alone.

McDaniel and Whetzel[73] make the point that measurements of practical intelligence are SJTs that measure multiple constructs, mostly *g* and personality, and have a long history of predicting job performance. They argue that SJTs do not measure a general factor as suggested by Sternberg, whether that factor is called practical intelligence or something else.[74] Practical intelligence remains an intriguing concept, and tests measuring it are likely most appropriate where new hires are expected to be "up and running" relatively quickly, with little mentoring or socialization. Such tests, however, do not substitute for GMA. Further, tests of practical intelligence are prone to candidates challenging the "right answers" (as what is deemed correct has been determined by a panel of people experienced in the job), unlike GMA, with definite correct answers.

A concept related to practical intelligence or tacit knowledge is **job knowledge**. In fact, Schmidt and Hunter[75] argue that practical intelligence is a narrow, specialized case of job knowledge, although Sternberg argues that, unlike job knowledge, which is simply declarative knowledge, practical knowledge is broader in that it includes procedural knowledge.[76] Job knowledge tests assess job applicants' or employees' knowledge of issues or procedures that are considered essential to successful job performance. Members of many professions must submit to an examination of their knowledge related to important professional practices and procedures before they are allowed entry into the profession. To practise law, a law school graduate must first have served a form of apprenticeship (articling) to gain knowledge and experience about legal procedures and then pass a written test that assesses these (known as the "bar" exam). Job knowledge tests have validities that average 0.45 with job performance. These types of tests tend to have higher validity when used to select people for high-complexity jobs. Clearly, they are most appropriate for use in selection where job knowledge requirements are expected to be fulfilled prior to hiring, and not learned on the job. It is not uncommon for job knowledge tests to be used to aid internal selection decisions, such as in lateral moves or promotions. Finally, job knowledge tests are more effective when they are job specific; that is, when a unique knowledge test is developed for each occupation or profession.[77]

Job knowledge
Knowledgeable of issues and/or procedures deemed essential for successful job performance.

EMOTIONAL INTELLIGENCE

The definition in the sidebar treats EQ as an ability; one of several intelligences. It is also multifaceted, in that it encompasses (1) the ability to perceive emotions; (2) the ability to use emotions to facilitate thought; (3) the ability to understand emotions; (4) and the ability to manage emotions.[78,79] This four-component ability-based model of EQ emphasizes information processing (consistent with the notion of EQ as reflecting an underlying intelligence). The Mayer-Salovey-Caruso **emotional intelligence** test (MSCEIT)[80] was developed to capture this conceptualization of EQ.

Emotional intelligence
The ability to accurately perceive and appraise emotion in oneself and others, and to appropriately regulate and express emotion.

Another popular EQ scale is the Emotional Quotient Inventory (EQ-i). It was intended as a broader ability-based measure than the MSCEIT, assessing both emotional *and* social intelligence across four main components (ability to be aware of, to understand, and to express oneself; the ability to be aware of, to understand, and relate to others; the ability to deal with strong emotions and control one's impulses; and the ability to adapt to change and to solve problems of a personal or social nature).[81,82]

The advantage of the MSCEIT over the EQ-i is that it has respondents complete a number of performance-based tasks reflecting its component parts (e.g., rating emotional facial expressions; choosing the most appropriate emotional responses in a variety of social situations presented in a series of vignettes). The EQ-i, on the other hand, is a self-report, consisting of items of the sort you would see on a personality inventory. There is considerable and compelling literature showing that people are biased when evaluating their own abilities.[83] For this reason, HR professionals do not ask job candidates to self-report on their GMA.

Many of the EQ-i factors themselves fall outside Mayer and Salovey's conceptions of EQ and are not much different from traditional personality factors. Newsome, Day, and Catano,[84] in fact, showed that there were moderate to high correlations between the EQ-i subscales and the five primary personality factors (known as the Big

Five–conscientiousness, extraversion, openness to experience, agreeableness, and emotional stability), similar to findings reported by Grubb and McDaniel.[85] These researchers accordingly viewed the EQ-i as an aggregate of the Big Five, and further showed that the EQ-i was highly "fakable." Actually, as noted by Mayer, Roberts, and Barsade,[86] the EQ-i measures a mix of constructs, including noncognitive capability, competency, or skill,[87] emotionally and socially intelligent behavior,[88] and personality dispositions.[89] A quantitative review of the EQ literature showed that measures reflecting mixed models of EQ overlap more with personality than with ability-based measures, while ability-based measures of EQ relate more highly to cognitive ability than to measures of mixed models.[90] Accordingly, if treating EQ as ability, the MSCEIT is recommended over the EQ-i. A review and guide to several other measures of EQ is provided by Mayer et al.

The usefulness of EQ measures in predicting job performance is best assessed through meta-analysis, which provides a quantitative assessment of the mean correlation reported between two or more variables derived from all independently executed studies. The most recent and most comprehensive meta-analysis of the EQ–job performance relationship was conducted by O'Boyle and his colleagues.[91] They sorted EQ studies into three primary groupings: (1) studies that used ability-based measures of EQ with objective test items; (2) studies that used self-report measures of EQ derived from Mayer and Salovey's four-component model of EQ[92]; and (3) studies that derived scores of EQ from measuring a mix of emotional and social competencies. They found that the studies from group 2 (self-report measures) and group 3 (mixed measures) offered the best prediction of job performance beyond measures of cognitive ability and the Big Five personality factors. These results are quite similar to those reported by Joseph and Newman.[93] O'Boyle et al. concluded that the approach to use in measuring EQ should be guided by the objectives underlying the assessment of EI, noting that objectively scored ability-based measures of EQ (group 1 measures, e.g., MSCEIT) may be best to use in selection because they are least susceptible to social desirability and faking.[94]

Joseph and Newman offer insights into the processes by which EQ impacts job performance.[95] Specifically, they found empirical support for a cascading (progressive) causal model, wherein accurate perceptions of one's own and others' emotion facilitates emotion understanding. Emotion understanding helps with emotion regulation, which in turn positively predicts job performance. Also, within their model, conscientiousness, cognitive ability, and emotional stability positively predicted perception of emotions, emotion understanding, and emotion regulation, respectively. This latter finding may help explain the predictive validity of mixed measures of EQ (which appear to have a heavy personality component). Importantly, Joseph and Newman found stronger EQ–performance relationships for jobs high in emotional labour ($r = .22$) than for jobs low in emotional labour ($r = .00$). Moreover, the incremental validity coefficient for EQ (beyond the Big Five and cognitive ability) was positive for high–emotional labour jobs, but negative for low–emotional labour jobs. Emotional labour refers to the demands a job places on the incumbent for managing/regulating one's own emotions. Jobs requiring a consistent presentation of positive emotion are considered high in emotional labour (e.g., flight attendants, sales agents, counsellors). Also, females scored higher on performance-based assessments of EQ than did men, and whites scored higher than blacks on both performance-based ability measures and self-report mixed measures of EQ.

The above research focuses on the potential work-related benefits of EQ. Other researchers, however, have considered the potential negative side of high EQ. Specifically, Kilduff, Chiaburu, and Menges[96] suggest that individuals high in EQ are likely better able to disguise and express emotions for personal gain, to stir and shape the emotions of others, and to control the flow of emotion-laden communication in ways that are detrimental to other employees and the organization overall. This, of course, suggests that whether EQ is likely to be used to the detriment or benefit of the organization may depend on other factors (e.g., personality disposition, personal virtues, and motives). As more primary studies of EQ–performance relationships become available that include different facets of performance (e.g., including OCB, prosocial behaviours), such potential moderators can be more thoroughly examined. A start in this direction is a study by Dion Greenidge and his colleagues.[97]

So, what conclusions can be drawn about the use of EQ for human resource selection? First, ability performance-based assessments of EQ best align with an ability/intelligence conceptualization of EQ. Self-reports of EQ, particularly those that are designed to measure a mix of personality, motivation, and social competencies, may be more difficult to defend when used in high-stakes decisions, as in selection. This is due to the construct ambiguity surrounding these assessments. Construct measurements used in selection must relate clearly to job requirements. This is very difficult to show for a measure of EQ that is so heterogeneous and ill defined. Second, the cascading model of EQ presented by Joseph and Newman suggests that emotion regulation is the component of EQ most directly related to job performance–that it is through the regulation of emotions that the other components of EQ influence performance.[98] This suggests that, for selection purposes, a measure of emotional regulation may be more efficient and effective in predicting performance than a broader EQ measure. There are ability-based assessments of emotion regulation, including situational judgment tests, either written or video based.[99] Third, while the empirical data suggest that EQ provides a statistically significant improvement in predicting performance over using measures of cognitive ability and personality, it is not yet clear that this improvement will be of practical significance. This is especially so when one considers that some elements of EQ, and certainly some aspects of social and emotional competencies, are (or can be) assessed through other means, such as structured interviews and/or reference checks. Fourth, the potential benefits of measuring EQ are likely to be maximal when selecting for jobs high in emotional labour. Fifth, we are only in the early stages of determining the potential adverse impact of using EQ assessments in selection.

Overall, the empirical literature is not yet at the point where measuring EQ to inform selection decisions can be confidently endorsed. Social and emotional competencies deemed relevant to a job, as determined through job analysis, can and should be mapped onto selection tools designed specifically to measure those competencies (including paper and pencil assessments, behavioural interviewing, situational judgment tests), rather than relying on measures of a heterogeneous ill-defined measured of EQ. Emotional intelligence is best assessed, if used for selection purposes, by use of ability-based measures of EQ.[100,101,102] However, there is yet a strong business case to be made for including assessments of EQ in employee selection processes, given scant empirical support for their predictive validity.[103]

PSYCHOMOTOR ABILITY TESTS

Psychomotor abilities involve controlled muscle movements that are necessary to complete a task. Examples of psychomotor abilities include finger dexterity, multilimb coordination, reaction time, arm–hand steadiness, and manual dexterity. Many tasks, from simple to complex, require coordinated movements for their success. Psychomotor abilities are often overlooked in selecting people for jobs. Consider a drummer who must independently move all four limbs and exercise hand–wrist coordination, all in a

Psychomotor abilities
Traits or characteristics that involve the control of muscle movements.

coordinated fashion; imagine an orchestra whose drummer had an extensive knowledge of music theory but little psychomotor ability. While GMA might predict ability to learn to read and understand music, it would not predict the level of motor coordination.

Canadian dental schools use tests of finger and manual dexterity as part of their selection process; all applicants are required to carve a tooth from a block of soap, which is then judged by a panel of dentists. The General Aptitude Test Battery (GATB) includes tests that involve apparatus that measure psychomotor ability in addition to cognitive and perceptual aptitudes (e.g., the Manual Dexterity and Finger Dexterity scales).

Although psychomotor tests can be quite successful in predicting performance in a number of jobs,[104,105,106] they are not as popular as cognitive tests. They involve individual testing on a specialized piece of equipment, and require more time and expense to administer. Nonetheless, they can improve predictions that are based only on cognitive ability. Johnston and Catano showed that the addition of psychomotor measures from the GATB significantly improved predictions of training success for mechanical jobs in the Canadian Forces by 5 percent when added to a cognitive ability measure.[107]

PHYSICAL AND SENSORY/PERCEPTUAL ABILITY TESTS

Physical abilities
Traits or characteristics that involve the use or application of muscle force over varying periods of time, either alone or in conjunction with an ability to maintain balance or gross body coordination.

Sensory/perceptual abilities
Traits or characteristics that involve different aspects of vision and audition, as well as the other senses.

Physical abilities are involved in the physical performance of a job or task. They generally involve use or application of muscle force over varying periods of time, either alone or in conjunction with an ability to maintain balance or gross body coordination. Physical abilities include both static and dynamic strength, body flexibility, balance, and stamina. Physical requirements for occupational tasks generally fall into three broad physical ability categories: strength, endurance, and quality of movement.[108]

Sensory/perceptual abilities involve different aspects of vision and audition. They include near and far vision, colour discrimination, sound localization, and speech recognition, among others.[109] Physical abilities and sensory/perceptual abilities are very similar in their relationship to job performance and in how they are assessed.

The performance of many jobs or tasks may require workers to possess one or more physical or sensory/perceptual abilities. A firefighter may need the strength to carry a body out of a burning building; a pilot may need adequate near and far vision to fly a plane; a soldier may need the strength and stamina to carry 100 kilograms of equipment for a long period of time and still be ready for combat; a construction worker may need strength to lift material and balance to keep from falling off a roof. People who possess greater amounts of these sensory/perceptual abilities perform better in jobs where such abilities are important.[110] Physical tests of strength and endurance are routinely used in selecting individuals for police officer and other protective services personnel such as firefighters.[111] As part of its comprehensive selection procedures, the Royal Canadian Mounted Police (RCMP) tests all applicants for physical ability.

Statistics from the National Institute of Occupational Safety and Health in the United States indicate that workers are three times more likely to be injured while performing jobs for which they have not demonstrated the required strength capabilities. Although medical and physical fitness exams (which are discussed later in this chapter) provide a measurement of wellness, they do not give sufficient indication of whether the candidate can perform the task requirements safely. Thus, more job-specific physical ability testing can help employers select workers who are capable of performing strenuous tasks, leading to fewer accidents, injuries, and associated costs, and increases in productivity.[112]

Tests of physical ability are quite varied but involve physical activity on the part of the applicant. Only a few physical ability tests require equipment. For example, a hand dynamometer is used to measure static strength. The hand dynamometer resembles the handgrips used in most gyms. The applicant squeezes the grips with full strength and the resultant force is measured by an attached scale. Pull-ups or push-ups are used to measure dynamic strength, sit-ups are used to assess body trunk strength, and 1500-metre runs, step tests, and treadmill tests are used to measure stamina and endurance.

Establishing cutoff scores on physical tests often leads to litigation, with unsuccessful applicants challenging the appropriateness of the scores that were chosen. This was precisely the situation that led to the Supreme Court's *Meiorin* decision we discussed in Recruitment and Selection Today 3.7, in which an employed forest firefighter lost her job because she failed to complete a 2.5-kilometre run in the required time, even though she had passed the other physical ability tests. The court upheld a labour arbitrator's decision to reinstate the dismissed firefighter. It held that the established cutoff had not taken into account differences in aerobic capacity between men and women and that most women could not raise their aerobic capacity to the required level even with training. The court found that the employer had not shown that the cutoff was reasonably necessary to identify individuals who could perform in a satisfactory manner as firefighters. Neither did the employer demonstrate that accommodating women would cause undue hardship.[113]

In some cases, physical standards, rather than physical ability or sensory/perceptual ability tests, are used for selection. A police department may require all applicants to meet certain height and weight requirements and to have uncorrected 20/20 vision. The physical standards are used as a substitute for actual physical testing. It is assumed that people who fall within the specified range should have the physical abilities required for successful job performance. It is often very difficult to justify that the physical standards in use meet legitimate job requirements. Indeed, many physical standards were set in the past to exclude members of certain groups, particularly women. When physical standards are set in such an arbitrary fashion, they are open to challenge before human rights tribunals, with employers subject to severe penalties. It is reasonable to set physical requirements for jobs as long as they are job related and nondiscriminatory. In its *Meiorin* decision, the Supreme Court upheld this position and laid out a series of important questions that must be answered in establishing physical or sensory/perceptual standards.

PHYSICAL FITNESS AND MEDICAL EXAMINATIONS

Many employers routinely administer physical fitness tests as part of their hiring process. Their intent is not to identify job-related physical abilities, but rather to screen out unhealthy or unfit individuals. The employer is concerned that placing physically non-fit people in jobs requiring some physical effort could lead to injury or illness, or that the work will be carried out in an unsafe manner. From the employer's view, hiring physically non-fit workers means lost productivity, replacement costs, and legal damages from coworkers and customers who have been injured through their actions.

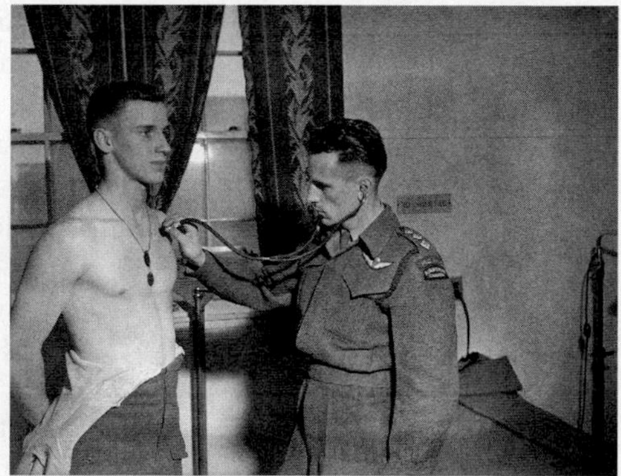
Capt. Frank Royal / Canada. Dept. of National Defence / Library and Archives Canada / PA-188829

The intent of physical fitness tests is to ensure that an applicant meets minimum standards of health to cope with the physical demands of the job. Canadian federal regulations also require physical or medical testing of applicants for certain dangerous occupations (e.g., deep-sea diver), or for jobs that may bring them into contact with dangerous chemical substances such as lead or asbestos. In addition to identifying any health problems, medical examinations provide baseline data for comparison of any job-related changes in the applicant's health that may be covered through Workers' Compensation or other insurance programs.

WHEN SHOULD PHYSICAL/MEDICAL EXAMS BE GIVEN?

Fitness testing or physical or medical examinations should be administered only after an offer of employment, which is made conditional on the applicant's passing the test. The physical or medical exam is generally the last step in selection. The employer must demonstrate that the health or fitness requirement is related to performing the job safely, reliably, and efficiently. Physical fitness testing is no different from any other assessment and must meet the same technical standards. In Canada, human rights acts require that medical or physical examinations of job candidates are job related.

PEOPLE WITH DISABILITIES

Requiring physical examinations before any offer of employment raises issues of privacy and also leaves the prospective employer open to charges of discrimination. This last concern is a major issue in hiring people who may have a disability. Canada was the first country to include equality rights for persons with mental or physical disabilities in its Constitution. Section 15.1 of the Canadian Charter of Rights and Freedoms provides for equal protection and equal benefit of the law without discrimination based on mental or physical disability. Every human rights act in Canada now includes protection against discrimination on the grounds of disability or handicap.

In Canada, the duty to accommodate people with disabilities in the workplace is much stronger. After the *Meiorin* decision, which we discussed in Chapter 3, there is a legal requirement for employers to work proactively, to the point of undue hardship, to eliminate policies, work rules, standards, or practices that discriminate against groups or individuals on the basis of physical or mental disability or handicap (there is no legal distinction between the terms "disability" and "handicap"). An employer, for example, could not refuse to hire an applicant with the strongest computer programming skills within the applicant pool for computer programmer on the basis of that person requiring special provisions because she was confined to a wheelchair. Reasonable accommodation short of "undue hardship" to the employer is necessary. The only exception is if the employer can establish that the mobility of the employee is a bona fide occupational requirement under the stringent test laid out in the *Meiorin* decision. The legal precedent established in *Meiorin* has been reinforced through many decisions rendered by human rights tribunals and the judiciary since then. Criteria for establishing a bona fide occupational requirement were presented in Chapter 3. Procedures following *Meiorin* for establishing reasonable accommodation were presented in Recruitment and Selection Notebook 3.4. The Canadian Human Rights Commission provides a template for developing organizational policy on workplace accommodation: http://www.chrc-ccdp.ca/eng/content/template-developing-workplace-accommodation-policy.

HIV AND AIDS TESTING

Employers are sensitive to hiring individuals with acquired immune deficiency syndrome (AIDS) or the human immunodeficiency virus (HIV). The current Canadian Human

Rights Commission policy, adopted in 1996, states, "The Commission will not accept being free from HIV/AIDS as a bona fide occupational requirement (BFOR) or a bona fide justification (BFJ) unless it can be proven that such a requirement is essential to the safe, efficient and reliable performance of the essential functions of a job or is a justified requirement for receiving programs or services."[114] The Commission cites policy statements of the Canadian Medical Association in support of its position. The Commission believes that "in the employment setting, medical testing should occur only where determination of the condition being assessed is necessary for the safe, efficient and reliable performance of the essential components of the job."[115] The Commission does not support pre- or post-employment testing for HIV. Decisions from the Canadian Human Rights Tribunal with respect to HIV/AIDS–related complaints can be found at http://decisions.chrt-tcdp.gc.ca/chrt-tcdp/en/d/s/index.do?cont=HIV.

GENETIC TESTING

The Health Law Institute at the University of Alberta reported that 24 percent of genetic specialists believed employers should have access to an employee's confidential medical records to determine whether the employee is likely to develop a genetic disease that could be costly to the employer.[116] Undoubtedly, many employers agree. **Genetic testing** is a controversial issue entailing job applicants. Genetic monitoring is used to detect exposure to workplace toxins or as an alert to workplace hazards. Genetic screening is also used to detect hereditary susceptibility to workplace toxins. The genetic screen could be used as a pre-employment test to reduce the risk of hiring someone likely to develop heredity-based adverse reactions to workplace toxins.[117] For example, applicants who have an inherited sensitivity to lead would not be hired for work in a lead battery plant.

Genetic testing
The testing or monitoring of genetic material to determine a genetic propensity or susceptibility to illness resulting from various workplace chemicals or substances.

Genetic screening raises many ethical and legal considerations.[118] MacDonald and Williams-Jones[119] argue that it is morally problematic to require employees to submit to genetic testing, as this would be an invasion of privacy and subject employees to a range of poorly understood tests. They propose that it is permissible to offer employees, on a voluntary basis, the opportunity for genetic testing only when certain conditions are met (see Recruitment and Selection Notebook 8.4), believing that no company should rush into genetic testing without considerable forethought because of the associated ethical problems. On the other hand, MacDonald and Williams-Jones argue that in some cases an employer is obligated to offer genetic testing when beneficial to employees. In addition to meeting the requirements specified in Recruitment and Selection Notebook 8.4, the results of genetic testing could impact employees' decisions to remain in their job.

The Human Genome Project, a $4 billion international effort to map all genetic material, has the potential to have a profound effect on how workers and their employers look at health hazards, privacy, and medical information. In the United States, where most health-care programs are privately funded by employers, there have been reports that applicants are being denied employment on the grounds that they are genetically more likely to develop cancer or environmentally related illnesses. In response to these concerns, the U.S. government amended the Americans with Disabilities Act to define genetic predisposition as a disability and to prohibit discrimination on the basis of genetic information. Over half of U.S. states have followed suit in banning the use of genetic information in making workplace decisions. There is less incentive for employers to do genetic screening in Canada to screen out individuals with certain genetic predispositions because of the availability of publicly funded health care in Canada.[120]

RECRUITMENT AND SELECTION NOTEBOOK 8.4

REQUIREMENTS THAT MUST BE MET IN THE UNITED STATES BEFORE OFFERING VOLUNTARY GENETIC TESTING TO EMPLOYEES

1. A genetic test is available that is highly specific and sensitive and has acceptably low false-positive and false-negative rates.
2. Tests must be carried out by an independent lab, with the results given directly to the worker by a genetic counsellor on a confidential basis and revealed to the employer only by the employee.
3. Pre- and post-test genetic counselling must be provided to the employees at the employer's expense.
4. The test must not focus on a gene that is predominantly associated with an identifiable and historically disadvantaged group.
5. Where relevant, the employer must guarantee continued access to group insurance regardless of the test outcome.
6. The employer must ensure that those employees who disclose that they have tested positive will retain a reasonable degree of job security.

Additional sources on the ethics of genetic testing can be found at http://www.genethics.ca.

Source: Adapted from C. MacDonald and B. Williams-Jones. 2002. "Ethics and Genetics: Susceptibility Testing in the Workplace," *Journal of Business Ethics*, 35: 235–41. Reproduced with permission of Kluwer Academic Publishers (Dordrecht) via Copyright Clearance Center.

At present, there is no ban on using genetic information to make employment decisions in Canada and it is probable that some use has occurred. It is very likely, however, that any workplace discrimination on the basis of genetic information would be excluded under existing provisions of the Charter of Rights and the various provincial human rights acts. A genetic predisposition would likely be considered a disability that would have to be reasonably accommodated by an employer.

REQUIREMENT TO ACCOMMODATE

Canadian employers cannot discriminate on the basis of a medical, genetic, or physical condition unless that condition poses a serious and demonstrable impediment to the conduct of the work or poses serious threats to the health and safety of people. Employers have an obligation to accommodate workers with medical or physical conditions on an *individual* basis. As stated by the Supreme Court of Canada in its *Meiorin* decision, "The legislatures have determined that the standards governing the performance of work should be designed to reflect all members of society, in so far as this is reasonably possible." The Court reinforced the need for accommodation by noting:

Courts and tribunals should be sensitive to the various ways in which individual capabilities may be accommodated. Apart from individual testing to determine whether the person has the aptitude or qualification that is necessary to perform the work, the possibility that there may be different ways to perform the job while still accomplishing the employer's legitimate work-related purpose should be considered in appropriate cases. The skills, capabilities and potential contributions of the individual claimants and others like him or her must be respected as much as possible. Employers, courts and tribunals should be innovative yet practical when considering how this may best be done in particular circumstances.[121]

DRUG AND ALCOHOL TESTING

Inevitably, societal changes find their way into the workplace. One of the most profound changes in North American society has been the increased use of drugs as a recreational activity that may carry over into the workplace. Employers often believe that workplace drug and alcohol use is an added expense through costs associated with employee accidents, absenteeism, turnover, and tardiness. Additionally, there may be costs associated with reduced product quality and productivity on the part of employees who use drugs and alcohol in the workplace. In some cases, drug or alcohol use by employees while working may result in threats to the safety of the public and coworkers. In the United States, where many workers receive health insurance through their employer, employers may face escalating costs of health-care insurance related to employee drug abuse.

For these reasons, many employers, with support from both their employees and the public, believe that employee screening for drug and alcohol use is warranted. The screening is then generally applied to all employees and job applicants, not just those in safety-sensitive positions. The intent is to deter individuals with substance abuse problems from applying for a position with the company.

Are these concerns justified? The evidence in support of alcohol and drug testing is far from clear. The relationship between drug use and turnover is relatively small, with correlations ranging from 0.04 to 0.08.[122] However, in a longitudinal study, employees who tested positive for drug use had a 59 percent higher absenteeism rate and a 47 percent higher involuntary turnover rate than those who tested negative.[123] While there are some links between drug and alcohol use and accidents and disciplinary measures,[124] the magnitude of the relationship is probably smaller than people have assumed. Self-reported drug use on the job does appear to be related to how workers behave in the workplace and interact with their coworkers, including antagonistic behaviours such as arguing with coworkers. In almost every workplace there is some expression of deviant behaviour, as noted in Chapter 5, that is not related to substance abuse, however. When this is taken into account the relationship between substance abuse and job performance becomes insignificant.[125]

Notwithstanding the empirical evidence, workplace drug and alcohol testing programs have become quite common in the United States. The Americans with Disabilities Act (ADA) stipulates that pre-employment alcohol testing is a medical examination and may be required only after a conditional offer of employment has been made and in accordance with ADA regulations on pre-employment physicals. However, it allows drug tests to be made before a conditional offer is made provided that the test:

1. accurately identifies only the use of illegal drugs;
2. is not given in conjunction with a pre-employment physical; and
3. does not require the applicant to disclose information about prescription drug use, unless a positive test result may be explained by use of a prescription drug.

DRUG TESTING IN CANADIAN ORGANIZATIONS

Richards Buell Sutton LLP, barristers and solicitors in Vancouver, provide an overview of the status of drug and alcohol testing in Canada in their July 18, 2013 newsletter to clients (http://www.rbs.ca/newsroom-publications-Employee-Drug-Alcohol-Testing-Canada.html). They note that uncertainty around the legality of testing employees for alcohol and drug use is prevalent among Canadian employers largely because there is no legislation specifically permitting or regulating such testing. Accordingly, employers are left to take guidance from court and tribunal decisions. With few exceptions, Canadian courts have generally decided that pre-employment drug or alcohol testing is prohibited as it is deemed discriminatory under human rights legislation. An exception to this is the Alberta Court of Appeal decision allowing for pre-employment drug testing for certain employers hiring for positions in an especially safety-sensitive work environment (Syncrude's Fort McMurray oil sands plant).[126] Following from this decision, the City of Calgary introduced a mandatory pre-employment drug-testing policy for "safety sensitive" jobs, including transit drivers, operators of heavy machinery, and water treatment plant workers. Job applicants, as of 2015, will be subjected to pre-employment testing for marijuana and cocaine.[127] See http://www.calgaryherald.com/health/City+draws+fire+employment+drug+testing/9815703/story.html.

Random drug or alcohol testing of individuals once employed is almost never permitted in Canada. The Supreme Court of Canada has ruled that such testing is not permitted, even in highly dangerous work environments, unless it can be established that there is a general problem of alcohol or drug abuse within the workplace.[128] However, employers are allowed to test for alcohol or drug levels where employees have been involved in a workplace accident and there are reasonable grounds to implicate drug or alcohol related impairment in the accident. Where evidence of impairment to the employee resulting from drug or alcohol consumption is so established, employees cannot be summarily dismissed; rather, they can be suspended or placed on leave to enroll in an employer-sponsored rehabilitation program. On return to work occasional testing is permitted for a period of time to ensure successful rehabilitation.

Notwithstanding the above, the legalities around workplace drug and alcohol testing by employers within Canada are complex, and employers should therefore seek legal counsel when developing a drug and alcohol testing policy, or before disciplining employees for suspected alcohol or drug abuse while on the job. For a more thorough and extensive review of the status of drug testing in Canada, see "Drug and Alcohol Testing: Recent Developments in the Law (May 2013), prepared by Blake, Cassels & Graydon LLP, Vancouver and Calgary (http://www.cle.bc.ca/PracticePoints/LABR/13-DrugandAlcoholTesting.pdf).

WORK SAMPLES AND SIMULATION TESTS

Work samples and simulations
Testing procedures that require job candidates to produce behaviours related to job performance under controlled conditions that approximate those found in the job.

Work samples and simulations are commonly used in selection to assess skills and competencies that are less amenable to traditional cognitive ability and personality testing. For example, written communication skills are best assessed by obtaining written samples from the candidate; oral communication skills may be assessed through an oral presentation; leadership and influence within teams can be assessed by observing the candidate participate in a simulated, unstructured group problem-solving task.

Work samples and simulations require candidates to produce behaviours related to job performance under controlled conditions that approximate those found in the actual job. The candidate is not asked to perform the actual job for several reasons. Actual job performance is affected by many factors other than the applicant's proficiency or aptitude for the job; these factors could impact candidates differentially, so that two applicants with the same proficiency might perform differently. Placing the applicant in the job may also be highly disruptive, costly, time consuming, and dangerous.

Work samples include major tasks taken from the job under consideration; these tasks are organized into an assignment, which the applicant completes. The work sample and the scoring are standardized, allowing for comparisons of skill or aptitude across candidates. Work samples can include both motor and verbal behaviours.[129] The former require applicants to physically manipulate machinery or tools; verbal work samples require the applicants to solve problems involving communication or interpersonal skills.

For example, a secretary's job might include using a computer and related software to type letters and reports, to manage the office budget, to track purchases, to send data files electronically to other people, together with operating the phone and voice-mail systems, scheduling appointments, and receiving people who visit the office. A work sample test given to applicants for this position might include both a motor work sample, using a computer to type and electronically transmit a standardized letter, and a verbal work sample, dealing with a message from the boss that asks the secretary to reschedule several important appointments to allow the boss to keep a dental appointment. The work sample test could be given to the candidate in the actual place of employment or in an off-site setting, and must use standardized instructions, conditions, and equipment.

Recall our discussion of typical versus maximum performance in Chapter 5; work sample performance is clearly a case of maximum performance, where the applicant's motivation may be quite different from that exhibited through typical, day-to-day job performance. Because they incorporate aspects of the job into selection, work samples attain relatively high levels of validity and garner positive applicant reactions.[130,131] In the most recent and most comprehensive meta-analysis of the relationship between work samples and measures of job performance, Roth, Bobko, McFarland, and Buster[132] reported a corrected mean validity of .33. These authors reported a mean observed correlation of .32 between work samples and tests of general cognitive ability, raising concerns about their potential adverse impact on racial and ethnic groups. For example, scores were higher for whites than for blacks on work sample tests that drew most heavily on cognitive ability and job knowledge skills.[133] Moreover, females tend to outperform males on work samples that draw most heavily on social skills and require written responses, while males tend to outperform females on work samples measuring technical skills.[134] Together, this research suggests that content and design of work samples figure importantly in their potential adverse impact on racial, ethnic, and gender groups. Of course, work samples with a heavy technical skills component will often reflect bona fide occupational requirements, with any potential adverse impact on females signalling the need for technical skills upgrading. Moreover, while cognitive ability–laden work samples may have an adverse impact on blacks, less adverse impact (and more favourable applicant reactions) is likely to result from using them in lieu of direct cognitive ability testing.[135] While the design and administration of work samples is certainly more costly for employers than off-the-shelf assessments (such as cognitive ability tests), they are associated with positive applicant reactions–important in tight labour markets.

Simulations, like work samples, attempt to duplicate salient features of the job. Candidates perform a set of designated tasks and are given an objective score based on their performance. The score is used to predict aptitude or proficiency for job performance. Unlike work samples, however, the tasks and the setting in which they are performed represent less of an approximation of the job. That is, the simulation involves a more artificial environment than work sample testing.

The most distinguishing feature of a simulation is its fidelity, the degree to which it represents the real environment. Simulations can range from those with lower fidelity (e.g., a computer simulation of an air traffic controller's function: http://www.atc-sim.com) to those with higher fidelity (e.g., a flight simulator that highly resembles a cockpit to predict pilot behaviour). High-fidelity simulations can be quite expensive, but in some cases there may be no alternative. The simulation allows a type of hands-on performance in an environment that provides substantial safety and cost benefits compared with allowing the applicant to perform in the actual job. While a computer-controlled flight simulator may cost several million dollars to develop and construct, it is far preferable to having prospective pilots demonstrate their flying proficiency in an actual aircraft where a mistake can be deadly, as well as much more costly.

High-fidelity computer-assisted flight simulators are normally used as part of training programs by Air Canada and other Canadian airlines. The Canadian Forces, however, is one of the few organizations to use a simulator in selecting candidates for flight school. The performance on their high-fidelity simulator is a much better predictor of the flying success of future pilots than is a battery of cognitive and psychomotor tests.[136] Generally, the savings from reductions in training failures and training time more than offset the initial cost of the simulator. Interactional multimedia simulations are increasingly used in employee selection, given their ease of administration and cost-effectiveness. For example, custom developed interactive multimedia simulations for call centre employees have shown substantial predictive validity on their own, as well as added prediction beyond the use of non-cognitive measures such as biodata and personality.[137]

Situational exercises are a form of work sample testing used in selecting managers or professionals. They attempt to assess aptitude or proficiency in performing important job tasks, but do so by using tasks that are more abstract and less realistic than those performed on the job. To a large extent, situational exercises are a form of low-fidelity simulation involving the types of skills called on by a job.

Situational exercises
Assess aptitude or proficiency in performing important job tasks by using tasks that are abstract and less realistic than those performed on the actual job.

Situational judgment test
Type of situational exercise designed to measure an applicant's judgment in workplace or professional situations.

Situational exercises have been designed to assess problem-solving ability, leadership potential, and communication skills. For example, at the women's prison in Kitchener, Ontario, a professional actor was hired to play the part of an inmate to assess a candidate's handling of difficult interpersonal situations.[138]

Situational judgment tests (SJTs), also known as *job situation exercises*, are a special type of situational exercise designed to measure an applicant's judgment in workplace or professional situations. They are normally paper-and-pencil tests that ask job candidates how they would respond in different workplace situations.[139,140] However, a variety of video-based SJTs have been developed for use in several occupations.[141,142,143] The situations are developed through interviews with subject-matter experts about critical incidents they have observed in their workplace. The critical incident technique, described in Chapter 4, is used to gather this information. The information is then transformed into items that constitute the SJT.

The number of items on a test may vary. Each situational question includes several response alternatives from which an applicant is asked to choose one. Generally, the candidate is asked to identify the "best" response that could be made in the situation; that is, what one "should do" in a situation. What constitutes the "best" course of action? Generally, after the questions have been developed, they are presented to a second panel of "subject-matter experts" who identify what, in their collective judgment, constitutes the best approach to solving the problem. Recruitment and Selection Today 8.3 presents a sample item on an SJT given to candidates for a managerial position.

RECRUITMENT AND SELECTION TODAY 8.3

A SAMPLE SITUATIONAL JUDGMENT TEST ITEM

You are the new supervisor of a 22-member department. The department is organized into two working groups of 10 members, plus a group leader. You have been on the job for less than a month but members from one working group have been dropping by your office to complain about their leader, Jane. They claim that she has been absent, on average, almost two days a week for the last three months and is not there to provide advice and help when they need it. Even when she is physically present, they claim that she is "not there." As a result, they believe that their own work is suffering. They demand that you take action to ensure that their group leader is performing her job.

Of the following options, which is the best course of action to take?

A. Inform Jane of the complaints made against her and encourage her to meet with her work group to resolve the problems between them.

B. Call Jane to a meeting and inform her that you have reviewed her absence record and that she has been missing two days a week for the last three months. Tell her that this must stop immediately and that any further missed time must be accompanied by a doctor's medical excuse or else she will be suspended.

C. Consult with your boss on how to handle the problem. Find out if Jane is "well connected" to minimize any problems for you in case you have to take action against her.

D. Review Jane's absence record to verify her work group's claims. Review her absence and performance record prior to the recent poor record of absence. Once you have completed the information, call Jane to a meeting, lay out your concerns, and try to determine the causes for her poor attendance. Help formulate a plan to help her overcome the obstacles to her attendance.

On an SJT, candidates could also be asked what they *would* do in the same situations. Ployhart and Ehrhart[144] showed that asking candidates to make "should do" or "would do" responses in SJTs alters both the reliability and validity of the test. They found that "should do" instructions produced outcomes with lower variability but also with lower reliabilities and criterion-related validities than "would do" instructions. However, one limitation of their study was that the SJT consisted of only five items developed for use with student samples, and the results may not apply to selecting employees in actual work situations. Nonetheless, the instructions used as part of the SJT must be carefully considered and match the purpose for which the test is used.

In addition to the response formats of "should do" and "would do," some ask for respondents to rate the degree of the appropriateness of a particular action; others ask the respondent to simply select the "best" and "worst" options, while still others ask for a ranking of best to worst response. Research based on 31,194 job applicants suggests that for non-cognitive constructs, such as integrity, the "rate response" format is superior. SJT scores using this format correlate higher with personality traits they are expected to correlate with, and lower with general mental ability.[145]

On the whole, SJTs are very good predictors of job performance. McDaniel, Morgeson, Finnegan, Campion, and Braverman[146] reported results from a meta-analysis that placed their validity coefficient in the population at 0.34 for predicting job performance. The correlation of SJTs with cognitive ability, $r = 0.36$, suggests that they are tapping into some aspect of general mental ability, which one would expect to see in a test of judgment. However, as Chan and Schmitt[147] showed when working with 164 civil service employees, SJTs measure a stable individual difference attribute that is distinct from cognitive ability and personality. In a series of meta-analyses, McDaniel and his colleagues reported moderate to strong positive correlations between SJTs and cognitive ability, agreeableness, conscientiousness, emotional stability, and extraversion.[148,149,150] In a more recent meta-analysis, SJTs were better predictors of overall job performance when measuring teamwork skills.[151] However, the predictive validity was highest when the predictor construct (e.g., interpersonal skills) was matched on relevance to the performance facet (e.g., contextual performance). Validities were also higher for video-based SJTs than for paper-and-pencil assessments.

Chan and Schmitt showed that SJTs predicted task and contextual performance, in addition to overall performance. Their SJT was based on "task statement and work-related competencies derived from the job analysis"[152] and most likely included items relevant to both task and contextual performance. Drasgow used the results from the McDaniel et al. meta-analysis to distinguish between SJTs that are highly correlated with cognitive ability and those that are lowly correlated.[153,154,155] He proposed that "high-*g*" SJTs primarily predict task performance, while "low-*g*" SJTs may primarily predict contextual behaviour. In their meta-analysis, Christian and his co-researchers found that most SJTs were designed to measure interpersonal skills, teamwork, and leadership, and that matching SJT constructs to performance criteria that are most likely related to such constructs improves predictive validity.[156]

SJTs appear to be a very promising assessment method. Interestingly, Ryan and Ployhart suggest that SJTs are "on a collision course" with the more elaborate digitalized hiring simulations that are becoming increasingly common today.[157] For more extensive reviews of the SJT literature, see Lievens, Peeters, and Schollaert,[158] Ployhart and MacKenzie,[159] and Whetzel and McDaniel.[160]

Leaderless group discussion
A simulation exercise designed to assess leadership, organizational, and communication skills.

In-basket test
A simulation exercise designed to assess organizational and problem-solving skills.

The two most prominent situational exercises are the leaderless group discussion and in-basket test. In a **leaderless group discussion**, a group of candidates for a managerial position might be asked to talk about or develop a position or statement on a job-related topic. In the leaderless group discussion used by IBM, candidates must advocate for the promotion of a staff member. In a leaderless group discussion, the group is not provided with any rules on how to conduct the discussion, nor is a structure imposed on the group. The primary purpose of the exercise is to see which of the candidates emerges as a leader by influencing other members of the group. Each candidate is assessed on a number of factors by a panel of judges, including, for example, communication and organizational skills, interpersonal skills, and leadership behaviour.

The **in-basket test** seeks to assess the applicant's organizational (e.g., planning, prioritizing, delegating, scheduling, appreciation for organizational hierarchy, etc.) and problem-solving skills. The Public Service Commission of Canada uses an in-basket test in selecting applicants for certain managerial and professional positions in the federal civil service (http://www.psc-cfp.gc.ca/ppc-cpp/psc-tests-cfp/in-basket-i-eng.htm). Each candidate is given a standardized set of short reports, notes, telephone messages, and memos of the type that most managers must deal with on a daily basis. Applicants must set priorities for the various tasks, determine which can be deferred or delegated, and which must be dealt with immediately. They must also indicate how they would approach the different problems the material suggests they will encounter as a manager. Each candidate's performance on the in-basket test is scored by a panel of judges.

The in-basket exercise has a great intuitive appeal as a selection test for managers because it resembles what managers actually do; unfortunately, empirical evidence suggests that it does not have high validity as a selection instrument.[161] In part, this may be due to the lack of agreed-on scoring procedures for the in-basket test; successful managers who complete the in-basket do not always arrive at the same conclusions. Also, those judging the in-basket performance often fail to distinguish among various target abilities that are supposed to be measured by the in-basket exercise, calling into question the accuracy of inferences of management potential made based on in-basket scores.[162]

Most types of work samples and situational tests discussed here are labour intensive and costly to develop and administer. However, the importance of making the right selection decision increases when organizations expect more from fewer employees. Particularly for small businesses, selecting the right individual is critical to their success. Additionally, because the relationship of work samples and situational tests to the job is so transparent, candidates from different gender and ethnic groups tend to perceive them as fair. This is highly desirable, given the growing minority segment of the workforce. For these reasons, the use of work samples and simulation tests is likely to increase in coming years, though they are increasingly likely to be delivered in digitalized form.

ASSESSMENT CENTRES

Although situational exercises can be used as stand-alone selection tests, they generally play a prominent role in testing that is part of an **assessment centre**. The term *assessment centre* (AC) is somewhat misleading in that it does not refer to a physical place. ACs evaluate individuals on a number of different performance dimensions (e.g., tact, written and oral fluency, decisiveness) over a sequence of different exercises (e.g., role-playing performance appraisal interview, leadership group discussion, in-basket), drawing on multiple raters (usually managers one level up from the position for which candidates are being considered). Such assessments are usually run over a one- to three-day period. The strength of the AC, as originally envisioned, is that it provides for multiple assessments (across exercises) of each of a number of performance dimensions, by different raters, in hopes of increasing the reliability and objectivity of the assessments. Individuals run through an AC generally receive a profile of their strengths and weaknesses across tasks and performance dimensions deemed relevant to the target position. ACs are used for external screening, development, internal promotion, early identification of potential, and certification of competence, mostly for managerial or administrative appointments.

Assessment centre
A standardized procedure that involves the use of multiple measurement techniques and multiple assessors to evaluate candidates for selection, classification, and promotion.

While ACs are administered to select external applicants, they are used mostly for internal selection (i.e., promotion). While some assessment exercises (e.g., an interview) may involve only one candidate, the vast majority of them entail group activities with candidates being evaluated by a panel of trained assessors. Managers serving as assessors are trained in the use of the assessment techniques and scoring procedures and are typically quite familiar with the position for which the candidate is being evaluated.[163] Key AC features are outlined in Recruitment and Selection Today 8.4.

ASSESSMENT CENTRE EVALUATIONS

While the specific assessments may vary from one AC to another, depending on its purpose, most include ability and aptitude tests, personality assessments, situational exercises, and interviews. After assessees complete all exercises in an AC the assessors come together to determine an overall dimension rating for each assessee on each performance dimension (allowing for profile scores across dimensions for each individual participant). Recall, dimension ratings are collected on each assessee across two or more AC exercises. At the end of the process, these multiple ratings on each dimension for each candidate must be consolidated so as to arrive at one overall dimension rating,

RECRUITMENT AND SELECTION TODAY 8.4

ESSENTIAL ELEMENTS OF AN ASSESSMENT CENTRE

According to the International Congress on Assessment Center Methods (http://www.assessmentcenters.org), assessment centres allow companies to meet their challenges by helping them:

- Identify, hire, and promote the most talented people.
- Improve bench strength and plan for succession.
- Provide candidates with realistic job previews.
- "Grow" their own leaders and accelerate leadership development.

Toward these goals, the International Congress has developed the following guidelines for effective assessment centres:

1. Job analysis is used to identify job dimensions, tasks, and attributes that are important to job success.
2. Behaviour displayed by candidates must be categorized by trained assessors and related to dimensions, aptitudes, attributes, or KSAOs.
3. Assessment techniques must provide information related to the dimensions and attributes identified in the job analysis.
4. Multiple assessment procedures are used to elicit a variety of behaviours and information relevant to the selected dimensions and attributes.
5. A sufficient number of job-related simulations must be included in the procedure to allow opportunities to observe behaviour on the selected dimensions.
6. Multiple assessors, diverse in ethnicity, age, gender, and functional work areas, are used to observe and assess each candidate.
7. Assessors must receive thorough training and meet performance standards before being allowed to evaluate candidates.
8. Systematic procedures must be used by assessors to record specific behavioural observations accurately at the time of their occurrence.
9. Assessors must prepare a report or record of observations made during each exercise in preparation for consolidating information across assessors.
10. Data from all assessor reports must be pooled or integrated either at a special meeting of assessors or through statistical methods.

Source: Guidelines and Ethical Considerations for Assessment Center Operations. 2000. *International Task Force on Assessment Center Guidelines:* http://www.assessmentcenters.org/pdf/00guidelines.pdf. Reprinted with permission from Development Dimensions International, Inc.

for each dimension, for each assessee. The performance dimensions typically include skills (administrative, problem solving, interpersonal), decision-making ability, leadership potential, motivation, resistance to stress, and flexibility.[164] The exercises typically include leaderless group discussion, a performance appraisal simulation, an in-basket, and a formal presentation. From the observations and ratings made over the period of the assessment, the team prepares a report summarizing all information obtained, providing assessees with a profile of scores across performance dimensions. Often the dimension ratings are summated to yield an overall AC score for each assessee, thereby allowing for a ranking of assessees, useful for selection.

To derive an overall dimension score, sometimes the ratings assigned to that dimension (from multiple assessors) within each exercise are summed within an exercise, and then across exercises. Summation may entail use of equal weights (i.e., unit weighting) or differential weights. Differential weights are applied to recognize that some AC exercises provide better assessments of some dimensions than of others; or that some performance dimensions are more important to the target job than are others. Evidence is mixed as to whether deriving dimension and overall AC scores through consensus-reaching discussions or through statistical aggregation results in better prediction of job performance criteria.[165] In any event, dimension scores are typically shared with the candidate, particularly when used for HR development and succession planning.

USE OF ASSESSMENT CENTRES IN CANADA

The Public Service Commission of Canada (PSC) uses ACs to select candidates for senior managerial positions in the federal civil service and as part of its executive development and education program. They are also used extensively by Ford Motor Company, General Motors, and Weyerhaeuser Canada, among many other organizations. The Canadian Forces use ACs to select applicants for training as naval officers and military police.

LOCATION AND COST OF THE ASSESSMENT CENTRE

ACs usually entail one to three days of assessment, several personnel, and considerable expense. They are often located on-site for large organizations that can afford developing and maintaining the necessary infrastructure because of the large number of individuals they process through the centre annually. Smaller organizations with fewer employees typically contract these assessments to be done off-site, or contract a firm such as Fenestra that specializes in providing remote, technology-enhanced assessment and development centres (http://fenestrainc.net).

EFFECTIVENESS OF ASSESSMENT CENTRES

A meta-analysis involving 50 ACs yielded a validity coefficient of 0.37,[166] while a study of one AC evaluated across 16 sites found a much lower validity of 0.08 to 0.16, depending on the criterion measure.[167] Another meta-analysis[168] that looked only at the ability of ACs to predict supervisory performance ratings found a "corrected" validity coefficient of 0.28. As well, AC ratings have provided prediction over both cognitive ability and personality.[169] The most comprehensive assessment of the incremental validity of AC scores is offered by Dilchert and Ones.[170] They used meta-analytically derived estimates to show that unit- and optimally weighted composites of construct-based AC dimensions predicted performance beyond that offered by personality and cognitive ability tests, whereas overall AC scores (i.e., aggregation across dimensions *and* exercises to arrive at one overall score per assessee) did not, whether the overall score was subjectively (through discussion-driven consensus) or arithmetically derived.

Variability in the mix, number of constructs assessed across ACs, and differences in the way similar constructs are operationalized from one AC to another can give rise to wide variation in the predictive validity of ACs. Researchers have attempted to specify the constructs most frequently measured in the AC process. In their meta-analysis, Arthur, Day, McNelly, and Edens[171] identified six dimensions common to most ACs: consideration/awareness of others, communication, drive, influencing others, organizing and planning, and problem solving. Mean statistically corrected criterion-related validities for these dimensions ranged from 0.25 to 0.39. Also, a composite score of four of the dimensions alone explained more of the variance in job performance (20 percent) than did the overall AC rating (14 percent).[172]

Collins and her colleagues[173] argued that assessments such as the in-basket rely mostly on cognitive ability, while leaderless group discussions favour personality variables. They performed a meta-analysis comparing overall assessment centre ratings (OARs) to cognitive ability and personality dimensions. OARs correlated 0.67 with cognitive ability. The correlations for the Big Five personality dimensions (discussed later in this chapter) were 0.50 for extraversion, 0.35 for emotional stability, 0.25 for openness, and 0.17 for agreeableness. These findings suggest that assessees' personality and cognitive ability substantially affect their OARs.

Bowler and Woehr found that both AC dimension scores and AC exercise scores figure importantly in the predictive validity of ACs. However, some dimensions and exercises contribute more than others to an OAR.[174] The strongest contributing dimensions are communication, influencing others, organizing and planning, and problem solving. The strongest contributing exercises are in-baskets, interviews, role-plays, case analysis, leaderless group discussions, and presentations. Though the exercise scores were more predictive of the OARs than were the dimension scores, both appear to be important to predicting OARs, which are used to predict performance.

ACs provide a wealth of information of potential benefit to the candidate and to the organization over the lifespan of a career. They identify candidate strengths and weaknesses, helpful to succession planning. Further, participants generally see ACs as fair and unbiased[175] and job relevant and realistic.[176] Indeed, several U.S. court decisions have recommended ACs as an alternative to measuring GMA.[177] Organizations have also used ACs to provide realistic job previews to job applicants.[178]

Cautions, however, are in order, and ACs may not be the best selection method in all cases. The worth of an AC, like any selection device, rests on an evaluation of its psychometric properties and its utility. An additional consideration is adverse impact. Dean, Roth, and Bobko[179] assessed the adverse impact of ACs through a meta-analysis of previous studies and found that ACs had more adverse impact on blacks than previously thought, but that they had less adverse impact on, and were "diversity friendly" toward, women and Hispanics. Other studies, not surprisingly, have shown that the degree of sub-group differences in AC performance will vary depending on the set of constructs assessed, with those more cognitively loaded constructs likely to adversely impact blacks, and those more interpersonally loaded constructs likely to favour women.[180,181]

The "Achilles' heel" of the AC method, however, is that while ACs were developed to provide objective assessments for performance dimensions deemed job relevant, there is little evidence to suggest that they can effectively do this (despite the predictive validity of overall AC scores). Specifically, the scores that candidates obtain on *different* dimensions within exercise correlate more highly than do scores obtained on the same dimension measured by different exercises. This finding (consistently obtained across studies and different ACs) is referred to as the exercise effect. Some scholars have suggested that overall AC scores are measures of a general ability to perform a job or set of jobs (i.e., general managerial ability, ability to assess situational demands).[182,183] They argue that a variety of different indicators of this general managerial ability arise from performance in the simulation exercises comprising the AC without reference to an intermediate set of variables such as dimensions, tasks, or exercises.[184] This would suggest that it is inappropriate to use ACs for providing dimension-specific or task-specific developmental feedback.[185] Still other AC experts attribute the cross-exercise inconsistency in assessee performance on a dimension to aspects of the exercise itself, arguing that some exercises are more potent in triggering or priming the particular trait underlying dimension performance than are other exercises.[186] For example, decisiveness is more directly primed in in-basket exercises that present multiple conflicting tasks to accomplish than in a leaderless group discussion where one ultimate, and shared, decision is made. In short, while ACs generally show good predictive validity for managerial and professional jobs, there is little consensus on why they work.

If the AC is being used for selection alone, and not for development, organizations would be best to simply use personality and cognitive ability assessments, supplemented by a structured interview and a work sample or two. Such an approach would involve fewer resources and yield comparable, if not higher, predictive validities. As noted previously, however, recently developed online versions of ACs can substantially reduce costs and increase efficiencies.[187] Still, more research on the predictive validity, cost-effectiveness, adverse impact, and candidate acceptability of such fully computerized systems is required before they can be recommended with confidence.

POLITICAL SKILL

Assessment centres are designed to be quite comprehensive in evaluating skills and abilities of job candidates and incumbents, and especially useful in succession planning programs, but knowledge, skills, and abilities are typically assessed outside the context of assessment centres for most organizations. One construct that has emerged and that is receiving increasing attention in the context of selection is political skill, defined essentially as being instrumental in facilitating social effectiveness in organizations. More specifically, one who is politically skilled is able to understand others in one's work environment and to leverage that understanding to get others to behave in ways that advance personal and organizational goals. Political skill is most commonly measured by the Political Skill Inventory (PSI), which relates positively with self-monitoring, politically savvy, emotional intelligence, extraversion, conscientiousness, self-efficacy, job satisfaction, organizational commitment, work productivity, and organizational citizenship behaviour; negatively with trait anxiety, neuroticism, and physiological strain; and does not correlate with general mental ability, psychological strain, or measures of social desirability.[188,189,190] A growing number of empirical studies show that political skills positively predict job performance, income, and promotability ratings.[191,192] Moreover, these relationships of political skill with job performance are stronger in work environments perceived to be *less* political.[193] Research also shows that political skill predicts job performance beyond the prediction offered by general mental ability and personality variables,[194] when the political skill and job performance were measured at the same time as well as when job performance was measured one year later.[195] Political skill has also been shown to offer predictive validity beyond other more traditional measures of managerial skills.[196] Mary Dana Laird and her colleagues showed that job performance associated positively with personal reputation for politically skilled employees, but not for their less politically skilled counterparts.[197] Other researchers showed that extraversion positively predicted sales for people high in political skill, but not for those low in political skill.[198] This accumulating research suggests value to organizations in assessing for political skill in some cases.

PERSONALITY INVENTORIES

In making hiring decisions, it is not unusual to hear a manager argue in support of one applicant over another because "she is the right type of assertive person we're looking for to sell cars," or "he is a very pleasant, outgoing person, the type that will do well as a receptionist." Generally, these sorts of comments are made following a job interview, when the manager has formed an impression of what the applicant is like as a person. The manager is stating a personal opinion, or "gut feeling," that the individual's characteristics or traits qualify the applicant for the job. This is the belief that some aspects of *personality* relate to job success. Indeed, given a choice, most managers would welcome employees who are hard working and well motivated, accept higher levels of initiative, fit into existing work groups, and are committed to the continuous development of their skills. Most managers and employees believe characteristics like these define the most effective employees.[199] Although these characteristics may be very appealing in an employee, more often than not managers may not succeed in hiring people with these characteristics or, if they do, the person may not turn out to be an effective employee.

There are two reasons for these failures. First, the specific personality traits that formed the manager's opinion of the applicant may not be job related; they may represent only the manager's opinion that they are necessary for effective job performance. Second, the manager's assessment of the applicant's personality may not be objective, reliable, or valid; it is only an opinion. In the next sections, we define personality, examine several measurement issues, and review personality as a predictor of job performance. As we go through this material, keep in mind the information in Recruitment and Selection Today 8.5: a poor personality measure will not offer any more value than a gut feeling.

Personality
A set of characteristics or properties that influence, or help to explain, an individual's behaviour.

Personality traits
Stable, measurable characteristics that help explain ways in which people vary.

DEFINING PERSONALITY

One of the major difficulties in using inventories for selection purposes is the lack of agreement on the definition of *personality*. **Personality** is comprised of a set of personal characteristics or properties that influence, or help to explain, a person's behaviour.[200]

Different personality theories may propose different ways in which people vary (e.g., aggressiveness, pleasantness). These variables are called **personality traits**, which are considered stable over time and measurable. Thus, if two people differ in aggressiveness or

RECRUITMENT AND SELECTION TODAY 8.5

BUYER BEWARE

Many personality tests are commercially available and have been used in personnel selection. We listed in Recruitment and Selection Notebook 8.3 some of the more commonly used personality tests, without comment on their validity or reliability. Many commercially available tests do not have credible supporting material on their reliability or validity or on how they assess faking and social desirability responding. Often, employers do not know where to begin in evaluating the merits of a personality test and in many cases end up paying large sums of money for no return. Recruitment and Selection Notebook 8.2 provides guidelines for choosing a test that should help an employer in making a choice among different personality tests.

Most important, before purchasing a personality test, have someone trained in testing issues review the test's technical manual. The lack of a technical manual tells you that there are no supporting data on the test's reliability and validity. It is not good enough to accept on faith testimonials from the test publisher that the supporting research has been done and is available. It is essential to ask for the technical manual.

pleasantness, appropriate measurements can be developed to reflect those differences. Traits are distinguished from personality *states*, which are more transitory or temporary. For example, an applicant may be very nervous in a job interview but calm otherwise (state), while another may always be anxious (trait).

Sets, collections, or patterns of traits and states define a personality *type*. A person whose behaviour reflects traits of extreme competitiveness, achievement, aggressiveness, haste, impatience, restlessness, hyper-alertness, explosiveness of speech, tenseness of facial musculature, and feelings of being under the pressure of time and under the challenge of responsibility is described as having a Type A personality.[201]

Self-report inventories are the most frequently used technique for measuring personality. A **self-report inventory** consists of sets of short, written statements related to various traits. For example, items such as "I constantly interrupt other people when they are speaking" or "I hate standing in line" might be used as part of an objective, self-report inventory to assess *time urgency*, a trait related to a Type A personality. The person responds by stating the extent to which they agree or disagree with each item using a rating scale much like those discussed in Chapter 5. Items included in the inventory relate to whatever trait is of interest and might include traits such as aggressiveness, competitiveness, and need for achievement, among others.

Self-report inventory
Short, written statements related to various personality traits.

A self-report inventory may measure only one trait or it may include subscales related to several different traits. A score for each trait assessed is determined by combining the ratings for those items that belong to a specific trait. These scores can be compared with normative data for populations of special interest. Patterns of scores across the measured traits are often used to derive statements about personality types. Self-report inventories are also called *objective techniques* because of their scoring methodology.

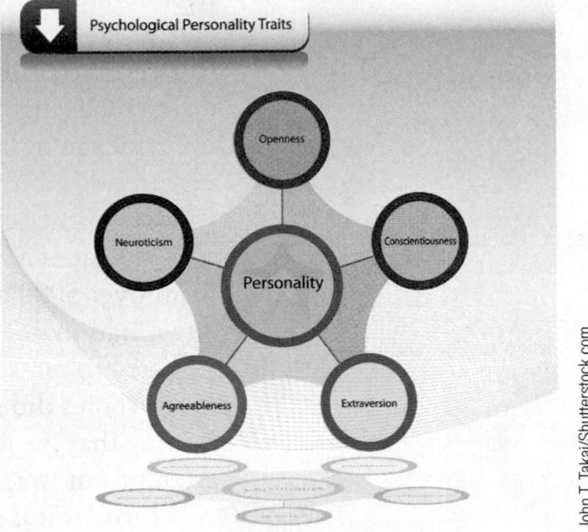

John T. Takai/Shutterstock.com

One criticism of these inventories is that they are prone to *faking* and *social desirability responses*. Faking occurs when individuals respond to inventory questions with answers that do not reflect their true beliefs or feelings. Social desirability responding is a form of faking, where individuals choose responses they believe will present them in a socially desirable way or in a positive light. For example, a person may endorse the item "I have never crossed a street on a red light" (or "told a lie"/"misrepresented the truth") to avoid being assessed as "deviant" (or untruthful). There is no doubt that individuals can distort their responses on self-report inventories in desired directions.[202,203] What is less clear is the impact of such distortions on employment decisions based on personality inventories.[204]

The major concern in using self-report inventories as part of personnel selection is that job applicants who distort their responses in a socially desirable manner will improve their chances of being hired.[205,206,207] Response distortion may cause a change in the rank-ordering of applicants at the upper end of a distribution of personality scores, leading to a loss of the best-qualified candidates.[208] This is why some researchers[209,210] argue that examining the effects of faking on validity coefficients, which has been the predominant method of investigating the effects of faking, is an inappropriate way to measure its impact on hiring decisions.

Not everyone agrees that faking and socially desirable responding have an impact on personality-based selection.[211,212] Ones and Viswesvaran,[213] using meta-analytic data, argue that socially desirable responding does not affect the validity of personality inventories, including integrity tests, that are used in work settings and go so far as to call the whole issue a "red herring." They argue that people respond to items to present an identity consistent with the way they see themselves. That is, individuals who view themselves as conscientious will portray themselves in a manner consistent with this trait when asked to complete a personality inventory.

Alliger and Dwight[214] challenged the methodological soundness of the meta-analyses conducted by Ones and Viswesvaran. Their own meta-analysis showed that respondents to self-report personality inventories could fake their way through a selection process, suggesting it is premature to make any conclusions about the impact of response distortion on self-report measures without additional empirical evidence. Donovan, Dwight, and Schneider took up this call for additional studies by collecting repeated self-reported measures for 162 individuals who applied for a pharmaceutical sales position and subsequent to hire. They also collected training performance measures and sales data five months post-training.[215] They found that faking not only was evident, but also negatively impacted the psychometric properties of the selection measure as well as the quality of hiring decisions, with fakers performing less well than non-fakers.

Clearly, people can distort their responses on self-report measures in laboratory settings when asked to do so. It is less certain what impact intentional distortion or faking may have in real-life settings where most of the evidence–based on change in validity coefficients–suggests that faking takes place but its impact is not as serious as shown in laboratory studies. This is especially so when job applicants are warned that faking can be detected and could have negative consequences for them.[216] While there are strategies to "correct" for response distortion, adjusting individual scores could lead to different hiring decisions unless all scores are adjusted, including those where there is no evidence of faking. Such corrections may be difficult to defend in a courtroom.[217]

In addition, procedures that correct for faking have little, if any, impact on the validity of the selection test, but they may have a significant impact on individual selection decisions.[218] Hogan, Barrett, and Hogan[219] examined personality test data taken from over 5000 applicants who had been rejected for customer service positions with a large, national U.S. company. The applicants had reapplied for the position and were required to retake the selection tests. Hogan and her associates concluded that the applicants' scores did not significantly change on the retest and argued that it is reasonable to assume that the applicants would have tried to improve their performance on the second attempt but were unable to do so substantially.

Perhaps it is simply best to warn job applicants that faking can be detected and that it will be taken into consideration when making hiring decisions.[220,221] Recent research suggests that faking while completing personality tests can also be detected via eye-tracking technology,[222] but its use in a selection context would need, of course, to be non-intrusive. Still, results from a self-report inventory should be considered in conjunction with a careful review of the candidate's complete file for evidence of distortion.[223]

PERSONALITY AS A PREDICTOR OF JOB PERFORMANCE

Historically, personality inventories were not considered good predictors of job performance. Guion[224,225] reviewed the technical and ethical problems associated with personality inventories and concluded that there was insufficient evidence to justify using them to inform employment decisions. Guion was concerned that they are too invasive of privacy, and not clearly job related.

The considerable body of research that is now available, however, shows that personality measures can predict a number of job-related criteria, including performance. This research has grouped related personality characteristics into a smaller number of dimensions, and empirically linked these dimensions to job performance. Accumulated research now shows that personality dimensions conceptually linked to job performance demands as determined from an analysis of job demands predict performance.[226–231]

THE BIG FIVE

So what are the key dimensions of personality? Personality traits cluster into five main categories, referred to as the Big Five: conscientiousness, emotional stability (also known as *neuroticism*), openness to experience, agreeableness, and extraversion.[232] Definitions for each of these five dimensions, along with their associated traits, are presented in Recruitment and Selection Notebook 8.5. While not everyone agrees with the Big Five model as the best way to categorize personality, it has become the most widely subscribed classification scheme in summarizing relationships between personality and job performance variables.[233]

RECRUITMENT AND SELECTION NOTEBOOK 8.5

THE BIG FIVE PERSONALITY DIMENSIONS

Conscientiousness is a general tendency to work hard and to be loyal, to give a full day's work each day, and to do one's best to perform well—following instructions and accepting organization goals, policies, and rules—even with little or no supervision. It is an approach to work characterized by industriousness, purposiveness, persistence, consistency, and punctuality. It also includes paying attention to every aspect of a task, including attention to details that might easily be overlooked.

Emotional stability reflects a calm, relaxed approach to situations, events, or people. It includes an emotionally controlled response to changes in the work environment or to emergency situations. It is an emotionally mature approach to potentially stressful situations, reflecting tolerance, optimism, a general sense of challenge rather than of crisis, and maturity in considering advice or criticism from others. (*Note:* "Emotional stability" is used in place of the older term *neuroticism* to describe this factor.)

Openness to experience reflects a preference for situations in which one can develop new things, ideas, or solutions to problems through creativity or insight. It includes trying new or innovative approaches to tasks or situations. It is a preference for original or unique ways of thinking about things. It is concerned with newness, originality, or creativity.

Agreeableness reflects a desire or willingness to work with others to achieve a common purpose and to be part of a group. It also includes a tendency to be a caring person in relation to other people, to be considerate and understanding, and to have genuine concern for the well-being of others; it is an awareness of the feelings and interests of others. It is the ability to work cooperatively and collaboratively either as part of a group or in the service of others. It is involved in assisting clients and customers as a regular function of one's work, or assisting coworkers to meet deadlines or to achieve work goals.

Extraversion reflects a tendency to be outgoing in association with other people, to seek and enjoy the company of others, to be gregarious, to interact easily and well with others, and to be likable and warmly approachable. It involves enjoying the company of others and a concern for their interests; it implies sociableness whether work is involved or not. *Extraversion* refers to being comfortable and friendly in virtually any sort of situation involving others.

Sources: M.R. Barrick and M.K. Mount. 1991. "The Big Five Personality Dimensions and Job Performance: A Meta-Analysis." *Personnel Psychology*, 44: 1–26; J.M. Digman. 1990. "Personality Structure: Emergence of the Five Factor Model." In M. Rosenzweig and L.W. Porter, eds., *Annual Review of Psychology*. Palo Alto, CA: Annual Reviews

Barrick and Mount found that each of the Big Five dimensions could predict at least one aspect of job performance with some degree of accuracy, while conscientiousness predicted several different aspects of job or training performance at moderate levels.[234] Recall that Campbell[235] believed that "demonstrating effort" and "maintaining personal discipline" were major performance components of every job (see Chapter 5). It is quite easy to see (from the definition given in Recruitment and Selection Notebook 8.5) how conscientiousness predicts these two job dimensions. Of the Big Five personality dimensions, it is the strongest and most consistent predictor of job performance across a wide range of jobs ($r = 0.31$).[236]

Other of these Big Five dimensions vary in ability to predict job success by occupational group. For example, extraversion predicts performance in occupations demanding social interaction, such as sales,[237] while openness to experience and extraversion predict training readiness and training success.[238] Moreover, conscientiousness and extraversion together predict job performance for managers in highly autonomous positions.[239] Agreeableness and emotional stability, in addition to conscientiousness, predict performance in jobs high in interpersonal interactions.[240]

Hough and Furnham[241] report the validity coefficients, based on meta-analytic studies, for each of the Big Five measures and overall job performance, contextual performance, and counterproductive behaviours. The validities varied over the different criteria, with conscientiousness correlating most highly with overall job performance for many jobs, but extraversion, openness to experience, and emotional stability correlated most highly with leadership in business settings. A more recent meta-analysis has shown emotional stability, extraversion, and openness to predict organizational citizenship behaviour beyond conscientiousness and agreeableness; whereas conscientiousness, emotional stability, and extraversion predict equally well both task performance and citizenship behaviour, openness and agreeableness have stronger relationships with citizenship behaviour than with task performance.[242]

Personality measures, while predictive of performance, are not as predictive as is cognitive ability. Even conscientiousness, the most stable and generalizable predictor among the Big Five, is less predictive of performance (with $r = 0.31$) than is cognitive ability ($r = 0.51$). Oh and Christopher,[243] however, show that meta-analysis may underestimate the predictive validity of personality because many of the primary studies used deficient criterion measures (relying entirely on ratings of overall performance provided by a single source–supervisors). They examined personality as a predictor of managerial performance (task and contextual) assessed through a 360-degree performance review (including peers *and* subordinate ratings), and showed improvements in prediction ranging from 50 to 70 percent across the Big Five factors.

The best use of a personality measurement may be as a supplement to cognitive ability testing. Conscientiousness when added to cognitive ability will improve the accuracy of predicting job performance by 18 percent.[244] Also, unlike GMA tests, personality measures have little to no adverse impact on protected groups.[245,246] Adding a personality measure to a cognitive ability–based selection system may weaken the adverse impact of the cognitive ability measure.[247] See Exhibit 5.1 in Oswald and Hough for a summary table of the empirical evidence supporting the predictive validity of personality measures across work-related criteria, including leadership and career success, job performance outcomes, contextual performance, counterproductive work behaviours, training outcomes, team performance, and job satisfaction.[248]

More recently, a sixth factor of personality has received much research attention, referred to as "Honesty-Humility" (H-H). This factor reflects individual differences in concern for fairness, greed avoidance, and modesty. For example, H-H scores correlate positively with supervisor ratings of overall job performance, and uniquely predict performance ratings beyond the Big Five.[249] A more in-depth coverage of honesty-integrity testing will be provided later in this chapter.

The personality inventories listed in Recruitment and Selection Notebook 8.3 are well established and widely used. For others, obtain objective arm's-length reviews from sources such as the Buros Mental Measurements Yearbook series. As noted earlier, you should also ask the commercial provider of the inventory for a technical manual.

SELECTING FOR WORK TEAMS

There are a growing number of studies on selecting people for teams to maximize team processes and outcomes, with personality figuring prominently in this research. Kichuk and Wiesner[250] asked teams of engineering students to design and construct a model bridge using limited resources. Teams whose members were more similar in their levels of conscientiousness did better than teams whose members differed more on this trait. Extraversion positively predicted team member satisfaction, which related positively to team longevity. Successful teams had higher levels of extraversion, emotional stability, and agreeableness than did teams judged as unsuccessful. Humphrey and his colleagues, using MBA project teams and a longitudinal design, showed that the highest levels of team performance (over the short and long term) were obtained through minimizing differences among team members in their levels of conscientiousness, and maximizing differences in team member extraversion.[251] Halfhill and his associates[252] studied the personalities of members of 47 intact military teams of the U.S. Air National Guard. They collected individual team member self-reported conscientiousness and agreeableness and also derived average personality scores for the teams. The latter correlated with the mean team performance ratings. Agreeableness and conscientiousness related positively to supervisory ratings of team-level performance. Teams high on *both* personality traits received the highest supervisory performance scores, perhaps because these traits play an important role in fostering and maintaining group harmony and effort. Specifically, meta-analysis shows that the validities for these two traits are higher for jobs high in interpersonal demands, particularly those requiring teamwork.[253] Together, these findings suggest benefits to using personality measures in putting together work teams. However, processes for assigning team membership to enhance team effectiveness are not straightforward. As noted by LePine and his colleagues[254]:

> *The research to date suggests that it is not enough to consider just measures of individual and team personality traits when using personality to predict performance. One must also consider situational factors such as the type of team that is being staffed, the nature of the task charged to the team, the level of autonomy given to the team, and the manner in which the individual members of the team will be rewarded. Without taking all of these variables into account, the use of personality measures to select individuals for teams will likely be ineffective. (p. 334)*

However, based on what we do know, one should avoid assigning individuals to teams who score low in agreeableness, conscientiousness, or emotional stability.[255] For most situations, it is best to select individuals who are conscientious, open to experience, emotionally stable, and high in agreeableness,[256] and to have a mixture of individuals high and low in extraversion.[257] Moreover, personality is likely to have its greatest impact on team effectiveness where the workflow within the team is reciprocal and intensive (i.e., where there is much active reciprocal exchange among team members versus team members working mostly independently and pooling the results of their efforts),[258] and where individual and team autonomy is high.[259] Where team activities are centred around, and directed by, a team leader, the personality profile of the team leader will likely substantially influence team effectiveness.[260]

BROAD VERSUS NARROW TRAITS

Some argue that narrower, more specific personality traits best predict specific facets of job performance.[261,262,263] For example "achievement," a narrow facet of conscientiousness, might be a better predictor of specific achievement outcomes than an overall measure of conscientiousness. Paunonen and Nicol point out that the relationship between a Big Five personality measure and job performance could be attributed to only one of the many facets defining that Big Five dimension.[264] Others have argued, and provided empirical support for, the Big Five personality measure offering better prediction of job performance than the more specific traits that define it.[265,266] In any event, purposeful behaviour at work can be viewed as resulting from one's personality attributes interacting with the motivational conditions of the workplace (or characteristics of one's job) that prime and engage personality–providing for its stimulation and expression.[267] While some jobs or work environments provide for considerable autonomy and discretion, allowing for a fuller expression of one's personality (e.g., sales agent; referred to as "low in situational strength"), others are more controlled and constraining, providing lesser opportunity for such expression (e.g., assembly line operation; referred to as "high in situational strength"). Situational strength has been shown empirically to interact with personality to predict voluntary work behaviour.[268]

Hough and Furnham[269] argue that whether Big Five measures, or the facets defining them, best predict performance depends on the nature of the criteria being predicted. If the criterion is narrow (e.g., "whistle-blowing"–making public the wrongdoings of one's organization), then a narrow trait may be best (e.g., the assertiveness facet of extraversion); however, if the focus is on broad workplace behaviours, such as overall job performance, then broad personality traits may be best (e.g., conscientiousness).

FUTURE DIRECTIONS ON THE BIG FIVE AND SELECTION

Penney, David, and Witt[270] reviewed empirical literature linking Big Five to the three primary dimensions of overall job performance: task performance, contextual performance, and counterproductive work behaviour. In so doing, they underscore the importance of validating measures of the Big Five against each of these criteria. They also review the emerging literature that has examined interactions among the Big Five as predictors of performance and call for more research of this kind. Interaction means that the relationship of one variable (e.g., conscientiousness) on another (e.g., job performance) depends on the value of a third variable (e.g., agreeableness). For example, Witt[271] found that conscientiousness related positively to job performance for individuals high in emotional stability but related negatively to job performance for individuals low in emotional stability. Personality also interacts with prior related work experience in predicting job performance,[272] and conscientiousness, openness to experience, and political skill interacted to predict performance, especially in highly complex jobs.[273] Another study showed that conscientiousness interacted with agreeableness to predict the job performance of bank employees in South Korea,[274] and another reported a curvilinear relationship between personality and performance, moderated by job complexity.[275]

Clearly, many possible interaction effects involving personality traits are emerging as predictors of job performance, and so this research needs an overarching guiding theoretical framing. Penney et al. provide a rationale in proposing predictive validities for various personality-performance combinations (i.e., extraversion × emotional stability; agreeableness × emotional stability; conscientiousness × agreeableness; and conscientiousness × extraversion).[276] They also identify moderators (e.g., task, social, and organizational demands) for both main and interactive effects, and call for research to develop typologies linking effect sizes across performance measures, particularly for those of growing importance (e.g., adaptability, taking initiative).

Finally, studies are also emerging showing that the predictive validity of personality assessments can be enhanced by contextualizing the items to the specific performance setting.[277] So, for example, rather than an item referring to general tendencies or preferences in one's life (e.g., prefer reading a book over going to a party), one would contextualize the item (e.g., prefer working alone than in teams).

THE BIG FIVE AND HR SELECTION: WHAT'S THE PRACTITIONER TO DO?

Personality assessment involving the Big Five and its facets should be considered as part of the HR selection toolkit for most jobs. Personality assessments should supplement measures of cognitive ability, a behavioural interview, one or more work samples, and perhaps EQ where practically and economically feasible. Generally speaking, the empirical evidence suggests that high conscientiousness and high emotional stability will be beneficial for most jobs. Add to these traits the importance of extraversion and agreeableness for service providers and for jobs with high teamwork demands. For leadership positions, extraversion, emotional stability, openness, and some key components of conscientiousness (e.g., achievement orientation, goal setting, persevering against adversity) are likely to improve selection decisions.

There are two special issues on the importance of personality to the world of work we recommend: *Human Resource Management Review* 21(4), December 2011, and *Industrial and Organizational Psychology* 1(3), September 2008. A 2014 comprehensive review of the literature on personality and cognitive ability as predictors of work performance is provided by Schmitt.[278]

FAIRNESS AND ADVERSE IMPACT

Fairness does not appear to be an issue concerning psychometrically sound personality inventories.[279] As noted earlier, adding personality assessment to a selection system that includes measures of cognitive ability can reduce adverse impact.[280]

POLYGRAPH TESTING

In many cases, organizational effectiveness may be limited by employee theft or misuse of organization's property or proprietary information, or other forms of dishonesty. This is one type of counterproductive work behaviour discussed in Chapter 5. The costs associated with such behaviour can run into many millions of dollars, as noted in Chapter 5. In response, many retailers have established "loss prevention" departments; they have emphasized employee training and workplace improvements as well as installing procedures for controlling inventory. Many organizations have also initiated programs designed to select people who not only are capable of doing the job but also are honest, reliable, or of high integrity.

Polygraph testing, otherwise known as using a lie detector, was once used extensively to check on employee honesty and to screen job applicants. It is based on the assumption that measurable, physiological changes (e.g., heart rate, breathing, blood pressure) occur when people lie regardless of how hard they try to control suppress these responses.

Although lie detectors enjoy a reputation among the public for being able to detect lies, empirical evidence shows that there are many unresolved issues about their reliability and validity. Polygraph results are mostly related to the skill of the polygraph operator, many of whom are poorly trained. Relatively few jurisdictions in either Canada or the United States have any licensing requirements for polygraph operators. Polygraph results are generally not accepted as evidence in North American courtrooms unless the test taker agrees to their admission. Many legislatures, including the U.S. Congress, which passed the 1988 Employee Polygraph Protection Act,[281] have banned the use of polygraph testing as part of most pre-employment screening procedures.[282] Subject to restrictions and strict standards for their use, the Act does allow employers to test applicants for security service firms and pharmaceutical-related industries. The test can also be given to employees who can reasonably be suspected of theft, embezzlement, or other crimes resulting in loss or injury. In Canada, Ontario has taken the lead in prohibiting the use of mandatory polygraph tests under its Employment Standards Act.

HONESTY/INTEGRITY TESTING

Restrictions placed on polygraph testing have led to an increase in the use of paper-and-pencil or computer administered **honesty or integrity tests**. These tests are personality-based measures.[283] They can easily be incorporated into a selection system, and they are inexpensive and inoffensive to most applicants. There are no legislative restrictions on their use; however, they must meet the same professional and scientific standards as any other type of employment test.

Honesty or integrity tests
Self-report inventories designed to assess employee honesty and reliability.

There are two general types of integrity tests. *Covert tests* are subtests or scales that are included in a general personality inventory; for example, the Reliability Scale of the Hogan Personality Inventory[284] is commonly used to assess employee honesty and reliability. *Overt honesty tests*, such as the Reid Report, ask very direct questions about the individual's attitude toward theft and other forms of dishonesty, as well as the person's prior involvement in theft or other illegal activities. With covert personality tests applicants may not be aware that their integrity is being assessed, in contrast to overt tests, which makes the later much more susceptible to faking.[285]

Dishonest applicants may be discouraged from applying for jobs when they know they will be tested for honesty. In the case of white-collar crime, personality-based integrity tests may be the best measure of psychological differences between white-collar criminals and honest employees.[286] After a chain of home improvement centres in Great Britain started using an honesty test as part of its selection procedures, inventory shrinkage dropped from 4 percent to less than 2.5 percent.[287]

A review of over 180 studies involving 25 different measures of honesty or integrity tests and a wide range of performance measures found integrity tests successfully predicted a wide range of dysfunctional job behaviours, including absenteeism, tardiness, violence, and substance abuse.[288] There is no evidence that integrity tests produce adverse impact. Ones and Viswesvaran[289] found trivial differences on integrity test outcomes when comparisons were made among whites, Asians, Native Americans, and blacks. Drawing on data from 2456 Israeli job applicants, Fine found scores on an overt integrity test correlated with self-reported counterproductive work behaviours across eight different industries (overall mean *r*, corrected for attenuation in criterion only, = .32; ranging from .21 to .38 across the eight industries), with no evidence of adverse impact by gender, age, or national origin.[290] Overall, a meta-analysis suggests that there are negligible race differences on scores of integrity tests.[291] Sturman and Sherwyn reported data from a large hotel chain that suggested the use of an integrity test for selection was responsible for significant savings in workers' compensation claims.[292] They estimated that the company experienced a 50 percent one-year return on investment from the test (benefit of $405,773 at a cost of $270,100, for cost reduction of $135,673).[293] Moreover, the test had no adverse impact across a variety of protected groups. Table 8.1 presents a summary of criterion-related validity data for both overt and covert integrity tests.[294,295]

A striking aspect of Table 8.1 is that integrity tests are more successful in predicting certain types of negative behaviours. They are much more successful at predicting property damage than detecting theft, although the latter is one of the main reasons for administering integrity tests to employees and job applicants. More recent and exhaustive reviews of psychological studies and law review articles on integrity tests, along with an examination of professional and legislative investigations of integrity tests, came to similar conclusions that honesty or integrity tests provide valid information about an applicant's potential to engage in certain types of dysfunctional job behaviours.[296,297]

Despite the accumulated empirical evidence for the predictive validity of integrity tests, research showing that they can add meaningful prediction of counterproductive work behaviour beyond the prediction offered by personality alone is not available, with the exception of Marcus and his co-investigators. Even here, however, integrity

TABLE 8.1

SUMMARY OF META-ANALYTIC INTEGRITY TEST CRITERION RELATED VALIDITIES

CRITERION	TYPE OF INTEGRITY TEST	MEAN OBSERVED VALIDITY COEFFICIENT, *r*	CORRECTED VALIDITY COEFFICIENT, ρ*
Detected theft	Overt	0.09	0.13
Admitted theft	Overt	0.30	0.42
Property damage	Overt and personality-based	0.50	0.69
Accidents on job	Overt and personality-based	0.37	0.52
Broad counterproductive behaviours	Overt	0.27	0.39
Broad counterproductive behaviours	Personality-based	0.20	0.29

* The mean observed validity coefficient, *r*, has been corrected for range restriction and unreliability in the criterion measure.

Source: Table 1 adapted from J.E. Wanek. 1999. "Integrity and Honesty Testing: What Do We Know? How Do We Use It?" *International Journal of Selection and Assessment*, 7: 183–95. Reproduced with permission from Blackwell Publishing Ltd. via Copyright Clearance Center.

test scores did not add meaningful incremental prediction when the Honesty-Humility scale of the HEXACO-Personality Inventory was added to data analyses.[298] Integrity measures correlate substantially with agreeableness, emotional stability, and especially conscientiousness (even though integrity measures on their own offer superior prediction of counterproductive work behaviours than do the Big Five, and the Big Five do not explain all the variance in integrity test scores).[299]

While integrity tests were developed specifically to predict theft and other counterproductive behaviours, they also predict overall job performance (corrected $r = .41$). In fact, measures of integrity offer the greatest incremental predication over cognitive ability tests than any other commonly used predictors of job performance.[300]

Furthermore, when statistically controlling for the effect of conscientiousness in the relationship between integrity and job performance there is only a small downward effect on the predictive validity of integrity, but when statistically controlling for the effect of integrity in the relationship between conscientiousness and job performance, the predictive validity of conscientiousness falls to nearly zero.[301] Ones[302] examined the incremental validity of integrity over all the Big Five and demonstrated that the multiple correlation resulting from regressing job performance on the Big Five was only .22, which rose to .46 when integrity was added to the equation. Not surprisingly, the Big Five best predicts covert (personality-based) versus overt measures of integrity.[303] Part of the variance in overt measures of personality not predicted by the Big Five can be explained by scores from the Honesty-Humility scale of the HEXACO-Personality Inventory (reflecting honesty, fairness, sincerity, and loyalty versus greed, conceit, pretentiousness, and slyness).[304] Also, there appear to be some facets of integrity that are predicted by cognitive ability.[305] Clearly, integrity is a multifaceted compound construct.

Some caveats exist in using integrity testing in HR selection (see Recruitment and Selection Today 8.6). Test scores from some honesty tests, like those from any personality measure, are open to misinterpretation and may constitute an invasion of the applicant's privacy. There is some evidence that job applicants do not hold favourable views of personality measures as selection instruments.[306] This suggests that some studies examining the applicant reactions to a wide range of selection devices suggest integrity tests fall somewhere close to the middle of the pack relative to other selection tools in garnering negative applicant reactions.[307] Data do suggest that honesty tests may have a high number of false positives; that is, they may tend to screen out a large number of applicants who are truly honest but do poorly on the test.[308] An applicant who is falsely rejected may feel stigmatized and take legal action.[309] Also, different measures of integrity show only low to moderate correlations with other measures of integrity, suggesting that these tests are not substitutable.[310] Accordingly, such tests should be used only where their psychometric properties and predictive validities are established.

One procedure that might reduce the false negative problem associated with integrity testing is to follow the practice used in drug testing, where a positive test is followed by an analysis of a holdout sample before any conclusions are drawn. In other words, when an integrity test suggests that the job candidate is prone to engaging in counterproductive work behaviours, the candidate should be given a second, and different, integrity test before any decision is made. Failing both integrity tests would reduce the probability that the results are false negatives. Although this procedure may be a bit more time consuming and expensive, it may spare an employer bad publicity and legal fees.

There is also a practical problem with using integrity tests. Most publishers of these tests require the proprietary testing forms to be returned to the publisher, which releases only an overall total score and subscale scores, though the publishers of the Reid Report have become more responsible about the administration and reporting of scores.[313] The HR

RECRUITMENT AND SELECTION TODAY 8.6

INTEGRITY AT THE CHECKOUT COUNTER

Sobeys operates a chain of food stores throughout Canada under several names. Sobeys' use of the Reid Report illustrates some of the pitfalls and negative publicity that may accompany integrity testing. The case involves a job applicant who failed the Reid Report. This applicant had worked for Sobeys for six years and had resigned her job to stay home and take care of her children for a year.

When she applied for a position with the company again, she was required to take the Reid Report, which had been introduced during her absence. She failed the integrity test. Since Sobeys' policy was to hire only those applicants who passed the test, her job application was rejected. The applicant questioned how she could have been rejected for failing the integrity test when she had worked without complaint for Sobeys for six years. The incident made local and national headlines and was the subject of a television feature on CBC. It also led to a great deal of discussion about the worth of integrity tests.

Sobeys was not alone in sharing the media spotlight over its use of integrity tests. A few years earlier, one of its main competitors, Loblaw's Real Canadian Superstore subsidiary, began using the Reid Report in its Vancouver operations. The British Columbia Civil Liberties Union became aware of the practice and publicly denounced the use of the test. It also called for legislation banning the practice as an invasion of privacy.

Even successful applicants may react negatively to an integrity test and the company using it.[311] David Lindsay wrote about his experience with an integrity test in *This Magazine*. He found the experience invasive and insulting, and failed to see the relevance of questions that involved statements such as "I like to take chances" and "I am afraid of fire." Neither did he see the value of answering questions such as "What drugs have you taken and how often?" He claims that he and his coworkers had all lied to achieve high "honesty" ratings: "Each of us had falsified a low-risk profile, feigning caution, docility, obedience, and inviolable, angelic truthfulness. We had denied all illegal activity, labour sympathies, and feelings of bitterness and alienation."[312]

Lindsay doubts that a quality such as honesty can be measured quantitatively. Sobeys, on the other hand, continues to see the merit in integrity testing and has not been deterred by the negative publicity arising from its assessing the honesty of job applicants. Sobeys continues to use the Reid Report in its hiring process. What do you think?

specialist is not able to review the correctness of the responses and must rely on the publisher's interpretation of the scores in the context of the publisher's proprietary normative data, which cannot be inspected.[314]

Should integrity tests be used to select employees? Table 8.1 shows that integrity tests are valid for a number of criteria. An HR practitioner must first decide on the negative behaviour that is of concern and then select an integrity test that predicts the behaviour with acceptable reliability and validity. These values can generally be found in the Buros Mental Measurements Yearbook or other sources of information on tests.

Catano and Prosser[315] reviewed some of the most popular integrity tests with respect to their psychometric properties. Table 8.2 summarizes these data, which should be considered when selecting an integrity test. Evaluate the test against the criteria presented in Recruitment and Selection Notebook 8.2. Never use an integrity test by itself–that is, as the sole selection test. Integrity testing is especially recommended for jobs in retail, banking, security/police services, and where safety is of paramount importance. The test should be used in conjunction with another test that is a valid predictor of job performance; for example, an integrity test added to a test of cognitive ability can raise the validity of the selection decisions from 0.51 to 0.65.[316] The integrity test should be given as the last hurdle in the selection procedure; that is, between two candidates who are equal in cognitive ability, selecting the candidate with the higher integrity test score

TABLE 8.2

COMPARISON OF INTEGRITY TESTS*

TEST	RELIABILITY	VALIDITY	FAKING POTENTIAL	AVAILABLE IN FRENCH	COMMENTS
London House Personnel Selection Inventory	0.85	Need for local validation studies	High	Yes	No technical data in manual. Only the Canadian version of the PSI that excludes drug avoidance scales can be used in Canada.
Reid Report	0.92	0.33	High	Yes	Uses category scoring that violates APA recommendations. Arbitrary cut points used to establish categories. Confusion over how scores are generated. Includes drug-use scale but that can be deleted in the abbreviated form.
Stanton Survey New Edition	0.92	Weakness in validation data	High	No	New edition presents scores in percentiles grouped, however, in categories. Includes a Social Desirability check. Cannot be used with current employees; only applicants.
Employee Reliability Inventory	Not technically well supported	Need for local validation studies	Moderate	No	No compelling evidence of validity. Uses category scoring that violates APA recommendations.
Personnel Reaction Blank	0.73	0.25/0.40 with work quality	High	No	Not recommended for use as it does not meet *Standards for Educational and Psychological Testing.*
Personnel Decisions Incorporated Employment Inventory	0.74	0.20–0.40 job performance and turnover	Low	No	Social desirability check. Evidence of dimensionality, reliability, and validity is weak. Many variables represented in the global score. Not good enough to warrant uncritical use.
Inwald Personality	0.92	0.41 with general performance	Moderate	No	Developed on obsolete procedures; no theoretical basis; does not measure conscientiousness.
Hogan Personality Inventory–Revised	0.80	0.40 (based on correlation of Prudence scale with absence criteria)	Low	Yes	Theoretically sound, carefully conceptualized, and well validated.

*All reliability and validity data were taken from reviews of the tests in Buros *Mental Measurements Yearbook.*

Almost all of these tests are available in a variety of formats: Paper-and-pencil, computer-administered, telephone-administered, and Internet-administered. While the tests may be administered by anyone, all of the proprietary tests require scoring by the test publisher. The report from the publisher may vary considerably in detail; however, all of these tests require a master's level person trained in assessment to score and/or interpret the results, even though some test manuals do not make this clear.

Source: Adapted from V.M. Catano and M.A. Prosser. 2007. "A Review of Integrity Tests and Their Implications for Selection of Security Personnel in a Canadian Context." The *Canadian Journal of Police & Security Services*, 5: 1–18. Reprinted with permission of V.M. Catano.

will likely lead to a workforce composed of employees who are more productive and less engaged in counterproductive behaviour.[317] Finally, given lower correlations between overt (versus covert/personality based) measures of integrity and the Big Five, the maximal value of the use of integrity tests will come from use of overt measures, except for predicting absenteeism.[318] For many measures of counterproductive work behaviours, there is scant compelling empirical evidence that covert measures of integrity will offer much in the way of practically meaningful prediction over and above a composite measure of conscientiousness, agreeableness, and emotional stability.

EVALUATING EFFECTIVENESS OF HR ASSESSMENTS

Throughout this chapter, we have emphasized that HR assessments used as part of selection procedures must exhibit sound psychometric properties, particularly reliability and validity. They must be constructed and used in accordance with accepted professional standards and meet legal requirements that govern their use. HR assessment systems involve the expenditure of time and money; in the case of assessment centres, the time and cost involved can be considerable. Therefore, it is not sufficient to demonstrate that a selection test or procedure has acceptable psychometric properties. A more important question is whether the new selection assessments improve on the benefits provided by those currently used by the organization.

COMPARING SELECTION PREDICTORS

With the exception of the employment interview, which will be discussed in the next chapter, we have reviewed the most commonly used predictors (knowledge, skills, abilities, traits and methods) that are used in personnel selection. Which, if any of these, work best? Which should be adopted as part of a selection system? In large part, the answers to these questions depend on the specific information being sought, as determined through a full understanding of the requirements of a job. Each predictor has different strengths and weaknesses and may be more suited to specific uses. Consideration must also be given to the type of criterion measure one wishes to predict (e.g., training performance, job tenure, task performance, citizenship behaviour, counterproductive work behaviour, promotion). Table 8.3 has been compiled from meta-analytic studies that have reviewed the validity of different selection measures. The validities reported here are averaged across job performance criteria and are presented in descending order based on their mean, corrected validity coefficient. Table 8.3 also presents data on the increase in validity expected from adding a second predictor to cognitive ability. Also, information is provided on the degree to which the selection tool is susceptible to producing adverse impact (noted by the index *d*). The greater the positive value of *d*, the greater the likelihood of adverse impact; a negative *d* value means the protected group has an advantage over the majority group on the selection device.[319]

Data are not available for all of the selection predictors we have discussed. As can be seen, adding a second predictor can provide a substantial increase in validity. While these validities may be influential, the difference in utility provided by different predictors may also influence choice of a measure. The potential net gains from using different predictors in the hiring situation should be compared before making any final decision on which predictor to use. As a rule of thumb, replacing a low-validity predictor with

TABLE 8.3

MEAN VALIDITIES FOR PREDICTORS USED IN SELECTION WITH OVERALL JOB PERFORMANCE AS THE CRITERION

PREDICTOR	MEAN VALIDITY WHEN USED BY ITSELF	MEAN VALIDITY WHEN USED TO SUPPLEMENT COGNITIVE ABILITY TEST*	SUBGROUP DIFFERENCES (*D*[a])
Cognitive ability[b]	0.51	—	
White–Black			0.99
White–Asian			–0.20
Male–Female			0.00
Work samples/SJTs[b]	0.54	0.63	
White–Black			0.40
White–Asian			0.49
Male–Female			–0.12
Interview—structured[b]	0.51	0.63	
White–Black			0.23
Job knowledge tests	0.48	0.58	
White–Black			0.48
Integrity tests[b]	0.41	0.65	—
White–Black			
White–Asian			
Male–Female			
Interview—unstructured[b]	0.38	0.55	—
Assessment centre[b]	0.37	0.53	—
White–Black			0.37
Biographical data[b]	0.35	0.52	
White–Black			0.33
Psychomotor ability[c]	0.35	—	—
White–Black			–0.72
Male–Female			–1.06
Perceptual ability[c]	0.34	—	—
White–Black			.66
Physical ability[d]	0.32	—	—
Male–Female			1.02 to 2.10
Conscientiousness[b]	0.31	0.60	—
White–Black			0.06

Continued

TABLE 8.3

CONTINUED

PREDICTOR	MEAN VALIDITY WHEN USED BY ITSELF	MEAN VALIDITY WHEN USED TO SUPPLEMENT COGNITIVE ABILITY TEST*	SUBGROUP DIFFERENCES (D^a)
White–Asian			0.08
Male–Female			–0.08
Reference checks[b]	0.26	0.57	—
Emotional stability[e]	0.12	—	—
White–Black			–0.04
White–Asian			–0.01
Male–Female			0.24
Extraversion[e]	0.12	—	
White–Black			0.10
White–Asian			0.08
Male–Female			.09
Agreeableness[e]	0.10	—	—
White–Black			0.02
White–Asian			0.01
Male–Female			–0.39
Openness to experience[e]	0.05	—	—
White–Black			0.21
White–Asian			0.18
Male–Female			0.07
Résumé components			
Grade point average[f]	0.32	—	—
Job experience[b]	0.18	—	—
Years of education[b]	0.10	0.52	—
Graphology[b]	0.02	0.51	—

(*Note:* The validity coefficients have been corrected for range restriction and unreliability in the criterion measures. The *d* values are uncorrected.)

Sources: [a] R.E. Ployhart and B.C. Holtz. 2008. "The Diversity-Validity Dilemma: Strategies for Reducing Racioethnic and Sex Subgroup Differences and Adverse Impact in Selection." *Personnel Psychology*, 6: 153–72;

[b] F.L Schmidt and J.E. Hunter. 1998. "The Validity and Utility of Selection Methods in Personnel Psychology: Practical and Theoretical Implications of 85 Years of Research Findings." *Psychological Bulletin*, 124: 262–74;

[c] J.E. Hunter and R.F. Hunter. 1984. "Validity and Utility of Alternative Predictors of Job Performance." *Psychological Bulletin*, 96: 72–98;

[d] N.A. Schmitt, R.Z. Gooding, R.D. Noe, and M. Kirsch. 1984. "Meta-Analyses of Validity Studies Published between 1964 and 1982 and lvestigation of Study Characteristics." *Personnel Psychology*, 37: 407–22;

[e] M.R. Barrick and M.K. Mount. 1991. "The Big Five Personality Dimensions and Job Performance: A Meta-Analysis." *Personnel Psychology*, 44: 1–26;

[f] P.L. Roth, C.A. BeVier, F.S. Switzer, III, and J.S. Schippmann. 1996. "Meta-Analyzing the Relationship between Grades and Job Performance." *Journal of Applied Psychology*, 81: 548–56

one of higher validity, at little or no cost, will lead to substantial benefits in terms of productivity for an organization.

The second point to note from Table 8.3 is that some of the most valid predictors, such as cognitive ability, have the most adverse impact on minorities. Accordingly, we must balance validity and diversity to obtain qualified employees who are representative of the general population. Recruitment and Selection Notebook 8.6 provides some guidelines for how organizations can minimize the validity–diversity dilemma.

APPLICANT REACTIONS

Recall from Chapter 2 that test fairness includes the reaction of applicants to selection procedures. Adverse reactions to selection tests and procedures may impair the ability of an organization to recruit and hire the best applicants. It may also lead to costly

RECRUITMENT AND SELECTION NOTEBOOK 8.6

GUIDELINES FOR BALANCING VALIDITY AND DIVERSITY IN SELECTION

1. Use job analysis to define carefully the nature of performance on the job, being sure to recognize both technical and nontechnical aspects of performance.
2. Use cognitive and noncognitive predictors to measure the full range of relevant cognitive and noncognitive KSAOs, as much as practically realistic.
3. Use alternative predictor measurement methods (interviews, SJTs, biodata, accomplishment record, assessment centres) when feasible. Supplementing a cognitive predictor with alternative predictor measurement methods can produce sizable reductions of adverse impact (if they are not too highly correlated), but the specific reductions are variable. Using alternative predictor measurement methods is costly but effective because they measure multiple KSAOs, reduce reading requirements, and have higher face validity. Among the best alternative predictor measures are interviews, SJTs, and assessment centres.
4. Decrease the cognitive loading of predictors and minimize verbal ability and reading requirements to the extent supported by a job analysis. For example, if a job analysis indicates the need for a high school reading level, ensure the predictors do not require a postsecondary reading level. Doing so may involve lowering the reading level of instructions and items, allowing constructed response options, or using video formats (but again, only if consistent with the job analysis findings).
5. Enhance applicant reactions. Although this strategy has only a minimal effect on subgroup differences, it does not reduce validity and is almost invariably beneficial from a public relations perspective. Simply using face valid predictors (such as interviews and assessment centres) goes a long way toward enhancing these perceptions. And some approaches are free (e.g., giving explanations for why the selection procedure is being used). Sensitivity review panels may help ensure content validity and legal defensibility.
6. *Consider* banding. We emphasize the word "consider" because this remains a controversial strategy among IO psychologists and will substantially reduce subgroup differences only when there is explicit racioethnic minority or female preference in final hiring decisions. [See Chapter 10]

Source: R.E. Ployhart and B.C. Holtz. 2008. "The Diversity-Validity Dilemma: Strategies for Reducing Racioethnic and Sex Subgroup Differences and Adverse Impact in Selection," *Personnel Psychology*, 61: 153–72. Reproduced with permission from Blackwell Publishing Ltd. via Copyright Clearance Center.

litigation. The most recent and comprehensive meta-analysis of applicant reactions to selection procedures, and the cross-cultural generalizability of these reactions, show that applicant overall reactions are quite similar across 17 countries (though some differences were found on dimension-specific perceptions of favourability).[320] This analysis also showed that applicant favourability ratings of selection tools clustered into three groups: most favoured were work samples and interviews; the second most favoured were résumés, cognitive tests, references, biodata, and personality inventories; and the least favoured were honesty tests, personal contacts, and graphology.[321] Encouragingly, favourability ratings correlated strongly and positively with international usage and with the predictive validity of the assessment. They concluded that applicant reactions were quite similar across countries and outweighed cross-cultural differences. They suggested that organizations engaged in international and expatriate selection should expect similar reactions from candidates to selection tools as reported in Table 8.4. While data for Canadian applicants are not available, there is no reason to believe that they would be substantially different from those summarized in Table 8.4. Canadian organizations that are considering using integrity tests, graphology, and personal contacts in their hiring process should consider the possible negative consequences on their ability to recruit and hire the best available people. The research literature also suggests, however, that applicant reactions to test procedures can be improved (i.e., greater perceived fairness) when employers provide a compelling rationale or explanation for why they are using the tool they are using, and that providing such explanations relates positively to cognitive ability test performance and test-taking motivation.[322]

TABLE 8.4

APPLICANT FAVOURABILITY PERCEPTIONS OF SELECTION METHODS

	RATING BY APPLICANTS	
SELECTION METHOD	**U.S.**	**FRENCH**
Interview	Good	Good
Résumé	Good	Good
Work samples	Good	Good
Biodata	Good	Medium
Ability tests	Medium	Medium–good
Reference checking	Medium	Medium
Personality tests	Medium	Medium–good
Honesty/integrity tests	Poor	Poor
Personal contacts	Poor	Poor
Graphology	Poor	Poor

Source: Adapted from D.D. Steiner and S.W. Gilliland. 2001. "Procedural Justice in Personnel Selection: International and Cross-Cultural Perspectives," *International Journal of Selection and Assessment*, 9: 124–37. Reproduced with permission from Blackwell Publishing Ltd. via Copyright Clearance Center.

// SUMMARY

Psychological assessments can be carried out for many purposes, including employee selection. Individual assessment in the context of employment must meet acceptable professional and legal standards and be carried out by professionals knowledgeable about tests and testing procedures. Only those assessments that are psychometrically sound should be used for employment purposes. The rights of job applicants asked to take employment assessments, including the right to privacy, must be respected at all times and balanced against the needs of the organization. A fundamental issue is whether the assessment provides information that is job-relevant, as systematically and objectively determined. A variety of tests can be used for selection purposes. Ability tests, both general cognitive ability and more specialized tests, consistently provide highly valid information about future job performance for a broad class of occupations. Cognitive ability tests are the primary predictor for almost every job. The addition of specific ability tests to a general cognitive ability test may increase the overall validity of the selection system. Tests of GMA may disadvantage members of some minority groups and should be supplemented with assessments known not to have adverse impact.

Work samples and simulations, particularly SJTs, attempt to base selection on the ability of job applicants to perform actual job components either directly or in some abstract form. Work samples have validity coefficients in the same range as cognitive ability tests and may be very appropriate to use in cases where cognitive ability testing might provoke a negative reaction; for example, in the selection of senior management and executives. Assessment centres appear to be well suited for selecting managers and professionals and provide a wealth of information, although some evidence suggests that these are elaborate means of assessing both cognitive ability and personality. All of these approaches are alternatives to more traditional selection procedures. Some of these new selection tools are expensive, and their costs may offset the benefits they provide. Before adopting specific tests, consideration must be given to their perceived fairness and utility.

Recent studies suggest a Big Five construction of personality may improve prediction of certain job performance dimensions. Adding personality tests to a selection system can improve overall validity and reduce adverse impact from testing for cognitive ability. Personality assessments are also increasingly used to assess honesty or integrity, with a considerable degree of predictive accuracy; however, their use may run the risk of inducing unfavourable reactions among job candidates, to the point where they will not consider employment with a company that uses honesty or integrity testing as part of selection. Employers are increasingly seeking information on applicant physical fitness and drug use. Collecting this information may pose a threat to privacy and therefore must conform to human rights guidelines and professional and ethical standards.

Overall, there are many benefits to both individuals and their organizations associated with using HR assessments in employee selection. Given these benefits, all organizations throughout Canada–small, medium, or large, public and private–should embrace the very best this field has to offer. The quality of the selection decisions made will reflect on the quality of the services and products provided, and overall organizational survival in an increasingly competitive economic landscape. Further, selection decisions that enhance person–organization fit nourish not only the economic well-being of the employing organization, but also the health and safety of employees. If you have worked in a job you felt ill-suited for you know the situation is not good for you, and not good for your employer.

For additional reviews of the studies, recommendations, latest advances, and future directions for employee selection, see Ryan and Ployhart (2014).[323] To determine where organizations operating in the United States have been most vulnerable legally concerning their selection tools and processes, see Williams, Schaffer, and Ellis.[324] Much of what they found in their review is certainly applicable to Canadian organizations.

KEY TERMS

Abilities, p. 331
Aptitude, p. 331
Assessment centre, p. 355
Cognitive abilities, p. 331
Emotional intelligence, p. 341
Genetic testing, p. 347
Honesty or integrity tests, p. 368
In-basket test, p. 354
Job knowledge, p. 341
Leaderless group discussion, p. 354
Personality, p. 360
Personality traits, p. 360
Physical abilities, p. 344
Practical intelligence, p. 340
Psychomotor abilities, p. 343
Self-report inventory, p. 361
Sensory/perceptual abilities, p. 344
Situational exercises, p. 352
Situational judgment test, p. 352
Skill, p. 331
Tacit knowledge, p. 340
Work samples and simulations, p. 350

WEB LINKS

The Personnel Psychology Centre's testing information and sample tests can be found at
http://www.psc-cfp.gc.ca/ppc-cpp/index-eng.htm

A wide variety of sample tests are available at
http://www.queendom.com

Buros Mental Measurements Yearbook is available at
http://www.unl.edu/buros

Examples and practice questions similar to those from the *Canadian Forces Aptitude Test* (CFAT) are available at
http://www.publicserviceprep.com/public/full_pkg_canadianforces.aspx

Sample questions from the Armed Services Vocational Aptitude Battery can be found at
http://usmilitary.about.com/od/joiningthemilitary/l/blasvabsample.htm

The HayGroup Emotional and Social Competency Inventory can be found at **http://www.haygroup.com/leadershipandtalentondemand/ourproducts/item_details.aspx?itemid=58&type=1**

Information on the Mayer-Salovey-Caruso Emotional Intelligence Test (MSCEIT) is available at
http://www.emotionaliq.com

The Treasury Board Secretariat's policy on the duty to accommodate persons with disabilities can be found at
http://www.tbs-sct.gc.ca/pol/doc-eng.aspx?id=12541

Additional sources on the ethics of genetic testing can be found at
http://www.genethics.ca

A computer simulation of an air traffic controller's function can be found at
http://www.atc-sim.com

The International Congress on Assessment Center Methods website is located at
http://www.assessmentcenters.org

DISCUSSION QUESTIONS

1. Why must anyone working in the area of HR be familiar with the professional and legal standards that govern the use of employment tests?
2. What are the limitations of cognitive ability testing? Do these limitations outweigh the advantages of selecting employees based on cognitive ability?
3. What is the Big Five model of personality and what is its relationship to employment testing?
4. If you planned to use a personality test as part of a selection program, what characteristics should the test have?
5. Why is honesty or integrity testing controversial? When and how should these tests be used?
6. Is an employer free to test for physical fitness or drug use before making a job offer? Explain your answer.
7. What is an assessment centre?
8. What is more important: the reliability and validity of a test or the applicant's perception of the test?

EXERCISES

1. Consult the government agency responsible for monitoring the use of selection tests, including physical fitness and drug testing, in your locality. This may be a human rights agency or other government body. Determine whether that agency has a policy on the use of selection tests. Compare that policy with the principles and standards identified in this chapter.

2. Survey 10 companies or organizations in your community to determine whether they use selection tests as part of their hiring procedures. List the tests that are used. Did any organization report using honesty, fitness, or drug tests? If the company did not use any type of testing, report the procedures it used and its reasons, if any, for not using selection tests.
3. Recruitment and Selection Today 8.3 presented a sample item from a situational judgment test for use in hiring a manager. We intentionally did not indicate which of the responses was the best course of action. Assume that you and some of your classmates are a group of subject-matter experts who have been brought together to develop the responses to items on an SJT, including the best option. In conjunction with your other SMEs, identify which of the four options a manager should do in the Recruitment and Selection Today 8.3 example. What do you think a manager would do in that situation? What do you think would be the worst thing for the manager to do in the situation?
4. Design an assessment centre that could be used to select teachers. Describe the rationale for selecting the various procedures that would be included in the centre. Could your centre be replaced by a cognitive ability test and a personality measure?
5. Your workplace, by the nature of the work performed there, has a high level of airborne dust particles. You are concerned about hiring people with environmental sensitivities. Assume that there is an accurate genetic screening device to identify people who might be susceptible to the dust particles. Under what circumstances should you institute the test as part of your hiring procedures? Should it be voluntary or mandatory? How would you implement the test? Who would have access to the results? What would you tell applicants who tested positive?
6. Recruitment and Selection Notebook 8.3 identified a number of tests for cognitive ability, personality, integrity, and so on. We also identified several Internet resources that could be used to obtain more information about a particular test. There are many more resources available on the Web from which you could obtain this information. All you need to do is enter the name of the test into your favourite search engine to find them. In the course of this chapter, we identified two measures of emotional intelligence: the MSCEIT and the Bar-On EQi measure. As well, we mentioned the MBTI in relation to personality measures listed in Recruitment and Selection Notebook 8.3.

   Choose either the two emotional intelligence measures or the MBTI and a personality test from Recruitment and Selection Notebook 8.3 and answer the following questions:

   a. What is the reliability and validity of your two measures?
   b. What is known about the use of your two measures in making employment decisions?
   c. Have the tests ever been the focus of legal proceedings?
   d. Are the tests defensible with respect to human rights issues?
7. Evaluate the two tests you chose in Exercise 6 against the criteria listed in Recruitment and Selection Notebook 8.2. If you were an HR manager and were asked to choose either one of your two tests for use in selecting employees, which one would you recommend, and why?

CASE

Applicants to the Royal Canadian Mounted Police must pass a written examination, an interview, and a physical ability test before being accepted for basic training at the RCMP's training centre in Regina. As a federally regulated agency, the RCMP falls under the jurisdiction of the Employment Equity Act, designed to further the employment of women, visible minorities, and other designated groups. The RCMP has had difficulty meeting recruiting targets of 20 percent women, 4.5 percent Aboriginals, and 8.3 percent visible minorities that were set in compliance with the objectives of the Act. A review of testing data showed that Aboriginal peoples and visible minorities scored slightly lower than other groups on the written tests and that 40–50 percent of women applicants fail the physical ability test, a rate considerably higher than that for men.

In response to concerns over failing to meet its recruiting objectives, the RCMP undertook a revision of the examination, which assesses cognitive ability. The new test retains "academic" items related to composition and computation, but it also has new items in the form of scenarios that are directed at problem solving. The new questions are more job directed and operational in nature. Test items were rewritten to minimize the impact of different regional language styles to ensure that the questions are fair and equitable for all applicants.

With respect to the physical ability test, women had particular difficulty with the upper-body strength requirements. To deal with this problem, the RCMP instituted a six-week pre-training fitness program to help women prepare for the fitness test. It also eased the physical standards for women.

These changes did not meet with unanimous approval, even from groups the changes were designed to help. A lawyer for the Federation of Saskatchewan Indian Nations is quoted as saying, "Instead of watering down their exams, the RCMP should try and change their relationship with Native people. The RCMP is trying to send the message that they want more Natives in the force, but the message to non-Natives is that the Indians are getting an easier ride. Indian people aren't stupid." An MP in Saskatchewan added that "the RCMP should set high physical standards and even higher intellectual standards for their recruits. Public safety should not be compromised for political correctness."

The changes, however, were applauded by members of Nova Scotia's black community, which sees more minority officers as necessary to preventing racial strife. A black leader said that while math may have clear-cut answers, "everyone's general knowledge is not exactly the same. . . . [General knowledge] is based on experience and exposure to certain things. I think our experiences are different in many respects." He noted that the black community was very different from the Aboriginal community.

Sources: *Alberta Report* (January 19, 1998); *Canadian Press Newswire* (August 11, 1996; January 4, 1998); *The Globe and Mail* (October 14, 1997).

QUESTIONS

1. Did the RCMP do the right thing in revising its written examination and fitness test? Did the RCMP reduce the rigour of its entrance

requirements? Base your response on what you have learned in this chapter.

2. It appears that the RCMP is trying to incorporate a "practical intelligence" component into its examinations. Is this appropriate? What type of "job knowledge" should be assessed of applicants?
3. If physical ability is a job requirement for police officers, is it appropriate to have different standards for male and female applicants to the RCMP? Argue your point.
4. Is the existing test fair and equitable for all candidates? Will the new procedures discriminate against white males?
5. Design and describe a recruiting campaign to attract more women and visible-minority applicants to the RCMP.
6. Chapter 10 looks at another method that can be used to improve the number of minority applicants: banding. This procedure is also controversial. You may want to read that section now and discuss this as an option. How would the public likely react to using banding?

// ENDNOTES

1 Johns, G. 1993. "Constraints on the Adoption of Psychology-Based Personnel Practices, Lessons from Organizational Innovation." *Personnel Psychology* 46: 569–92.

2 Catano, V.M. 2001. "Empirically Supported Interventions and HR Practice." *HRM Research Quarterly* 5: 1–5.

3 Rynes, S.L., A.E. Colbert, and K.G. Brown. 2003. "HR Professionals' Beliefs about Effective Human Resource Practices: Correspondence Between Research and Practice." *Human Resource Management* 41: 149–74.

4 Goffin, R.D. 2005, July 1. "Pre-employment Tests: Choosing the Best and Avoiding the Rest." HR.com. Retrieved January 12, 2012, from http://www.hr.com/en/communities/staffing_and_recruitment/pre-employment-tests-choosing-the-best-and-avoidi_eacv6z5i.html

5 Fleishman, E.A., and M.E. Reilly. 1992. *Handbook of Human Abilities*. Palo Alto, CA: Consulting Psychologists Press.

6 Fleishman, E.A., and M.K. Quaintance. 1984. *Taxonomies of Human Performance: The Description of Human Tasks*. Orlando, FL: Academic Press.

7 Schmidt, F.L. 2002. "The Role of General Cognitive Ability and Job Performance: Why There Cannot Be a Debate." *Human Performance* 15: 187–210.

8 Ree, M.J., and T.R. Carretta. 1998. "General Cognitive Ability and Occupational Performance." In C.L. Cooper and I.T. Robertson, eds., *International Review of Industrial and Organizational Psychology*, Vol. 13 (pp. 159–84). London: John Wiley and Sons.

9 Gottfredson, L. 1986. "Societal Consequences of the *g* Factor in Employment." *Journal of Vocational Behavior* 29: 379–411.

10 Bell, J. 1996. "Brain Power Counts, Too, When Evaluating Prospects." *USA Today* (April 10): 3C.

11 Barry, E. 1999. "Smarter Than the Average Cop." *The Boston Globe* (September 10): B1.

12 Lowman, R.L., ed. 1998. *The Ethical Practice of Psychology in Organizations.* Bowling Green, OH: Society for Industrial and Organizational Psychology.

13 Ree, M.J., and T.R. Carretta. 1998.

14 Gottfredson, L. 1997 "Why *g* Matters: The Complexity of Everyday Life." *Intelligence* 24: 79–132.

15 Ones, D.S., and S. Dilchert. 2004, October. *Practical vs. General Intelligence in Predicting Success in Work and Educational Settings.* Paper present at the University of Amsterdam.

16 Gottfredson, L. 2002. "Where and Why *g* Matters: Not a Mystery." *Human Performance* 15: 25–46.

17 Schmidt, F.L., and J.E. Hunter. 1998. "The Validity and Utility of Selection Methods in Personnel Psychology: Practical and Theoretical Implications of 85 Years of Research Findings." *Psychological Bulletin* 124: 262–74.

18 Lang, J.W.B., M. Kersting, U.R. Hulsheger, and J. Lang. 2010. "General Mental Ability, Narrower Cognitive Abilities, and Job Performance: The Perspective of the Nested-Factors Model of Cognitive Abilities." *Personnel Psychology* 63: 595–640.

19 Hartigan, J.A., and A.K. Wigdor. 1989. "Differential Validity and Differential Prediction." In J.A. Hartigan and A.K. Wigdor, eds. *Fairness in Employment Testing: Validity Generalization, Minority Issues, and the General Aptitude Test Battery* (pp. 172–188). Washington, DC: National Academy Press.

20 Berry, C.M., M.A. Clark, and T.K. McClure. 2011, March 28. "Racial/Ethnic Differences in the Criterion-Related Validity of Cognitive Ability Tests: A Qualitative and Quantitative Review." Journal of Applied Psychology, Advance online publication. doi: 10.1037/a0023222.

21 Schmidt, F.L., and J.E. Hunter. 1998.

22 Schmidt, F.L. 2002.

23 Salgado, J.F., N. Anderson, S. Moscoso, C. Bertua, and F. de Fruyt. 2003. "International Validity Generalization of GMA and Cognitive Abilities: A European Communities Meta-Analysis." *Personnel Psychology* 56: 573–605.

24 Bertua, C., N. Anderson, and J. F. Salgado. 2005. "The Predictive Ability of Cognitive Ability Tests: A UK Meta-Analysis." *Journal of Occupational and Organizational Psychology* 78: 387–409.

25 Gonzalez-Mulé, E., M. Mount, I-S Oh. In Press. "A Meta-Analysis of the Relationship between General Mental Ability and Non-Task Performance." *Journal of Applied Psychology.*

26 Sackett, P.R., M.J. Borneman, and B.S. Connelly. 2008. "High-Stakes Testing in Higher Education and Employment: Appraising the Evidence for Validity and Fairness." *American Psychologist* 63(4): 215–27.

27 Aguinis, H., S.A. Culpepper, and C.A. Pierce. 2010. "Revival of Test Bias Research in Preemployment Testing." *Journal of Applied Psychology* 95(4): 648–80.

28 Ibid.

29 Berry, C.M., M.A. Clark, and T.K. McClure. 2011, September. "Racial/Ethnic Differences in the Criterion-Related Validity of Cognitive Ability Tests: A Qualitative and Quantitative Review." *Journal of Applied Psychology* 96(5): 881–906.

30 Gottfredson, L. 1986.

31 Cronshaw, S.F. 1986.

32 Terpstra, D.E., A.A. Mohammed, and R.B. Kethley. 1999. "An Analysis of Federal Court Cases Involving Nine Selection Devices." *International Journal of Selection and Assessment* 7: 26–34.

33 Outtz, J.L. 2002. "The Role of Cognitive Ability Tests in Selection." *Human Performance* 15: 161–71.

34 Hausdorf, P.A., M.M. LeBlanc, and A. Chawla. 2003. "Cognitive Ability Testing and Employment Selection: Does Test Content Relate to Adverse Impact?" *Applied HRM Research* 7(2): 41–48.

35 Chung-Yan, G.A., P.A. Hausdorf, and S.F. Cronshaw. 2005. "A Criterion-Related Validation Study of Transit Operations." *International Journal of Selection and Assessment* 13(2): 172–77.

36 Jain, H.C., P. Singh, and C. Agocs. 2000. "Recruitment, Selection and Promotion of Visible Minority and Aboriginal Police Officers in Selected Canadian Police Services." *Canadian Public Administration* 43(1): 46–75.

37 Ng, E.S.W., and G.J. Sears. 2010. "The Effect of Adverse Impact in Selection Practices on Organizational Diversity: A Field Study." *The International Journal of Human Resource Management* 21(9): 1454–71.

38 Outtz, J.L. 2002.

39 Schmitt, N.A., W. Rogers, D. Chan, L. Sheppard, and D. Jennings. 1997. "Adverse Impact and Predictive Efficiency of Various Predictor Combinations." *Journal of Applied Psychology* 82: 719–30.

40 Cortina, J.M., N.B. Goldstein, S.C. Payne, H.K. Davison, and S.W. Gilliland. 2000. "The Incremental Validity of Interview Scores Over and Above Cognitive Ability and Conscientiousness Measures." *Personnel Psychology* 53: 325–51.

41 Newman, D.A., and J.S. Lyon. 2009. "Recruitment Efforts to Reduce Adverse Impact: Targeted Recruiting for Personality, Cognitive Ability, and Diversity." *Journal of Applied Psychology* 94(2): 298–317.

42 Vanderpool, M., and V.M. Catano. 2008. "Comparing the Performance of Native North American and Predominantly White Military Recruits on Verbal and Nonverbal Measures of Cognitive Ability." *International Journal of Selection and Assessment* 16: 239–48.

43 Hausdorf, P.A., M.M. LeBlanc, and A. Chawla. 2003. "Cognitive Ability Testing and Employment Selection: Does Test Content Relate to Adverse Impact?" *Applied HRM Research* 7(2): 41–48.

44 Judge, T.A., R.L. Klinger, and S.S. Lauren. 2010. "Time Is On My Side: Time, General Mental Ability, Human Capital, and Extrinsic Career Success." *Journal of Applied Psychology* 95(1): 92–107.

45 Ibid.

46 Fleishman, E.A., and M.E. Reilly. 1992.

47 Ree, M.J., and T.R. Carretta. 1998.

48 McHenry, J.J., L.M. Hough, J.L. Toquam, M.A. Hanson, and S. Ashworth. 1990. "Project A Validity Results: The Relationship between Predictor and Criterion Domains." *Personnel Psychology* 43: 335–54.

49 Levine, E.L., P.E. Spector, S. Menon, S. Narayanan, and J. Cannon-Bowers. 1996. "Validity Generalization for Cognitive, Psychomotor, and Perceptual Tests for Craft Jobs in the Utility Industry." *Human Performance* 9: 1–22.

50 Ree, M.J., and T.R. Carretta. 1998.

51 Carroll, J.B. 1993. *Human Cognitive Abilities: A Survey of Factor-Analytic Studies*. New York: Cambridge University Press.

52 Lang, J.W.B., M. Kersting, R.R. Hulsheger, and J. Lang. 2010.

53 Ibid.

54 Jonas, W.B., K.M. Lang, U.R. Hulsheger, and J. Lang. 2010. "General Mental Ability, Narrower Cognitive Abilities, and Job Performance: The Perspective of the Nested-Factors Model of Cognitive Abilities." *Personnel Psychology* 63(3): 595–640.

55 Ree, M.J., and T.R. Carretta. 1998.

56 Ree, M.J., and T.R. Carretta. 2002. "g2K." *Human Performance* 15: 2–23.

57 Johnston, P.J., and Catano, V.M. 2002.

58 Campbell, S., and V.M. Catano. 2004.

59 Lang, J.W.B., M. Kersting, U.R. Hulsheger, and J. Lang. 2010.

60 Murphy, K.R. 2009. "Content Validation Is Useful for Many Things, But Validity Isn't One of Them." *Industrial and Organizational Psychology* 2: 873–900.

61 Ones, D.S., C. Viswesvaran, and S. Dilchert. 2005. "Cognitive Ability in Personnel Selection Decisions." In A. Evers, O. Voskuijl, and N. Anderson, eds., *Handbook of Personnel Selection* (pp. 143–173). Oxford, UK: Blackwell.

62 Sternberg, R.J., G.B. Forsythe, J. Hedlund, J.A. Horvath, R.K. Wagner, W.M. Williams, et al. 2000. *Practical Intelligence in Everyday Life*. New York: Cambridge University Press.

63 Sternberg, R.J. 2002. "Practical Intelligence, *g*, and Work Psychology." *Human Performance* 15: 142–60.

64 Ibid.

65 Ibid.

66 McDaniel, M.A., and D.L. Whetzel. 2005. "Situational Judgment Test Research: Informing the Debate on Practical Intelligence Theory." *Intelligence* 33: 515–25.

67 Wagner, R.K., and R.J. Sternberg. 1985. "Practical Intelligence in Real-World Pursuits: The Role of Tacit Knowledge." *Journal of Personality and Social Psychology* 49: 436–58.

68 Wagner, R.K., H. Sujan, M. Sujan, C.A. Rashotte, and R.J. Sternberg. 1999. "Tacit Knowledge in Sales." In R.J. Sternberg and J.A. Horvath, eds., *Tacit Knowledge in Professional Practice* (pp. 155–82). Mahwah, NJ: Lawrence Erlbaum Associates.

69 Hedlund, J., R.J. Sternberg, and J. Psotka. 2000. *Tacit Knowledge for Military Leadership: Seeking Insight into the Acquisition and Use of Practical Knowledge* (Tech. Rep. No. ARI TR 1105). Alexandria, VA: U.S. Army Research Institute.

70 Gottfredson, L.S. 2003. "Dissecting Practical Intelligence Theory: Its Claims and Evidence." *Intelligence* 31(4): 343–97.

71 Taub, G.E. 1999. "Predicting Success: A Critical Analysis of R.J. Sternberg and R.K. Wagner's Theory of Practical Intelligence: Is This an Ability beyond *g*?" *Dissertation Abstracts International: Section B–The Sciences and Engineering* 60: 0863.

72 Lobsenz, R.E. 1999. "Do Measures of Tacit Knowledge Assess Psychological Phenomena Distinct from General Ability, Personality, and Social Knowledge?" *Dissertation Abstracts International: Section B–The Sciences and Engineering* 59: 05147.

73 McDaniel, M.A., and D.L. Whetzel. 2005.

74 Ibid.

75 Schmidt, F.L., and J.E. Hunter. 1993. "Tacit Knowledge, Practical Intelligence, General Mental Ability, and Job Knowledge." *Current Directions of Psychological Science* 2: 8–9.

76 Sternberg, R.J. 2002.

77 Dye, D.A., M. Reck, and M.A. McDaniel. 1993. "The Validity of Job Knowledge Measures." *International Journal of Selection and Assessment* 1: 153–57.

78 Consortium for Research on Emotional Intelligence in Organizations. The Mayer-Salovey-Caruso Emotional Intelligence Test (MSCEIT). Retrieved January 12, 2012, from http://www.eiconsortium.org/measures/msceit.html

79 Mayer, J.D., R.D. Roberts, and S.G. Barsade. 2008. "Human Abilities: Emotional Intelligence." *Annual Review of Psychology* 59: 507–36.

80 Mayer, J.D., and P. Salovey. 1997. "What Is Emotional Intelligence?" In P. Salovey, ed., *Emotional Development and Emotional Intelligence* (pp. 3–31). New York: Basic Books.

81 Bar-On, R. 1997. *Bar-On Emotional Quotient Inventory: User's Manual.* Toronto: Multi-Health Systems.

82 Bar-On, R. 2006. "The Bar-On Model of Emotional Social Intelligence (ESI)." *Psicothema* 18: 13–25.

83 Dunning, D., C. Heath, and J. Suls. 2004. "Flawed Self-Assessment: Implications for Health, Education and the Workplace." *Psychological Science in the Public Interest* 5: 69–106.

84 Newsome, S., A.L. Day, and V.M. Catano. 2000. "Assessing the Predictive Validity of Emotional Intelligence." *Personality and Individual Differences* 29: 1005–16.

85 Grubb, W.L., III, and M.A. McDaniel. 2007. "The Fakability of Bar-On's Emotional Quotient Inventory Short Form: Catch Me If You Can." *Human Performance* 20: 43–50.

86 Mayer, J.D., R.D. Roberts, and S.G. Barsade. 2008. "Human Abilities: Emotional Intelligence." *Annual Review of Psychology* 59: 507–36.

87 Bar-On, R. 1997. *Bar-On Emotional Quotient Inventory: Technical Manual.* Toronto: Multi-Health Systems.

88 Bar-On, R. 2004. "The Bar-On Emotional Quotient Inventory (EQi): Rationale, Description and Summary of Psychometric Properties." In G. Geher, ed., *Measuring Emotional Intelligence: Common Ground and Controversy* (pp. 115–22). New York: Nova Sci.

89 Petrides, K.V., and A. Furnham. 2003. "Trait Emotional Intelligence: Behavioral Validation in Two Studies of Emotion Recognition and Reactivity to Mood Induction." *European Journal of Personality* 17: 39–57.

90 Van Rooy, D.L., C. Viswesvaran, and P. Pluta. 2005. "An Examination of Construct Validity: What Is This Thing Called Emotional Intelligence?" *Human Performance* 18: 445–62.

91 O'Boyle, E.H. Jr., R.H. Humphrey, J.M. Pollack, T.H. Hawver, and P.A. Story. 2011. "The Relation Between Emotional Intelligence and Job Performance: A Meta-analysis." *Journal of Organizational Behavior* 32: 788–818.

92 Mayer, J.D., and P. Salovey. 1997. "What Is Emotional Intelligence?" In P. Salovey, ed., *Emotional Development and Emotional Intelligence* (pp. 3–31). New York: Basic Books.

93 Joseph, D.L., and Newman, D.A. 2010. "Emotional Intelligence: An Integrative Meta-Analysis and Cascading Model." *Journal of Applied Psychology* 95(1): 54–78.

94 O'Boyle, E.H., R.H. Humphrey, J.M. Pollack, T.H. Hawver, and P.A. Story. 2011. "The Relation Between Emotional Intelligence and Job Performance: A Meta-Analysis." *Journal of Organizational Behavior* 32(5): 788–818.

95 Joseph, D.L., and D.A. Newman. 2010.

96 Kilduff, M., D.S. Chiaburu, and J.I. Menges. 2010. "Strategic Use of Emotional Intelligence in Organizational Settings: Exploring the Dark Side." *Research in Organizational Behavior* 30: 129–52.

97 Greenidge, D., D. Devonish, and P. Alleyne. 2014. "The Relationship between Ability-Based Emotional Intelligence and Contextual Performance and Counterproductive Work Behaviours: A Test of the Medaing Effects of Job Satisfaction." *Human Performance* 27(3): 225–242.

98 Joseph, D.L., and D.A. Newman. 2010.

99 MacCaan, C., and R.D. Roberts. 2008. "Assessing Emotional Intelligence with Situational Judgment Tests Paradigms: Theory and Data." *Emotion* 8: 540–51.

100 Cherniss, C. 2010. "Emotional Intelligence: Toward Clarification of a Concept." *Industrial and Organizational Psychology* 3: 110–26.

101 Conte, J.M. 2005. "A Review and Critique of Emotional Intelligence Measures." *Journal of Organizational Behavior* 26: 433–40.

102 Cote, S. 2010. "Taking the 'Intelligence' in Emotional Intelligence Seriously." *Industrial and Organizational Psychology* 3: 127–30.

103 Sackett, P.R., and F. Lievens. 2008. "Personnel Selection." *Annual Review of Psychology* 59: 419–50.

104 Fleishman, E.A., and M.E. Reilly. 1992.

105 Levine, E.L., P.E. Spector, S. Menon, S. Narayanan, and J. Cannon-Bowers. 1996.

106 Johnston, P.J., and V.M. Catano. 2002.

107 Ibid.

108 Hogan, J. 1991. "Structure of Physical Performance in Occupational Tasks." *Journal of Applied Psychology* 76: 495–507.

109 Fleishman, E.A., and M.E. Reilly. 1992.

110 Campion, M.A. 1983. "Personnel Selection for Physically Demanding Jobs: Review and Recommendation." *Personnel Psychology* 36: 527–50.

111 Arvey, R.D., T.E. Landon, S.M. Nutting, and S.E. Maxwell. 1992. "Development of Physical Ability Tests for Police Officers: A Construct Validation Approach." *Journal of Applied Psychology* 77: 996–1009.

112 Dunn, K., and E. Dawson. 1994. "The Right Person for the Right Job." *Occupational Health and Safety Canada* 10: 28–31.

113 *British Columbia (Public Service Employee Relations Commission) v. BCGSEU.* Supreme Court of Canada decision rendered September 9, 1999.

114 Canadian Human Rights Commission. *Policy on HIV/AIDS.* Retrieved January 13, 2012, from http://www.chrc-ccdp.ca/legislation_policies/aids-en.asp

115 Ibid.

116 "Specialists Back Genetic Testing–Study." 1995. *Halifax Daily News* (December 23): 10.

117 MacDonald, C., and B. Williams-Jones. 2002. "Ethics and Genetics: Susceptibility Testing in the Workplace." *Journal of Business Ethics* 35: 235–41.

118 Yanchinski, S. 1990. "Employees under a Microscope." *The Globe and Mail* (January 3): D3.

119 MacDonald, C., and B. Williams-Jones. 2002.

120 Sabourin, M. 1999. "Bad Blood: Issues Surrounding Workplace Genetic Testing." *Occupational Health and Safety* 15: 34–41.

121 The Supreme Court of Canada. 1999. *British Columbia (Public Service Employee Relations Commission) v. BCGSEU.* Retrieved January 13, 2012, from http://scc.lexum.org/en/1999/1999scr3-3/1999scr3-3.html

122 Normand, J., S.D. Salyards, and J.J. Mahoney. 1990. "An Evaluation of Pre-Employment Drug Testing," *Journal of Applied Psychology* 75: 629–39.

123 Ibid.

124 Parish, D.C. 1989. "Relation of the Pre-employment Drug Testing Result to Employment Status: A One-Year Follow-up." *Journal of General Internal Medicine* 4: 44–47.

125 Harris, M.M., and M.L. Trusty. 1997. "Drug and Alcohol Programs in the Workplace: A Review of Recent Literature." In C.L. Cooper and I.T. Robertson, eds., *International Review of Industrial and Organizational Psychology*, Vol. 12 (pp. 289–315). London: John Wiley and Sons.

126 *Alberta (Human Rights and Citizenship Commission) v. Kellogg Brown & Root (Canada) Company,* 2007 ABCA 426, 425 AR 35 [Chiasson].

127 Krishnan, M. 2014, May 7. "City Draws Fire for Pre-Employment Drug Testing: Critics Call Program Unnecessary, Ineffective." *Calgary Herald.*

128 *Communications, Energy and Paperworkers Union of Canada, Local 30 v. Irving Pulp & Paper, Ltd.,* 2013 SCC 34 (CanLII).

129 Asher, J.J., and J.A. Sciarrino. 1974. "Realistic Work Sample Tests." *Personnel Psychology* 27: 519–33.

130 Ibid.

131 Hausknecht, J.P., D.V. Day, and S.C. Thomas. 2004. "Applicant Reactions to Selection Procedures: An Updated Model and Meta-Analysis." *Personnel Psychology* 57: 639–83.

132 Roth, P., P. Bobko, L.A. McFarland, and M. Buster. 2008. "Work Sample Tests in Personnel Selection: A Meta-Analysis of Black-White Differences in Overall and Exercise Scores." *Personnel Psychology* 61(3): 637–61.

133 Roth, P.L., M.A. Buster, and J.B. Barnes-Farrell. 2010. "Work Samples Exams and Gender Adverse Impact Potential: The Influence of Self-Concept, Social Skills, and Written Skills." *International Journal of Selection and Assessment* 18(2): 117–30.

134 Ployhart, R.E., and B.C. Holtz. 2008. "The Diversity-Validity Dilemma: Strategies for Reducing Racioethnic and Sex-Sub-Group Differences and Adverse Impact in Selection." *Personnel Psychology* 61: 153–72.

135 Ibid.

136 Spinner, B. 1990. *Predicting Success in Basic Flying Training from the Canadian Automated Pilot Selection System* (Working Paper 90-6). Willowdale, ON: Canadian Forces Personnel Applied Research Unit.

137 Fluckinger, C.D., N.M. Dudley, and M. Seeds. 2014. "Incremental Validity of Interactive Multimedia Simulations in Two Organizations." *International Journal of Selection and Assessment* 22(1): 108–112.

138 Thompson, C.T. 1995. "Actress to Help Test Applicants for Jobs at Prison." *Kitchener Record* (July 13): B1.

139 McDaniel, M.A., and N.T. Nguyen. 2001. "Situational Judgment Tests: A Review of Practice and Constructs Assessed." *International Journal of Selection and Assessment* 9: 103–13.

140 Weekley, J., and R. Ployhart, eds. 2006. *Situational Judgment Tests: Theory, Measurement, and Application.* Mahwah, NJ: Lawrence Erlbaum Associates.

141 Richman-Hirsch, W.L., J.B. Olson-Buchanan, and F. Drasgow. 2000. "Examining the Impact of Administration Medium on Examinee Perceptions and Attitudes. *Journal of Applied Psychology* 85: 880–87.

142 Weekly, J.A., and C. Jones. 1997. "Video-Based Situational Testing." *Personnel Psychology* 50: 25–49.

143 Chan, D., and N. Schmitt. 1997.

144 Ployhart, R.E., and M.G. Ehrhart. 2003. "Be Careful What You Ask For: Effects of Response Instructions on the Construct Validity and Reliability of Situational Judgment Tests." *International Journal of Selection and Assessment* 11: 1–16.

145 Arthur, W., Jr., R.M. Glaze, S.M. Jarrett, C.D. White, I. Schurig, and J.E. Taylor. 2014. "Comparative Evaluation of Three Situational Judgment Test Response Formats in Terms of Construct-Related Validity, Subgroup Differences and Susceptibility to Response Distortion." *Journal of Applied Psychology* 99(3): 535–545.

146 McDaniel, M.A., F.P. Morgeson, E.B. Finnegan, M.A. Campion, and E.P. Braverman. 2001. "Use of Situational Judgment Tests to Predict Job

Performance: A Clarification of the Literature." *Journal of Applied Psychology* 86: 730–40.

147 Chan, D., and N. Schmitt. 2002. "Situational Judgment and Job Performance." *Human Performance* 15: 233–54.

148 McDaniel M.A., F.P. Morgeson, E.B. Finnegan, M.A. Campion, and E.P. Braverman. 2001.

149 McDaniel, M.A., and N.T. Nguyen. 2001. "Situational Judgment Tests: A Review of Practice And Constructs Assessed." *International Journal of Selection and Assessment* 9: 103–13.

150 McDaniel M.A., N.S. Hartman, D.L. Whetzel, and W.L. Grubb. 2007. "Situational Judgment Tests, Response Instructions, and Validity: A Meta-Analysis." *Personnel Psychology 60*: 63–91.

151 Christian, M.S., B.D. Edwards, and J.C. Bradley. 2010. "Situational Judgment Tests: Constructs Assessed and a Meta-Analysis of Their Criterion-Related Validities." *Personnel Psychology* 63: 83–117.

152 Chan, D., and N. Schmitt. 2002, p. 240.

153 Drasgow, F. 2003.

154 Chan, D., and N. Schmitt. 2002, p. 240.

155 McDaniel, M.A., F.P. Morgeson, E.B. Finnegan, M.A. Campion, and E.P. Braverman. 2001.

156 Ibid.

157 Ryan, A.M., and R.E. Ployhart. 2014. "A Century of Selection." *Annual Review of Psychology* 65(20): 1–25.

158 Lievens, F., H. Peeters, and E. Schollaert. 2008. "Situational Judgment Tests: A Review of Recent Research." *Personnel Review* 37(4): 426–41.

159 Ployhart, R.E., and W.I. MacKenzie, Jr. 2011. "Situational Judgment Tests: A Critical Review and Agenda for the Future." In S. Zedeck, ed., *APA Handbook of Industrial and Organizational Psychology, Vol. 2: Selecting and Developing Members for the Organization* (pp. 237–52). American Psychological Association.

160 Whetzel, D., and M. McDaniel. 2009. "Situational Judgment Tests: An Overview of Current Research." *Human Resource Management Review 19*(3): 188–202.

161 Schippman, J.S., E.P. Prien, and J.A. Katz. 1990. "Reliability and Validity of In-Basket Performance." *Personnel Psychology* 43: 837–59.

162 Rolland, J.P. 1999. "Construct Validity of In-Basket Dimensions." *European Review of Applied Psychology* 49: 251–59.

163 Finkle, R.B. 1976. "Managerial Assessment Centers." In M.D. Dunnette, ed., *Handbook of Industrial and Organizational Psychology* (pp. 861–88). Chicago: Rand McNally.

164 Bray, D.W., R.J. Campbell, and D.L. Grant. 1974. *Formative Years in Business: A Long-Term AT&T Study of Managerial Lives*. New York: Wiley.

165 Thornton, III, G.D., and A.M. Gibbons. 2009. "Validity of Assessment Centers for Personnel Selection." *Human Resource Management Review* 19: 169–87.

166 Gaugler, B.B., D.B. Rosenthal, G.C. Thornton, and C. Bentson. 1987. "Meta-Analysis of Assessment Center Validity." *Journal of Applied Psychology* 72: 493–511.

167 Schmitt, N.A., J.R. Schneider, and S.A. Cohen. 1990. "Factors Affecting Validity of a Regionally Administered Assessment Center." *Personnel Psychology* 43: 2–11.

168 Hermelin, E., F. Lievens, and I.T. Robertson. 2007. "The Validity of Assessment Centers for the Prediction of Supervisory Performance Ratings: A Meta-Analysis." *International Journal of Selection and Assessment* 15: 405–11.

169 Thornton, III, G.D., and A.M. Gibbons. 2009.

170 Dilchert, S., and D.S. Ones. 2009. "Assessment Center Dimensions: Individual Differences Correlates and Meta-Analytic Incremental Validity." *International Journal of Selection and Assessment* 17(3): 254–70.

171 Arthur, W., Jr., E.A. Day, T.L. McNelly, and P.S. Edens. 2003. "A Meta-Analysis of the Criterion-Related Validity of Assessment Center Dimensions." *Personnel Psychology* 56: 125–54.

172 Gaugler, B.B., D.B. Rosenthal, G.C. Thornton, and C. Bentson. 1987.

173 Collins, J.D., F.L. Schmidt, M. Sanchez-Ku, L. Thomas, M.A. McDaniel, and H. Le. 2003. "Can Basic Individual Differences Shed Light on the Construct Meaning of Assessment Center Evaluations?" *International Journal of Selection and Assessment* 11: 17–29.

174 Bowler, M.C., and D.J. Woehr. 2006. "A Meta-Analytic Evaluation of the Impact of Dimension and Exercise Factors on Assessment Center Ratings." *Journal of Applied Psychology* 91: 1114–24.

175 Cascio, W.F., and H. Aguinis. 2005. "Test Development and Use: New Twists on Old Questions." *Human Resource Management* 44(3): 219–35.

176 Thornton, III, G.D., and A.M. Gibbons. 2009.

177 Ibid.

178 Howard, A. 1997. "A Reassessment of Assessment Centers: Challenges for the 21st Century." *Journal of Social Behavior and Personality* 12: 13–52.

179 Dean, M.E., P.L. Roth, and P. Bobko. 2008. "Ethnic and Subgroup Differences in Assessment Center Ratings: A Meta-Analysis." *Journal of Applied Psychology* 93: 685–91.

180 Andersen, N., F. Lievens, K. Van Dam, and M. Born. 2006. "A Construct Investigation of Gender Differences in a Leadership Role Assessment Center." *Journal of Applied Psychology* 91: 555–66.

181 Roth, P., P. Bobko, L.A. McFarland, and M. Buster. 2008. "Work Sample Tests in Personnel Selection: A Meta-Analysis of Black-White Differences in Overall and Exercise Scores." *Personnel Psychology* 61: 637–62.

182 Thornton, III, G.D., and A.M. Gibbons. 2009.

183 Jansen, A., K.G. Melchers, F. Lievens, M. Kleinmann, M. Brandi, L. Fraefel, and C.J. Konig. 2013. *Journal of Applied Psychology* 98(2): 326–341.

184 Ibid.

185 Kuncel, N.R., and P.R. Sackett. 2014. "Resolving the Assessment Centre Construct Validity Problem (as we know it)." *Journal of Applied Psychology* 99(1): 38–47.

186 Haaland, S., and N.D. Christiansen. 2002. "Implications of Trait-Activation Theory for Evaluating the Construct Validity of Assessment Center Ratings." *Personnel Psychology* 55: 137–163.

187 Lievens, F., E. Van Keer, and E. Volckaert. 2010. "Gathering Behavioral Samples through a Computerized and Standardized Assessment Center Exercise: Yes Is Possible." *Journal of Personnel Psychology* 9(2): 94–98.

188 Ferris, G.R., D.C. Treadway, R.W. Kolodinsky, W.A. Hochwarter, C.J. Kacmar, D. Ceasar, and D.F. Dwight. 2005. "Development and Validation of the Political Skill Inventory." *Journal of Management* 31(1): 126–152.

189 Blickle, G., G.R. Ferris, T.P. Munyon, T. Momm, I. Zettler, P.B. Schneider, and M.R. Buckley. 2011. "A Multi-Source, Multi-Study Investigation of Job Performance Prediction by Political Skill." *Applied Psychology, An International Review* 60(3): 449–474.

190 Munyon, T.P., J.K. Summers, K.M. Thompson, and G.R. Ferris. In Press. "Political Skill and Work Outcomes: A Theoretical Extension, Meta-Analytic Investigation, and Agenda for the Future." *Personnel Psychology*, doi: 10.1111/peps.12066

191 Ibid.

192 Gentry, W.A., D.C. Gilmore, M.L. Shuffler, and J.B. Leslie. 2011. "Political Skill as an Indicator of Promotability among Multiple Rater Sources." *Journal of Organizational Behavior* 33(1): 89–104.

193 Kapoutsis, I., A. Papalexandris, A. Nikolopoulos, W.A. Hochwarter, and G.R. Ferris. 2011. "Politics Perceptions as Moderator of the Political Skill-Job Performance Relationship: A Two-Study, Cross-National, Constructive Replication." *Journal of Vocational Behavior* 78(1): 123–135.

194 Munyon, T.P., et al. In Press.

195 Blickle, G., J. Kramer, P.B. Schneider, J.A. Meurs, G.R. Ferris, J. Mierke, A.H. Witzki, and T.D. Momm. 2011. "Role of Political Skill in Job Performance Prediction beyond General Mental Ability and Personality in Cross-Sectional and Predictive Studies." *Journal of Applied Social Psychology* 41(2): 488–514.

196 Snell, S.J., S. Tonidandel, P.W. Braddy, and J. Fleenor. 2014. "The Relative Importance of Political Skill Dimensions for Predicting Managerial Effectiveness." *European Journal of Work and Organizational Psychology* 23(6): 915–929.

197 Laird, M.D., J.J. Zboja, A.D. Martinez, and G.R. Ferris. 2013. "Performance and Political Skill in Personal Reputation Assessments." *Journal of Managerial Psychology* 28(6): 661–676.

198 Blickle, G., S. Wendel, and G.R. Ferris. 2010. "Political Skill as Moderator of Personality–Job Performance Relationships in Socioanalytic Theory: Test of the Getting Ahead Motive in Automobile Sales." *Journal of Vocational Behavior* 76(2): 326–335.

199 Hogan, R., J. Hogan, and B.W. Roberts. 1996. "Personality Measurement and Employment Decisions: Questions and Answers." *American Psychologist* 51: 469–77.

200 Hall, C.S., and G. Lindzey. 1970. *Theories of Personality*. New York: Wiley.

201 Jenkins, C.D., S.J. Zyzanski, and R.H. Rosenman. 1979. *Jenkins Activity Survey Manual.* New York: Psychological Corporation.

202 Hough, L.M. 1998. "Effects of Intentional Distortion in Personality Measurement and Evaluation of Suggested Palliatives." *Human Performance* 11: 209–44.

203 Ones, D., and C. Viswesvaran. 1998. "The Effects of Social Desirability and Faking on Personality and Integrity Testing for Personnel Selection." *Human Performance* 11: 245–69.

204 Oswald, F.L., and L.M. Hough. 2010. "Personality and Its Assessment in Organizations: Theoretical and Empirical Developments." In S. Zedeck, ed., *APA Handbook of Industrial and Organizational Psychology*, Vol. 2. American Psychological Association.

205 Hough, L.M. 1998.

206 Rosse, J.G., M.D. Steecher, J.L. Miller, and R.A Levin. 1998. "The Impact of Response Distortion on Preemployment Personality Testing and Hiring Decisions." *Journal of Applied Psychology* 83: 634–44.

207 Ellington, J.E., P.R. Sackett, and L.M. Hough. 1999. "Social Desirability Corrections in Personality Measurement: Issues of Applicant Comparison and Construct Validity." *Journal of Applied Psychology* 84: 155–66.

208 Zickar, M.J., and F. Drasgow. 1996. "Detecting Faking on a Personality Instrument Using Appropriateness Measurement." *Applied Psychological Measurement* 20: 71–87.

209 Zickar, M.J. 2001. "Conquering the Next Frontier: Modeling Personality Data with Item Response Theory." In B. Roberts and R.T. Hogan, eds., *Personality Psychology in the Workplace* (pp. 141–60). Washington, DC: American Psychological Association.

210 Zickar, M.J., and F. Drasgow. 1996.

211 Barrick, M.R., and M.K. Mount. 1991. "The Big Five Personality Dimensions and Job Performance: A Meta-Analysis." *Personnel Psychology* 44: 1–26.

212 Ones, D., and C. Viswesvaran. 1998.

213 Ibid.

214 Alliger, G.M., and S.A. Dwight. 2000. "A Meta-Analytic Investigation of the Susceptibility of Integrity Tests to Faking and Coaching." *Educational and Psychological Measurement* 60: 59–73.

215 Donovan, J.J., S.A. Dwight, and D. Schneider. 2014. "The Impact of Applicant Faking on Selection Measures, Hiring Decisions, and Employee Performance." *Journal of Business & Psychology* 29: 479–493.

216 Hough, L.M., and A. Furnham. 2003. "Use of Personality Variables in Work Settings." In W.C Borman, D.R. Ilgen, and R. Klimoski, eds., *Handbook of Psychology: Industrial and Organizational Psychology* 12 (pp. 131–69). New York: John Wiley and Sons.

217 Rosse, J.G., M.D. Steecher, J.L. Miller, and R.A Levin. 1998.

218 Schmitt, N., and F.L. Oswald. 2006. "The Impact of Corrections for Faking on the Validity of Noncognitive Measures in Selection Settings." *Journal of Applied Psychology* 91: 613–21.

219 Hogan, J., P. Barrett, and R. Hogan. 2007. "Personality Measurement, Faking, and Employment Selection." *Journal of Applied Psychology* 92: 1270–85.

220 Fan, J., D. Gao, S.A. Carroll, F.J. Lopez, T.S. Tian, and H. Heng. 2012. "Testing the Efficacy of a New Procedure for Reducing Faking on Personality Tests within Selection Contexts." *Journal of Applied Psychology* 97(4): 866–80.

221 Landers, R.N., P.R. Sackett, and K.A. Tuziniski. 2011. "Retesting after Initial Failure, Coaching Rumors, and Warnings against Faking in Online Personality Measures of Selection." *Journal of Applied Psychology* 96(1): 2012–10.

222 Van Hooft, E.A.J., and M.P. Born. 2012. "Intentional Response Distortion on Personality Tests: Using Eye-Tracking to Understand Response Processes when Faking." *Journal of Applied Psychology* 97(2): 301–16.

223 Rosse, J.G., M.D. Steecher, J.L. Miller, and R.A Levin. 1998.

224 Guion, R.M. 1965. *Personnel Testing*. New York: McGraw Hill.

225 Guion, R.M., and R.F. Gottier. 1965. "Validity of Personality Measures in Personnel Selection." *Personnel Psychology* 18: 135–64.

226 Tett, R.P., D.N. Jackson, and M. Rothstein. 1991. "Personality Measures as Predictors of Job Performance: A Meta-Analytic Review." *Personnel Psychology* 44: 703–42.

227 Salgado, J.F. 1997. "The Five Factor Model of Personality and Job Performance in the European Community." *Journal of Applied Psychology* 82: 30–43.

228 Salgado, J.F. 1998. "Big Five Personality Dimensions and Job Performance in Army and Civil Occupations: A European Perspective. *Human Performance* 11: 271–88.

229 McHenry, J.J., L.M. Hough, J.L. Toquam, M.A. Hanson, and S. Ashworth. 1990.

230 Hough, L.M., N.K. Eaton, M.D. Dunnette, J.D. Kamp, and R.A. McCloy. 1990. "Criterion-Related Validities of Personality Constructs and the Effect of Response Distortion on Those Validities." Monograph. *Journal of Applied Psychology* 75: 581–95.

231 Barrick, M.R., and M.K. Mount. 1991.

232 Digman, J.M. 1990. "Personality Structure: Emergence of the Five Factor Model." In M. Rosenzweig and L.W. Porter, eds., *Annual Review of Psychology* 41 (pp. 417–40). Palo Alto, CA: Annual Reviews.

233 Hough, L.M., and A. Furnham. 2003.

234 Barrick, M.R., and M.K. Mount. 1991.

235 Campbell, J.P. 1990. "Modeling the Performance Prediction Problem in Industrial and Organizational Psychology." In M.D. Dunnette and L.M. Hough, eds., *The Handbook of Industrial and Organizational Psychology*, Vol. 1, 2nd ed. (pp. 687–32). San Diego: Consulting Psychologists Press.

236 Mount, M.K., and M.R. Barrick. 1995. "The Big Five Personality Dimensions: Implications for Research and Practice in Human Resources Management. In G.R. Ferris, ed., *Research in Personnel and Human Resources Management*, Vol. 13 (pp. 153–200). Greenwich, CT: JAI Press.

237 McManus, M.A., and M.L. Kelly. 1999. "Personality Measures and Biodata: Evidence Regarding Their Incremental Predictive Value in the Life Insurance Industry." *Personnel Psychology* 52: 137–48.

238 Barrick, M.R., and M.K. Mount. 1991.

239 Ibid.

240 Mount, M.K., M.R. Barrick, and G.L. Stewart. 1998. "Five-Factor Model of Personality and Performance in Jobs Involving Interpersonal Interactions." *Human Performance* 11: 145–65.

241 Hough, L.M., and A. Furnham. 2003.

242 Chiaburu, D.S., O. In-Sue, C.M. Berry, L. Ning, and R.G. Gardner. 2011. "The Five-Factor Model of Personality Traits and Organizational Citizenship Behavior: A Meta-Analysis." *Journal of Applied Psychology* 96(6): 1140–1166.

243 Oh, I-S, and B.M. Christopher. 2009. "The Five-Factor Model of Personality and Managerial Performance: Validity Gains through the Use of 360 Degree Performance Ratings." *Journal of Applied Psychology* 94(6): 1498–513.

244 Schmidt, F.L., and J.E. Hunter. 1998. "The Validity and Utility of Selection Methods in Personnel Psychology: Practical and Theoretical Implications of 85 Years of Research Findings." *Psychological Bulletin* 124: 262–74.

245 Hogan, R., J. Hogan, and B.W. Roberts. 1996.

246 Oswald, F.L., and L.M. Hough. 2010. "Personality and Its Assessment in Organizations: Theoretical and Empirical Developments." In S. Zedeck, ed., *APA Handbook of Industrial and Organizational Psychology*, Vol. 2, American Psychological Association.

247 Outtz, J.L. 2002.

248 Oswald, F.L., and L.M. Hough. 2010.

249 Johnson, M.K., W.C. Rowatt, and L. Petrini. 2011. "A New Trait on the Market: Honesty-Humility as a Unique Predictor of Job Performance Ratings." *Personality and Individual Differences* 50(6): 857–862.

250 Kichuk, S.L., and W.H. Wiesner. 1998. "Work Teams: Selecting Members for Optimal Performance." *Canadian Psychology* 39: 23–32.

251 Humphrey, S.E., J.R. Hollenbeck, C.J. Meyer, and D.R. Ilgen. 2011. "Personality Configurations in Self-Managed Teams: A Natural Experiment on the Effects of Maximizing and Minimizing Variance in Traits." *Journal of Applied Social Psychology* 41(7): 1701–32.

252 Halfhill, T., T.M. Nielson, E. Sundstrom, and A. Weilbaecher. 2005. "Group Personality Composition and Performance in Military Service Teams." *Military Psychology* 17: 41–54.

253 Mount, M.K., M.R. Barrick, and G.L. Stewart. 1998. "Five Factor Model of Personality and Performance in Jobs Involving Interpersonal Interactions." *Human Performance* 11: 145–65.

254 LePine, J.A., B.R. Buckman, E.R. Crawford, and J.R. Methot. 2011. "A Review of Research on Personality in Teams: Accounting for Pathways Spanning Levels of Theory and Analysis." *Human Resource Management Review* 21: 311–30.

255 Stewart, G.L. 2003. "Toward an Understanding of the Multilevel Role of Personality in Teams." In M.R. Barrick and A.M. Ryan, eds., *Personality and Work: Reconsidering the Role of Personality in Organizations* (pp. 183–204). San Francisco: Jossey-Bass.

256 Bell, S.T. 2007. "Deep-Level Composition Variables as Predictors of Team Performance: A Meta-analysis." *Journal of Applied Psychology* 92: 595–615.

257 Humphrey, S.E., J.R. Hollenbeck, C.J. Meyer, and D.R. Ilgen. 2011. "Personality Configurations in Self-Managed Teams: A Natural Experiment on the Effects of Maximizing and Minimizing Variance in Traits." *Journal of Applied Social Psychology* 41(7): 1701–32.

258 Prewett, M.S., A.A.G. Walvoord, F.R.B. Stilson, M.E. Rossi, and M.T. Brannick. 2009. "The Team Personality–Team Performance Relationship Revisited: The Impact of Criterion Choice, Pattern of Workflow, and Method of Aggregation." *Human Performance* 22: 273–96.

259 LePine, J.A., B.R. Buckman, E.R. Crawford, and J.R. Methot. 2011. "A Review of Research on Personality in Teams: Accounting for Pathways Spanning Levels of Theory and Analysis." *Human Resource Management Review* 21: 311–30.

260 Ibid.

261 Tett, R.P., D.N. Jackson, and M. Rothstein. 1991. "Personality Measures as Predictors of Job Performance: A Meta-Analytic Review." *Personnel Psychology* 44(4): 703–742.

262 Paunonen, S.V., M.G. Rothstein, and D.N. Jackson. 1999. "Narrow Reasoning about the Use of Broad Personality Measures for Personnel Selection." *Journal of Organizational Behavior* 20: 389–405.

263 Ashton, M.C., S.V. Paunonen, and K. Lee. 2014. "On the Validity of Narrow and Broad Personality Traits: A Response to Salgado, Moscoso and Berges (2013)." *Personality and Individual Differences* 56: 24–28.

264 Paunonen, S.V., and A.A.A.M. Nicol. 2001. "The Personality Hierarchy and the Prediction of Work Behaviors." In B. Roberts and R.T. Hogan, eds., *Personality Psychology in the Workplace* (pp. 161–91). Washington, DC: American Psychological Association.

265 Ones, D., and C. Viswesvaran. 1996. "Bandwidth-Fidelity Dilemma in Personality Measurement for Personnel Selection." *Journal of Organizational Behavior* 17: 609–26.

266 Salgado, J.F., S. Moscoso, and A. Berges. 2013. "Conscientiousness, Its Facets, and the Prediction of Job Performance Ratings: Evidence against the Narrow Measures." *International Journal of Selection and Assessment* 21(1): 74–84.

267 Marick, M.R., M.K. Mount, and N. Li. 2013. "The Theory of Purposeful Work Behavior: The Role of Personality, Higher-Order Goals, and Job Characteristics." *Academy of Management Review* 38(1): 132–153.

268 Dalal, R.S., I.J. Jose, R. Hermida, T.R. Chen, and R.P. Vega. 2014. "Measuring Job-Related Situational Strength and Assessing Its Interactive Effects with Personality on Voluntary Work Behavior." *Journal of Management* 40(4): 1010–1041.

269 Hough, L.M., and A. Furnham. 2003.

270 Penney, L.M., E. David, and L.A. Witt. 2011. "A Review of Personality and Performance: Identifying Boundaries, Contingencies, and Future Research Directions." *Human Resource Management Review* 21: 297–310.

271 Witt, L.A. 2001, November. *Emotional Stability and Conscientiousness as Interactive Predictors of Job Performance.* Unpublished paper presented at the annual meeting of the Southern Management Association, New Orleans.

272 Uppal, N., S.K. Mishra, and N. Vohra. 2014. "Prior Related Work Experience and Job Performance: Role of Personality." *International Journal of Selection and Assessment* 22(1): 39–51.

273 Blickle, G., J.A. Meurs, A. Wihler, C. Ewen, A. Plies, and S. Gunther. 2013. "The Interactive Effects of Conscientiousness, Openness to Experience, and Political Skill on Job Performance in Complex Jobs: The Importance of Context." *Journal of Organizational Behavior* 34(8): 1145–1164.

274 Guay, R.P., I-S. Oh, D. Choi, M.S. Mitchell, M.K. Mount, and K. Shin. 2013. "The Interactive Effect of Conscientiousness and Agreeableness on Job Performance Dimensions in South Korea." *International Journal of Selection and Assessment* 21(2): 233–238.

275 Le, H., O. In-Sue, S.B. Robbins, I. Remus, E. Holland, and P. Westrick. 2011. "Too Much of a Good Thing: Curvilinear Relationships between Personality Traits and Job Performance." *Journal of Applied Psychology* 96(1): 113–133.

276 Penney, L.M., E. David, and L.A. Witt. 2011.

277 Bing, M.N., H.K. Davison, and J. Smothers. 2014. "Item-Level Frame-of-Reference Effects in Personality Testing: An Investigation of Incremental Validity in an Organizational Setting." *International Journal of Selection and Assessment* 22(2): 165–178.

278 Schmitt, N. 2014. "Personality and Cognitive Ability as Predictors of Effective Performance at Work." *Annual Review of Organizational Psychology and Organizational Behavior* 1: 45–65.

279 Ibid.

280 Ones, D., C. Viswesvaran, and F.L. Schmidt. 1993.

281 *Employee Polygraph Protection Act* (29 USC §2001 et seq.; 29 CFR 801).

282 Jones, J., ed. 1991. *Pre-Employment Honesty Testing: Current Research and Future Directions.* New York: Quorum Books.

283 Sackett, P.R., L.R. Burris, and C. Callahan. 1989. "Integrity Testing for Personnel Selection: An Update." *Personnel Psychology* 42: 491–529.

284 Hogan, J., and R. Hogan. 1989. "How to Measure Employee Reliability." *Journal of Applied Psychology* 74: 273–79.

285 Alliger, G.M., S.O. Lilienfeld, and K.E. Mitchell. 1996. "The Susceptibility of Overt and Covert Integrity Tests to Coaching and Faking." *Psychological Science* 7: 32–39.

286 Collins, J.D., and F.L. Schmidt. 1993. "Personality, Integrity, and White-Collar Crime: A Construct Validity Study." *Personnel Psychology* 46: 295–311.

287 Temple, W. 1992. "Counterproductive Behaviour Costs Millions." *British Journal of Administrative Management* (April/May): 20–21.

288 Ones, D., C. Viswesvaran, and F.L. Schmidt. 1993. "Comprehensive Meta-Analysis of Integrity Test Validities: Findings and Implications for Personnel Selection and Theories of Job Performance." *Journal of Applied Psychology* 78: 679–703.

289 Ones, D., and C. Viswesvaran. 1998.

290 Fine, S. 2010. "Pre-employment Integrity Testing across Multiple Industries." *Psychological Reports* 107(2): 607–10.

291 Ones, D.S., C. Viswesvaran, and F. Schmidt. 1993. "Comprehensive Meta-Analysis of Integrity Test Validities: Findings and Implications for Personnel Selection and Theories of Job Performance." *Journal of Applied Psychology Monograph* 78: 679–703.

292 Sturman, M.C., and D. Sherwyn. 2009. "The Utility of Integrity Testing for Controlling Workers' Compensation Costs." *Cornell Hospitality Quarterly* 50: 432–45.

293 Ibid.

294 Ones, D., C. Viswesvaran, and F.L. Schmidt. 1993.

295 Ones, D.S., and C. Viswesvaran. 1998. "Integrity Testing in Organizations." In R.W. Griffin, A. O'Leary, and J.M. Collins, eds., *Dysfunctional Behavior in Organizations: Vol. 2, Nonviolent Behaviors in Organizations* (pp. 243–76). Greenwich, CT: JAI Press.

296 Sackett, P.R., and J.E. Wanek. 1996. "New Developments in the Use of Measures of Honesty, Integrity, Conscientiousness, Dependability, Trustworthiness, and Reliability for Personnel Selection." *Personnel Psychology* 49: 787–827.

297 Berry, C.M., P.R. Sackett, and S. Wiemann. 2007. "A Review of Recent Developments in Integrity Test Research." *Personnel Psychology* 60: 271–301.

298 Marcus, B., M.C. Ashton, and K. Lee. 2013. "A Note on the Incremental Validity of Integrity Tests beyond Standard Personality Inventories for the Criterion of Counterproductive Behaviour." *Canadian Journal of Administrative Sciences* 30(1): 18–25.

299 Berry, C.M., P.R. Sackett, and S. Wiemann. 2007.

300 Schmidt, F.L., and Hunter, J.E. 1998. "The Validity and Utility of Personnel Selection Methods in Personnel Psychology: Practical and Theoretical Implications of 85 Years of Research Findings." *Psychological Bulletin* 124: 262–74.

301 Mumford, M.D., M.S. Connelly, W.B. Helton, J.M. Strange, and H.K. Osburn. 2001. "On the Construct Validity of Integrity Tests: Individual and Situational Factors as Predictors of Test Performance." *International Journal of Selection and Assessment* 9: 240–57.

302 Ones, D.S. 1993. The Construct Validity of Integrity Tests. Unpublished Ph.D. dissertation, University of Iowa.

303 See Marcus, B., K. Lee, and M.C. Ashton. 2007. "Personality Dimensions Explaining Relationships Between Integrity Tests and Counterproductive Behavior: Big Five, or One in Addition?" *Personnel Psychology* 60: 1–34.

304 Ibid.

305 Berry, C.M., P.R. Sackett, and S. Wiemann. 2007. "A Review of Recent Developments in Integrity Test Research." *Personnel Psychology* 60: 271–301.

306 Steiner, D.D., and S.W. Gilliland. 1996. "Fairness Reactions to Personnel Selection Techniques in France and the United States." *Journal of Applied Psychology* 81: 131–41.

307 Sackett, P.R., and J.E. Wanek. 1996. "New Developments in the Use of Measures of Honesty, Integrity, Conscientiousness, Dependability, Trustworthiness, and Reliability for Personnel Selection." *Personnel Psychology* 49: 787–829.

308 Camara, W.J., and D.L. Schneider. 1994.

309 Arnold, D.W. 1991. "To Test or Not to Test: Legal Issues in Integrity Testing." *Forensic Psychology* 4: 62–67.

310 Berry, C.M., P.R. Sackett, and S. Wiemann. 2007.

311 Neuman, G.A., and R. Baudoun. 1998. "An Empirical Examination of Overt and Covert Integrity Tests." *Journal of Business and Psychology* 13: 65–79.

312 D. Lindsay. 1998. "True Lies–An Applicant Writes an 'Integrity' Test," *This Magazine* 31: 4.

313 Neuman, G.A., and R. Baudoun. 1998. "An Empirical Examination of Overt and Covert Integrity Tests." *Journal of Business and Psychology* 13: 65–79.

314 Camara, W.J., and D.L. Schneider. 1994.

315 Catano, V.M., and M.A. Prosser. 2007. "A Review of Integrity Tests and Their Implications for Selection of Security Personnel in a Canadian Context." *The Canadian Journal of Police and Security Services* 5: 1–18.

316 Ones, D.S., and C. Viswesvaran. 1998.

317 Wanek, J.E. 1999. "Integrity and Honesty Testing: What Do We Know? How Do We Use It?" *International Journal of Selection and Assessment* 7: 183–95.

318 Ones, D.S., C. Viswesvaran, and F.L. Schmidt. 2003. "Personality and Absenteeism: A Meta-analysis of Integrity Tests." *European Journal of Personality* 17: S19–38.

319 Ployhart, R.E., and B.C. Holtz. 2008. "The Diversity–Validity Dilemma: Strategies for Reducing Racioethnic and Sex Subgroup Differences and Adverse Impact in Selection." *Personnel Psychology* 61: 153–72.

320 Anderson, N., J.F. Salgado, and U.R. Hulsheger. 2010. "Applicant Reactions in Selection: Comprehensive Meta-Analysis into Reaction Generalization versus Situational Specificity." *International Journal of Selection and Assessment* 18(3): 291–304.

321 Ibid.

322 Truxillo, D.M., T.E. Bodner, M. Bertolino, and T.N. Bauer. 2009. "Effects of Explanations on Applicant Reactions: A Meta-Analytic Review." *International Journal of Selection and Assessment* 17(4): 346–61.

323 Ryan, A.M., and R.E. Ployhart. 2014. "A Century of Selection." *Annual Review of Psychology* 65: 693–717.

324 Williams, K.Z., M.M. Schaffer, and L.E. Ellis. 2013. "Legal Risk in Selection: An Analysis of Processes and Tools." *Journal of Business and Psychology* 28: 401–410.

SELECTION III:
Interviewing

CHAPTER 9

CHAPTER LEARNING OUTCOMES

This chapter presents new and more effective alternatives to the traditional approaches to employment interviewing.

AFTER READING THIS CHAPTER YOU SHOULD:

- understand the purposes and uses of employment interviews;
- know the multiple phases of the employment interview and the factors affecting employment interview decisions;
- appreciate the selection errors associated with traditional approaches to employment interviewing;
- understand the elements of employment interview structuring;
- be aware of different structured interviewing techniques and their relative advantages and disadvantages;
- appreciate the legal and predictive advantages of structured employment interviewing methods;
- begin developing competence in the design of effective interview questions and scoring guides;
- know about innovations and future directions in interview research and practice; and
- appreciate the role of employment interviews in the changing organizational environment.

A TRADITIONAL INTERVIEW

The receptionist escorted Anita Job to the vice-president's office. The sign on the door read "M. Ployer." The receptionist knocked on the door and, upon hearing the invitation within, opened the door and introduced Anita to Mr. Ployer.

"Welcome, Anita!" said Mr. Ployer as he stood up, stepped forward, and shook Anita's hand. He motioned to a chair in front of his desk. "Please, have a seat."

As Anita sat down, Mr. Ployer stepped back, lowered himself into the chair behind his desk, and asked "How is the weather out there? Are the roads still slippery?"

"Oh, yes, I saw several cars in the ditch on the way here" replied Anita, "but I have an SUV with new snow tires, so I didn't have any problems. Say, that's a great painting behind you. Is that Algonquin Park?"

Mr. Ployer turned to look at the painting, "Yes, it's a painting by Ken Danby. It's called 'Algonquin (Homage to Tom Thomson).'"

Anita leaned forward, "Wow, it looks just like Algonquin! I love it there. We go just about every summer. I'm guessing, with that painting, you must go up there quite a bit too."

For the next 20 minutes Anita and Mr. Ployer had an enjoyable conversation about Algonquin Park, their favourite lakes, their favourite camp sites, and so forth. Then, during a lull in the conversation, Mr. Ployer recalled the purpose of their meeting, "I guess I need to ask you some questions related to the sales manager's position for which you've applied."

"Certainly," replied Anita.

"Anita, why did you apply for this position?" Mr. Ployer asked his first interview question.

Anita immediately offered her answer, "Well, I've heard a lot of good things about your company and I feel that this would be an excellent company to work for. When I saw the job posting, I thought that this would be a really good opportunity for a job change, to take on a new challenge, to grow my skills, and to contribute to your company. I'm really looking forward to it."

"How would you contribute to our company?" queried Mr. Ployer.

Anita was prepared. "I know I could at least double sales in the department in a very short time. I've had lots of experience selling and I'm very good at it. This position would give me the chance to demonstrate my leadership skills by getting your sales staff excited and up to speed and working with them to help them achieve the highest levels of success. I'm confident I could really get things moving."

"So, what do you consider to be your strengths?" asked Mr. Ployer.

Anita responded, "I'm a highly motivated go-getter. I never stop. When I set my mind to do something, I get it done. I enjoy challenges and I work well under pressure. I'm very success oriented and persistent. Also, I'm a great people person, I get along well with most people, and I have excellent communication skills. I also have very good customer service skills. I'm a natural leader. I'm good at seeing the 'big picture' and directing and motivating others to work with me to accomplish what needs to be done. People have told me I should be in management and that my skills are wasted in sales. I'm also a great problem solver, I'm good at making decisions, and I have a lot of great ideas. I'm a good planner. I carefully think through what I want to accomplish, I consider all the factors, and then I work hard to get the job done. And did I say I enjoy challenges?"

"That sounds great, Anita. What about your weaknesses?" inquired Mr. Ployer.

Anita thought for a moment, "Well, I'd have to say that I probably work too hard and get too involved in my work. I don't take enough time off for my personal life at home."

"Hmm . . . I'm not sure I would consider that a real weakness. I get pretty involved in my work myself. Can you think of something else about yourself that you would like to improve?" Mr. Ployer countered.

Anita thought again and then answered, "I haven't been as organized as I would like. However, I have been working to improve that. I worked out a new system using my new iPhone calendar app so that now I'm actually getting pretty good at organizing my work."

"O.K.," Mr. Ployer continued, "How do you think your current boss would describe you?"

Anita contemplated the question and responded, "Oh, I think she would see me as an excellent salesperson, a top performer. I think she would feel I have a lot of potential and that I'm someone who's very motivated and achievement oriented. She would probably describe me as a 'people person', someone with very good customer service skills, and a very valuable member of her sales team."

"Is there any area where your boss might feel you could improve?" asked Mr. Ployer.

Anita pondered, "Well, I guess she might say I sometimes I haven't paid enough attention to minor details. As I said, I'm a big-picture person. Anyway, I have been working on organizing myself better, so that's not really a problem for me anymore."

"That sounds wonderful," enthused Mr. Ployer, "Tell me, where do you see yourself five years from now?"

Anita replied, "I would like to prove myself in this job by taking the department to new levels of performance. With the opportunity to expand my knowledge and experience, I would look forward to taking on new challenges in three or four years. I can see myself moving into a district manager role in a few years."

"Thank you, Anita." Mr. Ployer smiled. "Do you have any questions for me?"

"Yes," answered Anita. "What do you see as my biggest challenge in raising the performance level of the department?"

Mr. Ployer discussed with Anita his perceptions of some of the challenges in the department and Anita assured him that she was more than capable of dealing with these challenges. At the conclusion of the interview, Mr. Ployer thanked Anita for the interview and indicated that she would hear from him within a week. Before she left, Anita asked Mr. Ployer when he was planning to go back to Algonquin Park. They had a brief discussion of their plans for the summer and Anita took her leave.

"That sounded like a really good interview." observed Mr. Ployer's receptionist.

"It was." Mr. Ployer smiled as he stepped back into his office.

The kind of interview illustrated in the opening vignette is not unusual. You may well encounter this kind of interview in your own job search. From this interview, how much accurate and useful information would Mr. M. Ployer have been able to obtain from Anita Job that would enable him to assess her ability to be an effective sales manager? The interview consisted of questions asking Anita to give her opinions about herself or her beliefs about her current boss's opinions of her. These opinions might or might not be accurate but they certainly reveal very little about Anita's knowledge, skills, abilities, or other attributes and competencies (KSAOs) or other qualities that would be important for the sales manager's position. Her answers reflect the advice found in numerous books and websites on how to answer such interview questions and she might well have memorized and rehearsed her answers from the material she read in preparing for this interview. Moreover, the discussion Mr. Ployer and Anita had about their shared love of Algonquin Park is likely to have biased Mr. Ployer's assessment of Anita's suitability for the job. Such interviews tend not to be very useful for selecting the best applicants for a job. The goal of this chapter is to provide insights into interviewing best practices that permit interviewers to be much more effective than the kind of interview illustrated in the opening vignette, which is used by far too many employers.

The employment interview is one of the oldest and most widely used of all selection procedures.[1,2] Data from Statistics Canada's Workplace and Employee Survey show that almost 80 percent of the firms that used pre-hiring selection relied on some type of interview.[3] Moreover, when making selection decisions, recruiters tend to have more confidence in the interview than in information provided from application forms, references, test results, or any other source of information about the applicant.[4,5,6] Given the interview's importance in the employee selection process, it is worth devoting close attention to this selection technique, particularly to relatively recent improvements in interview methods. Modern interview techniques, if used properly, can significantly improve the effectiveness of the traditional interview as a selection tool.

// PURPOSES AND USES OF THE INTERVIEW

© iStock.com/kupicoo

Except for screening interviews, interviews are usually conducted near the end of the selection process. Leaving the interview until the end allows the other selection instruments, such as tests, to screen out unqualified applicants and reduces the number of people who must be interviewed. It is usually desirable to reduce the number of interviewees because interviews are relatively expensive, compared with other selection instruments such as tests or the screening of résumés (i.e., the time spent by managers or supervisors interviewing applicants is one of the costs associated with the interview). However, interviews are often also used as preliminary screening devices (e.g., in recruitment centres, by campus recruiters, etc.). Therefore, in this chapter, we will examine the interview as both a screening device and a selection tool.

When used for screening purposes, the interview is often used to confirm or explore information provided in résumés or application forms and is also used as a recruitment tool. However, when used later in the selection process, the interview is best used to obtain information that has not been provided in the résumé or application form. Interviews are typically conducted by HR staff or by supervisors or line managers (who usually have little interview training).[7] They tend to have little time available for preparing interview questions and often use standard questions that they hear others using or that they remember having been asked when they were interviewees. In many organizations, applicants are interviewed by several interviewers, either simultaneously as part of panel or board interviews or in sequential or serial interviews.[8,9]

Although interviews can be and have been used to assess job knowledge and cognitive ability, they are probably best suited to the assessment of noncognitive attributes such as interpersonal relationships or social skills, initiative, dependability, perseverance, teamwork, leadership skills, adaptability or flexibility, organizational citizenship behaviour, and organizational fit.[10–16] As you may recognize from our discussion of personality in Chapter 8, several of these attributes are also measured by different personality inventories.

Interviews are also used to sell the job to the applicant. They provide applicants with an opportunity to ask questions about the job and the organization and to decide whether the job and the organization provide an appropriate fit. In fact, an interviewer's friendliness, warmth, and humour, as well as job knowledge and general competence, seem to increase applicant attraction to the organization and the likelihood that an applicant will accept a job offer.[17] However, interviewers' effects on applicant job choice are not as strong as factors such as pay, the job itself, promotion opportunities, or geographical location.[18,19] Moreover, when recruiters put too much effort into selling the job, rather than focusing on the selection function, they may actually reduce the attractiveness of the job for applicants.[20] It is possible that applicants become suspicious and back away when they perceive the recruiter trying too hard to convince them of the merits of the job or organization.

Interviews have also been used in the termination of employees. As organizations restructure, downsize, or "rightsize" and jobs are eliminated, employees must compete for a smaller number of redesigned jobs. The interview serves to assist in identifying employees who have the necessary KSAOs to perform well or are able to meet the new standards in the redesigned jobs. Those who do not have the necessary KSAOs or do not meet the new standards are let go. Although there is considerable debate about the merits of downsizing as a cure for ailing organizations, such interviews have become commonplace.[21]

Interviews are commonly used to determine who is best qualified when several employees are being considered for a promotion. Often *internal applicants* (employees) compete with *external applicants* for such positions. In such circumstances there might be concerns about how internal applicants will react if an external applicant is chosen over them. Conversely, there might be concerns about how internal applicants will respond if one of them is promoted to be the new supervisor over the others. Such decisions are not without political ramifications (which we will discuss later in the chapter). If there are substantial changes in how a job is performed (e.g., computer systems are introduced to a job that used to be largely manual), interviews can be used to help determine whether incumbents can meet the new standards required for the job. If retraining is not feasible in such circumstances, the incumbents could be reassigned or, in the absence of alternative positions, be let go. Interviews are also used to determine whether individuals who have been in a union job temporarily are able to meet the standards necessary to be hired into a permanent position.

THE COST OF INTERVIEWING

Interviews are a relatively expensive selection tool, even if they do not include travel. Costs include the time that supervisors or managers spend preparing for the interview and actually interviewing (as opposed to performing their usual tasks), time spent reflecting on interviewees' answers and comparing interviewees after the interviews, time spent by clerical staff on interview-related tasks, the use and/or reorganization of office space for the interview, and the use of equipment such as telephones, fax machines, and copiers for interview-related functions, not to mention the time spent in developing interview questions and scoring guides.

When the interview involves travel, the costs can rise dramatically. If candidates fly in (or drive) from another city, costs typically include the flight (or mileage), airport parking, meals, and taxi fares or parking fees. If the candidate needs to stay overnight because of when the interview is scheduled, the distance travelled, or the availability of transportation, costs include the hotel stay. Some organizations either make travel arrangements and pay for these expenses directly or reimburse the candidate for travel expenses related to the interview. When organizations shift these costs to the applicants, they risk losing many potential applicants because most applicants will be unwilling to incur travel costs given the risk of not getting a job offer, particularly as travel costs become high.

If recruiters or managers need to travel to conduct interviews, similar expenses are incurred, including flight costs or mileage, airport parking, hotel stay, meals, and taxi fare or parking fees. Because of the relatively high costs of interviewing, formal interviews are usually conducted near the end of the selection process, after the pool of applicants has been reduced by other selection instruments such as a review of application forms or résumés, administration of tests, and the use of preliminary screening interviews.

// SCREENING INTERVIEWS

In our discussion of recruitment in Chapter 6, we described how job applicants use their initial interview with a recruiter to obtain information about the organization. The interviewer takes the opportunity of this interview to find out information about the applicant that is not apparent from an application form or résumé. The interview has considerable value as a recruiting device and as a means of initiating a social relationship between a job applicant and an organization.[22] A selection interview provides the applicant with information, mostly favourable, about the organization as an employer, in the hope of increasing the odds that a desired applicant will accept a forthcoming job offer. The job applicant uses the interview to learn more about the organization as an employer and to make inferences about its values and philosophy in deciding whether there is a fit.[23]

Without a doubt, interviewing that is done as part of the recruitment process serves as a screening mechanism. Job applicants who do not meet the recruiter's standards do not proceed further. In fact, one of the main purposes of screening interviews is to narrow down the list of potential job applicants who proceed to subsequent stages of the selection system (such as testing and formal interviewing) and, therefore, help to increase the efficiency of the selection process. Goodyear Canada is among the organizations using an initial screening interview to determine whether job candidates possess competency in core performance areas related to corporate mission statements and strategic plans. Ford Motor Company selects students for sponsorship through universities and technical colleges on the basis of how well the students fit four competency dimensions related to successful job performance. These core competencies and performance areas are identified through procedures discussed in Chapters 4 and 5. This initial assessment also includes screening of values believed necessary to achieve the company's strategic goals.

Successful Canadian organizations recognize that selection and performance measurement go hand in hand. Moreover, the urgency to fill vacancies should not mean compromising rigour in screening and selection, as illustrated by Trevor Maurer, former executive director of sales for CIBA Vision, a U.S./Canadian contact lens and lens-care business, who had to hire 45 sales representatives within six weeks. Recruitment and Selection Today 9.1 outlines how he went about doing this.

RECRUITMENT AND SELECTION TODAY 9.1

HIRING SMART AND FAST AT CIBA VISION

Trevor Maurer, former executive director of sales for CIBA Vision, a U.S./Canadian contact lens and lens-care business, set out to establish a salesforce dedicated to selling a new product line that showed especially good promise. It was essential to get this new product to market as soon as possible, so he was given six weeks to hire 45 sales representatives. With help from his human resources group, he had developed the "perfect candidate profile" and hired four dedicated recruiters with whom he developed a five-stage sequential recruitment and screening process.

Stage 1 solicited basic information on previous experience, education, and salary expectations. Stage 2 involved telephone interviews in which the recruiter asked behavioural-based questions, with structured guidelines for scoring candidate responses. Stage 3 involved written responses to behavioural questions transmitted by e-mail. In Stage 4, a profile of each candidate was written and given to sales managers, who probed further in a telephone interview, using a structured template as their guide. Finally, in Stage 5 the remaining candidates were invited for an on-site structured interview.

The number of candidates was reduced in each sequential stage of the recruitment process, from an initial applicant pool of 2000. Given that time was of the essence, Maurer generated the original applicant pool through "Thingamajob" (http://www.thingamajob.com), an Internet-based sourcing program that placed the company's posting and searched other sites such as CareerBuilder (http://www.careerbuilder.ca) and Workopolis (www.workopolis.com).

Source: Adapted from T. Maurer. 2003. "Hiring Smart ... and Fast." *Sales and Marketing Management,* 155(5): 63–64.

THE TYPICAL SCREENING INTERVIEW

Screening interviews typically consist of a series of freewheeling, unstructured questions designed to fill gaps left on the candidate's application form or résumé. Such traditional interviews take on the qualities of a conversation and often revolve around a set of common questions like: "What is your greatest accomplishment?" These questions cover the applicant's personal history, attitudes and expectations, and skills and abilities.

Screening interviews
Preliminary interviews designed to fill gaps left on the candidate's application form or résumé, sometimes serving recruitment as well as selection functions.

The information obtained from many of these questions is often better collected through a well-constructed application form. Skilful interviewees know how to give socially desirable answers to many of these frequently asked questions. While some distortion is to be expected in the answers, there is no reason to believe these inaccuracies, intentional or otherwise, occur with greater frequency than do inaccuracies in biodata and résumé information. There is very little direct evidence on the rate or percentage of misinformation that takes place over the course of an interview. As with application forms and biodata, when interview questions focus on verifiable events related to past work or educational experiences, accuracy will likely increase.

SCREENING INTERVIEW FORMAT

The interviewer often obtains better information from a screening interview by following an interview guide. Following a set of preplanned questions or topics during the interview in addition to having reviewed the applicant's file before the interview begins will improve the reliability or consistency of information gathered.[24] The format for a screening interview begins with some opening remarks by the recruiter to put the applicant at ease. This generally involves an exchange of pleasantries and personal information, including information on the purpose of the interview and how the information will be used. The applicant is also advised whether any information presented during the interview will be held in confidence or shared with others. In addition, the interviewer informs the interviewee whether any notes or recordings will be made during the interview.

Following these clarifications, questions typically focus on the applicant's past work history, education and training, and general background. The interviewee is given an opportunity to ask questions about the job and company, as well as about issues raised during the interview. In closing, the interviewer outlines the timeline for the decision process and when applicants are likely to hear the outcome. After the applicant leaves, the interviewer prepares a summary of the interview by completing either a written narrative or a rating form. Often, in order to reduce the costs of the interview (e.g., travel, time, scheduling office space), screening interviews are conducted by telephone rather than face-to-face (see Recruitment and Selection Today 9.2). However, an increasing number of organizations are turning to computer-assisted interviewing (see Recruitment and Selection Today 9.3). Computer-assisted interviews can involve online videos of scenarios to which the candidate responds or online interview questions to which candidates can respond by submitting a video of themselves answering the questions, typing and submitting the answers, or selecting the answer from multiple-choice options. The multiple-choice response format is the least labour-intensive because the answers can be computer scored. However, this format could signal the best answer by allowing the candidates to view options they might not have thought of on their own. Moreover, it does not permit elaboration and and does not allow applicants to provide potentially superior answers that are not among the choices offered.

RECRUITMENT AND SELECTION TODAY 9.2

TELEPHONE SCREENING INTERVIEWS ARE COST-EFFECTIVE

Bob Markey, director of talent acquisition at Day & Zimmermann, a construction and engineering company with 23 000 employees headquartered in Philadelphia, receives more than 50 résumés from candidates for mid- or senior-level positions.

"Obviously, we're not going to bring them all in," Markey says. "By selecting the top five candidates and talking with them by phone to assess their interest and overall fit, the company can be more efficient with [its] time and money."

"Interviewing a candidate in person is a huge time commitment for our management team and the candidate," says Fran Peters, PHR, human resources manager at SWC Technology Partners Inc., a 150-employee IT consulting company in Oak Brook, Ill. Peters prescreens top candidates by phone to winnow the field. "We disqualify approximately *75* percent of candidates based on that initial phone screen."

A good initial phone screen can reveal a wealth of important information, including a candidate's skills, experience, motivation, professionalism, and salary expectations. Phone screens can also give under-the-radar applicants—those who might be overlooked if HR were doing only in-person interviews—an opportunity to shine. "Oftentimes, a candidate you see on paper may not hit all of the bullets, but there is something intriguing," according to Molly Brennan, managing partner at Koya Leadership Partners in Newburyport, Mass., a national recruiter for nonprofit organizations. "You don't want to miss a potentially good candidate, but you have to be sure the person is worth the investment of time to meet in person."

Pre-screenings can help HR professionals develop a rapport with the candidate before the in-person interview, adds Kelly Smith, a corporate recruiter consultant and author of *Corporate Recruiter Reveals Who Gets Hired and Why* (Excellent Enterprises LLC, 2013). Pre-screening also has the advantage of eliminating visual distractions. According to Rick Baron, SPHR, senior manager of HR operations for a global beverage company in Sarasota, Fla., "The power of the telephone interview, when done properly, is you can focus on what is being said."

Source: Originally published as "Be Well-Prepared to Pre-Screen Applicants by Telephone." by Kathryn Tyler, *HR Magazine*, 59(4).

RECRUITMENT AND SELECTION TODAY 9.3

COMPUTER-ASSISTED INTERVIEW SCREENING AT NIKE

Nike uses computer-assisted interviewing to hire employees for Niketowns, which are retail stores that showcase Nike products. For its Las Vegas store, Nike received 6000 responses to ads for 250 positions. The first cut was made by interactive voice-recognition (IVR) technology, with applicants responding to eight questions over the telephone. In this first stage, 3500 applicants were screened out for being unavailable when needed or for not having retail experience.

Candidates who passed this first assessment were then given a computer-assisted interview at the store, which identified individuals who had been in customer service environments, had a passion for sports, and would therefore probably be good Nike service representatives. They were then shown a video of three scenarios for helping a customer and asked to choose the "best one." A printout of applicant responses allowed interviewers to flag areas for further probing during the face-to-face interview that followed. The use of technology for screening interviews helped Nike speed up its staffing and reduce turnover in the retail division by 21 percent over two years.

Source: Adapted from L. Thornburg. 1998. "Computer-Assisted Interviewing Shortens Hiring Cycle." *HR Magazine*, 43(2): 73–9.

DECISIONS BASED ON THE SCREENING INTERVIEW

The interviewer is frequently required to make inferences about an applicant's personal qualities, motivation, overall ability, attitude toward work, and potential not only for doing the job but also for fitting into the organizational culture. Organizations that use screening interviews often require the interviewer to rate specific attributes or characteristics of the applicant either in addition to, or instead of, making an overall recommendation. Recruitment and Selection Notebook 9.1 presents a sample form used to rate applicants following a screening interview. The traits or attributes that interviewers are asked to rate vary among organizations. They range from the very specific (e.g., attitude toward working irregular hours) to the very general (e.g., initiative).

RECRUITMENT AND SELECTION NOTEBOOK 9.1

EXAMPLE OF A POST-INTERVIEW SUMMARY

Applicant's Name ______________________________ Date ____________

Position ______________________ Interviewed By ______________________

Ratings: 0–Unacceptable; 1–Poor; 2–Satisfactory; 3–Good; 4–Excellent

	RATING	COMMENTS
Previous Experience	0 1 2 3 4	
Communicating	0 1 2 3 4	
Interpersonal Skills	0 1 2 3 4	
Adaptability	0 1 2 3 4	
Emotional Stability	0 1 2 3 4	
Leadership Potential	0 1 2 3 4	
Ability to Work with Others	0 1 2 3 4	
Planning/Organizing	0 1 2 3 4	
Attitude toward Work Requirements	0 1 2 3 4	
Realistic Expectations	0 1 2 3 4	
Overall Impression	0 1 2 3 4	

Total Score ____________

Recommendation: ________ Unacceptable/Notify applicant of rejection ________ Applicant is acceptable for position

If acceptable, arrange for the following:

_______ Employment Testing

_______ Selection Interview

Microsoft Canada uses screening interviews to identify computer science graduates whose thinking is fast, flexible, and creative. The Microsoft interview includes questions related to computer science knowledge and brainteaser-type questions about balloons that move in mysterious ways. More than the right answer, Microsoft is looking for an ability to think creatively and an inquiring mind. Only about 25 percent of applicants from one of Canada's leading computer science programs made it through the final stages of one of these screening interviews.[25]

IMPRESSION FORMATION

Interviewers use both verbal and nonverbal behaviour of job applicants to form an impression of interviewees.[26,27] Similarly, applicants interpret the interviewer's verbal and nonverbal behaviours to form an impression of the organization and to judge whether they will accept any potentially forthcoming job offer. Recruitment and Selection Today 9.4 lists common behaviours of interviewees that leave the interviewer with either positive or negative impressions. While presenting all positive behaviours and avoiding the negative ones will not guarantee that candidates will move on to the next step in the selection process, it should certainly improve their odds.

VALUE OF THE SCREENING INTERVIEW

Much research has investigated the effectiveness of the selection interview, but much less has examined the interview used for employment screening. This may be because traditional interviews are resource intense (considering the time and labour). Advanced technology

RECRUITMENT AND SELECTION TODAY 9.4

INTERVIEWEE BEHAVIOURS THAT INFLUENCE INTERVIEWER IMPRESSIONS

- Find out where you are going beforehand so you can be on time for the interview.
- Wear appropriate clothing, a slight step up from what people normally wear to work for the job for which you are interviewing.
- Be prepared for the interview by having done homework on the company and anticipating common interview questions.
- Think about how you would answer the questions you might be asked—if possible, rehearse with a friend. Think of examples from your past experience that would illustrate your answers.
- Make direct eye contact with the interviewer.
- Remain confident and determined throughout the interview, regardless of how the interviewer's cues suggest the interview is going.
- Provide positive information about yourself when answering questions.
- Answer questions quickly and intelligently.
- Demonstrate interest in the position and organization.

Applicant Behaviours That Influence Negative Impressions

- Present a poor personal appearance or grooming.
- Display an overly aggressive, know-it-all attitude.
- Fail to communicate clearly (e.g., mumbling, poor grammar, use of slang).
- Lack career goals or career planning.
- Overemphasize monetary issues.
- Be evasive or do not answer questions completely.
- Show a lack of maturity, tact, courtesy, or social skills.

enables automatic administration and scoring of interview questions (e.g., interactive voice recognition), allowing for automatic assessment. There are, however, face-to-face screening interviews that can be cost effective. For example, it is common for graduating Ph.D. students seeking employment as university professors to be invited for a screening interview at academic/professional conferences. This is ideal for the hiring universities in that they do not incur costs for candidates' travel and accommodation, plus (in addition to the screening interview) they often have the opportunity to view candidates publicly presenting and defending their research (often a doctoral thesis)–a work sample of sorts, where the presentation and analytic skills of the aspiring professor can be assessed. Based on the screening interview (and research presentation), recruiters are then better positioned to determine whether (at their expense) to invite the candidate for an on-campus interview. Such prescreening is quite common for other professional groups as well.

Speed interviewing is now being used by recruiters who need to fill several positions as quickly and cost effectively as possible. Likened to speed dating, speed interviewing typically consists of a series of short (5–15 minute), consecutive interviews. For example, the University of Windsor hosted a recruitment fair for 14 law firms seeking to fill internship/articling positions. Candidates were processed through a four-hour circuit of 15-minute mini-interviews with firm representatives.[28]

Speed interviewing
A series of short (5–15 minute), consecutive interviews.

Speed interviews typically last less than 12 minutes. One of the largest forums for speed interviewing was held in Montreal in 2005, hosted by Videotron, a subsidiary of Quebecor Media Inc. Videotron held a job fair to hire 300 new employees, ranging from systems architects to technicians, analysts, and sales representatives, for its new Internet telephone service. The event attracted more than 2000 applicants who had already been pre-screened on the basis of résumés that they had submitted online. Each candidate was assigned to a circuit of five seven-minute interviews with recruiters and company officials of different specialty backgrounds. About 1000 applicants were retained based on their interview performance and given a half-hour test. Those making the short list following this testing were then given a second interview, lasting 15 minutes to an hour. By the end of the day, 200 of the 300 positions posted had been filled.[29]

Critics of speed interviewing question whether a 5–15 minute interview is sufficient to ascertain a candidate's fit with position requirements, while advocates argue that the speed interview is typically used as only a screening process, then followed by other more extensive assessments. Still, the concern remains that potentially very capable candidates could be screened out early based on such a brief encounter. Unlike the job fair hosted by the University of Windsor for law firms, where each candidate was given a 15-minute interview with each firm, Videotron had each candidate assessed in a *circuit* of several separate speed interviews conducted by different company representatives. Accordingly, a total interview score could be calculated across the different interviewers. It is argued that potential biases of any one interviewer are "cancelled" when scores are cumulated across assessors and interview questions, thereby providing a robust and accurate assessment of the candidate's job suitability. Another attractive attribute of the speed interview is that it enables recruiters to assess large number of candidates efficiently and cost effectively. McMaster University uses a version of the speed interview, which it refers to as the Multiple Mini-Interview (MMI), to screen applicants to its medical school. This approach will be discussed later in the chapter.

PREDICTIVE VALIDITY OF SCREENING INTERVIEWS

There is considerable research on the validity of interviews in employee selection. Meta-analyses report the validity for unstructured employment interviews, which is the type mostly used in screening, as approximately 0.20 (when corrected for statistical artifacts such as criterion unreliability and range restriction).[30,31] Even at 0.20, the validity of the screening interview is still low in comparison with other types of selection procedures. However, an interview will likely always play a role in hiring, regardless of its validity. Put simply, employers want to meet the prospective employee face-to-face before making a job offer. Later in the chapter we will examine ways of improving the interview by developing it from job analysis information. The improvements to the interview discussed later in the chapter should be incorporated into screening interviews as well as selection interviews. Properly developed interview questions have the potential to provide value-added screening. The reality is that, as currently done (e.g., unstructured, ad hoc, not directly linked to position or organizational requirements), most screening interviews fall short of achieving their full potential value.

CAUTIONS ON USING SCREENING INTERVIEWS

Using the interview as a screening device brings with it the potential for introducing discriminatory practices into the hiring process. Interviews, including those that are highly structured, are conversations between individuals. Something is said that provokes a response. In opening an interview with small talk or chitchat, interviewers often delve into the personal background of the applicant. They may ask questions about marital status, child-care arrangements, birthplace or birth date, or the applicant's name that relate to proscribed personal information and national or ethnic origin. Information of this type is clearly prohibited. If a job applicant who has been asked these questions is turned down, the onus will be on the employing organization to show that the reason was a lack of job-related requirements and not discriminatory hiring practices. Interview questions should follow the same rule of thumb as application blanks: Is the information obtained from this question job related? If the answer is "no," the question should not be asked.

A MODEL OF INFORMATION PROCESSING AND DECISION MAKING IN THE INTERVIEW

Employment interviews are complex interactions between applicants and interviewers that occur in the context of a larger selection system. That is, in addition to conducting interviews, employers collect information about the applicant from other sources, such as application blanks, résumés, reference checks, and tests. This information from other sources creates pre-interview impressions, which may influence the interview process and interview outcomes.[32,33,34] Moreover, the interviewee and interviewer generally have different objectives. The interviewee is motivated to create a positive impression with the objective of receiving a job offer. The interviewer, on the other hand, is motivated to get an accurate assessment of the interviewee in order to select the best candidate and avoid making a hiring mistake. In order to do this, the interviewer needs to process and make sense of a large amount of complex and often inconsistent or contradictory information.

Several models have been developed to help us better understand the information-processing and decision-making challenges faced by the interviewer. One such model, developed by Dipboye, is presented in Figure 9.1.[35] The model describes the interaction between applicant and interviewer during the interview, as well as the information processing and decision making engaged in by both interviewer and applicant before, during, and after the interview. However, it is important to keep in mind that these

FIGURE 9.1

A MODEL OF THE CORE PROCESSES OF THE INTERVIEW AND ITS CONTEXTS

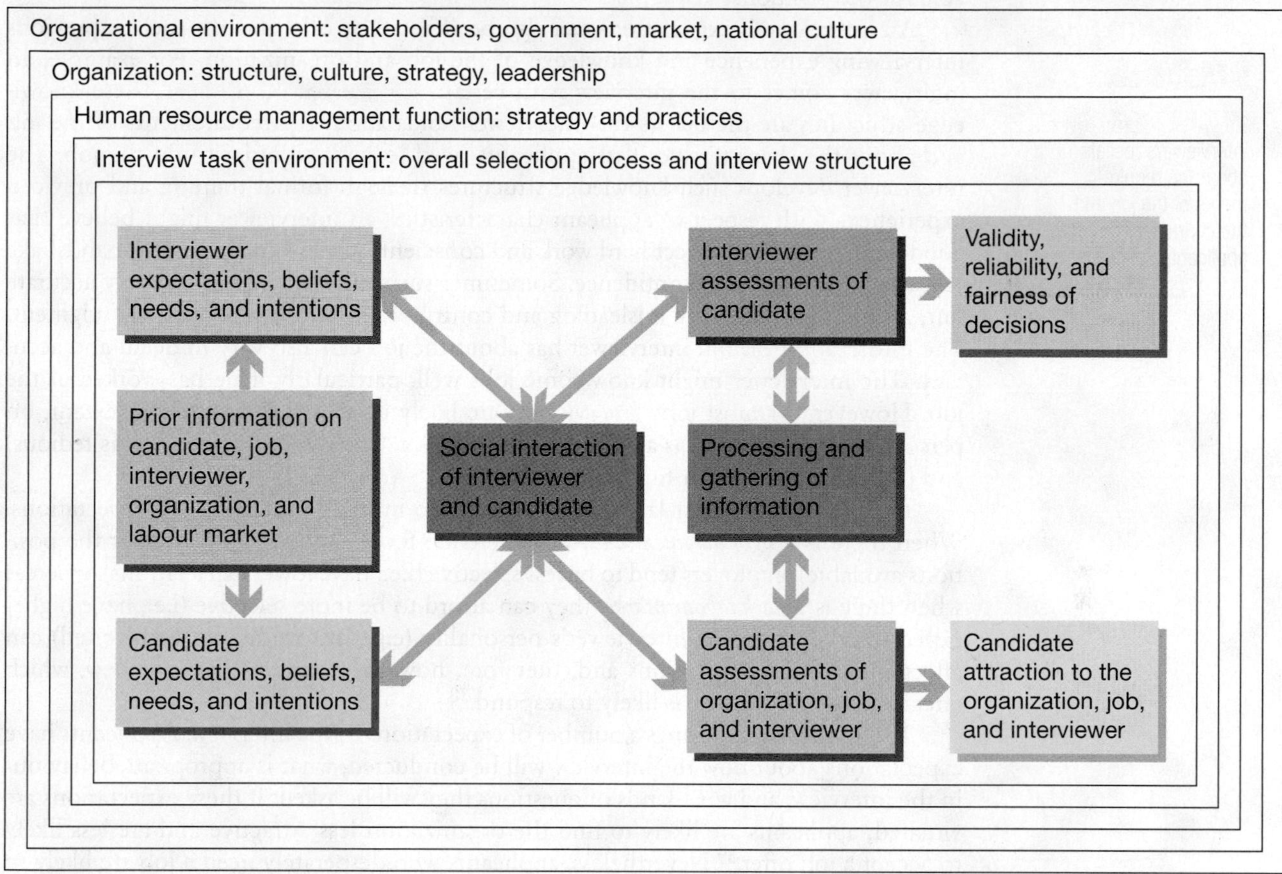

Source: Figure 1: Accuracy of Selection Methods (p. 3) in I.T. Robertson and M. Smith. 2001. "Personnel Selection," *Journal of Occupational and Organizational Psychology*, 74: 441–472. Reproduced with permission of British Psychological Society via Copyright Clearance Center.

processes occur in the context of an organization and its environment. Factors such as organizational culture, norms, strategy, market (e.g., supply of and demand for applicants), and government legislation will influence the interaction between the applicant and the interviewer and may affect the outcome of this interaction.[36]

PRIOR INFORMATION AND INTERVIEWER AND CANDIDATE EXPECTATIONS

According to Dipboye's model, both interviewers and applicants come to the interview with a variety of expectations, beliefs, needs, and intentions that not only influence the interview but also are affected by what happens in the interview. Interviewer expectations can be influenced by having access to *initial information* on the applicant before the interview. This information usually comes from the application form or résumé; sometimes, interviewers also have access to references, test scores, and other information.

This information, in combination with the interviewer's knowledge about the job and organization, contributes to the interviewer's *initial impressions of the applicant's qualifications*. That is, before the interview has begun, the interviewer already has an impression of the applicant and the degree to which the applicant appears to be suitable or unsuitable for the position.

An interviewer's expectations can also be affected by other factors such as previous interviewing experience and knowledge of the job and organization. For example, an interviewer comes to the interview with certain **knowledge structures**. These knowledge structures are the beliefs the interviewer holds about the requirements of the job and about the characteristics that applicants need to have in order to do the job. The interviewer develops such knowledge structures through formal training and previous experience. With respect to applicant characteristics, an interviewer might believe that good grades in school reflect hard work and conscientiousness, or that a firm handshake reveals assertiveness and confidence. Sometimes such beliefs can be reasonably accurate but, all too often, they are misleading and contribute to error in interviewer judgment. The information that an interviewer has about the job can also vary in detail and accuracy. The interviewer might know some jobs well, particularly if he has worked at the job. However, for most jobs, interviewers are likely to rely, at least to some extent, on personal beliefs (e.g., this is a "male" job or this is a "female" job, or this job is tedious) and these beliefs might or might not be accurate.

Knowledge structures Interviewers' beliefs about the requirements of the job and the characteristics of applicants.

The applicant pool or labour market can also influence interviewers' expectations. When there is a *tight labour market* (i.e., there are few qualified applicants for the positions available) employers tend to be less selective (i.e., have lower expectations), whereas when there is a *slack labour market* they can afford to be more selective (i.e., have higher expectations).[37] Even an interviewer's personality (e.g., introverted vs. extraverted) can affect interviewer expectations and, therefore, how she conducts the interview, which affects how the applicant is likely to respond.[38]

The applicant also brings a number of expectations to the interview. Applicants have expectations about how the interview will be conducted, what is appropriate behaviour in the interview, and what kinds of questions they will be asked. If these expectations are violated, applicants are likely to find the organization less attractive and are less likely to accept a job offer.[39] Nevertheless, applicants who desperately need a job are likely to process what happens in the interview differently and to behave differently than those who have other options or are not interested in the position.[40] A desperate applicant might thus accept a job despite negative impressions of the interview, the interviewer, or the organization. However, individuals who accept jobs under such conditions are likely to leave as soon as another job opportunity presents itself.

THE SOCIAL INTERACTION OF INTERVIEWER AND CANDIDATE

The expectations that both interviewers and applicants have can influence the *social interaction in the interview*.[41] An interviewer may be more attentive and supportive with applicants evaluated more positively than with applicants deemed to be unsuitable. Moreover, interviewers tend to seek information that will confirm their initial impressions; they will shape the interview with the kinds of questions they ask and how these questions are phrased. Thus, while interviewers' initial impressions may be supplemented or modified by impressions gained during the interview, there is a strong tendency for interviewers to seek and to find support for their initial impressions. In addition, factors such as the applicant's physical appearance and nonverbal behaviours during the interview, as well as responses to the interview questions, can affect the interviewer's evaluation of the applicant and the interviewer's responses to the applicant.

How the interviewer behaves can affect the applicant's performance in the interview.[42] Applicants who sense that the interview is not going well or that the interviewer has developed a negative impression of them may experience greater anxiety, which might negatively affect their performance. The applicants might come to believe that there is little likelihood of obtaining a job offer and, therefore, reduce their efforts in the interview. Conversely, an applicant who senses that things are going well or that the interviewer is interested and supportive is likely to respond in a more positive manner, with greater composure, enthusiasm, and effort. Thus, the applicant and interviewer continue to influence each other throughout the interview, so that there is a tendency to perpetuate, if not intensify, initial negative or positive impressions.

Applicant responses to the interviewer appear to be related to interview outcomes. Those applicants who end up receiving job offers tend to respond to interview questions more quickly or with less hesitancy. They spend more time in conversations unrelated to answering interview questions and are interrupted less frequently. They also have more positive nonverbal behaviour and less negative nonverbal behaviour.[43] In other words, when the interviewer and applicant develop a positive relationship during the interview, the applicant is more likely to receive a job offer. Applicants can also take an active role during the interview by using impression management tactics such as self-promotion or ingratiation. These will be discussed later in the chapter.

INTERVIEWER AND CANDIDATE INFORMATION PROCESSING AND ASSESSMENTS

Both the interviewer and the applicant gather and process information during the interview and continue to process information after the interview. The interviewer is collecting and processing information in order to assess the applicant's qualifications for the job and whether the applicant is a good fit for the organization. The applicant collects and processes information about the job and the organization (and the interviewer, as a representative of the organization) to determine whether they are sufficiently attractive (and the interviewer sufficiently trustworthy and compatible) to accept a job offer. The interviewer's processing of data from the interview is very much influenced by the knowledge structures, as well as by the initial impressions he has of the applicant. The knowledge structures assist the interviewer in categorizing or stereotyping applicants (e.g., as highly motivated but lacking common sense, as a homemaker who wishes to resume her career, as an elderly person who needs the money, etc.). Through the course of the interview, the interviewer may recategorize an applicant several times. The interviewer's knowledge structures also influence the interviewer's attributions of applicant behaviour. That is, the interviewer makes determinations as to the extent to which the behaviours described or exhibited by the applicant are caused by stable personal traits or by situational circumstances. For example, an interviewer might regard an applicant's description of a successful accomplishment as indicative of the applicant's capabilities and perseverance, while a similar description from another applicant might be attributed to an easy task or luck or exaggeration on the part of the applicant. Interviewers may adjust their attributions several times during the interview as more information is obtained. Thus, the interviewer's knowledge structures guide the interviewer in both shaping and interpreting the data collected in the interview.[44]

During the interview a number of factors that are considered unrelated to the applicant's qualifications can influence the assessments made by the interviewer. These factors can include verbal expressiveness or speech style, nonverbal behaviours, race, ethnicity, sex, age, disability, attractiveness, and impression management tactics used by the applicant. These will be discussed in more detail later in the chapter. Similarly, the applicant's assessment can be influenced by these same factors (e.g., the interviewer's attractiveness) as well as by impression management tactics that might be used by the interviewer to make the job or organization sound more attractive. Although such factors are typically considered biases that contribute to lower quality assessments, Dipboye and others argue that they can sometimes be positively related to job performance (i.e., they can actually improve interview validity and reliability) and, therefore, should not necessarily be considered biases.[45,46,47,48] However, a recent meta-analysis suggests that such results are likely because the same biases that can affect interview ratings (e.g., nonverbal behaviours or impression tactics) can also affect job performance ratings.[49,50]

INTERVIEWER AND APPLICANT DECISIONS

After the interview, the interviewer evaluates the applicant's qualifications and then makes a final assessment or decision about the applicant. In most situations, the interviewer needs to recall and compare the applicants who were interviewed and select the one(s) considered best qualified. In such situations, contrast effects come into play. Applicants may benefit or suffer in these comparisons, depending on whether their competitors are deemed more or less qualified than they are. In making comparisons, the interviewer may rely to some degree on a memory of what was said in the interview. Unfortunately, the interviewer's memory can be faulty or biased.[51] In fact, we have witnessed interviewers becoming confused as to which applicant said what after interviewing a series of applicants. This is not surprising, given the large amount of complex information interviewers must process and make sense of in making a selection decision. The interviewer's decisions can be evaluated in terms of their *validity, reliability, and fairness* and in terms of success in attracting the desired applicants to accept job offers from the organization. Similarly, the *applicants assess the organization, job, and interviewer* to determine whether they are sufficiently attracted to accept a job offer. Applicants who have job offers from other organizations have the option of selecting the job they feel best meets their requirements. Thus, there can often be a mismatch between the organization's first choice and the applicant's first choice.

THE CONTEXT OF THE INTERVIEW

It's important to keep in mind that selection interviews are conducted in the *context* of the overall selection process (i.e., along with tests, references, etc.) and how the interview is structured; the strategy and practices of the Human Resources function; the structure, culture, strategy, and leadership of the organization; and, more broadly, the stakeholders, government legislation, the labour market, and national culture. These contextual factors can influence and, in some instances, determine how the interview is conducted and how selection decisions are made. For example, in some organizations interviews are conducted by HR staff; in others, interviews are conducted by supervisors and/or line managers; and in still others, interviews are conducted by both. In some organizations, HR staff make the final hiring decision; in others, the supervisor or line manager has the final say. Thus, the interview can involve interactions among members of the organization as well as interactions between the applicant and the interviewer(s) and can sometimes be affected by authority structures, interdepartmental politics, and power games.[52] On the other hand, the interview process and decisions can be affected by the supply of and demand for applicants. When unemployment rates are low and it is more difficult to find suitable applicants, interviewers tend to be more lenient, whereas when applicants are plentiful, they can be more selective.[53]

The interviewer's final selection decision is influenced by various factors, such as pressure to hire quickly, hiring quotas, as well as interdepartmental or intradepartmental politics. Concerns such as how internal candidates will respond if someone is hired from outside the organization, or whether an internal candidate will be accepted by individuals who used to be his peers if he is promoted to a supervisory position over them, can influence the selection decision.[54] Sometimes personal motivations influence an interviewer's decisions, particularly when he or she knows one of the applicants (or one of the applicant's referees), or has something in common with an applicant. Thus, a wide variety of contextual factors can influence both the interview processes and selection decisions.

The model described in this section presents the difficult challenges faced by interviewers in trying to make accurate assessments of applicants in the interview. It very much reflects the processes taking place in traditional, unstructured approaches to employment interviewing. Over the last three decades efforts to structure employment interviews have substantially reduced the effects of the idiosyncratic interview processes described in this model and have improved the accuracy of interview assessments.[55] However, because many employers continue to use unstructured interviews, it is worth examining these traditional interviews before turning to the more valid, structured interviewing techniques.

UNSTRUCTURED INTERVIEWS

The traditional approach to employment interviewing is one that has become known as an **unstructured interview**. In such interviews, the interviewer typically engages in an open-ended conversation with the interviewee. There are few constraints on the kinds of questions that may be asked, and furthermore, many of the questions used in the interview may not occur to the interviewer until partway through the interview. Most interviewers, however, appear to rely on a common set of questions, often ones that they have heard others use. Recruitment and Selection Today 9.5 presents a list of questions often used by interviewers. These types of questions invite applicants to evaluate themselves or to describe the evaluations of others. You may recall that these are the kinds of questions that were asked in the vignette at the beginning of this chapter. Naturally, applicants who want to create a positive impression are likely to evaluate themselves much more favourably than perhaps they should.

Unstructured interview
A traditional method of interviewing that involves no constraints on the questions asked, no requirements for standardization, and a subjective assessment of the candidate.

Moreover, many interviewees have learned to respond to such questions with standard answers. For example, common responses to the question, "What are your weaknesses?" include "I get too involved in my work" and "I'm too much of a perfectionist." Answers to such questions reveal very little useful information about the applicant. The interviewer is forced to take on the role of an amateur psychologist trying to read meaning into vague self-evaluations, verbal expressiveness, or body language. Sometimes, as Recruitment and Selection Today 9.6 shows, the questions that interviewers ask suggest that they may need to see a clinical psychologist for help!

RECRUITMENT AND SELECTION TODAY 9.5

COMMONLY USED INTERVIEW QUESTIONS

1. Why did you leave your last job? Why do you want to leave your current job?
2. What do you consider to be your strengths? What are your weaknesses?
3. What were your strongest/weakest subjects at school? What did you learn in school that you could use in this job?
4. How would other people [*or* someone who knows you or worked with you] describe you as an individual?
5. What is your greatest accomplishment [*or* most meaningful work experience]?
6. What were the most enjoyable aspects of your last job? What were the least enjoyable aspects?
7. Why do you want this job? What are you looking for from this job [*or* from us]?
8. Why should we hire you? What can you do for us? [*or* Why are you the best candidate for this position?]
9. What are your long-range plans or goals? [Where do you plan to be five years from now?]
10. Tell me about yourself.

Impression management
Attempts by applicants to create a favourable impression by monitoring interviewer reactions and responding accordingly.

Some interviewees are particularly skilled at **impression management**–that is, creating a favourable impression of themselves by picking up cues from the interviewer concerning what answers the interviewer wishes to hear. They are able to monitor and change their own responses and behaviours in order to align them with those they perceive to be desired by the interviewer. By artfully guiding the conversation and making effective use of nonverbal behaviours, the polished interviewee is able to impress the interviewer and obfuscate the true purpose of the interview.[56,57] Thus, instead of hiring the best *candidate*, the interviewer is likely to hire the most skilful *interviewee*.

In fact, skilful interviewees can divert the conversation from relevant and important interview topics to topics that result in pleasant but uninformative conversations that cast themselves in a more favourable light. For example, on noticing the golf trophy (or a painting of Algonquin Park) in an interviewer's office, such an interviewee may engage the interviewer in an amiable conversation about the game of golf (or Algonquin Park) that lasts most of the interview. The interviewer, left with a good feeling about the applicant, is likely to hire the applicant without actually having obtained any job-relevant information during the interview.

Research suggests that more than 90 percent of applicants make use of impression management tactics or "faking" during the interview but most of them do not resort to outright invention or lying.[58] Rather, most exaggerate slightly or tailor their answers to make their experiences seem more positive or relevant to the job. Many also try to ingratiate themselves with the interviewer by appearing to agree with the interviewer's views or complimenting the interviewer or the organization. Good impression managers are somewhat more likely to get a job offer than applicants who do not engage in impression management or are less effective at impression management.[59,60] However, research indicates that the kind of impression management that is likely to result in positive interview ratings and a job offer does not involve deception. It consists of self-promotion which is defined as highlighting one's job-relevant abilities, accomplishments, and experiences.[61,62] In contrast, deceptive impression management tactics, which include tailoring or distorting answers to please the interviewer, exaggeration, and making up

RECRUITMENT AND SELECTION TODAY 9.6

EXCERPTS FROM DON'T GET STUMPED BY OFF-THE-WALL JOB INTERVIEW QUESTIONS

Although not as common as the interview questions listed in Recruitment and Selection Today 9.5, the questions or comments listed below must certainly rank among the most off-the-wall questions used in employment interviews:

- If you could be any character in fiction, who would you be?
- If Hollywood made a movie about your life, who would you like to see play the lead role as you?
- If you could be a superhero, what would you want your superpowers to be?
- If someone wrote a biography about you, what do you think the title should be?
- If you were shipwrecked on a deserted island, but all your human needs—such as food and water—were taken care of, what two items would you want to have with you?
- If you had six months with no obligations or financial constraints, what would you do with your time?
- If you had only six months left to live, what would you do with your time?
- If you could have dinner with anyone in history, who would it be and why?
- If you could compare yourself to any animal, which would it be and why?
- If you were a type of food, what type of food would you be?
- If you won $20 million in a lottery, what would you do with the money?
- If you were a salad, what kind of dressing would you have?
- How do I rate as an interviewer?
- If you were a car, what kind would you be?
- Whom do you admire the most and why?
- In the news story of your life, what would the headline say?
- If aliens landed in front of you and, in exchange for anything you desire, offered you any position on their planet, what would you want?
- What would I find in your refrigerator?
- If you had the opportunity to switch to the opposite gender for just a week, would you do it? Why or why not?

Source: Adapted from Katherine Hansen, Ph.D. 2008. "Don't Get Stumped by Off-the-Wall Job Interview Questions." *Quintessential Careers*: http://www.quintcareers.com/wild_card_interview_questions.html.

stories or lying, are likely to result in lower interview ratings and, therefore, reduce the likelihood of receiving a job offer.

As Recruitment and Selection Today 9.7 and 9.8 show, however, not all job candidates are skilled at impression management and some behave in ways that guarantee they will not receive a job offer. Several websites provide interviewing tips for applicants, including http://www.careercc.com/interv3.shtml, http://www.quintcareers.com/intvres.html, and http://www.ctdol.state.ct.us/progsupt/jobsrvce/intervie.htm.

Another characteristic typical of unstructured interviews is that no systematic rating procedure is used. Interviewers are free to interpret interviewee responses in any manner they choose, as there are no guidelines for evaluating the responses. Rather than evaluating responses or answers to interview questions, the interviewer, in fact, uses the interview to get a "feeling" or a "hunch" about the applicant. The interviewer emerges from the interview with a global, subjective evaluation of the applicant, which is biased by

RECRUITMENT AND SELECTION TODAY 9.7

SARAH'S JOB INTERVIEW

A woman (we'll call her "Sarah") who interviewed for an assistant's job referred to herself in the third person through the entire interview:

"Sarah could do that for you with no problem." "Sarah likes working hard to get the job done." "Well, Sarah would never let that happen."

It was too much for the interviewer, who started laughing. When Sarah asked what was so funny, he told her. Upset, she grabbed her purse, stood up and, before stomping out of the office, sputtered, "Sarah doesn't have to put up with this."

Source: Originally published as "Interview Answers Get Weirder, Wackier." by K. Gurchiek, *HR Magazine*, 50(June): 44–46. © 2005, Society for Human Resource Management, Alexandria, VA. Used with permission. All rights reserved.

RECRUITMENT AND SELECTION TODAY 9.8

OTHER JOB INTERVIEWS THAT DIDN'T GO WELL

Interviewers are not the only ones who mishandle interviews—applicants do their share of bungling as well. A survey conducted by a Canadian recruitment firm, Office Team, asked 150 executives and HR managers about unusual interview experiences. Below are some of the responses.

- After answering the first few questions, the candidate picked up his cell phone and called his parents to tell them that the interview was going well.
- At the end of the interview, the candidate expressed her interest in getting the position, but only if her boyfriend liked the company and the hiring manager. She then said, "He's waiting outside. Can I bring him in to say hello?"
- When asked why he wanted to work for the company, the applicant responded, "That's a good question. I really haven't given it much thought."
- When asked how the candidate would improve sales if hired for the position, he replied, "I'll have to think about that and get back to you." He then stood up, walked out, and never came back.
- When asked by the hiring manager why she was leaving her current job, the applicant said, "My manager is a jerk. All managers are jerks."
- A candidate disparaged his former boss during the interview, not realizing the boss and the interviewer had the same last name—and were related.
- When asked what he liked least in his current job, the applicant replied, "Staff management." He was interviewing for a management position.
- After being complimented on his choice of college and the grade point average he achieved, the candidate replied, "I'm glad that got your attention. I didn't really go there."
- When asked by the hiring manager if he had any questions, the candidate replied by telling a knock-knock joke.
- When asked by the manager about his goals, the job seeker said, "To work in this position for the least amount of time possible until I can get your job."

Source: Reprinted by permission of *Canadian HR Reporter*. © Copyright Thomson Reuters Canada Ltd., 2002, Toronto, Ontario. 1-800-387-5164. Web: www.hrreporter.com

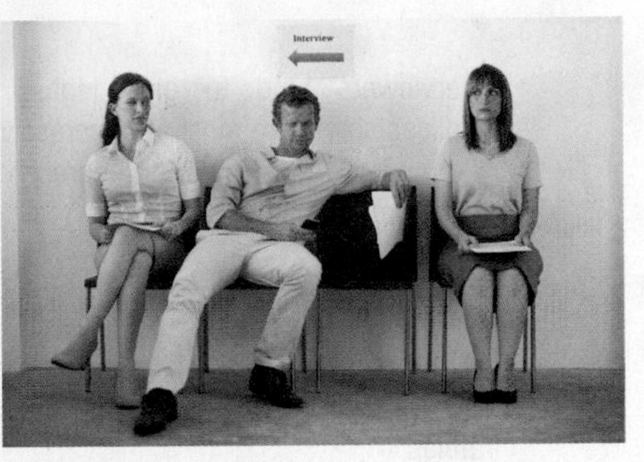

© iStock.com/PeopleImages

personal views and preferences and likely to be inaccurate. In fact, many interviewers report that they rely on such "gut feelings" in making their hiring decisions. Worse yet, some writers are still recommending such practices.[63,64]

Webster[65,66] and his colleagues at McGill University, along with Dipboye,[67] Jelf,[68] Posthuma,[69] Macan,[70] and others, have documented the numerous biases and perceptual and information-processing errors that have plagued the unstructured employment interview (see Recruitment and Selection Notebook 9.2). For example, interviewers rate applicants more favourably if the applicants are perceived as being similar to themselves.[71,72] Moreover, interview ratings are susceptible to first impressions.[73,74] That is, an interviewer's initial impression of an applicant, such as might be formed upon reading the résumé, affects the way the interview is conducted, the questions asked, and the evaluation of the candidate's answers. In addition, interview ratings are influenced by visual cues such as physical attractiveness of the applicant, eye contact, body orientation, smiling, and hand gestures, as well as vocal cues such as rate of speaking, number and duration of pauses, variability in loudness, and pitch (e.g., lower voices tend to be rated more positively than higher voices for management positions).[75,76] Recruitment and Selection Notebook 9.2 summarizes some of the research findings pertaining to the unstructured employment interview.

RECRUITMENT AND SELECTION NOTEBOOK 9.2

SOME RESEARCH FINDINGS ON THE UNSTRUCTURED INTERVIEW

Interview Decisions

- Interviewers tend to make a hire/not hire decision before completing the interview (i.e., before all the information has been collected).[77,78]
- Unfavourable information provided by the applicant tends to have greater impact on interview ratings than favourable information.[79,80]
- Once interviewers have formed an impression of an applicant, they tend to look for information that will confirm their impression.[81,82]

Order Effects

- Interviewers tend to remember information provided at the beginning of the interview better than information provided in the middle (primacy effect).[83,84]
- Information provided at the end of the interview tends to be remembered better than information provided in the middle (recency effect).[85,86]
- An applicant's interview rating can be affected by the preceding applicant (contrast effects); the applicant tends to benefit if the preceding applicant was relatively poor but suffer if the preceding applicant was relatively good.[87,88]

Effects of Information

- Impressions formed by the interviewer as a result of information obtained about the applicant prior to the interview (e.g., by reading the résumé) affect how the applicant is treated and rated in the interview.[89,90]
- Interviewers who have more information about the job tend to have a more accurate perception (template) of what the "ideal" applicant should look like.[91,92]

Demographic Characteristics

- Minority applicants tend to receive lower interview ratings than nonminority applicants.[93]

- Interviewers tend to give higher ratings to applicants who are most like themselves (similar-to-me effect) in terms of demographic characteristics or in terms of attitudes.[94,95]

Verbal/Nonverbal Behaviour

- An applicant's verbal skills and expressiveness and attractiveness of voice can affect interview ratings.[96,97]
- An applicant's mannerisms can affect interview ratings.[98,99]
- An applicant's appearance (e.g., physical attractiveness, posture, age, clothing) can affect interview ratings.[100,101]

Reliability and Validity

- Agreement on ratings among interviewers interviewing the same applicants tends to be quite low (low reliability).[102,103]
- Correlations between interview scores and job performance ratings (for those hired) tend to be fairly low (low criterion validity).[104,105,106]

(Descriptions of additional interview biases can be found at http://www.indiana.edu/~uhrs/employment/best.html.) Such biases and errors contribute to the poor reliability and validity of unstructured interviews.

// ATTEMPTS TO IMPROVE INTERVIEW EFFECTIVENESS

Given the research on the biases and errors inherent in the unstructured interview, past reviews of employment interview research have, understandably, been rather pessimistic concerning the reliability and validity of the interview as a selection instrument.[107] Nevertheless, the interview has remained popular among employers, who seem to have considerable confidence in its usefulness for employee selection. However, developments in interview research over the last three decades will give those employers even more reason for confidence. In the early 1980s, a number of researchers, notably Janz and Latham, began working on new approaches to employment interviewing, which have become known as **structured interviews.**[108,109,110]

Structured interview
An interview consisting of a standardized set of job-relevant questions; a scoring guide is used.

Reviews of the employment interview literature some 30 or more years ago indicated that structuring an interview appeared to contribute to increased interview reliability and validity.[111,112,113] In fact, today, meta-analytic investigations of interview validity reveal that structured selection interviews do indeed have significantly greater reliability and predictive validity than traditional, unstructured interviews.[114,115] In particular, the criterion-related validity of highly structured interviews is about three times that of completely unstructured interviews. For example, Huffcutt and Arthur found that unstructured interviews have an average validity coefficient of .11 (.20 when corrected for criterion unreliability and range restriction), whereas highly structured interviews have an average validity coefficient of .34 (.57 when corrected for criterion unreliability and range restriction).[116]

References to interview structure in selection interview literature tend to give the impression that structure is a dichotomous variable (i.e., that interviews are either structured or unstructured). Interview structure, however, is a function of several factors and it can vary along a continuum, ranging from very unstructured to highly structured.

In fact, Huffcutt and Arthur found that interview validity increases as the degree of interview structure increases so that even moderate levels of structure can contribute to relatively high interview validity.[117] It is therefore useful to gain an understanding of what is meant by interview "structure."

STRUCTURING EMPLOYMENT INTERVIEWS

The development of structured employment interview techniques is due to the contributions of numerous researchers over more than half a century. These researchers sought to address what were perceived as the shortcomings of the traditional, unstructured interview by applying psychometric principles to employment interview design. Over time, these researchers uncovered a number of structuring elements that seemed to contribute to interview reliability and validity. Although not all interviews referred to as "structured" make use of all elements, the more of these elements that are part of the interview, the more structured it is. In other words, employment interviews can be structured in a number of ways and to varying degrees. Below is a summary of components that can contribute to employment interview structure, extracted from a detailed review provided by Campion, Palmer, and Campion[118]:

1. Interview questions are derived from a job analysis (they are job related).
2. Interview questions are standardized (all applicants are asked the same questions).
3. Prompting, follow-up questioning, probing, and/or elaboration on questions are limited.
4. Interview questions focus on behaviours or work samples rather than opinions or self-evaluations.
5. Interviewer access to ancillary information (e.g., résumés, letters of reference, test scores, transcripts) is controlled.
6. Questions from the candidate are not allowed until after the interview.
7. Each answer is rated during the interview using a rating scale tailored to the question (this is preferable to rating dimensions at the end of the interview and certainly preferable to making an overall rating or ranking at the end).
8. Rating scales are "anchored" with behavioural examples to illustrate scale points (e.g., examples of a "1," "3," or "5" answer).
9. Total interview score is obtained by summing across scores for each of the questions.
10. Detailed notes are taken during the interview (such notes should be a record of applicants' actual words and behaviours as related in the interview rather than evaluations of applicants).[119]

In addition, Campion and his colleagues recommend using the same interviewer(s) across all candidates for greater standardization, not permitting interviewers to discuss candidates or answers between interviews, and providing interviewers with extensive training.[120] Recruitment and Selection Notebook 9.3 provides some guidelines for building more structure into an interview. A more detailed discussion of how structured interviews are developed can be found in "Structured Employment Interview Techniques" later in this chapter.

RECRUITMENT AND SELECTION NOTEBOOK 9.3

THE STRUCTURED INTERVIEWING PROCESS

Preparing for the Interview

1. Determine the amount of time available for the interview and how many questions you will be able to ask, without rushing, in that length of time.
2. Make a standardized list of interview questions so that all applicants are asked the same questions, in the same order. If possible, the questions should be based on a job analysis (such as the critical incident technique). At very least, they should deal with situations or behaviours that are important to job performance.
3. Develop a scoring guide with benchmark or sample answers. Ideally, these answers should come from a job analysis. If that is not possible, meet with relevant subject-matter experts (i.e., employees, supervisors, and/or managers familiar with the job) and jointly determine what would be an ideal, an acceptable, and a poor answer for each question. Allow space in the guide or have a notepad for taking notes.
4. Use an office or arrange for an interview room where you can have privacy, freedom from distractions, and quiet. Ensure good lighting and ventilation, a comfortable temperature, and comfortable seating for yourself and the applicant (as well as any other interviewers who may be present).
5. Schedule the interviews with sufficient time for a brief break between interviews and to allow for some interviews to run a little over. If more than one interviewer is involved, this time can be used to discuss the applicant's answers and reach consensus on the ratings.
6. Arrange to hold all calls and prevent interruptions during the interview. If you are interrupted to attend to a critical matter, apologize to the applicant and resolve the matter as quickly as possible, delegating it if you can.

Conducting the Interview

1. Spend a few minutes at the beginning of the interview putting the applicant at ease. Greet the applicant by name. Introduce yourself and other interview panel members (if there are others). Indicate where the applicant is to sit. Provide the applicant with an overview of the interview process.
2. Ask each question in turn without omitting or skipping any. Let the candidate know she has lots of time to answer and you don't mind her taking time to think. Allow silence. If the applicant seems confused or stuck, rephrase the question but don't do so too quickly. If the applicant still has difficulty, indicate you will come back to the question later.
3. Take detailed notes of the applicant's responses, focusing on recording what the applicant says. Your notes should not be evaluative (i.e., do *not* record your opinions or impressions; e.g., "the applicant seems unmotivated"). Use the scoring guide to score the answers to interview questions as soon as possible.
4. Allow the applicant to ask questions at the end of the interview and answer them to the best of your ability without committing to a decision or indicating any kind of preference.
5. Follow the same procedures for each applicant and retain interview documentation for future reference.

Closing the Interview

1. Tell the candidate when he should expect to hear from you, or someone else in your organization, and how you will communicate your decision (e.g., telephone, e-mail, letter).
2. If you are likely to contact references or call the applicant back for a second interview, inform the applicant.
3. Thank the applicant for coming in for the interview. Escort her to the door and take your leave.
4. Review your notes and make your ratings (if you have not already done so). If the interview was conducted by a panel, briefly meet with the panel and compare your ratings. Discuss and resolve large discrepancies. Either average the ratings (if discrepancies are not large) or arrive at a consensus rating.

5. Make sure you inform all candidates of your decision when you have made it. It's a common practice to hold back on informing second- or third-choice candidates in case the first- and/or second-choice candidates turn down the offer. If you do so, inform the remaining candidates as soon as the offer has been accepted. Thank the candidates who were not accepted for their interest in the job and the organization.

PANEL AND SERIAL INTERVIEWS

Among their recommendations, Campion and his colleagues[121] advocate using panel or serial interviews. **Panel interviews**, also known as *board interviews*, are interviews conducted by two or more interviewers together at the same time. Although panel or board interviews appear to be most common in the public sector, notably for civil service jobs, police, and military positions,[122] a survey of Canadian HR practitioners suggests that almost two-thirds of Canadian organizations use panel interviews.[123] These interview panels operate in various ways. One member of the panel may ask all the questions or panel members may take turns asking questions. In some panels, one member is assigned the task of taking notes, while in other panels several or all members take notes. Some panels consist of only two members, while others may have many members.

Panel interview
An interview conducted by two or more interviewers together at one time.

Unfortunately, there has not been much research on the relative effectiveness of these different approaches and the little research that has been done has provided largely inconclusive results.[124,125] While panel interviews offer an efficient way for several interviewers to interview applicants, they require considerable coordination of schedules to permit all interviewers to attend, particularly as the number of interviewers increases. Moreover, panel interviews can be quite intimidating to applicants and may negatively affect their performance in the interview.

Serial interviews, also known as *sequential interviews*, are interviews conducted by two or more interviewers separately or in sequence. That is, the applicant is usually interviewed individually by the first interviewer, then by the second interviewer, and so on until all interviewers have interviewed the applicant. The applicant may move from office to office for each interview or stay in one interview room while each interviewer visits in turn. The interviewers usually get together, either after they have all interviewed each applicant or after they have interviewed all applicants, in order to discuss and evaluate the applicant(s) and make a decision.

Serial interviews
A series of interviews where the applicant is interviewed separately by each of two or more interviewers.

Scheduling interviewers is less of a problem with serial interviews than with panel interviews as there is greater flexibility in scheduling a particular interviewer. Also, serial interviews are not as intimidating as panel interviews[126] but they can be quite exhausting, as the applicant may spend many hours in a series of interviews. Moreover, the questions and answers can become somewhat repetitious from one interview to the next, and applicants may lose track of what they have or have not said by the fifth or sixth interview.

Despite their problems, panel and serial interviews should reduce the impact of biases held by an individual interviewer because interviewers are accountable to each other and provide a check on each other to ensure irrelevant information does not enter the decision. Each interviewer contributes a different perspective that should increase accuracy, and the aggregation of multiple judgments should cancel out random errors. The recall of information should also be better with multiple interviewers.[127]

Conway, Jako, and Goodman[128] found that panel interviews are more reliable than individual interviews, and Wiesner and Cronshaw[129] found that panel interviews have greater validity than individual interviews when the interview is unstructured, but did not find a difference for structured interviews. However, other meta-analyses have produced inconsistent results with respect to the reliability and validity of panel versus individual interviews.[130,131] These inconsistencies could be the result of factors such as inadequate controls for structure in the analyses, the fact that most panel interviews occur in public-sector settings, the possibility of group process losses in interview panels (e.g., conformity, conflict, loafing), differences in training of interviewers, and the type of interview questions used, all of which might reduce the advantages in some applications.[132,133] Moreover, there is some evidence that there is a complex interaction of structure and the use of panel interviews that needs to be more fully explored in future research.[134]

Nevertheless, the use of panel or serial interviews appears to be viewed favourably by courts and, therefore, gives some measure of protection from discrimination suits.[135,136] In addition, interview panels can include representation from different gender or ethnic groups, thus contributing to perceptions of fairness. More information on panel interviews can be found at http://www.liscareer.com/peters_interviews.htm and http://sciencecareers.sciencemag.org/career_magazine/previous_issues/articles/2000_12_15/noDOI.13270463381342766512.

STRUCTURED EMPLOYMENT INTERVIEW TECHNIQUES

THE SITUATIONAL INTERVIEW

Situational interview
A highly structured interview in which important or decisive situations employees are likely to encounter on the job are described and applicants are asked what they would do in these situations.

Dilemma
A choice in an interview question between two alternatives that appear equally desirable or undesirable.

Scoring guide
A behavioural rating scale consisting of sample answers to each question that is used by the interviewer to evaluate and score the applicant's answers.

One of the approaches to structured interviewing is the **situational interview** (SI) developed by Latham and his colleagues.[137,138] The interviewer describes to the applicant important or decisive situations that are likely to be encountered on the job and asks the applicant what he would do in the situations. Importantly, SI questions should be posed in the form of **dilemmas** (i.e., the applicant is placed in the position of choosing between two competing alternatives that appear equally desirable or undesirable).[139] Thus, the "correct" answers should not be readily apparent to applicants and their answers should reflect their predominant behavioural tendencies or values. For example, a question might place applicants in a situation where they have to make a choice between showing up for work to complete a project with urgent deadlines and caring for their sick family.

The interviewer then uses a **scoring guide** consisting of sample answers to each question to evaluate and score the applicant's answers. The scoring guide is designed using the critical incidents technique,[140] in which examples of actual job-related behaviours that varied in effectiveness in particular situations are collected and refined to serve as sample answers. Thus, numerical values on the scale are illustrated with examples of answers that would be worth a 1 or a 3 or a 5. An example of an SI question is provided in Table 9.1. Please note that the scoring guide is visible only to the interviewer(s), not to the interviewee. Cover up the scoring guide in Table 9.1 with your hand and try answering the question. Once you have answered the question, compare your answer with the scoring guide.

The scoring guide for an SI question should be based on behaviours that have been shown to be either effective or ineffective in that situation in the past. However, because organizations differ, what is an effective response in one organization might not be effective in another. Thus, the scoring guide might differ from one company to another. In the example in Table 9.1, applicants who indicate that they would ignore the supervisor's suggestion and insist on following through on the initial decision would be ignoring potentially important information. The result might be a serious mistake, which could cost the company considerable money. Such a response would not score

TABLE 9.1

EXAMPLE OF A SITUATIONAL INTERVIEW QUESTION

You have just been hired as the manager of our purchasing department and it's your first day on the job. After carefully reviewing product and price information, you make a decision to purchase parts from a particular supplier. Your immediate subordinate, an experienced supervisor who is considerably older than you, questions your judgment in front of other employees and suggests that another supplier would be better. He seems quite convinced that you are making a mistake. The employees look to you for a response, some of them smirking. What would you do?

Scoring Guide

1—I would tell the supervisor that I'm in charge and I am going with my initial decision.

3—I would do what the supervisor suggests, as he knows the suppliers and materials better than I do, *or* I would openly discuss the merits of his suggestion versus my own judgment.

5—I would take the supervisor to a private place, thank him for the information, but instruct him never to question me in front of the employees again. Then, after asking him for information on the best supplier and dismissing him, I would think about the options again and after a brief period announce *my* decision to go with the supplier suggested in our private conversation.

well. Doing what the supervisor suggests or openly discussing the merits of the supervisor's suggestion might result in a good decision being made. However, this course of action would likely undermine the new manager's authority.

The ideal answer does not have to be given exactly as written in the scoring guide. However, the interviewer would be looking for evidence that the applicant recognizes the dynamics at play in the situation and understands basic principles of human behaviour. First, it is important to recognize that there is the potential for a serious mistake if the manager persists in the original course of action. Second, the applicant should recognize that the manager's authority is being undermined, whether intentionally or not. The fact that the supervisor raises the issue in front of the employees and some of them are smirking suggests that there might be a test of leadership going on. Thus, the manager needs to determine the validity of the supervisor's suggestion but also to assert authority. Recognizing that these objectives would best be accomplished in a private conversation reveals an understanding of human nature. Confronting the supervisor in public might make the supervisor defensive and evoke a need for him to "save face" in front of the employees. As much as possible, the manager needs to claim the final decision as his or her own.

The interviewer's task is to compare the applicant's answers with the examples on the scoring guides and to score the answers accordingly. There may be instances where an answer falls somewhere between two scoring guide examples (e.g., better than a 3 answer but not as good as a 5 answer). Under such circumstances, the interviewer has the discretion of assigning an intermediate score (e.g., a 4 or even a 4.5). However, there is some evidence that using rating scales where example answers are used for all five anchor points on the scoring guide might reduce interview bias more than when example answers are used for only three of the anchor points.[141]

The assumption underlying the SI approach is that intentions are related to subsequent behaviours.[142] Critics of this approach have argued that what applicants say they would do in a given situation and what they actually do may be quite different. However, a convincing counterargument is that just *knowing* what the appropriate response should be can differentiate effective from ineffective performers. Latham and Sue-Chan conducted a meta-analysis of the SI based on 20 coefficients and obtained a mean criterion validity coefficient of 0.29 (0.39 corrected for criterion unreliability and range restriction).[143] The mean validity coefficient increased to 0.35 (0.47 corrected) when they removed one very large study and one "outlier" (i.e., a study with extremely different results from the remaining studies) from their analysis.

Two more recent meta-analyses both obtained a mean criterion validity coefficient of 0.26 (between 0.43 and 0.47 with corrections for criterion unreliability and range restriction) based on 29 and 32 coefficients, respectively, for the SI.[144,145] One of these meta-analyses reported a mean inter-rater reliability of 0.79 for the SI. Although there is some disagreement among these meta-analyses as to the precise validity coefficient attributable to the SI, it is clear that the SI is a valid predictor of job performance. Additional information on SIs can be found at http://www.job-interview-site.com/situational-interview-questions-and-answers.html and https://na.theiia.org/iiarf/Public%20Documents/Situational%20Interviewing%20-%20Chattanooga.pdf.

THE BEHAVIOURAL INTERVIEW

Janz,[146,147] following up on a suggestion made by Latham et al.[148] and based on Ghiselli's findings,[149] used another approach, which he referred to as the patterned behaviour description interview. More recent variations of this approach are called behaviour description interview, past behaviour interview, or, simply, **behavioural interview** (BI). The interviewer is asked to predict the interviewee's behaviours in a given job situation based on the interviewee's descriptions of her behaviours in similar situations in the past. Table 9.2 provides an example of a BI question based on the same critical incidents, and thus the same dynamics, as were used in the development of the SI question in Table 9.1. However, because BI questions are concerned with past behaviours in a potentially wide variety of settings, their scope is more general. Therefore, one of the goals in designing BI questions is to make the questions apply to a wide variety of previous experiences or situations.

Behaviour description interview
A structured interview in which the applicant is asked to describe what he did in given situations in the past.

Comparison of the questions in Tables 9.1 and 9.2 suggests that the BI question is likely to generate responses with considerably broader scope than the SI question. Whereas the SI question relates to a very specific situation, the BI could elicit descriptions of a wide variety of situations, depending on the applicants' experiences. In response to the same question, one applicant might relate an experience as the chair on the board of directors of an organization, whereas another applicant might discuss her experience as a member of a group working on an assignment at school.

The broad nature of BI questions and probable responses makes it likely that the interviewer will need to clarify the applicant's answers in order to allow them to be scored accurately. Follow-up questions or **probes** are used to guide the applicant's descriptions of situations or events until sufficient information is obtained to permit scoring. Some probes are written in advance, as in the example in Table 9.2, in anticipation of probable responses and with consideration of the information that will be required for scoring. However, the interviewer is permitted to supplement the list of probes with additional probes during the interview if the information obtained is insufficient to make a rating. Probing questions allow the interviewer to explore in more depth how the applicant responded to various situations in the past, the reasons or thinking behind his actions,

Probes
Follow-up questions or prompts used by the interviewer to guide the applicant's descriptions of situations or events or to provide scorable elaboration of answers.

TABLE 9.2

EXAMPLE OF A BEHAVIOUR INTERVIEW QUESTION

We all encounter situations in which our judgment is challenged. Tell me about a time when you were not certain you had made the right decision and then someone openly challenged your decision. What did you do?

Probes:

What aspect of your decision were you uncertain about?
Did the person who challenged you have essential information that you did not possess?
Could anyone overhear the person's challenge?
What issues and possible consequences did you consider in responding to this person's challenge?
What was your final decision and what was the outcome?

Scoring Guide

1—I told the person that I was in charge and I was sticking with my decision.
3—I changed my mind and did what the person suggested *or* I openly discussed the merits of his/her suggestion (in front of others).
5—I took the person to a private place and thanked him for the advice but asked not to be questioned in front of other people. Then, after asking the person for suggestions, I took some time to reconsider the options and consequences. I made the decision that had the greatest probability of success, regardless of where the ideas came from, but made it clear it was *my* decision.

how he interacted and communicated with others, their values or beliefs, and the outcomes of their behaviours. However, it is important for interviewers to keep the level of probing relatively consistent across applicants so that they do not introduce bias into the interview process. Probing to obtain required information without treating applicants differently or giving away the content of the ideal answer requires considerable skill on the part of the interviewer. The concern that unplanned, spontaneous probing could bias the interview has led some researchers to recommend that only preplanned, neutral probes should be used.[150]

The example in Table 9.2 contains a scoring guide similar to the one used for the SI question. Initial approaches to BI did not include the use of scoring guides but, rather, had interviewers rate applicants on various dimensions or traits (e.g., motivation, communication skills) based on their responses to interview questions.[151] The process of translating answers to dimension ratings was a rather subjective one, for scores would be derived on the basis of impressions gained by interviewers listening to answers to various questions. There was no direct correspondence between any one question and any one dimension. Such an approach would be expected to compromise interview reliability and validity (this is discussed in the next section). More recent approaches to the BI have incorporated scoring guides.[152,153,154]

Note that the BI question in Table 9.2 requests information that the applicant might construe as negative and might thus be reluctant to provide. When asking questions that might be viewed as requesting negative information, it is helpful to begin the question with what is called a *disarming statement*. In the example, the disarming statement communicates to the applicant that it is normal and perfectly acceptable to have had one's judgment challenged. The disarming statement is intended to reduce the likelihood that the applicant will deny having experienced this situation and to set the applicant at ease about discussing it freely. Table 9.3 provides additional examples of BI questions that request both positive and negative information.

Like the SI, the BI is an attempt to apply Wernimont and Campbell's suggestion that a predictor should sample behaviours that are representative of criterion behaviours (i.e., a work sample).[155] However, in contrast to the SI, the BI approach is based on the premise that the best predictor of future behaviour is past behaviour. Critics of this approach have argued that people learn from past mistakes and that situational factors (e.g., relationships with supervisors, tasks, organizational norms) constrain behaviour; therefore, past behaviours will not necessarily be repeated in the future, particularly if the situation is somewhat different or if learning has taken place. After describing negative experiences, applicants can be asked, however, to indicate if they would repeat the behaviour next time or to relate an experience where they were successful in a similar situation.

An additional concern with the BI is that applicants could make up stories about events that never happened. However, this is very difficult to do convincingly, given the amount of detail solicited in the probes. Moreover, one approach that is very effective at maximizing accuracy in BIs is to indicate to applicants at the beginning of the interview that, after each answer, the interviewer will be asking for names and contact information of individuals who could verify the answer, and to alert the applicants that some of these individuals might be contacted after the interview for verification. Under such circumstances, applicants are likely to endeavour to be as accurate as possible in their answers.

Taylor and Small report a mean criterion validity coefficient of 0.26 (0.47 with corrections for criterion unreliability and range restriction) for the BI when no descriptively anchored scoring guides were used (across 8 coefficients), but a mean criterion validity coefficient of 0.35 (0.63 with corrections for criterion unreliability and range restriction) when scoring guides were used (across 11 coefficients).[156] Inter-rater reliability was 0.73 without scoring guides and 0.77 with scoring guides.[157] Clearly, the use of scoring guides has improved the reliability and validity of the BI. Huffcutt et al. obtained similar results for the BI (based on 22 coefficients), with a mean criterion validity coefficient of 0.31 (0.51 corrected).[158] For more information on different aspects of the BI approach to interviewing, see http://www.jobinterviewquestions.org/questions/behavioral-interview.asp. Further information on both SI and BI interviews as well as on developing interview questions is provided at http://apps.opm.gov/ADT/ContentFiles/SIGuide09.08.08.pdf.

THE EXPERIENCE-BASED INTERVIEW

Experience-based interview
Experience-based interviews assess applicant qualifications such as work experience and education using job knowledge or work sample questions.

Campion and others have developed an approach now referred to as the **experience-based interview** (EBI).[159,160] Experience-based interviews assess applicant qualifications such as work experience and education by asking questions about job knowledge or using work sample questions. Job knowledge questions assess the degree to which the applicant possesses relevant job knowledge (e.g., "When putting a piece of machinery back together after repairing it, why would you clean all the parts first?"). Work sample questions require the applicant to demonstrate a skill or competence (i.e., provide a work sample) during the interview (e.g., "If this item costs $5.67 and I give you $10, how much change should I get?" or "Show me how to wire these two three-way switches"). EBIs differ from SIs and BIs in that interviewers can choose questions from a predetermined set of questions instead of asking each applicant the exact same set of questions. This flexibility is necessary because different applicants are likely to bring somewhat different experience and knowledge to the interview.

TABLE 9.3

ADDITIONAL EXAMPLES OF BEHAVIOUR INTERVIEW QUESTIONS

These BI questions are based on the SI question in Table 9.1.

1. Sometimes we encounter individuals who seem to avoid us when we try to conduct personal or corporate business with them. Tell me about a time you were trying to contact an individual who seemed to be avoiding you or not answering your calls.

Probes:

What efforts did you make to contact this person?
How long did you keep trying?
Were you successful? What happened?
If you were not successful, what did you do?
What was the outcome?

1—I stopped calling or trying to make contact. There was no point in continuing because the individual was clearly not interested.
3—I continued trying to contact the individual. I left messages until I was successful.
5—I tried to contact the individual in person. I tried to discover what the problem was and why the individual was avoiding me. I tried to rectify the situation, if possible.

2. Sometimes we find ourselves in situations where something is wrong or out of place, that nobody else seems to notice, and which could have serious consequences or hurt someone if not corrected. Tell me about a time where you experienced such a situation and tell me what you did.

Probes:

What about the situation seemed dangerous or potentially harmful?
What steps did you take to ensure those nearby would be safe?
What did you do to reduce the danger or resolve the situation?
What was the outcome?

1—I left things well enough alone. Nobody else seemed concerned, so I wasn't going to get involved.
3—I took some steps to fix the situation *or* I reported the situation to someone in authority.
5—I reported the situation to those nearby as well as to someone in authority. I recommended that appropriate action be taken to keep everyone safe. I tried to fix the problem or assisted in trying to fix it to the extent possible.

3. Sometimes we are asked to settle disputes between conflicting parties concerning limited resources. In fact, sometimes the settlement has a personal cost for us. Tell me about a time when you were asked to help resolve a conflict over resources between two other individuals, especially one where there was some potential cost to you.

Probes:

Who were the participants in the conflict and what was the conflict about?
What did you do to facilitate the discussion?
How did you help the parties resolve the conflict?
What potential cost was there to you in the process or the resolution?
What was the outcome?

1—I refused to get involved.
3—I supported one of the sides (based on friendship, my sense of who had the stronger case, etc.) *or* I told them to work it out between themselves.
5—I tried to help them resolve the issue by seeking a compromise. I tried to discover what the factors were and to consider them as objectively as possible. If no solution was reached, I arbitrated based on the merits of each position.

Several approaches have been taken to EBIs, but they all involve assessing job knowledge and work experience.[161,162,163] A related approach to work sample interviewing involves role-playing. One of the interviewers or an assistant plays a foil to the role played by the applicant, while the interviewer or others observe and evaluate. The Edmonton Police Service has used such role-play to assess assertiveness in candidates. For example, the applicant is asked to assume he has just set up a chair to watch a parade. The chair happens to be similar to ones set up by the city for public use. The applicant is told to assume that he has left the chair unattended in order to get a drink and returns to find the chair occupied (by the foil). The applicant's task is to convince the foil to vacate the chair without resorting to aggressive behaviour (physical or verbal).

Another approach to the EBI is the walk-through interview used by Hedge and Teachout and also by Ree, Earles, and Teachout to select U.S. Air Force enlistees.[164,165] The walk-through interview involves asking the interviewees to describe in detail, step by step, how they perform a job-related task while visualizing themselves performing the task.

Like the SI and BI, the EBI can be derived from critical incidents through focus-group sessions. Scoring guides should also be developed using the procedures described for the SI and BI. However, in some respects, the EBI may be a little more difficult to construct than either the SI or BI. Care must be taken when simulating situations in the interview setting to ensure fidelity to the actual situation. Due to the length of time required to administer some of the EBI questions, fewer of them are likely to be usable in one session. They should therefore be selected judiciously to assess the most important performance domains. Nevertheless, the EBI offers an alternative approach for predicting job performance.

Campion and his associates were able to predict job performance as well using this approach ($r = 0.56$ with corrections for criterion unreliability and range restriction, $r = 0.34$, uncorrected; reliability is estimated at 0.88).[166] For more information on job knowledge questions, as well as SI and BI questions, see http://www.psc-cfp.gc.ca/plcy-pltq/guides/structured-structuree/downloads/app-e/abbr-eng.pdf.

COMPARISON OF THE STRUCTURED INTERVIEW APPROACHES

According to the research evidence available to date (see above), validity coefficients for the situational interview, experience-based interview, and behaviour description interview seem to be reasonably similar. However, these comparisons are indirect because, in most studies, researchers examined either the SI or the BI (there are very few studies of the EBI). A few competitive tests of the BI and SI approaches have been conducted.[167,168,169] Unfortunately, the results of these studies are conflicting and inconclusive and, taken together, do not suggest that either approach has a strong advantage in terms of predictive validity.[170,171] There is some evidence that the BI might be a bit better than the SI for highly complex jobs (e.g., management positions).[172,173] However, there are also conflicting findings in this regard. That is, if the SI is properly designed with questions that contain a dilemma and are pilot tested to reduce the effects of impression management, it appears to be at least as effective as the BI for complex jobs.[174]

The conclusion that the SI and BI are equally effective is evident in a comparative study. Day and Carroll used critical incidents to generate related SI and BI questions like those in Tables 9.1 and 9.3, with accompanying scoring guides.[175] The resultant questions were then used to interview undergraduate students for admission into a fictitious academic program. Two trained interviewers conducted the interviews. In some cases, the applicants had been given the interview questions to study prior to the interview.

Day and Carroll also obtained the students' grade point averages, their past academic experience, a measurement of cognitive ability, and their perceptions of the fairness of the questions.

Both types of structured interview questions predicted academic success and accounted for incremental validity over and above that provided by cognitive ability and experience. They also found that knowing the interview questions beforehand led to significantly higher interview scores. Neither the SI nor the BI elicited differing perceptions of fairness; however, interviews were perceived as more fair when the interview questions had been provided ahead of time to participants. Overall, Day and Carroll concluded that neither the SI nor the BI produced significantly different results in their ability to predict performance.[176]

Other research has addressed the question of whether there are differences in the constructs measured by SI and BI interviews. Berry, Sackett, and Landers found that BIs have a lower correlation with cognitive ability than SIs (0.12 for the BI and 0.26 for the SI, uncorrected).[177] In fact, overall, the correlation of cognitive ability with structured interviews seems to be somewhat higher than with unstructured interviews, which suggests that structured interviews do measure cognitive ability to a moderate degree.[178] However, structured interviews also have incremental validity over cognitive ability (see Chapter 10), which means that they have greater potential to predict components of job performance that are not predicted by cognitive ability and, therefore, increase the accuracy of our predictions of job performance.[179]

Correlations between structured interviews and personality measurements are also quite modest.[180,181,182,183] Both the BI and the SI have modest correlations with Conscientiousness (0.12 and 0.10, respectively), but the BI appears to also correlate with Extraversion (0.12), while the SI seems to correlate negatively with Neuroticism (–0.12).[184]

In fact, the constructs best measured by structured interviews, whether SI or BI, seem to be job experience, job knowledge, situational judgment, social skills, and organizational fit.[185,186] These constructs are multidimensional and it is likely that good interview questions are multidimensional as well. For example, answering the question in Table 9.1 (and behaving appropriately in such a situation) likely involves not just one but several constructs, such as motivation to lead, understanding human motivation and behaviour, situational judgment, rational and analytical thinking, social skills, self-control, and self-confidence. Thus, it should not be surprising that interview questions often do not correlate highly with measurements of the single constructs they are supposed to assess or with other interview questions ostensibly measuring the same single construct.[187] Recently, some researchers have suggested using multidimensional scoring guides in order to accommodate the multidimensional nature of responses to interview questions.[188,189] However, having to rate several dimensions or constructs for each answer would be very cognitively demanding for interviewers and would likely disrupt the flow of the interview.

Some researchers have explored how applicants use impression management tactics in the SI and BI. They found that applicants tend to use more ingratiation tactics (e.g., complimenting the interviewer or organization) in the SI, while they tend to use more self-focused and defensive tactics (e.g., self-promotion, explaining mistakes or failures) in the BI.[190,191] The latter finding should not be surprising, given that the BI requires applicants to discuss past situations where they have either been successful or where they have encountered difficulty or failure. However, in another study, researchers found that applicants also used more ingratiation tactics in the BI than in the SI.[192]

Other researchers have compared BI questions with SI questions in terms of how much effect applicant impression management tactics actually have on interview ratings.

Although some researchers found that SI questions are less susceptible to impression management behaviour,[193] others found that BI questions are more resistant to faking,[194] and still others found no difference.[195] Thus, again, the evidence is inconclusive. Nevertheless, regardless of the type of questions used, it is clear that the more structured an interview becomes, the less effect impression management tactics will have on interview ratings.[196,197]

Validity and other issues notwithstanding, the BI might be more appropriate in some selection situations, whereas the SI might be more appropriate in others. In particular, the BI seems best suited to the selection of candidates who have had prior work experience (especially in related areas of work) or have been engaged in relevant volunteer activities or hobbies. However, the SI is useful with both experienced and inexperienced applicants. Experienced applicants may still have some advantage over inexperienced applicants competing for the same job when situational questions are asked, but the difference would likely be reduced.

As noted above, interviewers appear to require a fair degree of skill in order to conduct the BI effectively. The SI might therefore be more foolproof in the hands of supervisors and line managers when they do the interviewing. The SI seems to require less skill or training because the interviewer simply reads the questions and compares the answers given with the scoring guide examples. Probing is not permitted. A thorough training program is highly recommended for all interviewers but it becomes particularly important if the BI is to be used.

It is important to recognize that the above discussion of the relative merits of the two approaches is somewhat speculative. More research is needed to investigate the relative merits of the BI and the SI in various situations and with varying degrees of interviewer training and experience. In addition to addressing the theoretical questions surrounding the relationships of past behaviour and behavioural intentions with subsequent behaviour, such research would provide highly useful information for improving the design of structured interviews. In fact, researchers increasingly recommend using both SI and BI questions in the same interview sessions because they tend to measure somewhat different constructs and may complement each other.[198] Moreover, applicants who have difficulty answering a BI question because of a lack of relevant work experience could be asked a corresponding SI question. Alternatively, SI questions could be followed by corresponding BI questions in order to determine whether the behavioural intentions are consistent with past behaviours. For more information on situational and behavioural questions, visit https://www.jobsetc.gc.ca/pieces.jsp?category_id=1501.

STRUCTURED INTERVIEWS IN PRACTICE

SCORING STRUCTURED EMPLOYMENT INTERVIEWS

As noted above, an interviewing best practice is for interviewers to score the answer to each interview question as soon as it has been given.[199] Normally, each interview question would take up between half a page to a full page, including the question and the scoring guide (as illustrated in Tables 9.1, 9.2, and 9.3), as well as some space for recording notes. The interviewer's task is to compare the applicant's response to the scoring guide and assign an appropriate score (e.g., by circling the corresponding number on the scoring guide). The scores for each question should be combined at the end of the interview to yield a total interview score. Recruitment and Selection Notebook 9.4 provides an example of a scoring summary that could be used for this purpose (as well

RECRUITMENT AND SELECTION NOTEBOOK 9.4

EXAMPLE OF A STRUCTURED INTERVIEW SCORING SUMMARY

INTERVIEW QUESTION	SCORE
Question 1 When someone is in charge of others, he/she often has to delegate work to them and hope that they will do a good job. Tell me about the last time you asked someone to do a task for you and you personally got in trouble because this person messed up.	3
Question 2 When making difficult decisions it's natural to ask others for information and advice but sometimes we just don't have the time to do that because the decision has to be made quickly or sometimes there's no one around that we can ask. Tell me about the last time you had to make a very difficult decision quickly and you really couldn't rely on anyone else for information or advice.	4
Question 3 Tell me about a time when you were working toward an important deadline and you started to realize, as the deadline approached, that you wouldn't be able to meet the deadline by working as you had been up to that point.	2
Question 4 We all make mistakes at one time or another. Sometimes we're in too much of a hurry, sometimes we're tired, sometimes we haven't got enough information or materials to do the job right, and sometimes others let us down. Tell me about the mistake you made which you would most like to have a second chance at doing right.	3
Question 5 Tell me about the last time you worked in a group with someone who was not doing his or her fair share of the work.	2
Question 6 Some people seem to find fault with just about everything that we do. Tell me about the last time you worked with or for someone who was like that.	5
Question 7 Sometimes unanticipated events get in the way of our carefully laid plans. Tell me about a time when you had made some plans and something equally important which also required your time and attention came up unexpectedly.	3
Question 8 Tell me about a time when you were trying to explain something to someone and the person seemed to be having trouble understanding what you were telling him or her.	4
Question 9 Tell me about the last time you were in charge of a group and you and your group seemed to have an enormous amount of work to do in order to achieve a difficult goal or objective.	1
Question 10 In almost any group there are bound to be individuals who don't get along with each other at one time or another. Tell me about a time when you were in a group in which two or more members were having a disagreement and it looked like their behaviour was having a negative effect on the whole group.	4
TOTAL INTERVIEW SCORE	31

as providing additional examples of BI questions). Of course, in this example, the scores are purely hypothetical. In practice, these scores would come from the scoring guides that accompany each of the interview questions (see Tables 9.1, 9.2, and 9.3).

INTERVIEWING FOR ORGANIZATIONAL FIT

Structured interviews are particularly useful in assessing organizational fit.[200,201] Rather than determining organizational fit by assessing an applicant's stated attitudes or values, structured interviews can assess the applicant's behaviours in situations or contexts that reflect organizational values or norms. Characteristics such as integrity, customer service orientation, teamwork orientation, tolerance for stress, initiative, openness to learning, flexibility/adaptability, and other characteristics that reflect organizational norms and values can all be assessed in both SI and BI interviews. For example, to assess integrity, the interviewer might ask a question such as, "Tell me about a time when your supervisor asked you to do something that you felt was inappropriate or unethical. Describe the situation and tell me what you did. What did you learn from this event?" To assess customer service orientation, an interviewer might ask a question such as, "Tell me about a time you had to deal with a customer who was upset but, in this situation, you knew the customer was wrong. Describe the situation and tell me what you did. Has this experience changed how you respond in such situations? If so, how?" The answers to questions such as these can be compared with how employees in the organization are expected to behave in such situations and would, therefore, reflect the fit between the applicant and the organization.

EMPLOYER REACTIONS TO INTERVIEW STRUCTURE

When employers were first exposed to structured interview methods a few decades ago, they tended to be somewhat suspicious of them. Most felt more comfortable with unstructured approaches that relied to a large extent on "gut feelings." Moreover, many interviewers prefer the greater discretion, personal contact, and ease of preparation provided by unstructured interviews.[202] However, it appears that most employers have begun using interviews with at least moderate levels of structure.[203,204,205]

In the most recent survey by Simola, Tagger, and Smith, more than 48.2 percent of Canadian HR practitioners reported always using behaviour description questions, while another 37.5 percent reported using them most of the time.[206] Situational questions were used less frequently, with 17.6 percent reporting always using them and another 26.6 percent reporting using them most of the time.[207] However, it is not clear whether these interviews are being used appropriately. The survey suggests that most HR practitioners do not have a strong understanding of best practices concerning employment interviewing. Only 34.6 percent reported basing interview questions on a job analysis and more than 75 percent reported that they add questions during the interview.

These disturbing findings are supported by those of Chapman and Zweig, who found that interviewers tend not to use formal rating systems to rate applicant answers and generally do not even have an ideal response in mind with which to compare applicant answers. Moreover, they tend to use their global impressions of the applicant rather than combining scores statistically to come to a selection decision (see the following section and Chapter 10).[208] Providing interviewers with training concerning structured interviewing techniques and strong organization support for the use of structured interviews seem to be effective ways of increasing the likelihood that structured interviews will be used correctly.[209,210, 211]

APPLICANT REACTIONS TO INTERVIEW STRUCTURE

Applicants seem to like interviews more than any other selection devices such as cognitive ability tests, personality tests, biodata inventories, or work samples, and consistently rate interviews very favourably.[212,213] They perceive them to be fairer and more valid than other selection methods, and minority applicants in particular seem to prefer interviews to other selection methods.[214] Nevertheless, applicant reactions to structured interviewing techniques have been mixed. Wagner found that using structured techniques did not affect applicants' impressions of the company or the likelihood of accepting a job offer.[215] Chapman and Zweig found that applicants perceive structured interview questions as more difficult than typical questions, but interview structure is not related to perceptions of interview fairness nor is it related to whether applicants are likely to accept a job offer.[216] However, Seijts and Kyei-Poku found that applicants perceived the structured interview to be fairer than the unstructured interview in an organization that had adopted an employment equity program.[217]

On the other hand, Chapman and Rowe[218] and Kohn and Dipboye[219] found that applicants are most attracted to organizations that use less structured interviews. Kohn and Dipboye found that, when structured interviews were used, participants were less likely to accept a job offer and rated the organization as less attractive, less social, and more authoritarian, and the interviewer as less fair and less likable than when unstructured interviews were used.[220] Structuring an interview may reduce applicants' perceptions of rapport with the interviewer and provide less opportunity to develop positive feelings about the interviewer and the organization. It also provides less opportunity for applicants to use impression management tactics and may, therefore, be frustrating for some applicants.[221]

Interviews serve both a recruitment and a selection function. Unfortunately, these two purposes may conflict in that factors related to improved validity (e.g., interview structure) might result in negative applicant reactions. Kohn and Dipboye found that the negative effect of structure on applicant attraction to the organization could be reduced if the interviewer provided more information about the job and organization in the interview.[222] Moreover, as pointed out at the beginning of this chapter, compared with factors such as pay, promotion opportunities, or geographical location, interviewers' effects on applicant job choice are minimal.[223] Nevertheless, some time should be taken during the interview to put the applicants at ease and build rapport. The nature of the questions and the interview process can be explained and opportunities should be given for the applicants to ask questions. These steps should not only reduce possible negative reactions but also contribute to a less stressful interview situation, which should allow interviewees to perform at their best when answering the questions.

INTERVIEW PRACTICE AND HUMAN RIGHTS

As noted above, one of the hallmarks of structured interviews is the standardization of interview questions. When interviews are standardized, applicants can be compared on the basis of the same criteria and the interviewer obtains a better picture of the merits of each applicant relative to other applicants. In fact, a number of researchers have suggested that standardization is an important factor in increasing interview reliability and validity.[224]

Equally if not more important, the standardized treatment of applicants is generally perceived as being fairer than non-standardized treatment. The likelihood of organizations that use standardized interview questions becoming embroiled in selection-related litigation is therefore reduced. Moreover, when such organizations do go to court, the courts tend to rule in their favour.[225,226,227] Standardization therefore gives the interviewer and organization some measure of protection from discrimination suits.

Another aspect of structured interviews that appears to have a strong impact on the organization's ability to defend itself against litigation is the exclusive use of job-related questions (i.e., questions based on a formal job analysis). Questions that probe areas not directly relevant to the job run the risk of being interpreted as having discriminatory intent by the applicant and by the courts.[228,229,230] In fact, structured interviews meet the requirements of federal and provincial privacy legislation because they only collect information that is directly relevant to the job. A question such as "Do you plan to have children?" which is frequently posed to female but not to male applicants, is not only unrelated to job requirements but treats male and female applicants differently (i.e., is not standardized). Such questions are particularly troublesome from a human rights perspective. Such questions also result in negative applicant reactions to the interview and the interviewer and a decreased likelihood that they will accept a job offer or recommend the organization to others.[231]

The job relevance of interview questions has a significant impact on interview validity as well.[232] Structured interviews may have greater predictive validity, in part, because structuring an interview increases its reliability and accuracy in differentiating between applicant competencies on job-relevant dimensions. Moreover, the greater job relevance of structured interview questions may direct the interviewer's attention away from irrelevant information and focus it on job-relevant information. This focusing of interviewer attention may reduce the potential effects of the biases and processing errors inherent in the unstructured interview. Therefore, the degree to which structured interview questions are job relevant and interview ratings are reliable appears to contribute to the validity of the interview.

However, the job relevance of interview questions does not, by itself, guarantee the reliability of interview ratings. Interviewers often disagree in their ratings of the same dimensions or characteristics for a given applicant and even give different ratings for the same answer to an interview question. Therefore, some kind of job-relevant rating or scoring guide is essential if high reliability among raters is to be achieved and if the interview ratings are to be based on job-relevant criteria. In fact, such scoring guides appear to reduce the effects of bias and increase interview reliability, and therefore validity, particularly when they are used to assess the answers given by interviewees rather than trait dimensions.[233,234,235,236] The use of a standardized, job-relevant scoring system for assessing and comparing candidates may also contribute to an effective defence against litigation.[237,238] The courts have been particularly concerned when there is evidence that applicants giving the same responses are treated differently on the basis of gender or race or any other grounds on which discrimination is forbidden. To build on a previous example, it is insufficient for an employer to standardize the interview by asking both male and female applicants whether they intend to have children if a male's response to the question is irrelevant to the selection decision whereas a female's response might determine whether or not she is offered the job (i.e., the *scoring* of responses is not standardized).

Latham and his colleagues' approach requires interviewers to sum the scores given for each individual question to give an overall interview score, rather than permitting interviewers to make global judgments.[239] The final score can then be used to make the selection decision by ranking candidates or by determining cutoff scores, which must be exceeded by candidates if they are to qualify for the job. In essence, this approach relieves the interviewer of much of the decision-making function and isolates the selection decision from the interviewer's biases and stereotypes.[240] The selection decision, then, is a statistical or actuarial process that has greater criterion-related validity than the error-prone judgmental processes typically engaged in by interviewers when they make overall ratings or recommendations.[241]

This advantage for the statistical combination of scores does not appear to hold, however, when interview questions with low job-relevance are used. Rather than evaluating behaviours, interviewers using such questions make subjective judgments with respect to each answer given.[242] The total interview score for such questions therefore represents the sum of several subjective judgments, which do not differ significantly from a single overall subjective rating.

Day and Carroll's study also raises an important point about access to the interview questions.[243] Knowing the questions in advance, whether they are SI or BI, will lead to higher interview scores. Strict control must be maintained of all questions or the interview questions must be given to all candidates beforehand to remove the possibility of some candidates having an advantage through prior knowledge of the questions. As Day and Carroll show, knowing the questions beforehand does not lead to every applicant giving brilliant answers; there is still a distribution of scores. All applicants must be treated fairly with respect to access to the interview questions.

It should be emphasized, with respect to the discussion above, that interview validity and reliability issues are very much related, in that reliability can place an upper limit on validity.[244] Conditions that serve to make interviews more reliable should therefore be the same as those that make them more valid.[245]

Although unstructured interviews are vulnerable targets of potential litigation, there is comparatively little evidence of bias in structured interviews. Arvey and Campion found no evidence of age or gender bias in their semistructured interviews.[246] Similarly, in their investigation of over 27 000 structured interviews for 18 different jobs, Blankenship and Cesare found no evidence of bias on the basis of age.[247] Although Lin, Dobbins, and Farh also found no evidence of age bias in their structured interview, they found a very small effect for a same-race bias.[248] More recent studies have also found no evidence of age or gender bias, although a very small same-race bias was found.[249,250] In particular, interview panels or boards consisting of all black or mostly black interviewers were found to give slightly higher scores to black applicants than panels or boards made up of all white or mostly white interviewers (ratings did not differ for white or Hispanic applicants).[251] However, Lin, Dobbins, and Farh found less evidence of race bias when structured interviews were used than when unstructured interviews were used.[252] Moreover, they note that the true performance levels of the applicants are unknown. Nevertheless, they recommended the use of mixed-race interview boards to reduce the potential for bias.

Paullin[253] reviewed seven studies, including four conducted by Motowidlo et al.,[254] and found no consistent trends for bias with respect to gender or race or ethnic group. Any differences that do exist tend to be less than half a standard deviation and do not consistently favour any group. Huffcutt and Roth conducted a meta-analysis of 31 studies to assess racial group differences in employment interview scores.[255] Like Lin, Dobbins, and Farh,[256] they found differences in ratings were quite small for structured interviews and much less than for unstructured interviews. The studies represent a variety of jobs including marketing, entry-level management, nonmanagerial telecommunications jobs, and firefighting. Finally, McCarthy, Van Iddekinge, and Campion, in a large study involving almost 20 000 applicants for a managerial-level position, found no evidence of gender or race bias or applicant–interviewer similarity effects with respect to gender or race when highly structured interviews were used.[257]

Brecher, Bragger, and Kutcher found that, compared to unstructured interviews, structured interviews reduce bias with respect to physical disability.[258] In addition, Reilly and her colleagues found that using behaviourally anchored scoring guides is effective in removing bias with respect to disability in structured interviews.[259] Not only are structured interviews less vulnerable to bias than unstructured interviews, but applicants perceive them as more job related and, thus, fairer.[260,261,262] Consequently, applicants are less likely to be concerned about decisions made on the basis of structured interviews.

There is an important caveat that we have to make with respect to the defensibility of structured interviews. The improved reliability, validity, and lack of bias occur in structured interviews that have been developed from the principles presented in this chapter. Too often we have seen HR practitioners use shortcuts to develop a set of structured interview questions or to simply choose questions off the shelf from books on structured interviews. In our practice, we have seen HR practitioners screen out candidates on answers to one question rather than the total score. They often fail to ensure that questions were job related, fail to develop appropriate scoring keys, and fail to properly train those who will be doing the interviews. As with any tool, to get the best results, interviews must be properly used. Failure to follow the "best practices" with respect to structured interviews will undermine their defensibility. Information on structured interviewing and human rights concerns can be found at http://www.canadavisa.com/canada-immigration-employment-interviews.html.

DESIGNING INTERVIEW QUESTIONS

Although a variety of job analysis methods can be used to develop structured interview questions, the most common is the critical incidents technique.[263] The critical incidents technique has been the basis of both the SI and the BI. Examples of effective and ineffective as well as typical behaviours that contributed to the success or failure of employees in particular job-related situations or tasks are collected. Each important task or situation is thus linked with several examples of typical, effective, and ineffective behaviours. This information can be obtained from incumbents and their supervisors through interviews, focus group sessions, and questionnaires.

Once the critical incidents have been collected, the situations on which they are based can be turned into EBI, BI, or SI questions. For SI questions, the situation should be described in sufficient detail to allow an applicant to visualize it accurately and should be followed by a "What would you do?" question. For each situation, the best critical incidents (i.e., most representative and most likely to be used as answers by interviewees) demonstrating effective, typical, and ineffective behaviours can serve as behavioural anchors for the scoring guide (i.e., poor, average, and good answer, respectively). Scores are typically assigned so that 1 represents the poor answer, 3 an average answer, and 5 a good answer.

Care should be taken to select situations and to phrase questions in a way that does not make the best answer readily apparent to the applicant. Situations where there is tension between competing demands or options are ideal if the options appear equally aversive or attractive to inexperienced individuals (i.e., there is a dilemma). Questions and scoring guides should be pre-tested on a group of applicants or recently hired employees to ensure that the questions are clear and elicit a range of responses. For example, if the poor answer is never given, the answers that are given should be examined to determine whether some of them reflect an alternative critical incident representing ineffective performance. Alternatively, the question should be reworked to create more tension.

BI questions are designed by examining each task or situation in order to identify the behavioural dimension underlying the situation (e.g., meeting deadlines). The dimensions are turned into BI questions, which retain the essence rather than the details of the original situation. In other words, the BI question applies to a variety of situations that share the underlying behavioural dimension (e.g., meeting deadlines in a job, at school, when sending birthday cards, etc.). As with the SI, critical incidents are used to develop a scoring guide. However, the scoring guide anchors also need to be rephrased to make them more generally applicable to a variety of situations. The underlying behavioural dimensions rather than the actual incidents serve as anchors (e.g., "planning ahead, setting up contingency plans, monitoring progress" instead of "working long hours at the last minute, asking for extensions, missing the deadline").

Probes are developed by anticipating the kinds of responses that applicants from different backgrounds, or with different levels of experience, are likely to give to a BI question. For example, applicants with limited work experience might never have been in a situation where they disagreed with a superior. A probe might then focus on responses to a disagreement with parents or friends in a situation similar to the one of relevance to the job. The probes should provide a clear understanding of the situation, the behaviour, and the outcome so that the applicant's response can be accurately scored. General probes such as "What led up to the situation?" "What did you do?" "What happened?" "What was your reason for . . .?" or "Can you tell me more about . . .?" seem to apply in most circumstances.

Job knowledge or work sample questions can also be derived from critical incidents. The situations that lead to ineffective or effective behaviours can be simulated during the interview. For example, if problems have occurred on the job because solvents have been mixed or used inappropriately and if a contributing factor is functional illiteracy, applicants could be asked to read the directions on a solvent container aloud and then to explain in their own words what the directions mean. Similarly, an applicant for a sales position could be asked to "sell" a product to interviewers playing the roles of the kinds of customers who have been challenging for salespeople in the past. Additional information on the development of structured interview questions and scoring guides can be found at http://www.psc-cfp.gc.ca/plcy-pltq/guides/structured-structuree/index-eng.htm.

INTERVIEWER TRAINING

Interviewer training has tended to focus on reducing common sources of bias and inaccuracy such as halo error, similar-to-me effects, contrast effects, and leniency and severity errors. Interviewers are also taught to put the applicant at ease, ask open-ended questions, develop good listening skills, maintain control of the interview, take appropriate notes, and ignore or interpret correctly the nonverbal behaviours occurring in the interview. Unfortunately, such training efforts have achieved mixed results at best.[264,265] Most studies report that interviewer training designed to eliminate halo and other rating biases has minimal effect on interviewer behaviour and interview outcomes, particularly when shorter training programs are examined.

Training interviewers to administer a structured interview is a considerably different endeavour than training them to avoid errors and biases or develop good listening skills.

Although rapport building is an important skill, interviewers using structured interviews need to also learn how to ask questions, evaluate answers, and use scoring guides, as well as how to take notes.[266] For example, interviewers require training on how to score an answer when it does not match the examples in the scoring guide. The training should provide interviewers with decision rules to use in such circumstances.

Interviewers using techniques that allow more discretion, such as the BI, might require more extensive training than those using more standardized approaches, such as the SI. When using their discretion, interviewers need to learn how to select questions or probes and when to probe. They need to learn how to use probes effectively without giving away the ideal answer. Demonstrations, behavioural role modelling, and opportunities for active practice are likely to be essential training techniques in any such training program.[267,268] Training that focuses on the evaluation and scoring of applicant answers has been found to contribute to higher interview reliability and validity.[269,270] Frame-of-reference (FOR) training, which involves helping interviewers understand the performance dimensions they are assessing, defines and describes behavioural examples of different performance levels for each dimension or interview question, and provides opportunity for practice and feedback, has been found to contribute significantly to inter-rater reliability and rating accuracy.[271]

INTERVIEW COACHING FOR APPLICANTS

Being interviewed for a job can be an anxiety-arousing situation for applicants.[272,273] Interview anxiety is negatively related to interview performance and, as a result, anxious applicants are less likely to be hired, even though their interview anxiety might be unrelated to job performance.[274] Such applicants can benefit from coaching to help them handle employment interviews more effectively. In fact, most applicants can benefit from some interview coaching, but those who have not been interviewed for a long time, those who have not experienced structured approaches to interviewing, and those who have experienced ongoing difficulty doing well in interviews stand to gain the most from such coaching.

Coaching applicants for structured employment interviews generally involves explaining the purpose of the interview, suggestions and advice on how to do well in the interview, exposing applicants to different kinds of questions, discussing the nature of responses interviewers are looking for with illustrations of how to perform, providing opportunities for role-play or practice, providing feedback to applicants, and providing reinforcement for appropriate interview behaviours.[275] Attributional retraining, which involves helping applicants perceive repeated failure in interviews as a temporary condition and encourages them to take control over their reactions to such events, can be effective in changing applicant motivations and behaviours.[276] Providing applicants with interview coaching increases their interview self-efficacy (reducing their anxiety) and improves their performance in interviews.[277,278,279] Coaching applicants to improve their interview performance might seem counterintuitive, given the interviewer's objective of selecting the best job candidates rather than the most polished interviewees. However, the interview coaching described here appears to actually increase the validity of structured interviews.[280] This may be because coaching helps applicants to focus their answers, describing more job-relevant behaviours more clearly, thus helping the interviewer obtain a more accurate perspective of the applicant's capabilities. Additional information and tips about preparing for interviews as an applicant can be found at http://www.ctdol.state.ct.us/progsupt/jobsrvce/intervie.htm.

OTHER APPROACHES TO INTERVIEWING

LONG-DISTANCE INTERVIEWS

Many organizations recruit candidates across the country or internationally, necessitating the use of **long-distance interviews**. However, as discussed at the beginning of the chapter, the costs of flying candidates in for interviews and paying for their accommodations or, conversely, flying recruiters across the country or overseas can be prohibitive. Moreover, there has been an increased concern in recent years about the safety of air travel and associated inconveniences, such as additional time spent at airports, as well as concerns about invasion of privacy and health with the introduction of airport body scanners. As a result, some organizations have turned to telephone interviews, videoconference interviews, Internet interviews, or computerized interviews as alternatives to face-to-face interviews.[281] Although preliminary evidence suggests that long-distance, structured interviews can be valid predictors of job performance,[282] there is also evidence that the use of technology can, in some circumstances, make the interview an unsatisfying, or even unpleasant, experience for both the applicant and the interviewer.[283,284,285] Moreover, there are a number of obstacles, such as limited access to videoconferencing facilities, high costs, and technical limitations (e.g., picture and sound quality) that must be overcome if such technology is to be used effectively.[286]

Long-distance interviews
Interviews conducted over a long distance, including telephone interviews, videoconference interviews, Internet interviews, or computerized interviews, which serve as alternatives to face-to-face interviews.

Ldprod/Shutterstock.com

Some preliminary research suggests that applicants interviewed using videoconference technology receive higher ratings than those interviewed face-to-face.[287,288] However, other researchers found the reverse.[289] Although the research evidence to date is inconclusive concerning who receives higher ratings, any differences in ratings of applicants are of considerable concern if an organization interviews some applicants in face-to-face situations while others are interviewed using interview technology, because one group might be disadvantaged. There is also some evidence that interview technology interacts with interview structure in complex ways.[290,291] Clearly, more research is needed on applicant and interviewer reactions to interview technology, as well as on the validity of such technology-dependent interviews compared with face-to-face interviews.

PUZZLE INTERVIEWS

Puzzle interviews ask applicants to solve puzzles or unusual problems. These interviews require applicants to use their creativity and problem-solving skills, demonstrate quick thinking, and even show a sense of humour. Puzzle interviews are usually administered in an unstructured format and do not use formal scoring keys. The approach was popularized by Microsoft in the 1990s but has now spread to many other organizations, particularly those in the high-tech sector such as Google or IBM. Puzzle interviews can include questions that some applicants should be able to solve in the interview (e.g., "Why are manhole covers round?", "How would you weigh an elephant without a scale?", "How can four employees calculate the average of their salaries without knowing each other's salary?"). However, they can also include questions that are not solvable in the context of an interview without access to the Internet (e.g., "How many gas stations are there in Canada?", "How many golf balls can fit in a school bus?", "How long would it take to move Mount Fuji?"). When the latter kind of questions are asked, interviewers

Puzzle interviews
Puzzle interviews are usually unstructured interviews that ask applicants to solve puzzles or unusual problems.

are usually looking for evidence in the applicant's answer of logical thought and an awareness of the variables that need to be considered to solve the problem. Thus, the applicant is not expected to solve the problem accurately but, rather, to think aloud about the solution to the problem, discussing the variables, the measurement methods that could be used, voicing assumptions, and making estimates based on information that the applicant does possess.

To date, only two studies have investigated puzzle interviews, either using undergraduate students as interviewees participating in mock interviews or having undergraduate students watch and rate videotaped interviews.[292,293] The puzzle questions used were of both the solvable and the non-solvable varieties. Although the researchers were not able to obtain data relating to the criterion validity of these interviews, the researchers in one of the studies found high levels of inter-rater reliability (.88 across five questions). They also found that the interview scores were moderately correlated with cognitive ability (.45).[294] Interviewee reactions to the interviews in this study were mixed. Not surprisingly, those interviewees who did well, or perceived themselves as having done well, felt that the interview was fairer than those who did not do well or did not perceive themselves as having done well. In the other study, participants perceived the puzzle interviews less favourably than behavioural interviews.[295] In particular, they believed that puzzle interviews had lower validity, were less fair, were less likely to result in them being hired, and were less transparent than behavioural interviews.

Given the scant amount of research available on the properties of puzzle interviews, we cannot recommend their use at this time. Their unstructured nature and the difficulty in scoring the less solvable problems give cause for concern. If organizations wish to measure general intelligence or problem-solving ability, they would be better off using established paper-and-pencil measures of cognitive ability or problem solving. Considerably more research needs to be done before puzzle interviews can be recommended for employee selection.

MULTIPLE MINI-INTERVIEWS

Multiple Mini-Interviews
A version of the speed interview where applicants participate in a circuit of 12 eight-minute interviews with 12 different interviewers at 12 different interview stations.

In 2002, to select applicants to its medical school, researchers at McMaster University pioneered a version of the speed interview that has become known as the **Multiple Mini-Interview** (MMI).[296,297] Each spring, candidates pre-screened on the basis of their GPA and autobiographical profile are invited to participate in a circuit of 12 eight-minute MMIs. Each applicant visits an interviewing "station" where she is asked a single question by the interviewer. At the end of eight minutes a buzzer sounds and the applicant moves on to the second station where she is asked a second question by a different interviewer. This process continues until the applicant has visited all 12 stations. These MMIs, some consisting of role-playing exercises and simulations, assess a variety of attributes deemed essential for Canadian physicians, including communication, collaboration, critical thinking, ethics, personal statement, and understanding of the health-care system. The 12 ratings for each applicant, one from each station, are pooled at the end of the interview process to yield a total score for the interview. Admission decisions are then made based on a combination of scores from the MMI, autobiographical profile, and GPA. Over the past several years, other Canadian, American, and international medical schools as well as schools of nursing, dentistry, pharmacy, and veterinary science have also begun using the MMI as part of their selection process.[298]

McMaster's MMI was developed to better assess noncognitive (e.g., interpersonal) skills and to augment predictions afforded by GPA and SAT scores. Previously, pre-screened applicants were given one-on-one interviews, but this proved too resource intense, requiring an unsustainable commitment of labour hours and causing logistical difficulties and inconvenience to both interviewers and candidates. With the MMI, McMaster University is able to evaluate more than 500 applicants over two days.[299] Although the MMI procedure requires considerable attention to organization and scheduling, it is able to process hundreds of applicants much more efficiently than is possible with one-on-one interviews.

Research on the MMI indicates that the reliability of the MMI (generalizability coefficients) ranges from .69 to .79, with a mean of .73.[300] This level of reliability is acceptable given that it reflects different interviewers asking different questions (or administering different kinds of simulations) at different stations. The validity coefficients obtained range from .15 to .57, depending on the criterion used.[301,302,303] However, MMI scores appear to correlate more highly with performance in clerkship rotations (supervised practice in the hospital) than with exams, exceeding correlations of .50. Given MMIs are designed to assess noncognitive (e.g., interpersonal) skills, higher correlations with medical practice than with exams are to be expected. This level of prediction is in line with the criterion validity of structured interviews.

In studies designed to assess the constructs measured by the MMI, researchers found that the MMI does not correlate significantly with undergraduate GPA, the Medical College Admissions Test (MCAT), measures of logical reasoning ability, or measures of nonverbal reasoning.[304,305,306] Given the low correlations with the MCAT and the measures of reasoning ability, these results suggests that the MMI does not measure cognitive ability.[307] However, the MMI does appear to be moderately correlated with some of the Big Five measures of personality, namely Extraversion (mean $r = .26$), Conscientiousness (mean $r = .20$), Agreeableness (mean $r = .16$), and Openness (mean $r = .14$). In particular, the MMI is correlated with the personality facets of Activity (mean $r = .22$), Friendliness (mean $r = .21$), Assertiveness (mean $r = .20$), Gregariousness (mean $r = .19$), Achievement (mean $r = .24$), Self-Discipline (mean $r = .19$), Cautiousness (mean $r = .19$), Altruism (mean $r = .18$), Sympathy (mean $r = .16$), and is negatively correlated with Self Consciousness (mean $r = -.21$).[308] The MMI is also significantly correlated with a situational judgment test of interpersonal understanding (mean $r = .18$), but is not correlated with a measure of emotional intelligence.[309,310] Although the MMI appears to measure personality factors to a moderate degree, personality accounts for only about 10 percent of the variance in MMI scores.[311] More research is needed to identify some of the other factors measured in the MMI. One recent study found fairly strong correlations between the MMI and the SI ($r = .45$, uncorrected) and the BI ($r = .57$, uncorrected), suggesting considerable overlap in the constructs measured by these interviews.[312]

Although the MMI has been used almost exclusively for admission to schools for the health professions, it has potential usefulness for employee selection in organizations in general. This approach would most likely be useful when an organization needs to interview a large number of applicants in a short time. However, more research needs to be done on the effectiveness of the MMI for predicting job performance in organizational settings before any strong recommendations can be made.

RESEARCH ISSUES

Although there is indisputable evidence that SIs are good predictors of job performance, we still do not have a clear understanding of *why* they predict.[313,314] More research based on good theoretical models of the SI is needed to provide a better understanding of the mechanisms responsible for interview effectiveness. Such research would contribute greatly to improvements in interview design and performance.

Despite the predictive validity of SIs, many employers and applicants have responded negatively to them. Some employers resist using SIs or modify them, possibly because these employees don't fully understand how to use SIs or because they want more control of the interview process. Likewise, some applicants do not like SIs, possibly because they find them more difficult or because the applicants have less influence on the interview process. Research is needed to find ways of improving user reactions to structured interviews and making them easier to use.

// SUMMARY

Employment interviews are the most popular selection procedure among employers and employees. Over the past two decades, many Canadian employers have abandoned traditional, unstructured approaches to interviewing in favour of structured interviews, notably behavioural interviews. However, most do not seem to be following best practices in implementing structured interview techniques. Moreover, many employers continue to use unstructured interviews, which have been plagued by poor reliability and validity and have placed the employers in a legally vulnerable position.

Dipboye's model of information processing and decision making in the interview was presented in this chapter.[315] This model is particularly relevant to unstructured interviews, although it applies, to a lesser degree, to structured interviews as well. According to the model, interviewers and applicants bring expectations, beliefs, needs, intentions, and initial information to the interview situation. These expectations and the preliminary information contribute to pre-interview impressions that can influence the interviewer's attributions and behaviour in the interview. The interviewer's behaviour, in turn, influences the applicant's behaviour. The interviewer emerges from the interaction with global impressions of the applicant that are influenced by his expectations, an emotional response to the applicant (i.e., liking of the applicant), and the first impressions carried through the interview and sometimes intensified by the interview experience. Various factors, including time pressures, quotas, and politics, can affect the final decision.

Structured approaches to employment interviewing were developed to address the shortcomings of the unstructured interview. Structuring factors include standardization, job-relatedness of interview questions, and standardized scoring systems. Such interviews need to be based on a job analysis so that they assess only job-relevant attributes. Interview questions should be non-transparent and tend to be most effective when they centre on situations involving dilemmas or tension between competing demands. Appropriate scoring guides and rater training are essential to maintaining high rating accuracy.

Various approaches to constructing structured interviews are available, including situational interviews, behaviour description interviews, and experience-based interviews. Structured interviews provide improved reliability and predictive validity and are more legally defensible than unstructured interviews. However, interviewers should be trained in the proper administration and scoring of the interview. Although the evidence is not clear on whether panel or serial interviews contribute to interview reliability and validity, they do appear to provide some degree of protection from discrimination suits.

As job requirements change in response to the ever-changing workplace, organizations are beginning to shift the focus of selection from specific job skills to organizational fit, transferable skills, and personality attributes. Structured employment interviews are well suited to assessing such attributes and will continue to play an important role in selection for the workplace of tomorrow. New approaches to interviewing involving the use of technology, such as videoconferencing and Internet interviews, puzzle interviews, and the Multiple Mini-Interview (MMI), are also being adopted by employers or, in the case of the MMI, schools for health professions. However, considerable research remains to be done to determine the effects of technology and other approaches to interviewing on interview validity, as well as on interviewer and applicant responses.

KEY TERMS

Behaviour description interview, p. 428
Dilemma, p. 426
Experience-based interview, p. 430
Impression management, p. 418
Knowledge structures, p. 414
Long-distance interviews, p. 443
Multiple Mini-Interviews, p. 444
Panel interview, p. 425
Probes, p. 428
Puzzle interviews, p. 443
Scoring guide, p. 426
Screening interviews, p. 407
Serial interviews, p. 425
Situational interview, p. 426
Speed interviewing, p. 411
Structured interview, p. 422
Unstructured interview, p. 417

WEB LINKS

Examples of bad interviews as well as links for interviewees can be found at **http://www.quintcareers.com/wild_card_interview_questions.html and http://www.garywill.com/worksearch/worst.htm**

For interviewing tips for applicants, go to **http://www.careercc.com/interv3.shtml, http://www.quintcareers.com/intvres.html, and http://www.ctdol.state.ct.us/progsupt/jobsrvce/intervie.htm**

A summary of common biases in the unstructured interview is at **http://www.indiana.edu/~uhrs/employment/best.html**

More panel interview information can be found at **http://www.liscareer.com/peters_interviews.htm and http://sciencecareers.sciencemag.org/career_magazine/previous_issues/articles/2000_12_15/noDOI.13270463381342766512**

For more information on situational interviews, visit **http://www.job-interview-site.com/situational-interview-questions-and-answers.html and https://na.theiia.org/iiarf/Public%20Documents/Situational%20Interviewing%20-%20Chattanooga.pdf**

Behavioural interviews are discussed at
http://www.jobinterviewquestions.org/questions/behavioral-interview.asp

Further information on both SI and BI interviews and on developing interview questions is found at
http://apps.opm.gov/ADT/ContentFiles/SIGuide09.08.08.pdf

More information on job knowledge questions, as well as SI and BI questions, can be found at
http://www.psc-cfp.gc.ca/ppc-cpp/acs-cmptnc-evl-cmptnc/strctr-slctn-eng.htm and http://mmsearch.com/inc/landing_pages/int_prep/main.php

For more information on employment interviewing and human rights in Canada, visit
http://www.canadavisa.com/canada-immigration-employment-interviews.html

DISCUSSION QUESTIONS

1. Describe the multiple phases of the employment interview.
2. What factors affect employment interview decisions?
3. What are the different errors or biases that commonly occur as part of a traditional employment interview?
4. What is a situational interview? What role does a critical incident play in formulating situational questions?
5. What is a behaviour description interview? What does it have in common with a situational interview? How does it differ?
6. What is an experience-based interview? How do experience-based interviews differ from behaviour description interviews?
7. How do structured interviews compare to traditional interviews in terms of reliability and validity?
8. Why is a scoring guide crucial to the success of a structured interview?
9. Why is a structured employment interview likely to be more defensible than other types of employment interviews?
10. Which is more effective–a situational interview or a behaviour description interview?
11. Why do many high-tech organizations use puzzle interviews? Are puzzle interviews effective for employee selection? Why or why not?
12. How might Multiple Mini-Interviews be used effectively by employers? In what situations are they most likely to be most effective?
13. Why do many employers resist using structured interviews? How would you encourage more employers to use structured interview techniques?

EXERCISES

INTERVIEW CONSTRUCTION

1. Several of the websites that are listed in this chapter provide guidance on how to write SI and BI questions (e.g., http://apps.opm.gov/ADT/ContentFiles/

SIGuide09.08.08.pdf). You might find these sites helpful for the following exercises.

a. Select a job you have done or know well. Identify the five most important tasks for this job.
b. For each of the five tasks, think of examples of both effective and ineffective performance that you have observed or have been a part of (e.g., critical incidents).
c. For each task, write an SI or a BI question. Use the critical incidents to develop a three-point scoring guide (example of a poor answer, a typical answer, and a good answer).

This exercise can be completed individually or in small groups of three to five. The product of the exercise is used in the role-play that follows below. An alternative to selecting a job with which participants are familiar is to have participants develop an interview for the job of "Course Instructor."

INTERVIEW QUESTION WRITING

2. Are the following good interview questions? If not, how would you change them?
   a. "How did you get along with your supervisor?"
   b. "Do you follow policies, rules, and procedures carefully?"
3. "Are you an organized worker?" is obviously not a good interview question because it is transparent and requests a self-evaluation. Is the following wording satisfactory? If not, why not, and how would you change it? "Can you give me an example of how organized you are?"
4. Rewrite the following questions to make them more effective.
   a. "Are you able to handle stress?"
   b. "How are you at meeting deadlines?"
   c. "Do you have problems working closely with others?"
   d. "When you make a mistake, what do you do to fix it?"
   e. "How are you at solving problems?"
   f. "Do have any problems communicating with people?"
   g. "How do you feel about staying late to finish a project?"
   h. "Are you a good leader? Can you motivate others?"
   i. "What do you do when you encounter obstacles to meeting your goals?"
   j. "Are you a good planner?"

PERSONALITY CHARACTERISTICS ASSESSMENT

5. Organizations exist in an increasingly dynamic environment. As a result, jobs change and employees are required to move around the organization, to do a variety of tasks, to develop multiple skills, and to "retool" or upgrade themselves on an ongoing basis. Employees are being hired less for specific job skills and more for their abilities to fit themselves to the needs of the organization. Organizations are looking for employees

who are innovative, flexible, willing to learn, and conscientious, and who fit into the organizational culture–in other words, those who are good organizational citizens. (You may want to review the sections "Job Performance as a Multidimensional Concept," "A Multidimensional Model of Job Performance," and "Predicting Task, Contextual, and Counterproductive Job Performance" in Chapter 5, which address these issues.)

a. Can the employment interview be used to assess such personality characteristics effectively? How?

b. Are there better selection tools than the interview for assessing these characteristics? If so, what are they and why are they superior? If not, why not?

c. Does the assessment of organizational fit and relevant personality attributes pose a danger to human rights? If so, how? If not, why not? How might you reduce the dangers of human rights violations while still pursuing employees who fit into the organizational culture?

INTERVIEW ROLE-PLAY

6. a. Form small groups of between three and five. Assign the role of applicant to one group member and the role of interviewer to another. The remaining members of the group serve as observers. The applicant is to be interviewed for one of the jobs selected for the Interview Construction exercise (pages 448–449).

   b. As a group, select five self-evaluation questions from the list in Recruitment and Selection Today 9.5 (page 418). The interviewer is to use these questions to begin interviewing the applicant for the job.

   c. Next, the interviewer is to use the five job-relevant questions developed in the Interview Construction exercise (pages 448–449).

   d. While the interviewer is conducting the interview, the observers should record their answers to the following questions:

      i. How do the answers to the first five questions differ from the answers to the second five questions?

      ii. Does one set of questions provide better information on which to base a selection decision? If so, which one?

      iii. Is there a difference between the two question sets in terms of how much time the applicant spends talking? If so, which takes more time and why?

      iv. Of the second set of questions, are there any questions that don't seem to work as well as they should? If so, why? How would you improve these questions?

      v. How useful is the scoring guide? Would you recommend any modifications to the scoring guide? If so, how would you change it?

   e. After the interview, the observers are to debrief the interviewer and the applicant. How did they perceive the relative effectiveness of the two sets of questions? Where did they experience difficulties? The observers should also provide feedback to both the interviewer and the applicant as to how they might improve their interview performance.

This role-play can be conducted as a class demonstration with one interviewer and one applicant as role-players and the remainder of the class as observers. A discussion of the relative effectiveness of the two question sets and the effectiveness of the interviewer and applicant can be held with the entire class.

CASE

Cango Distribution (not the actual name) is a large, rapidly growing, multi-national transportation logistics and delivery company. The company has administrative offices in Toronto and New York with about 150 and 500 administrative employees, respectively. In addition, the company has delivery depots in over 200 cities in North America (as well as other depots around the world). There are about 1500 employees distributed in depots across Canada and another 6500 employees across the U.S. (and a total of about 30 000 employees worldwide). Hiring for field operations (e.g., linehaul drivers, couriers, dispatchers, customer service agents, data systems agents, customs brokerage agents, package handling/sorting, warehouse operations, etc.) is done at the local depots, although policies and procedures are developed at the head offices and recruitment is also centralized (e.g., websites, advertising, posting jobs).

Job listings are up 186 percent in the transportation/logistics industry as a whole and, given the rapid growth of the company and industry demand, Cango will have strong competition from other organizations in recruiting new talent and they expect the bulk of new hires to come from the "millennial" generation (i.e., those born between the early 1980s and the early 2000s). In addition to the recruitment challenge, Cango is concerned about maximizing retention. Retention is an important concern because preliminary research suggests that millennials are likely to be "job hoppers." According to the U.S. Department of Labor statistics, most millennials will have ten jobs by the time they turn 38. Expending resources to hire employees who only stay a short time is not cost-effective.

A related concern is the reputation millennials have as the "instant gratification generation." According to a survey conducted by *I Love Rewards*,[316] two-thirds of respondents indicated they want to be rewarded early and often for their individual efforts. Razor Suleman, the chief executive and founder of *I Love Rewards*, indicates that the expectations of millennials will likely exceed the reality of entry-level jobs. That leaves recruiters with the challenge of getting potential hires excited about the company without painting too rosy a picture.

Until now Cango has left the hiring process to the local depots. However, the company is concerned that this has resulted in rather haphazard selection procedures which often result in poor hiring decisions. Cango wants to standardize selection procedures by implementing new testing procedures as well as structured interviews that would be used across all depots. The company hopes that the new selection procedures will not only improve its ability to select better performers but will also reduce the likelihood of turnover among its employees.

QUESTIONS

1. Do you agree with the findings of the *I Love Rewards* survey and the comments by the chief executive and founder of *I Love Rewards*, Razor Suleman, concerning the motivation and attitudes of millennials? Why or why not? In what other ways do you think millennials differ from older employees?
2. What measures can Cango take to maximize the likelihood of attracting and retaining millinial employees? What part would the selection system play in these measures?

3. Does the fact that millennials are a major recruitment target of Cango now and in the future have implications for how structured interviews should be developed and/or used with this cohort? If not, why not? If so, how might structured interviews be adapted for this group?
4. Select one of the occupations available at Cango (i.e., linehaul drivers, couriers, dispatchers, customer service agents, data systems agents, customs brokerage agents, package handling/sorting, warehouse operations) and locate the summary report for the tasks performed and the KSAOs required for the occupation at http://www.onetonline.org. Develop five SI and five BI questions to assess some of the KSAOs relevant to the occupation you selected.
5. One of the concerns at Cango is employee retention. Develop two or three interview questions that would allow you to assess the likelihood that an applicant is likely to stay at Cango for a longer period of time. Do you believe the questions you developed will result in an honest answer from the applicants? If so, why? If not, why not? How might you assess the concern about employee retention in a less transparent way?

// ENDNOTES

1 Rowe, P.M., M.C. Williams, and A.L. Day. 1994. "Selection Procedures in North America." *International Journal of Selection and Assessment* 2: 74–79.

2 Levashina, J., C.J. Hartwell, F.P. Morgeson, and M.A. Campion. 2014. "The Structured Employment Interview: Narrative and Quantitative Review of the Research Literature." *Personnel Psychology* 67: 241–93.

3 Mann, S.M., and J. Chowhan. 2011. "Selection Practices in Canadian Firms: An Empirical Investigation." *International Journal of Selection and Assessment* 19: 435–37.

4 Kinicki, A.J., C.A. Lockwood, P.W. Hom, and R.W. Griffeth. 1990. "Interviewer Predictions of Applicant Qualifications and Interviewer Validity: Aggregate and Individual Analysis." *Journal of Applied Psychology* 75: 477–86.

5 Sanyal, R., and T. Guvenli. 2004. "Personnel Selection in a Comparative Setting: Evidence from Israel, Slovenia, and the USA." *Journal of East–West Business* 10: 5–27.

6 Macan, T. 2009. "The Employment Interview: A Review of Current Studies and Directions for Future Research." *Human Resource Management Review* 19: 203–18.

7 Di Milia, L. 2004. "Australian Management Selection Practices: Closing the Gap between Research Findings and Practice." *Asia Pacific Journal of Human Resources* 42: 214–28.

8 Simola, S.K., S. Taggar, and G.W. Smith. 2007. "The Employment Selection Interview: Disparity among Research-Based Recommendation, Current Practices and What Matters to Human Rights Tribunals." *Canadian Journal of Administrative Sciences* 24: 30–44.

9 Dixon, M., S. Wang, J. Calvin, B. Dineen, and E. Tomlinson. 2002. "The Panel Interview: A Review of Empirical Research and Guidelines for Practice." *Public Personnel Management* 31: 397–428.

10 Motowidlo, S.J., G.W. Carter, M.D. Dunnette, N. Tippins, S. Werner, J.R. Burnett, and M.J. Vaughan. 1992. "Studies of the Structured Behavioral Interview." *Journal of Applied Psychology* 77: 571–87.

11 Latham, G.P., and D.P. Skarlicki. 1995. "Criterion-Related Validity of the Situational and Patterned Behavior Description Interviews with Organizational Citizenship Behavior." *Human Performance* 8: 67–80.

12 Pulakos, E.D., and N. Schmitt. 1995. "Experience-Based and Situational Interview Questions: Studies of Validity." *Personnel Psychology* 48: 289–308.

13 Huffcutt, A., J.M. Conway, J.P.I. Roth, and N.S. Stone. 2001. "Identification and Meta-Analytic Assessment of Psychological Constructs Measured in Employment Interviews." *Journal of Applied Psychology* 86: 897–913.

14 Posthuma, R.A., F.P. Morgeson, and M.A. Campion. 2002. "Beyond Employment Interview Validity: A Comprehensive Narrative Review of Recent Research and Trends over Time." *Personnel Psychology* 55: 1–81.

15 Sue-Chan, C., and G.P. Latham. 2004. "The Situational Interview as a Predictor of Academic and Team Performance: A Study of the Mediating Effects of Cognitive Ability and Emotional Intelligence." *International Journal of Selection and Assessment* 12: 312–20.

16 Maurer, S.D. 2006. "Using Situational Interviews to Assess Engineering Applicant Fit to Work Group, Job, and Organizational Requirements." *Engineering Management Journal* 18: 27–35.

17 Carless, S.A., and A. Imber. 2007. "The Influence of Perceived Interviewer and Job and Organizational Characteristics on Applicant Attraction and Job Choice Intentions: The Role of Applicant Anxiety." *International Journal of Selection and Assessment* 15: 359–71.

18 Posthuma, R.A., F.P. Morgeson, and M.A. Campion. 2002.

19 Rynes, S.L., and D. Cable. 2003. "Recruitment Research in the Twenty-First Century." In W.C. Borman, D.R. Ilgen, and R.J. Klimoski, eds., *Industrial–Organizational Psychology*; I.B. Weiner, ed., *Handbook of Psychology* 12: 55–76. Hoboken, NJ: John Wiley and Sons.

20 Rynes, S. L., and D. Cable. 2003.

21 Cascio, W.F. 2005. "Strategies for Responsible Restructuring." *The Academy of Management Executive* 19: 39–50.

22 Rowe, P.M., M.C. Williams, and A.L. Day. 1994. "Selection Procedures in North America." *International Journal of Selection and Assessment* 2: 74–79.

23 Kutcher, E.J., J.D. Bragger, and J.L. Masco. 2013. "How Interviewees Consider Content and Context Cues to Person–Organization Fit." *International Journal of Selection and Assessment* 27: 294–308.

24 Schwab, D.P., and G.G. Henneman, III. 1969. "Relationship between Interview Structure and Interviewer Reliability in an Employment Interview Situation." *Journal of Applied Psychology* 53: 214–17.

25 Carpenter, R. 1995. "Geek Logic." *Canadian Business* 68: 57–58.

26 Dipboye, R.L. 2005. "The Selection/Recruitment Interview: Core Processes and Contexts." In A. Evers, N. Anderson, and O. Voskuijl, eds., *The Blackwell Handbook of Personnel Selection* (pp. 121—142). Malden, MA: Blackwell Publishing.

27 Webster, E.C. 1982. *The Employment Interview: A Social Judgement Process*. Schomberg, ON: S.I.P. Publications.

28 Immen, W. 2006. "Quick Encounters of the Hiring Kind." *The Globe and Mail* (February 8): C1.

29 Immen, W. 2006.

30 Wiesner, W.H., and S.F. Cronshaw. 1988. "A Meta-Analytic Investigation of the Impact of Interview Format and Degree of Structure on the Validity of the Employment Interview." *Journal of Occupational Psychology* 61: 275–90.

31 Huffcutt, A.I., and W. Arthur, Jr. 1994. "Hunter and Hunter (1984) Revisited: Interview Validity for Entry-Level Jobs." *Journal of Applied Psychology* 79: 184–90.

32 Dougherty, T.W., D.B. Turban, and J.C. Callender. 1994. "Confirming First Impressions in the Employment Interview: A Field Study of Interviewer Behavior." *Journal of Applied Psychology* 79: 659–65.

33 Macan, T.H., and R.L. Dipboye. 1990. "The Relationship of Pre-Interview Impressions to Selection and Recruitment Outcomes." *Personnel Psychology* 43: 745–68.

34 Reilly, N.P., S.P. Bocketti, S.A. Maser, and C.L. Wennet. 2006. "Benchmarks Affect Perceptions of Prior Disability in a Structured Interview." *Journal of Business and Psychology* 20: 489–500.

35 Dipboye, R.L. 2005. "The Selection/Recruitment Interview: Core Processes and Contexts." In A. Evers, N. Anderson, and O. Voskuijl, eds., *The Blackwell Handbook of Personnel Selection* (pp. 121—142). Malden, MA: Blackwell Publishing.

36 Dipboye, R.L. 2005.

37 Latham, G.P., and Z. Millman. 2001. "Context and the Employment Interview." In J.F. Gubrium and J.A. Holstein, eds., *Handbook of Interview Research: Context and Method*. Thousand Oaks, CA: Sage Publications.

38 Huffcutt, A.I., C.H. Van Iddekinge, and P.L. Roth. 2011. "Understanding Applicant Behavior in Employment Interviews: A Theoretical Model of Interviewee Performance." *Human Resource Management Review* 21: 353–67.

39 Kohn, L.S., and R.L. Dipboye. 1998. "The Effects of Interview Structure on Recruiting Outcomes." *Journal of Applied Social Psychology* 28: 821–43.

40 Huffcutt, A.I., C.H. Van Iddekinge, and P.L. Roth. 2011.

41 Ibid.

42 Ibid.

43 Liden, R.C., C.L. Martin, and C.K. Parsons. 1993. "Interviewer and Applicant Behaviors in Employment Interviews." *Academy of Management Journal* 36: 372–86.

44 Liden, R.C., C.L. Martin, and C.K. Parsons. 1993.

45 Huffcutt, A.I., C.H. Van Iddekinge, and P.L. Roth. 2011.

46 DeGroot, T., and J. Gooty. 2009. "Can Nonverbal Cues Be Used to Make Meaningful Personality Attributions in Employment Interviews?" *Journal of Business and Psychology* 24: 179–192.

47 Sears, G.J., and P.M. Rowe. 2003. "A Personality-Based Similar-to-Me Effect in the Employment Interview: Conscientiousness, Affect-Versus Competence-Mediates Interpretations, and the Role of Job Relevance." *Canadian Journal of Behavioural Science* 35: 13–24.

48 Sheppard, L.D., R.D. Goffin, R.J. Lewis, and J. Olson. 2011. "The Effect of Target Attractiveness and Rating Method on the Accuracy of Trait Ratings." *Journal of Personnel Psychology* 10(1): 24–33.

49 Barrick, M.R., J. Shaffer, and S.D. DeGrassi. 2009. "What You See May Not Be What You Get: Relationships among Self-Presentation Tactics and Ratings of Interview and Job Performance. *Journal of Applied Psychology* 94, 1394–1412.

50 Huffcutt, A.I. 2011. "An Empirical Review of the Employment Interview Construct Literature." *International Journal of Selection and Assessment* 19: 62–81.

51 Middendorf, C.H., and T.H. Macan. 2002. "Note-Taking in the Employment Interview: Effects on Recall and Judgments." *Journal of Applied Psychology* 87: 293–303.

52 Bozionelos, N. 2005. "When the Inferior Candidate Is Offered the Job: The Selection Interview as a Political and Power Game." *Human Relations* 58: 1605–31.

53 Latham, G.P., and Z. Millman. 2001. "Context and the Employment Interview." In J.F. Gubrium and J.A. Holstein, eds., *Handbook of Interview Research: Context and Method*. Thousand Oaks, CA: Sage Publications.

54 Billsberry, J. 2007. *Experiencing Recruitment and Selection*. Chichester, England: John Wiley and Sons.

55 Campion, M.A., D.K. Palmer, and J.E. Campion. 1997. "A Review of Structure in the Selection Interview." *Personnel Psychology* 50: 655–702.

56 Goldberg, C., and D.J. Cohen. 2004. "Walking the Walk and Talking the Talk: Gender Differences in the Impact of Interviewing Skills on Applicant Assessments." *Group & Organization Management* 29: 369–84.

57 Barrick, M.R., J. Shaffer, and S.D. DeGrassi. 2009.

58 Levashina, J., and M.A. Campion. 2007. "Measuring Faking in the Employment Interview: Development and Validation on an Interview Faking Behavior Scale." *Journal of Applied Psychology* 92: 1638–56.

59 Levashina, J., and M.A. Campion. 2007.

60 Huffcutt, A.I. 2011.

61 Swider, B.W., M.R. Barrick, T.B. Harris, and A.C. Stoverink. 2011. "Managing and Creating an Image in the Interview: The Role of Interviewee Initial Impressions." Journal of Applied Psychology 96: 1275–88.

62 Roulin, N., A. Bangerter, and J. Levashina. 2014. "Interviewers' Perceptions of Impression Management in Employment Interviews." Journal of Managerial Psychology 29: 141–63.

63 Buhler, P. 2007. "Managing in the New Millennium: Ten Keys to Better Hiring." *SuperVision* 68 (November): 17–20.

64 Ramsey, R.D. 2011, January. "The Art of Interviewing Final Job Candidates." *Supervision* 72: 3–5.

65 Webster, E.C. 1964. *Decision Making in the Employment Interview*. Montreal: Industrial Relations Centre, McGill University.

66 Webster, E.C. 1982.

67 Dipboye, R.L. 1992. *Selection Interviews: Core Process Perspectives*. Cincinnati, OH: South-Western Publishing.

68 Jelf, G.S. 1999. "A Narrative Review of Post-1989 Employment Interview Research." *Journal of Business and Psychology* 14: 25–58.

69 Posthuma, R.A., F.P. Morgeson, and M.A. Campion. 2002.

70 Macan, T. 2009.

71 Garcia, M.F., R.A. Posthuma, and A. Colella. 2008. "Fit Perceptions in the Employment Interview: The Role of Similarity, Liking, and Expectations." *Journal of Occupational and Organizational Psychology* 81: 173–89.

72 Sears, G.J., and P.M. Rowe. 2003.

73 Dougherty, T.W., D.B. Turban, and J.C. Callender. 1994.

74 Macan, T.H., and R.L. Dipboye. 1990.

75 DeGroot, T., and S.J. Motowidlo. 1999.

76 Macan, T. 2009.

77 Tucker, D.H., and P.M. Rowe. 1977. "Consulting the Application Form Prior to the Interview: An Essential Step in the Selection Process." *Journal of Applied Psychology* 62: 283–88.

78 Tullar, W.L., T.W. Mullins, and S.A. Caldwell. 1979. "Relational Control in the Employment Interview." *Journal of Applied Psychology* 64: 669–74.

79 Dipboye, R.L., C. Stramler, and G.A. Fontenelle. 1984. "The Effects of Application on Recall of Information from the Interview." *Academy of Management Journal* 27: 561–75.

80 Rowe, P.M. 1963. "Individual Differences in Selection Decisions." *Journal of Applied Psychology* 47: 986–93.

81 Dougherty, T.W., D.B. Turban, and J.C. Callender. 1994.

82 Macan, T.H., and R.L. Dipboye. 1990.

83 Dipboye, R.L., C. Stramler, and G.A. Fontenelle. 1984.

84 Farr, J.L., and C.M. York. 1975. "The Amount of Information and Primacy–Recency Effects in Recruitment Decisions." *Personnel Psychology* 28: 233–38.

85 Dipboye, R.L., C. Stramler, and G.A. Fontenelle. 1984.

86 Farr, J.L., and C.M. York. 1975.

87 Rowe, P.M. 1963.

88 Wexley, K.N., G.A. Yukl, S.Z. Kovacs, and R.E. Saunders. 1972. "Importance of Contrast Effects in Employment Interviews." *Journal of Applied Psychology* 56: 45–48.

89 Dougherty, T.W., D.B. Turban, and J.C. Callender. 1994.

90 Macan, T.H., and R.L. Dipboye. 1990.

91 Dipboye, R.L. 1992. *Selection Interviews: Process Perspectives*. Cincinnati, OH: South-Western Publishing.

92 Rowe, P.M. 1984. "Decision Processes in Personnel Selection." *Canadian Journal of Behavioural Science* 16: 326–37.

93 Huffcutt, A.I., and P.L. Roth. 1998. "Racial Group Differences in Employment Interview Evaluations." *Journal of Applied Psychology* 83: 179–89.

94 Graves, L.M., and G.N. Powell. 1996. "Sex Similarity, Quality of the Employment Interview and Recruiters' Evaluation of Actual Applicants." *Journal of Occupational and Organizational Psychology* 69: 243–61.

95 Howard, J.L., and G.R. Ferris. 1996. "The Employment Interview Context: Social and Situational Influences on Interviewer Decisions." *Journal of Applied Social Psychology* 26: 112–36.

96 DeGroot, T., and S.J. Motowidlo. 1999. "Why Visual and Vocal Interview Cues Can Affect Interviewers' Judgments and Predict Job Performance." *Journal of Applied Psychology* 84: 986–93.

97 DeGroot, T., and D. Kluemper. 2007. "Evidence of Predictive and Incremental Validity of Personality Factors, Vocal Attractiveness and the Situational Interview." *International Journal of Selection and Assessment* 15: 30–39.

98 Liden, R.C., C.L. Martin, and C.K. Parsons. 1993.

99 Deprez-Sims, A.S., and S.B. Morris. 2010. "Accents in the Workplace: Their Effects during a Job Interview." *International Journal of Psychology* 45: 417–26.

100 Morrow, P.C. 1990. "Physical Attractiveness and Selection Decision Making." *Journal of Management* 16(1): 45–60.

101 Sheppard, L.D., R.D. Goffin, R.J. Lewis, and J. Olson. 2011.

102 McDaniel, M.A., D.L. Whetzel, F.L. Schmidt, and S.D. Maurer. 1994. "The Validity of Employment Interviews: A Comprehensive Review and Meta-Analysis." *Journal of Applied Psychology* 79: 599–616.

103 Wiesner, W.H., and S.F. Cronshaw. 1988.

104 Huffcutt, A.I., and W. Arthur, Jr. 1994.

105 McDaniel, M.A., D.L. Whetzel, F.L. Schmidt, and S.D. Maurer. 1994.

106 Wiesner, W.H., and S.F. Cronshaw. 1988.

107 Schmitt, N. 1976. "Social and Situational Determinants of Interview Decisions: Implications for the Employment Interview." *Personnel Psychology* 29: 79–101.

108 Janz, T. 1982. "Initial Comparisons of Patterned Behavior Description Interviews versus Unstructured Interviews." *Journal of Applied Psychology* 67: 577–80.

109 Latham, G.P., L.M. Saari, E.D. Pursell, and M.A. Campion. 1980. "The Situational Interview." *Journal of Applied Psychology* 65: 422–27.

110 Latham, G.P., and L.M. Saari. 1984. "Do People Do What They Say? Further Studies on the Situational Interview." *Journal of Applied Psychology* 69: 569–73.

111 Arvey, R.D., and J.E. Campion. 1982. "The Employment Interview: A Summary and Review of Recent Research." *Personnel Psychology* 35: 281–322.

112 Harris, M.M. 1989. "Reconsidering the Employment Interview: A Review of Recent Literature and Suggestions for Future Research." *Personnel Psychology* 42: 691–726.

113 Webster, E.C. 1964.

114 Levashina, J., C.J. Hartwell, F.P. Morgeson, and M.A. Campion. 2014. "The Structured Employment Interview: Narrative and Quantitative Review of the Research Literature." *Personnel Psychology* 67: 241–93.

115 Huffcutt, A.I., S.S. Culbertson, and W.S. Weyhrauch. 2013. "Employment Interview Reliability: New Meta-Analytic Estimates by Structure and Format." *International Journal of Selection and Assessment* 21: 264–76.

116 Huffcutt, A.I., and W. Arthur, Jr. 1994.

117 Ibid.

118 Campion, M.A., D.K. Palmer, and J.E. Campion. 1997.

119 Burnett, J.R., C. Fan, S.J. Motowidlo, and T. DeGroot. 1998. "Interview Notes and Validity." *Personnel Psychology* 51: 375–96.

120 Campion, M.A., D.K. Palmer, and J.E. Campion. 1997.

121 Ibid.

122 Dixon, M., S. Wang, J. Calvin, B. Dineen, and E. Tomlinson. 2002.

123 Simola, S.K., S. Taggar, and G.W. Smith. 2007.

124 Dixon, M., S. Wang, J. Calvin, B. Dineen, and E. Tomlinson. 2002.

125 Van Iddekinge, C.H., C.E. Sager, J.L. Burnfield, and T.S. Heffener. 2006. "The Variability of Criterion-Related Validity Estimates among Interviewers and Interview Panels." *International Journal of Selection and Assessment* 14: 193–205.

126 Bayne, R., C. Fletcher, and J. Colwell. 1983. "Board and Sequential Interviews in Selection: An Experimental Study of Their Comparative Effectiveness." *Personnel Review* 12: 14–19.

127 Arvey, R.D., and J.E. Campion. 1982.

128 Conway, J.M., R.A. Jako, and D.F. Goodman. 1995. "A Meta-Analysis of Inter-Rater and Internal Consistency Reliability of Selection Interviews." *Journal of Applied Psychology* 80: 565–79.

129 Wiesner, W.H., and S.F. Cronshaw. 1988.

130 Dixon, M., S. Wang, J. Calvin, B. Dineen, and E. Tomlinson. 2002.

131 Huffcutt, A.I., S.S. Culbertson, and W.S. Weyhrauch. 2013.

132 Campion, M.A., D.K. Palmer, and J.E. Campion. 1997.

133 Macan, T. 2009.

134 Huffcutt, A.I., S.S. Culbertson, and W.S. Weyhrauch. 2013.

135 Hackett, R.D., L.M. Lapierre, and H.P. Gardiner. 2004. "A Review of Canadian Human Rights Cases Involving the Employment Interview." *Canadian Journal of Administrative Sciences* 21: 215–28.

136 Hackett, R.D., J.B. Rose, and J. Pyper. 2000. "The Employment Interview: An Analysis of Canadian Labour Arbitration Decisions." In K. Whitaker, J. Sack, M. Gunderson, R. Filion, and B. Bohuslawsy, eds., *Labour Arbitration Yearbook 1999–2000,* Vol. 1 (pp. 233–250). Toronto: Lancaster House.

137 Latham, G.P., L.M. Saari, E.D. Purcell, and M.A. Campion. 1980.

138 Latham, G.P., and L.M. Saari. 1984.

139 Latham, G.P., and C. Sue-Chan. 1999. "A Meta-Analysis of the Situational Interview: An Enumerative Review of Reasons for Its Validity." *Canadian Psychology* 40: 56–67.

140 Flanagan, J.C. 1954. "The Critical Incident Technique." *Psychological Bulletin* 51: 327–58.

141 Reilly, N.P., S.P. Bocketti, S.A. Maser, and C.L. Wennet. 2006.

142 Fishbein, M., and I. Ajzen. 1975. *Belief, Attitude, Intention, and Behavior: An Introduction to Theory and Research*. Reading, MA: Addison-Wesley.

143 Latham, G.P., and C. Sue-Chan. 1999. "A Meta-Analysis of the Situational Interview: An Enumerative Review of Reasons for Its Validity." *Canadian Psychology* 40: 56–67.

144 Taylor, P.J., and B. Small. 2002. "Asking Applicants What They Would Do versus What They Did Do: A Meta-Analytic Comparison of Situational and Past Behaviour Employment Interview Questions." *Journal of Occupational and Organizational Psychology* 75: 277–94.

145 Huffcutt, A.I., J.M. Conway, P.L. Roth, and U.C. Klehe. 2004. "The Impact of Job Complexity and Study Design on Situational and Behavior Description Interview Validity." *International Journal of Selection and Assessment* 12: 262–73.

146 Janz, T. 1982.

147 Janz, T. 1989. "The Patterned Behavior Description Interview: The Best Prophet of the Future Is the Past." In R.W. Eder and G.R. Ferris, eds., *The Employment Interview: Theory, Research, and Practice* (pp. 158–168). Newbury Park, CA: Sage Publications.

148 Latham, G.P., L.M. Saari, E.D. Pursell, and M.A. Campion. 1980.

149 Ghiselli, E.E. 1966. "The Validity of the Personnel Interview." *Personnel Psychology* 19: 389–94.

150 Levashina, J., C.J. Hartwell, F.P. Morgeson, and M.A. Campion. 2014.

151 Janz, T., L. Hellervik, and D.C. Gilmore. 1986. *Behavior Description Interviewing: New, Accurate, Cost-Effective*. Boston, MA: Allyn and Bacon.

152 Campion, M.A., D.K. Palmer, and J.E. Campion. 1997.

153 Taylor, P.J., and B. Small. 2002.

154 Levashina, J., C.J. Hartwell, F.P. Morgeson, and M.A. Campion. 2014.

155 Wernimont, P.F., and J.P. Campbell. 1968. "Signs, Samples, and Criteria." *Journal of Applied Psychology* 52: 372–76.

156 Taylor, P.J., and B. Small. 2002.

157 Ibid.

158 Huffcutt, A.I., J.M. Conway, P.L. Roth, and U.C. Klehe. 2004.

159 Campion, M.A., E.D. Pursell, and B.K. Brown. 1988. "Structured Interviewing: Raising the Psychometric Properties of the Employment Interview." *Personnel Psychology* 41: 25–42.

160 McCarthy, J.M., C.H. Van Iddekinge, and M.A Campion. 2010. "Are Highly Structured Job Interviews Resistant to Demographic Similarity Effects?" *Personnel Psychology* 63: 325–59.

161 Campion, M.A., E.D. Pursell, and B.K. Brown. 1988.

162 Wright, P.M., P.A. Lichtenfels, and E.D. Pursell. 1989. "The Structured Interview: Additional Studies and a Meta-Analysis." *Journal of Occupational Psychology* 62: 191–99.

163 Kennedy, R. 1985. "Validation of Five Structured Interviews." Unpublished master's thesis. East Carolina University.

164 Hedge, J.W., and M.S. Teachout. 1992. "An Interview Approach to Work Sample Criterion Measurement." *Journal of Applied Psychology* 77: 453–61.

165 Ree, M.J., J.A. Earles, and M.S. Teachout. 1994. "Predicting Job Performance: Not Much More Than *g*." *Journal of Applied Psychology* 79: 518–24.

166 Campion, M.A., E.D. Pursell, and B.K. Brown. 1988.

167 Klehe, U.C., and G.P. Latham. 2006. "What Would You Do–Really or Ideally? Constructs Underlying the Behavior Description Interview and the Situational Interview in Predicting Typical Versus Maximum Performance." *Human Performance* 19: 357–82.

168 Krajewski, H.T., R.D. Goffin, J.M. McCarthy, M.G. Rothstein, and N. Johnston. 2006. "Comparing the Validity of Structured Interviews for Managerial-Level Employees: Should We Look to the Past or Focus on the Future?" *Journal of Occupational and Organizational Psychology* 79: 411–32.

169 Taylor, P.J., and B. Small. 2002.

170 Ibid.

171 Levashina, J., C.J. Hartwell, F.P. Morgeson, and M.A. Campion. 2014.

172 Huffcutt, A.I., J. Weekley, W.H. Wiesner, T. DeGroot, and C. Jones. 2001. "Comparison of Situational and Behavior Description Interview Questions for Higher Level Positions." *Personnel Psychology* 54: 619–44.

173 Huffcutt, A.I., J.M. Conway, P.L. Roth, and U.C. Klehe. 2004.

174 Klehe, U.C., and G.P. Latham. 2005. "The Predictive and Incremental Validity of the Situational and Patterned Behavior Description Interviews for Teamplaying Behavior." *International Journal of Selection and Assessment* 13: 108–15.

175 Day, A.L., and S.A. Carroll. 2003.

176 Ibid.

177 Berry, C.M., P.R. Sackett, and R.N. Landers. 2007. "Revisiting Interview–Cognitive Ability Relationships: Attending to Specific Range Restriction Mechanism in Meta-Analysis." *Personnel Psychology* 60: 837–74.

178 Cortina, J.M., N.B. Goldstein, S.C. Payne, H.K. Davison, and S.W. Gilliland. 2000. "The Incremental Validity of Interview Scores Over and Above Cognitive Ability and Conscientiousness Scores." *Personnel Psychology* 53: 325–51.

179 Ibid.

180 Huffcutt, A., J.M. Conway, J.P.I. Roth, and N.S. Stone. 2001.

181 Salgado, J.S., and S. Moscoso. 2002. "Comprehensive Meta-Analysis of the Construct Validity of the Employment Interview." *European Journal of Work and Organizational Psychology* 11: 299–324.

182 Roth, P.L., C.H. Van Iddekinge, A.I. Huffcutt, and M.J. Schmit. 2005. "Personality Saturation in Structured Interviews." *International Journal of Selection and Assessment* 13: 261–73.

183 Van Iddekinge, C.H., P.H. Raymark, and P.L. Roth. 2005. "Assessing Personality with a Structured Employment Interview: Construct-Related Validity and Susceptibility to Response Inflation." *Journal of Applied Psychology* 90: 536–52.

184 Roth, P.L., C.H. Van Iddekinge, A.I. Huffcutt, and M.J. Schmit. 2005.

185 Huffcutt, A., J.M. Conway, J.P.I. Roth, and N.S. Stone. 2001.

186 Salgado, J.S., and S. Moscoso. 2002.

187 Huffcutt, A.I., J. Weekley, W.H. Wiesner, T. DeGroot, and C. Jones. 2001.

188 Huffcutt, A.I., S.S. Culbertson, and W.S. Weyhrauch. 2013.

189 Hamdani, M.R., S. Valcea, and M.R. Buckley. 2014. "The Relentless Pursuit of Construct Validity in the Design of Employment Interviews." *Human Resource Management Review* 24: 160–76.

190 Ellis, A.P.J., B.J. West, A.M. Ryan, and R.P DeShon. 2002. "The Use of Impression Management Tactics in Structured Interviews: A Function of Question Type." *Journal of Applied Psychology* 87: 1200–08.

191 Peeters, H., and F. Lievens. 2006. "Verbal and Nonverbal Impression Management Tactics in Behavior Description and Situational Interviews." *International Journal of Selection and Assessment* 14: 206–22.

192 Kleinmann, M., and U.-C. Klehe. 2011. "Selling Oneself: Construct and Criterion-Related Validity of Impression Management in Structured Interviews." *Human Performance* 24: 29–46.

193 Van Iddekinge, C.H., L.A. McFarland, and P.H. Raymark. 2007. "Antecedents of Impression Management Use and Effectiveness in a Structured Interview." *Journal of Management* 33: 752–73.

194 Levashina, J., and M.A. Campion. 2007.

195 Kleinmann, M., and U.-C. Klehe. 2011.

196 Tsai, W.C., C.C. Chen, and S.F. Chiu. 2005. "Exploring Boundaries of the Effects of Applicant Impression Management Tactics in Job Interviews." *Journal of Management* 31: 108–25.

197 Barrick, M.R., J. Shaffer, and S.D. DeGrassi. 2009.

198 Levashina, J., C.J. Hartwell, F.P. Morgeson, and M.A. Campion. 2014.

199 Ibid.

200 Huffcutt, A., J.M. Conway, J.P.I. Roth, and N.S. Stone. 2001.

201 Maurer, S.D. 2006.

202 Lievens, F., and A. De Paepe. 2004. "An Empirical Investigation of Interviewer-Related Factors That Discourage the Use of High Structure Interviews." *Journal of Organizational Behavior* 25: 29–46.

203 Simola, S.K., S. Taggar, and G.W. Smith. 2007.

204 Lievens, F., and A. De Paepe. 2004.

205 Way, S.A., and J.W. Thacker. 1999. "Selection Practices: Where Are Canadian Organizations?" *HR Professional* 16: 33–37.

206 Simola, S.K., S. Taggar, and G.W. Smith. 2007.

207 Ibid.

208 Chapman, D.S., and D.I. Zweig. 2005. "Developing a Nomological Network for Interview Structure: Antecedents and Consequences of the Structured Selection Interview." *Personnel Psychology* 58: 673–702.

209 Chapman, D.S., and D.I. Zweig. 2005.

210 Chen, Y.C., W.C. Tsai, and C. Hu. 2008. "The Influences of Interviewer-Related and Situational Factors on Interviewer Reactions to High Structured Job Interviews." *The International Journal of Human Resource Management* 19: 1056–71.

211 Lievens, F., and A. De Paepe. 2004.

212 Posthuma, R.A., F.P. Morgeson, and M.A. Campion. 2002.

213 Hausknecht, J.P., D.V. Day, and S.C. Thomas. 2004. "Applicant Reactions to Selection Procedures: An Updated Model and Meta-Analysis." *Personnel Psychology* 57: 639–83.

214 Becton, J.B., H.S. Feild, W.F. Giles, and A. Jones-Farmer. 2008. "Racial Differences in Promotion Candidate Performance and Reactions to Selection Procedures: A Field Study in a Diverse Top-Management Context." *Journal of Organizational Behavior* 29: 265–85.

215 Cited in Posthuma, R.A., F.P. Morgeson, and M.A. Campion. 2002.

216 Chapman, D.S., and D.I. Zweig. 2005.

217 Seijts, G.H., and I. Kyei-Poku. 2010. "The Role of Situational Interviews in Fostering Positive Reactions to Selection Decisions." *Applied Psychology: An International Review* 59: 431–53.

218 Chapman, D.S., and P.M. Rowe. 2001. "The Impact of Videoconference Technology, Interview Structure, and Interviewer Gender on Interviewer Evaluations in the Employment Interview: A Field Experiment." *Journal of Occupational and Organizational Psychology* 74: 279–98.

219 Kohn, L.S., and R.L. Dipboye. 1998. "The Effects of Interview Structure on Recruiting Outcomes." *Journal of Applied Social Psychology* 28: 821–43.

220 Kohn, L.S., and R.L. Dipboye. 1998.

221 Tsai, W.C., C.C. Chen, and S.F. Chiu. 2005.

222 Kohn, L.S., and R.L. Dipboye. 1998.

223 Posthuma, R.A., F.P. Morgeson, and M.A. Campion. 2002.

224 Campion, M.A., D.K. Palmer, and J.E. Campion. 1997.

225 Hackett, R.D., L.M. Lapierre, and H.P. Gardiner. 2004.

226 Hackett, R.D., J.B. Rose, and J. Pyper. 2000.

227 Williamson, L.G., J.E. Campion, S.B. Malos, M.V. Roehling, and M.A. Campion. 1997. "Employment Interview on Trial: Linking Interview Structure with Litigation Outcomes." *Journal of Applied Psychology* 82: 900–12.

228 Hackett, R.D., L.M. Lapierre, and H.P. Gardiner. 2004.

229 Hackett, R.D., J.B. Rose, and J. Pyper. 2000.

230 Williamson, L.G., J.E. Campion, S.B. Malos, M.V. Roehling, and M.A. Campion. 1997.

231 Saks, A.M., and J.M. McCarthy. 2006. "Effects of Discriminatory Interview Questions and Gender on Applicant Reactions." *Journal of Business and Psychology* 21: 175–91.

232 Campion, M.A., D.K. Palmer, and J.E. Campion. 1997.

233 Ibid.

234 Maurer, S.D. 2002. "A Practitioner-Based Analysis of Interviewer Job Expertise and Scale Format as Contextual Factors in Situational Interviews." *Personnel Psychology* 55: 307–27.

235 Reilly, N.P, S.P. Bocketti, S.A. Maser, and C.L. Wennet. 2006.

236 Melchers, K.G., N. Lienhardt, M. Von Aarburg, and M. Kleinmann. 2011. "Is More Structure Really Better? A Comparison of Frame-of-Reference Training and Descriptively Anchored Rating Scales to Improve Interviewers' Rating Quality." *Personnel Psychology* 64: 53–87.

237 Hackett, R.D., L.M. Lapierre, and H.P. Gardiner. 2004.

238 Hackett, R.D., J.B. Rose, and J. Pyper. 2000.

239 Latham, G.P., L.M. Saari, E.D. Pursell, and M.A. Campion. 1980.

240 Webster, E.C. 1964.

241 Campion, M.A., D.K. Palmer, and J.E. Campion. 1997.

242 Wiesner, W.H. 1989. "The Contributions of Job Relevance, Timing, and Rating Scale to the Validity of the Employment Interview." In S.F. Cronshaw, chair, *Improving Interview Validity and Legal Defensibility through Structuring.* Symposium conducted at the 50th Annual Convention of the Canadian Psychological Association.

243 Day, A.L., and S.A. Carroll. 2003.

244 Nunnally, J.C., and I.H. Bernstein. 1994. *Psychometric Theory*, 3rd ed., New York: McGraw-Hill.

245 Schmidt, F.L., and R.D. Zimmerman. 2004. "A Counterintuitive Hypothesis about Employment Interview Validity and Some Supporting Evidence." *Journal of Applied Psychology* 89: 553–61.

246 Arvey, R.D., and J.E. Campion. 1982.

247 Blankenship, M.H., and S.J. Cesare. 1993. "Age Fairness in the Employment Interview: A Field Study." In R.D. Arvey, chair, *Perceptions, Theories, and Issues of Fairness in the Employment Interview.* Symposium presented at the 101st Annual Convention of the Psychological Association, Toronto.

248 Lin, T.R., G.H. Dobbins, and J.L. Farh. 1992. "A Field Study of Age and Race Similarity Effects on Interview Ratings in Conventional and Situational Interviews." *Journal of Applied Psychology* 77: 363–71.

249 Buckley, M.R., K.A. Jackson, M.C. Bolino, J.G. Veres, III, and H.S. Feild. 2007. "The Influence of Relational Demography on Panel Interview Ratings: A Field Experiment." *Personnel Psychology* 60: 627–46.

250 McFarland, L.A., A.M. Ryan, J.M. Sacco, and S.D. Kriska. 2004. "Examination of Structured Interview Ratings across Time: The Effects of Applicant Race, Rater Race, and Panel Composition." *Journal of Management* 30: 435–52.

251 McFarland, L.A., A.M. Ryan, J.M. Sacco, and S.D. Kriska. 2004.

252 Lin, T.R., G.H. Dobbins, and J.L. Farh. 1992.

253 Paullin, C. 1993. "Features of Structured Interviews Which Enhance Perceptions of Fairness." In R.D. Arvey, chair, *Perceptions, Theories, and Issues of Fairness in the Employment Interview.* Symposium presented at the 101st Annual Convention of the American Psychological Association, Toronto.

254 Motowidlo, S.J., G.W. Carter, M.D. Dunnette, N. Tippins, S. Werner, J.R. Burnett, and M.J. Vaughan. 1992.

255 Huffcutt, A.I., and P.L. Roth. 1998. "Racial and Group Differences in Employment Interview Evaluations." *Journal of Applied Psychology* 83: 179–89.

256 Lin, T.R., G.H. Dobbins, and J.L. Farh. 1992.

257 McCarthy, J.M., C.H. Van Iddekinge, and M.A Campion. 2010.

258 Brecher, E., J. Bragger, and E. Kutcher. 2006. "The Structured Interview: Reducing Bias toward Applicants with Disabilities." *Employee Responsibilities and Rights Journal* 18: 155–70.

259 Reilly, N.P., S.P. Bocketti, S.A. Maser, and C.L. Wennet. 2006.

260 Harris, M.M. 1993. "Fair or Foul: How Interview Questions Are Perceived." In R.D. Arvey, chair, *Perceptions, Theories, and Issues of Fairness in the Employment Interview*. Symposium presented at the 101st Annual Convention of the American Psychological Association, Toronto.

261 Williamson, L.G., J.E. Campion, S.B. Malos, M.V. Roehling, and M.A. Campion. 1997.

262 Seijts, G.H., and I. Kyei-Poku. 2010.

263 Campion, M.A., D.K. Palmer, and J.E. Campion. 1997.

264 Dipboye, R.L. 1992.

265 Posthuma, R.A., F.P. Morgeson, and M.A. Campion. 2002.

266 Campion, M.A., D.K. Palmer, and J.E. Campion. 1997.

267 Ibid.

268 Dipboye, R.L. 1992.

269 Conway, J.M., R.A. Jako, and D.F. Goodman. 1995.

270 Huffcutt, A.I., and D.J. Woehr. 1999. "Further Analysis of Employment Interview Validity: A Quantitative Evaluation of Interviewer-Related Structuring Methods." *Journal of Organizational Behavior* 20: 549–60.

271 Melchers, K.G., N. Lienhardt, M. Von Aarburg, and M. Kleinmann. 2011.

272 Carless, S.A., and A. Imber. 2007.

273 McCarthy, J., and R. Goffin. 2004. "Measuring Job Interview Anxiety: Beyond Weak Knees and Sweaty Palms." *Personnel Psychology* 57: 607–37.

274 McCarthy, J., and R. Goffin. 2004.

275 Maurer, T.J., and J.M. Solamon. 2006. "The Science and Practice of a Structured Employment Interview Coaching Program." *Personnel Psychology* 59: 433–56.

276 Jackson, S.E., P.M. Rowe, N.C. Hall, and L.M. Daniels. 2009. "Getting the Job: Attributional Retraining and the Employment Interview." *Journal of Applied Social Psychology* 39: 973–98.

277 Latham, G.P., and M.H. Budworth. 2006. "The Effect of Training in Verbal Self-Guidance on the Self-Efficacy and Performance of Native North Americans in the Selection Interview." *Journal of Vocational Behavior* 68: 516–23.

278 Maurer, T.J., J.M. Solamon, and M. Lippstreu. 2008. "How Does Coaching Interviewees Affect the Validity of a Structured Interview?" *Journal of Organizational Behavior* 29: 355–71.

279 Jackson, S.E., P.M. Rowe, N.C. Hall, and L.M. Daniels. 2009.

280 Maurer, T.J., J.M. Solamon, and M. Lippstreu. 2008.

281 Chapman, D.S., and P.M. Rowe. 2001.

282 Schmidt, F.L., and M. Rader. 1999. "Exploring the Boundary Conditions for Interview Validity: Meta-Analytic Validity Findings for a New Interview Type." *Personnel Psychology* 52: 445–64.

283 Chapman, D.S., and P.M. Rowe. 2002.

284 Martin, C.L., and D.H. Nagao. 1989. "Some Effects of Computerized Interviews on Job Applicant Responses." *Journal of Applied Psychology* 74: 72–80.

285 Sears, G.J., H. Zhang, W.H. Wiesner, R.D. Hackett, and Y. Yuan. 2013. "A Comparative Assessment of Videoconference and Face-to-Face Employment Interviews." *Management Decision* 51(8): 1733–52.

286 Meckenbach, G. 1997. "Your Next Job Interview Might Be at Home." *Computing Canada* 16: 1–4.

287 Chapman, D.S., and P.M. Rowe. 2001.

288 Van Iddekinge, C.H., P.H. Raymark, P.L. Roth, and H.S. Payne. 2006. "Comparing the Psychometric Characteristics of Ratings of Face-to-Face and Videotaped Structured Interviews." *International Journal of Selection and Assessment* 14: 347–59.

289 Sears, G.J., H. Zhang, W.H. Wiesner, R.D. Hackett, and Y. Yuan. 2013.

290 Chapman, D.S., and P.M. Rowe. 2002.

291 Chapman, D.S., and P.M. Rowe. 2001.

292 Honer, J., C.W. Wright, and C.J. Sablynski. 2006. "Puzzle Interviews: What Are They and What Do They Measure?" *Applied HRM Research* 11: 79–96.

293 Wright, C.W., C.J. Sablynski, T.M. Manson, and S. Oshiro. 2012. "Why Are Manhole Covers Round? A Laboratory Study of Reactions to Puzzle Interviews." *Journal of Applied Social Psychology* 42: 2834–57.

294 Honer, J., C.W. Wright, and C.J. Sablynski. 2006.

295 Wright, C.W., C.J. Sablynski, T.M. Manson, and S. Oshiro. 2012.

296 Eva, K.W., H.I. Reiter, J. Rosenfeld, and G.R. Norman. 2004. "The Relationship between Interviewers' Characteristics and Ratings Assigned during a Multiple Mini-Interview." *Academic Medicine* 79: 602–609.

297 Reiter, H.I., J. Rosenfeld, and L. Giordano. 2004. "Selection of Medical Students at McMaster University: A Quarter Century Later." *McMaster University Medical Journal* 2: 41–45.

298 Pau, A., K. Jeevaratnam, Y.S. Chen, A.A. Fall, C. Khoo, and V.D. Nadarajah. 2013. "The Multiple Mini-Interview (MMI) for Student Selection in Health Professions Training–A Systematic Review." *Medical Teacher* 35: 1027–41.

299 Kulasegaram, K., H.I. Reiter, W.H. Wiesner, R.D. Hackett, and G.R. Norman. 2010. "Non-association between Neo-5 Personality Tests and Multiple Mini-Interview." *Advances in Health Sciences Education* 15: 415–23.

300 Eva, K.W., H.I. Reiter, K. Trinh, P. Wasi, J. Rosenfeld, and G.R. Norman. 2009. "Predictive Validity of the Multiple Mini-Interview for Selecting Medical Trainees." *Medical Education* 43: 767–75.

301 Hofmeister, M., J. Lockyer, and R. Crutcher. 2009. "The Multiple Mini-Interview for Selection of International Medical Graduates into Family Medicine Residency Education." *Medical Education* 4: 573–79.

302 Reiter, H.I., K.W. Eva, J. Rosenfeld, and G.R. Norman. 2007. "Multiple Mini-Interviews Predict Clerkship and Licensing Examination Performance." *Medical Education* 4: 378–84.

303 Husbands, A., and J. Dowell. 2013. "The Predictive Validity of the Dundee Multiple Mini-Interview." *Medical Education* 47: 717–25.

304 Kulasegaram, K., H.I. Reiter, W.H. Wiesner, R.D. Hackett, and G.R. Norman. 2010.

305 Griffin, B., and I. Wilson. 2012. "Associations between the Big Five Personality Factors and Multiple Mini-Interviews." *Advances in Health Sciences Education* 17: 377–88.

306 Jerant, A., E. Griffin, J. Rainwater, M. Henderson, F. Sousa, K.D. Berkatis, J.J. Fenton, and P. Franks. 2012. "Does Applicant Personality Influence Multiple Mini-Interview Performance and Medical School Acceptance Offers?" *Academic Medicine* 87: 1250–59.

307 Shen, H., and A.L. Comrey. 1997. "Predicting Medical Students' Academic Performances by Their Cognitive Abilities and Personality Characteristics" *Academic Medicine* 72: 781–86.

308 Griffin, B., and I. Wilson. 2012.

309 Ibid.

310 Yen, W., R. Hovey, K. Hodowitz, and S. Zhang. 2011. "An Exploration of the Relationship between Emotional Intelligence (EI) and the Multiple Mini-Interview (MMI)." *Advances in Health Sciences Education* 16: 59–67.

311 Jerant, A., E. Griffin, J. Rainwater, M. Henderson, F. Sousa, K.D. Berkatis, J.J. Fenton, and P. Franks. 2012.

312 Eva, K.W., and C. Macala. 2014. "Multiple Mini-Interview Test Characteristics: 'Tis Better to Ask Candidates to Recall Than to Imagine." *Medical Education* 48: 604–13.

313 Buckley, R.M., A.M. Norris, and D.S. Wiese. 2000. "A Brief History of the Selection Interview: May the Next 100 Years Be More Fruitful." *Journal of Management History* 6: 113–26.

314 Levashina, J., C.J. Hartwell, F.P. Morgeson, and M.A. Campion. 2014.

315 Dipboye, R.L. 2005.

316 Covert, K. 2010, March 24. "Recruiting the Recruiter." *Financial Post*. Retrieved from http://www2.canada.com/news/women+risk+averse+study+finds/5331026/story.html?id=2718808&p=2

CHAPTER 10

DECISION MAKING

CHAPTER LEARNING OUTCOMES

This chapter considers ways of reducing subjectivity and error in making selection decisions by using scientific methods that maximize selection effectiveness and efficiency. It also discusses statistical methods of accomplishing employment equity objectives while maintaining the validity of the selection system.

AFTER READING THIS CHAPTER YOU SHOULD:

- appreciate the complexity of decision making in the employee selection context;
- be familiar with the sources of common decision-making errors in employee selection;
- understand the distinction between judgmental and statistical approaches to the collection and combination of applicant information;
- understand the advantages and disadvantages of various decision-making models;
- appreciate issues involved with group decision making;
- know the basic principles in the application of cutoff scores, banding, and top-down selection;
- understand the factors that need to be considered in making a job offer;
- understand the role of letters of employment and employment contracts in the job offer process;
- understand the issues and legal concerns, as well as potential dangers, that need to be considered in drafting and/or signing letters of employment or employment contracts; and
- be able to discuss the benefits of using best practices in recruitment and selection.

SELECTION DECISIONS: GUT FEELINGS OR HARD NUMBERS?

Mike Brydon and Peter Tingling are decision theory specialists at Simon Fraser University's Faculty of Business, and they have a question they like to ask when giving presentations to senior management groups, especially to human resources managers. "How many here have taken golf lessons to improve their game?" A lot of hands go up. Then they ask: "How many have had instruction to improve their decision making?" No one raises a hand because, as Brydon and Tingling have discovered, all managers, but especially those in HR, consider themselves to be expert decision makers already.

We all tend to judge others intuitively, having "evolved to take the measure of people quickly," Brydon says. But in recruiting, it can be a costly practice, as anyone knows who's hired someone they liked after a few interviews, only to find that person couldn't do the job.

This happens because of the many biases that affect our decisions about people. We are instinctive pattern matchers, for example, judging character by a person's shoes or tattoos. This tendency affects even companies like General Electric (long a bastion of analytic management), whose outgoing CEO Jack Welch wrote that his successor, Jeffery Immelt, met with his approval because the man seemed "comfortable in his own skin." Was that a job requirement? In which case, did Welch really know what it meant or how to measure it?

Equally common are selection process biases. Brydon and Tingling cite "first-date interviews," where banal questions elicit no useful information. Or the study-proven phenomenon that applicants who let their interviewers do most of the talking tend to earn higher rankings. Likewise similarity, such as coming from the same school as your interviewer, is known to create what's called an "association" bias.

Do politeness and alma mater–overlap correlate in any way with likely future performance? Probably not. But plenty of people get hired because of them.

Information asymmetries are an even bigger issue in hiring, Tingling says. If you don't have a rigorous way of measuring candidates against job-relevant attributes—such as leadership skills or analytical abilities, market profile, or sales results in the previous quarter—then there are all kinds of ways applicants can game the system. They can pump up their résumés. They can hide jobs from which they were fired. They can train themselves to give a great interview using guides available on the Internet. These tactics make candidates more attractive and articulate to the boss who goes with the gut, but this doesn't mean that the person will be any good at the job.

The question for the HR manager, then, is how to make the selection process more analytical. To help, Brydon and Tingling have developed a sophisticated decision-making software called Amadeus SRA. They refer to it as "*Moneyball* for the rest of us," a nod to Michael Lewis's book [recently made into a movie] about [Major League Baseball's] 2002 Oakland A's under manager Billy Beane. That team won its division with a payroll of $41 million (U.S.), a third of what the New York Yankees shelled out in the same year. The A's success hinged on Beane's radically non-traditional recruiting practices. He set aside the standard measures of a player's offensive success—stolen bases, RBIs, and batting average—in favour of on-base percentage and slugging average. Beane was convinced that those two statistics, while undervalued in the marketplace, were more indicative of a player's potential.

That mentality, Tingling and Brydon assert, is critical in non-sports management, too, and their software guides every aspect of the interviewing and hiring process. It sets the desired attributes and considers exactly what the successful applicant must bring to the table relative to company objectives. It provides interview and testing methods by which those attributes will be measured in each case, and compiles the input of however many interviewers are involved. It then produces rankings, and slices and dices the data in inventive (and patented) ways.

Compared with traditional blunt measures, this new rigour gives company directors a new way of assessing how well the HR department is doing its job.

As Tingling says: "I've never met an HR manager who didn't know his company's attrition rate. But I've never met one who knew his company's regrettable attrition rate." That latter stat is the one that matters, of course.

The Amadeus software is currently being tested by several educational institutions and is being considered by at least one unnamed security agency. Those employers who are attracted to the software, Tingling says, appreciate the words of W. Edwards Deming: "In God we trust. All others bring data."

Source: Timothy Taylor. 2011. "Hiring: Gut Feelings or Hard Numbers." *The Globe and Mail* (February 18): Retrieved from http://www.theglobeandmail.com/report-on-business/rob-magazine/hiring-gut-feelings-or-hard-numbers/article1913575/ Reproduced by permission of the author.

The purpose of selection is to discriminate. This statement may sound strange in the context of our discussion of human rights and employment equity in Chapter 3. Unfortunately, the term "discrimination" has acquired a negative connotation because of its frequent association with the word "unfair." In fact, we do not want to discriminate illegally or unfairly, but we do want to differentiate on the basis of applicants' abilities to do the work. Just as we differentiate in the grocery store between the desirable fruit or vegetables and those we do not want, our task in employee selection is to differentiate between those applicants we believe will become effective employees and those who will not. Thus, selection involves making decisions about which applicants to hire and which not to hire, based on the information available.

Unfortunately, as indicated in *The Globe and Mail* article in the chapter-opening vignette, humans are imperfect decision makers.[1] The use of phrases such as "I'm only human" as justification for having made mistakes reflects our common understanding of this principle. Factors other than logic typically enter into our HR decisions–emotional reactions to applicants or gut feelings, pressures to hire, political motives, and a variety of constraints.[2,3,4] Decision makers often make decisions based on inadequate or erroneous information. As a result, employers frequently make poor hiring decisions. The purpose of this chapter is to provide information and tools that can assist employers in making better selection decisions.

The chapter-opening vignette highlights some of the issues that we will discuss here. It is not simply a case of using proper selection tools. HR professionals must know how to integrate data from the different assessments that they have obtained from job candidates. They must understand the advantages and limitations of the different procedures that they might use and recognize that the recommended list of candidates may change, depending on the method they used to integrate the information. As explained in the chapter-opening vignette, Brydon and Tingling, decision theory specialists at Simon Fraser University's Faculty of Business, have developed software to assist human resources managers in integrating selection information to make selection decisions. Their software compiles and analyzes data from the various selection tools used and then produces rankings of the applicants based on predetermined criteria, making the selection decisions relatively straightforward. Although such software can certainly be helpful, it is not necessary and, in fact, can sometimes have disadvantages such as employer acceptance and adverse impact against protected groups.[5] HR managers or others involved in making selection decisions can make effective use of various statistically based methods of decision making, provided they have some mathematical background. In this chapter we advocate the use of statistically based decision-making models and illustrate how they are used to make selection decisions.

// THE CONTEXT OF SELECTION DECISIONS

Employers typically have to contend with a number of constraints and competing demands when making selection decisions. Often, time pressures prevent them from making logical or objective choices. If they need to fill vacant positions quickly, they tend to **satisfice**.[6] That is, rather than searching for the best candidates, they will select the first applicants they encounter who meet the minimum qualifications or levels of acceptability.[7] Similarly, if an insufficient number of suitable applicants are available or if the level of applicant qualifications is quite low, employers' standards of acceptability tend to drop.[8] They will often accept less-qualified applicants rather than continue their recruitment efforts in order to generate applications from better-qualified candidates.

Satisficing
Making an acceptable or adequate choice rather than the best or optimal choice.

Often, rather than selecting for a specific job, employers select applicants for the organization. Their selection decisions are based on perceptions of the applicants' overall suitability for the organization, or **organizational fit**, particularly during the interview stages of the selection process.[9] In fact, according to Waterstone Human Capital's 2011 Corporate Culture Study, 85 percent of Canadian managers feel cultural fit is more important than job-specific skills when hiring candidates for their organization.[10] Often, organizations that hire for cultural or organizational fit do not concern themselves with which job a candidate should be placed in until after the hiring decision has been made. Such organizations tend to have *promote-from-within* policies, flexible job descriptions, or jobs that change rapidly, or they tend to practise job rotation or rapid promotion. Hiring for organizational fit is a reasonable strategy if, in a relatively short time, new employees end up doing considerably different work than what they were hired to do. However, organizations using such a strategy need to ensure that they accurately measure the organization's corporate culture, that they can accurately assess applicants' fit to that culture, and that organization fit is predictive of performance or tenure in the organization or other criterion measures.

Organizational fit
Applicants' overall suitability for the organization and its culture.

Another form of selection involves promotion or transfer. Although promotions or transfers are often made on the basis of seniority or merit, they are most effective if treated as selection decisions. The candidates selected should be those most qualified for the vacant positions. When candidates are selected on the basis of merit or good job performance, the selection decision is based on the assumption that good performance in one job is indicative of good performance in another. However, the best salesperson or machinist will not necessarily make the best sales manager or shop supervisor. In fact, that person might be quite incompetent in the new job. On the other hand, promotions based on seniority are based on the assumption that the most experienced employee would be most effective. But the most experienced salesperson might not even be the best salesperson, let alone the best sales manager. Therefore, just as in other selection decisions, candidates for promotion or transfer should be assessed in terms of the knowledge, skills, abilities, or other attributes and competencies (KSAOs) they possess relevant to the positions for which they are being considered.

// SELECTION ERRORS

Many employers believe they have a knack for making good selection decisions. Some look for a firm handshake, unwavering eye contact, or upright posture in an applicant. Others look for confidence, enthusiasm, or personality (see Recruitment and Selection Today 10.1). Most employers hold **implicit theories** about how certain behaviours, mannerisms, or personality characteristics go together.[11] Implicit theories are personal beliefs that are held about how people or things function, without objective evidence and often without conscious awareness. For example, an employer might believe that unwavering eye contact reveals honesty, directness, and confidence. However, such an assumption is not necessarily warranted. Maintaining eye contact could be an interview tactic learned by the applicant or it could even reflect hostility. Moreover, in some cultures maintaining direct eye contact is considered rude and inappropriate behaviour. Applicants from these cultures would be disadvantaged if eye contact was a factor in the selection decision.

Implicit theories
Personal beliefs that are held about how people or things function, without objective evidence and often without conscious awareness.

RECRUITMENT AND SELECTION TODAY 10.1

WHAT DO EMPLOYERS LOOK FOR IN AN APPLICANT?

Employers have long hired applicants for a variety of reasons that do not appear to be job related. You be the judge as to the merits of the selection techniques described below.

- One employer asked applicants to lunch in order to observe them eating. The employer believed that those who eat quickly are energetic workers, that they eat quickly in order to be able to get on with their work. Conversely, those who eat slowly are expected to take longer at lunch and coffee breaks, as well as to work more slowly. It appears the employer believed in a variation of the well-known maxim "You are *how* you eat."
- Another employer looked for the same characteristic by observing how applicants walked into the office for their interviews. Those who had a spry, determined step were more likely to be hired than those who ambled into the office or those who seemed hesitant as they entered. The employer believed that an energetic, determined walk is indicative of an energetic, determined worker.
- Yet another employer didn't like to hire applicants with a lot of hobbies or those involved in a lot of extracurricular activities. The employer reasoned that people who are active outside of work or who have a lot of nonwork interests will be too distracted by their hobbies to sufficiently devote themselves to their work and that they might use some of their work time to pursue their own interests.
- Finally, one employer had a tendency to hire applicants who seemed to desperately need the job. It appears the applicants' needs triggered the employer's sense of social responsibility and compassion. The employer felt good about being able to help these needy individuals and reasoned that the more capable applicants can easily find employment elsewhere.

What advice would you have for each of these employers?

Many employers have implicit theories about what characteristics or qualities are important or necessary for particular kinds of work. For example, some employers might believe that someone who is extraverted or outgoing would not make a good accountant. Many employers believe certain jobs are best suited for males (e.g., construction work) whereas other jobs are best suited for females (e.g., secretary).[12,13] In a study by Ng and Wiesner, even commerce students who had been exposed to lectures on human rights and employment equity issues expressed a preference for hiring male police officers and female nurses.[14] Only when they were reminded of employment equity considerations did a relatively small majority of the students indicate they would be willing to hire female police officers or male nurses, although not under all conditions. Many of these students are likely to have carried their implicit theories about gender-appropriate jobs (or job sex-typing) into the workplace upon graduation and these theories are likely to influence their decisions should they be involved in employee selection.[15]

Many other employers make subjective decisions based on gut feelings about the applicant. They hire applicants simply because they like them or seem to get along well with them, at least based on the few minutes they spend together in an interview. Invariably, such gut feelings, as well as implicit theories, lead to poor selection decisions, as we discussed in Chapter 2.

Although employers assess a considerable amount of often complex information about each candidate, they must simplify this information to produce a dichotomous decision. Candidates are classified as either acceptable or unacceptable and hired or not hired on the basis of this assessment. Sometimes these decisions turn out to be correct, and the applicant who is hired becomes a productive and valued employee. Other times (more often than many employers care to admit), employers make mistakes by hiring individuals who turn out to be unsuitable. The four possible outcomes of a selection decision are presented in Figure 10.1.

Two of the outcomes in Figure 10.1, the true positive and the true negative, are correct decisions, or "hits." In the *true positive* outcome, the employer has hired an applicant who turns out to be a successful employee. In the *true negative* outcome, the employer did not hire an applicant who would have been considered a failure as an employee if hired. Obviously, an employer would want to maximize both these "hits" or correct predictions but, as we will demonstrate later in this chapter, that can be quite difficult to accomplish. The two other outcomes represent selection errors or "misses."

False positive error
Occurs when an applicant who is assessed favourably turns out to be a poor choice.

A **false positive error** occurs when an applicant is assessed favourably and is hired, but proves to be unsuccessful on the job. This is a costly error and may even be disastrous in some jobs. Productivity, profits, and the company's reputation may suffer when such errors are made. It may be difficult to terminate the employees once hired, termination can be costly, and grievance proceedings could result from the termination. Moreover, a replacement for the unsuccessful employee must be recruited, selected, and trained, all at additional cost. Some organizations use probationary periods (e.g., between one and six months) for new employees in order to reduce the costs of false positive errors. In fact, tenure for professors is really a probationary system–in this case, the probationary period is five or six years.

FIGURE 10.1

OUTCOMES OF THE SELECTION PROCESS

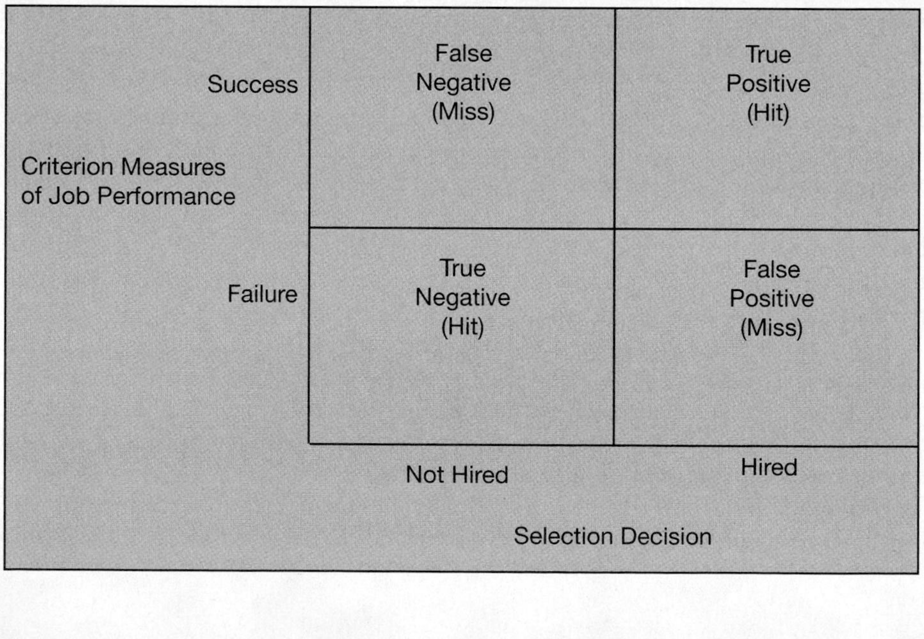

Criterion Measures of Job Performance	Not Hired	Hired
Success	False Negative (Miss)	True Positive (Hit)
Failure	True Negative (Hit)	False Positive (Miss)

Selection Decision

A **false negative error** is one in which the applicant is assessed unfavourably and is not hired but would have been successful if hired. Such errors tend to go unnoticed because there are usually no obvious negative consequences for the employer as there are with false positive errors. The employer rarely finds out about the quality of the applicant who was not hired. Only in high-profile occupations such as professional sports does a false negative error become readily apparent. When an athlete who is turned down by one team becomes a star pitcher, goalie, or fullback with a competing team, the first team is constantly faced with its mistake.

False negative error
Occurs when an applicant who is rejected would have been a good choice.

Even though false negative errors are rarely that obvious in most organizations, they can be costly. Applicants for key jobs (e.g., software designer) might develop highly successful products for the competing organization that did hire them. Furthermore, when an organization turns down a number of good candidates who are then hired by a competitor, even for non-key jobs, the competitor could gain a significant advantage in productivity. In addition, false negative errors might adversely affect minority applicants and could result in human rights litigation.

Although it is not possible to entirely avoid or even recognize all errors when making selection decisions, they can be minimized. Valid selection methods and systematic procedures will serve to improve the probability of making correct selection decisions. One particular challenge faced by employers is how to make sense of the various, and sometimes conflicting, sources of information about applicants in order to make an informed decision. The next section considers different ways of combining complex information and suggests some systematic procedures for making selection decisions.

// COLLECTION AND COMBINATION OF INFORMATION

Before a selection decision can be made, information about the applicants must be collected from various sources and combined in an effective way. Typically, employers collect this information on application forms or from résumés, in employment interviews, and through reference checks. Many employers also administer ability, personality, and/or other tests; collect and score biographical information; or make use of assessment centres. These methods of collecting applicant information are discussed in detail in Chapters 7, 8, and 9.

Sometimes all information is in agreement and the decision can be straightforward. Other times, the information is contradictory and the decision is more difficult. For example, if one applicant looks very good on paper (i.e., on the application form or résumé), has a high score on a cognitive ability test, and receives glowing recommendations from the references, but does poorly in the interview, while another applicant does well on everything except the cognitive ability test, what is the appropriate decision? Unfortunately, in such circumstances employers tend to emphasize one of the sources of information, often the interview, while giving relatively little consideration to the other information available.[16,17] The employer must find some way of making sense of all this information and combining it effectively so that the best possible selection decision can be made. We will therefore explore the effectiveness of different of ways of collecting and combining selection information.

Information collected from some sources, such as test scores, tends to be more objective. A good test result provides a reliable and valid measurement of some attribute, which can be readily used to compare applicants on a numerical or statistical basis. That is, no (or very little) human judgment is involved in collecting this score. We will refer to these methods of collecting applicant information or data as *statistical*. Information collected from more subjective sources, such as unstructured interviews, relies much more, or even exclusively, on human judgment. We will refer to these methods of collecting applicant information or data as *judgmental* (some authors refer to these as "clinical" methods).

Just as applicant data can be collected statistically or judgmentally, the data can be *combined* using statistical and judgmental methods. Data combined mathematically, using a formula, has been synthesized in a more objective fashion, which we will call *statistical* combination. Combining data through human judgment or an overall impression is a more subjective process, which we will refer to as *judgmental* combination. So, a number of permutations are possible. Judgmentally collected data can be combined in either a judgmental or statistical manner, and statistically collected data can be combined in either a judgmental or a statistical manner. Moreover, it is possible that some of the data are collected judgmentally (e.g., an unstructured interview), whereas other data are collected statistically (e.g., test scores). This composite of judgmental and statistical data can also be combined in either a judgmental or statistical manner. The possible permutations of methods of data collection and combination are presented in Table 10.1.

Pure judgment approach
An approach in which judgmental data are combined in a judgmental manner.

In the **pure judgment approach**, judgmental data are collected and combined in a judgmental manner. The decision maker forms an overall impression of the applicant based on gut feeling or implicit theories rather than explicit, objective criteria. In this approach, the decision maker both collects information and makes a decision about the applicant. An employer making a selection decision based on an unstructured interview is representative of this approach. The employer who hires applicants because he feels sorry for them is using intuition or pure judgment to make his decisions.

Trait rating approach
An approach in which judgmental data are combined statistically.

The **trait rating approach** is one in which judgmental data are combined statistically. A number of judgmental ratings are made (e.g., based on interviews, application forms or résumés, or reference checks). The ratings are combined using a mathematical formula, which produces an overall score for each applicant. Although the decision makers collect the information and make ratings on each of the components, the decision is based on the overall score generated by the mathematical formula.

TABLE 10.1

METHODS OF COLLECTING AND COMBINING APPLICANT INFORMATION

METHOD OF COLLECTING DATA	METHOD OF COMBINING DATA	
	JUDGMENTAL	STATISTICAL
Judgmental	Pure judgment	Trait ratings
Statistical	Profile interpretation	Pure statistical
Both	Judgmental composite	Statistical composite

Source: Adapted from J. Sawyer. 1966. "Measurement and Prediction, Clinical and Statistical." *Psychological Bulletin* 66: 178–200. Copyright © 1966 by the American Psychological Association.

The **profile interpretation** strategy involves combining statistical data in a judgmental manner. Data are collected from objective sources such as tests or biographical inventories. The decision maker examines these data to form an overall, subjective impression of the applicant's suitability for the job. The selection decision is based on this overall impression or gut feeling.

In the **pure statistical approach**, statistically collected data are combined statistically. Test scores or scores from other objective sources such as biographical inventories or weighted application blanks are fed into a formula or regression equation, which produces an overall combined score. Applicants are then selected in order of their scores (i.e., the top scorer, then the second-highest, and so on, until the desired number of applicants has been selected).

The **judgmental composite** involves collecting both judgmental and statistical data and then combining them judgmentally. A decision maker might conduct unstructured interviews and reference checks (judgmental data) and have access to test scores (statistical data). The decision maker then examines the test scores and considers the impressions of the applicants gained from the interviews and reference checks in order to form an overall impression and make a decision concerning who should be hired. This is probably the most common method used by employers to make selection decisions.

The **statistical composite** also involves collecting both judgmental and statistical data, but the data are combined statistically. Ratings or scores are given or obtained from each component, such as an interview, a reference check, a personality test, and a mental ability test. The ratings or scores are combined in a formula or regression equation to produce an overall score for each applicant. Selection decisions are thus based on the applicants' scores.

Profile interpretation
An approach in which statistical data are combined in a judgmental manner.

Pure statistical approach
An approach in which data are combined statistically.

Judgmental composite
An approach in which judgmental and statistical data are combined in a judgmental manner.

Statistical composite
An approach in which judgmental and statistical data are combined statistically.

Although all six of the basic decision-making approaches described above have been used in employee selection, they are not equally effective. A considerable body of research indicates that the pure statistical and the statistical composite approaches are generally superior to the other methods in predicting performance.[18,19,20] Both of these approaches involve combining information in a statistical manner.

There are several possible explanations for the superiority of statistical methods over judgmental methods of combining information.[21] First, as noted previously, implicit theories are more likely to bias evaluations and contribute to error when judgmental methods are used. Irrelevant factors such as the applicant's appearance or mannerisms are likely to unduly influence the decision. Second, it is difficult for decision makers to take into account the complexity of all of the information available to them when they use judgmental processes to make decisions. Because the ability to remember and process information is easily overloaded, decision makers tend to oversimplify or inappropriately simplify information, resulting in applicant summaries that are inaccurate.[22]

Third, it is virtually impossible to assign appropriate weights to all of the selection instruments when judgmental procedures are used. How important should reference checks be in comparison to ability tests or interviews? It is difficult to give even equal weighting to all selection information in a subjective manner. Generally, particular applicant data, such as test scores, are largely ignored in favour of impressions based on other sources, such as the interview.[23,24] Statistical approaches are likely to provide better decisions, even when scores from all of the selection instruments are weighted equally, because all applicant information is taken into consideration in a systematic manner.[25] In fact, a recent meta-analysis reveals that, in comparison to judgmental methods, using statistical data combination improves the prediction of job performance by more than 50 percent.[26]

It is worth noting that statistical approaches are compromised when poor-quality information goes into the selection equation. The maxim "garbage in, garbage out" applies just as well to employee selection methods as it does to computer programming. Erroneous or irrelevant information, such as might be obtained from bad interview questions, invalid tests, or inaccurate references, will contribute error variance to the equation and reduce the likelihood of making good selection decisions. It is therefore important to ensure that only data coming from reliable and valid selection measures are combined to yield an overall score for each applicant.

// WHY DO EMPLOYERS RESIST USING STATISTICAL APPROACHES?

Although statistical approaches to decision making are clearly superior to judgmental approaches, employers tend to resist them.[27,28] They prefer relying on gut feelings or instinct. There are probably several reasons that employers cling to judgmental approaches. Some employers might find it difficult to give up the personal control that judgmental approaches give them.[29] They can choose to ignore or discount information that is at odds with gut feelings and they can emphasize or rely solely on information that is in accord with their feelings. When they use statistical approaches, their role becomes simply that of information collectors rather than decision makers.

Employers also tend to be overconfident in their decision-making abilities.[30,31] They generally believe that they are quite successful in selecting good job candidates. Unfortunately, few employers bother to keep track of their success or "hit" rates by reviewing the job performance of those they hired. If they did, they would become much more concerned about their abilities to judge applicant competence. Granted, there might be a very small minority of employers who are be able to assess job applicants with reasonable accuracy, but even they are outperformed by statistical models based on their own decision rules (known as *bootstrapping*).[32] Unfortunately, most employers are not very good judges of job applicant potential.

There is research evidence that not all employers respond the same way to statistical approaches. That is, employers differ in their preferences for using judgmental versus statistical approaches based on their decision style. In particular, employers who have a holistic, intuitive decision-making style (i.e., like to make decisions quickly, based on hunches and emotions) are more likely to prefer judgmental approaches than employers who have an analytical, rule-based decision making style (i.e., like to take time to use logic and step-by-step analysis).[33] Thus, the more intuitive decision makers might require more evidence and training to convince them to use statistical approaches.

Finally, some employers use judgmental approaches because they feel they can't afford the time or money required to develop a statistical selection model. However, statistical models can be quite simple and need not be expensive. Moreover, any costs incurred can be more than recouped in savings generated by an effective selection system.

It is important to note that HR professionals are responsible for collection, management, protection, and disposition of all HR information within the parameters of professional practice, organizational policy, and the applicable legislative and regulatory framework. They are responsible for the effective and efficient provision of HR information systems for the benefit of the organization or any other party that is legally entitled to that information. This involves the development, maintenance, and use of manual and/or automated systems.

Most organizations, even small businesses, have the capability to collect and integrate data through specialized or enterprise software. PeopleSoft, one of the more ubiquitous systems, has the capability for storing competency or other KSAO data for use in selection and promotion decisions. The Amadeus software described in the chapter-opening vignette is another example of such software. HR-Guide.com lists many software packages and consultants that can provide specialized selection software. These systems can assist in the efficient collection and integration of assessment data for statistical decision-making purposes.

One method we have used quite effectively in workshops to demonstrate to managers the inaccuracy of their judgments is to show them videotapes of actual employment interviews. In fact, the applicants appearing on the videotapes had been hired and we had obtained job performance ratings from their supervisors after they had been working at least half a year. We asked the managers attending the workshops to rate the applicants and predict their job performance. We were then able to compare the managers' ratings and predictions with the applicants' actual job performance ratings. It was quite a surprise for many of the managers at the workshops to discover how badly they had misjudged the applicants. The experience made them much more receptive to a statistical approach to decision making.

// GROUP DECISION MAKING

Although most employee selection research has explored individual models of decision making, several surveys indicate that in most organizations, selection decisions are made by groups. Some researchers suggest that groups can be poor decision makers. Power motives, politics, conformity to the group, and lack of information sharing serve to reduce the objectivity of group decisions.[34,35] However, in spite of all of the potential problems encountered in group decision making, many researchers conclude that groups are generally better at problem solving and decision making than the average individual.[36]

In most organizations, there appears to be an intuitive understanding that groups might make better selection decisions than individuals; thus, selection teams or panels are commonplace. For example, in a large company, the immediate supervisor, a member from the HR department, and a support staff person might all be involved in the hiring of a data entry clerk. In hiring the data entry clerk's supervisor, the group charged with making the decision might include the supervisor's manager, a more senior HR person, and an experienced data entry clerk. Having two or more individuals make the selection decision can reduce the effects of the biases that any one individual might have. Selection team or panel members are more likely to be careful in their assessments when they have to justify their ratings to other team members. The fact that differences of opinion concerning an applicant must be resolved to everyone's satisfaction will tend to reduce the impact of biases. Also, with more individuals examining applicant information, it is less likely that particular information will be overlooked or distorted.

A less commendable reason for organizations to use selection teams or panels is that such teams make it easier to share the blame for poor decisions. Individual members might be somewhat less conscientious than they should be because they can evade personal responsibility and consequences for their decisions. Nevertheless, based on the research evidence, it is advisable that any judgmental information be collected by

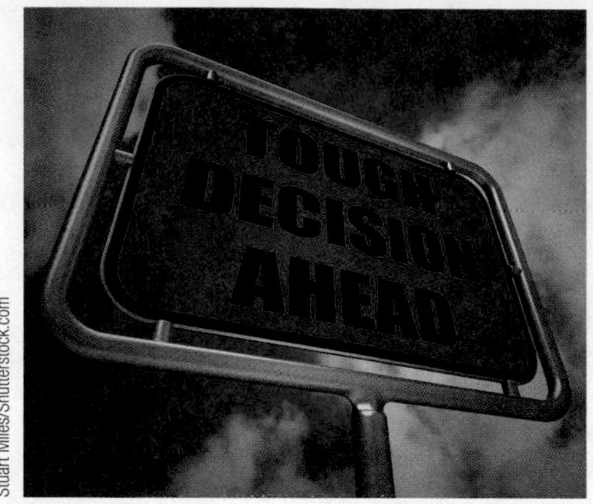

Stuart Miles/Shutterstock.com

a selection team or panel. In fact, numerous Canadian human rights tribunals have cited the use of selection panels as an important factor in defending against discrimination suits.[37,38]

One recent development in the Canadian workplace is the increasing use of teams to do work. Selecting appropriate team members has thus become an important challenge and research focus.[39,40,41] Not only job-related abilities but also personality and interpersonal factors must be taken into consideration when selecting for a team.

When teams make selection decisions (see Recruitment and Selection Today 10.2 for an example of team decision making at SC Johnson Ltd.), there are often disagreements among team members as to appropriate ratings or who should be hired. It is important that such differences be resolved as objectively as possible. The easiest way to resolve differences is to average the team members' individual scores to arrive at a combined score for each applicant (this is analogous to statistical combination).

However, as noted when we discussed the collection and combination of information, such combinations can be misleading if some of the team members submit erroneous or biased ratings. As a general rule, when there is close agreement among team members' ratings, the individual ratings can be safely averaged. But when there is disagreement (e.g., a range of two or more points), team members should discuss the reasons for their ratings until they arrive at a consensus. By discussing their rationales

RECRUITMENT AND SELECTION TODAY 10.2

TEAM DECISION MAKING AT SC JOHNSON LTD.

SC Johnson Ltd. (http://www.scjohnson.ca) produces a wide variety of products, including Pledge furniture polishes, Glade air fresheners, Windex glass and surface cleaners, Raid insecticides, Off insect repellents, Edge shaving gels, Ziploc bags, Saran Wrap, Shout stain remover, and Scrubbing Bubbles bathroom cleaners. The Canadian plant, located in Brantford, Ontario, was at one time one of the poorest-producing plants in the Johnson family. However, management and employees at the plant were able to turn the plant into one of Johnson's star performers. They attribute much of their success to the implementation of a team-based manufacturing process.

Teams at the Brantford plant construct and take apart assembly lines as needed to manufacture seasonal products such as insect repellents and citronella candles. The team members may choose who does what tasks on the assembly line, may rotate tasks, may elect their team leader, and may also interview and select new members. The teams use a semistructured interview focusing primarily on assessing factors that have to do with working in a team environment, such as cooperation, conscientiousness, and other aspects of contextual performance. While they do make occasional hiring errors, for the most part, the teams seem to enjoy good success in selecting individuals who fit well into the team environment. The existing team members seem to have a good sense of the personal qualities that will contribute to effective team membership. Moreover, given that the team is responsible for selecting the new member, the team members all tend to take responsibility for ensuring that the new member receives sufficient direction, correction, and encouragement to become an effective team member and productive employee.

for the ratings, team members are likely to uncover some of the misperceptions, biases, and errors in recollection that can contribute to differences in scores.

// INCREMENTAL VALIDITY

As pointed out earlier in this chapter, employers typically rely on various sources of information about applicants in making selection decisions. Sometimes each source of information (e.g., test score, interview, reference check) provides unique information which, taken together, gives a more complete picture of the applicant's capabilities. Often, different sources provide considerable redundant information and, therefore, do not add value to the selection process. For example, if an interview collected information only about where the applicant had worked, how long he worked for each employer, and what education he had received, the interview would be useless because all of this information could be found in the résumé or application form.

Predictors that are highly correlated with each other (e.g., measurements of cognitive ability and university admission test scores) provide considerable redundant information and, therefore, there is little value in using both. Instead, employers benefit by using predictors that have low intercorrelations. When predictors are used that are relatively uncorrelated with each other but that are correlated with the criterion (e.g., job performance), they assess different aspects of the KSAOs needed for the job and, therefore, each predictor provides **incremental validity**. That is, each predictor adds value to the selection system, and the validity of the system increases.

Incremental validity
The value in terms of increased validity of adding a particular predictor to an existing selection system.

Figure 10.2 provides an illustration of incremental validity using hypothetical data. Each predictor is represented by a circle (P1 and P2, respectively) and the criterion is also represented by a circle (C). In Figure 10.2(a), the correlation between the two predictors is 0.8 and the correlation between each predictor and the criterion is 0.5. As the figure demonstrates, there is considerable overlap between the parts of the predictors (P1 and P2) that overlap with the criterion (C) and there is a relatively small area of unique overlap between P2 and C once the overlap between P1 and C is taken into account. As you can see, the second predictor provides relatively little incremental validity when two predictors are highly correlated.

In Figure 10.2(b), there is a zero correlation between the two predictors and the correlation between each predictor and the criterion is 0.5. Each predictor (P1 and P2) overlaps with a completely different part of the criterion (C) and provides incremental validity over the other predictor. In the example in Figure 10.2(b), P1 accounts for 25 percent of the variance in C and P2 accounts for an additional 25 percent of the variance in C (variance is the square of the correlation). Thus, P1 and P2 together account for 50 percent of the variance in C.

When employers use selection instruments (predictors) that are uncorrelated or have low intercorrelations with each other but are correlated with job performance (the criterion), these selection instruments provide better prediction as a group than each instrument provides on its own (i.e., they have incremental validity). Often, scores are collected from each selection instrument and entered into a regression equation to provide a composite score for each applicant that reflects the information provided by each of the components of the selection system (see the section on decision-making models in this chapter).

FIGURE 10.2

AN ILLUSTRATION OF INCREMENTAL VALIDITY: CORRELATED AND UNCORRELATED PREDICTORS

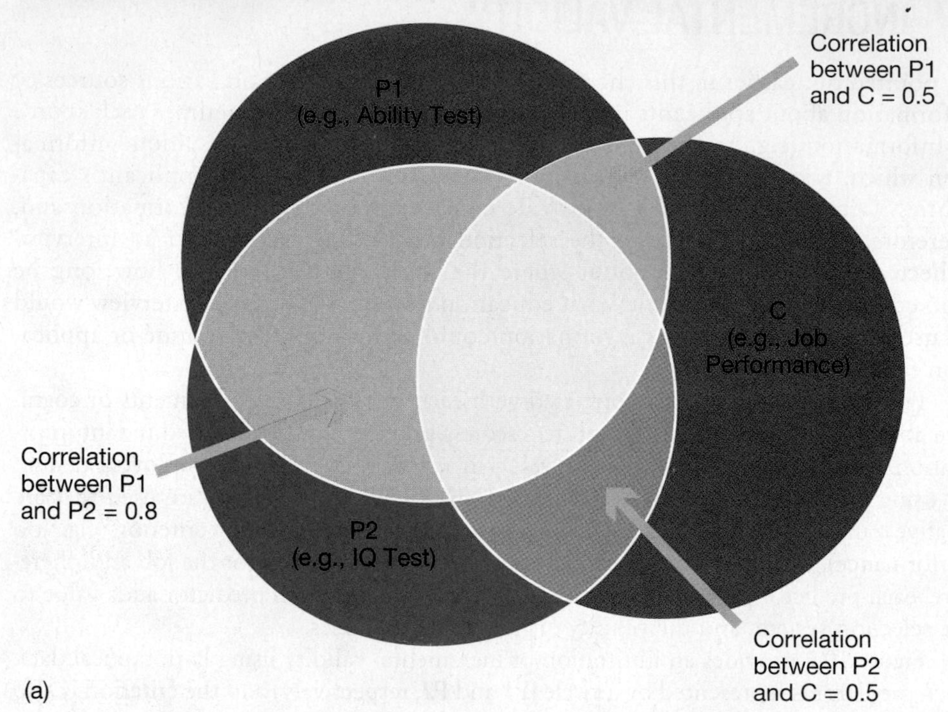

(a)

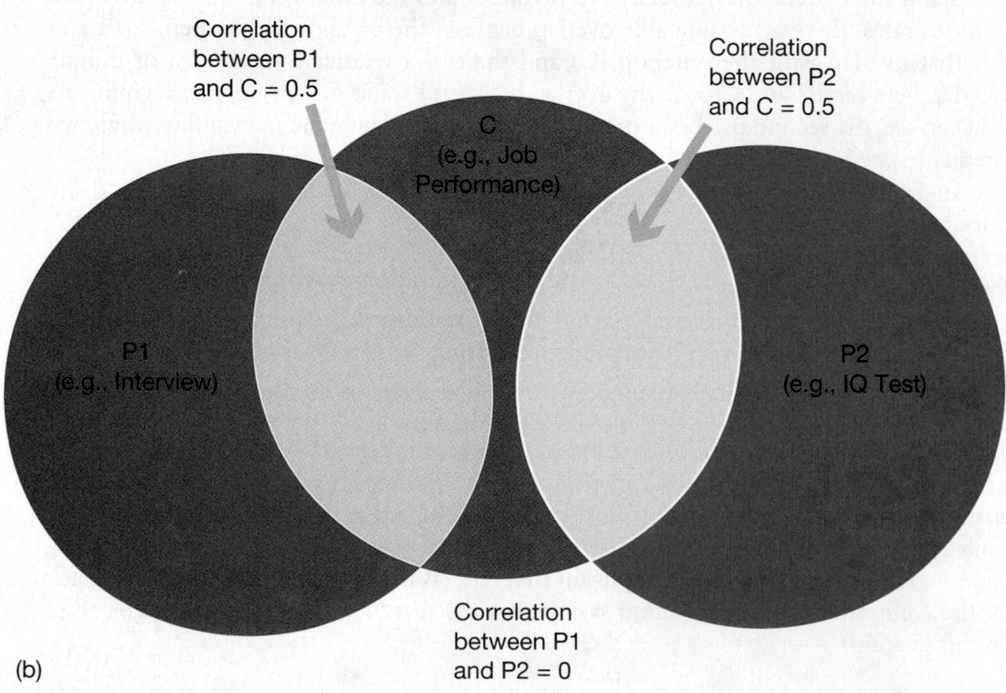

(b)

// SETTING CUTOFF SCORES

In the next section we will consider different models of decision making. Several of these models make use of a *cutoff score*, so it is necessary to understand cutoff scores before we discuss the models. **Cutoff scores** serve as criteria or thresholds in selection decisions. Applicants who score below the cutoff on a given predictor (e.g., test, interview) are rejected. Thus, cutoff scores ensure that applicants meet some minimum level of ability or qualification to be considered for a job. In college or university, a grade of 50 percent often serves as a cutoff. A student whose mark is lower than 50 percent fails the course. This cutoff has been established by convention. In most organizations, cutoffs are established based on the predictor scores of individuals who are successful in the job being selected for, or based on expert judgments concerning the difficulty of the predictor items.[42]

Cutoff score
A threshold; those scoring at or above the cutoff score pass, those scoring below fail.

One method of establishing cutoff scores involves identifying the proportion of applicants who are to be hired and determining how stringent the cutoff score should be to select only the desired number of applicants. First, the expected **selection ratio** is calculated (number of individuals to be hired divided by the expected number of applicants). Next, the distribution of the applicants' scores on the predictor is estimated by examining the predictor score distributions of past groups of applicants or of current employees (i.e., predictive or concurrent validation data). Finally, the cutoff score is established by applying the selection ratio to the predictor score distribution in order to determine the score that only the top applicants (the proportion to be hired) would attain.

Selection ratio
The proportion of applicants for one or more positions who are hired.

For example, if a fire department seeks to hire five firefighters and 150 people are expected to apply, the selection ratio will be 0.03 (5/150). About 3 percent of expected applicants will be accepted or, conversely, about 97 percent of expected applicants will have to be rejected. The cutoff score should therefore be set at the 97th percentile of the distribution of predictor scores (plus or minus one standard error of measurement). That is, the cutoff score is set so that only 3 percent of applicants would be expected to meet or exceed the score (or 97 percent would fall below it). This approach is limited to setting cutoffs for a single predictor. When more than one predictor is to be used, it is common to use expert judges, although computational methods have been developed to facilitate the setting of multiple cutoffs.[43]

There are several ways in which expert judges can be used to establish cutoffs, but they differ only slightly in their methods. We will consider the general approach; consult Cascio and Aguinis[44] or Gatewood, Feild, and Barrick[45] for more detailed treatments of the various methods. Experienced employees, supervisors, or managers who know the job well, or industrial psychologists, typically serve as expert judges. Essentially, the expert judges are asked to rate the difficulty of test items (or interview questions) and to indicate what score on each item should be attained by a minimally competent applicant. These ratings are summed for all items to yield a pass threshold or cutoff score. Cutoff scores can be established in this manner for each of the predictors used in the selection process.

The procedures used by the Public Service Commission of Canada to establish cutoff scores can be found at http://www.psc-cfp.gc.ca/ppc-cpp/acs-cmptnc-evl-cmptnc/ct-off-scrs-pnts-cpr-eng.htm.

// DECISION-MAKING MODELS

Several different decision-making models involve combining applicant information statistically (regardless of how that information was collected). These models are unit and rational weighting, multiple regression, multiple cutoffs, multiple hurdle, combination, and profile matching.[46] We will consider the models in terms of their usefulness for different purposes and under different conditions.

UNIT AND RATIONAL WEIGHTING

The simplest way of combining applicant information is to simply add together the scores applicants received on the various selection tools that were used and to give each score the same weighting (e.g., a value of 1.0). This approach is known as *unit weighting*. However, scores on different selection instruments likely reflect different scales of measurement. For example, let's assume we're going to use a cognitive ability test, an extraversion scale, a 12-question structured interview, and a reference check to select applicants for a retail sales position. The cognitive ability test might be out of 50 (i.e., the maximum score is 50), the extraversion scale out of 40, the interview out of 60 (e.g., 12 questions at 5 points per question), and the reference check out of 10. By simply adding applicant scores on these instruments, we would be giving the greatest weight to the interview score and the least weight to the reference check score by default. Thus, we would not actually be using unit weighting. If we wish to weight all of the scores equally, we need to standardize or convert all the scores to equal units (e.g., make them all out of 50).

Table 10.2 provides the hypothetical scores of four applicants for a retail sales position on each of four predictors–a cognitive ability test, an extraversion personality scale,

TABLE 10.2

EXAMPLES OF SALES APPLICANT DATA

	PREDICTOR SCORES			
APPLICANT	COGNITIVE ABILITY TEST	EXTRAVERSION SCALE	STRUCTURED INTERVIEW	REFERENCE CHECK
Mr. A	26	42	45	37
Ms. B	23	46	27	33
Mr. C	33	31	40	43
Ms. D	29	37	47	47
MAXIMUM POSSIBLE				
Scores	50	50	50	50
Regression Weights	0.5	0.1	0.5	0.25
Cutoff Scores	20	33	30	33
Mean Scores	24	37	38	37

Predicted job performance = 1.1 + 0.5 Cognitive ability score + 0.1 Extraversion score + 0.5 Interview score + 0.25 Reference check score. A predicted job performance score can thus be calculated for each applicant.

a structured interview, and a reference check. Maximum scores, regression weights, cutoff scores, and mean (or average) scores for each predictor are also given. We have standardized all the scores in the table so they are all out of 50. We can now add each applicant's scores to obtain a unit weighted total: 150 for Mr. A (26 + 42 + 45 + 37), 129 for Ms. B (23 + 36 + 27 + 33), 147 for Mr. C (33 + 31 + 40 + 43), and 160 for Ms. D (29 + 37 + 47 + 47). The applicants can now be ranked based on their total scores: (1) Ms. D, (2) Mr. A, (3) Mr. C, and (4) Ms. B. They can be selected on a top-down basis until the desired number of candidates has been obtained. If we needed to hire only two candidates, Ms. D and Mr. A would be selected.

Although unit weighting is simple and easy to use, the method assumes that each predictor is equally important or contributes equally to predicting job performance. This is rarely the case. As you have discovered in this text, selection instruments vary in terms of criterion validity–some predict better than others. Therefore, in most instances, we need to weight the scores on the different predictors according to their importance or validity. The simplest way of doing this is to have managers or other subject-matter experts determine the appropriate weights in a rational or logical way based on their experience. This approach is known as *rational weighting*. For example, the managers might decide they have the greatest confidence in the interview scores, slightly less confidence in reference checks, and the least confidence in the test scores. They might therefore assign a weight of 1 to the cognitive ability test as well as to the extraversion test, a weight of 3 to the interview, and a weight of 2 to the reference check. Applying these weights to the scores in Table 10.2 results in a score of 277 for Mr. A [(1 × 26) + (1 × 42) + (3 × 45) + (2 × 37)], 216 for Ms. B [(1 × 23) + (1 × 46) + (3 × 27) + (2 × 33)], 270 for Mr. C [(1 × 33) + (1 × 31) + (3 × 40) +(2 × 43)], and 301 for Ms. D [(1 × 29) + (1 × 37) + (3 × 47) + (2 × 47)]. Thus, the rankings would be: (1) Ms. D, (2) Mr. A, (3) Mr. C, and (4) Ms. B. In this example, the rankings are the same as for the unit weighting approach but the rankings can differ, depending on the obtained distribution of scores and the weightings applied.

The rational weighting approach requires managers to think about the relative importance of each predictor and, therefore, makes the weighting process explicit. However, assigning weights in this manner is a fairly subjective process. For example, why would the managers assign a weight of 3 to the interview? Why not a weight of 2 or 4? Based on their different experiences and knowledge, managers are likely to disagree on what the appropriate weights should be. Moreover, the managers' levels of confidence in the various predictors might be unjustified, particularly if their judgments are not based on research evidence. The multiple regression model provides a more scientific and defensible approach to weighting predictor scores.

MULTIPLE REGRESSION MODEL

In the multiple regression model, the applicant's scores on each predictor (e.g., tests, interviews, reference checks) are also weighted and summed to yield a total score (e.g., predicted job performance). However, unlike rational weighting, the appropriate regression weights or b values are determined through prior research, where the unique contributions of each predictor (X) to predicting job performance (Y) are investigated. Although, over time and with a sufficiently large number of hires, an organization could collect enough data to determine the appropriate weights for each of the selection instruments, it is more efficient to use the validity coefficients obtained in meta-analytic studies of various predictors (see "Validity Generalization" on pages 49–51). That is, the validity coefficients from relevant meta-analyses can be used as regression weights or *b* values in the regression equation. For example, based on meta-analytic findings, measures of cognitive ability have an average validity coefficient of 0.50 (see Chapter 8). Therefore, a regression weight or *b* value of 0.50 can be applied to an applicant's cognitive ability score. Similarly, validity coefficients from meta-analytic studies related to the other predictors can be used to assign appropriate regression weights for those predictors.

Table 10.2 provides regression weights for each of the predictors roughly based on their respective validity coefficients. Thus, the regression weight (b_1) for the cognitive ability test (X_1) is 0.5, the regression weight (b_2) for the extraversion scale (X_2) is 0.1, the regression weight (b_3) for the interview score (X_3) is 0.5, and the regression weight (b_4) for the reference check score (X_4) is 0.25. The regression equation for predicting job performance in this case is:

$$Y = a + b_1X_1 + b_2X_2 + b_3X_3 + b_4X_4$$

The "*a*" in the equation is the intercept, the point where the regression line intersects the *Y*-axis. We do not need to concern ourselves with the calculation of intercepts for purposes of this illustration. The intercept value will change the magnitude of all the scores equally, so it will not change their relative standing or ranking. In this example, the intercept has been arbitrarily set to 1.1.

Applying the regression equation to the data in Table 10.2 yields a total predicted score of 50.1 for Mr. A, 39.0 for Ms. B, 51.5 for Mr. C, and 54.6 for Ms. D. The applicants can now be ranked based on their total predicted scores: (1) Ms. D, (2) Mr. C, (3) Mr. A, and (4) Ms. B (see Table 10.3). If two candidates are needed, Ms. D and Mr. C would be selected. Although this result is different from the one obtained by rational weighting (and unit weighting), whether the different methods produce the same or different rakings depends on the distribution of scores and how large the differences in weightings are. However, given the regression weights are based on research findings rather than on subjective judgments or estimates (which are the basis of the rational weights), we should have more confidence in the regression weights than in subjective weighting methods.

The multiple regression model assumes that the predictors are linearly related to the criterion and that a low score on one predictor can be compensated for by a high score on another predictor. An applicant could do very poorly in the interview (e.g., receive a score of zero) and still do well if he or she received high scores on the tests and the reference check. However, the assumptions made by the multiple regression model are not necessarily warranted. First, very high scores on some predictors might be as undesirable as very low scores. For example, while an extreme introvert might have difficulty relating to customers in a retail sales position, an extreme extravert might annoy them and drive them away.

Second, there might be a minimum level of competence required on each of the predictors for the individual to perform acceptably in the job. For example, a very low interview score might indicate that the applicant has such poor interpersonal and communication skills that she cannot function acceptably in retail sales, regardless of high cognitive ability and extraversion scores. The multiple regression approach also has the disadvantage of being expensive, particularly for large applicant pools, because all applicants must be assessed on all predictors.

Nevertheless, the multiple regression approach does have several advantages. It is an efficient method of combining multiple predictors in an optimal manner and it minimizes errors in prediction. Moreover, by assigning different weights, different regression

TABLE 10.3

EXAMPLES OF RESULTS FOR SALES APPLICANT DATA IN TABLE 10.2

MULTIPLE REGRESSION MODEL

APPLICANT		RANK
Mr. A	$Y = 1.1 + (0.5)26 + (0.1)42 + (0.5)45 + (0.25)37 = 50.1$	3
Ms. B	$Y = 1.1 + (0.5)23 + (0.1)46 + (0.5)27 + (0.25)33 = 39.0$	4
Mr. C	$Y = 1.1 + (0.5)33 + (0.1)31 + (0.5)40 + (0.25)43 = 51.5$	2
Ms. D	$Y = 1.1 + (0.5)29 + (0.1)37 + (0.5)47 + (0.25)47 = 54.6$	1

MULTIPLE CUTOFF MODEL

APPLICANT	COGNITIVE ABILITY TEST (CUTOFF = 20)	EXTRAVERSION SCALE (CUTOFF = 33)	STRUCTURED INTERVIEW (CUTOFF = 30)	REFERENCE CHECK (CUTOFF = 33)	DECISION
Mr. A	26 (above)	42 (above)	45 (above)	37 (above)	accept
Ms. B	23 (above)	46 (above)	27 (below)	33 (at cutoff)	reject
Mr. C	33 (above)	31 (below)	40 (above)	43 (above)	reject
Ms. D	29 (above)	37 (above)	47 (above)	47 (above)	accept

MULTIPLE HURDLE MODEL

APPLICANT	STAGE 1 COGNITIVE ABILITY TEST (CUTOFF = 20)	STAGE 2 EXTRAVERSION SCALE (CUTOFF = 33)	STAGE 3 STRUCTURED INTERVIEW (CUTOFF = 30)	STAGE 4 REFERENCE CHECK (CUTOFF = 33)	RESULT
Mr. A	26 (pass)	42 (pass)	45 (pass)	37 (pass)	pass
Ms. B	23 (pass)	46 (pass)	27 (fail)		fail
Mr. C	33 (pass)	31 (fail)			fail
Ms. D	29 (pass)	37 (pass)	47 (pass)	47 (pass)	pass

MULTIPLE CUTOFF COMBINATION MODEL

Only Mr. A and Ms. D meet all cutoff requirements (see results for multiple hurdle model above). So, Ms. B and Mr. C are rejected.

APPLICANT		RANK
Mr. A	$Y = 1.1 + (0.5)26 + (0.1)420 + (0.5)45 + (0.6)37 = 50.1$	2
Ms. D	$Y = 1.1 + (0.5)29 + (0.1)37 + (0.5)47 + (0.6)47 = 54.6$	1

Continued

TABLE 10.3 CONTINUED		
MULTIPLE HURDLE COMBINATION MODEL		
Mr. C does not meet the cutoff requirements for stages 1 and 2 so he is rejected (see results for multiple hurdle model above).		
APPLICANT		**RANK**
Mr. A	$Y = 1.1 + (0.5)26 + (0.1)420 + (0.5)45 + (0.6)37 = 50.1$	2
Ms. B	$Y = 1.1 + (0.5)23 + (0.1)46 + (0.5)27 + (0.25)33 = 39.0$	3
Ms. D	$Y = 1.1 + (0.5)29 + (0.1)37 + (0.5)47 + (0.6)47 = 54.6$	1
PROFILE MATCHING MODEL		
APPLICANT		**RANK**
Mr. A	$D^2 = (26 - 24)^2 + (42 - 37)^2 + (45 - 38)^2 + (37 - 37)^2 = 78$	1
Ms. B	$D^2 = (23 - 24)^2 + (46 - 37)^2 + (27 - 38)^2 + (33 - 37)^2 = 219$	4
Mr. C	$D^2 = (33 - 24)^2 + (31 - 37)^2 + (40 - 38)^2 + (43 - 37)^2 = 157$	2
Ms. D	$D^2 = (29 - 24)^2 + (37 - 37)^2 + (47 - 38)^2 + (47 - 37)^2 = 206$	3

equations can be produced for different jobs, even if the same predictors are used for all jobs. So, if applicants are being selected for more than one job, they can be placed in the job for which their total score is the highest or they can be placed in the job where their total score is the farthest above the minimum score necessary for acceptable job performance. The multiple regression approach is probably the most efficient decision-making approach if the assumptions underlying the model are not violated.[47]

MULTIPLE CUTOFF MODEL

In the multiple cutoff model, scores on all predictors are obtained for all applicants, just as in the multiple regression model. Using the data in Table 10.2, all applicants would write the cognitive ability and extraversion tests, all would be interviewed, and reference check information would be scored for all. However, in this model, applicants are rejected if their scores on any of the predictors fall below the cutoff scores. In our example, both Mr. A and Ms. D score above the cutoffs on all four predictors. Ms. B's score falls below the cutoff on the structured interview, and Mr. C's score falls below the cutoff on the extraversion scale. Ms. B and Mr. C would thus be rejected. Note that this is quite a different result from the multiple regression approach, where Mr. C obtained the second-highest score and would have been selected (see Table 10.3).

The multiple cutoff model assumes that a minimum level is required on each of the attributes measured by the predictors for successful job performance (i.e., there is a nonlinear relationship among the predictors and job performance). The model also assumes that the predictors are not compensatory–it is not possible to compensate for a low score on one predictor with a high score on another predictor.

A disadvantage of the multiple cutoff model is that, just like the multiple regression approach, it requires that all applicants be assessed on all procedures. This requirement makes it expensive to administer. Another disadvantage is that the model identifies only those applicants who have minimum qualifications for the job. There is no way of distinguishing among those who have surpassed the minimum cutoffs. If 10 applicants have passed the cutoffs but the employer wants to select only five candidates, how would the employer decide which ones to select?

In spite of its disadvantages, the multiple cutoff model does serve to narrow the pool of applicants to a smaller set of minimally qualified candidates and it is an easy model for managers to understand. It is probably most useful when minimum levels of certain physical abilities are required for job performance.[48] For example, some occupations such as law enforcement, firefighting, or heavy manufacturing have minimum specifications for eyesight, colour vision, or strength.

MULTIPLE HURDLE MODEL

In the multiple hurdle model, applicants must pass the minimum cutoff for each predictor, in turn, before being assessed on the next predictor. As soon as an applicant has failed to meet the cutoff on a given predictor, the applicant ceases to be a candidate for the job and is not assessed on any of the remaining predictors. In Chapter 2, Recruitment and Selection Today 2.2 (page 33) described the selection procedures used to hire Toronto police constables; this was an example of a multiple-hurdle procedure. Applicants had to pass the current step in the process before moving on to the next; those applicants who failed a step are screened out of the process (see http://www.torontopolice.on.ca/careers/uni_become_officer.php). In our example in Table 10.2, all four applicants pass the cognitive ability test and go on to write the extraversion scale. Mr. C fails to meet the cutoff on the extraversion scale and is dropped from further consideration. Only Mr. A, Ms. B, and Ms. D go on to the structured interview, where Ms. B fails to meet the cutoff and is rejected. Reference checks are performed only for Mr. A and Ms. D, who both pass and become candidates for the job (see Table 10.3).

The result is identical to the one for the multiple cutoff model but the approach is less expensive because fewer applicants need to be assessed at each stage of the selection process. Both models make the same assumptions but differ in the procedure used for collecting predictor information. The multiple cutoff approach uses a nonsequential procedure, whereas the multiple hurdle procedure is sequential (i.e., applicants must pass each predictor cutoff, in sequence, before going on to the next predictor). Like the multiple cutoff approach, the multiple hurdle model narrows the pool of applicants to a smaller set of candidates who meet minimum qualifications and is also an easy model to understand.

The multiple hurdle approach has the disadvantage of being more time consuming than the multiple regression or multiple cutoff approaches. Applicants need to be assessed and scored on one predictor before a decision can be made on whether to assess them on the next predictor. It also makes it difficult to estimate the validity of each procedure, particularly in later stages of the selection process. Relatively fewer applicants are being assessed on predictors toward the end of the sequence (e.g., interview and reference check, in our example), so restriction of range becomes a problem for estimating the validity of these predictors. One other disadvantage is that, like the multiple cutoff model, this model identifies only those applicants who have minimum qualifications for the job and does not distinguish among those who have surpassed all of the cutoffs.

Like the multiple cutoff approach, the multiple hurdle approach is most appropriate when minimum levels of particular KSAOs are necessary for job performance and cannot be compensated for by higher levels on other KSAOs. Moreover, the multiple hurdle approach is most useful when the applicant pool is large and some of the selection procedures are expensive.[49] In such circumstances, the less-expensive procedures (e.g., tests) can be used as hurdles at the beginning in order to screen out inappropriate applicants and reduce the applicant pool. Thus, the more expensive procedures (e.g., interviews) are used on a smaller pool of select applicants. More information on the multiple hurdles approach, as well as other methods for integrating selection data, can be found at http://www.hr-guide.com/data/G366.htm

COMBINATION MODELS

There are two possible combination models. One model involves a combination of the multiple cutoff approach and the multiple regression approach. We'll refer to this as the *multiple cutoff combination model.* The other model involves a combination of the multiple hurdle approach and the regression approach, so we will refer to this as the *multiple hurdle combination model.*

Multiple cutoff combination model
A combination of multiple cutoff and regression approaches.

In the **multiple cutoff combination model**, all applicants are measured on all predictors and those falling below the cutoff on any of the predictors are rejected, just as in the multiple cutoff model. Then, multiple regression is used to calculate the total scores of those applicants who surpass the cutoff scores. The applicants are ranked by total score and selected on a top-down basis, as in the multiple regression method. The multiple cutoff combination model is therefore a mixture of the multiple cutoff and multiple regression approaches. If we apply this model to the data in Table 10.2, Ms. B and Mr. C would be rejected because they do not surpass all the cutoff scores. So far, this result is identical to the result for the multiple cutoff model. Now the regression equation is applied to the remaining applicants, Mr. A and Ms. D. Recall from our discussion of the multiple regression model that Mr. A's total score is 50.1 and Ms. D's total score is 54.6. Ms. D is therefore ranked first and Mr. A ranked second. If we were hiring only one candidate, Ms. D would be selected (see Table 10.3).

Like the multiple cutoff model, the multiple cutoff combination model assumes that a minimum level of each of the KSAOs is required for effective job performance. A further assumption is that, once minimum levels have been reached, high scores on one predictor can compensate for low scores on another predictor. As might be expected, the multiple cutoff combination model has the same advantages as the multiple cutoff model but has the additional advantage of providing a means of selecting from among those candidates who surpass all of the cutoff scores. However, the multiple cutoff combination approach is just as expensive as the multiple cutoff approach because all applicants are assessed on all predictors.

Obviously, the multiple cutoff combination model is useful as long as the assumptions underlying the approach hold. It is an appropriate model when selection instruments do not vary greatly in cost and is particularly useful when a considerable number of applicants tend to surpass all of the cutoffs. When more applicants than can be hired surpass the cutoff scores, the multiple cutoff combination model facilitates selection among those applicants.

Multiple hurdle combination model
A combination of multiple hurdle and regression approaches.

In the **multiple hurdle combination model**, a multiple hurdle approach is used in the early stages of the selection process but then a multiple regression approach is used in the later stages of the selection process. Applicants must pass each of the minimum cutoffs, in turn, for predictors used early in the selection process, as in the multiple hurdle model. However, the regression approach is applied to predictors used later in the selection process. Normally, we would use the multiple hurdle approach with the less expensive predictors at the beginning of the selection process to reduce the number of applicants, particularly if the number of applicants is large. For the relatively smaller number of applicants who proceed to the subsequent and, likely, more expensive predictors, the multiple regression method would be applied. Moreover, the multiple hurdle component of this model should include predictors with minimum requirements or scores (e.g., evidence of appropriate certification, required levels of physical fitness, etc.) which cannot be compensated for by higher scores on other predictors. Thus, the regression component should only include compensatory predictors.[50]

Let's assume that we have applied the multiple hurdle approach to the cognitive ability test and the extraversion scale and the regression approach to the interview and reference check in our example in Table 10.3. Mr. C would be rejected because he does not pass the cutoff score on the extraversion scale at stage 2. So far, this result is identical to the result for the multiple hurdle model. Now the regression equation is applied to the remaining applicants, Mr. A, Ms. B, and Ms. D. Based on the regression results, Ms. D. would be ranked first (54.6), Mr. A would be ranked second (50.1), and Ms. B would be ranked third (39.0). If we were hiring two candidates, Ms. D and Mr. A would be selected (see Table 10.3). The result in this example is the same as with the multiple hurdle approach, but it could have been different depending on the scores achieved in the stage 3 and 4 predictors.

The multiple hurdle combination model assumes that some of predictors are linearly related to the criterion while other predictors do not have a linear relationship with the criterion (i.e., a minimum level is required on these predictors). The model also assumes that some predictors are compensatory while others are not. These assumptions are very reasonable in most selection contexts.[51] Moreover, the multiple hurdle combination model combines some of the advantages and disadvantages of both multiple hurdle and the multiple regression models. It is less expensive than the regression or multiple cutoff models, though more expensive than the simple multiple hurdle model, because not all applicants need to be assessed on all predictors. This model is not as time consuming as the multiple hurdle model because there is no need to wait for the scoring of later stage predictors, but it is more time consuming than the multiple regression or multiple cutoff approaches. The model ensures that minimum qualifications are met while also permitting the combination of later stage predictors in regression equations, which provide for the rank ordering of finalists. In short, the multiple hurdle combination model provides a good compromise with more nuanced and, likely, more realistic assumptions concerning the predictors used to select applicants than most of the other models.[52]

PROFILE MATCHING MODEL

In the profile matching model, current employees who are considered successful on the job are assessed on several predictors. Their average scores on each predictor are used to form an *ideal* profile of scores required for successful job performance. One should also try to obtain average predictor scores for current employees who are considered poor or marginal performers. Obtaining scores for poor or marginal employees is not always easy because such employees are often dismissed or leave of their own accord soon after being hired or, if a valid selection system is used, tend not to be hired in the first place.

If it is possible to obtain scores for poor performers, their average predictor scores should be compared with the average predictor scores of good performers to ensure that the predictors differentiate between good and poor performers. Those predictors that do not differentiate should not be included in the ideal profile of scores.

Once an ideal profile of scores has been established, applicants' predictor scores can be compared with the ideal profile. Those applicants whose profiles are most similar to the ideal profile can then be selected. One of two methods can be used to determine the degree of similarity between applicant profiles and the ideal profile: the correlation method and the D^2 method. The correlation method involves correlating an applicant's scores on the predictors with the predictor scores of the ideal profile. The higher the correlation, the greater the similarity between the applicant's profile and the ideal profile. The D^2 method involves calculating differences between an applicant's scores and ideal profile scores on each predictor, squaring the differences, and summing the squared differences to yield D^2. The larger D^2 is, the poorer the match is between the applicant's profile and the ideal profile. The D^2 method is preferred because it considers the magnitude of applicants' mean scores across the predictors, the degree to which applicant scores differ from the ideal scores, and the pattern or shape of applicant scores relative to the ideal profile. The correlation method considers only the pattern or shape of the scores.[53]

In our example in Table 10.2, let's assume the mean scores across the predictors represent the ideal profile. These can be correlated with the applicants' scores across the predictors to produce a correlation coefficient for each of the applicants. The resulting correlation coefficients are as follows: Mr. A ($r = 0.938$), Ms. B ($r = 0.571$), Mr. C ($r = 0.457$), and Ms. D ($r = 0.858$). Therefore, our applicants would be ranked accordingly: (1) Mr. A, (2) Ms. D, (3) Ms. B, and (4) Mr. C. Using the D^2 method requires the subtraction of the mean score for each predictor from each applicant's score on that predictor to obtain a difference. The resulting differences are squared and the squares summed across predictors for each applicant to obtain a D^2 score. Our applicants in Table 10.2 obtained the following D^2 scores: Mr. A ($D^2 = 78$), Ms. B ($D^2 = 219$), Mr. C ($D^2 = 157$), and Ms. D ($D^2 = 206$). Recall that the smaller the D^2 score is, the better the match. Accordingly, the rankings would be (1) Mr. A, (2) Mr. C, (3) Ms. D, and (4) Ms. B (see Table 10.3). Thus, in this example, the rank orders for the correlation and D^2 method are different. If we were hiring only two applicants, Mr. A and Ms. D would have been hired using the correlation method whereas Mr. A and Mr. C would have been hired using the D^2 method.

Although the two methods produced different rank orders in this example, the resulting rank orders can sometimes be the same. Nevertheless, the correlation method often yields very high correlation coefficients, which barely differentiate applicants from each other. The D^2 method can also produce misleading results. An applicant whose scores substantially *exceed* the mean scores will have a high D^2 score and rank below an applicant whose scores fall close to the mean scores (whether slightly above or even below the means). Thus, this model is based on the assumption that scores that are higher than the ideal are as undesirable as scores that are lower than the ideal. In fact, the model assumes that there is one best profile, whereas there could be several profiles that predict success just as well.

As noted previously, the profile matching model cannot be implemented if the predictors do not differentiate between employees who are poor performers and those who are good performers. Moreover, restriction of range can be a problem because truly poor performers are often difficult to find (i.e., they are asked to leave or are not hired in the first place). Also, because the profiles of successful employees could change over time, ideal profiles need to be checked periodically.

Profile matching does have the advantage of permitting the ranking of applicants based on their similarities to the ideal profile. It is an appropriate method to use when there is clearly a best profile for employees in a job and when it is known that poor employees tend to score higher as well as lower on the predictors than good employees (i.e., there is a curvilinear relationship between predictor scores and job performance). As these conditions rarely apply, multiple regression or multiple hurdle combination remain more appropriate approaches in virtually all circumstances.[54,55]

// MAKING SELECTION DECISIONS

Regardless of which decision-making model is used, the eventual aim of the selection process is to decide which applicants to hire. The models described in the previous sections lend themselves to one of two basic approaches: *top-down selection* and *banding*. Each method is based on particular assumptions and has certain advantages and disadvantages.

TOP-DOWN SELECTION

Top-down selection involves ranking applicants on the basis of their total scores and selecting from the top down until the desired number of candidates has been selected. This approach is based on the assumption that individuals scoring higher on the predictors will be better performers on the job than individuals scoring lower on the predictors (i.e., there is a linear relationship between predictor scores and job performance). As long as this assumption is not violated, top-down selection is considered the best approach for maximizing organizational performance.[56] Only those who are likely to be the top performers are hired.

Top-down selection
Ranking applicants on the basis of their total scores and selecting from the top down until the desired number of candidates has been selected.

One difficulty with using top-down selection is that it can have adverse impact against certain minority groups. For example, black applicants tend to have slightly lower average scores than white applicants on certain tests. Selecting from the top down could therefore result in disproportionately more white than black applicants being hired. *Race norming* or *within-group scoring* has been suggested as a method of preventing such adverse impact. Applicants can be ranked on their predictor scores within their relevant minority groups. For example, white applicants could be ranked on their predictor scores relative to other white applicants, and black applicants could be rank-ordered on their predictor scores relative to other black applicants. Then the top-ranking black candidate and the top-ranking white candidate could be selected, followed by the black and white candidates ranking second, and so on until the desired number of candidates is selected. Although top-down selection across all groups would result in the best-quality candidates being hired, on average, ranking within groups permits employers to achieve employment equity goals while still hiring high-quality applicants.[57]

Although the American Civil Rights Act of 1991 prohibits race norming (the adjustment of scores, or the use of different cutoff scores for different minority groups in the United States), there is no such legislation in Canada. Nevertheless, employment equity initiatives can be difficult to implement, as one Canadian fire department discovered. In Ontario, the Kitchener Fire Department attempted to increase minority representation in the department by reducing the cutoff score for women. Whereas male applicants needed a score of 85 to pass, the cutoff score for females was set at 70. The public outcry was so great that the department had to abandon this approach. Many individuals perceived this method as an example of reverse discrimination–discrimination against the white male applicants.

BANDING

Banding
Grouping applicants based on ranges of scores.

An alternative approach to accomplishing employment equity is banding. **Banding** involves grouping applicants based on ranges of scores. In fact, cutoff scores are actually a form of banding where there are two bands (i.e., those above the cutoff score are in one band and those below the cutoff score are in another band). Sometimes bands are devised in a subjective manner through expert or managerial judgment. For example, applicants can be grouped into "Top Choice," Very Good," "Acceptable," and "Unacceptable" candidates. However, the term *banding* usually refers to a grouping process that takes into account the concept of *standard error of measurement* (from classical test theory).

Essentially, the standard error of measurement (SEM) reflects the fact that almost any measurement contains an error as well as a true score component. For example, if you obtain a score of 83 percent on an exam, part of that score reflects your true knowledge of the material tested but part of it reflects other factors such as your level of alertness during testing, level of stress, distractions, and luck. Not sleeping well the night before the test, experiencing personal problems, or spending considerable time studying material that turns out to be a very small component of the exam can reduce your test score so that it underrepresents your true knowledge. On the other hand, if you study only some of the course material but, as luck would have it, that very material constitutes most of the test, or if you obtain some advance knowledge of test content, or if you simply make some lucky guesses, your test score overrepresents your true knowledge. Such errors of measurement are taken into account by the SEM, a statistic that reflects the reliability of an individual's score. In banding, SEM is used to calculate the *standard error of difference* (SED) using the formula SED = $\sqrt{2}$ SEM. SED is the standard deviation associated with the difference in two independent scores.[58]

Bands around a given score are calculated as 1.96 × the standard error of difference (i.e., ±1.96 $\sqrt{2}$ SEM). Assuming that the error is randomly distributed, we would be correct 95 percent of the time in asserting that an individual's true score lies within the band defined by ±1.96 SED. If the SEM in our example above is 2.03, we can establish a band of 5.63 points (1.96 × $\sqrt{2}$ × 2.03) around your score of 83. That is, there is a 95 percent probability that your true score is somewhere between 77.37 and 88.63 (i.e., 83 ± 5.63).

Now, let's assume you have a friend who wrote the same exam and scored 80 percent. Before you belittle your friend's lower grade, consider the effects of measurement error. If we construct a band around your friend's score of 80, we discover that his or her true score is somewhere between 74.37 and 85.63 (with a 95 percent probability). It is therefore possible that your friend's true score is higher than yours! Because there is an overlap in the bands around your scores, we can assert that your scores are not statistically different from each other. From a measurement perspective, both of you can be viewed as being at the same level of proficiency with respect to the course material. In fact, in this example, both of you would receive a grade of A–. Of course, SED is not used to differentiate grades of A– from B+, or B+ from B, but such grades are a form of banding.

Banding is applied to selection decisions by calculating a band from the top score downward. If the top score on a test is 96 and the 1.96 × SED is 5, then the band extends from 96 down to 91 (96 – 5). There is no need to extend the band above 96, as 96 is the top score. Any scores falling within the band from 91 to 96 are considered equal because the differences among them are not statistically significant. We are therefore free to select any applicants we wish within the band. In fact, as long as their scores fall within the same band, we could select minority applicants ahead of nonminority applicants in order to accomplish employment equity objectives.

Bands can be constructed in one of two ways: fixed or sliding. *Fixed bands* are calculated starting at the top score, as described above. All of the applicants within the band must be selected before a new band can be calculated. A new band is calculated starting from the highest score among those applicants who were not included in the first band. This process continues until the desired number of applicants has been hired.

Figure 10.3 illustrates both fixed and sliding bands with hypothetical data. The scores of 19 applicants have been ranked and some of them have been identified as minority applicants. If we assume that the 1.96 × SED is 5, then the first band ranges from 91 to 96 (as described above). Using the fixed bands approach, we would select the applicants scoring 93 and 96 and then construct a second fixed band from 89 (the new highest

FIGURE 10.3

FIXED VERSUS SLIDING BANDS FOR THE SELECTION OF MINORITY APPLICANTS

Fixed Bands	Applicant Scores and Minority Status	
Band 1	96	
	93	Minority
Band 2	89	
	89	Minority
	87	
	86	
	85	
	85	Minority
	85	Minority
	84	
Band 3	82	Minority
	82	
	81	
	80	
	80	
	79	Minority
	78	Minority
	78	
	77	

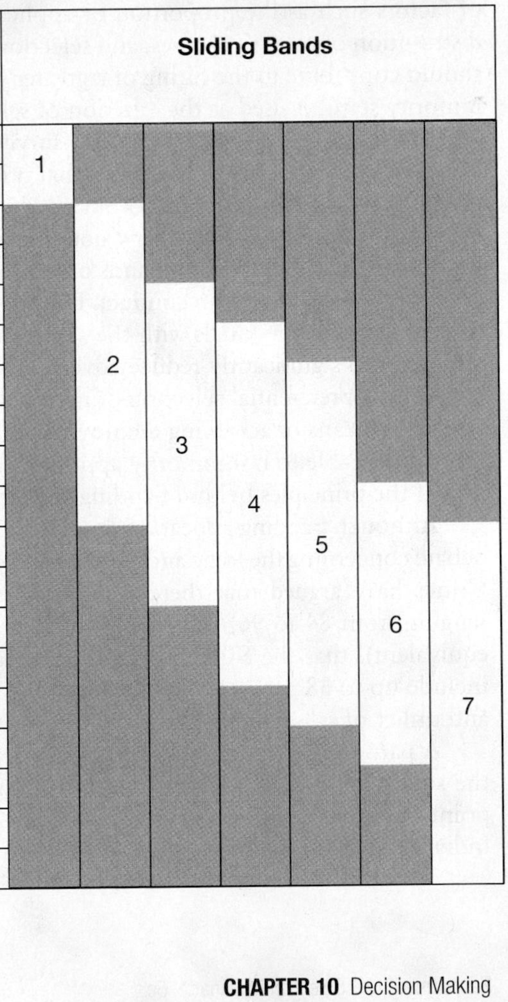

score) down to 84. Within the second fixed band, we would select the minority applicants first and then the remainder of the applicants until all of the required applicants who scored within the band have been selected. If we required additional candidates, we would construct a third fixed band from 82 down to 77.

With *sliding bands*, not every applicant in the band needs to be selected before the next band is constructed. Once the top scorer in the band has been selected, a new band is constructed from the next highest score. In this manner, the band slides down each time the top scorer within the band is selected. Applying the sliding band approach to the data in Figure 10.3, we would first select the minority applicant scoring 93 and then the applicant scoring 96. Once we've selected the top scorer (96), we would construct the second sliding band from 84 to 89. Within this band we would select the three minority applicants and then the highest remaining scorer (89). Once the highest scorer has been selected, we would construct the third sliding band from 82 to 87 and so on.

The sliding band approach provides a larger number of bands to select from than does the fixed band approach and therefore provides greater likelihood of selecting minority applicants. To illustrate, assume we want to select seven candidates from among the applicants represented in Figure 10.3. Using the traditional top-down approach, we would select as few as two and at the most three minority applicants. The fixed band approach would result in the selection of four minority candidates, whereas the sliding band approach would result in the selection of five minority applicants. Of course, the number of minority applicants selected in any particular situation depends on a number of factors such as the proportion of applicants who are minority group members, the distribution of minority scores, and selection ratios.[59] Nevertheless, on average, banding should contribute to the hiring of a greater proportion of minority applicants, provided minority status is used as the criterion of selection within bands.

The principle of banding has survived legal scrutiny in the United States. Nevertheless, U.S. courts have ruled that it is not permissible to use minority status as a primary criterion for selection within bands because the U.S. courts consider that a form of race norming (see http://www.siop.org/tip/backissues/tipjul97/Gutman.aspx).[60,61,62] Employers may select within bands on the basis of secondary criteria such as education, experience, or professional conduct. However, minority status may be used only as a tie-breaker among individuals with the same scores. Under such circumstances, banding is not likely to significantly reduce adverse impact.[63,64] In Canada, there is no legislation prohibiting preferential selection of minority applicants. As a result, banding could be a workable means of achieving employment equity objectives in a manner that might be more acceptable to nonminority applicants and employees than race norming, particularly if the principles behind banding are explained to them.[65]

Although banding appears to be permissible in Canada, there has been considerable debate concerning the logic and psychometric soundness of SED-based banding.[66,67,68,69] Critics have argued that there are logical inconsistencies in banding (e.g., in a band ranging from 84 to 96, 84 and 96 are considered equivalent while 83 and 84 are not equivalent), that the SED approach leads to very wide bands (i.e., the first band can include up to 38 percent of applicants), and that banding negatively affects the validity and utility of selection instruments.[70,71]

A particularly troubling criticism involves the fact that the SEM is derived from all the scores in an applicant group but is applied to the top-scoring individual(s). Critics point out that the SEM is usually much smaller for top-scoring individuals than it is for individuals in the middle of the distribution. Therefore, if bands are calculated from the top score down, using the group-based SEM is inappropriate. However, if bands are calculated using the SEM of top-scoring individuals, the bands become so narrow that they are not likely to be of much help for employment equity purposes.[72,73]

Given these concerns about banding, many researchers recommend other approaches to help achieve employment equity objectives.[74,75,76] For example, greater effort can be made to recruit members of minority groups or to better prepare minority applicants for testing (e.g., through training on test taking). Also, selection tools such as structured interviews, personality scales, or biodata inventories, which have less adverse impact on minority applicants, should be used for this purpose.

PRACTICAL CONSIDERATIONS

A variety of decision-making models and methods are available for making selection decisions. Which model or method is best in a given situation depends on a number of factors. The number of applicants expected, the amount of time available before selection decisions have to be made, and the costs associated with the selection instruments all have to be considered in making a choice. However, whenever they are feasible, linear models appear to outperform other approaches to decision making.

Many of the models discussed in this chapter assume large applicant pools or frequent and regular selection activity. Yet small businesses, which constitute a growing proportion of the Canadian economy, often hire small numbers of applicants on an infrequent basis. How can selection decisions in such small businesses be made more effectively?

Most of the rating procedures described in this chapter can be simplified to serve the needs of a small-business owner or manager.[77] The owner or manager can conduct an "armchair" job analysis by considering what tasks the employee would be expected to perform and how job performance would be assessed. As well, the owner or manager could consult the NOC or O*NET (see Chapter 4) for tasks related to similar jobs and the stated job requirements for those jobs.

Next the owner or manager should determine what behaviours related to these tasks could best be assessed in an interview and/or in simulations. Subjective weights could be attached, in advance, to each of the behaviours assessed, and the owner or manager should ensure that all applicants are evaluated systematically and fairly on the same criteria. Thus, although applicant information may be collected in a judgmental fashion or in a judgmental and statistical fashion, the information is combined statistically (i.e., trait rating or statistical composite) to yield a total score for each applicant. This total score can then be used to make the selection decisions.

Increasingly, small businesses are recognizing that they need to improve their human resources. Small-business associations have started to provide information on a vast array of topics, including the latest developments in human resources and how they can be adapted to a small-business environment. Many HR personnel now see the provision of HR services to small businesses on a consulting basis as a viable alternative to working in the HR department of a large firm.

Recruitment and Selection Notebook 10.1 provides guidelines that should help the HR professional in making a selection decision. Although the processes outlined here may seem intimidating, use of these procedures, with some practice, should lead to the selection of the best candidates who will, in turn, be more productive and effective.

RECRUITMENT AND SELECTION NOTEBOOK 10.1

MAKING THE SELECTION DECISION

1. Identify all of the sources of information about the applicant available to you (résumés, references, tests, interviews, etc.).
2. Use reliable, valid selection instruments whenever possible (e.g., structured interviews, reliable tests). Apply standardized criteria to the assessment of résumés, references, and other nonstandardized instruments so that they can be scored.
3. Determine which decision-making model you will use (taking into account the number of applicants, number and nature of predictors, cost factors, etc.).
4. If using the regression or combination models, collect and save data over a period of time for all predictors as well as job performance data for those applicants who are hired. When sufficient data have been collected, compute a regression equation, regressing job performance on the predictors. Determine the appropriate weights for each predictor.
5. If using multiple cutoff or multiple hurdle models, determine appropriate cutoff scores for each predictor.
6. Combine data from different predictors statistically to yield an overall score.
7. Offer the position(s) to the candidate(s) with the highest overall score(s).

© iStock.com/fotostorm

MAKING SELECTION DECISIONS: CONCLUSIONS

Although valid selection instruments are necessary for making good selection decisions, they are not sufficient. Good selection procedures must be used as well. Selection systems can be made more effective if some of the following recommendations are followed[78]:

1. Use valid selection instruments.
2. Dissuade managers from making selection decisions based on gut feelings or intuition.
3. Encourage managers to keep track of their own selection "hits" and "misses."
4. Train managers to make systematic selection decisions using one of the approaches described in this chapter.
5. Periodically evaluate or audit selection decisions in order to identify areas needing improvement.

// HIRING SELECTED APPLICANT(S)

Once employers have decided which applicant(s) they wish to hire, they need to move as quickly as possible to make the job offer(s). Top applicants are often considering offers from other organizations and, even if a particular employer is their first choice, they will usually accept one of the other offers if they have reached the offer deadline and their preferred employer is not yet ready to make an offer.[79] Therefore, any delay in contacting the selected applicants carries a high risk of losing them to competing organizations.

Nevertheless, employers need to ensure the hiring process is carried out carefully, with attention to detail, because errors made during the hiring process can result in very costly remediation once the applicant has been hired. In the following subsections we will discuss important factors employers need to consider in making a job offer.

PREPARING TO MAKE A JOB OFFER

Before a job offer can be made a number of preparatory steps are needed. These steps should culminate in an employment letter or contract, which we will discuss later in this section. In most large organizations there are HR policies in place that regulate the nature and content of employment offers. In smaller organizations offers are often constructed on an individual, case-by-case basis, though previous offers for the same or similar positions usually serve as templates. In essence, preparing to make a job offer involves ensuring all the details of the offer have been approved by the ultimate decision maker(s) in the organization and are known by the individual who will be communicating the offer to the applicant. If individuals communicating the offer have some leeway for negotiating with the applicant, their limits in negotiating an agreement should be clearly spelled out in advance. The following are questions that need to be resolved before making the job offer:

1. What will be the compensation package (base pay, commission, bonuses, stock options, perks, etc.)? In large or unionized organizations, the answer to this question will usually be determined by HR policies or collective agreements. These policies or agreements typically take into consideration what competing organizations are paying for similar occupations. In small non-unionized organizations, employers need to conduct a wage survey (which can be informal): what are competing organizations offering for similar skills? Both large and small organizations also need to determine whether they are able and willing to pay above, at, or below the average pay rate of competing organizations. This decision is based on the organization's budget but has implications for the organization's ability to attract top talent.
2. What will be the benefits package (medical, dental, vision, disability, life insurance, pension, etc.)? In most large or unionized organizations there is a standard benefits package for most employees or for particular subsets of employees, usually in accord with the benefits provided by competing organizations. Some large organizations are able to afford cafeteria-style benefits packages which are an attractive feature because they better serve the needs of employees. Small organizations are well advised to also strive to offer competitive benefits packages that will attract top employees.
3. Is the job offer conditional and, if so, what conditions need to be met (verification of qualifications, health screening and drug tests, criminal record check, satisfactory references, proof of eligibility to work in Canada, etc.)? Of course, any conditions need to be bona fide occupational requirements and must not violate human rights or employment standards. Applicants will need to be informed when the offer is made that failure to meet the conditions will void the job offer.
4. Will there be a probationary period (if so, how long?), a termination and/or resignation clause, a non-competition agreement or other restrictive agreements in the offer letter or contract that the applicant will be asked to sign (see the subsection on employment letters and contracts below for more information)?

If so, these details need to be made known to the applicant at the time the offer is made. That allows the applicants to reject the offer if they cannot accept particular clauses and if a mutually acceptable solution cannot be found. Failure to fully inform the applicants can make an employer liable for misleading them.

5. Does the individual making the job offer have authorization to negotiate with the applicant and, if so, what are the limits with respect to salary, perks, stock options, benefits, relocation costs, flexible work schedule, early salary review, bonuses/incentives, paid time off, work hours per week, vacation, educational assistance, start date, etc.? If there is some leeway in terms of the offer, it is most efficient to authorize the individual making the offer to negotiate with the applicant (within stated limits) to expedite the hiring process.
6. Does the individual making the job offer have authorization to proceed to the second or third-choice candidate should the first-choice candidate turn down the offer? If the top-choice candidate turns down the offer it's important to contact the next candidate as quickly as possible. Delays in moving down the list of acceptable candidates risk losing them to competing organizations.

MAKING A JOB OFFER

The selection process culminates in a two-way decision. The employers identify their preferred candidates, but most top candidates are also in the position of being able to identify their preferred employers. Unfortunately, there is not always a match between employer and candidate preferences. Often an employer's top-choice candidate identifies another organization as the top choice. In such circumstances, a timely, attractive job offer can often entice the candidate to accept, particularly if the competing organization is unable to match the offer or not yet ready to make an offer.[80] In any case, the content of the offer and the manner in which it is made are important not only to increasing the likelihood that the candidate will accept, but also to establishing a positive relationship between the new employee and the organization. Recruitment and Selection Notebook 10.2 provides recommendations that will help to make the job offer a positive experience for the candidate and increase the likelihood of job acceptance.

RECRUITMENT AND SELECTION NOTEBOOK 10.2

MAKING A JOB OFFER

1. Move quickly. The selected candidate should be contacted as soon as the selection decision has been made and approved. Delay in contacting the candidate risks losing the candidate to a competing organization.
2. Hold off on contacting the second-choice, third-choice, or possibly even fourth- or subsequent-choice candidates in case the first-choice candidate (or second-choice candidate) turns down the offer. Candidates will usually not appreciate knowing they are second or third choice and letting them know that can undermine their relationship with the organization. If these candidates inquire about the status of their applications, they can simply be told that the selection decisions are still being made.
3. Contact the top candidate by telephone rather than by e-mail or surface mail. A telephone conversation is more personal and allows the employer to convey enthusiasm, gauge the candidate's reaction, and respond accordingly.

4. Be enthusiastic and positive. Letting candidates know they are the organization's first choice and conveying excitement will increase the attractiveness of the organization to the candidate and increase the likelihood of job offer acceptance.
5. Ensure the job offer is attractive. Providing an offer that is competitive with those that an applicant is likely to receive from competing organizations will enhance the likelihood of offer acceptance. To ensure that an applicant fully appreciates the offer, it is important to thoroughly explain the details of the offer, including pay, benefits, perks, moving allowance, etc. Employers should be enthusiastic in outlining the offer but ensure that everything they say is accurate.
6. Try to get an oral commitment, even if it's tentative. It's normal for candidates to ask for time to consider a job offer but it can be very helpful for the employer to ask them what they think about the offer so that he can get a sense of any hesitation and try to answer any questions or concerns the candidate might have. However, it's important not to be too pushy in asking for the candidate's feedback. If the applicant clearly does not wish to discuss the offer at this time, the employer should drop the topic.
7. Be ready to negotiate, if necessary, and be as flexible as possible. Usually employers are constrained in what they can offer, either because of budget limitations or the inequities that can result with existing employees if excessive concessions are made for new employees. However, within these constraints, anything an employer can do to satisfy a candidate's requests will increase the likelihood of job acceptance. Some concessions, such as reserving a particular week for an already-booked vacation or altering the employment start date, need not be costly or inequitable. In fact, research indicates that flexibility with start dates is significantly related to likelihood of offer acceptance.[81]
8. If the candidate will be leaving a current employer to accept your offer, provide support and advice, if needed. Leaving an employer for a new job can be intimidating and stressful for job candidates. Allowing them to express their feelings and concerns and to ask questions about the process can help them with the transition. Job candidates might seek advice on what to say to their current employer, how much notice they need to give, how to deal with possible gaps in income, etc. Providing advice and guidance on these questions can allay their concerns and ease the transition.
9. Follow up in writing as soon as you have completed your telephone conversation with the candidate. The written communication can take the form of an offer of employment letter or a formal contract. It should include all the elements of the job offer, including job title, pay, benefits, vacation, holidays, perks, moving expenses, start date of employment, etc. Whatever form the written document takes, the applicant should be asked to sign off on acceptance of the job offer and return the document. Applicants are well-advised to retain a copy for their own records.
10. Set a deadline for the candidate to accept the offer. Three days is a typical length of time given for candidates to review the offer and make a decision. According to research, giving applicants a deadline does not result in negative reactions.[82] However, sometimes candidates ask for deadline extensions. Often such requests signal that the applicants are negotiating competing offers or hoping to hear from a competing organization.
11. If the candidate drags out the decision for too long, tell her that you need an answer so you can inform some of the other excellent candidates whether the job has been filled. How much time is "too long" depends on how desperately the organization wants to hire a particular candidate and the quality of the other candidates. The employer must also take into consideration the likelihood that second- and third-choice candidates could accept job offers from other organizations and would no longer be available, should the top-choice candidate eventually decline the offer.
12. If the candidate has a better offer from a competitor, make a counter-offer, if you are able. The extent of the counter-offer will depend on budgetary and other constraints, as noted above, and might be insufficient to sway the candidate but, if it is successful, it's worth the effort.
13. Never push a candidate to renege on acceptance of an offer from another employer. It is unethical for an employer to undermine a commitment that a candidate has made to another employer and no employers would want others to do that to them. However, if candidates who have made commitments to an employer wish to be released from that commitment, it is better

for that employer to let them go than have disgruntled employees working for him. Sometimes candidates will alert a prospective employer that they have received an offer from a competing organization and they have to make a decision by a certain deadline. If the prospective employer is not yet ready to make a decision, inform the candidate of that, and indicate when a decision is likely to be forthcoming. It is then up to the candidate to negotiate a new deadline with the competing organization or to accept or decline that company's offer.

14. If you are unable to negotiate further (keeping in mind budgetary and other constraints), inform the candidate that this is your final offer and, if it is not acceptable, you will need to withdraw the offer. Some candidates will keep asking for concessions, even if they would accept the job offer without those concessions, simply because they want to get as much as they can from the employer. Such candidates will accept the offer at this point. It is best that candidates who are still not satisfied with everything the employer has to offer find employment elsewhere, and that the employer withdraw the offer.

15. If your final offer fails, move on to your second-choice candidate as quickly as possible (or to the third choice, if the second-choice candidate is no longer available). Depending on the job market, the size of the organization, and the number of qualified candidates in the applicant pool, some organizations might have to restart the recruitment process at this point.[83] That is a costly, time-consuming outcome of an excessively slow selection process, which can be avoided by streamlining the decision and job offer process and expanding the applicant pool as much as possible. However, rather than restarting the recruitment process, some organizations settle for a mediocre or even poor candidate.[84] This is a poor selection decision, which is likely to be very costly to the organization in the end and lead to bad hiring decisions.

16. Once you have received a signed acceptance of the written offer, inform the remaining job candidates that the position has been filled. This can be done by telephone but is usually done by e-mail or surface mail, particularly if there are a large number of candidates to be contacted. In communicating with the candidates, the employer should acknowledge their strong job-related qualities and convey appreciation for their candidacy. It is important to leave a positive impression of the organization with these candidates because it's quite possible that they will again become candidates in future job competitions and they will certainly communicate their opinions about the organization, whether positive or negative, to others who might be customers or employees of the organization, or future job applicants.

So far, we have considered job offers from the perspective of the employer. Recruitment and Selection Notebook 10.3 provides advice for negotiating a job offer from the perspective of the applicant.

RECRUITMENT AND SELECTION NOTEBOOK 10.3

FIFTEEN RULES FOR NEGOTIATING A JOB OFFER

Job-offer negotiations are rarely easy. Consider three typical scenarios:

1. You're in a third-round interview for a job at a company you like, but a firm you admire even more just invited you in. Suddenly the first hiring manager cuts to the chase: "As you know, we're considering many candidates. We like you, and we hope the feeling is mutual. If we make you a competitive offer, will you accept it?"

2. You've received an offer for a job you'll enjoy, but the salary is lower than you think you deserve. You ask your potential boss whether she has any flexibility. "We typically don't hire people with your background,

and we have a different culture here," she responds. "This job isn't just about the money. Are you saying you won't take it unless we increase the pay?"

3. You've been working happily at your company for three years, but a recruiter has been calling, insisting that you could earn much more elsewhere. You don't want to quit, but you expect to be compensated fairly, so you'd like to ask for a raise. Unfortunately, budgets are tight, and your boss doesn't react well when people try to leverage outside offers. What do you do?

Each of these situations is difficult in its own way—and emblematic of how complex job negotiations can be. At many companies, compensation increasingly comes in the form of stock, options, and bonuses linked to both personal and group performance. In MBA recruitment, more companies are using "exploding" offers or sliding-scale signing bonuses based on when a candidate accepts the job, complicating attempts to compare offers. With executive mobility on the rise, people vying for similar positions often have vastly different backgrounds, strengths, and salary histories, making it hard for employers to set benchmarks or create standard packages.

In some industries a weak labour market has also left candidates with fewer options and less leverage, and employers better positioned to dictate terms. Those who are unemployed, or whose current job seems shaky, have seen their bargaining power further reduced.

But job market complexity creates opportunities for people who can skilfully negotiate the terms and conditions of employment. After all, negotiation matters most when there is a broad range of possible outcomes.

As a professor who studies and teaches the subject, I frequently advise current and former students on navigating this terrain. For several years I have been offering a presentation on the topic to current students. (To see a video of this talk, go to www.NegotiateYourOffer.com.) Every situation is unique, but some strategies, tactics, and principles can help you address many of the issues people face in negotiating with employers. Here are 15 rules to guide you in these discussions.

The Rules

Don't underestimate the importance of likability. This sounds basic, but it's crucial: People are going to fight for you only if they like you. Anything you do in a negotiation that makes you less likable reduces the chances that the other side will work to get you a better offer. This is about more than being polite; it's about managing some inevitable tensions in negotiation, such as asking for what you deserve without seeming greedy, pointing out deficiencies in the offer without seeming petty, and being persistent without being a nuisance. Negotiators can typically avoid these pitfalls by evaluating (for example, in practice interviews with friends) how others are likely to perceive their approach.

Help them understand why you deserve what you're requesting. It's not enough for them to like you. They also have to believe you're worth the offer you want. Never let your proposal speak for itself—always tell the story that goes with it. Don't just state your desire (a 15% higher salary, say, or permission to work from home one day a week); explain precisely why it's justified (the reasons you deserve more money than others they may have hired, or that your children come home from school early on Fridays). If you have no justification for a demand, it may be unwise to make it. Again, keep in mind the inherent tension between being likable and explaining why you deserve more: Suggesting that you're especially valuable can make you sound arrogant if you haven't thought through how best to communicate the message.

Make it clear they can get you. People won't want to expend political or social capital to get approval for a strong or improved offer if they suspect that at the end of the day, you're still going to say, "No, thanks." Who wants to be the stalking horse for another company? If you intend to negotiate for a better package, make it clear that you're serious about working for this employer. Sometimes you get people to want you by explaining that *everybody* wants you. But the more strongly you play that hand, the more they may think that they're not going to get you anyway, so why bother jumping through hoops? If you're planning to mention all the options you have as leverage, you should balance that by saying why—or under what conditions—you would be happy to forgo those options and accept an offer.

Understand the person across the table. Companies don't negotiate; people do. And before you can influence the person sitting opposite you, you have to understand her. What are her interests and individual concerns? For example, negotiating with a prospective boss is very different from negotiating with an HR representative. You can perhaps afford to pepper the latter with questions regarding details of the offer, but you don't want to annoy someone who may become your manager with seemingly petty demands. On the flip side, HR may be responsible for hiring 10 people and therefore reluctant to break precedent, whereas the boss, who will benefit more directly from your joining the company, may go to bat for you with a special request.

Understand their constraints. They may like you. They may think you deserve everything you want. But they still may not give it to you. Why? Because they may have certain ironclad constraints, such as salary caps, that no amount of negotiation can loosen. Your job is to figure out where they're flexible and where they're not. If, for example, you're talking to a large company that's hiring 20 similar people at the same time, it probably can't give you a higher salary than everyone else. But it may be flexible on start dates, vacation time, and signing bonuses. On the other hand, if you're negotiating with a smaller company that has never hired someone in your role, there may be room to adjust the initial salary offer or job title but not other things. The better you understand the constraints, the more likely it is that you'll be able to propose options that solve both sides' problems.

Be prepared for tough questions. Many job candidates have been hit with difficult questions they were hoping not to face: Do you have any other offers? If we make you an offer tomorrow, will you say yes? Are we your top choice? If you're unprepared, you might say something inelegantly evasive or, worse, untrue. My advice is to never lie in a negotiation. It frequently comes back to harm you, but even if it doesn't, it's unethical. The other risk is that, faced with a tough question, you may try too hard to please and end up losing leverage. The point is this: You need to prepare for questions and issues that would put you on the defensive, make you feel uncomfortable, or expose your weaknesses. Your goal is to answer honestly without looking like an unattractive candidate—and without giving up too much bargaining power. If you have thought in advance about how to answer difficult questions, you probably won't forfeit one of those objectives.

Focus on the questioner's intent, not on the question. If, despite your preparation, someone comes at you from an angle you didn't expect, remember this simple rule: It's not the question that matters but the questioner's intent. Often the question is challenging but the questioner's intent is benign. An employer who asks whether you would immediately accept an offer tomorrow may simply be interested in knowing if you are genuinely excited about the job, not trying to box you into a corner. A question about whether you have other offers may be designed not to expose your weak alternatives but simply to learn what type of job search you're conducting and whether this company has a chance of getting you. If you don't like the question, don't assume the worst. Rather, answer in a way that addresses what you think is the intent, or ask for a clarification of the problem the interviewer is trying to solve. If you engage in a genuine conversation about what he's after, and show a willingness to help him resolve whatever issue he has, both of you will be better off.

Consider the whole deal. Sadly, to many people, "negotiating a job offer" and "negotiating a salary" are synonymous. But much of your satisfaction from the job will come from other factors you can negotiate—perhaps even more easily than salary. Don't get fixated on money. Focus on the value of the entire deal: responsibilities, location, travel, flexibility in work hours, opportunities for growth and promotion, perks, support for continued education, and so forth. Think not just about *how* you're willing to be rewarded but also *when*. You may decide to chart a course that pays less handsomely now but will put you in a stronger position later.

Negotiate multiple issues simultaneously, not serially. If someone makes you an offer and you're legitimately concerned about parts of it, you're usually better off proposing all your changes at once. Don't say, "The salary is a bit low. Could you do something about it?" and then, once she's worked on it, come back with "Thanks. Now here are two other things I'd like..." If you ask for only one thing initially, she may assume that getting it will make you ready to accept the offer (or at least to make a decision). If you keep saying "and one more thing...," she is unlikely to remain in a generous or understanding mood. Furthermore, if you have more than one request, don't simply mention all the things you want—A, B, C, and D; also signal the relative importance of each to you. Otherwise, she may pick the two things you value least, because they're pretty easy to give you, and feel she's met you halfway. Then you'll have an offer that's not much better and a negotiating partner who thinks her job is done.

Don't negotiate just to negotiate. Resist the temptation to prove that you are a great negotiator. MBA students who have just taken a class on negotiation are plagued by this problem: They go bargaining berserk the first chance they get, which is with a prospective employer. My advice: If something is important to you, absolutely negotiate. But don't haggle over every little thing. Fighting to get just a bit more can rub people the wrong way—and can limit your ability to negotiate with the company later in your career, when it may matter more.

Think through the timing of offers. At the beginning of a job hunt, you often want to get at least one offer in order to feel secure. This is especially true for people finishing a degree program, when everyone is interviewing and some are celebrating early victories. Ironically, getting an early offer can be problematic: Once a company has made an offer, it will expect an answer reasonably soon. If you want to consider multiple jobs, it's useful to have all your offers arrive close together. So don't be afraid to slow down the process with one potential employer or to speed it up with another, in order to have all your options laid out at one time. This, too, is a balancing act: If you pull back too much—or push too hard—a company may lose interest and hire someone else. But there are subtle ways to solve such problems. For example, if you want to delay an offer, you might ask for a later second- or third-round interview.

Avoid, ignore, or downplay ultimatums of any kind. People don't like being told "Do this or else." So avoid giving ultimatums. Sometimes we do so inadvertently—we're just trying to show strength, or we're frustrated, and it comes off the wrong way. Your counterpart may do the same. My personal approach when at the receiving end of an ultimatum is to simply ignore it, because at some point the person who gave it might realize that it could scuttle the deal and will want to take it back. He can do that much more easily without losing face if it's never been discussed. If someone tells you, "We'll never do this," don't dwell on it or make her repeat it. Instead you might say, "I can see how that might be difficult, given where we are today. Perhaps we can talk about X, Y, and Z." Pretend the ultimatum was never given and keep her from becoming wedded to it. If it's real, she'll make that clear over time.

Remember, they're not out to get you. Tough salary negotiations or long delays in the confirmation of a formal offer can make it seem that potential employers have it in for you. But if you're far enough along in the process, these people like you and want to continue liking you. Unwillingness to move on a particular issue may simply reflect constraints that you don't fully appreciate. A delay in getting an offer letter may just mean that you're not the only concern the hiring manager has in life. Stay in touch, but be patient. And if you can't be patient, don't call up in frustration or anger; better to start by asking for a clarification on timing and whether there's anything you can do to help move things along.

Stay at the table. Remember: What's not negotiable today may be negotiable tomorrow. Over time, interests and constraints change. When someone says no, what he's saying is "No—given how I see the world today." A month later that same person may be able to do something he couldn't do before, whether it's extending an offer deadline or increasing your salary. Suppose a potential boss denies your request to work from home on Fridays. Maybe that's because he has no flexibility on the issue. But it's also possible that you haven't yet built up the trust required to make him feel comfortable with that arrangement. Six months in, you'll probably be in a better position to persuade him that you'll work conscientiously away from the office. Be willing to continue the conversation and to encourage others to revisit issues that were left unaddressed or unresolved.

Maintain a sense of perspective. This is the final and most important point. You can negotiate like a pro and still lose out if the negotiation you're in is the wrong one. Ultimately, your satisfaction hinges less on getting the *negotiation* right and more on getting the *job* right. Experience and research demonstrate that the industry and function in which you choose to work, your career trajectory, and the day-to-day influences on you (such as bosses and coworkers) can be vastly more important to satisfaction than the particulars of an offer. These guidelines should help you negotiate effectively and get the offer you deserve, but they should come into play only after a thoughtful, holistic job hunt designed to ensure that the path you're choosing will lead you where you want to go.

Sources: Deepak Malhotra. "15 Rules for Negotiating a Job Offer." *Harvard Business Review* (April 2014): Retrieved from http://hbr.org/2014/04/15-rules-for-negotiating-a-job-offer/ar/1. Reprinted by permission of *Harvard Business Review.*

Brian A Jackson/Shutterstock.com

EMPLOYMENT LETTERS AND CONTRACTS

Offers of employment can be made verbally, by letter, or by contract. Letters and verbal offers of employment are typically used for lower-level employees and, generally, are less detailed than employment contracts. They serve to make a job offer and outline the basic terms of employment, as well as to inform the candidates of the general expectations that the employer has of the candidates, should they accept the offer. In workplaces covered by a collective agreement with a union, the candidate is usually given a letter setting out important clauses in the collective agreement that apply to their work along with a copy of the collective agreement. Verbal offers of employment are just as binding as written offers. However, it is in the interests of both employers and employees to have a signed written agreement as evidence in the event of disagreements about the employment relationship.

Employment contracts are much more detailed and formal than job offer letters and they are generally used for professionals, managers, and other high-level employees. These employees typically have access to corporate strategy, proprietary information, and clients and client lists. As a result, they pose potential risks to the organization, which the contracts seek to mitigate.

Regardless of whether the offer is made verbally, by letter, or by contract, there are certain requirements for an offer of employment to be legally valid and enforceable. There must be an offer and an acceptance of the offer of employment, in return for which the job candidate is promised some form of compensation. This promise of compensation is referred to as **consideration** by the courts. Moreover, the employment offer must not be unconscionable (e.g., exploitative, coercive, misleading, etc.) or illegal. All employment offers must comply with federal and provincial human rights legislation, workplace safety legislation, and employment standards. Anything that is not specified in the employment agreement becomes subject to common law. That is, if a disagreement between an employer and a candidate or employee is brought before the courts, the case would be decided based on legal precedent. The implications of common law for employment contracts will be discussed in more detail below. Recruitment and Selection Today 10.3 and 10.4, respectively, provide examples of an offer of employment letter and a template for an employment contract.

Consideration
A promise of compensation by the employer in return for the prospective employee's services.

RECRUITMENT AND SELECTION TODAY 10.3

EXAMPLE OF AN OFFER OF EMPLOYMENT LETTER

Miss Steak 'N Identity Restaurant
123 Porterhouse Street, Angus, Ontario

September 11, 2014
Ms. Leigh Vatip
456 Porterhouse Street, Angus, Ontario

Dear Ms. Vatip,

I am pleased to offer you the position of waitress at Miss Steak 'N Identity Restaurant effective September 30, 2014. We are proud of our restaurant and hope you will enjoy working with our team.

Your duties in our restaurant will include presenting menus to patrons, answering questions about menu items, and making recommendations upon request; taking orders from patrons for food or beverages; checking patrons' identification to ensure that they meet minimum age requirements for consumption of alcoholic beverages; writing patrons' food orders on order slips or memorizing orders, and entering orders into computers for transmittal to kitchen staff; serving food or beverages to patrons, and preparing or serving specialty dishes at tables as required; checking with customers to ensure that they are enjoying their meals and taking action to correct any problems; collecting payments from customers; and clearing and cleaning tables or counters after patrons have finished dining.

You will be reporting to Ms. May Tredee, our head waitress, and your starting pay will be $11.00 per hour plus any tips you collect. Your hours of work will vary from day-to-day, in accordance with our needs and the hours of operation of the restaurant, but they will amount to at least 40 hours per week, including evenings and weekends, as needed. Please note that our restaurant hours are 11 a.m. to 11 p.m., Tuesdays to Sundays (we are closed on Mondays). You are entitled to two weeks' paid vacation effective October 1, 2015, as well as public holiday pay plus overtime pay for any public (statutory) holidays that you work. An optional benefits package is also available (please see the enclosed benefits information).

Your employment with us is subject to a probationary period of 3 months beginning September 30, 2014. This probationary period will be subject to the Ontario Employment Standards Act, 2000.

Please sign the enclosed copy of this letter and return it to me by September 16, 2014 to indicate your acceptance of this offer.

Sincerely,

Ms. Sally Sperry-Steak, Owner
Miss Steak 'N Identity Restaurant

I understand the terms of this agreement and accept the offer outlined above.

Name: ______________________________ Date: ____________________
Signature: ___________________________

RECRUITMENT AND SELECTION TODAY 10.4

TEMPLATE FOR AN EMPLOYMENT CONTRACT

Employment agreements

The purpose of an employment agreement is to set out the terms and conditions of the relationship between an employer and an employee. It states the obligations they have to each other and the benefits they will receive from each other. Each agreement must be tailored to suit an individual employment relationship.

Employment agreements do not need to repeat terms and conditions set out in the organization's policies. Employment agreements may need to be more detailed if policies are not in place or if the particular position has specific requirements. For example, overtime rules may be specific to the position, or the employee may have access to confidential information because of the work they do.

This template is a guide. It is not a substitute for information about the laws and standards of practice that apply in any specific situation.

Sample content for an employment agreement

According to the terms of this agreement, (*Organization*) will employ (*Individual*) in the position (*Title*) beginning on (*Start Date*) OR from (*Start Date*) to (*End Date*).

> *Without an end date, the agreement will remain in effect until it is cancelled by one of the parties. Terms for canceling the agreement are part of the agreement (see below).*
>
> *A "fixed term" agreement should include terms for renewing it. For example, you can state that the agreement is automatically renewed at the end of each period unless one of the parties cancels it. If you opt for automatic renewal, you should also specify that neither party can refuse to renew; that is, the contract ends only when one of the parties cancel it.*

Duties and responsibilities

> *Duties and responsibilities can be described in an attached position description, which should be referred to as "part of this agreement". Or a description of the duties and responsibilities can be incorporated into the body of this agreement.*

Reporting lines

The (Title) reports to (Title of supervisor).

Compensation

SALARY:

The annual salary of the (*Title*) is $_____ for the first year.
The annual salary will be increased by ___% effective on (date).
OR
Salary increases will be negotiated to take effect at the beginning of each renewal period.

GROUP INSURANCE:

The (*Title*) is eligible for coverage under the organization's Group Insurance plan (*refer to policy or description of plan*).
OR
The (*Title*) will receive payment equivalent to ___% of salary in lieu of benefits.
The cost of group insurance will be paid by the organization with the exception of the cost of the premium for Long Term Disability insurance, which will be deducted from the employee's pay.
OR
The cost of group insurance will be shared; 50% will be paid by the organization and 50% will be deducted from the employee's pay.

RETIREMENT BENEFITS:

The organization will make a contribution on behalf of (*employee*) to (*name of Retirement Savings Plan*) equal to ___% of (*employee*)'s annual salary.

OTHER BENEFITS:

Mention any other benefits that apply to this position.

PAY SCHEDULE:

The (*Title*) will be paid according to organization's established pay schedule.
OR
The (*Title*) will be paid as follows: Monthly direct deposit of salary and quarterly cheques for contribution to retirement savings plan.

Reimbursement of expenses

The employee will be reimbursed for travel and other expenses incurred to while carrying out their responsibilities on behalf of (*organization*) provided these expenses are approved in advance by (*Title of position with the authority to approve expenses*).

The organization may also cover fees for membership in professional associations

Allowances

For example, if the organization pays an allowance to the employee for use of the employee's car for business purposes, the terms should be spelled out.

Work hours/schedule

The (*organization*)'s policies on standard hours, overtime and compensatory time, *and other related topics* apply to this position.
OR
The standard hours of work for (*organization*) are ___ hours per week. Employees are compensated for work time that exceeds standard hours with time off at a rate of 1.5 hours off per extra hour worked.
OR
The standard hours of work for (*organization*) are ___ hours per week. Employees are compensated for work time that exceeds standard hours at a rate of 1.5 times their regular hourly rate provided that overtime work is approved in advance by (*Title of position with the authority to approve overtime*).

Annual leave

(*Title*) is entitled to annual leave (vacation with pay) in accordance with (*organization*)'s policy.
OR
(*Title*) is entitled to annual leave (*vacation with pay*) as follows: (FOR EXAMPLE)

YEARS OF SERVICE COMPLETED	ANNUAL LEAVE
1–3 years	3 weeks
4–6 years	4 weeks
7+ years	5 weeks

It is helpful to clarify vacation entitlements for the first year. Can vacation be taken as it accumulates? Or will the employee be entitled to vacation at the end of the first year?

Other leave

If the employee is entitled to other leave (for example, sabbatical or leave for personal reasons) mention it here.

Annual performance review

The performance of the (Title) will be reviewed annually by (Title of supervisor or manager with responsibility for conducting the review) based on criteria agreed upon by the (Employee's Title) and (Supervisor, manager, or committee acting on behalf of the organization) at the beginning of the period subject to review.

Settlement of disagreements

Describe the process or procedure that will be used to settle disagreements between the employer and the employee when they cannot resolve the disagreement themselves.

Cancellation of this agreement

This agreement can be cancelled only as follows:

By the employer, in the event of the employee's death or "with cause:" Under these circumstances, no compensation will be paid to the employee after the agreement is cancelled.

By the employer "without cause:" The employer will give ___ weeks written notice to the employee and pay salary and benefits in respect of the notice period as agreed or negotiated.

By the employee: The employee will give ___ weeks notice. The employer will pay salary and benefits in respect of the notice period as agreed or negotiated.

Other provisions

Some employment agreements also include provisions to deal with matters such as: Ownership of intellectual property, Confidentiality, Terms of departure, Non-competition in the period after employment ends, Non-solicitation of the organization's employees, Indemnification of the employee or Limitations on other employment or activities with other organization

---

A national organization agreed to post this policy on www.hrcouncil.ca as part of the HR Toolkit. Sample policies are provided for reference only. Always consult current legislation in your jurisdiction to create policies and procedures for your organization

Source: Courtesy of Community Foundations of Canada/HR Council of Canada.

Employment contracts can be for a definite term or for an indefinite term. Definite-term contracts pertain to a fixed period of employment (e.g., six months) or to the completion of a specific task. If an employer terminates an employee before the term or task is completed, the employee can sue for damages (such as loss of income) as a consequence of being prevented from fulfilling the contract. Employers need to be aware that stringing a series of short-term contracts together can be deemed by the courts to be indefinite employment. For example, the Ontario Employment Standards Act, 2000 indicates that a term or task agreement that exceeds 12 months (whether as one contract or a series of contracts) is deemed to be indefinite employment. Indefinite-term contracts have no fixed termination date or task. In an indefinite employment agreement, the employee is entitled to notice of termination or payment in lieu of notice in accordance with provincial employment standards, should the employee be terminated.

Employment contracts provide protection for both the employer and the job candidate or employee. They are a written record of the employment agreement and are legally binding. However, the effectiveness of employment contracts is limited by what is and what is not included. Both employers and applicants need to be vigilant to ensure that the contract documents clearly all of their requirements, rights, and obligations. Many employers seek legal advice in drafting employment contracts and, particularly for complex contracts, it is advisable that applicants also seek legal advice before signing. Employment contracts can include just about anything deemed by either party to be important to the employment relationship and the contents can be negotiated. However, there are common elements in most employment contracts. These common elements are discussed below. Although these elements are discussed in the context of employment contracts, they apply equally to offer of employment letters.

EMPLOYMENT DETAILS

The contract should include details of employment such as the start date, the position title, work location, reporting relationships, hours of work, and be accompanied by a document detailing all rules and regulations. The starting date is important because it defines when the employment relationship begins and has implications for other aspects of the employment agreement such as the commencement of benefits and the conclusion of probationary periods. Normally the start date should permit the applicant to give a current employer at least two weeks' notice of resignation (assuming the applicant is currently employed). It is also advisable to provide employees with copies of an employee handbook, or collective agreement, containing all rules and regulations to clearly communicate the expectations of the employer and reduce the likelihood of employees unknowingly committing infractions or injuring themselves in the first few days of work. Moreover, applicants who might object to particular regulations are forewarned and can choose to decline the offer if they feel they cannot adhere to the regulations.

COMPENSATION AND BENEFITS

The details of the compensation package (salaried, wage-based, piece rate, or other) should be made clear, including components like bonuses, commissions, stock options, company cars, etc. Contingencies should also be outlined. For example, if bonuses are part of the pay package, there should be an indication that a particular level of performance is required to obtain the bonus (i.e., the bonus is not guaranteed). If the compensation information is complex, it might be preferable to include a separate document outlining the compensation plan and to simply refer to it in the contract. Most employers who provide benefits have a brochure or document which outlines their benefits package (sometimes with options). If the employer provides a benefits package, the relevant brochure or document should accompany the contract rather than attempting to summarize the benefits in the contract. By having the contract simply refer to the enclosed document, there is less risk of making inaccurate promises or inadvertently contradicting the benefits plan. The employer might also wish to include a clause in the contract reserving the right to modify or discontinue benefits plans, should the need arise (e.g., if a plan becomes too expensive), without any obligation to replace them or compensate affected employees.

HIRING INCENTIVES

Sometimes organizations provide special incentives to attract applicants and increase the likelihood of job offer acceptance. Hiring incentives can include hiring bonuses, accelerated promotion opportunities, relocation assistance, housing subsidies, and any other incentives of value to prospective employees. These hiring incentives should be specified in the contract but, if the related regulations or conditions are complex, it is advisable to provide the details in a separate document which accompanies the contract. Hiring bonuses are a way of attracting employees in tight job markets without incurring a permanent increase in an employee's base pay and, thereby, potentially creating internal inequities. It's advisable to pay the bonus in installments and to indicate in the contract that the employee will not receive the full bonus unless she remains with the organization a minimum length of time (e.g., one year) to prevent an employee from collecting the bonus and leaving within the first weeks of employment. Some organizations also make the bonus contingent on the employee meeting certain performance goals. If an applicant needs to move to another geographic location in order to work for an employer, the employer can provide relocation assistance. This can involve partially or totally defraying the applicant's moving costs, arranging the applicant's move, helping with house hunting, providing mortgage subsidies, guaranteeing the purchase of the applicant's old house, and providing cost-of-living adjustments if the applicant is moving to a high-cost area. Some organizations simply provide new employees with a lump-sum relocation allowance and let the employee work out the details of her move. Conditions or regulations pertaining to relocation assistance should be also spelled out in the contract or in a separate document if they are complex.

CONDITIONAL OFFERS

If the job offer is conditional upon the fulfillment of particular requirements, such as completion of a degree, diploma, or other qualifications, health screening or drug tests, background checks, satisfactory references, or proof of eligibility to work in Canada, this should be specified in the contract. The contract should indicate that failure to meet any of the conditions to the employer's satisfaction voids the job offer. If any of the checks require the employer to obtain information from third parties, a consent form should be included with the offer for the applicant's signature. In all cases, the conditions must not violate human rights, workplace safety standards, or employment standards.

PROBATIONARY PERIOD

Contrary to popular misconception, employees are not automatically subject to a probationary period. For example, although the Ontario Employment Standards Act, 2000 indicates that no minimum pay in lieu of notice is required for employees with less than three months of service, it does not specify that employees with less than three months of service have probationary status. Therefore, in the absence of a probationary clause in the contract, common law applies. Some employees with less than three months of service have been awarded significant pay in lieu of notice, sometimes amounting to more than the actual earnings of the employee during the period of employment (typically based on factors such as the employee's age, managerial level, and probability of re-employment). Therefore, if an employer wishes to have a probationary period, a probationary clause must be included in the contract. Although it is common for employers to choose a three-month probationary period, the law does not impose a limit on how long a probationary period may be. Thus, an employer is free to have a probationary period of six months or longer (recall that, for university professors, tenure involves a probationary period that lasts five or six years). However, after three months the employer must provide notice or payment in lieu of notice at least in accordance with employment standards. In any case, it is advisable that the contract specify the applicability of the relevant employment standards to avoid appeals to common law.

TERMINATION

Termination of employment can occur for many reasons including just cause, without cause, resignation, and retirement. Termination with just cause involves the dismissal of an employee for an action or omission by the employee that has irreparably damaged the relationship between the employer and the employee. Just cause typically involves serious misconduct such as theft, workplace violence, breaches of confidentiality obligations, conflict of interest, or any illegal activity, but can also involve poor performance that persists despite warnings and corrective efforts by the employer. It is prudent to specify in the contract that the employee can be terminated for just cause without notice or pay in lieu of notice. Providing a non-exhaustive list of examples of just cause in the contract is also advisable. Termination without cause involves reasons that are not related to misconduct such as layoffs, job redundancy, economic reorganization, and mergers but can also include poor performance. Termination without cause requires the employer to give the employee notice or pay in lieu of notice at least in accordance with employment standards. However, in certain circumstances (e.g., senior employees, a large number of employees laid off at the same time) terminated employees have successfully invoked common law to obtain substantially larger severance packages than specified by the employment standards. To protect themselves, employers can specify in the contract that, in case of dismissal without cause, the minimum payments required by employment standards legislation will apply. Resignation can occur for many reasons including a new job offer, a spouse's transfer, a career change, or returning to school. Because resignations often leave employers scurrying to hire and train a replacement for the employee who leaves, it helps them to have some advance warning. Although, as a courtesy, most employees will provide at least two weeks' notice if they are leaving, that is not always the case. Therefore, employers may wish to include in the contract a clause specifying that the employee agrees to give a specific amount of advance written notice (e.g., two weeks) when leaving. The employer might also reserve the right to pay the employee in lieu of the employee reporting to work for any part of the notice period. Whether the termination is for cause, without cause, or due to resignation or retirement, the contract should also specify when benefits, bonuses, commissions, and other compensation cease. For example, an employer might specify that the employee is not entitled to bonuses and commissions that might accrue beyond the end of the statutory notice period.

RESTRICTIVE AGREEMENTS

Employers sometimes insert restrictive agreements into contracts to protect the interests of the organization. These restrictive agreements can include confidentiality clauses, non-solicitation clauses, and non-competition clauses. Confidentiality clauses usually prohibit current or departing employees from divulging confidential information such as secret formulas, manufacturing processes, client lists, or the business strategy of the organization. Non-solicitation clauses prohibit departing employees from soliciting or recruiting the organization's employees or clients for their new employer. Non-competition clauses prohibit the departing employee from setting up a business that competes with the organization or from joining a competing organization. Generally, courts have struck down such clauses if they are overly restrictive because they could prohibit the employee from making a living. For example, software developers working for a software company are not likely to find work suited to their training and experience except with another software company that develops similar software. Restrictive agreements are not likely to be enforceable unless it is clear that they protect legitimate proprietary interests of the organization, and even in those circumstances the organization needs to make a case by describing specifically why it needs protection (e.g., because it is new to the marketplace, because the marketplace is very competitive, because the organization is specialized, because the employee holds a critical role or has critical information). Moreover, the agreement needs to have reasonable limits in terms of the duration of the restriction, the geographic area of the restriction, and the level of the restriction (e.g., a non-solicitation clause might be more appropriate in most circumstances than a non-competition clause).

Additional information about employment contracts is available at http://www.gowlings.com/KnowledgeCentre/article.asp?pubID=2908, http://www.nelligan.ca/e/pdf/Employment_Contracts.pdf, and http://managingtheworkplace.com/materials/2013/introducing-and-enforcing-employment-contracts.pdf.

ACCEPTANCE AND IMPLEMENTATION OF EMPLOYMENT LETTERS AND CONTRACTS

The offer letter or contract should specify the date when the offer will lapse to prevent applicants who have not responded from claiming a right to the job long after the offer was made. Applicants should signify their acceptance of the job offer by signing a copy of the offer letter or contract and returning it to the employer. If candidates wish to make changes to the contract, they cannot do so by modifying and signing the contract. A revised contract, including the requested changes, would need to be drawn up by the employer and signed by the applicant. If the employer does not accept the requested modifications, the applicant can either accept the original contract or reject the offer (or the offer expires).

If an applicant signs the offer letter or contract the day he starts work, or anytime thereafter, the contract is not enforceable because the applicant is already employed under an oral agreement at the time he signs the written contract. The contract should be signed and returned to the employer before the employee starts work. Moreover, the employee should be given sufficient time before the start date to review the contract and seek advice if desired. Also, the applicant should be given an opportunity to ask questions of the employer concerning the contract. Otherwise, the employee can make the claim that he did not understand parts of the contract and was not given an opportunity to discover the implications of the contract before he signed. Once the signed contract has been received by the employer, a copy should be given to employees for their records.

Most of our discussion of offer letters and employment contracts has been from the perspective of the employer. Recruitment and Selection Notebook 10.4 provides advice for job candidates on reviewing employment contracts.

RECRUITMENT AND SELECTION NOTEBOOK 10.4

WHAT YOU NEED TO KNOW ABOUT EMPLOYMENT CONTRACTS

Congratulations. After countless interviews, you've finally been offered your dream job. All that's left to do now, you're told, is sign the company's employment contract. You scan the document, and are quickly overwhelmed by the legalese. What to do? Do you sign now or risk losing the job if you don't?

Such scenarios are playing out across Canadian workplaces. Written employment contracts are a standard practice for high-level executive positions, but experts say they are increasingly becoming a condition of hire for every level of worker. What's more, such contracts are becoming more complex as employers seek to protect themselves from potential damages should the relationship go sour.

Blame it partly on the recession. A weak economy and the resulting layoffs had many companies paying out hefty severance packages, says Daniel Lublin, a workplace lawyer and partner with Whitten & Lublin LLP in Toronto who specializes in hiring and dismissals.

"It's a factor of experience. They're waking up to what can happen and they want to protect themselves and reduce the expense of terminations," he says.

"It's also just good employment hygiene," says Janice Rubin, a partner with Rubin Thomlinson LLP in Toronto. "[A written employment contract] sets out clearly what the deal is. It may not eliminate misunderstandings, but it certainly reduces them."

Typically an employment contract outlines both party's rights, duties and obligations. It can be a one-page offer or a 10-page tome, Ms. Rubin says.

Whatever form it takes, an employment contract can be intimidating. Here's what you need to know before you sign on the dotted line:

Review, review, review

Employment contracts are by nature filled with legal jargon difficult for the average person to comprehend. "Never sign anything you don't understand," Ms. Rubin advises.

But when presented with a contract, people often feel they are under pressure to act quickly or perhaps lose the job. "It's extremely hard to say no to a potential employer, because you want the job," Mr. Lublin says. What you need to remember, he adds, is that the company spent a lot of time and resources wooing you. It's unlikely that it will rescind the job offer if you ask for time to review the contract.

While there are no provisions in law that give you a grace period to examine the document, "it's a reasonable request to ask for time to review a contract, and obtain legal advice," Ms. Rubin notes. "If they say, 'No, you must sign now,' that should give you pause. That should tell you a lot about your prospective employer."

What the contract should cover

Besides basic elements such as your starting date, job title and duties and responsibilities, all aspects of your financial compensation should be clearly documented, particularly if your salary structure is complex, Ms. Rubin says. This includes base salary, raises you're promised, commissions, bonuses, stock options, profit sharing and how you will be compensated for overtime. "If you look at commission, for example, you want to know not just how much but when it's triggered; is it upon payment or when the deal is signed?" she says.

Make sure that the contract includes any special promises or considerations made to you. If you are being orally promised a promotion six months down the road along with a pay increase, or perhaps a move to the firm's New York office within the year, get it in writing. "Figure out what is important to you and make sure it's in the contract," Ms. Rubin says.

Other clauses that an employer will likely include are terms of termination, including severance and any post-employment restrictions.

Negotiate for better terms

Employment contracts often don't sufficiently protect an employee's interests, Mr. Lublin says. Worse, a contract might reduce or remove rights you are entitled to under law. "Oftentimes employers will say, 'This is the standard deal that everyone has to sign,'" he notes. But as with any contract, employment agreements can be negotiated, depending on the issue and whether you have leverage in the form of in-demand skills or experience or specialized knowledge. If there is something you don't like or is missing in the contract, ask for changes, Mr. Lublin says. "It can never hurt to try."

Red flags

One area to pay close attention to in a contract is the termination clause. Mr. Lublin says that many employers typically offer departing staff only the minimum severance required under the law. "However, without a contract, the vast majority of employees are entitled to more than the minimum and in some cases far greater than the minimum," he says.

Another area is post-employment restrictions, which can prevent you from competing with your former employer or soliciting customers, suppliers or former colleagues if your employment is terminated. Many employees unwittingly agree to unfavourable restrictions on their activities after they leave a company, Mr. Lublin says.

Alarm bells should also ring if you're asked to sign a new contract mid-stream, Ms. Rubin says. "If your employer presents you with a new contract, whether it's six months or a year later, be very careful to ensure that it doesn't take away something you're already entitled to."

Ties that bind

How binding is an employment contract? That depends. Generally, a written employment contract will be enforceable by both parties if it is fair and properly drafted, Mr. Lublin says.

Not surprisingly, Ms. Rubin says, "the provisions that generate the most traffic are what employees are entitled to upon termination and restrictive covenants post-employment."

Many factors can render a contract unenforceable by Canadian courts, she adds, including language deemed to be ambiguous or unclear, or if it can be shown that the employee signed the contract under duress.

If you're unsure of, or uneasy about, the terms of a contract, seek appropriate advice. "Much of my work is dedicated to undoing a bad contract that someone unknowingly signed years earlier," Mr. Lublin says.

Source: Jennifer Myers. 2011. "What You Need to Know About Employment Contracts." *The Globe and Mail* (January 7): Retrieved from http://www.theglobeandmail.com/report-on-business/careers/career-advice/what-you-need-to-know-about-employment-contracts/article560882/. Reproduced with permission of the author.

// SUMMARY

Employers face a difficult task in trying to combine and make sense of complex applicant information in order to make selection decisions. They are vulnerable to numerous biases and errors and they often oversimplify information because their information processing abilities are overloaded. Unfortunately, many employers prefer to rely on their gut instincts rather than on more objective sources of information.

In many organizations, selection decisions are made by groups rather than by individuals. There is some evidence that groups can make better decisions and the use of selection panels has been supported in Canadian human rights tribunals.

Although several approaches to making selection decisions can be used, methods that involve combining applicant information in a statistical manner are generally superior to other methods in reducing errors and predicting job performance.

Various decision-making models, such as multiple regression, multiple cutoff, multiple hurdle, combination, and profile matching, can help in making effective selection decisions when used under appropriate conditions. The multiple regression and multiple hurdle combination approaches are probably the most efficient decision-making models if the assumptions underlying the models are not violated. These models produce a total score, which can be used to rank candidates and select them from the top down until the desired number of candidates has been selected. However, banding is suggested as an alternative to conventional top-down selection because banding satisfies employment equity objectives, while still enabling the hiring of top-quality applicants.

Once the most suitable candidates have been selected, a job offer is made, preferably in writing. A number of legal and practical details and implications need to be considered in making the offers and drafting job offer letters or contracts. Importantly, candidates should sign the offer letters or contracts before they commence working for the organization.

Today's organizations are undergoing rapid change and, to survive, must adapt to unanticipated innovations in technology, global competition, changing labour force demographics, and increasing government regulation and societal pressures for conformity to ethical, environmental, and human rights standards. Best practices in recruitment and selection are part of an organization's survival tools. The procedures we have outlined in this text address the need for reliable, valid, and legally defensible staffing procedures that provide a return on their investment and enhance a firm's productivity.

KEY TERMS

Banding, p. 492
Consideration, p. 504
Cutoff score, p. 481
False negative error, p. 473
False positive error, p. 472
Implicit theories, p. 470
Incremental validity, p. 479
Judgmental composite, p. 475
Multiple cutoff combination model, p. 488
Multiple hurdle combination model, p. 488
Organizational fit, p. 470
Profile interpretation, p. 475
Pure judgment approach, p. 474
Pure statistical approach, p. 475
Satisficing, p. 469
Selection ratio, p. 481
Statistical composite, p. 475
Top-down selection, p. 491
Trait rating approach, p. 474

WEB LINKS

Information on setting cutoff scores for tests, as developed by the Public Service Commission of Canada, is available at
http://www.psc-cfp.gc.ca/ppc-cpp/acs-cmptnc-evl-cmptnc/ct-off-scrs-pnts-cpr-eng.htm

An example of a multiple hurdle approach can be found at the Toronto Police Service website at
http://www.torontopolice.on.ca/careers/uni_become_officer.php

For more information on the multiple hurdles approach, as well as other methods for integrating selection data, go to
http://www.hr-guide.com/data/G366.htm

The status of banding is discussed at
http://www.siop.org/tip/backissues/tipjul97/Gutman.aspx

Information on offer of employment letters and contracts is available at
http://www.gowlings.com/KnowledgeCentre/article.asp?pubID=2908,
http://www.nelligan.ca/e/pdf/Employment_Contracts.pdf, and
http://managingtheworkplace.com/materials/2013/introducing-and-enforcing-employment-contracts.pdf.

DISCUSSION QUESTIONS

1. What are the common decision-making errors made in employee selection? Can these be eliminated? If so, how? If they cannot be eliminated, can they be reduced? If so, how?
2. What is the difference between judgmental and statistical approaches to the collection and combination of applicant information?
3. What are the advantages and disadvantages of the following decision-making models?
    a. Rational weighting
    b. Regression models
    c. Multiple hurdle
    d. Multiple cutoff
    e. Profile matching
4. Why do organizations tend to use groups to make selection decisions? What are the advantages and disadvantages of group decision making?
5. Why is it better to use predictors that are uncorrelated or that have a low correlation with each other than predictors that are highly correlated with each other?
6. Discuss the differences among cutoff scores, banding, and top-down selection. Is any one of these more advantageous to use than the others? If so, under what circumstances?
7. What are the biggest pitfalls employers need to be concerned about when drafting offer of employment letters or contracts? What steps can be taken to avoid or minimize the likelihood of problems with offers of employment?
8. Discuss the benefits of using best practices in recruitment and selection.

EXERCISES

1. Assume that you occasionally hire cashiers for a small store. You generally do not hire more than two or three at a time. You have five applicants for two positions. You have obtained information from all of the applicants on a set of five predictors, as follows (the regressions weights are validity coefficients multiplied by two):

Predictor Scores

Applicant	Cognitive Test	Conscientious-ness Scale	Biodata Form	Structured Interview	Reference Check
Ms. Z	47	26	18	47	6
Mr. Y	36	36	15	45	8
Ms. W	46	36	16	32	9
Ms. V	44	30	10	36	7
Mr. U	39	38	14	41	10
Maximum Possible					
Scores	50	40	20	50	10
Regression weights	1.1	0.4	0.8	1.0	0.5
Cutoff scores	36	27	12	35	7
Mean scores	40	35	16	39	8

a. Using the information presented in the table, determine which of the applicants would be selected and, where appropriate, what their rank would be under each of the following decision-making models:
   i. Multiple regression
   ii. Multiple cutoff
   iii. Multiple hurdle combination
   iv. Profile matching (D^2 only)

b. Which of the selection models discussed do you believe is best suited to this situation? Why?

2. If the regression weights were 1.2, 0.7, 0.3, 1.5, and 0.5 for the five measures, respectively, who would now be selected (the cutoff scores remain unchanged from the original)? What would be the rank-order under each of the four decision-making models?
3. If the cutoffs were 30, 30, 15, 40, and 6, respectively, for the five measures, who would now be selected (the regression weights remain unchanged from the originals)? What would be the rank-order under each of the four decision-making models?
4. Discuss the impact that both cutoff scores and regression weights may have on selection decisions.
5. You are an HR practitioner trying to improve selection procedures in your organization. Under the current system, application forms are screened by relevant department managers to determine who should be interviewed. References are also collected. The managers do their own interviewing using individual, unstructured interviews and base their selection decisions almost exclusively on these interviews.

They tend to have a lot of confidence in their gut feelings about candidates and believe they've been doing a pretty good job of selecting the right applicants.

a. How would you go about trying to convince them that they should adopt a more structured, objective (i.e., statistical) decision-making system?
b. What objections to your suggestion do you anticipate would be raised by the managers?
c. How would you address these objections?

6. Table 10.2 on page 482 presented hypothetical data for four predictors used to hire sales representatives. For the purpose of the illustration, arbitrary cutoffs were set for each of the predictors. For this exercise, we want you to develop actual cutoff scores that you might assign to each of the four measures. Retain the maximum possible score stated in Table 10.2 for each measure.

   First, obtain the requirements for a sales representative by going to the National Occupational Classification or other job analysis procedure discussed in Chapter 4. Next, follow the Public Service of Canada guidelines to develop cutoff scores for each measure. The cognitive ability and extraversion measures are generic; however, you may want to use the resources identified in Chapter 8 (e.g., Buros Mental Measurements Yearbook) to select specific cognitive ability and personality measures. Use the information from these specific tests, such as any normative data that is provided, to help set your cutoffs.

   a. What are your new cutoffs for each of the tests?
   b. Using your new cutoffs, reanalyze the data in Table 10.2, following the procedures in Table 10.3 (page 485), for each of the decision-making models. Compare your rank-ordering of the four candidates under each model to that obtained from using the Table 10.2 cutoffs. Are there differences in who would be hired?
   c. Discuss the importance of setting cutoffs with respect to hiring decisions.

CASE

The Google organization is best known for its Web search engine, which now accounts for over 90 percent of worldwide market share, to the point that the term "Googling" has become synonymous with Web browsing.[85] Actually, the name "Google" was derived from the word "googol," a mathematical term for the number 1 followed by 100 zeros, which was intended to convey Google's mission to organize the huge amount of information on the Web.[86] Of course, Google offers a wide variety of other products and services, including Gmail, Google Calendar, Blogger, Google Docs, Google Maps, Google Groups, and others. Google's official mission is to "organize the world's information and make it universally accessible and useful."[87]

Google was founded in 1998 by Larry Page and Sergey Brin, three years after they met at Stanford University. They started working out of a garage with one employee in 1998 but the Google corporation has now grown to almost 30 000 employees internationally, including Canadian offices in Kitchener-Waterloo, Montreal, Ottawa, and Toronto. Although Google has grown a lot since 1998, it strives to maintain a small-company feel. Google needs to innovate in order to survive and depends on its employees to provide the necessary innovation.

Casual interactions among employees and the sharing of ideas and opinions at the office café or break rooms are strongly encouraged. Every employee is expected to contribute in a variety of ways, often wearing several hats. In turn, Google treats its employees very well, providing a wide variety of perquisites and generous compensation and benefits packages for its employees. It is therefore understandable that Google was ranked first in the most recent Fortune's "100 Best Companies to Work For."[88]

Given its reputation, it is not surprising that Google attracts more than 100 000 job applications every month. Although this number of applications provides great opportunity for Google to be highly selective, it also creates a challenge in terms of how to efficiently sort through the more than one million applications every year to determine which applicants are most suitable. Fortunately, Google has been able to apply search algorithms, similar to the ones it uses for Web searches, to its online job applications. This automated system makes the selection process much easier and also more effective.[89]

In the past, Google's selection system required successful applicants to have a grade-point average of at least 3.7 and to go through more than half a dozen interviews. However, management at Google was not satisfied with the outcomes of this system. In addition to seeking greater efficiency, they were interested in hiring more "well-rounded" candidates who demonstrated abilities in leadership, teamwork, creativity, and other areas, not just those who did well academically.

To accomplish its objectives, Google developed an online biographical information blank (BIB) or biodata form (see "Biographical Data" on pages 289–294 in Chapter 7). Every employee who had worked with the company for at least five months was asked to fill out a 300-question survey. The survey included questions about what programming languages employees were familiar with, what Internet mailing lists they subscribed to, what magazines they subscribed to, whether their workplace was messy or neat, whether they were introverts or extraverts, whether they preferred working alone or in groups, whether they had ever tutored, what pets they had, whether they had ever made a profit from activities such as a catering business or dog walking, whether they had ever set a world record, etc. Data from the initial survey were compared with 25 separate measures of job performance, including supervisors' ratings, peer ratings, and measures of organizational citizenship. Eventually, patterns of responses were identified that predicted performance in various areas such as engineering, sales, finance, or human resources. The resulting online biodata form is now completed by applicants and their responses are sorted by Google's algorithm to identify which applicants are best suited to the various positions available.[90]

The online application form has not eliminated the interview as part of the selection process but it seems to have reduced the number of interviews in which successful candidates participate. Now, applicants who are identified as possible match for a position by Google's algorithm are contacted by a recruiter for a 30–40 minute telephone screening interview. The recruiter makes a preliminary assessment of their technical skills and proficiency, and determines whether they should be brought in for in-person interviews.

Applicants who proceed to an on-site interview are further assessed in terms of their job-relevant skills. For example, applicants for a technical position would be evaluated in terms of their core software engineering skills including coding, algorithm development, data structures, design patterns, and analytical thinking skills. Applicants for business and general positions are evaluated with respect to their problem solving and behavioural abilities. Google's interviews include puzzle interview questions (see "Puzzle Interviews" on pages 443–444 in Chapter 9). However, Google's instructions make it clear that the interviewers are not so much concerned with whether applicants get the answers right or wrong, but with what processes they use to solve the questions. They are especially looking for evidence of creativity.[91]

The onsite visits include interviews with at least four interviewers, including both managers and potential colleagues. Applicants are also given a tour of the facilities and exposed to various work activities at the site during their visit. Following the interviews, the interviewers deliberate in order to arrive at a consensus-based decision. This process means that it can take up to two additional weeks for hiring decisions to be made. However, the people at Google believe it helps them make the most effective decisions possible.

QUESTIONS

1. Why did Google change its selection system? How was the selection system changed?
2. Do you think the changes are an improvement compared with Google's previous selection system? Why or why not?
3. Do you agree that using an online biographical information blank (BIB) is the best way for Google to manage the large volume of applications? Why or why not?
4. Is invasion of privacy a concern with the kinds of questions used in Google's online BIB (e.g., "Is your workplace messy or neat?")? Why or why not?
5. Do you think the online BIB could have adverse impact on minority applicants? If so, why? If not, why not?
6. What alternatives can you suggest for an organization such as Google to manage a large number of applications?
7. Do you think the new system will be more effective at helping Google to hire candidates who will be more "well rounded" (i.e., have demonstrated abilities in leadership, teamwork, creativity, etc.)? Why or why not?
8. What alternative ways are there of identifying the kind of "well-rounded" candidates Google is looking for?
9. Do you recommend that Google continue using puzzle interviews (see "Puzzle Interviews" on pages 443–444 in Chapter 9) as part of its selection system? Why or why not? How would you assess technical skills?
10. Pretend you have been put in charge of staffing at Google. Your job is to review the new selection system and to explore ways of improving the system.

a. How would you determine whether the online BIB and interviews are helping Google accomplish its employee selection objectives?

b. If you found that the BIB has adverse impact on minority applicants, what would you do to address the problem?

c. What suggestions would you make to help Google further improve its selection system? How would you determine whether these suggested changes are effective?

d. What decision-making model (e.g., multiple regression, multiple cutoff, multiple hurdle, combination, profile matching) is currently being used by Google? Is this the most appropriate model? If so, why? If not, why not and what alternative model would you recommend? Why?

// ENDNOTES

1 Simon, H.A. 1957. *Administrative Behavior,* 2nd ed. New York: Free Press.

2 Bazerman, M.H. 1986. *Judgment in Managerial Decision Making.* New York: Wiley.

3 Janis, I.L., and L. Mann. 1977. *Decision Making: A Psychological Analysis of Conflict, Choice, and Commitment.* New York: Free Press.

4 Huber, V.L., M.A. Neale, and G.B. Northcraft. 1987. "Decision Bias and Personnel Selection Strategies." *Organizational Behavior and Human Decision Processes* 40: 136–47.

5 Stone, D.L., K.M. Lukaszewski, E.F. Stone-Romero, and T.L. Johnson. 2013. "Factors Affecting the Effectiveness and Acceptance of Electronic Selection Systems." *Human Resource Management Review* 23: 50–70.

6 Simon, H.A. 1957.

7 Scullen, S.E. 2013. "What If the Preferred Applicant Rejects a Job Offer? A Look at Smaller Applicant Pools." *Journal of Business Psychology* 28: 331–44.

8 Ross, M., and J.H. Ellard. 1986. "On Winnowing: The Impact of Scarcity on Allocators' Evaluations of Candidates for a Resource." *Journal of Experimental Social Psychology* 22: 374–88.

9 Chuang, A., and P.R. Sackett. 2005. "The Perceived Importance of Person–Job Fit and Person–Organization Fit Between and Within Interview Stages." *Social Behaviour and Personality* 33: 209–26.

10 Parker, M. 2012, February 27. "Recruiting for Fit: 7 Steps to Ensure Candidate's Success." *Canadian HR Reporter.* Retrieved August 2014 from http://www.waterstonehc.com/sites/default/files/Recruiting%20for%20fit%20-%20Marty%20Parker%20%282%29.pdf

11 Highhouse, S. 2008. "Stubborn Reliance on Intuition and Subjectivity in Employee Selection." *Industrial and Organizational Psychology: Perspectives on Science and Practice* 1: 333–42.

12 Davison, H.K., and M.J. Burke. 2000. "Sex Discrimination in Simulated Employment Contexts: A Meta-Analytic Investigation." *Journal of Vocational Behavior* 56: 225–48.

13 Luzadis, R., M. Wesolowski, and B.K. Snavely. 2008. "Understanding Criterion Choice in Hiring Decisions from a Prescriptive Gender Bias Perspective." *Journal of Managerial Issues* 20: 468–84.

14 Ng, E.S., and W.H. Wiesner. 2007. "Are Men Always Picked Over Women? The Effects of Employment Equity Directives on Selection Decisions." *Journal of Business Ethics* 76: 177–87.

15 Luzadis, R., M. Wesolowski, and B.K. Snavely. 2008.

16 Lievens, F., S. Highhouse, and W. DeCorte. 2005. "The Importance of Traits and Abilities in Supervisors' Hirability Decisions as a Function of Method of Assessment." *Journal of Occupational and Organizational Psychology* 78: 453–70.

17 Tews, M.J., K. Stafford, and J.B. Tracey. 2011. "What Matters Most? The Perceived Importance of Ability and Personality for Hiring Decisions." *Human Resources Management* 52: 94–101.

18 Meehl, P.E. 1954. *Clinical versus Statistical Prediction: A Theoretical Analysis and a Review of the Evidence.* Minneapolis, MN: University of Minnesota Press.

19 Sawyer, J. 1966. "Measurement and Prediction, Clinical and Statistical." *Psychological Bulletin* 66: 178–200.

20 Kuncel, N.R., D.M. Klieger, B.S. Connelly, and D.S. Ones. 2013. "Mechanical versus Clinical Data Combination in Selection and Admissions Decisions: A Meta-Analysis." *Journal of Applied Psychology* 98: 1060–72.

21 Kleinmuntz, B. 1990. "Why We Still Use Our Heads Instead of Formulas: Toward an Integrative Approach." *Psychological Bulletin* 107: 296–310.

22 Highhouse, S. 2008.

23 Lievens, F., S. Highhouse, and W. DeCorte. 2005.

24 Tews, M.J., K. Stafford, and J.B. Tracey. 2011.

25 Kleinmuntz, B. 1990.

26 Kuncel, N.R., D.M. Klieger, B.S. Connelly, and D.S. Ones. 2013.

27 Diab, D.L., S-Y. Pui, M. Yankelevich, and S. Highhouse. 2011. "Lay Perceptions of Selection Decision Aids in US and Non-US Samples." *International Journal of Selection and Assessment* 19: 209–16.

28 Lodato, M.A., S. Highhouse, and M.E. Brooks. 2011. "Predicting Professional Preferences for Intuition-Based Hiring." *Journal of Managerial Psychology* 26: 352–65.

29 Highhouse, S. 2008.

30 Kleinmuntz, B. 1990.

31 Diab, D.L., S-Y. Pui, M. Yankelevich, and S. Highhouse. 2011.

32 Kleinmuntz, B. 1990.

33 Lodato, M.A., S. Highhouse, and M.E. Brooks. 2011.

34 Dose, J.J. 2003. "Information Exchange in Personnel Selection Decisions." *Applied Psychology: An International Review* 52: 237–52.

35 Slaughter, J.E., J. Bagger, and A. Li. 2006. "Context Effects on Group-Based Employee Selection Decisions." *Organizational Behavior and Human Decision Processes* 100: 47–59.

36 Guzzo, R., and E. Salas, eds. 1997. *Team Effectiveness and Decision Making in Organizations.* San Francisco: Jossey-Bass.

37 Hackett, R.D., J.B. Rose, and J. Pyper. 2000. "The Employment Interview: An Analysis of Canadian Labour Arbitration Decisions." In K. Whitaker, J. Sack, M. Gunderson, R. Filion, and B. Bohuslawsy, eds. *Labour Arbitration Yearbook 1999–2000,* Vol. 1. Toronto: Lancaster House.

38 Hackett, R.D., L.M. Lapierre, and H.P. Gardiner. 2004. "A Review of Canadian Human Rights Cases Involving the Employment Interview." *Canadian Journal of Administrative Sciences* 21: 215–28.

39 Kichuk, S.L., and W.H. Wiesner. 1998. "Work Teams: Selecting Members for Optimal Performance." *Canadian Psychology* 39: 23–32.

40 Stevens, M.J., and M.A. Campion. 1994. "The Knowledge, Skill, and Ability Requirements for Teamwork: Implications for Human Resource Management." *Journal of Management* 20: 503–30.

41 Burch, G.S.J., P. Christos Pavelis, and R.L. Port. 2008. "Selecting for Creativity and Innovation: The Relationship between the Innovation Potential Indicator and the Team Selection Inventory." *International Journal of Selection and Assessment* 16: 177–81.

42 Saks, A.M., N. Schmitt, and R.J. Klimoski. 2000. *Research, Measurement, and Evaluation of Human Resources*. Scarborough, ON: Nelson.

43 Drezner, Z., G.O. Wesolowsky, and W.H. Wiesner. 1999. "A Computational Procedure for Setting Multiple Cutoff Scores." *Journal of Business and Management* 6: 86–98.

44 Cascio, W.F., and H. Aguinis. 2010. *Applied Psychology in Human Resource Management*, 7th ed. Englewood Cliffs, NJ: Prentice-Hall.

45 Gatewood, R.D., H.S. Feild, and M. Barrick. 2011. *Human Resource Selection*, 7th ed. Mason, OH: Thomson/Southwestern.

46 Ibid.

47 Cascio, W.F., and H. Aguinis. 2010

48 Gatewood, R.D., H.S. Feild, and M. Barrick. 2011.

49 Ibid.

50 Stone, D.L., K.M. Lukaszewski, E.F. Stone-Romero, and T.L. Johnson. 2013.

51 Ibid.

52 Ibid.

53 Nunnally, J.C., and I.H. Bernstein. 1994. *Psychometric Theory*, 3rd ed. New York: McGraw-Hill.

54 Stone, D.L., K.M. Lukaszewski, E.F. Stone-Romero, and T.L. Johnson. 2013.

55 Gatewood, R.D., H.S. Feild, and M. Barrick. 2011.

56 Ibid.

57 Ibid.

58 Cascio, F.W., J. Outtz, S. Zedeck, and I.L. Goldstein. 1991. "Six Methods of Test Score Use in Personnel Selection." *Human Performance* 4: 233–64.

59 Murphy, K.R., K. Osten, and B. Myors. 1995. "Modeling the Effects of Banding in Personnel Selection." *Personnel Psychology* 48: 61–84.

60 Gutman, A., and N. Christiansen. 1997. "Further Clarification of the Judicial Status of Banding." *The Industrial–Organizational Psychologist* 35: 75–81: http://siop.org/tip/backissues/tipjul97/Gutman.aspx

61 Barrett, G.V., and S.B. Lueke. 2004. "Legal and Practical Implications of Banding for Personnel Selection." In H. Aguinis, ed., *Test Score Banding in Human Resource Selection: Technical, Legal, and Societal Issues.* Westport, CT: Praeger Publishers.

62 Henle, C.A. 2004. "Case Review of the Legal Status of Banding." *Human Performance* 17: 415–32.

63 Murphy, K.R., K. Osten, and B. Myors. 1995.

64 Campion, M.A., J.L. Outtz, S. Zedeck, F.L. Schmidt, J.F. Kehoe, K.R. Murphy, and R.M. Guion. 2001. "The Controversy Over Score Banding in Personnel Selection: Answers to 10 Key Questions." *Personnel Psychology* 54: 149–85.

65 Truxillo, D.M., and T.N. Bauer. 1999. "Applicant Reactions to Test Score Banding in Entry-Level and Promotional Contexts." *Journal of Applied Psychology* 84: 322–39.

66 Cascio, W.F., J. Outtz, S. Zedeck, and I.L. Goldstein. 1995. "Statistical Implications of Six Methods of Test Score Use in Personnel Selection." *Human Performance* 8: 133–64.

67 Schmidt, F.L. 1995. "Why All Banding Procedures in Personnel Selection Are Logically Flawed." *Human Performance* 8: 165–77.

68 Murphy, K.R., and B. Myors. 1995.

69 Campion, M.A., J.L. Outtz, S. Zedeck, F.L. Schmidt, J.F. Kehoe, K.R. Murphy, and R.M. Guion. 2001.

70 Ibid.

71 Bobko, P., P.L. Roth, and A. Nicewander. 2005. "Banding Selection Scores in Human Resource Management Decisions: Current Inaccuracies and the Effect of Conditional Standard Errors." *Organizational Research Methods* 8: 259–73.

72 Bobko, P., and P.L. Roth. 2004. "Personnel Selection with Top-Score-Referenced Banding: On the Inappropriateness of Current Procedures." *International Journal of Selection and Assessment* 12: 291–98.

73 Bobko, P., P.L. Roth, and A. Nicewander. 2005.

74 Campion, M.A., J.L. Outtz, S. Zedeck, F.L. Schmidt, J.F. Kehoe, K.R. Murphy, and R.M. Guion. 2001.

75 Bobko, P., and P.L. Roth. 2004.

76 Kehoe, J.F. 2008. "Commentary on Pareto-Optimality as a Rationale for Adverse Impact Reduction: What Would Organizations Do?" *International Journal of Selection and Assessment* 16: 195–200.

77 Schneider, B., and N.W. Schmitt. 1986. *Staffing Organizations.* Glenview, IL: Scott Foresmann.

78 Gatewood, R.D., H.S. Feild, and M. Barrick. 2011. *Human Resource Selection,* 7th ed. Mason, OH: Thomson/Southwestern.

79 Breaugh, J.A. 2013. "Employee Recruitment." *Annual Review of Psychology* 64: 389–416.

80 Scullen, S.E. 2013.

81 Breaugh, J.A. 2013.

82 Ibid.

83 Scullen, S.E. 2013.

84 Ibid.

85 StatCounter Global Stats, "Top 5 Search Engines from August 2013 to July 2014." Retrieved August 15, 2014. http http://gs.statcounter.com/#search_engine-ww-monthly-201308-201407

86 Google: Company. Retrieved August 2014 from http://www.google.com/about/corporate/company/index.html

87 Ibid.

88 Fortune, "100 Best Companies to Work For, 2014." Retrieved August 2014 from http://archive.fortune.com/magazines/fortune/best-companies/2014/list/

89 Hansell, S. 2007, January 3. "Google Answer to Filling Jobs is an Algorithm," *New York Times*. Retrieved from http://www.nytimes.com/2007/01/03/technology/03google.html?pagewanted=all&_r=0

90 Ibid.

91 Google: Hiring Process. Retrieved August 2014 from http://www.google.com/about/careers/lifeatgoogle/hiringprocess/

GLOSSARY

A

Abilities
Enduring, general traits or characteristics on which people differ and which they bring to a work situation. (p. 331)

Absolute rating systems
Compare the performance of one worker with an absolute standard of performance; can be used to assess performance on one dimension or to provide an overall assessment. (p. 206)

Accommodation
The duty of an employer to put in place modifications to discriminatory employment practices or procedures to meet the needs of members of a protected group being affected by the employment practice or procedure. As part of a BFOR defence, an employer must demonstrate that such accommodation is impossible to achieve without incurring undue hardship in terms of the organization's expense or operations. (p. 94)

Adaptive performance
A worker's behavioural reactions to changes in a work system or work role. (p. 179)

Adverse effect discrimination
Refers to a situation where an employer, in good faith, adopts a policy or practice that has an unintended, negative impact on members of a protected group. (p. 87)

Adverse impact
Occurs when the selection rate for a protected group is lower than that for the relevant comparison group. (p. 88)

Applicant pool
The set of potential candidates who may be interested in, and who are likely to apply for, a specific job. (p. 226)

Application blank
A form completed by job candidates that provides a prospective employer with basic information concerning such things as applicant knowledge, skills, education, and previous work experience. (p. 285)

Aptitude
A specific, narrow ability or skill that may be used to predict job performance. (p. 331)

Assessment centre
A standardized procedure that involves the use of multiple measurement techniques and multiple assessors to evaluate candidates for selection, classification, and promotion. (p. 355)

B

Banding
Grouping applicants based on ranges of scores. (p. 492)

Behaviour description interview
A structured interview in which the applicant is asked to describe what he did in given situations in the past. (p. 428)

Bias
Systematic errors in measurement, or inferences made from those measurements, that are related to different identifiable group membership characteristics such as age, sex, or race. (p. 55)

Biodata
Biographical data gathered from applicant BIBs, application blanks, or other sources. (p. 291)

Biographical information blank (BIB)
A pre-selection questionnaire that requires applicants to provide detailed job-related information concerning their personal background and life experiences. (p. 289)

Bona fide occupational requirement (BFOR)
A procedure used to defend a discriminatory employment practice or policy on the grounds that the policy or practice was adopted in an honest and good-faith belief that it was reasonably necessary to assure the efficient and economical performance of the job without endangering employees or the general public. BFORs are sometimes referred to as bona fide occupational qualifications (BFOQs). (p. 92)

C

Cognitive abilities
Intelligence, general mental ability, or intellectual ability. (p. 331)

Competencies
Groups of related behaviours or attributes that are needed for successful job performance in an organization. (p. 151)

Competency dictionary
A listing of all of the competencies required by an organization to achieve its mandate, along with the proficiency level required to perform successfully in different functional groups or positions. (p. 153)

Competency framework
A broad framework for integrating, organizing, and aligning various competency models that are based on an organization's strategy and vision. (p. 152)

Competency model
A collection of competencies that are relevant to performance in a particular job, job family, or functional area. (p. 152)

Competency profile
A set of proficiency ratings related to a function, job, or employee. (p. 156)

Concurrent validation
Strategies in which evidence is obtained about a correlation between predictor and criteria scores from information that is collected at approximately the same time from a specific group of workers. (p. 48)

Consideration
A promise of compensation by the employer in return for the prospective employee's services. (p. 504)

Construct validity
The degree to which a test or procedure assesses an underlying theoretical construct it is supposed to measure; assessed through multiple sources of evidence showing that it measures what it purports to measure and not other constructs. For example, an IQ test must measure intelligence and not personality. (p. 45)

Content validity
Whether the items on a test appear to match the content or subject matter they are intended to assess; assessed through the judgments of experts in the subject area. A related concept is face validity, which is the degree to which test users or other non-experts believe that the test measures the content area. (p. 45)

Contextual performance
The activities or behaviours that are not part of a worker's formal job description but that remain important for organizational effectiveness. (p. 179)

Core competencies
Characteristics that every member of an organization, regardless of position, function, job, or level of responsibility within the organization, is expected to possess. (p. 153)

Counterproductive work behaviours
Voluntary behaviours that violate significant organizational norms and in so doing threaten the well-being of an organization, its members, or both. (p. 179)

Criteria
Measures of job performance that attempt to capture individual differences among employees with respect to job-related behaviours. (p. 178)

Criterion contamination
The degree to which the criterion measure is influenced by, or measures, behaviours or competencies that are not part of job performance. (p. 198)

Criterion deficiency
Those job performance behaviours or competencies that are not measured by the criterion. (p. 198)

Criterion measures
Measures of employee job-related outcomes important to the employer (e.g., absenteeism, turnover, supervisory ratings of performance) used to establish the validity (i.e., the appropriateness and meaningfulness) of screening and selection tools. (p. 288)

Criterion relevance
The degree to which the criterion measure captures behaviours or competencies that constitute job performance. (p. 198)

Criterion-related validity
The relationship between a predictor (test score) and an outcome measure; assessed by obtaining the correlation between the predictor and outcome scores. (p. 45)

Cutoff score
A threshold; those scoring at or above the cutoff score pass, those scoring below fail. (p. 481)

D

Designated targeted groups
The four groups (women, visible minorities, Aboriginal peoples, and people with disabilities) designated in the federal government's Employment Equity Act that receive legal "protection" in employment policies and practices because of their underrepresentation in the workforce. (p. 284)

Dilemma
A choice in an interview question between two alternatives that appear equally desirable or undesirable. (p. 426)

Discrimination
In employment, any refusal to employ or to continue to employ any person, or to adversely affect any current employee, on the basis of that individual's membership in a protected group. All Canadian jurisdictions prohibit discrimination at least on the basis of race or colour, religion or creed, age, sex, marital status, and physical or mental disability. (p. 67)

E

Emotional intelligence
The ability to accurately perceive and appraise emotion in oneself and others, and to appropriately regulate and express emotion. (p. 341)

Employment equity
Policies and practices designed to increase the presence of qualified women, visible minorities, Aboriginal people, and people with disabilities in the workforce; the elimination of discriminatory practices that prevent the entry or retention of members from designated groups in the workplace, and the elimination of unequal treatment in the workplace related to membership in a designated group. (p. 270)

Error score
The hypothetical difference between an observed score and a true score. (p. 39)

Ethics
The determination of right and wrong; the standards of appropriate conduct or behaviour for members of a profession: what those members may or may not do. (p. 17)

Experience-based interview
Assess applicant qualifications such as work experience and education using job knowledge or work sample questions. (p. 430)

F

Fairness
The principle that every test taker should be assessed in an equitable manner. (p. 56)

False negative error
Occurs when an applicant who is rejected would have been a good choice. (p. 473)

False negatives
Individuals who, based on their screening outcomes, are expected to be unsuccessful in the job, but who nonetheless would have performed satisfactorily if given the chance. (p. 285)

False positive error
Occurs when an applicant who is assessed favourably turns out to be a poor choice. (p. 472)

False positives
Individuals who, based on their screening outcomes, are expected to perform well in the target job, but who do not. (p. 284)

Functional competencies
Characteristics shared by different positions within an organization (i.e., a group of related or similar jobs). Only those members of an organization in these positions are expected to possess these competencies. (p. 153)

G

Genetic testing
The testing or monitoring of genetic material to determine a genetic propensity or susceptibility to illness resulting from various workplace chemicals or substances. (p. 347)

H

Honesty or integrity tests
Self-report inventories designed to assess employee honesty and reliability. (p. 368)

Human Resources Information Systems
Computer-based systems that track employee data, the needs of HR, and the requirements and competencies needed for different positions, among other functions. (p. 3)

I

Image advertising
Advertising designed to raise an organization's profile in a positive manner in order to attract job seekers' interest. (p. 261)

Implicit theories
Personal beliefs that are held about how people or things function, without objective evidence and often without conscious awareness. (p. 470)

Impression management
Attempts by applicants to create a favourable impression by monitoring interviewer reactions and responding accordingly. (p. 418)

In-basket test
A simulation exercise designed to assess organizational and problem-solving skills. (p. 354)

Incremental validity
The value in terms of increased validity of adding a particular predictor to an existing selection system. (p. 479)

Interests and values
An individual's likes and dislikes and the importance or priorities attached to those likes and dislikes. (p. 259)

Internet recruiting
The use of the Internet to match candidates to jobs through electronic databases that store information on jobs and job candidates. (p. 246)

J

Job
A collection of positions that are similar in their significant duties. (p. 115)

Job description
A written description of what job occupants are required to do, how they are supposed to do it, and the rationale for any required job procedures. (p. 115)

Job family
A set of different, but related, jobs that rely on the same set of KSAOs. (p. 115)

Job knowledge
Knowledgeable of issues and/or procedures deemed essential for successful job performance. (p. 341)

Job performance
Behaviour (the observable things people do) that is relevant to accomplishing the goals of an organization. (p. 178)

Job performance domain
The set of job performance dimensions (i.e., behaviours) that is relevant to the goals of the organization, or the unit, in which a person works. (p. 181)

Job search
The strategies, techniques, and practices an individual uses in looking for a job. (p. 259)

Job specification
The knowledge, skills, abilities, and other attributes or competencies that are needed by a job incumbent to perform well on the job. (p. 115)

Job-specific competencies
Characteristics that apply only to specific positions within the organization. Only those people in the position are expected to possess these competencies. (p. 153)

Judgmental composite
An approach in which judgmental and statistical data are combined in a judgmental manner. (p. 475)

K

Knowledge structures
Interviewers' beliefs about the requirements of the job and the characteristics of applicants. (p. 414)

KSAOs
The knowledge, skills, abilities, and other attributes necessary for a new incumbent to do well on the job; also referred to as *job, employment,* or *worker specifications.* (p. 29)

L

Leaderless group discussion
A simulation exercise designed to assess leadership, organizational, and communication skills. (p. 354)

Long-distance interviews
Interviews conducted over a long distance, including telephone interviews, videoconference interviews, Internet interviews, or computerized interviews, which serve as alternatives to face-to-face interviews. (p. 443)

M

Measurement error
The hypothetical difference between an observed score and a true score; comprises both random error and systematic error. (p. 40)

Minimum qualifications (MQ)
Knowledge, skills, abilities, and experience, deemed necessary for minimally acceptable performance in one or more positions; designed for making the "first cut" in screening applicants, and sometimes referred to as *selection criteria.* (p. 284)

Multiple cutoff combination model
A combination of multiple cutoff and regression approaches. (p. 488)

Multiple hurdle combination model
A combination of multiple hurdle and regression approaches. (p. 488)

Multiple Mini-Interviews
A version of the speed interview where applicants participate in a circuit of 12 eight-minute interviews with 12 different interviewers at 12 different interview stations. (p. 444)

Objective performance measures
Production, sales, and personnel data used in assessing individual job performance. (p. 203)

Organization analysis
An important step in the recruitment and selection process in which human resources specialists consider the design and structure, functions and processes, and strategies and missions of organizations to highlight areas of strength and weakness useful to human resources planning. (p. 233)

Organizational fit
Applicants' overall suitability for the organization and its culture. (p. 470)

Outreach recruiting
A recruitment practice where the employing organization makes a determined and persistent effort to make potential job applicants, including designated group members, aware of available positions within the employing organization. (p. 101)

Outsourcing
Contracting with an outside agent to take over specified HR functions. (p. 229)

Panel interview
An interview conducted by two or more interviewers together at one time. (p. 425)

Performance dimensions
Sets of related behaviours that are derived from an organization's goals and linked to successful job performance. (p. 181)

Person–job fit
Occurs when a job candidate has the knowledge, skills, abilities, or other attributes and competencies required by the job in question. (p. 262)

Person–organization fit
Occurs when a job candidate fits the organization's values and culture and has the contextual attributes desired by the organization. (p. 262)

Personality
A set of characteristics or properties that influence, or help to explain, an individual's behaviour. (p. 360)

Personality traits
Stable, measurable characteristics that help explain ways in which people vary. (p. 360)

Physical abilities
Traits or characteristics that involve the use or application of muscle force over varying periods of time, either alone or in conjunction with an ability to maintain balance or gross body coordination. (p. 344)

Position
A collection of duties assigned to individuals in an organization at a given time. (p. 115)

Practical intelligence
The ability to apply ideas in "real world" contexts. (p. 340)

Practicality
The degree to which a criterion measure is available, plausible, and acceptable to organizational decision makers. (p. 199)

Predictive validation
Strategies in which evidence is obtained about a correlation between predictor scores that are obtained before an applicant is hired and criterion scores that are obtained at a later time, usually after an applicant is employed. (p. 48)

Probes
Follow-up questions or prompts used by the interviewer to guide the applicant's descriptions of situations or events or to provide scorable elaboration of answers. (p. 428)

Professional standards
Professional standards provide guidance on how HR professionals should behave in certain situations including the use of employment tests. (p. 18)

Proficiency level
The level at which competency must be performed to ensure success in a given functional group or position. (p. 154)

Proficiency scale
A series of behavioural indicators expected at specific levels of a competency. (p. 155)

Profile interpretation
An approach in which statistical data are combined in a judgmental manner. (p. 475)

Psychomotor abilities
Traits or characteristics that involve the control of muscle movements. (p. 343)

Pure judgment approach
An approach in which judgmental data are combined in a judgmental manner. (p. 474)

Pure statistical approach
An approach in which data are combined statistically. (p. 475)

Puzzle interviews
Usually unstructured interviews that ask applicants to solve puzzles or unusual problems. (p. 443)

Realistic job preview
A procedure designed to reduce turnover and increase satisfaction among newcomers to an organization by providing job candidates with accurate information about the job and the organization. (p. 266)

Recruitment
The generation of an applicant pool for a position or job in order to provide the required number of candidates for a subsequent selection or promotion program. (p. 4, 226)

Reference check
Information gathered about a job candidate from supervisors, coworkers, clients, or other people named as references by the candidate. The information is usually collected from the written references and/or from contacts over the phone. (p. 303)

Relative rating system
A subjective measurement system that compares the overall performance of one employee to that of others to establish a rank order of employee performance. (p. 204)

Reliability
The degree to which observed scores are free from random measurement errors. Reliability is an indication of the stability or dependability of a set of measurements over repeated applications of the measurement procedure. (p. 37)

S

Satisficing
Making an acceptable or adequate choice rather than the best or optimal choice. (p. 469)

Scoring guide
A behavioural rating scale consisting of sample answers to each question that is used by the interviewer to evaluate and score the applicant's answers. (p. 426)

Screening
The first step of the selection process; involves identifying individuals from the applicant pool who lack the minimum qualifications for the target position(s). Candidates "passing" this first hurdle then undergo more extensive assessment. (p. 284)

Screening interviews
Preliminary interviews designed to fill gaps left on the candidate's application form or résumé, sometimes serving recruitment as well as selection functions. (p. 407)

Selection
The choice of job candidates from a previously generated applicant pool in a way that will meet management goals and objectives as well as current legal requirements. (p. 5)

Selection ratio
The proportion of applicants for one or more positions who are hired. (p. 284, 481)

Self-report inventory
Short, written statements related to various personality traits. (p. 361)

Self-selecting out
Occurs during the recruitment and selection process when candidates form the opinion that they do not want to work in the organization for which they are being recruited. (p. 257)

Sensory/perceptual abilities
Traits or characteristics that involve different aspects of vision and audition, as well as the other senses. (p. 344)

Serial interviews
A series of interviews where the applicant is interviewed separately by each of two or more interviewers. (p. 425)

Situational exercises
Assess aptitude or proficiency in performing important job tasks by using tasks that are abstract and less realistic than those performed on the actual job. (p. 352)

Situational interview
A highly structured interview in which important or decisive situations employees are likely to encounter on the job are described and applicants are asked what they would do in these situations. (p. 426)

Situational judgment tests
Type of situational exercise designed to measure an applicant's judgment in workplace or professional situations. (p. 352)

Skill
An individual's degree of proficiency or competency on a given task, which develops through performing the task. (p. 331)

Social networks
Internet sites that allow users to post a profile with a certain amount of information that is visible to the public. (p. 252)

Speed interviewing
A series of short (5–15 minute), consecutive interviews. (p. 411)

Statistical composite
An approach in which judgmental and statistical data are combined statistically. (p. 475)

Structured interview
An interview consisting of a standardized set of job-relevant questions; a scoring guide is used. (p. 422)

Subject-matter experts (SMEs)
People who are most knowledgeable about a job and how it is currently performed; generally job incumbents and their supervisors. (p. 116)

Subjective performance measures
Ratings or rankings made by supervisors, peers, or others that are used in assessing individual job performance. (p. 203)

Sufficient risk
As part of a BFOR defence, an employer may argue that an occupational requirement that discriminates against a protected group is reasonably necessary to ensure that work will be performed successfully and in a manner that will not pose harm or danger to employees or the public. (p. 98)

Systemic discrimination
In employment, the intentional or unintentional exclusion of members of groups that are protected under human rights legislation through recruiting, selection, or other personnel practices or policies. (p. 230)

T

Tacit knowledge
Knowledge that is derived from experience when learning is not the primary objective. (p. 340)

Talent management
An organization's commitment to recruit, retain, and develop the most talented and superior employees. (p. 3)

Task inventories
Work-oriented surveys that break down jobs into their component tasks. (p. 133)

Task performance
Duties related to the direct production of goods and services and to the direct contribution to the efficient functioning of the organization that form part of a job. These duties are part of the worker's formal job description. (p. 179)

Task statement
A discrete sentence containing one action verb that concisely describes a single observable activity performed by a job incumbent. (p. 129)

Top-down selection
Ranking applicants on the basis of their total scores and selecting from the top down until the desired number of candidates has been selected. (p. 491)

Trait rating approach
An approach in which judgmental data are combined statistically. (p. 474)

True score
The average score that an individual would earn on an infinite number of administrations of the same test or parallel versions of the same test. (p. 39)

U

Ultimate criterion
The concept that a single criterion measure reflects overall job success. (p. 200)

Unstructured interview
A traditional method of interviewing that involves no constraints on the questions asked, no requirements for standardization, and a subjective assessment of the candidate. (p. 417)

V

Validity
The degree to which accumulated evidence and theory support specific interpretations of test scores in the context of the test's proposed use. (p. 45)

Validity coefficient
The correlation between assessment scores and job performance measures. (p. 294)

Validity generalization
The application of validity evidence, obtained through meta-analysis of data obtained from many situations, to other situations that are similar to those on which the meta-analysis is based. (p. 50)

W

Weighted application blank (WAB)
A formal method for quantitatively combining information from application blank items by assigning weights that reflect the value of each item in the prediction of job success. (p. 288)

Work samples and simulations
Testing procedures that require job candidates to produce behaviours related to job performance under controlled conditions that approximate those found in the job. (p. 350)

Work-oriented job analysis
Job analysis techniques that emphasize work outcomes and descriptions of the various tasks performed to accomplish those outcomes. (p. 123)

Worker-oriented job analysis
Job analysis techniques that emphasize general aspects of jobs, describing perceptual, interpersonal, sensory, cognitive, and physical activities. (p. 123)

Worker traits inventories
Methods used to infer employee specifications from job analysis data. (p. 140)

INDEX